P9-EJY-774

THE
THOMAS JEFFERSON
READER

THE
THOMAS JEFFERSON
READER

KONECKY&KONECKY

Konecky & Konecky
72 Ayers Point Rd.
Old Saybrook, Ct 06475

ALL RIGHTS RESERVED

ISBN: 1-56852-587-7

PRINTED IN THE U.S.A.

CONTENTS

Part I

Major Writings Other Than Letters

THE
THOMAS JEFFERSON
READER

ThoWharton

A
SUMMARY VIEW
OF THE
RIGHTS
OF
BRITISH AMERICA.
SET FORTH IN SOME
RESOLUTIONS
INTENDED FOR THE
INSPECTION
OF THE PRESENT
DELEGATES
OF THE
PEOPLE OF VIRGINIA.
NOW IN
CONVENTION.

By Thomas Jefferson

BY A NATIVE, AND MEMBER OF THE
HOUSE OF BURGESSES.

WILLIAMSBURG:
PRINTED BY CLEMENTINA RIND.

TITLE PAGE, FIRST EDITION

THE PREFACE OF THE EDITORS.

THE *following piece was intended to convey to the late meeting of* DELEGATES *the sentiments of one of their body, whose personal attendance was prevented by an accidental illness. In it the sources of our present unhappy differences are traced with such faithful accuracy, and the opinions entertained by every free American expressed with such a manly firmness, that it must be pleasing to the present, and may be useful to future ages. It will evince to the world the moderation of our late convention, who have only touched with tenderness many of the claims insisted on in this pamphlet, though every heart acknowledged their justice. Without the knowledge of the author, we have ventured to communicate his sentiments to the public; who have certainly a right to know what the best and wisest of their members have thought on a subject in which they are so deeply interested.*

PREFACE BY ARTHUR LEE, LONDON EDITION (1774)

MANUSCRIPT CORRECTIONS BY JEFFERSON IN HIS
COPY OF THE "SUMMARY VIEW"

Page 8, footnote. *This is rewritten to read:*

> In 1621 Nova Scotia was granted by James I. to Sir Wm. Alexander. In 1632 Maryland was granted by Charles II. to D. of York: as also New Jersey, which the D. of York conveied again to Ld. Berkeley & Sr Geo. Carteret. So also were the Delaware counties, which the same Duke conveied again to Wm. Penn. In 1665 the country including North and South Carolina, Georgia & the Floridas was granted by Charles II. to the E. of Clarendon, D. of Albemarle, E. of Craven, Ld Berkely, Ld Ashley, Sir George Carteret, Sr John Coleton, & Sr. Wm. Berkely. In 1681 Pennsylvania was granted by Charles II. to Wm. Penn.

Page 18, note 3 On the passage "his majesty possessed no such power by the Constitution," Jefferson annotates, in addition to note present: "On further inquiry I find two instances of dissolution before the Parliament would, of itself, have been at an end: Viz., the Parliament called to meet August 24, 1698, was dissolved by King William, Dec. 19, 1700, and a new one called, to meet February 6, 1701, which was also dissolved November 11, 1701, and a new one met Dec. 30, 1701."

A SUMMARY VIEW OF THE RIGHTS
OF BRITISH AMERICA [1]
August, 1774

The Legislature of Virginia happened to be in session, in Williamsburg, when news was received of the passage, by the British Parliament, of the Boston Port Bill, which was to take effect on the first day of June then ensuing. The House of Burgesses, thereupon passed a resolution, recommending to their fellow-citizens, that that day should be set apart for fasting and prayer to the Supreme Being, imploring him to avert the calamities then threatening us, and to give us one heart and one mind to oppose every invasion of our liberties. The next day, May the 20th, 1774, the Governor dissolved us. We immediately repaired to a room in the Raleigh tavern, about one hundred paces distant from the Capitol, formed ourselves into a meeting, Peyton Randolph in the chair, and came to resolutions, declaring, that an attack on one colony, to enforce arbitrary acts, ought to be considered as an attack on all, and to be opposed by the united wisdom of all. We, therefore, appointed a Committee of correspondence, to address letters to the Speakers of the several Houses of Representatives of the colonies, proposing the appointment of deputies from each, to meet annually in a General Congress, to deliberate on their common interests, and on the measures to be pursued in common. The members then separated to their several homes, except those of the Committee, who met the next day, prepared letters according to instructions, and despatched them by messengers express, to their several destinations. It had been agreed, also, by the meeting, that the Burgesses, who should be elected under the writs then issuing, should be requested to meet in Convention, on a certain day in August, to learn the results of these letters, and to appoint delegates to a Congress, should that measure be approved by the other colonies. At the election, the people re-elected every man of the former Assembly, as a proof of their approbation of what they had done.

Before I left home, to attend the Convention, I prepared what I thought might be given, in instruction, to the Delegates who should be appointed to attend the General Congress proposed. They were drawn in haste, with a number of blanks,

---

[1] The "Summary View" was first called "Bill of Rights" and was originally referred to by Jefferson as "Instructions." It was first printed in Williamsburgh by subscription by "several of the author's admirers" and quickly ran through several editions. It was printed in London soon after it was written and created considerable discussion throughout England. The paper did not bear Jefferson's name, simply stating that it was "By a Native and Member of the House of Burgesses." But everyone in the Continental Congress knew who had written it. The text in this book is from the Congress Edition of Jefferson's *Writings* Volume 1. pp. 181-211. For an excellent discussion of the "Summary View," see *A Summary View of the Rights of British America with an introduction and a Bibliographical Note* by Thomas P. Abernathy (Scholars Facsimiles and Reprints, New York, 1943).

with some uncertainties and inaccuracies of historical facts, which I neglected at the moment, knowing they could be readily corrected at the meeting. I set out on my journey, but was taken sick on the road, and was unable to proceed. I therefore sent on, by express, two copies, one under cover to Patrick Henry, the other to Peyton Randolph, who I knew would be in the chair of the Convention. Of the former, no more was ever heard or known. Mr. Henry probably thought it too bold, as a first measure, as the majority of the members did. On the other copy being laid on the table of the Convention, by Peyton Randolph, as the proposition of a member, who was prevented from attendance by sickness on the road, tamer sentiments were preferred, and, I believe, wisely preferred; the leap I proposed being too long, as yet, for the mass of our citizens. The distance between these, and the instructions actually adopted, is of some curiosity, however, as it shews the inequality of pace with which we moved, and the prudence required to keep front and rear together. My creed had been formed on unsheathing the sword at Lexington. They printed the paper, however, and gave it the title of "A Summary view of the rights of British America." In this form it got to London, where the opposition took it up, shaped it to opposition views, and, in that form, it ran rapidly through several editions: [1]

Resolved, That it be an instruction to the said deputies, when assembled in General Congress, with the deputies from the other states of British America, to propose to the said Congress, that an humble and dutiful address be presented to his Majesty, begging leave to lay before him, as Chief Magistrate of the British empire, the united complaints of his Majesty's subjects in America; complaints which are excited by many unwarrantable encroachments and usurpations, attempted to be made by the legislature of one part of the empire, upon the rights which God, and the laws, have given equally and independently to all. To represent to his Majesty that these, his States, have often individually made humble application to his imperial Throne, to obtain, through its intervention, some redress of their injured rights; to none of which, was ever even an answer condescended. Humbly to hope that this, their joint address, penned in the language of truth, and divested of those expressions of servility, which would persuade his Majesty that we are asking favors, and not rights, shall obtain from his Majesty a more respectful acceptance; and this his Majesty will think we have reason to expect, when he reflects that he is no more than the chief officer of the people, appointed by the laws, and circumscribed with definite powers, to assist in working the great machine of government, erected for their use, and, consequently, subject to their superintendence; and, in order that these, our rights, as well as the invasions of them, may be laid more fully before his Majesty, to take a view of them, from the origin and first settlement of these countries.

[1] From Jefferson's *Autobiography*, Appendix.

To remind him that our ancestors, before their emigration to America, were the free inhabitants of the British dominions in Europe, and possessed a right, which nature has given to all men, of departing from the country in which chance, not choice, has placed them, of going in quest of new habitations, and of there establishing new societies, under such laws and regulations as, to them, shall seem most likely to promote public happiness. That their Saxon ancestors had, under this universal law, in like manner, left their native wilds and woods in the North of Europe, had possessed themselves of the Island of Britain, then less charged with inhabitants, and had established there that system of laws which has so long been the glory and protection of that country. Nor was ever any claim of superiority or dependence asserted over them, by that mother country from which they had migrated: and were such a claim made, it is believed his Majesty's subjects in Great Britain have too firm a feeling of the rights derived to them from their ancestors, to bow down the sovereignty of their state before such visionary pretensions. And it is thought that no circumstance has occurred to distinguish, materially, the British from the Saxon emigration. America was conquered, and her settlements made and firmly established, at the expense of individuals, and not of the British public. Their own blood was spilt in acquiring lands for their settlement, their own fortunes expended in making that settlement effectual. For themselves they fought, for themselves they conquered, and for themselves alone they have right to hold. Not a shilling was ever issued from the public treasures of his Majesty, or his ancestors, for their assistance, till of very late times, after the colonies had become established on a firm and permanent footing. That then, indeed, having become valuable to Great Britain for her commercial purposes, his Parliament was pleased to lend them assistance against an enemy who would fain have drawn to herself the benefits of their commerce, to the great aggrandisement of herself, and danger of Great Britain. Such assistance, and in such circumstances, they had often before given to Portugal and other allied states, with whom they carry on a commercial intercourse. Yet these states never supposed, that by calling in her aid, they thereby submitted themselves to her sovereignty. Had such terms been proposed, they would have rejected them with disdain, and trusted for better, to the moderation of their enemies, or to a vigorous exertion of their own force. We do not, however, mean to underrate those aids, which, to us, were doubtless valuable, on whatever principles granted: but we would shew that they cannot give a title to that authority which the British Parliament would arrogate over us; and that may amply be repaid by our giving to the inhabitants of Great Britain such exclusive privileges in trade as may be advantageous to them, and, at the same time, not too restrictive to ourselves. That settlement having been thus effected in the wilds of America, the emigrants thought proper to adopt that system of laws, under which they had hitherto lived in the mother country, and to continue their union with her, by submitting themselves to the same common sovereign, who was thereby made the central link, connecting the several parts of the empire thus newly multiplied.

But that not long were they permitted, however far they thought themselves removed from the hand of oppression, to hold undisturbed the rights thus acquired at the hazard of their lives and loss of their fortunes. A family of Princes was then on the British throne, whose treasonable crimes against their people, brought on them, afterwards, the exertion of those sacred and sovereign rights of punishment, reserved in the hands of the people for cases of extreme necessity, and judged by the constitution unsafe to be delegated to any other judicature. While every day brought forth some new and unjustifiable exertion of power over their subjects on that side of the water, it was not to be expected that those here, much less able at that time to oppose the designs of despotism, should be exempted from injury. Accordingly, that country, which had been acquired by the lives, the labors, and fortunes of individual adventurers, was by these Princes, several times, parted out and distributed among the favorites and followers of their fortunes; and, by an assumed right of the Crown alone, were erected into distinct and independent governments; a measure, which it is believed, his Majesty's prudence and understanding would prevent him from imitating at this day; as no exercise of such power, of dividing and dismembering a country, has ever occurred in his Majesty's realm of England, though now of very ancient standing; nor could it be justified or acquiesced under there, or in any part of his Majesty's empire.

That the exercise of a free trade with all parts of the world, possessed by the American colonists, as of natural right, and which no law of their own had taken away or abridged, was next the object of unjust encroachment. Some of the colonies having thought proper to continue the administration of their government in the name and under the authority of his Majesty, King Charles the first, whom, notwithstanding his late deposition by the Commonwealth of England, they continued in the sovereignty of their State, the Parliament, for the Commonwealth, took the same in high offence, and assumed upon themselves the power of prohibiting their trade with all other parts of the world, except the Island of Great Britain. This arbitrary act, however, they soon recalled, and by solemn treaty entered into on the 12th day of March, 1651, between the said Commonwealth, by their Commissioners, and the colony of Virginia by their House of Burgesses, it was expressly stipulated by the eight article of the said treaty, that they should have "free trade as the people of England do enjoy to all places and with all nations, according to the laws of that Commonwealth." But that, upon the restoration of his Majesty, King Charles the second, their rights of free commerce fell once more a victim to arbitrary power; and by several acts of his reign, as well as of some of his successors, the trade of the colonies was laid under such restrictions, as show what hopes they might form from the justice of a British Parliament, were its uncontrolled power admitted over these States. History has informed us, that bodies of men as well as of individuals, are susceptible of the spirit of tyranny. A view of these acts of Parliament for regulation, as it has been affectedly called, of the American trade, if all other evidences were removed out of the case, would undeniably evince the truth of this observation. Besides the duties they impose on our articles of export and import, they prohibit our going to any markets Northward of Cape Finisterra, in the kingdom of Spain, for the sale of commodities which Great Britain will not take from us, and for the purchase of others, with which she cannot supply us; and that, for no other than the arbitrary purpose of purchasing for themselves, by a sacrifice of our rights and interests, certain privileges in their commerce with an allied state, who, in confidence, that their exclusive trade with America will be continued, while the principles and power of the British Parliament be the same, have indulged themselves in every exorbitance which their avarice could dictate or our necessity extort: have raised their commodities called for in America, to the double and treble of what they sold for, before such exclusive privileges were given them, and of what better commodities of the same kind would cost us elsewhere; and, at the same time, give us much less for what we carry thither, than might be had at more convenient ports. That these acts prohibit us from carrying, in quest of other purchasers, the surplus of our tobaccos, remaining after the consumption of Great Britain is supplied: so that we must leave them with the British merchant, for whatever he will please to allow us, to be by him re-shipped to foreign markets, where he will reap the benefits of making sale of them for full value. That, to heighten still the idea of Parliamentary justice, and to show with what moderation they are like to exercise power, where themselves are to feel no part of its weight, we take leave to mention to his Majesty, certain other acts of the British Parliament, by which they would prohibit us from manufacturing, for our own use, the articles we raise on our own lands, with our own labor. By an act passed in the fifth year of the reign of his late Majesty, King George the second, an American subject is forbidden to make a hat for himself, of the fur which he has taken, perhaps, on his own soil; an instance of despotism, to which no parallel can be produced in the most arbitrary ages of British history. By one other act, passed in the twenty-third year of the same reign, the iron which we make, we are forbidden to manufacture; and, heavy as that article is, and necessary in every branch of husbandry, besides commission and insurance, we are to pay freight for it to Great Britain, and freight for it back again, for the purpose of supporting, not men, but machines, in the island of Great Britain. In the same spirit of equal and impartial legislation, is to be viewed the act of Parliament, passed in the fifth year of the same reign, by which American lands are made subject to the demands of British creditors, while their own lands were still continued unanswerable for their debts; from which, one of these conclusions must necessarily follow, either that justice is not the same thing in America as in Britain, or else, that the British Parliament pay less regard to it here than there. But, that we do not point out to his Majesty the injustice of these acts, with intent to rest on that principle the cause of their nullity; but to show that experience confirms the propriety of those political principles, which exempt us from the jurisdiction of the British Parliament. The true ground on which we declare these acts void, is, that the British Parliament has no right to exercise authority over us.

That these exercises of usurped power have not been confined to instances alone, in which themselves were interested; but they have also intermeddled with the regulation of the internal affairs of the colonies. The act of the 9th of Anne for establishing a post office in America, seems to have had little connection with British convenience, except that of accommodating his Majesty's ministers and favorites with the sale of a lucrative and easy office.

That thus have we hastened through the reigns which preceded his Majesty's, during which the violation of our rights were less alarming, because repeated at more distant intervals, than that rapid and bold succession of injuries, which is likely to distinguish the present from all other periods of American story. Scarcely have our minds been able to emerge from the astonishment into which one stroke of Parliamentary thunder has involved us, before another more heavy and more alarming is fallen on us. Single acts of tryanny may be ascribed to the accidental opinion of the day; but a series of oppressions, begun at a distinguished period, and pursued unalterably through every change of ministers, too plainly prove a deliberate, systematical plan of reducing us to slavery.

That the act passed in the fourth year of his Majesty's reign, entitled "an act for granting certain duties in the British colonies and plantations in America, etc."

One other act passed in the fifth year of his reign, entitled "an act for granting and applying certain stamp duties and other duties in the British colonies and plantations in America, etc."

One other act passed in the sixth year of his reign, entitled "an act for the better securing the dependency of his Majesty's dominions in America upon the crown and parliament of Great Britain."

And one other act passed in the seventh year of his reign, entitled "an act for granting duties on paper, tea, etc." form that connected chain of Parliamentary usurpation, which has already been the subject of frequent applications to his Majesty, and the Houses of Lords and Commons of Great Britain; and, no answers having yet been condescended to any of these, we shall not trouble his Majesty with a repetition of the matters they contained.

But that one other act passed in the same seventh year of his reign, having been a peculiar attempt, must ever require peculiar mention. It is entitled "an act for suspending the legislature of New York." One free and independent legislature, hereby takes upon itself to suspend the powers of another, free and independent as itself, thus exhibiting a phenomenon unknown in nature, the creator, and creature of its own power. Not only the principles of common sense, but the common feelings of human nature must be surrendered up, before his Majesty's subjects here, can be persuaded to believe, that they hold their political existence at the will of a British Parliament. Shall these governments be dissolved, their property annihilated, and their people reduced to a state of nature, at the imperious breath of a body of men whom they never saw, in whom they never confided, and over whom they have no powers of punishment or removal, let their crimes against the American public be ever so great? Can any one reason be assigned, why one hundred and sixty thousand electors in the island of Great Britain, should give law to four millions in the States of America, every individual of whom is equal to every individual of them in virtue, in understanding, and in bodily strength? Were this to be admitted, instead of being a free people, as we have hitherto supposed, and mean to continue ourselves, we should suddenly be found the slaves, not of one, but of one hundred and sixty thousand tyrants; distinguished, too, from all others, by this singular circumstance, that they are removed from the reach of fear, the only restraining motive which may hold the hand of a tyrant.

That, by "an act to discontinue in such manner, and for such time as are therein mentioned, the landing and discharging, lading or shipping of goods, wares and merchandize, at the town and within the harbor of Boston, in the province of Massachusetts bay, in North America," which was past at the last session of the British Parliament, a large and populous town, whose trade was their sole subsistence, was deprived of that trade, and involved in utter ruin. Let us for a while, suppose the question of right suspended, in order to examine this act on principles of justice. An act of Parliament had been passed, imposing duties on teas, to be paid in America, against which act the Americans had protested, as inauthoritative. The East

India Company, who till that time, had never sent a pound of tea to America on their own account, step forth on that occasion, the asserters of Parliamentary right, and send hither many ship loads of that obnoxious commodity. The masters of their several vessels, however, on their arrival in America, wisely attended to admonition, and returned with their cargoes. In the province of New-England alone, the remonstrances of the people were disregarded, and a compliance, after being many days waited for, was flatly refused. Whether in this, the master of the vessel was governed by his obstinancy, or his instructions, let those who know, say. There are extraordinary situations which require extraordinary interposition. An exasperated people, who feel that they possess power, are not easily restrained within limits strictly regular. A number of them assembled in the town of Boston, threw the tea into the ocean, and dispersed without doing any other act of violence. If in this they did wrong, they were known, and were amenable to the laws of the land; against which, it could not be objected, that they had ever, in any instance, been obstructed or diverted from the regular course, in favor of popular offenders. They should, therefore, not have been distrusted on this occasion. But that ill-fated colony had formerly been bold in their enmities against the House of Stuart, and were now devoted to ruin, by that unseen hand which governs the momentous affairs of this great empire. On the partial representations of a few worthless ministerial dependants, whose constant office it has been to keep that government embroiled, and who, by their treacheries, hope to obtain the dignity of British knighthood, without calling for a party accused, without asking a proof, without attempting a distinction between the guilty and the innocent, the whole of that ancient and wealthy town, is in a moment reduced from opulence to beggary. Men who had spent their lives in extending the British commerce, who had invested, in that place, the wealth their honest endeavors had merited, found themselves and their families, thrown at once on the world, for subsistence by its charities. Not the hundredth part of the inhabitants of that town, had been concerned in the act complained of; many of them were in Great Britain, and in other parts beyond sea; yet all were involved in one indiscriminate ruin, by a new executive power, unheard of till then, that of a British Parliament. A property of the value of many millions of money, was sacrificed to revenge, not repay, the loss of a few thousands. This is administering justice with a heavy hand indeed! And when is this tempest to be arrested in its course? Two wharves are to be opened again when his Majesty shall think proper: the residue, which lined the extensive shores of the bay of Boston, are forever interdicted the exercise of commerce. This little exception seems to have been thrown in for no other purpose, than that of setting a precedent for investing his Majesty with legislative powers.

If the pulse of his people shall beat calmly under this experiment, another and another will be tried, till the measure of despotism be filled up. It would be an insult on common sense, to pretend that this exception was made, in order to restore its commerce to that great town. The trade, which cannot be received at two wharves alone, must of necessity be transferred to some other place; to which it will soon be followed by that of the two wharves. Considered in this light, it would be an insolent and cruel mockery at the annihilation of the town of Boston. By the act for the suppression of riots and tumults in the town of Boston, passed also in the last session of Parliament, a murder committed there, is, if the Governor pleases, to be tried in the court of King's bench, in the island of Great Britain, by a jury of Middlesex. The witnesses, too, on receipt of such a sum as the Governor shall think it reasonable for them to expend, are to enter into recognizance to appear at the trial. This is, in other words, taxing them to the amount of their recognizance; and that amount may be whatever a Governor pleases. For who does his Majesty think can be prevailed on to cross the Atlantic for the sole purpose of bearing evidence to a fact? His expenses are to be borne, indeed, as they shall be estimated by a Governor; but who are to feed the wife and children whom he leaves behind, and who have had no other subsistence but his daily labor? Those epidemical disorders, too, so terrible in a foreign climate, is the cure of them to be estimated among the articles of expense, and their danger to be warded off by the Almighty power of a Parliament? And the wretched criminal, if he happen to have offended on the American side, stripped of his privilege of trial by peers of his vicinage, removed from the place where alone full evidence could be obtained, without money, without counsel, without friends, without exculpatory proof, is tried before Judges predetermined to condemn. The cowards who would suffer a countryman to be torn from the bowels of their society, in order to be thus offered a sacrifice to Parliamentary tyranny, would merit that everlasting infamy now fixed on the authors of the act! A clause, for a similar purpose, had been introduced into an act passed in the twelfth year of his Majesty's reign, entitled, "an act for the better securing and preserving his Majesty's Dock-yards, Magazines, Ships, Ammunition and Stores"; against which, as meriting the same censures, the several colonies have already protested.

That these are the acts of power, assumed by a body of men foreign to our constitutions, and unacknowledged by our laws; against which we do, on behalf of the inhabitants of British America, enter this, our solemn and determined protest. And we do earnestly intreat his Majesty, as yet the only mediatory power between the several States of the British empire, to recommend to his Parliament of Great Britain, the total revocation of these acts, which, however nugatory they may be, may yet prove the cause of further discontents and jealousies among us.

That we next proceed to consider the conduct of his Majesty, as holding the Executive powers of the laws of these States, and mark out his deviations from the line of duty. By the Constitution of Great Britain, as well as of the several American States, his Majesty possesses the power of refusing to pass into a law, any bill which has already passed the other two branches of the legislature. His Majesty, however, and his ancestors, conscious of the impropriety of opposing their single opinion to the united wisdom of two Houses of Parliament, while their proceedings were unbiassed by interested principles, for several ages past, have modestly declined the exercise of this power, in that part of his empire called Great Britain. But, by change of circumstances, other principles than those of justice simply, have obtained an influence on their determinations. The addition of new States to the British empire has produced an addition of new, and, sometimes, opposite interests. It is now, therefore, the great office of his Majesty to resume the exercise of his negative power, and to prevent the passage of laws by any one legislature of the empire, which might bear injuriously on the rights and interests of another. Yet this will not excuse the wanton exercise of this power, which we have seen his Majesty practice on the laws of the American legislature. For the most trifling reasons, and, sometimes for no conceivable reason at all, his Majesty has rejected laws of the most salutary tendency. The abolition of domestic slavery is the great object of desire in those colonies, where it was, unhappily, introduced in their infant state. But previous to the enfranchisement of the slaves we have, it is necessary to exclude all further importations from Africa. Yet our repeated attempts to effect this, by prohibitions, and by imposing duties which might amount to a prohibition, having been hitherto defeated by his Majesty's negative: thus preferring the immediate advantages of a few African corsairs, to the lasting interests of the American States, and to the rights of human nature, deeply wounded by this infamous practice. Nay, the single interposition of an interested individual against a law was scarcely ever known to fail of success, though, in the opposite scale, were placed the interests of a whole country. That this is so shameful an abuse of a power, trusted with his Majesty for other purposes, as if, not reformed, would call for some legal restrictions.

With equal inattention to the necessities of his people here has his Majesty permitted our laws to lie neglected, in England, for years, neither confirming them by his assent, nor annulling them by his negative: so, that such of them as have no suspending clause, we hold on the most precarious of all tenures, his Majesty's will; and such of them as suspend themselves till his Majesty's assent be obtained, we have feared might be called into existence at some future and distant period, when time and change of circumstances shall have rendered them destructive to his people here. And, to render this grievance still more oppressive, his Majesty, by his instructions, has laid his Governors under such restrictions, that they can pass no law, of any moment, unless it have such suspending clause: so that, however immediate may be the call for legislative interposition, the law cannot be executed, till it has twice crossed the Atlantic, by which time the evil may have spent its whole force.

But in what terms reconcilable to Majesty, and at the same time to truth, shall we speak of a late instruction to his Majesty's Governor of the colony of Virginia, by which he is forbidden to assent to any law for the division of a county, unless the new county will consent to have no representative in Assembly? That colony has as yet affixed no boundary to the Westward. Their Western counties, therefore, are of an indefinite extent. Some of them are actually seated many hundred miles from their Eastern limits. Is it possible, then, that his Majesty can have bestowed a single thought on the situation of those people, who in order to obtain justice for injuries, however great or small, must, by the laws of that colony, attend their county court at such a distance, with all their witnesses, monthly, till their litigation be determined? Or does his Majesty seriously wish, and publish it to the world, that his subjects should give up the glorious right of representation, with all the benefits derived from that, and submit themselves the absolute slaves of his sovereign will? Or is it rather meant to confine the legislative body to their present numbers, that they may be the cheaper bargain, whenever they shall become worth a purchase?

One of the articles of impeachment against Tresilian, and the other Judges of Westminster Hall, in the reign of Richard the Second, for which they suffered death, as traitors to their country, was, that they had advised the King, that he might dissolve his Parliament at any time; and succeeding kings have adopted the opinion of these unjust Judges. Since the establishment, however, of the British constitution, at the glorious Revolution, on its free and ancient principles, neither his Majesty, nor his ancestors, have exercised such a power of dissolution in the island of Great Britain;[1] and when his Majesty was petitioned, by the united voice of his people there, to dissolve the present Parliament, who had become obnoxious to them, his Ministers were heard to declare, in open Parliament, that his Majesty possessed no such power by the constitution. But how different their language,

[1] On further inquiry, I find two instances of dissolution before the Parliament would, of itself, have been at an end: viz., the Parliament called to meet August 24, 1698, was dissolved by King William, December 19, 1700, and a new one called, to meet February 6, 1701, which was also dissolved, November 11, 1701, and a new one met December 30, 1701.—T. J.

and his practice, here! To declare, as their duty required, the known rights of their country, to oppose the usurpation of every foreign judicature, to disregard the imperious mandates of a Minister or Governor, have been the avowed causes of dissolving Houses of Representatives in America. But if such powers be really vested in his Majesty, can he suppose they are there placed to awe the members from such purposes as these? When the representative body have lost the confidence of their constitutents, when they have notoriously made sale of their most valuable rights, when they have assumed to themselves powers which the people never put into their hands, then, indeed, their continuing in office becomes dangerous to the State, and calls for an exercise of the power of dissolution. Such being the cause for which the representative body should, and should not, be dissolved, will it not appear strange, to an unbiassed observer, that that of Great Britain was not dissolved, while those of the colonies have repeatedly incurred that sentence?

But your Majesty, or your Governors, have carried this power beyond every limit known or provided for by the laws. After dissolving one House of Representatives, they have refused to call another, so that, for a great length of time, the legislature provided by the laws, has been out of existence. From the nature of things, every society must, at all times, possess within itself the sovereign powers of legislation. The feelings of human nature revolt against the supposition of a State so situated, as that it may not, in any emergency, provide against dangers which, perhaps, threaten immediate ruin. While those bodies are in existence to whom the people have delegated the powers of legislation, they alone possess, and may exercise, those powers. But when they are dissolved, by the lopping off one or more of their branches, the power reverts to the people, who may use it to unlimited extent, either assembling together in person, sending deputies, or in any other way they may think proper. We forbear to trace consequences further; the dangers are conspicuous with which this practice is replete.

That we shall, at this time also, take notice of an error in the nature of our land holdings, which crept in at a very early period of our settlement. The introduction of the feudal tenures into the kingdom of England, though ancient, is well enough understood to set this matter in a proper light. In the earlier ages of the Saxon settlement, feudal holdings were certainly altogether unknown, and very few, if any, had been introduced at the time of the Norman conquests. Our Saxon ancestors held their lands, as they did their personal property, in absolute dominion, disincumbered with any superior, answering nearly to the nature of those possessions which the feudalist term Allodial. William the Norman, first introduced that system generally. The lands which had belonged to those who fell in the battle of Hastings, and in the subsequent insurrections of his reign, formed a considerable proportion of the lands of the whole kingdom. These he granted out, subject to feudal duties, as did he also those of a great number of his new subjects, who, by persuasions or threats, were induced to surrender them for that purpose. But still, much was left in the hands of his Saxon subjects, held of no superior, and not subject to feudal conditions. These, therefore, by express laws, enacted to render uniform the system of military defence, were made liable to the same military duties as if they had been feuds; and the Norman lawyers soon found means to saddle them, also, with the other feudal burthens. But still they had not been surrendered to the King, they were not derived from his grant, and therefore they were not holden of him. A general principle was introduced, that "all lands in England were held either mediately or immediately of the Crown"; but this was borrowed from those holdings which were truly feudal, and only applied to others for the purposes of illustration. Feudal holdings were, therefore, but exceptions out of the Saxon laws of possession, under which all lands were held in absolute right. These, therefore, still form the basis or groundwork of the Common law, to prevail wheresoever the exceptions have not taken place. America was not conquered by William the Norman, nor its lands surrendered to him or any of his successors. Possessions there are, undoubtedly, of the Allodial nature. Our ancestors, however, who migrated hither, were farmers, not lawyers. The fictitious principle, that all lands belong originally to the King, they were early persuaded to believe real, and accordingly took grants of their own lands from the Crown. And while the Crown continued to grant for small sums and on reasonable rents, there was no inducement to arrest the error, and lay it open to public view. But his Majesty has lately taken on him to advance the terms of purchase and of holding, to the double of what they were; by which means, the acquisition of lands being rendered difficult, the population of our country is likely to be checked. It is time, therefore, for us to lay this matter before his Majesty, and to declare, that he has no right to grant lands of himself. From the nature and purpose of civil institutions, all the lands within the limits, which any particular party has circumscribed around itself, are assumed by that society, and subject to their allotment; this may be done by themselves assembled collectively, or by their legislature, to whom they may have delegated sovereign authority; and, if they are allotted in neither of these ways, each individual of the society, may appropriate to himself such lands as he finds vacant, and occupancy will give him title.

That, in order to enforce the arbitrary measures before complained of, his Majesty has, from time to time, sent among us large bodies of armed forces, not made up of the people here, nor raised by the authority of our laws. Did his Majesty possess such a right as this, it might swallow up all our other rights, whenever he should think proper. But his Majesty has no right to land a single armed man on our shores; and those whom he sends here are liable to our laws, for the suppression and punishment of riots, routs, and unlawful assemblies, or are hostile bodies invading us in defiance of law. When, in the course of the late war, it became expedient that a body of Hanoverian troops should be brought over for the defence of Great Britain, his Majesty's grandfather, our late sovereign, did not pretend to introduce them under any authority he possessed. Such a measure would have given just alarm to his subjects of Great Britain, whose liberties would not be safe if armed men of another country, and of another spirit, might be brought into the realm at any time, without the consent of their legislature. He, therefore, applied to Parliament, who passed an act for that purpose, limiting the number to be brought in, and the time they were to continue. In like manner is his Majesty restrained in every part of the empire. He possesses indeed the executive power of the laws in every State; but they are the laws of the particular State, which he is to administer within that State, and not those of any one within the limits of another. Every State must judge for itself, the number of armed men which they may safely trust among them, of whom they are to consist, and under what restrictions they are to be laid. To render these proceedings still more criminal against our laws, instead of subjecting the military to the civil power, his majesty has expressly made the civil subordinate to the military. But can his Majesty thus put down all law under his feet? Can he erect a power superior to that which erected himself? He has done it indeed by force; but let him remember that force cannot give right.

That these are our grievances, which we have thus laid before his Majesty, with that freedom of language and sentiment which becomes a free people, claiming their rights as derived from the laws of nature, and not as the gift of their Chief Magistrate. Let those flatter, who fear: it is not an American art. To give praise where it is not due might be well from the venal, but would ill beseem those who are asserting the rights of human nature. They know, and will, therefore, say, that Kings are the servants, not the proprietors of the people. Open your breast, Sire, to liberal and expanded thought. Let not the name of George the third, be a blot on the page of history. You are surrounded by British counsellors, but remember that they are parties. You have no ministers for American affairs, because you have none taken from among us, nor amenable to the laws on which they are to give you advice. It behooves you, therefore, to think and to act for yourself and your people. The great principles of right and wrong are legible to every reader; to pursue them, requires not the aid of many counsellors. The whole art of government consists in the art of being honest. Only aim to do your duty, and mankind will give you credit where you fail. No longer persevere in sacrificing the rights of one part of the empire to the inordinate desires of another; but deal out to all, equal and impartial right. Let no act be passed by any one legislature, which may infringe on the rights and liberties of another. This is the important post in which fortune has placed you, holding the balance of a great, if a well-poised empire. This, Sire, is the advice of your great American council, on the observance of which may perhaps depend your felicity and future fame, and the preservation of that harmony which alone can continue, both to Great Britain and America, the reciprocal advantages of their connection. It is neither our wish nor our interest to separate from her. We are willing, on our part, to sacrifice everything which reason can ask, to the restoration of that tranquillity for which all must wish. On their part, let them be ready to establish union and a generous plan. Let them name their terms, but let them be just. Accept of every commercial preference it is in our power to give, for such things as we can raise for their use, or they make for ours. But let them not think to exclude us from going to other markets to dispose of those commodities which they cannot use, nor to supply those wants which they cannot supply. Still less, let it be proposed, that our properties, within our own territories, shall be taxed or regulated by any power on earth, but our own. The God who gave us life, gave us liberty at the same time: the hand of force may destroy, but cannot disjoin them. This, Sire, is our last, our determined resolution. And that you will be pleased to interpose, with that efficacy which your earnest endeavors may insure, to procure redress of these our great grievances, to quiet the minds of your subjects in British America against any apprehensions of future encroachment, to establish fraternal love and harmony through the whole empire, and that that may continue to the latest ages of time, is the fervent prayer of all British America.

COPY OF DECLARATION MADE BY JEFFERSON FOR MADISON

A DECLARATION BY THE REPRESENTATIVES OF THE UNITED STATES OF AMERICA, IN GENERAL CONGRESS ASSEMBLED [1]

July 4, 1776

When, in the course of human events, it becomes necessary for one people to dissolve the political bands which have connected them with another, and to assume among the powers of the earth the separate and equal station to which the laws of nature and of nature's God entitle them, a decent respect to the opinions of mankind requires that they should declare the causes which impel them to the separation.

We hold these truths to be self-evident; that all men are created equal; that they are endowed by their creator with [*inherent and*] inalienable rights; that among these certain are life, liberty, and the pursuit of happiness; that to secure these rights, governments are instituted among men, deriving their just powers from the consent of the governed; that whenever any form of government becomes destructive of these ends, it is the right of the people to alter or to abolish it, and to institute new government, laying its foundation on such principles, and organizing its powers in such form, as to them shall seem most likely to effect their safety and happiness. Prudence, indeed, will dictate that governments long established should not be changed for light and transient causes; and accordingly all experience hath shown that mankind are more disposed to suffer while evils are sufferable, than to right themselves by abolishing the forms to which they are accustomed. But when a long train of abuses and usurpations [*begun at a distinguished period and*] pursuing invariably the same object, evinces a design to reduce them under absolute despotism, it is

[1] Jefferson's title was changed by Congress on July 19, 1776, to read "The Unanimous Declaration of the thirteen United States of America." The text used here is from a copy of the Declaration made by Jefferson for James Madison in the spring of 1783. In it the changes made by Congress are clearly marked by Jefferson himself. The parts stricken out by Congress are shown in brackets and in italics. Insertions are shown in the margin or in a parallel column.

21

their right, it is their duty to throw off such government, and to provide new guards for their future security. Such has been the patient sufferance of these
Colonies; and such is now the necessity which constrains

alter   them to [*expunge*] their former systems of government.
The history of the present King of Great Britain is a his-

repeated   tory of [*unremitting*] injuries and usurpations, [*among
which appears no solitary fact to contradict the uniform*

all having   *tenor of the rest, but all have*] in direct object the establishment of an absolute tyranny over these States. To
prove this, let facts be submitted to a candid world [*for
the truth of which we pledge a faith yet unsullied by
falsehood*].

He has refused his assent to laws the most wholesome
and necessary for the public good.

He has forbidden his governors to pass laws of immediate and pressing importance, unless suspended in
their operation till his assent should be obtained; and,
when so suspended, he has utterly neglected to attend to
them.

He has refused to pass other laws for the accommodation of large districts of people, unless those people
would relinquish the right of representation in the Legislature, a right inestimable to them, and formidable to
tyrants only.

He has called together legislative bodies at places unusual, uncomfortable, and distant from the depository of
their public records, for the sole purpose of fatiguing
them into compliance with his measures.

He has dissolved representative houses repeatedly [*and
continually*] for opposing with manly firmness his invasions on the rights of the people.

He has refused for a long time after such dissolutions
to cause others to be elected, whereby the legislative
powers, incapable of annihilation, have returned to the
people at large for their exercise, the State remaining,
in the meantime, exposed to all the dangers of invasion
from without and convulsions within.

He has endeavored to prevent the population of these
States; for that purpose obstructing the laws for naturalization of foreigners, refusing to pass others to en-

courage their migrations hither, and raising the conditions of new appropriations of lands.

He has [*suffered*] the administration of justice [*totally to cease in some of these States*] refusing his assent to laws for establishing judiciary powers.   *obstructed by*

He has made [*our*] judges dependent on his will alone for the tenure of their offices, and the amount and payment of their salaries.

He has erected a multitude of new offices, [*by a self-assumed power*] and sent hither swarms of new officers to harass our people and eat out their substance.

He has kept among us in times of peace standing armies [*and ships of war*] without the consent of our Legislatures.

He has affected to render the military independent of, and superior to, the civil power.

He has combined with others to subject us to a jurisdiction foreign to our constitutions and unacknowledged by our laws, giving his assent to their acts of pretended legislation for quartering large bodies of armed troops among us; for protecting them by a mock trial from punishment for any murders which they should commit on the inhabitants of these States; for cutting off our trade with all parts of the world; for imposing taxes on us without our consent; for depriving us [   ] of the   *in many cases* benefits of trial by jury; for transporting us beyond seas to be tried for pretended offences; for abolishing the free system of English laws in a neighboring province, establishing therein an arbitrary government, and enlarging its boundaries, so as to render it at once an example and fit instrument for introducing the same absolute rule into these [*States*]; for taking away our charters,   *Colonies* abolishing our most valuable laws, and altering fundamentally the forms of our governments; for suspending our own Legislatures, and declaring themselves invested with power to legislate for us in all cases whatsoever.

He has abdicated government here [*withdrawing his governors, and declaring us out of his allegiance and protection*].   *by declaring us out of his protection, and waging war against us.*

He has plundered our seas, ravaged our coasts, burnt our towns, and destroyed the lives of our people.

He is at this time transporting large armies of foreign mercenaries to complete the works of death, desolation, and tyranny already begun with circumstances of cruelty and perfidy [   ] unworthy the head of a civilized nation.

scarcely paralleled in the most barbarous ages, and totally

He has constrained our fellow-citizens taken captive on the high seas to bear arms against their country, to become the executioners of their friends and brethren, or to fall themselves by their hands.

·He has [   ] endeavored to bring on the inhabitants of our frontiers the merciless Indian savages, whose known rule of warfare is an undistinguished destruction of all ages, sexes, and conditions [of existence].

excited domestic in- surrection among us, and has

[He has incited treasonable insurrections of our fellow- citizens, with the allurements of forfeiture and confisca- tion of our property.

He has waged cruel war against human nature itself, violating its most sacred rights of life and liberty in the persons of a distant people who never offended him, captivating and carrying them into slavery in another hemisphere, or to incur miserable death in their trans- portation thither. This piratical warfare, the opprobrium of INFIDEL powers, is the warfare of the CHRISTIAN King of Great Britain. Determined to keep open a market where MEN should be bought and sold, he has prosti- tuted his negative for suppressing every legislative at- tempt to prohibit or to restrain this execrable commerce. And that this assemblage of horrors might want no fact of distinguished die, he is now exciting those very people to rise in arms among us, and to purchase that liberty of which he has deprived them, by murdering the people on whom he also obtruded them: thus paying off former crimes committed against the LIBERTIES of one people with crimes which he urges them to commit against the LIVES of another.]

In every stage of these oppressions we have petitioned for redress in the most humble terms: our repeated peti- tions have been answered only by repeated injuries.

A Prince whose character is thus marked by every act which may define a tyrant is unfit to be the ruler of a

free   [   ] people [who mean to be free. Future ages will scarcely believe that the hardiness of one man adven-

tured, within the short compass of twelve years only, to lay a foundation so broad and so undisguised for tyranny over a people fostered and fixed in principles of freedom.]

Nor have we been wanting in attentions to our British brethren. We have warned them from time to time of attempts by their legislature to extend [*a*] jurisdiction over [*these our States*]. We have reminded them of the circumstances of our emigration and settlement here, [*no one of which could warrant so strange a pretension: that these were effected at the expense of our own blood and treasure, unassisted by the wealth or the strength of Great Britain: that in constituting indeed our several forms of government, we had adopted one common king, thereby laying a foundation for perpetual league and amity with them: but that submission to their parliament was no part of our Constitution, nor ever in idea, if history may be credited: and,*] we [   ] appealed to their native justice and magnanimity [*as well as to*] the ties of our common kindred to disavow these usurpations which [*were likely to*] interrupt our connection and correspondence. They too have been deaf to the voice of justice and of consanguinity, [*and when occasions have been given them, by the regular course of their laws, of removing from their councils the disturbers of our harmony, they have, by their free election, re-established them in power. At this very time too, they are permitting their chief magistrate to send over not only soldiers of our common blood, but Scotch and foreign mercenaries to invade and destroy us. These facts have given the last stab to agonizing affection, and manly spirit bids us to renounce forever these unfeeling brethren. We must endeavor to forget our former love for them, and hold them as we hold the rest of mankind, enemies in war, in peace friends. We might have been a free and a great people together; but a communication of grandeur and of freedom, it seems, is below their dignity. Be it so, since they will have it. The road to happiness and to glory is open to us too. We will tread it apart from them, and*] acquiesce in the necessity which denounces our [*eternal*] separation [   ]!

an unwarrantable
us

have
and we have conjured them by

would inevitably

We must therefore and hold them as we hold the rest of mankind, enemies in war, in peace friends.

We therefore the representatives of the United States of America in General Congress assembled, appealing to the supreme judge of the world for the rectitude of our intentions, do in the name, and by the authority of the good people of these Colonies, solemnly publish and declare, that these united Colonies are, and of right ought to be, free and independent States; that they are absolved from all allegiance to the British crown, and that all political connection between them and the state of Great Britain is, and ought to be, totally dissolved; and that as free and independent States, they have full power to levy war, conclude peace, contract alliances, establish commerce, and to do all other acts and things which independent States may of right do.

And for the support of this declaration, with a firm reliance on the protection of divine providence, we mutually pledge to each other our lives, our fortunes, and our sacred honor.

We therefore the representatives of the United States of America in General Congress assembled, do in the name, and by the authority of the good people of these [*States reject and renounce all allegiance and subjection to the kings of Great Britain and all others who may hereafter claim by, through, or under them; we utterly dissolve all political connection which may heretofore have subsisted between us and the people or parliament of Great Britain: and finally we do assert and declare these Colonies to be free and independent States,*] and that as free and independent States, they have full power to levy war, conclude peace, contract alliances, establish commerce, and to do all other acts and things which independent States may of right do.

And for the support of this declaration, we mutually pledge to each other our lives, our fortunes, and our sacred honor.

BILL TO ABOLISH ENTAILS

1776

A BILL TO ENABLE TENANTS IN TAIL TO CONVEY THEIR LANDS IN FEE-SIMPLE

Whereas the perpetuation of property in certain families by means of gifts made to them in fee-simple is contrary to good policy, tends to deceive fair traders who give credit on the visible possession of such estates, discourages the holder thereof from taking care and improving the same, and sometimes does injury to the morals of youth by rendering them independent of, and disobedient to, their parents; and whereas the former method of docking such estates tail by special act of assembly formed for every particular case employed very much time of the legislature, was burthensome to the public, and also to the individual who made application for such acts:

Be it therefore enacted by—

and it is hereby enacted by authority of the same that any person who now hath, or hereafter may have any estate in fee tail general or special in any lands or slaves in possession, or who now is or hereafter may be entitled to any such estate tail in reversion or remainder after the determination of any estate for life or lives or of any lesser estate, whether such estate hath been or shall be created by deed, will, act of assembly, or any other ways or means shall have full power to pass, convey, or assure in fee-simple or for any lesser estate the said lands or slaves, or use in lands or slaves or such reversion or remainder therein, or any part or parcel thereof, to any person or persons whatsoever by deed or deeds of feoffment, gift, grant, exchange, partition, lease, release, bargain, and sale, covenant to stand seized to uses, deed to lead uses, or by his last will and testament, or by any other mode or form of conveyance or assurance by which such lands or slaves, or use in lands or slaves, or such reversion or remainder therein might have been passed, conveyed or assured had the same been held in fee-simple by the person so passing, conveying or assuring the same: and such deed, will or other conveyance shall be good and effectual to bar the issue in tail and those in remainder and revert as to such estate or estates so passed, conveyed, or assured by such deed, will, or other conveyance.

Provided nevertheless that such deed, will, or other conveyance shall be executed, acknowledged, or proved, and recorded in like manner as, and in all cases where, the same should have been done, had the person or persons

27

so conveying or assuring held the said lands or slaves, or use of lands and slaves or such reversion or remainder in fee-simple.

A BILL CONCERNING SLAVES

1779

SECTION I. Be it enacted by the General Assembly, that no persons shall, henceforth, be slaves within this commonwealth, except such as were so on the first day of this present session of Assembly, and the descendants of the females of them.

SECTION II. Negroes and mulattoes which shall hereafter be brought into this commonwealth and kept therein one whole year, together, or so long at different times as shall amount to one year, shall be free. But if they shall not depart the commonwealth within one year thereafter they shall be out of the protection of the laws.

SECTION III. Those which shall come into this commonwealth of their own accord shall be out of the protection of the laws; save only such as being seafaring persons and navigating vessels hither, shall not leave the same while here more than twenty four hours together.

SECTION IV. It shall not be lawful for any person to emancipate a slave but by deed executed, proved and recorded as is required by law in the case of a conveyance of goods and chattels, on consideration not deemed valuable in law, or by last will and testament, and with the free consent of such slave, expressed in presence of the court of the county wherein he resides. And if such slave, so emancipated, shall not within one year thereafter, depart the commonwealth, he shall be out of the protection of the laws. All conditions, restrictions and limitations annexed to any act of emancipation shall be void from the time such emancipation is to take place.

SECTION V. If any white woman shall have a child by a Negro or mulatto, she and her child shall depart the commonwealth within one year thereafter. If they shall fail so to do, the woman shall be out of the protection of the laws, and the child shall be bound out by the Aldermen of the county, in like manner as poor orphans are by law directed to be, and within one year after its terms of service expired shall depart the commonwealth, or on failure so to do, shall be out of the protection of the laws.

SECTION VI. Where any of the persons before described shall be disabled from departing the commonwealth by grievous sickness, the protection of the law shall be continued to him until such disability be removed: And if the county shall in the meantime, incur any expense in taking care of him, as of other county poor, the Aldermen shall be entitled to recover the same from his master, if he had one, his heirs, executors and administrators.

SECTION VII. No Negro or mulatto shall be a witness except in pleas of the commonwealth against Negroes or mulattoes, or in civil pleas wherein Negroes or mulattoes alone shall be parties.

SECTION VIII. No slave shall go from the tenements of his master, or other person with whom he lives, without a pass, or some letter or token whereby it may appear that he is proceeding by authority from his master, employer, or overseer: If he does, it shall be lawful for any person to apprehend and carry him before a Justice of the Peace, to be by his order punished with stripes, or not in his direction.

SECTION IX. No slaves shall keep any arms whatever, nor pass, unless with written orders from his master or employer, or in his company, with arms from one place to another. Arms in possession of a slave contrary to this prohibition shall be forfeited to him who will seize them.

SECTION X. Riots, routs, unlawful assemblies, trespasses and seditious speeches by a Negro or mulatto shall be punished with stripes at the discretion of a Justice of the Peace; and he who will may apprehend and carry him before such a Justice.

A BILL FOR PROPORTIONING CRIMES AND PUNISHMENTS
1779

Whereas, it frequently happens that wicked and dissolute men, resigning themselves to the dominion of inordinate passions, commit violations on the lives, liberties, and property of others, and, the secure enjoyment of these having principally induced men to enter into society, government would be defective in its principal purpose, were it not to restrain such criminal acts, by inflicting due punishments on those who perpetrate them; but it appears, at the same time, equally deducible from the purposes of society, that a member thereof, committing an inferior injury, does not wholly forfeit the protection of his fellow citizens, but, after suffering a punishment in proportion to his offence, is entitled to their protection from all greater pain, so that it becomes a duty in the legislature to arrange, in a proper scale, the crimes which it may be necessary for them to repress, and to adjust thereto a corresponding gradation of punishments.

And whereas, the reformation of offenders, though an object worthy the attention of the laws, is not effected at all by capital punishments, which exterminate instead of reforming, and should be the last melancholy resource against those whose existence is become inconsistent with the safety of their fellow citizens, which also weaken the State, by cutting off so many who, if reformed, might be restored sound members to society, who, even under a course of correction, might be rendered useful in various labors for the public, and would be living and long-continued spectacles to deter others from committing the like offences.

And forasmuch as the experience of all ages and countries hath shown, that cruel and sanguinary laws defeat their own purpose, by engaging the benevolence of mankind to withhold prosecutions, to smother testimony, or to listen to it with bias, when, if the punishment were only proportioned to the injury, men would feel it their inclination, as well as their duty, to see the laws observed.

For rendering crimes and punishments, therefore, more proportionate to each other:

Be it enacted by the General Assembly, that no crime shall be henceforth punished by the deprivation of life or limb,[1] except those hereinafter ordained to be so punished.

[2] If a man do levy war[3] against the Commonwealth [*in the same*], or be adherent to the enemies of the Commonwealth [*within the same*],[4] giving to them aid or comfort in the Commonwealth, or elsewhere, and thereof be convicted of open deed, by the evidence of two sufficient witnesses, or his own voluntary confession, the said cases, and no[5] other, shall be adjudged

---

[1] This takes away the punishment of cutting off the hand of a person striking another, or drawing his sword in one of the superior courts of justice. Stamf. P. C. 38. 33. H. 8. c. 12. In an earlier stage of the Common law, it was death. Gif hwa gefeohte on Cyninges huse sy he scyldig ealles his yrfes, and sy on Cyninges dome hwæther he lif age de nage: *si quis in regis domo pugnet, perdat omnem suam haereditatem, et in regis sit arbitrio, possideat vitam an non possideat.* Ll. Inae. 6. Gif hwa on Cyninges healle gefeohte, oththe his wæpne gebrede, and hine mon gefo, sy thæt on Cyninges dome swa death, swa lif, swa he him forgyfan wille: *si quis in aula regia pugnet, vel arma sua extrahat et capiatur, sit in regis arbitrio tam mors quam vita, sicut ei condonare voluerit.* Ll. Alfr. 7. Gif hwa on Cyninges hirede gefeohte tholige thæt lifes, buton se Cyning him gearian wille: *si quis in regia dimicat, perdat vitam, nisi rex hoc illi condonare velit.* Ll. Cnuti. 56. 4. Bl. 125.—T. J.

[2] 25. E. 3. st. 5. c. 2. 7. W. 3. c. 3. § 2.—T. J.

[3] Though the crime of an accomplice in treason is not here described, yet, Lord Coke says, the partaking and maintaining a treason herein described, makes him a principal in that treason: it being a rule that in treason all are principals. 3 Inst. 138. 2 Inst. 590. 1 H. 6. 5.—T. J.

[4] These words in the English statute narrow its operation. A man adhering to the enemies of the Commonwealth, in a foreign country, would certainly not be guilty of treason with us, if these words be retained. The convictions of treason of that kind in England have been under that branch of the statute which makes the compassing the king's death treason. Foster 196. 197. But as we omit that branch, we must by other means reach this flagrant case.—T. J.

[5] The stat. 25. E. 3. directs all other cases of treasons to await the opinion of Parliament. This has the effect of negative words, excluding all other treasons. As we drop that part of the statute, we must, by negative words, prevent an inundation of common law treasons. I strike out the word "it," therefore, and insert "the said cases, and no others." Quære, how far those negative words may affect the case of accomplices above mentioned? Though if their case was within the statute, so as that it needed not await the opinion of Parliament, it should seem to be also within our act, so as not to be ousted by the negative words.—T. J.

treasons which extend to the Commonwealth, and the person so convicted shall suffer death, by hanging,[1] and shall forfeit his lands and goods to the Commonwealth.

If any person commit petty treason, or a husband murder his wife, a parent[2] his child, or a child his parent, he shall suffer death by hanging, and his body be delivered to anatomists to be dissected.

Whosoever committeth murder by poisoning shall suffer death by poison.

Whosoever committeth murder by way of duel shall suffer death by hanging; and if he were the challenger, his body, after death, shall be gibbetted.[3] He who removeth it from the gibbet shall be guilty of a misdemeanor; and the officer shall see that it be replaced.

Whosoever shall commit murder in any other way shall suffer death by hanging.

And in all cases of petty treason and murder, one half of the lands and goods of the offender, shall be forfeited to the next of kin to the person killed, and the other half descend and go to his own representatives. Save only, where one shall slay the challenger in a duel,[4] in which case, no part

---

[1] This implies "by the neck." See 2 Hawk. 544. notes n. o.—T. J.

[2] By the stat. 21. Jac. 1. c. 27. and Act Ass. 1170. c. 12. concealment by the mother of the death of a bastard child is made murder. In justification of this, it is said, that shame is a feeling which operates so strongly on the mind, as frequently to induce the mother of such a child to murder it, in order to conceal her disgrace. The act of concealment, therefore, proves she was influenced by shame, and that influence produces a presumption that she murdered the child. The effect of this law then is, to make what, in its nature, is only presumptive evidence of a murder conclusive of that fact. To this I answer, 1. So many children die before or soon after birth, that to presume all those murdered who are found dead, is a presumption which will lead us oftener wrong than right, and consequently would shed more blood than it would save. 2. If the child were born dead, the mother would naturally choose rather to conceal it, in hopes of still keeping a good character in the neighborhood. So that the act of concealment is far from proving the guilt of murder on the mother. 3. If shame be a powerful affection of the mind, is not parental love also? Is it not the strongest affection known? Is it not greater than even that of self-preservation? While we draw presumptions from shame, one affection of the mind, against the life of the prisoner, should we not give some weight to presumptions from parental love, an affection at least as strong, in favor of life? If concealment of the fact is a presumptive evidence of murder, so strong as to overbalance all other evidence that may possibly be produced to take away the presumption, why not trust the force of this incontestable presumption to the jury, who are, in a regular course, to hear presumptive, as well as positive testimony? If the presumption arising from the act of concealment, may be destroyed by proof positive or circumstantial to the contrary, why should the legislature preclude that contrary proof? Objection. The crime is difficult to prove, being usually committed in secret. Answer. But circumstantial proof will do; for example, marks of violence, the behavior, countenance, &c. of the prisoner, &c. And if conclusive proof be difficult to be obtained, shall we therefore fasten irremovably upon equivocal proof? Can we change the nature of what is contestable, and make it incontestable? Can we make that conclusive which God and nature have made inconclusive? Solon made no law against parricide, supposing it impossible that anyone could be guilty of it; and the Persians, from the same opinion, adjudged all who killed their reputed parents to be bastards; and although parental be yet stronger than filial affection, we admit saticide proved on the most equivocal testimony, whilst they rejected all proof of an act certainly not more repugnant to nature, as of a thing impossible, unprovable. See Beccaria, § 31.—T. J.

[3] 25. G. 2. c. 37.—T. J.

[4] Quære, if the estates of both parties in a duel, should not be forfeited? The deceased is equally guilty with a suicide.—T. J.

of his lands or goods shall be forfeited to the kindred of the party slain, but, instead thereof, a moiety shall go to the Commonwealth.

The same evidence[1] shall suffice, and order and course[2] of trial be observed in cases of petty treason, as in those of other[3] murders.

Whosoever shall be guilty of manslaughter,[4] shall, for the first offence, be condemned to hard[5] labor for seven years in the public works, shall forfeit one half of his lands and goods to the next of kin to the person slain; the other half to be sequestered during such term, in the hands and to the use of the Commonwealth, allowing a reasonable part of the profits for the support of his family. The second offence shall be deemed murder.

And where persons, meaning to commit a trespass[6] only, or larceny, or other unlawful deed, and doing an act from which involuntary homicide hath ensued, have heretofore been adjudged guilty of manslaughter, or of murder, by transferring such their unlawful intention to an act, much more penal than they could have in probable contemplation; no such case shall hereafter be deemed manslaughter, unless manslaughter was intended, nor murder, unless murder was intended.

In other cases of homicide, the law will not add to the misteries of the party, by punishments and forfeitures.[7]

---

[1] Quære, if these words may not be omitted? By the Common law, one witness in treason was sufficient. Foster 233. Plowd. 8. a. Mirror c. 3. § 34. Waterhouse on Fortesc. de laud. 252. Carth. 144. per. Holt. But Lord Coke, contra 3 inst. 26. The stat. 1. E. 6. c. 12. & 5. E. 6. c. 11. first required two witnesses in treason. The clause against high treason supra, does the same as to high treason; but it seems if 1st and 5th E. 6. are dropped, Petty treason will be tried and proved, as at Common law, by one witness. But quære, Lord Coke being contra, whose opinion it is ever dangerous to neglect.—T. J.

[2] These words are intended to take away the peremptory challenge of thirty-five jurors. The same words being used 1. 2. Ph. & M. c. 10. are deemed to have restored the peremptory challenge in high treason; and consequently are sufficient to take it away. Foster 237.—T. J.

[3] Petty treason is considered in law only as an aggravated murder. Foster 107. 323. A pardon of all murders, pardons petty treason. 1 Hale P. C. 378. see 2 H. P. C. 340. 342. It is also included in the word "felony," so that a pardon of all felonies, pardons petty treason.—T. J.

[4] Manslaughter is punishable at law, by burning in the hands, and forfeiture of chattels.—T. J.

[5] It is best, in this act, to lay down principles only, in order that it may not forever be undergoing change; and, to carry into effect the minuter parts of it, frame a bill "for the employment and government of felons, or malefactors, condemned to labor for the Commonwealth," which may serve as an Appendix to this, and in which all the particulars requisite may be directed; and as experience will, from time to time, be pointing out amendments, these may be made without touching this fundamental act. See More's Utopia p. 50. for some good hints. Fugitives might, in such a bill, be obliged to work two days for every one they absent themselves.—T. J.

[6] The shooting at a wild fowl, and killing a man, is homicide by misadventure. Shooting at a pullet, without any design to take it away, is manslaughter; and with a design to take it away, is murder. 6 Sta. tr. 222. To shoot at the poultry of another, and thereby set fire to his house, is arson, in the opinion of some. Dalt. c. 116. 1. Hale's P. C. 569. c. contra.—T. J.

[7] Beccaria. § 32. Suicide. Homicides are, 1. Justifiable. 2. Excusable. 3. Felonious. For the last, punishments have been already provided. The first are held to be totally without guilt, or rather commendable. The second are in some cases not quite unblamable. These should subject the party to marks of contrition; viz., the killing of a man in defence of property; so also in defence of one's person, which is a species of excusable homicide; because, although cases may happen where these also are commendable, yet most frequently they are done on too slight appearance of danger; as in return for a blow, kick, fillip, &c.; or on a person's getting into a house, not

Whenever sentence of death shall have been pronounced against any person for treason or murder, execution shall be done on the next day but one after such sentence, unless it be Sunday, and then on the Monday following.[1]

Whosoever shall be guilty of rape,[2] polygamy,[3] or sodomy[4] with man

animo furandi, but perhaps *veneris causa*, &c. Bracton says, *"si quis furem nocturnum occident, ita demum impune foret, si parcere ei sine periculo suo non potuit, si autem potuit, aliter erit. Item erit si quis hamsokne quae dicitur invasio domus contra pacem domini regis in domo sua se defenderit, et invasor occisus fuerit; impersecutus et insultus remanebit, si ille quem invasit aliter se defendere non potuit; dicitur enim quod non est dignus habere pacem qui non vult observare eam."* L. 3. c. 23. § 3. *"Qui latronem occiderit, non tenetur, nocturnum vel diurnum, si aliter periculum evadere non possit; tenetur tamen si possit. Item non tenetur si per infortunium, et non animo et voluntate occidendi, nec dolus, nec culpa ejus inveniatur."* L. 3. c. 36. § 1. The stat. 24. H. 8. c. 5. is therefore merely declaratory of the Common law. See on the general subject Puffend. 2. 5. § 10. 11. 12. 16. 17. Excusable homicides are by misadventure, or in self-defence. It is the opinion of some lawyers, that the Common law punished these with death, and that the statute of Marlbridge, c. 26. and Gloucester, c. 9. first took away this by giving them title to a pardon, as matter of right, and a writ of restitution of their goods. See 2. Inst. 148. 315. 3. Inst. 55. Bracton L. 3. c. 4. § 2. Fleta L. 1. c. 23. § 14. 15. 21. E. 3. 23. But it is believed never to have been capital. 1. H. P. C. 425. 1 Hawk. 75. Foster, 282. 4. Bl. 188. It seems doubtful also, whether at Common law, the party forfeited all his chattels in this case, or only paid a weregild. Foster, *ubi supra*, doubts, and thinks it of no consequence, as the statute of Gloucester entitles the party to Royal grace, which goes as well to forfeiture as life. To me there seems no reason for calling these excusable homicides, and the killing a man in defence of property, a justifiable homicide. The latter is less guiltless than misadventure or self-defence.

Suicide is by law punishable by forfeiture of chattels. This bill exempts it from forfeiture. The suicide injures the State less than he who leaves it with his effects. If the latter then be not punished, the former should not. As to the example, we need not fear its influence. Men are too much attached to life, to exhibit frequent instances of depriving themselves of it. At any rate, the quasi-punishment of confiscation will not prevent it. For if one be found who can calmly determine to renounce life, who is so weary of his existence here, as rather to make experiment of what is beyond the grave, can we suppose him, in such a state of mind, susceptible of influence from the losses to his family from confiscation? That men in general, too, disapprove of this severity, is apparent from the constant practice of juries finding the suicide in a state of insanity; because they have no other way of saving the forfeiture. Let it then be done away. —T. J.

[1] Beccaria. § 19. 25. G. 2. c. 37.—T. J.

[2] 13. E. 1. c. 34. Forcible abduction of a woman having substance, is felony by 3. H. 7. c. 2. 3. Inst. 61. 4. Bl. 208. If goods be taken, it will be felony as to them, without this statute; and as to the abduction of the woman, quære if not better to leave that, and also kidnapping, 4 Bl. 219. to the Common law remedies, *viz.*, fine, imprisonment, and pillory, Raym. 474. 2 Show. 221. Skin. 47. Comb. 10. the writs of Homine replegiando, Capias in Withernam, Habeas corpus, and the action of trespass? Rape was felony at the Common law. 3. Inst. 60. but see 2. Inst. 181. further—for its definition see 2. Inst. 180. Bracton, L. 3. c. 28. § 1. says the punishment of rape is *"amissio membrorum, ut sit membrum pro membro, quia virgo, cum corrumpitur, membrum amittit, et ideo corruptor puniatur in eo in quo deliquit; oculos igitur amittat propter aspectum decoris quo virginem concupivit; amittat et testiculos qui calorem stupri induxerunt. Olim quidem corruptores virginitatis et castitatis suspendebantur et eorum fautores, &c.* Modernis tamen temporibus aliter observatur,"* &c. And Fleta, *"solet justiciarius pro quolibet mahemio ad amissionem testiculorum vel oculorum convictum condemnare, sed non sine errore, eo quod id judicium nisi in corruptione virginum tantum competebat; nam pro virginitatis corruptione solebant abscidi et merito judicari, ut sic pro membro quod abstulit, membrum per quod deliquit amitteret, viz., testiculos, qui calorem stupri induxerunt,"* &c. Fleta, L. 1. c. 40. § 4. "Gif theow man theowne to nydhed genyde, gabte mid his eowende:" *"Si servus sarvam ad stuprum coegerit, compenset hoc virga sua virili. Si quis puellam,"* &c. Ll. Aelfridi. 25. *"Hi purgist femme per forze forfait ad les membres."* Ll. Gul. conq. 19. In Dyer, 305, a man was indicted, and found guilty of a rape on a girl of seven years old. The court "doubted of the rape of so tender a girl; but if she had been nine years old, it would have been otherwise." 14. Eliz. Therefore the statute 18. Eliz. c. 6. says, "For plain declaration of law, be it enacted, that if any

or woman, shall be punished, if a man, by castration,[1] if a woman, by cutting through the cartilage of her nose a hole of one half inch in diameter at the least.

But no one shall be punished for polygamy, who shall have married after probable information of the death of his or her husband or wife, or after his or her husband or wife, hath absented him or herself, so that no notice of his or her being alive hath reached such person for seven years together, or hath suffered the punishments before prescribed for rape, polygamy, or sodomy.

Whosoever on purpose, and of malice forethought, shall maim[2] another, or shall disfigure him, by cutting out or disabling the tongue, slitting or cutting off a nose, lip, or ear, branding, or otherwise, shall be maimed, or disfigured in like[3] sort: or if that cannot be, for want of the same part, then as nearly as may be, in some other part of at least equal value and estimation, in the opinion of a jury, and moreovevr, shall forfeit one half of his lands and goods to the sufferer.

---

person shall unlawfully and carnally know and abuse any woman child, under the age of ten years, &c., he shall suffer as a felon, without allowance of clergy." Lord Hale, however, 1. P. C. 630. thinks it rape independent of that statute, to know carnally, a girl under twelve, the age of consent. Yet 4. Bl. 212. seems to neglect this opinion; and as it was founded on the words of 3. E. 1. c. 13. and this is with us omitted, the offence of carnally knowing a girl under twelve, or ten years of age, will not be distinguished from that of any other.—T. J.

³ 1. Jac. 1. c. 11. Polygamy was not penal till the statute 1. Jac. The law contented itself with the nullity of the act. 4. Bl. 163. 3. Inst. 88.—T. J.

⁴ 25. H. 8. c. 6. Buggery is twofold. 1. With mankind, 2. with beasts. Buggery is the genus, of which sodomy and bestiality, are the species. 12. Co. 37. says, "note that sodomy is with mankind." But Finch's L. B. 3. c. 24. "Sodomiary is a carnal copulation against nature, to wit, of man or woman in the same sex, or of either of them with beasts." 12. Co. 36. says, "it appears by the ancient authorities of the law that this was felony." Yet the 25. H. 8. declares it felony, as if supposed not to be so. Britton, c. 9. says, that sodomites are to be burnt. F.N.B. 269. b. Fleta, L. 1. c. 37. says, *"pecorantes et Sodomitae in terra vivi confodiantur."* The Mirror makes it treason. Bestiality can never make any progress; it cannot therefore be injurious to society in any great degree, which is the true measure of criminality in *foro civili*, and will ever be properly and severely punished, by universal derision. It may, therefore, be omitted. It was anciently punished with death, as it has been latterly. Ll. Aelfrid. 31. and 25. H. 8. c. 6. see Beccaria. § 31. Montesq.—T. J.

¹ Bracton, Fleta, &c.—T. J.

² 22. 23. Car. 2. c. 1. Maiming was felony at the Common law. Britton, c. 25. *"Mahemium autem dici poteri, aubi aliquis in aliqua parte sui corparis laesionem acceperit, per quam affectus sit inutilis ad pugnandum: ut si manus amputetur, vel pes, oculus privetur, vel scerda de osse capitis laveter, vel si quis dentes praecisores amiserit, vel castratus fuerit, et talis pro mahemiato poterit adjudicari."* Fleta L. 1. c. 40. *"Et volons que nul maheme ne soit tenus forsque de membre tollet dount home est plus feble a combatre, sicome del oyl, ou de la mayn, ou del pie, ou de la tete debruse, ou de les dentz devant."* Britton, c. 25. For further definitions, see Bracton, L. 3. c. 24. § 3. 4. Finch L. B. 3. c. 12. Co. L. 126. a. b. 288. a. 3. Bl. 121. 4. Bl. 205. Stamf. P. C. L. 1. c. 41. I do not find any of these definitions confine the offence to wilful and malicious perpetrations of it. 22. 23. Car. 2. c. 1. called the Coventry act, has the words "on purpose and of malice forethought." Nor does the Common law prescribe the same punishment for disfiguring, as for maiming.—T. J.

³ The punishment was by retaliation. *"Et come ascun appele serra de tele felonie atteint et attende le jugement, si soit le jugement tiel que il perde autriel membre come il avera tollet al pleintyfe. Et sy la pleynte soi faite de femme que avera tollet a home ses membres, en tiel cas perdra la femme la une meyn par jugement, come le membre dount ele axera trespasse."* Britton, c. 25. Fleta, B. 1. c. 40. Ll. Aelfr. 19. 40.—T. J.

Whosoever shall counterfeit [1] any coin, current by law within this Commonwealth, or any paper bills issued in the nature of money, or of certificates of loan on the credit of this Commonwealth, or of all or any of the United States of America, or any Inspector's notes for tobacco, or shall pass any such counterfeit coin, paper, bills, or notes, knowing them to be counterfeit; or, for the sake of lucre, shall diminish,[2] case, or wash any such coin, shall be condemned to hard labor six years in the public works, and shall forfeit all his lands and goods to the Commonwealth.

[3] Whosoever committeth arson, shall be condemned to hard labor five years in the public works, and shall make good the loss of the sufferers threefold.[4]

If any person shall, within this Commonwealth, or being a citizen thereof,

[1] 25. E. 3. st. 5. c. 2, 5. El. c. 11. 18. El. c. 1. 8. 9. W. 3. c. 26. 15. 16. G. 2. c. 28. 7. Ann. c. 25. By the laws of Aethelstan and Canute, this was punished by cutting off the hand. "Gif se mynetere ful wurthe slea man tha hand of, the he that ful mid worthe and sette uppon tha mynet smiththan." In English characters and words "if the minter foul [criminal] wert, slay the hand off, that he the foul [crime] with wrought, and set upon the mint-smithery." Ll. Aethelst. 14. "Et si quis praeter hanc, falsam fecerit, perdat manum quacum falsam confecit." Ll. Cnuti. 8. It had been death by the Ll. Aethelredi sub fine. By those of H. 1. "siquis cum falso denario inventus fuerit—fiat justitia mea, saltem de dextro pugno et de testiculis." Anno 1108. "Operae pretium vero est audire quam severus rex fuerit in pravos. Monetarios enim fere omnes totius Angliae fecit ementulari, et manus dextras abscindi, quia monetam furtive corruperant." Wilkins ib. et anno 1125. When the Common law became settled, it appears to have been punishable by death. "Est aliud genus criminis quod sub nomine falsi continetur, et tangit coronam domini regis, et ultimum inducit supplicium, sicut de illis qui falsam fabricant monetam, et qui de re non reproba, faciunt reprobam; sicut sunt retonsores denariorum." Bract. L. 3. c. § 2. Fleta, L. 1. c. 22. § 4. Lord Hale thinks it was deemed petty treason at common law. 1. H. P. C. 220. 224. The bringing in false money with intent to merchandize, and make payment of it, is treason, by 25. E. 3. But the best proof of the intention, is the act of passing it, and why not leave room for repentance here, as in other cases of felonies intended? 1. H. P. C. 229. —T. J.

[2] Clipping, filing, rounding, impairing, scaling, lightening, (the words in the statues) are included in "diminishing"; gilding, in the word "casing"; coloring in the word "washing"; and falsifying, or making, is "counterfeiting."—T. J.

[3] 43. L. c. 13. confined to four counties. 22. 23. Car. 2. c. 7. 9. G. 1. c. 22. 9. G, 3. c. 29. —T. J.

[4] Arson was a felony at Common law—3. Insti. 66; punished by a fine, Ll. Aethelst. 6. But Ll. Cnuti, 61. make it a "scelus inexpiable." "Hus brec and bærnet and open thyfth æberemorth and hlaford swice æfter woruld laga is botleds." Word for word, "house break and burnt, and open theft, and manifest murther, and lord-treachery, afterworld's law is bootless." Bracton says it was punished by death. "Si quis turbida seditione incendium fecerit nequiter et in felonia, vel ob inimicitias, vel praedandi causa, capitali puniatur poena vel sententia." Bract. L. 3. 27. He defines it as commissible by burning "aedes alienas.'" Ib. Britton, c. 9. "Ausi soit enquis de ceux que felonisement en temps de pees eient autre blees ou autre mesons ars, et ceux que serrount de ceo atteyntz, soient ars issint que eux soient punys par mesme cele chose dount ilz pecherent." Fleta, L. 1. c. 37. is a copy of Bracton. The Mirror c. 1. § 8. says, "Ardours sont que ardent citie, ville, maison home, maison beast, ou auters chatelx, de lour felonie en temps de pace pour haine ou vengeance." Again, c. 2. § 11. pointing out the words of the appellor "jeo dise que Sebright, &c., entiel meason ou biens mist de feu." Coke 3. Inst. 67. says, "the ancient authors extended this felony further than houses, viz., to sacks of corn, waynes or carts of coal, wood or other goods." He denies it as commissible, not only on the inset house, parcel of the mansion house, but the outset also, as barn, stable, cowhouse, sheep house, dairy house, mill house, and the like, parcel of the mansion house. But "burning of a barn, being no parcel of a mansion house, is no felony," unless there be corn or hay within it. Ib. The 22. 23. Car. 2. and 9. G. 1. are the principal statutes against arson. They extend the offence beyond the Common law.—T. J.

shall without the same, wilfully destroy,[1] or run[2] away with any sea-vessel, or goods laden on board thereof, or plunder or pilfer any wreck, he shall be condemned to hard labor five years in the public works, and shall make good the loss of the sufferers threefold.

Whosoever committeth Robbery,[3] shall be condemned to hard labor four years in the public works, and shall make double reparation to the persons injured.

Whatsoever act, if committed on any Mansion house, would be deemed Burglary,[4] shall be Burglary, if committed on any other house; and he, who is guilty of Burglary, shall be condemned to hard labor four years in the public works, and shall make double reparation to the persons injured.

Whatsoever act, if committed in the night time, shall constitute the crime of Burglary, shall, if committed in the day, be deemed House-breaking;[5]

---

[1] Ann. st. 2. c. 9. 12. Ann. c. 18. 4. G. 1. c. 12. 26. G. 2. c. 19.—T. J.

[2] 11. 12. W. 3. c. 7.—T. J.

[3] Robbery was a felony at Common law. 3 Inst. 68. "*Scelus inexpiable*," by the Ll. Cnuti. 61. [See before in Arson.] It was punished with death. Britt. c. 15, "*de robbours et de larouns et de semblables mesfesours, soit ausi ententivement enquis—et tauntost soient ceux robbours juges a la mort.*" Fleta says, "*si quis convictus fuerit de bonis viri robbatis vel asportatis ad sectam regis judicium capitale subibit.*" L. 1. c. 39. See also Bract. L. 3. c. 32. § 1.—T. J.

[4] Burglary was felony at the Common law. 3 Inst. 63. It was not distinguished by ancient authors, except the Mirror, from simple House-breaking, ib. 65. Burglary and House-breaking were called "*Hamsockne diximus etiam de pacis violatione et de immunitatibus domus, si quis hoc in posterum fecerit ut perdat omne quod habet, et sit in regis arbitrio utrum vitam habeat. Eac we quædon be mundbryce and be ham socnum, sethe hit ofer this do thæt he dolie ealles thæes the age, and sy on Cyninges dome hwæther he life age; and we quoth of mound-breach, and of home-seeking he who it after this do, that he dole all that he owe [owns], and is in king's doom whether he life owes [owns.]*" Ll. Eadmundi. c. 6. and see Ll. Cnuti. 61. "hus brec," in notes on Arson. ante. A Burglar was also called a Burgessor. "*Et soit enquis de Burgessours et sunt tenus Burgessours trestous ceux que* feloniement *en temps de pees debrusont esglises ou auter mesons, ou murs ou portes de nos cytes, ou de nos Burghes.*" Britt. c. 10. "*Burglaria est nocturna diruptio habitaculi alicujus, vel ecclesiae, etiam murorum, partarumve civitatis aut burgi, ad feloniam aliquam perpetrandam.* Noctanter *dico, recentiores secutus; veteres enim hoc non adjungunt.* Spelm. gloss. verb. *Burglaria.*" It was punished with death. Ib. citn. from the office of a Coronet. It may be committed in the outset houses, as well as inset. 3 Inst. 65. though not under the same roof or contiguous, provided they be within the Curtilage or Homestall. 4 Bl. 225. As by the Common law, all felonies were clergiable, the stat. 23 H. 8. c. 1. 5. E. 6. c. 9. and 18 El. c. 7. first distinguished them, by taking the clerical privilege of impunity from the principals, and 3. 4. W. M. c. 9. from accessories before the fact. No *statute* defines what Burglary is. The 12 Ann. c. 7. decides the doubt whether, where breaking is subsequent to entry, it is Burglary. Bacon's Elements had affirmed, and 1 H. P. C. 554. had denied it. Our bill must distinguish them by different degrees of punishment.—T. J.

[5] At the Common law, the offence of Housebreaking was not distinguished from Burglary, and neither of them from any other larceny. The statutes at first took away clergy from Burglary, which made a leading distinction between the two offences. Latter statutes, however, have taken clergy from so many cases of Housebreaking, as nearly to bring the offences together again. These are 23 H. 8. c. 1. 1. E. 6. c. 12. 5 and 6 E. 6. c. 9. 3 and 4 W. M. c. 9. 39 El. c. 15. 10 and 11 W. 3 c. 23. 12 Ann. c. 7. See Barr. 428. 4 Bl. 240. The circumstances which in these statutes characterize the offence, seem to have been occasional and unsystematical. The houses on which Burglary may be committed, and the circumstances which constitute that crime being ascertained, it will be better to define Housebreaking by the same subjects and circumstances, and let the crimes be distinguished only by the hour at which they are committed, and the degree of punishment.—T. J.

and whosoever is guilty thereof, shall be condemned to hard labor three years in the public works, and shall make reparation to the persons injured.

Whosoever shall be guilty of Horse-stealing,[1] shall be condemned to hard labor three years in the public works, and shall make reparation to the person injured.

Grand Larceny[2] shall be where the goods stolen are of the value of five dollars; and whosoever shall be guilty thereof, shall be forthwith put in the pillory for one half hour, shall be condemned to hard labor[3] two years in the public works, and shall make reparation to the person injured.

Petty Larceny shall be, where the goods stolen are of less value than five dollars; and whosoever shall be guilty thereof, shall be forthwith put in the pillory for a quarter of an hour, shall be condemned to hard labor one year in the public works, and shall make reparation to the person injured.

Robbery[4] or larceny of bonds, bills obligatory, bills of exchange, or promissory notes for the payment of money or tobacco, lottery tickets, paper bills issued in the nature of money, or of certificates of loan on the credit of this Commonwealth, or of all or any of the United States of America, or In-

---

[1] The offence of Horse-stealing seems properly distinguishable from other larcenies, here, where these animals generally run at large, the temptation being so great and frequent, and the facility of commission so remarkable. See 1 E. 6. c. 12. 23 E. 6. c. 33. 31 El. c. 12.—T. J.

[2] The distinction between grand and petty larceny is very ancient. At first 8d. was the sum which constituted grand larceny. Ll. Aethelst. c. 1. *"Ne parcatur ulli furi, qui furtum manutenens captus sit, supra 12. annos nato, et supra 8. denarios."* Afterwards, in the same king's reign it was raised to 12d. *"non parcatur alicui furi ultra 12 denarios, et ultra 12 annos nato—ut occidemus illum et capiamus omne quod possidet, et imprimis sumamus rei furto ablatae pretium ab haerede, ac dividatur postea reliquum in duas partes, una pars uxori, si munda, et facinoris conscia non sit; et residuum in duo, dimidium capiat rex, dimidium societas."* Ll. Aethelst. Wilkins, p. 65.—T. J.

[3] Ll. Inae. c. 7. *"Si quis furetur ita ut uxor ejus et infans ipsius nesciant, solvat 60. solidos poenae loco. Si autem furetur testantibus omnibus haeredibus suis, abeant omnes in servitutem."* Ina was king of the West-Saxons, and began to reign A. C. 688. After the union of the Heptarchy, i. e. temp. Aethelst. inter 924 and 940, we find it punishable with death as above. So it was inter 1017 and 1035, i. e. temp. Cnuti. Ll. Cnuti 61. cited in notes on Arson. In the time of William the conqueror, it seems to have been made punishable by fine only. Ll. Gul. conq. apud Wilk. p. 218, 220. This commutation, however, was taken away by Ll. H. 1. anno 1108. *"Si quis in furto vel latrocinio deprehensus fuisset, suspenderetur; sublata wirgildorum, id est. pecuniarae redemptionis lege."* Larceny is the felonious taking and carrying away of the personal goods of another. 1. As to the taking, the 3. 4. W. M. c. 9 § 5. is not additional to the Common law, but declaratory of it; because where only the care or use, and not the possession, of things is delivered, to take them was larceny at the Common law. The 33. H. 6. c. 1. and 21 H. 8. c. 7. indeed, have added to the Common law, by making it larceny in a servant to convert things of his master's. But quære, if they should be imitated more than as to other breaches of trust in general. 2. As to the subject of larceny, 4 G. 2. c. 32. 6 G. 3. c. 36. 48. 43. El. c. 7. 15. Car. 2. 3. 2. 23. G. 2. c. 26. 31. G. 2. c. 35. 9. G. 3. c. 41. 25. G. 2. c. 10. have extended larceny to things of various sorts either real, or fixed to the reality. But the enumeration is unsystematical, and in this country, where the produce of the earth is so spontaneous, as to have rendered things of this kind scarcely a breach of civility or good manners, in the eyes of the people, quære, if it would not too much enlarge the field of Criminal law? The same may be questioned of 9 G. 1. c. 22. 13 Car. 2. c. 10. 10 G. 2. c. 32. 5 G. 3. c. 14. 22 and 23 Car. 2. c. 25. 37 E. 3. c. 19. making it felony to steal animals feræ naturæ.—T. J.

[4] 2 G. 2. c. 25 § 3. 7 G. 3. c. 50.—T. J.

spectors' notes for tobacco, shall be punished in the same manner as robbery or larceny of the money or tobacco due on, or represented by such papers.

Buyers [1] and receivers of goods taken by way of robbery or larceny, knowing them to have been so taken, shall be deemed accessaries to such robbery or larceny after the fact.

Prison-breakers,[2] also, shall be deemed accessaries after the fact, to traitors or felons whom they enlarge from prison.[3]

All attempts to delude the people, or to abuse their understanding by exercise of the pretended arts of witchcraft, conjuration, enchantment, or sorcery, or by pretended prophecies, shall be punished by ducking and whipping, at the discretion of a jury, not exceeding fifteen stripes.[4]

If the principal offenders be fled,[5] or secreted from justice, in any case not touching life or member, the accessaries may, notwithstanding, be prosecuted as if their principal were convicted.[6]

[1] 3. 4. W. M. c. 9. § 4. 5 Ann. c. 31 § 5. 4 G. 1. c. 11. § 1.—T. J.

[2] 1 E. 2.—T. J.

[3] Breach of prison at the Common law was capital, without regard to the crime for which the party was committed. *"Cum pro criminis qualitate in carcerem recepti fuerint, conspiraverint (ut ruptis vinculis aut fracto carcere) evadant, amplius (quam causa pro qua recepti sunt exposeit) puniendi sunt, videlicet ultimo supplicio, quamvis ex eo crimine innocentes inveniantur, propter quod inducti sunt in carcerem et imparcati."* Bracton L. 3. c. 9. § 4. Britt. c. 11. Fleta, L. 1. c. 26. § 4. Yet in the Y. B. Hill. 1. H. 7. 2. Hussey says, that by the opinion of Billing and Choke, and all the justices, it was a felony in strangers only, but not in the prisoner himself. S. C. Fitz. Abr. Coron. 48. They are principal felons, not accessaries. *ib.* Whether it was felony in the prisoner at Common law, is doubted. Stam. P. C. 30. b. The Mirror c. 5. § 1, says, *"abusion est a tener escape de prisoner, ou de bruserie del gaole pur peche mortell, car cel usage nest garrant per nul ley, ne in nul part est use forsque in cest realme, et en France, eins [mais] est leu garrantie de ceo faire per la ley de nature."* 2 Inst. 589. The stat. 1. E. 2. *de fraugentibus prisonam,* restrained the judgment of life and limb for prison breaking, to cases where the offence of the prisoner required such judgment.

It is not only vain, but wicked, in a legislator to frame laws in opposition to the laws of nature, and to arm them with the terrors of death. This is truly creating crimes in order to punish them. The law of nature impels everyone to escape from confinement; it should not, therefore, be subjected to punishment. Let the legislator restrain his criminal by walls, not by parchment. As to strangers breaking prison to enlarge an offender, they should, and may be fairly considered as accessaries after the fact. This bill says nothing of the prisoner releasing himself by breach of jail, he will have the benefit of the first section of the bill, which repeals the judgment of life and death at the common law.—T. J.

[4] Gif wiccan owwe wigleras nansworan, owwe morthwyrhtan owwe fule afylede æbere horcwenan ahwhar on lande wurthan agytene, thonne fyrsie man of earde and clænsie tha theode, owwe on earde forfare hi mid ealle, buton hi geswican and the deoper gebetan: if witches, or weirds, man-swearers, or murther-wroughters, or foul, defiled, open whore-queens, aywhere in the land were gotten, then force them off earth, and cleanse the nation, or in earth forth-fare them withal, buton they beseech, and deeply better. Ll. Ed. et Guthr. c. 11. *"Sagae, mulieres barbara, factitantes sacrificia, aut pestiferi, si cui mortem intulerint, neque id inficiari poterint, capitis poena esto."* Ll. Aethelst. c. 6. apud Lambard. Ll. Aelfr. 30. Ll. Cnuti. c. 4. *"Mesme cel jugement (d'etrears) eyent sorcers, et sorceresses, &c. ut supra. Fleta ut et ubi supra."* 3. Inst. 44. Trial of witches before Hale in 1664. The statutes 33 H. 8. c. 8. 5. El. c. 16 and 1. Jac. 1. c. 12. seem to be only in confirmation of the Common law. 9. G. 2. c. 25. punishes them with pillory, and a year's imprisonment. 3 E. 6. c. 15. 5 El. c. 15. punish fond, fantastical and false prophecies, by fine and imprisonment.—T. J.

[5] 1 Ann. c. 9. § 2.—T. J.

[6] As every treason includes within it a misprision of treason, so every felony includes a mis-

If any offender stand mute of obstinacy,[1] or challenge peremptorily more of the jurors than by law he may, being first warned of the consequence thereof, the court shall proceed at if he had confessed the charge.[2]

Pardon and Privilege of clergy, shall henceforth be abolished, that none may be induced to injure through hope of impunity. But if the verdict be against the defendant, and the court before whom the offence is heard and determined, shall doubt that it may be untrue for defect of testimony, or other cause, they may direct a new trial to be had.[3]

No attainder shall work corruption of blood in any case.

In all cases of forfeiture, the widow's dower shall be saved to her, during her title thereto; after which it shall be disposed of as if no such saving had been.

---

prision, or misdemeanor. 1 Hale P. C. 652. 708. *"Licet fuerit felonia, tamen in eo continetur misprisio."* 2 R. 3 10. Both principal and accessary, therefore, may be proceeded against in any case, either for felony or misprision, at the Common law. Capital cases not being mentioned here, accessaries to them will of course be triable for misprisions, if the offender flies.—T. J.

[1] E. 1. c. 12.—T. J.

[2] Whether the judgment of penance lay at Common law. See 2 Inst. 178. 2 H. P. C. 321. 4 Bl. 322. It was given on standing mute; but on challenging more than the legal number, whether that sentence, or sentence of death is to be given, seems doubtful. 2 H. P. C. 316. Quære, whether it would not be better to consider the supernumerary challenge as merely void, and to proceed in the trial? Quære too, in case of silence?—T. J.

[3] *"Cum Clericus sic de crimine convictus degradetur non sequitur alia poena pro uno delicto, vel pluribus ante degradationem perpetratis. Satis enim sufficit ei pro poena degradatio, quae est magna capitis diminutio, nisi forte convictus fuerit de apostatia, quia hinc primo degradetur, et postea per manum laicalem comburetur, secundum quod accidit in concilio Oxoni celebrato a bonae memoriae S. Cantuanen. Archiepiscopo de quodam diacono, qui se apostatavit pro quadam Judaea; qui cum esset per episcopum degradatus, statim fuit igni traditus per manum laicalem."* Bract. L. 3. c. 9. § 2. *"Et mesme cel jugement* (i.e., *qui ils soient ars) eyent sorcers et sorceresses, et sodomites et mescreauntz apertement atteyntz."* Britt. c. 9. *"Christiani autem Apostatae, sortilegii, et hujusmodi detractari debent et comburi."* Fleta, L. 1. c. 37. § 2. see 3. Inst. 39. 12. Rep. 92. 1. H. P. C. 393. The extent of the clerical privilege at the Common law. 1. As to the crimes, seems very obscure and uncertain. It extended to no case where the judgment was not of life, or limb. Note in 2. H. P. C. 326. This therefore excluded it in trespass, petty larceny, or killing *se defendendo*. In high treason against the person of the King, it seems not to have been allowed. Note 1. H. P. C. 185. Treasons, therefore, not against the King's person immediately, petty treasons and felonies, seem to have been the cases where it was allowed; and even of those, not for *insidiatio varium, depopulation agrorum*, or *combustio domorum*. The statute de Clero, 25. E. 3. st. 3. c. 4. settled the law on this head. 2. As to the persons, it extended to all clerks, always, and *toties quoties*. 2. H. P. C. 374. To nuns also. Fitz. Abr. Corone. 461. 22. E. 3. The clerical habit and tonsure were considered as evidence of the person being clerical. 26. Assiz. 19. 20. E. 2. Fitz. Corone. 233. By the 9. E. 4. 28. b. 34. H. N. 49 a. b. simple reading became the evidence. This extended impunity to a great number of laymen, and *toties quoties*. The stat. 4. H. 7. c. 13. directed that real clerks should, upon a second arraignment, produce their orders, and all others to be burnt in the hand with M. or T. on the first allowance of clergy, and not to be admitted to it a second time. A heretic, Jew, or Turk (as being incapable of orders) could not have clergy. 11. Co. Rep. 29 b. But a Greek, or other alien, reading in a book of his own country, might. Bro. Clergie. 20. So a blind man, if he could speak Latin. Ib. 21. qu. 11. Rep. 29. b. The orders entitling the party, were bishops, priests, deacons and subdeacons, the inferior being reckoned *Clerici in minoribus*. 2. H. P. C. 373. Quære, however, if this distinction is not founded on the stat. 23. H. 8. c. 1. 25. H. 8. c. 32. By merely dropping all the statutes, it should seem that none but clerks would be entitled to this privilege, and that they would, *toties quoties*.—T. J.

The aid of Counsel,[1] and examination of their witnesses on oath, shall be allowed to defendants in criminal prosecutions.

Slaves guilty of any offense[2] punishable in others by labor in the public works, shall be transported to such parts in the West Indies, South America, or Africa, as the Governor shall direct, there to be continued in slavery.

A BILL FOR THE MORE GENERAL DIFFUSION OF KNOWLEDGE

1779

SECTION I. Whereas it appeareth that however certain forms of government are better calculated than others to protect individuals in the free exercise of their natural rights, and are at the same time themselves better guarded against degeneracy, yet experience hath shewn, that even under the best forms, those entrusted with power have, in time, and by slow operations, perverted it into tyranny; and it is believed that the most effectual means of preventing this would be, to illuminate, as far as practicable, the minds of the people at large, and more especially to give them knowledge of those facts, which history exhibiteth, that, possessed thereby of the experience of other ages and countries, they may be enabled to know ambition under all its shapes, and prompt to exert their natural powers to defeat its purposes; And whereas it is generally true that that people will be happiest whose laws are best, and are best administered, and that laws will be wisely formed, and honestly administered, in proportion as those who form and administer them are wise and honest; whence it becomes expedient for promoting the publick happiness that those persons, whom nature hath endowed with genius and virtue, should be rendered by liberal education worthy to receive, and able to guard the sacred deposit of the rights and liberties of their fellow citizens, and that they should be called to that charge without regard to wealth, birth or other accidental condition or circumstance; but the indigence of the greater number disabling them from so educating, at their own expence, those of their children whom nature hath fitly formed and disposed to become useful instruments for the public, it is better that such should be sought for and educated at the common expence of all, than that the happiness of all should be confined to the weak or wicked:

SECTION II. Be it therefore enacted by the General Assembly, that in every

---

[1] I. Ann. c. 9.—T. J.

[2] Manslaughter, counterfeiting, arson, asportation of vessels, robbery, burglary, house-breaking, horse-stealing, larceny.—T. J.

county within this commonwealth, there shall be chosen annually, by the electors qualified to vote for Delegates, three of the most honest and able men of their county, to be called the Alderman of the county; and that the election of the said Aldermen shall be held at the same time and place, before the same persons, and notified and conducted in the same manner as by law is directed, for the annual election of Delegates for the county.

SECTION III. The person before whom such election is holden shall certify to the court of the said county the names of the Aldermen chosen, in order that the same may be entered of record, and shall give notice of their election to the said Aldermen within a fortnight after such election.

SECTION IV. The said Aldermen on the first Monday in October, if it be fair, and if not, then on the next fair day, excluding Sunday, shall meet at the court-house of their county, and proceed to divide their said county into hundreds, bounding the same by water courses, mountains, or limits, to be run and marked, if they think necessary, by the county surveyor, and at the county expence, regulating the size of the said hundreds, according to the best of their discretion, so as that they may contain a convenient number of children to make up a school, and be of such convenient size that all the children within each hundred may daily attend the school to be established therein, and distinguishing each hundred by a particular name; which division, with the names of the several hundreds, shall be returned to the court of the county and be entered of record, and shall remain unaltered until the increase or decrease of inhabitants shall render an alteration necessary, if the opinion of any succeeding Alderman, and also in the opinion of the court of the county.

SECTION V. The electors aforesaid residing within every hundred shall meet on the third Monday in October after the first election of Aldermen, at such place. within their hundred, as the said Aldermen shall direct, notice thereof being previously given to them by such person residing within the hundred as the said Aldermen shall require who is hereby enjoined to obey such requisition, on pain of being punished by amercement and imprisonment. The electors being so assembled shall choose the most convenient place within their hundred for building a school-house. If two or more places, having a greater number of votes than any others, shall yet be equal between themselves, the Aldermen, or such of them as are not of the same hundred, on information thereof, shall decide between them. The said Aldermen shall forthwith proceed to have a school-house built at the said place, and shall see that the same shall be kept in repair, and, when necessary, that it be rebuilt; but whenever they shall think necessary that it be rebuilt, they shall give notice as before directed, to the electors of the hundred to meet at the said school-house on such a day as they shall appoint, to determine by vote, in the manner before directed, whether it shall be rebuilt at the same, or what other place in the hundred.

SECTION VI. At every of those schools shall be taught reading, writing, and common arithmetick, and the books which shall be used therein for instructing the children to read shall be such as will at the same time make them acquainted with Græcian, Roman, English, and American history. At these schools all the free children, male and female, resident within the respective hundred, shall be intitled to receive tuition gratis, for the term of three years, and as much longer, at their private expence, as their parents, guardians, or friends shall think proper.

SECTION VII. Over every ten of these schools (or such other number nearest thereto, as the number of hundreds in the county will admit, without fractional divisions) an overseer shall be appointed annually by the aldermen at their first meeting, eminent for his learning, integrity, and fidelity to the commonwealth, whose business and duty it shall be, from time to time, to appoint a teacher to each school, who shall give assurance of fidelity to the commonwealth, and to remove him as he shall see cause; to visit every school once in every half year at the least; to examine the scholars; see that any general plan of reading and instruction recommended by the visitors of William and Mary College shall be observed; and to superintend the conduct of the teacher in everything relative to his school.

SECTION VIII. Every teacher shall receive a salary of ———— by the year, which, with the expences of building and repairing the school-houses, shall be provided in such manner as other county expences are by law directed to be provided and shall also have his diet, lodging, and washing found him, to be levied in like manner, save only that such levy shall be on the inhabitants of each hundred for the board of their own teacher only.

SECTION IX. And in order that grammer schools may be rendered convenient to the youth in every part of the commonwealth, be it therefore enacted, that on the first Monday in November, after the first appointment of overseers for the hundred schools, if fair, and if not, then on the next fair day, excluding Sunday, after the hour of one in the afternoon, the said overseers appointed for the schools in the counties of Princess Ann, Norfolk, Nansemond and Isle-of-Wight, shall meet at Nansemond court-house; those for the counties of Southampton, Sussex, Surry and Prince George, shall meet at Sussex court-house; those for the counties of Brunswick, Mecklenburg and Lunenburg, shall meet at Lunenburg court-house; those for the counties of Dinwiddie, Amelia and Chesterfield, shall meet at Chesterfield court-house; those for the counties of Powhatan, Cumberland, Goochland, Henrico and Hanover, shall meet at Henrico court-house; those for the counties of Prince Edward, Charlotte and Halifax, shall meet at Charlotte court-house; those for the counties of Henry, Pittsylvania and Bedford, shall meet at Pittsylvania court-house; those for the counties of Buckingham, Amherst, Albemarle and Fluvanna, shall meet at Albemarle court-house; those for the counties of Botetourt, Rockbridge, Montgomery, Washington and Kentucky, shall meet at Botetourt court-house; those for the counties of Augusta, Rockingham and Greenbriar, shall meet at Augusta court-house; those for the counties of Accomack and Northampton, shall meet at Accomack court-house; those for the counties of Elizabeth City, Warwick, York, Gloucester, James City, Charles City and New-Kent, shall meet at James City court-house; those for the counties of Middlesex, Essex, King and Queen, King William and Caroline, shall meet at King and Queen court-house; those for the counties of Lancaster, Northumberland, Richmond and Westmoreland, shall meet at Richmond court-house; those for the counties of King George, Stafford, Spotsylvania, Prince William and Fairfax, shall meet at Spotsylvania court-house; those for the counties of Loudoun and Fauquier, shall meet at Loudoun court-house; those for the countiess of Culpeper, Orange and Louisa, shall meet at Orange court-house; those for the county of Shenandoah and Frederick, shall meet at Frederick court-house; those for the counties of Hampshire and Berkeley, shall meet at Berkeley court-house; and those for the counties of Yohogania, Monongalia, and Ohio, shall meet at the Monongalia court-house; and shall fix on such place in some one of the counties in their district as shall be most proper for situating a grammer school-house, endeavoring that the situation be as central as may be to the inhabitants of the said counties, that it be furnished with good water, convenient to plentiful supplies of provision and fuel, and more than all things that it be healthy. And if a majority of the overseers present should not concur in their choice of any one place proposed, the method of determining shall be as follows: If two places only were proposed, and the votes be divided, they shall decide between them by fair and equal lot; if more than two places were proposed, the question shall be put on those two which on the first division had the greater number of votes; or if no two places had a greater number of votes than the others, then it shall be decided by fair and equal lot (unless it can be agreed by a majority of votes) which of the places having equal numbers shall be thrown out of the competition, so that the question shall be put on the remaining two, and if on this ultimate question the votes shall be equally divided, it shall then be decided finally by lot.

SECTION X. The said overseers having determined the place at which the grammer school for their district shall be built, shall forthwith (unless they can otherwise agree with the proprietors of the circumjacent lands as to location and price) make application to the clerk of the county in which the said house is to be situated, who shall thereupon issue a writ, in the nature of a writ of ad quod damnum, directed to the sheriff of the said county commanding him to summon and impannel twelve fit persons to meet at the place, so destined for the grammer school-house, on a certain day, to be named in the said writ, not less than five, nor more than ten, days from the date thereof; and also to give notice of the same to the proprietors and tenants of the lands to be viewed if they be found within the county, and if not, then to their agents therein if any they have. Which freeholders shall be charged by the said sheriff impartially, and to the best of their skill and judgment to view the lands round about the said place and to locate and circumscribe, by certain meets and bounds, one hundred acres thereof, having regard therein principally to the benefit and convenience of the said school, but respecting in some measure also the convenience of the said proprietors, and to value and appraise the same in so many several and distinct parcels as shall be owned or held by several and distinct owners or tenants, and according to their respective interests and estates therein. And after such location and appraisement so made, the said sheriff shall forthwith return the same under the hands and seals of the said jurors, together with the writ, to the clerk's office of the said county and the right and property of the said proprietors and tenants in the said lands so circumscribed shall be immediately devested and be transferred to the commonwealth for the use of the said grammer school, in full and absolute dominion, any want of consent or disability to consent in the said owners or tenants notwithstanding. But it shall not be lawful for the said overseers so to situate the grammer school-house, nor to the said jurors so to locate the said lands, as to include the mansion-house of the proprietor of the lands, nor the offices, curtilage, or garden, thereunto immediately belonging.

SECTION XI. The said overseers shall forthwith proceed to have a house of brick or stone, for the said grammer school, with necessary offices, built on the said lands, which grammer school-house shall contain a room for the school, a hall to dine in, four rooms for a master and usher, and ten or twelve lodging rooms for the scholars.

SECTION XII. To each of the said grammer schools shall be allowed out of the public treasury, the sum of   pounds, out of which shall be paid by the Treasurer, on warrant from the Auditors, to the proprietors or tenants of the lands located, the value of their several interests as fixed by the jury, and the balance thereof shall be delivered to the said overseers to defray the expense of the said buildings.

SECTION XIII. In either of these grammer schools shall be taught the Latin and Greek languages, English Grammer, geography, and the higher part of numerical arithmetick, to wit, vulgar and decimal fractions, and the extrication of the square and cube roots.

SECTION XIV. A visiter from each county constituting the district shall be appointed, by the overseers, for the county, in the month of October annually, either from their own body or from their county at large, which visiters, or the greater part of them, meeting together at the said grammer school on the first Monday in November, if fair, and if not, then on the next fair day, excluding Sunday, shall have power to choose their own Rector, who shall call and preside at future meetings, to employ from time to time a master, and if necessary, an usher, for the said school, to remove them at their will, and to settle the price of tuition to be paid by the scholars. They shall also visit the school twice in every year at the least, either together or separately at their discretion, examine the scholars, and see that any general plan of instruction recommended by the visiters, of William and Mary College shall be observed. The said masters and ushers, before they enter on the execution of their office, shall give assurance of fidelity to the commonwealth.

SECTION XV. A steward shall be employed, and removed at will by the master, on such wages as the visiters shall direct; which steward shall see to the procuring provisions, fuel, servants for cooking, waiting, house cleaning, washing, mending, and gardening on the most reasonable terms; the expence of which, together with the steward's wages, shall be divided equally among all the scholars boarding either on the public or private expence. And the part of those who are on private expence, and also the price of their tuitions due to the master or usher, shall be paid quarterly by the respective scholars, their parents, or guardians, and shall be recoverable, if withheld, together with costs, on motion in any Court of Record, ten days notice thereof being previously given to the party, and a jury impannelled to try the issue joined, or enquire of the damages. The said steward shall also, under the direction of the visiters, see that the houses be kept in repair, and necessary enclosures be made and repaired, the accounts for which, shall, from time to time, be submitted to the Auditors, and on their warrant paid by the Treasurer.

SECTION XVI. Every overseer of the hundred schools shall, in the month of September annually, after the most diligent and impartial examination and inquiry, appoint from among the boys who shall have been two years at the least at some one of the schools under his superintendance, and whose parents are too poor to give them farther education, some one of the best and most promising genius and disposition, to proceed to the grammer school of his district; which appointment shall be made in the court-house of the county, and on the court day for that month if fair, and if not, then on the next fair day, excluding Sunday, in the presence of the Aldermen, or two of them at the least, assembled on the bench for that purpose, the said overseer being previously sworn by them to make such appointment, without favor or affection, according to the best of his skill and judgment, and being interrogated by the said Aldermen, either on their own motion, or on suggestions from their parents, guardians, friends, or teachers of the children, competitors for such appointment; which teachers the parents shall attend for the information of the Aldermen. On which interrogatories the said Aldermen, if they be not satisfied with the appointment proposed, shall have right to negative it; whereupon the said visiter may proceed to make a new appointment, and the said Aldermen again to interrogate and negative, and so toties quoties until an appointment be approved.

SECTION XVII. Every boy so appointed shall be authorized to proceed to the grammer school of his district, there to be educated and boarded during such time as is hereafter limited; and his quota of the expences of the house together with a compensation to the master or usher for his tuition, at the rate of twenty dollars by the year, shall be paid by the Treasurer quarterly on warrant from the Auditors.

SECTION XVIII. A visitation shall be held, for the purpose of probation, annually at the said grammer school on the last Monday in September, if fair, and if not, then on the next fair day, excluding Sunday, at which one third of the boys sent thither by appointment of the said overseers, and who shall have been there one year only, shall be discontinued as public foundationers, being those who, on the most diligent examination and enquiry, shall be thought to be the least promising genius and disposition; and of those who shall have been there two years, all shall be discontinued save one only the best in genius and disposition, who shall be at liberty to continue there four years longer on the public foundation, and shall thence forward be deemed a senior.

SECTION XIX. The visiters for the districts which, or any part of which, be southward and westward of James river, as known by that name, or by the names of Fluvanna and Jackson's river, in every other year, to wit, at the probation meetings held in the years, distinguished in the Christian computation by odd numbers, and the visiters for all the other districts at their said meetings to be held in those years, distinguished by even numbers, after diligent examination and enquiry as before directed, shall chuse one among the said seniors, of the best learning and most hopeful genius and disposition, who shall be authorized by them to proceed to William and Mary College; there to be educated, boarded, and clothed, three years; the expence of which annually shall be paid by the Treasurer on warrant from the Auditors.

A BILL FOR ESTABLISHING A PUBLIC LIBRARY

1779

SECTION I. Be it enacted by the General Assembly, that on the first day of January, in every year, there shall be paid out of the treasury the sum of two thousand pound, to be laid out in such books and maps as may be proper to be preserved in a public library, and in defraying the expences necessary for the care and preservation thereof; which library shall be established at the town of Richmond.

SECTION II. The two houses of Assembly shall appoint three persons of learning and attention to literary matters, to be visiters of the said library, and shall remove them, and fill any vacancies, from time to time, as they shall think fit; which visiters shall have power to receive the annual sum before-mentioned, and therewith to procure such books and maps as aforesaid, and shall superintend the preservation thereof. Whensoever a keeper shall be found necessary they shall appoint such keeper, from time to time, at their will, on such annual salary (not exceeding one hundred pounds) as they shall think reasonable.

SECTION III. If during the time of war the importation of books and maps shall be hazardous, or if the rate of exchange between this commonwealth and any state from which such articles are wanted, shall from any cause be such that they cannot be imported to such advantage as may be hoped at a future day, the visiters shall place the annual sums, as they become due, in the public loan office, if any there be, for the benefit of interest, or otherwise shall suffer them to remain in the treasury until fit occasions shall occur of employing them.

SECTION IV. It shall not be lawful for the said keeper, or the visiters themselves, or any other person to remove any book or map out of the said library, unless it be for the necessary repair thereof; but the same be made useful by indulging the researches of the learned and curious, within the said library, without fee or reward, and under such rules for preserving them safe and in good order and condition as the visiters shall constitute.

SECTION V. The visiters shall annually settle their accounts with the Auditors and leave with them the vouchers for the expenditure of the monies put into their hands.

A BILL FOR ESTABLISHING RELIGIOUS FREEDOM [1]

1779

SECTION I. Well aware that the opinions and belief of men depend on their own will, but follow involuntarily the evidence proposed to their minds; that Almighty God hath created the mind free, and manifested his supreme will that free it shall remain by making it altogether insusceptible of restraint; that all attempts to influence it by temporal punishments, or burthens, or by civil incapacitations, tend only to beget habits of hypocrisy and meanness, and are a departure from the plan of the holy author of our religion, who being lord both of body and mind, yet choose not to propagate it by coercions on either, as was in his Almighty power to do, but to exalt it by its influence on reason alone; that the impious presumption of legislature and ruler, civil as well as ecclesiastical, who, being themselves but fallible and uninspired men, have assumed dominion over the faith of others, setting up their own opinions and modes of thinking as the only true and infallible, and as such endeavoring to impose them on others, hath established and maintained false religions over the greatest part of the world and through all time: That to compel a man to furnish contributions of money for the propagation of opinions which he disbelieves and abhors, is sinful and tyrannical; that even the forcing him to support this or that teacher of his own religious persuasion, is depriving him of the comfortable liberty of giving his contributions to the particular pastor whose morals he would make his pattern, and whose powers he feels most persuasive to righteousness; and is withdrawing from the ministry those temporary rewards, which proceeding from an approbation of their personal conduct, are an additional incitement to earnest and unremitting labours for the instruction of mankind; that our civil rights have no dependance on our religious opinions, any more than our opinions in physics or geometry; and therefore the proscribing any citizen as unworthy the public confidence by laying upon him an incapacity of being called to offices of trust or emolument, unless he profess or renounce this or that religious opinion, is depriving him injudiciously of those privileges and advantages to which, in common with his fellow-citizens, he has a natural right; that it tends also to corrupt the principles of that very religion it is meant to encourage, by bribing with a monopoly of worldly honours and emoluments, those who will externally profess and conform to it; that though indeed these are criminals who do not withstand such

---

[1] To Jefferson this bill ranked with the Declaration of Independence as his greatest achievement, and prior to his death he asked that it be noted on his tombstone that he was its author.

temptation, yet neither are those innocent who lay the bait in their way; that the opinions of men are not the object of civil government, nor under its jurisdiction; that to suffer the civil magistrate to intrude his powers into the field of opinion and to restrain the profession or propagation of principles on supposition of their ill tendency is a dangerous fallacy, which at once destroys all religious liberty, because he being of course judge of that tendency will make his opinions the rule of judgment, and approve or condemn the sentiments of others only as they shall square with or suffer from his own; that it is time enough for the rightful purposes of civil government for its officers to interfere when principles break out into overt acts against peace and good order; and finally, that truth is great and will prevail if left to herself; that she is the proper and sufficient antagonist to error, and has nothing to fear from the conflict unless by human interposition disarmed of her natural weapons, free argument and debate; errors ceasing to be dangerous when it is permitted freely to contradict them.

SECTION II. We the General Assembly of Virginia do enact that no man shall be compelled to frequent or support any religious worship, place, or ministry whatsoever, nor shall be enforced, restrained, molested, or burthened in his body or goods, or shall otherwise suffer, on account of his religious opinions or belief; but that all men shall be free to profess, and by argument to maintain, their opinions in matters of religion, and that the same shall in no wise diminish, enlarge, or affect their civil capacities.

SECTION III. And though we well know that this Assembly, elected by the people for their ordinary purposes of legislation only, have no power to restrain the acts of succeeding Assemblies, constituted with powers equal to our own, and that therefore to declare this act to be irrevocable would be of no effect in law; yet we are free to declare, and do declare, that the rights hereby asserted are of the natural rights of mankind, and that if any act shall be hereafter passed to repeal the present or to narrow its operations, such act will be an infringement of natural right.

NOTES on the ſtate of VIRGINIA;

written in the year 1781, ſomewhat corrected and enlarged in the winter of 1782,
for the uſe of a Foreigner of diſtinction, in
anſwer to certain queries propoſed by him
reſpecting

MDCCLXXXII.

TITLE PAGE, ORIGINAL EDITION

NOTES ON THE STATE OF VIRGINIA [1]

1781-1785

QUERY I

An exact description of the limits and boundaries of the State of Virginia

Virginia is bounded on the east by the Atlantic; on the north by a line of latitude crossing the eastern shore through Watkin's Point, being about 37° 57′ north latitude; from thence by a straight line to Cinquac, near the mouth of Potomac; thence by the Potomac, which is common to Virginia and Maryland, to the first fountain of its northern branch; thence by a meridian line, passing through that fountain till it intersects a line running east and west, in latitude 39° 43′ 42.4″ which divides Maryland from Pennsylvania, and which was marked by Messrs. Mason and Dixon; thence by that line, and a continuation of it westwardly to the completion of five degrees of longitude from the eastern boundary of Pennsylvania, in the same latitude, and thence by a meridian line to the Ohio; on the west by the Ohio and Mississippi, to latitude 36° 30′ north, and on the south by the line of latitude last mentioned. By admeasurements through nearly the whole of this last line, and supplying the unmeasured parts from good data, the Atlantic and Mississippi are found in this latitude to be seven hundred and fifty-eight miles distant, equal to 30° 38′ of longitude, reckoning fifty-five miles and three thousand one hundred and forty-four feet to the degree. This being our comprehension of longitude, that of our latitude, taken between this and Mason and Dixon's line, is 3° 13′ 42.4″ equal to two hundred and twenty-three and one-third miles, supposing a degree of a great

---

[1] In his "Autobiography" Jefferson stated that in the year 1781, "I had received a letter from M. de Marbois, of the French legation in Philadelphia, informing me he had been instructed by his government to obtain such statistical accounts of the different states of our Union, as might be useful for their information; and addressing to me a number of queries relative to the state of Virginia. I had always made it a practice whenever an opportunity occurred of obtaining any information of our country, which might be of use to me in any station public or private, to commit it to writing. These memoranda were on loose papers, bundled up without order, and difficult of recurrence when I had occasion for a particular one. I thought this a good occasion to embody their substance, which I did in the order of M. Marbois' queries, so to answer his wish and to arrange them for my own use. Such friends to whom they were occasionally communicated wished for copies; but their volume rendering this too laborious by hand, I proposed to get a few printed for their gratification. . . ."

Notes on the State of Virginia was published in Paris in the year 1785. It appeared without name of author, place of printing, or printer, carrying on its novel title page the date MDCCLXXXII. In letters to friends to whom he sent copies of the book, Jefferson requested them to keep the name of the author secret. "My reason," he wrote to James Monroe on June 17, 1775, "is that I fear the terms in which I speak of slavery and of our Constitution may produce an irritation which will revolt the minds of our countrymen against reformation in these two articles, and thus do more harm than good." Jefferson's *Works*, Edited by Paul Leceister Ford, New York, 1904, Federal edition, vol. IV, pp. 418-419.

circle to be sixty-nine miles, eight hundred and sixty-four feet, as computed by Cassina. These boundaries include an area somewhat triangular of one hundred and twenty-one thousand five hundred and twenty-five square miles, whereof seventy-nine thousand six hundred and fifty lie westward of the Alleghany mountains, and fifty-seven thousand and thirty-four westward of the meridian of the mouth of the Great Kanhaway. This State is therefore one-third larger than the islands of Great Britain and Ireland, which are reckoned at eighty-eight thousand three hundred and fifty-seven square miles.

These limits result from, 1. The ancient charters from the crown of England. 2. The grant of Maryland to the Lord Baltimore, and the subsequent determinations of the British court as to the extent of that grant. 3. The grant of Pennsylvania to William Penn, and a compact between the general assemblies of the commonwealths of Virginia and Pennsylvania as to the extent of that grant. 4. The grant of Carolina, and actual location of its northern boundary, by consent of both parties. 5. The treaty of Paris of 1763. 6. The confirmation of the charters of the neighboring States by the convention of *Virginia* at the time of constituting their commonwealth. 7. The cession made by *Virginia* to Congress of all the lands to which they had title on the north side of the Ohio.

QUERY II

A notice of its rivers, rivulets, and how far they are navigable

An inspection of a map of *Virginia*, will give a better idea of the geography of its rivers, than any description in writing. Their navigation may be imperfectly noted.

Roanoke, so far as it lies within the State, is nowhere navigable but for canoes, or light batteaux; and even for these in such detached parcels as to have prevented the inhabitants from availing themselves of it at all.

James River, and its waters, afford navigation as follows:

The whole of *Elizabeth River,* the lowest of those which run into James River, is a harbor, and would contain upwards of three hundred ships. The channel is from one hundred and fifty to two hundred fathoms wide, and at common flood tide affords eighteen feet water to Norfolk. The Stafford, a sixty gun ship, went there, lightening herself to cross the bar at Sowel's Point. The Fier Rodrigue, pierced for sixty-four guns, and carrying fifty, went there without lightening. Craney Island, at the mouth of this river, commands its channel tolerably well.

Nansemond River is navigable to Sleepy Hole for vessels of two hundred and fifty tons; to Suffolk for those of one hundred tons; and to Milner's for those of twenty-five.

Pagan Creek affords eight or ten feet water to Smithfield, which admits vessels of twenty tons.

Chickahominy has at its mouth a bar, on which is only twelve feet water at common flood tide. Vessels passing that, may go eight miles up the river; those of ten feet draught may go four miles further, and those of six tons burden twenty miles further.

Appamattox may be navigated as far as Broadways, by any vessel which has crossed Harrison's bar in James River; it keeps eight or ten feet water a mile or two higher up to Fisher's bar, and four feet on that and upwards to Petersburg, where all navigation ceases.

James River itself affords a harbor for vessels of any size in Hampton Road, but not in safety through the whole winter; and there is navigable water for them as far as Mulberry Island. A forty gun ship goes to Jamestown, and, lightening herself, may pass Harrison's bar; on which there is only fifteen feet water. Vessels of two hundred and fifty tons may go to Warwick; those of one hundred and twenty-five go to Rocket's, a mile below Richmond; from thence is about seven feet water to Richmond; and about the centre of the town, four feet and a half, where the navigation is interrupted by falls, which in a course of six miles, descend about eighty-eight feet perpendicular; above these it is resumed in canoes and batteaux, and is prosecuted safely and advantageously to within ten miles of the Blue Ridge and even through the Blue Ridge a ton weight has been brought and the expense would not be great, when compared with its object, to open a tolerable navigation up Jackson's river and Carpenter's creek, to within twenty-five miles of Howard's creek of Green Briar, both of which have then water enough to float vessels into the Great Kanhaway. In some future state of population I think it possible that its navigation may also be made to interlock with that of the Potomac, and through that to communicate by a short portage with the Ohio. It is to be noted that this river is called in the maps *James River,* only to its confluence with the Rivanna; thence to the Blue Ridge it is called the Fluvanna; and thence to its source Jackson's river. But in common speech, it is called James River to its source.

The *Rivanna,* a branch of James River, is navigable for canoes and batteaux to its intersection with the South-West mountains, which is about twenty-two miles; and may easily be opened to navigation through these mountains to its fork about Charlottesville.

York River, at Yorktown, affords the best harbor in the State for vessels of the largest size. The river there narrows to the width of a mile, and is contained within very high banks, close under which vessels may ride. It holds four fathom water at high tide for twenty-five miles above York to the mouth of Poropotank, where the river is a mile and a half wide, and the channel only seventy-five fathom, and passing under a high bank. At the confluence of *Pamunkey* and *Mattapony,* it is reduced to three fathom depth, which continues up Pamunkey to Cumberland, where the width is one hundred yards, and up Mattapony to within two miles of Frazier's ferry, where it becomes two and a half fathom deep, and holds that about five miles. Pamunkey is then capable of navigation for loaded flats to Brockman's bridge, fifty miles above Hanover town, and Mattapony to Downer's bridge, seventy miles above its mouth.

Piankatank, the little rivers making out of *Mobjack Bay* and those of the eastern shore, receive only very small vessels, and these can but enter them.

Rappahannock affords four fathom water to Hobb's hole, and two fathom from thence to Fredericksburg.

Potomac is seven and a half miles wide at the mouth; four and a half at Nomony bay; three at Aquia; one and a half at Hallowing point; one and a quarter at Alexandria. Its soundings are seven fathom at the mouth; five at St. George's island; four and a half at Lower Matchodic; three at Swan's point, and thence up to Alexandria; thence ten feet water to the falls, which are thirteen miles above Alexandria. These falls are fifteen miles in length, and of very great descent, and the navigation above them for batteaux and canoes is so much interrupted as to be little used. It is, however, used in a small degree up the Cohongoronta branch as far as fort Cumberland, which was at the mouth of Willis's creek; and is capable, at no great expense, of being rendered very practicable. The Shenandoah branch interlocks with James river about the Blue Ridge, and may perhaps in future be opened.

The *Mississippi* will be one of the principal channels of future commerce for the country westward of the Alleghany. From the mouth of this river to where it receives the Ohio, is one thousand miles by water, but only five hundred by land, passing through the Chickasaw country. From the mouth of the Ohio to that of the Missouri, is two hundred and thirty miles by water, and one hundred and forty by land, from thence to the mouth of the Illinois river, is about twenty-five miles. The Mississippi, below the mouth of the Missouri, is always muddy, and abounding with sand bars, which frequently change their places. However, it carries fifteen feet water to the mouth of the Ohio, to which place it is from one and a half to two miles wide, and thence to Kaskaskia from one mile to a mile and a quarter wide. Its current is so rapid, that it never can be stemmed by the force of the wind alone, acting on sails. Any vessel, however, navigated with oars, may come up at any time, and receive much aid from the wind. A batteau passes from the mouth of Ohio to the mouth of Mississippi in three weeks, and is from two to three months getting up again. During its floods, which are periodical as those of the Nile, the largest vessels may pass down it, if their steerage can be insured. These floods begin in April, and the river returns into its banks early in August. The inundation extends further on the western than eastern side, covering the lands in some places for fifty miles from its banks. Above the mouth of the Missouri it becomes much such a river as the Ohio, like it clear and gentle in its current, not quite so wide, the period of its floods nearly the same, but not rising to so great a height. The streets of the village at Cohoes are not more than ten feet above the ordinary level of the water, and yet were never overflowed. Its bed deepens every year. Cohoes, in the memory of many people now living, was insulated by every flood of the river. What was the eastern channel has now become a lake, nine miles in length and one in width, into which the river at this day never flows. This river yields turtle of a peculiar kind, perch, trout, gar, pike, mullets, herrings, carp, spatula-fish of fifty pounds weight, cat-fish of one hundred pounds weight, buffalo fish, and sturgeon. Alligators or crocodiles have been seen as high up as the Acansas. It also abounds in herons, cranes, ducks, brant, geese, and swans. Its passage is commanded by a fort established by this State, five miles below the mouth of the Ohio, and ten miles above the Carolina boundary.

The Missouri, since the treaty of Paris, the Illinois and northern branches of the Ohio, since the cession to Congress, are no longer within our limits. Yet having been so heretofore, and still opening to us channels of extensive communication with the western and north-western country, they shall be noted in their order.

The *Missouri* is, in fact, the principal river, contributing more to the common stream than does the Mississippi, even after its junction with the Illinois. It is remarkably cold, muddy, and rapid. Its overflowings are considerable. They happen during the months of June and July. Their commencement being so much later than those of the Mississippi, would induce a belief that the sources of the Missouri are northward of those of the Mississippi, unless we suppose that the cold increases again with the ascent of the land from the Mississippi westwardly. That this ascent is great, is proved by the rapidity of the river. Six miles above the mouth, it is brought within the compass of a quarter of a mile's width; yet the Spanish merchants at Pancore, or St. Louis, say they go two thousand miles up to it. It heads far westward of the Rio Norte, or North River. There is, in the village of Kaskaskia, Cohoes, and St. Vincennes, no inconsiderable quantity of plate, said to have been plundered during the last war by the Indians from the churches and private houses of Santa Fé, on the North river, and brought to the villages for sale. From the mouth of the Ohio to Santa Fé are forty days journey, or about one thousand miles. What is the shortest distance between the navigable waters of the Missouri, and those of the North river, or how far this is navigable above Santa Fé, I could never learn. From Santa Fé to its mouth in the Gulf of Mexico is about twelve hundred miles. The road from New Orleans to Mexico crosses this river at the post of Rio Norte, eight hundred miles below Santa Fé, and from this post to New Orleans is about twelve hundred miles; thus making two thousand miles between Santa Fé and New Orleans, passing down the North river, Red river, and Mississippi; whereas it is two thousand two hundred and thirty through the Missouri and Mississippi. From the same post of Rio Norte, passing near the mines of La Sierra and Laiguana, which are between the North river, and the river Salina to Sartilla, is three hundred and seventy-five miles, and from thence, passing the mines of Charcas, Zaccatecas, and Potosi, to the city of Mexico, is three hundred and seventy-five miles; in all, one thousand five hundred and fifty miles from Santa Fé to the city of Mexico. From New Orleans to the city of Mexico is about one thousand nine hundred and fifty miles; the roads after setting out from the Red river, near Natchitoches, keeping generally parallel with the coast, and about two hundred miles from it, till it enters the city of Mexico.

The *Illinois* is a fine river, clear, gentle, and without rapids; insomuch that it is navigable for batteaux to its source. From thence is a portage of two miles only to the Chicago, which affords a batteau navigation of sixteen miles to its entrance into lake Michigan. The Illinois, about ten miles above its mouth, is three hundred yards wide.

The *Kaskaskia* is one hundred yards wide at its entrance into the Mississippi, and preserves that breadth to the Buffalo plains, seventy miles above. So far, also, it is navigable for loaded batteaux, and perhaps much further. It is not rapid.

The *Ohio* is the most beautiful river on earth. Its current gentle, waters clear, and bosom smooth and unbroken by rocks and rapids, a single instance only excepted.

It is one-quarter of a mile wide at Fort Pitt, five hundred yards at the mouth of the Great Kanhaway, one mile and twenty-five poles at Louisville, one-quarter of a mile on the rapids three or four miles below Louisville, half a mile where the low country begins, which is twenty miles above Green river, a mile and a quarter at the receipt of the Tennessee, and a mile wide at the mouth.

Its length, as measured according to its meanders by Captain Hutchins, is as follows:

From Fort Pitt

To Log's Town	18½	Licking Creek	8
Big Beaver Creek	10¾	Great Miami	26¾
Little Beaver Creek	13½	Big Bones	32½
Yellow Creek	11¾	Kentucky	44¼
Two Creeks	21¾	Rapids	77¼
Long Reach	53¾	Low Country	155¾
Eng Long Reach	16½	Buffalo River	64½
Muskingum	25½	Wabash	97¼
Little Kanhaway	12¼	Big Cave	42¾
Hockhocking	16	Shawanee River	52½
Great Kanhaway	82½	Cherokee River	13
Guiandot	43¾	Massac	11
Sandy Creek	14½	Mississippi	46
Sioto	48¼		
Little Miami	126¼		1188

In common winter and spring tides it affords fifteen feet water to Louisville, ten feet to Le Tarte's rapids, forty miles above the mouth of the great Kanhaway, and a sufficiency at all times for light batteaux and canoes to Fort Pitt. The rapids are in latitude 38° 8′. The inundations of this river begin about the last of March, and subside in July. During these, a first-rate man-of-war may be carried from Louisville to New Orleans, if the sudden turns of the river and the strength of its current will admit a safe steerage. The rapids at Louisville descend about thirty feet in a length of a mile and a half. The bed of the river there is a solid rock, and is divided by an island into two branches, the southern of which is about two hundred yards wide, and is dry four months in the year. The bed of the northern branch is worn into channels by the constant course of the water, and attrition of the pebble stones carried on with that, so as to be passable for batteaux through the greater part of the year. Yet it is thought that the southern arm may be the most easily opened for constant navigation. The rise of the waters in these rapids does not exceed ten or twelve feet. A part of this island is so high as to have been never overflowed, and to command the settlement at Louisville, which is opposite to it. The fort, however, is situated at the head of the falls. The ground on the south side rises very gradually.

The *Tennessee,* Cherokee, or Hogohege river, is six hundred yards wide at its mouth, a quarter of a mile at the mouth of Holston, and two hundred yards at Chotee, which is twenty miles above Holston, and three hundred miles above the mouth of the Tennessee. This river crosses the southern boundary of Virginia, fifty-eight miles from the Mississippi. Its current is moderate. It is navigable for loaded boats of any burden to the Muscle shoals, where the river passes through the Cumberland mountain. These shoals are six or eight miles long, passable downwards for loaded canoes, but not upwards, unless there be a swell in the river. Above these the navigation for loaded canoes and batteaux continues to the Long island. This river has its inundations also. Above the Chickamogga towns is a whirlpool called the Sucking-pot, which takes in trunks of trees or boats, and throws them out again half a mile below. It is avoided by keeping very close to the bank, on the south side. There are but a few miles portage between a branch of this river and the navigable waters of the river Mobile, which runs into the Gulf of Mexico.

Cumberland, or Shawanee river, intersects the boundary between Virginia and North Carolina sixty-seven miles from the Mississippi, and again one hundred and ninety-eight miles from the same river, a little above the entrance of Obey's river into the Cumberland. Its Clear fork crosses the same boundary about three hundred miles from the Mississippi. Cumberland is a very gentle stream, navigable for loaded batteaux eight hundred miles, without interruption; then intervene some rapids of fifteen miles in length, after which it is again navigable seventy miles upwards, which brings you within ten miles of the Cumberland mountains. It is about one hundred and twenty yards wide through its whole course, from the head of its navigation to its mouth.

The *Wabash* is a very beautiful river, four hundred yards wide at the mouth, and three hundred at St. Vincennes, which is a post one hundred miles above the mouth, in a direct line. Within this space there are two small rapids, which give very little obstruction to the navigation. It is four hundred yards wide at the mouth, and navigable thirty leagues upward for canoes and small boats. From the mouth of Maple river to that of Eel river is about eighty miles in a direct line, the river continuing navigable, and from one to two hundred yards in width. The Eel river is one hundred and fifty yards wide, and affords at all times navigation for periaguas, to within eighteen miles of the Miami of the Lake. The Wabash, from the mouth of Eel river to Little river, a distance of fifty miles direct, is interrupted with frequent rapids and shoals, which obstruct the navigation, except in a swell. Little river affords navigation during a swell to within three miles of the Miami, which thence affords a similar navigation into Lake Erie, one hundred miles distant in a direct line. The Wabash overflows periodically in correspondence with the Ohio, and in some places two leagues from its banks.

Green River is navigable for loaded batteaux at all times fifty miles upwards; but it is then interrupted by impassable rapids, above which the navigation again commences and continues good thirty or forty miles to the mouth of Barren river.

Kentucky River is ninety yards wide at the mouth, and also at Boonsborough, eighty miles above. It affords a navigation for loaded batteaux one hundred and eighty miles in a direct line, in the winter tides.

The *Great Miami* of the Ohio, is two hundred yards wide at the mouth. At the Piccawee towns, seventy-five miles above, it is reduced to thirty yards; it is, nevertheless, navigable for loaded canoes fifty miles above these towns. The portage from its western branch into the Miami of Lake Erie, is five miles; that from its eastern branch into Sandusky river, is of nine miles.

Salt River is at all times navigable for loaded batteaux seventy or eighty miles. It is eighty yards wide at its mouth, and keeps that width to its fork, twenty-five miles above.

The *Little Miami* of the Ohio, is sixty or seventy yards wide at its mouth, sixty miles to its source, and affords no navigation.

The *Sioto* is two hundred and fifty yards wide at its mouth, which is in latitude 38° 22′, and at the Saltlick towns, two hundred miles above the mouth, it is yet one hundred yards wide. To these towns it is navigable for loaded batteaux, and its eastern branch affords navigation almost to its source.

Great Sandy River is about sixty yards wide, and navigable sixty miles for loaded batteaux.

Guiandot is about the width of the river last mentioned, but is more rapid. It may be navigated by canoes sixty miles.

The *Great Kanhaway* is a river of considerable note for the fertility of its lands, and still more, as leading towards the head waters of James river. Nevertheless, it is doubtful whether its great and numerous rapids will admit a navigation, but at an expense to which it will require ages to render its inhabitants equal. The great obstacles begin at what are called the Great Falls, ninety miles above the mouth, below which are only five or six rapids, and these passable, with some difficulty, even at low water. From the falls to the mouth of Greenbriar is one hundred miles, and thence to the lead mines one hundred and twenty. It is two hundred and eighty yards wide at its mouth.

Hockhocking is eighty yards wide at its mouth, and yields navigation for loaded batteaux to the Press-place, sixty miles above its mouth.

The *Little Kanhaway* is one hundred and fifty yards wide at the mouth. It yields a navigation of ten miles only. Perhaps its northern branch, called Junius' creek, which interlocks with the western of Monongahela, may one day admit a shorter passage from the latter into the Ohio.

The *Muskingum* is two hundred and eighty yards wide at its mouth, and two hundred yards at the lower Indian towns, one hundred and fifty miles upwards. It is navigable for small batteaux to within one mile of a navigable part of Cuyahoga river, which runs into Lake Erie.

At Fort Pitt the river Ohio loses its name, branching into the Monongahela and Alleghany.

The *Monongahela* is four hundred yards wide at its mouth. From thence is twelve or fifteen miles to the mouth of Yohogany, where it is three hundred yards wide. Thence to Redstone by water is fifty miles, by land thirty. Then to the mouth of Cheat river by water forty miles, by land twenty-eight, the width continuing at three hundred yards, and the navigation good for boats. Thence the width is about two hundred yards to the western fork, fifty miles higher, and the navigation frequently interrupted by rapids, which, however, with a swell of two or three feet, become very passable for boats. It then admits light boats, except in dry seasons, sixty-five miles further to the head of Tygart's valley, presenting only some small rapids and falls of one or two feet perpendicular, and lessening in its width to twenty yards. The *Western fork* is navigable in the winter ten or fifteen miles towards the northern of the Little Kanhaway, and will admit a good wagon road to it. The *Yohogany* is the principal branch of this river. It passes through the Laurel mountain, about thirty miles from its mouth; is so far from three hundred to one hundred and fifty yards wide, and the navigation much obstructed in dry weather by rapids and shoals. In its passages through the mountain it makes very great falls, admitting no navigation for ten miles to the Turkey Foot. Thence to the Great Crossing, about twenty miles, it is again navigable, except in dry seasons, and at this place is two hundred yards wide. The sources of this river are divided from those of the Potomac by the Alleghany mountain. From the falls, where it intersects the Laurel mountain, to Fort Cumberland, the head of the navigation on the Potomac, is forty miles of very mountainous road. Willis' creek, at the mouth of which was Fort Cumberland, is thirty or forty yards wide, but affords no navigation as yet. *Cheat* river, another considerable branch of the Monongahela, is two hundred yards wide at its mouth, and one hundred yards at the *Dunkard's* settlement, fifty miles higher. It is navigable for boats, except in dry seasons. The boundary between Virginia and Pennsylvania crosses it about three or four miles above its mouth.

The *Alleghany* river, with a slight swell, affords navigation for light batteaux to Venango, at the mouth of French Creek, where it is two hundred yards wide, and is practised even to Le Bœuf, from whence there is a portage of fifteen miles to Presque Isle on the Lake Erie.

The country watered by the Mississippi and its eastern branches, constitutes five-eighths of the United States, two of which five-eighths are occupied by the Ohio and its waters; the residuary streams which run into the Gulf of Mexico, the Atlantic, and the St. Lawrence, water the remaining three-eighths.

Before we quit the subject of the western waters, we will take a view of their principal connections with the Atlantic. These are three; the Hudson river, the Potomac, and the Mississippi itself. Down the last will pass all heavy commodities. But the navigation through the Gulf of Mexico is so dangerous, and that up the Mississippi so difficult and tedious, that it is thought probable that European merchandise will not return through that channel. It is most likely that flour, timber, and other heavy articles will be floated on rafts, which will themselves be an article for sale as well as their loading, the navigators returning by land, or in light batteaux. There will, therefore, be a competition between the Hudson and Potomac rivers for the residue of the commerce of all the country westward of Lake Erie, on the waters of the lakes, of the Ohio, and upper parts of the Mississippi. To go to New York, that part of the trade which comes from the lakes or their waters, must first be brought into Lake Erie. Between Lake Superior and its waters and Huron, are the rapids of St. Mary, which will permit boats to pass, but not larger vessels. Lakes Huron and Michigan afford communication with Lake Erie by vessels of eight feet draught. That part of the trade which comes from the waters of the Mississippi must pass from them through some portage into the waters of the lakes. The portage from the Illinois river into a water of Michigan is of one mile only. From the Wabash, Miami, Muskingum, or Alleghany, are portages into the waters of Lake Erie, of from one to fifteen miles. When the commodities are brought into, and have passed through Lake Erie, there is between that and Ontario an interruption by the falls of Niagara, where the portage is of eight miles; and between Ontario and the Hudson river are portages at the falls of Onondago, a little above Oswego, of a quarter of a mile; from Wood creek to the Mohawks river two miles; at the little falls of the Mohawks river half a mile; and from Schenectady to Albany sixteen miles. Besides the increase of expense occasioned by frequent change of carriage, there is an increased risk of pillage produced by committing merchandise to a greater number of hands successively. The Potomac offers itself under the following circumstances: For the trade of the lakes and their waters westward of Lake Erie, when it shall have entered that lake, it must coast along its southern shore, on account of the number and excellence of its harbors; the northern, though shortest, having few harbors, and these unsafe. Having reached Cuyahoga, to proceed on to New York it will have eight hundred and twenty-five miles and five portages; whereas it is but four hundred and twenty-five miles to Alexandria, its emporium on the Potomac, if it turns into the Cuyahoga, and passes through that, Big Beaver, Ohio, Yohogany (or Monongahela and Cheat), and Potomac, and there are but two portages; the first of which, between Cuyahoga and Beaver, may be removed by uniting the sources of these waters, which are lakes in the neighborhood of each other, and in a champaign country; the other from the waters of Ohio to Potomac will be from fifteen to forty miles, according to the trouble which shall be taken to approach the two navigations. For the trade of the Ohio, or that which shall come into it from its own waters or the Mississippi, it is nearer through the Potomac to Alexandria than to New York by five hundred and eighty miles, and it is interrupted by one portage only. There is another circumstance of difference too. The lakes themselves never freeze, but the communications between them freeze, and the Hudson river is itself shut up by the ice three months in the year; whereas the channel to the Chesapeake leads directly into a warmer climate. The southern parts of it very rarely freeze at all, and whenever the northern do, it is so near the sources of the rivers, that the frequent floods to which they are there liable, break up the ice immediately, so that vessels may pass through the whole winter, subject only to accidental and short delays. Add to all this, that in case of war with our neighbors, the Anglo-Americans or the Indians, the route to New York becomes a frontier through almost its whole length, and all commerce through it ceases from that moment. But the channel to New York is already known to practice, whereas the upper waters of the Ohio and the Potomac, and the great falls of the latter, are yet to be cleared of their fixed obstructions. (A.)

QUERY III

A notice of the best Seaports of the State, and how big are the vessels they can receive?

Having no ports but our rivers and creeks, this *Query* has been answered under the preceding one.

QUERY IV

A notice of its Mountains

For the particular geography of our mountains I must refer to Fry and Jefferson's map of Virginia; and to Evans' analysis of this map of America, for a more philosophical view of them than is to be found in any other work. It is worthy of notice, that our mountains are not solitary and scattered confusedly over the face of the country; but that they commence at about one hundred and fifty miles from the sea-coast, are disposed in ridges, one behind another, running nearly parallel with the sea-coast, though rather approaching it as they advance north-eastwardly. To the south-west, as the tract of country between the sea-coast and the Mississippi becomes narrower, the mountains converge into a single ridge, which, as it approaches the Gulf of Mexico, subsides into plain country, and gives rise to some of the waters of that gulf, and particularly to a river called the Apalachicola, probably from the Apalachies, an Indian nation formerly residing on it. Hence the mountains giving rise to that river, and seen from its various parts, were called the Appalachian mountains, being in fact the end or termination only of the great ridges passing through the continent. European geographers, however, extended the name northwardly as far as the mountains extended; some giving it, after their separation into different ridges, to the Blue Ridge, others to the North Mountain, others to the Alleghany, others to the Laurel Ridge, as may be seen by their different maps. But the fact I believe is, that none of these ridges were ever known by that name to the inhabitants, either native or emigrant, but as they saw them so called in European maps. In the same direction, generally, are the veins of limestone, coal, and other minerals hitherto discovered; and so range the falls of our great rivers. But the courses of the great rivers are at right angles with these. James and Potomac penetrate through all the ridges of mountains eastward of the Alleghany; that is, broken by no water course. It is in fact the spine of the country between the Atlantic on one side, and the Mississippi and St. Lawrence on the other. The passage of the Potomac through the Blue Ridge is, perhaps, one of the most stupendous scenes in nature. You stand on a very high point of land. On your right comes up the Shenandoah, having ranged along the foot of the mountain an hundred miles to seek a vent. On your left approaches the Potomac, in quest of a passage also. In the moment of their junction, they rush together against the mountain, rend it asunder, and pass off to the sea. The first glance of this scene hurries our senses into the opinion, that this earth has been created in time, that the mountains were formed first, that the rivers began to flow afterwards, that in this place, particularly, they have been dammed up by the Blue Ridge of mountains, and have formed an ocean which filled the whole valley; that continuing to rise they have at length broken over at this spot, and have torn the mountain down from its summit to its base. The piles of rock on each hand, but particularly on the Shenandoah, the evident marks of their disrupture and avulsion from their beds by the most powerful agents of nature, corroborate the impression. But the distant finishing which nature has given to the picture, is of a very different character. It is a true contrast to the foreground. It is as placid and delightful as that is wild and tremendous. For the mountain being cloven asunder, she presents to your eye, through the cleft, a small catch of smooth blue horizon, at an infinite distance in the plain country, inviting you, as it were, from the riot and tumult roaring around, to pass through the breach and participate of the calm below. Here the eye ultimately composes itself; and that way, too, the road happens actually to lead. You cross the Potomac above the junction, pass along its side through the base of the mountain for three miles, its terrible precipices hanging in fragments over you, and within about twenty miles reach Fredericktown, and the fine country round that. This scene is worth a voyage across the Atlantic. Yet here, as in the neighborhood of the Natural Bridge, are people who have passed their lives within half a dozen miles, and have never been to survey these monuments of a war between rivers and mountains, which must have shaken the earth itself to its centre. (B.)

The height of our mountains has not yet been estimated with any degree of exactness. The Alleghany being the great ridge which divides the waters of the Atlantic from those of the Mississippi, its summit is doubtless more elevated above the ocean than that of any other mountain. But its relative height, compared with the base on which it stands, is not so great as that of some others, the country rising behind the successive ridges like the steps of stairs. The mountains of the Blue Ridge, and of these the Peaks of Otter, are thought to be of a greater height, measured from their base, than any others in our country, and perhaps in North America. From data, which may found a tolerable conjecture, we suppose the highest peak to be about four thousand feet perpendicular, which is not a fifth part of the height of the mountains of South America, nor one-third of the height which would be necessary in our latitude to preserve ice in the open air unmelted through the year. The ridge of mountains next beyond the Blue Ridge, called by us the North mountain, is of the greatest extent; for which reason they were named by the Indians the endless mountains.

A substance supposed to be Pumice, found floating on the Mississippi, has induced a conjecture that there is a volcano on some of its waters; and as these are mostly known to their sources, except the Missouri, our expectations of verifying the conjecture would of course be led to the mountains which divide the waters of the Mexican Gulf from those of the South Sea; but no volcano having ever yet been known at such a distance from the sea, we must rather suppose that this floating substance has been erroneously deemed Pumice.

QUERY V

Its Cascades and Caverns

The only remarkable cascade in this country is that of the Falling Spring in Augusta. It is a water of James' river where it is called Jackson's river, rising in the warm spring mountains, about twenty miles south west of the warm spring, and flowing into that valley. About three-quarters of a mile from its source it falls over a rock two hundred feet into the valley below. The sheet of water is broken in its breadth by the rock, in two or three places, but not at all in its height. Between the sheet and the rock, at the bottom, you may walk across dry. This cataract will bear no comparison with that of Niagara as to the quantity of water composing it; the sheet being only twelve or fifteen feet wide above and somewhat more spread below; but it is half as high again, the latter being only one hundred and fifty-six feet, according to the mensuration made by order

An eye draught of Madison's cave on a scale of 67 feet to the inch. The arrows show where it descends or ascends.

of M. Vaudreuil, Governor of Canada, and one hundred and thirty according to a more recent account.

In the lime-stone country there are many caverns of very considerable extent.

The most noted is called Madison's Cave, and is on the north side of the Blue Ridge, near the intersection of the Rockingham and Augusta line with the south fork of the southern river of Shenandoah. It is in a hill of about two hundred feet perpendicular height, the ascent of which, on one side, is so steep that you may pitch a biscuit from its summit into the river which washes its base. The entrance of the cave is, in this side, about two-thirds of the way up. It extends into the earth about three hundred feet, branching into subordinate caverns, sometimes ascending a little, but more generally descending, and at length terminates, in two different places, at basons of water of unknown extent, and which I should judge to be nearly on a level with the water of the river; however, I do not think they are formed by refluent water from that, because they are never turbid; because they do not rise and fall in correspondence with that in times of flood or of drought; and because the water is always cool. It is probably one of the many reservoirs with which the interior parts of the earth are supposed to abound, and yield supplies to the fountains of water, distinguished from others only by being accessible. The vault of this cave is of solid lime-stone, from twenty to forty or fifty feet high; through which water is continually percolating. This, trickling down the sides of the cave, has incrusted them over in the form of elegant drapery; and dripping from the top of the vault generates on that and on the base below, stalactites of a conical form, some of which have met and formed massive columns.

Another of these caves is near the north mountain, in the county of Frederic, on the lands of Mr. Zane. The entrance into this is on the top of an extensive ridge. You descend thirty or forty feet, as into a well, from whence the cave extends, nearly horizontally, four hundred feet into the earth, preserving a breadth of from twenty to fifty feet, and a height of from five to twelve feet. After entering this cave a few feet, the mercury, which in the open air was 50°, rose to 57° of Fahrenheit's thermometer, answering to 11° of Reaumur's, and it continued at that to the remotest parts of the cave. The uniform temperature of the cellars of the observatory of Paris, which are ninety feet deep, and of all subterraneous cavities of any depth, where no chemical agencies may be supposed to produce a factitious heat, has been found to be 10° of Reaumur, equal to 54½° of Fahrenheit. The temperature of the cave above mentioned so nearly corresponds with this, that the difference may be ascribed to a difference of instruments.

At the Panther gap, in the ridge which divides the waters of the Crow and the Calf pasture, is what is called the *Blowing Cave*. It is in the side of a hill, is of about one hundred feet diameter, and emits constantly a current of air of such force as to keep the weeds prostrate to the distance of twenty yards before it. This current is strongest in dry, frosty weather, and in long spells of rain weakest. Regular inspirations and expirations of air, by caverns and fissures, have been probably enough accounted for by supposing them combined with intermitting fountains; as they must of course inhale air while their reservoirs are emptying themselves, and again emit it while they are filling. But a constant issue of air, only varying in its force as the weather is drier or damper, will re-

quire a new hypothesis. There is another blowing cave in the Cumberland mountain, about a mile from where it crosses the Carolina line. All we know of this
is, that it is not constant, and that a fountain of water issues from it.

The *Natural Bridge,* the most sublime of nature's works, though not comprehended under the present head, must not be pretermitted. It is on the ascent of
a hill, which seems to have been cloven through its length by some great convulsion. The fissure, just at the bridge, is, by some admeasurements, two hundred and seventy feet deep, by others only two hundred and five. It is about
forty-five feet wide at the bottom and ninety feet at the top; this of course determines the length of the bridge, and its height from the water. Its breadth in
the middle is about sixty feet, but more at the ends, and the thickness of the
mass, at the summit of the arch, about forty feet. A part of this thickness is
constituted by a coat of earth, which gives growth to many large trees. The
residue, with the hill on both sides, is one solid rock of lime-stone. The arch
approaches the semi-elliptical form; but the larger axis of the ellipsis, which
would be the cord of the arch, is many times longer than the transverse. Though
the sides of this bridge are provided in some parts with a parapet of fixed rocks,
yet few men have resolution to walk to them, and look over into the abyss. You
involuntarily fall on your hands and feet, creep to the parapet, and peep over
it. Looking down from this height about a minute, gave me a violent head-ache.
If the view from the top be painful and intolerable, that from below is delightful in an equal extreme. It is impossible for the emotions arising from the sublime to be felt beyond what they are here; so beautiful an arch, so elevated, so
light, and springing as it were up to heaven! the rapture of the spectator is really
indescribable! The fissure continuing narrow, deep, and straight, for a considerable distance above and below the bridge, opens a short but very pleasing view
of the North mountain on one side and the Blue Ridge on the other, at the distance each of them of about five miles. This bridge is in the county of Rockbridge, to which it has given name, and affords a public and commodious passage over a valley which cannot be crossed elsewhere for a considerable distance.
The stream passing under it is called Cedar-creek. It is a water of James' river,
and sufficient in the driest seasons to turn a grist-mill, though its fountain is
not more than two miles above.[1]

[1] Don Ulloa mentions a break, similar to this, in the province of Angaraez, in South America. It is from sixteen to twenty-two feet wide, one hundred and eleven feet deep, and of 1.3
miles continuance, English measure. Its breadth at top is not sensibly greater than at bottom.
But the following fact is remarkable, and will furnish some light for conjecturing the probable
origin of our natural bridge. "*Esta caxa, ó cauce está cortada en péna viva con tanta precision,
que las desigualdades del un lado entrantes, corresponden á las del otro lado salientes, como si
aquella altura se hubiese abierto expresamente, con sus bueltas y tortuosidades, para darle transito
á los aguas por entre los dos morallones que la forman; siendo tal su igualdad, que si llegasen
á juntarse se endentarian uno con otro sin dextar hueco.*" Not. Amer. ii. § 10. Don Ulloa in-
clines to the opinion that this channel has been effected by the wearing of the water which runs
through it, rather than that the mountain should have been broken open by any convulsion of
nature. But if it had been worn by the running of water, would not the rocks which form the
sides, have been worn plain? or if, meeting in some parts with veins of harder stone, the water
had left prominences on the one side, would not the same cause have sometimes, or perhaps
generally, occasioned prominences on the other side also? Yet Don Ulloa tells us, that on the

QUERY VI

A notice of the mines and other subterraneous riches; its trees, plants, fruits, &c.

I knew a single instance of gold found in this State. It was interspersed in small specks through a lump of ore of about four pounds weight, which yielded seventeen pennyweights of gold, of extraordinary ductility. This ore was found on the north side of Rappahanock, about four miles below the falls. I never heard of any other indication of gold in its neighborhood.

On the Great Kanhaway, opposite to the mouth of Cripple creek, and about twenty-five miles from our southern boundary, in the county of Montgomery, are mines of lead. The metal is mixed, sometimes with earth, and sometimes with rock, which requires the force of gunpowder to open it; and is accompanied with a portion of silver too small to be worth separation under any process hitherto attempted there. The proportion yielded is from fifty to eighty pounds of pure metal from one hundred pounds of washed ore. The most common is that of sixty to one hundred pounds. The veins are sometimes most flattering, at others they disappear suddenly and totally. They enter the side of the hill and proceed horizontally. Two of them are wrought at present by the public, the best of which is one hundred yards under the hill. These would employ about fifty laborers to advantage. We have not, however, more than thirty generally, and these cultivate their own corn. They have produced sixty tons of lead in the year; but the general quantity is from twenty to twenty-five tons. The present furnace is a mile from the ore bank and on the opposite side of the river. The ore is first wagoned to the river, a quarter of a mile, then laden on board of canoes and carried across the river, which is there about two hundred yards wide, and then again taken into wagons and carried to the furnace. This mode was originally adopted that they might avail themselves of a good situation on a creek for pounding mill; but it would be easy to have the furnace and pounding mill on the same side of the river, which would yield water, without any dam, by a canal of about half a mile in length. From the furnace the lead is transported one hundred and thirty miles along a good road, leading through the peaks of Otter to Lynch's ferry, or Winston's on James' river, from whence it is carried by water about the same distance to Westham. This land carriage may be greatly shortened, by delivering the lead on James' river, above the Blue Ridge, from whence a ton weight has been brought on two canoes. The Great Kanhaway has considerable falls in the neighborhood of the mines. About seven

---

other side there are always corresponding cavities, and that these tally with the prominences so perfectly, that, were the two sides to come together they would fit in all their indentures, without leaving any void. I think that this does not resemble the effect of running water, but looks rather as if the two sides had parted asunder. The sides of the break, over which is the natural bridge of Virginia, consisting of a veiny rock which yields to time, the correspondence between the salient and re-entering inequalities, if it existed at all, has now disappeared. This break has the advantage of the one described by Don Ulloa in its finest circumstance; no portion in that instance having held together, during the separation of the other parts, so as to form a bridge over the abyss.—T. J.

miles below are three falls, of three or four feet perpendicular each; and three miles above is a rapid of three miles continuance, which has been compared in its descent to the great falls of James' river. Yet it is the opinion, that they may be laid open for useful navigation, so as to reduce very much the portage between the Kanhaway and James' river.

A valuable lead mine is said to have been lately discovered in Cumberland, below the mouth of Red river. The greatest, however, known in the western country, are on the Mississippi, extending from the mouth of Rock river one hundred and fifty miles upwards. These are not wrought, the lead used in that country being from the banks on the Spanish side of the Mississippi, opposite to Kaskaskia.

A mine of copper was once opened in the county of Amherst, on the north side of James' river, and another in the opposite country, on the south side. However, either from bad management or the poverty of the veins, they were discontinued. We are told of a rich mine of native copper on the Ouabache, below the upper Wiaw.

The mines of iron worked at present are Callaway's, Ross's, and Ballendine's, on the south side of James' river; Old's on the north side, in Albemarle; Miller's in Augusta, and Zane's in Frederic. These two last are in the valley between the Blue Ridge and North mountain. Callaway's, Ross's, Miller's, and Zane's make about one hundred and fifty tons of bar iron each, in the year. Ross's makes also about sixteen hundred tons of pig iron annually; Ballendine's one thousand; Callaway's, Miller's, and Zane's, about six hundred each. Besides these, a forge of Mr. Hunter's, at Fredericksburg, makes about three hundred tons a year of bar iron, from pigs imported from Maryland; and Taylor's forge on Neapsco of Potomac, works in the same way, but to what extent I am not informed. The indications of iron in other places are numerous, and dispersed through all the middle country. The toughness of the cast iron of Ross's and Zane's furnaces is very remarkable. Pots and other utensils, cast thinner than usual, of this iron, may be safely thrown into, or out of the wagons in which they are transported. Salt-pans made of the same, and no longer wanted for that purpose, cannot be broken up, in order to be melted again, unless previously drilled in many parts.

In the western country, we are told of iron mines between the Muskingum and Ohio; of others on Kentucky, between the Cumberland and Barren rivers, between Cumberland and Tennessee, on Reedy creek, near the Long Island, and on Chesnut creek, a branch of the Great Kanhaway, near where it crosses the Carolina line. What are called the iron banks, on the Mississippi, are believed, by a good judge, to have no iron in them. In general, from what is hitherto known of that country, it seems to want iron.

Considerable quantities of black lead are taken occasionally for use from Winterham in the county of Amelia. I am not able, however, to give a particular state of the mine. There is no work established at it; those who want, going and procuring it for themselves.

The country on James' river, from fifteen to twenty miles above Richmond, and for several miles northward and southward, is replete with mineral coal of a very excellent quality. Being in the hands of many proprietors, pits have been opened, and, before the interruption of our commerce, were worked to an extent equal to the demand.

In the western country coal is known to be in so many places, as to have induced an opinion, that the whole tract between the Laurel mountain, Mississippi, and Ohio, yields coal. It is also known in many places on the north side of the Ohio. The coal at Pittsburg is of very superior quality. A bed of it at that place has been a-fire since the year 1765. Another coal-hill on the Pike-run of Monongahela has been a-fire ten years; yet it has burnt away about twenty yards only.

I have known one instance of an emerald found in this country. Amethysts have been frequent, and crystals common; yet not in such numbers any of them as to be worth seeking.

There is very good marble, and in very great abundance, on James' river, at the mouth of Rockfish. The samples I have seen, were some of them of a white as pure as one might expect to find on the surface of the earth; but most of them were variegated with red, blue, and purple. None of it has been ever worked. It forms a very large precipice, which hangs over a navigable part of the river. It is said there is marble at Kentucky.

But one vein of limestone is known below the Blue Ridge. Its first appearance, in our country, is in Prince William, two miles below the Pignut ridge of mountains; thence it passes on nearly parallel with that, and crosses the Rivanna about five miles below it, where it is called the South-west ridge. It then crosses Hard-ware, above the mouth of Hudson's creek, James' river at the mouth of Rockfish, at the marble quarry before spoken of, probably runs up that river to where it appears again at Ross's iron-works, and so passes off south-westwardly by Flat Creek of Otter river. It is never more than one hundred yards wide. From the Blue Ridge westwardly, the whole country seems to be founded on a rock of limestone, besides infinite quantities on the surface, both loose and fixed. This is cut into beds, which range, as the mountains and sea-coast do, from south-west to north-east, the lamina of each bed declining from the horizon towards a parallelism with the axis of the earth. Being struck with this observation, I made, with a quadrant, a great number of trials on the angles of their declination, and found them to vary from 22° to 60°; but averaging all my trials, the result was within one-third of a degree of the elevation of the pole or latitude of the place, and much the greatest part of them taken separately were little different from that; by which it appears, that these lamina are, in the main, parallel with the axis of the earth. In some instances, indeed, I found them perpendicular, and even reclining the other way; but these were extremely rare, and always attended with signs of convulsion, or other circumstances of singularity, which admitted a possibility of removal from their original position. These trials were made between Madison's cave and the Potomac. We hear of limestone on the Misssissippi and Ohio, and in all the mountainous country between the eastern and western waters, not on the mountains themselves, but occupying the valleys between them.

Near the eastern foot of the North mountain are immense bodies of *Schist*, containing impressions of shells in a variety of forms. I have received petrified shells of very different kinds from the first sources of Kentucky, which bear no resemblance to any I have ever seen on the tide-waters. It is said that shells are found in the Andes, in South America, fifteen thousand feet above the level of the ocean. This is considered by many, both of the learned and unlearned, as a proof of an universal deluge. To the many considerations opposiing this opinion, the following may be added: The atmosphere, and all its contents, whether of water, air, or other matter, gravitate to the earth; that is to say, they have weight. Experience tells us, that the weight of all these together never exceeds that of a column of mercury of thirty-one inches height, which is equal to one of rain water of thirty-five feet high. If the whole contents of the atmosphere, then, were water, instead of what they are, it would cover the globe but thirty-five feet deep; but as these waters, as they fell, would run into the seas, the superficial measure of which is to that of the dry parts of the globe, as two to one, the seas would be raised only fifty-two and a half feet above their present level, and of course would overflow the lands to that height only. In Virginia this would be a very small proportion even of the champaign country, the banks of our tide-waters being frequently, if not generally, of a greater height. Deluges beyond this extent, then, as for instance, to the North mountain or to Kentucky, seem out of the laws of nature. But within it they may have taken place to a greater or less degree, in proportion to the combination of natural causes which may be supposed to have produced them. History renders probably some instances of a partial deluge in the country lying round the Mediterranean sea. It has been often [1] supposed, and it is not unlikely, that that sea was once a lake. While such, let us admit an extraordinary collection of the waters of the atmosphere from the other parts of the globe to have been discharged over that and the countries whose waters run into it. Or without supposing it a lake, admit such an extraordinary collection of the waters of the atmosphere, and an influx from the Atlantic ocean, forced by long-continued western winds. The lake, or that sea, may thus have been so raised as to overflow the low lands adjacent to it, as those of Egypt and Armenia, which, according to a tradition of the Egyptians and Hebrews, were overflowed about two thousand three hundred years before the Christian era; those of Attica, said to have been overflowed in the time of Ogyges, about five hundred years later; and those of Thessaly, in the time of Deucalion, still three hundred years posterior. But such deluges as these will not account for the shells found in the higher lands. A second opinion has been entertained, which is, that in times anterior to the records either of history or tradition, the bed of the ocean, the principal residence of the shelled tribe, has, by some great convulsion of nature, been heaved to the heights at which we now find shells and other marine animals. The favorers of this opinion do well to suppose the great events on which it rests to have taken place beyond all the

[1] Buffon Époques, 96.—T. J.

eras of history; for within these, certainly, none such are to be found; and we may venture to say farther, that no fact has taken place, either in our own days, or in the thousands of years recorded in history, which proves the existence of any natural agents, within or without the bowels of the earth, of force sufficient to heave, to the height of fifteen thousand feet, such masses as the Andes. The difference between the power necessary to produce such an effect, and that which shuffled together the different parts of Calabria in our days, is so immense, that from the existence of the latter, we are not authorized to infer that of the former.

M. de Voltaire has suggested a third solution of this difficulty. (Quest. Encycl. Coquilles.) He cites an instance in Touraine, where, in the space of eighty years, a particular spot of earth had been twice metamorphosed into soft stone, which had become hard when employed in building. In this stone shells of various kinds were produced, discoverable at first only with a microscope, but afterwards growing with the stone. From this fact, I suppose, he would have us infer, that, besides the usual process for generating shells by the elaboration of earth and water in animal vessels, nature may have provided an equivalent operation, by passing the same materials through the pores of calcareous earth and stones; as we see calcareous drop-stones generating every day, by the percolation of water through lime-stone, and new marble forming in the quarries from which the old has been taken out. And it might be asked, whether is it more difficult for nature to shoot the calcareous juice into the form of a shell, than other juices into the forms of crystals, plants, animals, according to the construction of the vessels through which they pass? There is a wonder somewhere. Is it greatest on this branch of the dilemma; on that which supposes the existence of a power, of which we have no evidence in any other case; or on the first, which requires us to believe the creation of a body of water and its subsequent annihilation? The establishment of the instance, cited by M. de Voltaire, of the growth of shells unattached to animal bodies, would have been that of his theory. But he has not established it. He has not even left it on ground so respectable as to have rendered it an object of inquiry to the *literati* of his own country. Abandoning this fact, therefore, the three hypotheses are equally unsatisfactory; and we must be contented to acknowledge, that this great phenomenon is as yet unsolved. Ignorance is preferable to error; and he is less remote from the truth who believes nothing, than he who believes what is wrong.

There is great abundance (more especially when you approach the mountains) of stone, white, blue, brown, &c., fit for the chisel, good mill-stone, such also as stands the fire, and slate stone. We are told of flint, fit for gun-flints, on the Meherrin in Brunswick, on the Mississippi between the mouth of the Ohio and Kaskaskia, and on others of the western waters. Isinglass or mica is in several places; loadstone also; and an Asbestos of a ligneous texture, is sometimes to be met with.

Marle abounds generally. A clay, of which, like the Sturbridge in England, bricks are made, which will resist long the violent action of fire, has been found on Tuckahoe creek of James' river, and no doubt will be found in other places.

Chalk is said to be in Botetourt and Bedford. In the latter county is some earth believed to be gypseous. Ochres are found in various parts.

In the lime-stone country are many caves, the earthy floors of which are impregnated with nitre. On Rich creek, a branch of the Great Kanhaway, about sixty miles below the lead mines, is a very large one, about twenty yards wide, and entering a hill a quarter or half a mile. The vault is of rock, from nine to fifteen or twenty feet above the floor. A Mr. Lynch, who gives me this account, undertook to extract the nitre. Besides a coat of the salt which had formed on the vault and floor, he found the earth highly impregnated to the depth of seven feet in some places, and generally of three, every bushel yielding on an average three pounds of nitre. Mr. Lynch having made about ten hundred pounds of the salt from it, consigned it to some others, who have since made ten thousand pounds. They have done this by pursuing the cave into the hill, never trying a second time the earth they have once exhausted, to see how far or soon it receives another impregnation. At least fifty of these caves are worked on the Greenbriar. There are many of them known on Cumberland river.

The country westward of the Alleghany abounds with springs of common salt. The most remarkable we have heard of are at Bullet's-lick, the Big-bones, the Blue-licks, and on the north fork of Holston. The area of Bullet's-lick is of many acres. Digging the earth to the depth of three feet the water begins to boil up, and the deeper you go and the drier the weather, the stronger is the brine. A thousand gallons of water yield from a bushel to a bushel and a half of salt, which is about eighty pounds of water to one pound of salt. So that sea-water is more than three times as strong as that of these springs. A salt spring has been lately discovered at the Turkey foot on Yohogany, by which river it is overflowed, except at very low water. Its merit is not yet known. Dunning's lick is also as yet untried, but it is supposed to be the best on this side the Ohio. The salt springs on the margin of the Onondago lake are said to give a saline taste to the waters of the lake.

There are several medicinal springs, some of which are indubitably efficacious, while others seem to owe their reputation as much to fancy and change of air and regimen, as to their real virtues. None of them having undergone a chemical analysis in skilful hands, nor been so far the subject of observations as to have produced a reduction into classes of the disorders which they relieve; it is in my power to give little more than an enumeration of them.

The most efficacious of these are two springs in Augusta near the first sources of James' river, where it is called Jackson's river. They rise near the foot of the ridge of mountains generally called the Warm spring mountains, but in the maps Jackson's mountains. The one distinguished by the name of the Warm spring, and the other of the Hot spring. The Warm spring issues with a very bold stream, sufficient to work a grist mill and to keep the waters of its basin, which is thirty feet in diameter, at the vital warmth, *viz.* 96° of Fahrenheit's thermometer. The matter with which these waters is allied is very volatile; its smell indicates it to be sulphureous, as also does the circumstance of its turning silver black. They relieve rheumatisms. Others complaints also of very different natures have been removed or lessened by them. It rains here four or five days in every week.

The *Hot* spring is about six miles from the Warm, is much smaller, and has been so hot as to have boiled an egg. Some believe its degree of heat to be lessened. It raises the mercury in Fahrenheit's thermometer to 112 degrees, which is fever heat. It sometimes relieves where the Warm fails. A fountain of common water, issuing within a few inches of its margin, gives it a singular appearance. Comparing the temperature of these with that of the Hot springs of Kamschatka, of which Krachininnikow gives an account, the difference is very great, the latter raising the mercury to 200° which is within 12° of boiling water. These springs are very much resorted to in spite of a total want of accommodation for the sick. Their waters are strongest in the hottest months, which occasions their being visited in July and August principally.

The Sweet springs are in the county of Botetourt, at the eastern foot of the Alleghany, about forty-two miles from the Warm springs. They are still less known. Having been found to relieve cases in which the others had been ineffectually tried, it is probable their compositions is different. They are different also in their temperature, being as cold as common water; which is not mentioned, however, as a proof of a distinct impregnation. This is among the first sources of James' river.

On Potomac river, in Berkley county, above the North mountain, are medicinal springs, much more frequented than those of Augusta. Their powers, however, are less, the waters weakly mineralized, and scarcely warm. They are more visited, because situated in a fertile, plentiful, and populous country, better provided with accommodations, always safe from the Indians, and nearest to the more populous States.

In Louisa county, on the head waters of the South Ann branch of York river, are springs of some medicinal virtue. They are not much used however. There is a weak chalybeate at Richmond; and many others in various parts of the country, which are of too little worth, or too little note, to be enumerated after those before mentioned.

We are told of a sulphur spring on Howard's creek of Greenbriar, and another at Boonsborough on Kentucky.

In the low grounds of the Great Kanhaway, seven miles above the mouth of Elk river, and sixty-seven above that of the Kanhaway itself, is a hole in the earth of the capacity of thirty or forty gallons, from which issues constantly a bituminous vapor, in so strong a current as to give to the sand about its orifice the motion which it has in a boiling spring. On presenting a lighted candle or torch within eighteen inches of the hole it flames up in a column of eighteen inches in diameter, and four or five feet height, which sometimes burns out within twenty minutes, and at other times has been known to continue three days, and then has been still left burning. The flame is unsteady, of the density of that of burning spirits, and smells like burning pit coal. Water sometimes collects in the basin, which is remarkably cold, and is kept in ebullition by the vapor issuing through it. If the vapor be fired in that state, the water soon becomes so warm that the hand cannot bear it, and evaporates wholly in a short time. This, with the circumjacent lands, is the property of His Excellency General Washington and of General Lewis.

There is a similar one on Sandy river, the flame of which is a column of about twelve inches diameter, and three feet high. General Clarke, who informs me of it, kindled the vapor, staid about an hour, and left it burning.

The mention of uncommon springs leads me to that of Syphon fountains. There is one of these near the intersection of the Lord Fairfax's boundary with the North mountain, not far from Brock's gap, on the stream of which is a grist mill, which grinds two bushels of grain at every flood of the spring; another near Cow-pasture river, a mile and a half below its confluence with the Bull-pasture river, and sixteen or seventeen miles from Hot springs, which intermits once in every twelve hours; one also near the mouth of the north Holston.

After these may be mentioned the *Natural Well,* on the lands of a Mr. Lewis in Frederick county. It is somewhat larger than a common well; the water rises in it as near the surface of the earth as in the neighboring artificial wells, and is of a depth as yet unknown. It is said there is a current in it tending sensibly downwards. If this be true, it probably feeds some fountain, of which it is the natural reservoir, distinguished from others, like that of Madison's cave, by being accessible. It is used with a bucket and windlass as an ordinary well.

A complete catalogue of the trees, plants, fruits, &c., is probably not desired. I will sketch out those which would principally attract notice, as being first, Medicinal; second, Esculent; third, Ornamental; or four, useful for fabrication; adding the Linnæan to the popular names, as the latter might not convey precise information to a foreigner. I shall confine myself too to native plants.

1. Senna. Cassia ligustrina.
   Arsmart. Polygonum Sagittatum.
   Clivers, or goose-grass. Galium spurium.
   Lobelia of several species.
   Palma Christi. Ricinus.
   (3) Jamestown weed. Datura Stramonium.
   Mallow. Malva rotundafolia.
   Syrian mallow. Hibiscus moschentos.
   Hibiscus Virginicus.
   Indian mallow. Sida rhombifolia.
   Sida abutilon.
   Virginia marshmallow. Napæa hermaphrodita.
   Napæa dioica.
   Indian physic. Spiria trifoliata.
   Euphorbia Ipecacuanhæ.
   Pleurisy root. Asclepias decumbens.
   Virginia snake-root. Aristolochia serpentaria.

Black snake-root. Actæ racemosa.
Seneca rattlesnake-root. Polygala Senega.
Valerian. Valeriana locusta radiata.
Gentiana, Saponaria, Villosa & Centaurium.
Ginseng. Panax quinquefolium.
Angelica. Angelica sylvestris.
Cassava. Jatropha urens.

2. Tuckahoe. Lycoperdon tuber.
   Jerusalem artichoke. Helianthus tuberosus.
   Long potatoes. Convolvulas batatas.
   Granadillas. Maycocks, Maracocks, Passiflora incarnata.
   Panic. Panicum of many species.
   Indian millet. Holcus laxus.
   Indian millet. Holcus striosus.
   Wild oat. Zizania aquaticia.
   Wild pea. Dolichos of Clayton.

Lupine. Lupinus perennis.

Wild hop. Humulus lupulus.

Wild cherry. Prunus Virginiana.

Cherokee plum. Prunus sylvestris fructu majori. Clayton.

Wild plum. Prunus sylvestris fructu minori. Clayton.

Wild crab apple. Pyrus coronaria.

Red mulberry. Morus rubra.

Persimmon. Diospiros Virginiana.

Sugar maple. Acer saccarinum.

Scaly bark hiccory. Juglans alba cortice squamoso. Clayton.

Common hiccory. Juglans alba, fructu minore rancido. Clayton.

Paccan, or Illinois nut. Not described by Linnæus, Millar, or Clayton. Were I to venture to describe this, speaking of the fruit from memory, and of the leaf from plants of two years' growth, I should specify it as Juglans alba, foliolis lanceolatis, acuminatus, serratis, tomentosis, fructu minore, ovato, compresso, vix insculpto, dulci, putamine tenerrimo. It grows on the Illinois, Wabash, Ohio, and Mississippi. It is spoken of by Don Ulloa under the name of Pacanos, in his Noticias Americanas. Entret. 6.

Black walnut. Juglans nigra.

White walnut. Juglans alba.

Chesnut. Fagus castanea.

Chinquapin. Fagus pumila.

Hazlenut. Corylus avellana.

Grapes. Vitis. Various kinds; though only three described by Clayton.

Scarlet strawberries. Fragaria Virginiana of Millar.

Whortleberries. Vaccinium uliginosum.

Wild gooseberries. Ribes grossularia.

Cranberries. Vaccinium oxycoccos.

Black raspberries. Rubus occidentalis.

Blackberries. Rubus fructicosus.

Dewberries. Rubus cæsius.

Cloudberries. Rubus Chamæmorus.

3. Plane tree. Platanus occidentalis.

Poplar. Liriodenadron tulipifera.
       Populus heterophylla.

Black poplar. Populus nigra.

Aspen. Populus tremula.

Linden, or lime. Telia Americana.

Red flowering maple. Acer rubrum.

Horse-chesnut, or buck's-eye. Æsculus pavia.

Catalpa. Bignonia catalpa.

Umbrella. Magnolia tripetala.

Swamp laurel. Magnolia glauca.

Cucumber-tree. Magnolia acuminata.

Portugal bay. Laurus indica.

Red bay. Laurus borbonia.

Dwarf-rose bay. Rhododendron maximum.

Laurel of the western country. Qu. species?

Wild pimento. Laurus benzoin.

Sassafras. Laurus sassafras.

Locust. Robinia pseudo-acacia.

Honey-locust. Gleditsia. 1. 6

Dogwood. Cornus florida.

Fringe, or snow-drop tree. Chionanthus Virginica.

Barberry. Barberis vulgaris.

Redbud, or Judas-tree. Cercis Canadensis.

Holly. Ilex aquifolium.

Cockspur hawthorn. Cratægus coccinea.

Spindle-tree. Euonymus Europæus.

Evergreen spindle-tree. Euonymus Americanus.

Itea Virginica.

Elder. Sambucus nigra.

Papaw. Annona triloba.

Candleberry myrtle. Myrica cerifera.

Dwarf laurel. Kalmia angustifolia, Kalmia latifolia (called ivy with us).

Ivy. Hedera quinquefolia.

Trumpet honeysuckle. Lonicera sempervirens.

Upright honeysuckle. Azalea nudiflora.

Yellow jasmine. Bignonia sempervirens.

Calycanthus floridus.
American aloe. Agave Virginica.
Sumach. Rhus. Qu. species?
Poke. Phytolacca decandra.
Long moss. Tillandsia Usneoides.

4. Reed. Aruudo phragmitis.
Virginia hemp. Acnida cannabina.
Flax. Linum Virginianum.
Black, or pitch-pine. Pinus tæda.
White pine. Pinus strobus.
Yellow pine. Pinus Virginica.
Spruce pine. Pinus foliis singularibus. Clayton.
Hemlock spruce Fir. Pinus Canadensis.
Abor vitæ. Thuya occidentalis.
Juniper. Juniperus Virginica (called cedar with us).
Cypress. Cupressus disticha.

White cedar. Cupressus Thyoides.
Black oak. Quercus nigra.
White oak. Quercus alba.
Red oak. Quercus rubra.
Willow oak. Quercus phellos.
Chesnut oak. Quercus prinus.
Black jack oak. Quercus aquatica. Clayton.
Ground oak. Quercus pumila. Clayton.
Live oak. Quercus Virginiana. Millar.
Black birch. Betula nigra.
White birch. Betula alba.
Beach. Fagus sylvatica.
Ash. Fraxinus Americana.
    Fraxinus Novæ Angliæ. Millar.
Elm. Ulmus Americana.
Willow. Salix. Qu. species?
Sweet gum. Liquidambar styraciflua.

The following were found in Virginia when first visited by the English; but it is not said whether of spontaneous growth, or by cultivation only. Most probably they were natives of more southern climates, and handed along the continent from one nation to another of the savages.

Tobacco. Nicotiana.
Maize. Zea mays.
Round potatoes. Solanum tuberosum.

Pumpkins. Cucurbita pepo.
Cymlings. Cucurbita verrucosa.
Squashes. Cucurbita melopepo.

There is an infinitude of other plants and flowers, for an enumeration and scientific description of which I must refer to the Flora Virginica of our great botanist, Dr. Clayton, published by Gronovius at Leyden, in 1762. This accurate observer was a native and resident of this State, passed a long life in exploring and describing its plants, and is supposed to have enlarged the botanical catalogue as much as almost any man who has lived.

Besides these plants, which are native, our *farms* produce wheat, rye, barley, oats, buck-wheat, broom corn, and Indian corn. The climate suits rice well enough, wherever the lands do. Tobacco, hemp, flax, and cotton, are staple commodities. Indigo yields two cuttings. The silk-worm is a native, and the mulberry, proper for its food, grows kindly.

We cultivate, also, potatoes, both the long and the round, turnips, carrots, parsnips, pumpkins, and ground nuts (Arachis.) Our grasses are lucerne, st. foin, burnet, timothy, ray, and orchard grass; red, white, and yellow clover; greensward, blue grass, and crab grass.

The *gardens* yield musk-melons, water-melons, tomatoes, okra, pomegranates, figs, and the esculant plants of Europe.

The *orchards* produce apples, pears, cherries, quinces, peaches, nectarines, apricots, almonds, and plums.

Our quadrupeds have been mostly described by Linnæus and Mons. de Buffon. Of these the mammoth, or big buffalo, as called by the Indians, must certainly have been the largest. Their tradition is, that he was carnivorous, and still exists in the northern parts of America. A delegation of warriors from the Delaware tribe having visited the Governor of Virginia, during the revolution, on matters of business, after these had been discussed and settled in council, the Governor asked them some questions relative to their country, and among others, what they knew or had heard of the animal whose bones were found at the Saltlicks on the Ohio. Their chief speaker immediately put himself into an attitude of oratory, and with a pomp suited to what he conceived the elevation of his subject, informed him that it was a tradition handed down from their fathers, "That in ancient times a herd of these tremendous animals came to the Big-bone licks, and began an universal destruction of the bear, deer, elks, buffaloes, and other animals which had been created for the use of the Indians; that the Great Man above, looking down and seeing this, was so enraged that he seized his lightning, descended on the earth, seated himself on a neighboring mountain, on a rock of which his seat and the print of his feet are still to be seen, and hurled his bolts among them till the whole were slaughtered, except the big bull, who presenting his forehead to the shafts, shook them off as they fell; but missing one at length, it wounded him in the side; whereon, springing round, he bounded over the Ohio, over the Wabash, the Illinois, and finally over the great lakes, where he is living at this day." It is well known, that on the Ohio, and in many parts of America further north, tusks, grinders, and skeletons of unparalleled magnitude, are found in great numbers, some lying on the surface of the earth, and some a little below it. A Mr. Stanley, taken prisoner near the mouth of the Tennessee, relates, that after being transferred through several tribes, from one to another, he was at length carried over the mountains west of the Missouri to a river which runs westwardly; that these bones abounded there, and that the natives described to him the animal to which they belonged as still existing in the northern parts of their country; from which description he judged it to be an elephant. Bones of the same kind have been lately found, some feet below the surface of the earth, in salines opened on the North Holston, a branch of the Tennessee, about the latitude of 36½° north. From the accounts published in Europe, I suppose it to be decided that these are of the same kind with those found in Siberia. Instances are mentioned of like animal remains found in the more southern climates of both hemispheres; but they are either so loosely mentioned as to leave a doubt of the fact, so inaccurately described as not to authorize the classing them with the great northern bones, or so rare as to found a suspicion that they have been carried thither as curiosities from the northern regions. So that, on the whole, there seem to be no certain vestiges of the existence of this animal farther south than the salines just mentioned. It is remarkable that the tusks and skeletons have been ascribed by the naturalists of Europe to the elephant, while the grinders have been given to the hippopotamus, or river horse. Yet it is acknowledged, that the tusks and skeletons are much larger than those of the elephant, and the grinders many times greater than those of the hippopotamus, and essentially different in form. Wherever these grinders are found, there also we find the tusks and skeleton; but no skeleton of the hippopotamus nor grinders of the elephant. It will not be said that the hippopotamus and elephant came always to the same spot, the former to deposit his grinders, and the latter his tusks and skeleton. For what became of the parts not deposited there? We must agree then, that these remains belong to each other, that they are of one and the same animal, that this was not a hippopotamus, because the hippopotamus had no tusks, nor such a frame, and because the grinders differ in their size as well as in the number and form of their points. That this was not an elephant, I think ascertained by proofs equally decisive. I will not avail myself of the authority of the celebrated[1] anatomist, who, from an examination of the form and structure of the tusks, has declared they were essentially different from those of the elephant; because another[2] anatomist, equally celebrated, has declared, on a like examination, that they are precisely the same. Between two such authorities I will suppose this circumstance equivocal. But, 1. The skeleton of the mammoth (for so the incognitum has been called) bespeaks an animal of five or six times the cubic volume of the elephant, as Mons. de Buffon has admitted. 2. The grinders are five times as large, are square, and the grinding surface studded with four or five rows of blunt points; whereas those of the elephant are broad and thin, and their grinding surface flat. 3. I have never heard an instance, and suppose there has been none, of the grinder of an elephant being found in America. 4. From the known temperature and constitution of the elephant, he could never have existed in those regions where the remains of the mammoth have been found. The elephant is a native only of the torrid zone and its vicinities; if, with the assistance of warm apartments and warm clothing, he has been preserved in the temperate climates of Europe, it has only been for a small portion of what would have been his natural period, and no instance of his multiplication in them has ever been known. But no bones of the mammoth, as I have before observed, have been ever found further south than the salines of Holston, and they have been found as far north as the Arctic circle. Those, therefore, who are of opinion that the elephant and mammoth are the same, must believe, 1. That the elephant known to us can exist and multiply in the frozen zone; or, 2. That an eternal fire may once have warmed those regions, and since abandoned them, of which, however, the globe exhibits no unequivocal indications; or, 3. That the obliquity of the ecliptic, when these elephants lived, was no great as to include within the tropics all those regions in which the bones are found; the tropics being, as is before observed, the natural limits of habitation for the elephant. But if it be admitted that this obliquity has really decreased, and we adopt the highest rate of decrease yet pretended, that is, of one minute in a century, to transfer the northern tropic to the Arctic circle, would carry the existence of these sup-

[1] Hunter.—T. J.   [2] D'Aubenton.—T. J.

posed elephants two hundred and fifty thousand years back; a period far beyond our conception of the duration of animal bones less exposed to the open air than these are in many instances. Besides, though these regions would then be supposed within the tropics, yet their winters would have been too severe for the sensibility of the elephant. They would have had, too, but one day and one night in the year, a circumstance to which we have no reason to suppose the nature of the elephant fitted. However, it has been demonstrated, that, if a variation of obliquity in the ecliptic takes place at all, it is vibratory, and never exceeds the limits of nine degrees, which is not sufficient to bring these bones within the tropics. One of these hypotheses, or some other equally voluntary and inadmissable to cautious philosophy, must be adopted to support the opinion that these are the bones of the elephant. For my own part, I find it easier to believe that an animal may have existed, resembling the elephant in his tusks, and general anatomy, while his nature was in other respects extremely different. From the 30th degree of south latitude to the 30th degree of north, are nearly the limits which nature has fixed for the existence and multiplication of the elephant known to us. Proceeding thence northwardly to 36½ degrees, we enter those assigned to the mammoth. The farther we advance north, the more their vestiges multiply as far as the earth has been explored in that direction; and it is as probable as otherwise, that this progression continues to the pole itself, if land extends so far. The centre of the frozen zone, then, may be the acmé of their vigor, as that of the torrid is of the elephant. Thus nature seems to have drawn a belt of separation between these two tremendous animals, whose breadth, indeed, is not precisely known, though at present we may suppose it about 6½ degrees of latitude; to have assigned to the elephant the regions south of these confines, and those north to the mammoth, founding the constitution of the one in her extreme of heat, and that of the other in the extreme of cold. When the Creator has therefore separated their nature as far as the extent of the scale of animal life allowed to this planet would permit, it seems perverse to declare it the same, from a partial resemblance of their tusks and bones. But to whatever animal we ascribe these remains, it is certain such a one has existed in America, and that it has been the largest of all terrestrial beings. It should have sufficed to have rescued the earth it inhabited, and the atmosphere it breathed, from the imputation of impotence in the conception and nourishment of animal life on a large scale; to have stifled, in its birth, the opinion of a writer, the most learned, too, of all others in the science of animal history, that in the new world, *"La nature vivante est beaucoup moins agissante, beaucoup moins forte."* [1] that nature is less active, less energetic on one side of the globe than she is on the other. As if both sides were not warmed by the same genial sun; as if a soil of the same chemical composition was less capable of elaboration into animal nutriment; as if the fruits and grains from that soil and sun yielded a less rich chyle, gave less extension to the solids and fluids of the body, or produced sooner in the cartilages, membranes, and fibres, that rigidity which restrains all further extension, and terminates animal growth.

[1] Buffon, xviii, 112 edit. Paris, 1764.—T. J.

The truth is, that a pigmy and a Patagonian, a mouse and a mammoth, derive their dimensions from the same nutritive juices. The difference of increment depends on circumstances unsearchable to beings with our capacities. Every race of animals seems to have received from their Maker certains laws of extension at the time of their formation. Their elaborate organs were formed to produce this, while proper obstacles were opposed to its further progress. Below these limits they cannot fall, nor rise above them. What intermediate station they shall take may depend on soil, on climate, on food, on a careful choice of breeders. But all the manna of heaven would never raise the mouse to the bulk of the mammoth.

The opinion advanced by the Count de Buffon,[1] is 1. That the animals common both to the old and new world are smaller in the latter. 2. That those peculiar to the new are on a smaller scale. 3. That those which have been domesticated in both have degenerated in America; and 4. That on the whole it exhibits fewer species. And the reason he thinks is, that the heats of America are less; that more waters are spread over its surface by nature, and fewer of these drained off by the hand of man. In other words, that *heat* is friendly, and *moisture* adverse to the production and development of large quadrupeds. I will not meet this hypothesis on its first doubtful ground, whether the climate of America be comparatively more humid? Because we are not furnished with observations sufficient to decide this question. And though, till it be decided, we are as free to deny as others are to affirm the fact, yet for a moment let it be supposed. The hypothesis, after this supposition, proceeds to another; that *moisture* is unfriendly to animal growth. The truth of this is inscrutable to us by reasonings *à priori*. Nature has hidden from us her *modus agendi*. Our only appeal on such questions is to experience; and I think that experience is against the supposition. It is by the assistance of *heat* and *moisture* that vegetables are elaborated from the elements of earth, air, water, and fire. We accordingly see the more humid climates produce the greater quantity of vegetables. Vegetables are mediately or immediately the food of every animal; and in proportion to the quantity of food, we see animals not only multiplied in their numbers, but improved in their bulk, as far as the laws of their nature will admit. Of this opinion is the Count de Buffon himself in another part of his work;[2] *"en general il paroit ques les pays un peu* froids *conviennent mieux à nos boeufs que les pays chauds, et qu'ils sont d'autant plus gross et plus grands que le climat est plus* humide *et plus abondans en paturages. Les boeufs de Danemarck, de la Podolie, de l'Ulkraine et de la Tartarie qu habitent les Calmouques sont les plus grands de tous."* Here then a race of animals, and one of the largest too, has been increased in its dimensions by *cold* and *moisture,* in direct opposition to the hypothesis, which supposes that these two circumstances diminish animal bulk, and that it is their contraries *heat* and *dryness* which enlarge it. But when we appeal to experience we are not to rest satisfied with a single fact. Let us, therefore, try our question on more general ground. Let us take two portions of the earth, Europe and America for instance, sufficiently extensive to give opera-

[1] Buffon, xviii. 100, 156.—т. ј.   [2] viii. 134.—т. ј.

tion to general causes; let us consider the circumstances peculiar to each, and observe their effect on animal nature. America, running through the torrid as well as temperate zone, has more *heat* collectively taken, than Europe. But Europe, according to our hypothesis, is the *dryest*. They are equally adapted then to animal productions; each being endowed with one of those causes which befriend animal growth, and with one which opposes it. If it be thought unequal to compare Europe with America, which is so much larger, I answer, not more so than to compare America with the whole world. Besides, the purpose of the comparison is to try an hypothesis, which makes the size of animals depend on the *heat* and *moisture* of climate. If, therefore, we take a region so extensive as to comprehend a sensible distinction of climate, and so extensive too as that local accidents, or the intercourse of animals on its borders, may not materially affect the size of those in its interior parts, we shall comply with those conditions which the hypothesis may reasonably demand. The objection would be the weaker in the present case, because any intercourse of animals

A COMPARATIVE VIEW OF THE QUADRUPEDS OF EUROPE AND OF AMERICA

I. ABORIGINALS OF BOTH

	EUROPE LB.	AMERICA LB.
Mammoth		
Buffalo. Bison		* 1800
White Bear. Ours blanc		
Carribou. Renne		
Bear. Ours	153.7	* 410
Elk. Elan. Original palmated		
Red deer. Cerf	288.8	* 273
Fallow Deer. Daim	167.8	
Wolf. Loup	69.8	
Roe. Chevreuil	56.7	
Glutton. Glouton. Carcajou		
Wild cat. Chat sauvage		† 30
Lynx. Loup cervier	25.	
Beaver. Castor	18.5	* 45
Badger Blaireau	13.6	
Red fox. Renard	13.5	
Gray fox. Isatis		
Otter. Loutre	8.9	† 12
Monax. Marmotte	6.5	
Vison. Fouine	2.8	
Hedgehog. Herisson	2.2	
Marten. Marte	1.9	† 6
	oz.	
Water rat. Rat d'eau	7.5	
Weasel. Belette	2.2	oz.
Flying squirrel. Polatouche	2.2	† 4
Shrew moseu Musaraigne	1.	

which may take place on the confines of Europe and Asia, is to the advantage of the former, Asia producing certainly larger animals than Europe. Let us then take a comparative view of the quadrupeds of Europe and America, presenting them to the eye in three different tables, in one of which shall be enumerated those found in both countries; in a second, those found in one only; in a third, those which have been domesticated in both. To facilitate the comparison, let those of each table be arranged in gradation according to their sizes, from the greatest to the smallest, so far as their sizes can be conjectured. The weights of the large animals shall be expressed in the English avoirdupois and its decimals; those of the smaller, in the same ounce and its decimals. Those which are marked thus *, are actual weights of particular subjects, deemed among the largest of their species. Those marked thus †, are furnished by judicious persons, well acquainted with the species, and saying, from conjecture only, what the largest individual they had seen would probably have weighed. The other weights are taken from Messrs. Buffon and D'Aubenton, and are of such subjects as came casually to their hands for dissection. This circumstance must be remembered where their weights and mine stand opposed; the latter being stated not to produce a conclusion in favor of the American species, but to justify a suspension of opinion until we are better informed, and a suspicion, in the meantime, that there is no uniform difference in favor of either; which is all I pretend.

II. ABORIGINALS OF ONE ONLY

Europe	LB.
Sanglier. Wild boar	280.
Mouflon. Wild sheep	56.
Bouquetin. Wild goat	
Lievre. Hare	7.6
Lapin. Rabbit	3.4
Putois. Polecat	3.3
Genette	3.1
Desman. Muskrat	OZ.
Ecureuil. Squirrel	12.

America	LB.
Tapir	534.
Elk, round horned	†450.
Puma	
Jaguar	218.
Cabiai	109.
Tamanoir	109.
Tammandua	65.4
Cougar of North-America	75.
Cougar of South-America	59.4

Europe	LB.
Hermine. Ermin	8.2
Rat. Rat	7.5

	LB.
Loirs	3.1
Lerot. Dormouse	1.8
Taupe. Mole	1.2
Hampster	.6
Zisel	
Leming	
Souris. Mouse	.6

America	LB.
Ocelot	
Pecari	46.3
Jaguaret	43.6
Alco	
Lama	
Paco	
Paca	32.7
Serval	
Sloth. Unau	27.25
Saricovienne	
Kincajou	
Tatou Kabassou	21.8
Urson. Urchin	
Raccoon. Raton	16.5
Coati	
Coendou	16.3

Sloth. Aï	13.	Fox squirrel of Virginia	† 2.625
Sapajou Ouarini		Surikate	2.
Sapajou Coaita	9.8	Mink	† 2.
Tatou Encubert		Sapajou. Sajou	1.8
Tatou Apar		Indian pig. Cochon d'Inde	1.6
Tatou Cachica	7.	Sapajou Saïmiri	1.5
Little Coendou	6.5		
Opossum. Sarigu		*America*	LB.
Tapeti		Phalanger	
Margay		Coqualain	
Crabier		Lesser gray squirrel	† 1.5
Agouti	4.2	Black squirrel	† 1.5
Sapajou Saï	3.5	Red squirrel	10.oz.
Tatou Cirquinçon		Sagoin Saki	
Tatou Tatouate	3.3	Sagoin Pinche	
Mouffette Squash		Sagoin Tamarin	oz.
Mouffette Chinche		Sagoin Ouistiti	4.4
Mouffette Conepate		Sagoin Marakine	
Scunk		Sagoin Mico	
Mouffette. Zorilla		Cayopollin	
Whabus. Hare. Rabbit.		Fourmillier	
Aperea		Marmose	
Akouchi		Sarigue of Cayenne	
Ondatra. Muskrat		Tucan	
Pilori		Red mole	oz.
Great gray squirrel	† 2.7	Ground squirrel	4.

III. DOMESTICATED IN BOTH

	EUROPE LB.	AMERICA LB.
Cow	765.	* 2500
Horse		* 1366
Ass		
Hog		* 1200
Sheep		* 125
Goat		* 80
Dog	67.6	
Cat	7.	

I have not inserted in the first table the Phoca,[1] nor leather-winged bat, because the one living half the year in the water, and the other being a winged animal, the individuals of each species may visit both continents.

Of the animals in the first table, Monsieur de Buffon himself informs us,

[1] It is said that this animal is seldom seen above thirty miles from shore, or beyond the 56th degree of latitude. The interjacent islands between Asia and America admit his passing from one continent to the other without exceeding these bounds. And in fact, travellers tell us that these islands are places of principal resort for them, and especially in the season of bringing forth their young.—T. J.

[xxvii. 130, xxx. 213,] that the beaver, the otter, and shrew mouse, though of the same species, are larger in America than in Europe. This should therefore have corrected the generality of his expressions, xviii. 145, and elsewhere, that the animals common to the two countries, are considerably less in America than in Europe, *"et cela sans aucune exception."* He tells us too, [Quadrup. viii. 334, edit. Paris 1777,] that on examining a bear from America, he remarked no difference, *"dans* la forme *de cet ours d'Amerique comparé a celui d'Europe,"* but adds from Bartram's journal, that an American bear weighed four hundred pounds, English, equal to three hundred and sixty-seven pounds French; whereas we find the European bear examined by Mons. D'Aubenton [xvii. 82], weighed but one hundred and forty-one pounds French. That the palmated elk is larger in America than in Europe, we are informed by Kalm,[1] a naturalist, who visited the former by public appointment, for the express purpose of examining the subjects of natural history. In this fact Pennant concurs with him. [Barrington's Miscellanies.] The same Kalm tells us[2] that the black moose, or renne of America, is as high as a tall horse; and Catesby,[3] that it is about the bigness of a middle-sized ox. The same account of their size has been given me by many who have seen them. But Monsieur D'Aubenton says[4] that the renne of Europe is about the size of a red deer. The weasel is larger in America than in Europe, as may be seen by comparing its dimensions as reported by Monsieur D'Aubenton[5] and Kalm. The latter tells us,[6] that the lynx, badger, red fox, and flying squirrel, are the *same* in America as in Europe; by which expression I understand, they are the same in all material circumstances, in size as well as others; for if they were smaller, they would differ from the European. Our gray fox is, by Catesby's account,[7] little different in sizes and shape from the European fox. I presume he means the red fox of Europe, as does Kalm, where he says,[8] that in size "they do not quite come up to our foxes." For proceeding next to the red fox of America, he says, "they are entirely the same with the European sort"; which shows he had in view one European sort only, which was the red. So that the result of their testimony is, that the American gray fox is somewhat less than the European red; which is equally true of the gray fox of Europe, as may be seen by comparing the measures of the Count de Buffon and Monseiur D'Aubenton.[9] The white bear of America is as large as that of Europe. The bones of the mammoth which has been found in America, are as large as those found in the old world. It may be asked, why I insert the mammoth, as if it still existed? I ask in return, why I should omit it, as if it did not exist? Such is the economy of nature, that no instance can be produced, of her having permitted any one race of her animals to become extinct; of her having formed any link in her great work so weak as to be broken. To add to this, the traditionary testimony of the Indians, that this animal still exists in the northern and western parts of America, would be adding the light of a

[1] I. 233, Lon. 1772.—T. J.   [2] Ib. 233.—T. J.   [3] I. xxvii.—T. J.
[4] XXIV. 162.—T. J.   [5] XV. 42.—T. J.   [6] I. 359. I. 48, 221, 251. II. 52.—T. J.
[7] II. 78.—T. J.   [8] I. 220.—T. J.
[9] XXVII. 63. XIV. 119. Harris, II. 387. Buffon, Quad. IX. 1.—T. J.

taper to that of the meridian sun. Those parts still remain in their aboriginal state, unexplored and undisturbed by us, or by others for us. He may as well exist there now, as he did formerly where we find his bones. If he be a carnivorous animal, as some anatomists have conjectured, and the Indians affirm, his early retirement may be accounted for from the general destruction of the wild game by the Indians, which commences in the first instant of their connection with us, for the purpose of purchasing match-coats, hatchets, and firelocks, with their skins. There remain then the buffalo, red deer, fallow deer, wolf, roe, glutton, wild cat, monax, bison, hedgehog, marten, and water-rat, of the comparative sizes of which we have not sufficient testimony. It does not appear that Messieurs de Buffon and D'Aubenton have measured, weighed, or seen those of America. It is said of some of them, by some travellers, that they are smaller than the European. But who were these travellers? Have they not been men of a very different description from those who have laid open to us the other three quarters of the world? Was natural history the object of their travels? Did they measure or weigh the animals they speak of? or did they not judge of them by sight, or perhaps even from report only? Were they acquainted with the animals of their own country, with which they undertake to compare them? Have they not been so ignorant as often to mistake the species? A true answer to these questions would probably lighten their authority, so as to render it insufficient for the foundation of an hypothesis. How unripe we yet are, for an accurate comparison of the animals of the two countries, will appear from the work of Monsieur de Buffon. The ideas we should have formed of the sizes of some animals, from the information he had received at his first publications concerning them, are very different from what his subsequent communications give us. And indeed his candor in this can never be too much praised. One sentence of his book must do him immortal honor. *"J'aime autant une personne qui me releve d'une erreur, qu'une autre qui m'apprend une verité parce qu'en effet une erreur corrigée est une verité."* [1] He seems to have thought the cabiai he first exclaimed wanted little of its full growth. *"Il n'etoit pas encore tout-a-fait adulte."* [2] Yet he weighed but forty-six and a half pounds, and he found afterwards,[3] that these animals, when full grown, weigh one hundred pounds. He had supposed, from the examination of a jaguar,[4] said to be two years old, which weighed but sixteen pounds twelve ounces, that when he should have acquired his full growth, he would not be larger than a middle-sized dog. But a subsequent account[5] raises his weight to two hundred pounds. Further information will, doubtless, produce further corrections. The wonder is, not that there is yet something in this great work to correct, but that there is so little. The result of this view then is, that of twenty-six quadrupeds common to both countries, seven are said to be larger in America, seven of equal size, and twelve not sufficiently examined. So that the first table impeaches the first member of the assertion, that of the animals common to both countries, the American are smallest, *"et cela sans aucune exception."* It

---

[1] Quad. IX. 158.—T. J.　　[2] XXV. 184.—T. J.　　[3] Quad. IX. 132.—T. J.
[4] XIX. 2.—T. J.　　[5] Quad. IX. 41.—T. J.

shows it is not just, in all the latitude in which its author has advanced it, and probably not to such a degree as to found a distinction between the two countries.

Proceeding to the second table, which arranges the animals found in one of the two countries only, Monsieur de Buffon observes, that the tapir, the elephant of America, is but of the size of a small cow. To preserve our comparison, I will add, that the wild boar, the elephant of Europe, is little more than half that size. I have made an elk with round or cylindrical horns an animal of America, and peculiar to it; because I have seen many of them myself, and more of their horns; and because I can say, from the best information, that, in Virginia, this kind of elk has abounded much, and still exists in smaller numbers; and I could never learn that the palmated kind had been seen here at all. I suppose this confined to the more northern latitudes.[1] I have made our hare or rabbit peculiar, believing it to be different from both the European animals of those denominations, and calling it therefore by its Algonquin name, Whabus, to keep it distinct from these. Kalm is of the same opinion.[2] I have enumerated the squirrels according to our own knowledge, derived from daily sight of them, because I am not able to reconcile with that the European appellations and descriptions. I have heard of other species, but they have never come within my own notice. These, I think, are the only instances in which I

[1] The descriptions of Theodat, Denys and La Honton, cited by Monsieur de Buffon, under the article Elan, authorize the supposition, that the flat-horned elk is found in the northern parts of America. It has not however extended to our latitudes. On the other hand, I could never learn that the round-horned elk has been seen further north than the Hudson's river. This agrees with the former elk in its general character, being, like that, when compared with a deer, very much larger, its ears longer, broader, and thicker in proportion, its hair much longer, neck and tail shorter, having a dewlap before the breast (caruncula gutturalis Linnæi) a white spot often, if not always, of a foot diameter, on the hinder part of the buttocks round the tail; its gait a trot, and attended with a rattling of the hoofs; but distinguished from that decisively by its horns, which are not palmated, but round and pointed. This is the animal described by Catesby as the Cervus major Americanus, the stag of America, le Cerf de l'Amerique. But it differs from the Cervus as totally as does the palmated elk from the dama. And in fact it seems to stand in the same relation to the palmated elk, as the red deer does to the fallow. It has abounded in Virginia, has been seen, within my knowledge, on the eastern side of the Blue Ridge since the year 1765, is now common beyond those mountains, has been often brought to us and tamed, and its horns are in the hands of many. I should designate it as the *"Alces Americanus cornibus teretibus."* It were to be wished, that naturalists, who are acquainted with the renne and elk of Europe, and who may hereafter visit the northern parts of America, would examine well the animals called there by the names of gray and black moose, caribou, original and elk. Monsieur de Buffon has done what could be done from the materials in his hands, toward clearing up the confusion introduced by the loose application of these names among the animals they are meant to designate. He reduces the whole to the renne and flat-horned elk. From all the information I have been able to collect, I strongly suspect they will be found to cover three, if not four distinct species of animals. I have seen skins of a moose, and of the caribou: they differ more from each other, and from that of the round-horned elk, than I ever saw two skins differ which belonged to different individuals of any wild species. These differences are in the color, length, and coarseness of the hair, and in the size, texture, and marks of the skin. Perhaps it will be found that there is, 1, the moose, black and gray, the former being said to be the male, and the latter the female; 2, the caribou or renne; 3, the flat-horned elk, or original; 4, the round-horned elk. Should this last, though possessing so nearly the characters of the elk, be found to be the same with the Cerf d'Ardennes or Brandhitz of Germany, still there will remain the three species first enumerated.—T. J.

[2] Kalm II. 340, I. 82.—T. J.

have departed from the authority of Monsieur de Buffon in the construction of this table. I take him for my ground work, because I think him the best informed of any naturalist who has ever written. The result is, that there are eighteen quadrupeds peculiar to Europe; more than four times as many, to wit, seventy four, peculiar to America; that the[1] first of these seventy-four weighs more than the whole column of Europeans; and consequently this second table disproves the second member of the assertion, that the animals peculiar to the new world are on a smaller scale, so far as that assertion relied on European animals for support; and it is in full opposition to the theory which makes the animal volume to depend on the circumstances of *heat* and *moisture*.

The third table comprehends those quadrupeds only which are domestic in both countries. That some of these, in some parts of America, have become less than their original stock, is doubtless true; and the reason is very obvious. In a thinly-peopled country, the spontaneous productions of the forests, and waste fields, are sufficient to support indifferently the domestic animals of the farmer, with a very little aid from him, in the severest and sarcest season. He therefore finds it more convenient to receive them from the hand of nature in that indifferent state, than to keep up their size by a care and nourishment which would cost him much labor. If, on this low fare, these animals dwindle, it is no more than they do in those parts of Europe where the poverty of the soil, or the poverty of the owner, reduces them to the same scanty subsistence. It is the uniform effect of one and the same cause, whether acting on this or that side of the globe. It would be erring, therefore, against this rule of philosophy, which teaches us to ascribe like effects to like causes, should we impute this diminution of size in America to any imbecility or want of uniformity in the operations of nature. It may be affirmed with truth, that, in those countries, and with those individuals in America, where necessity or curiosity has produced equal attention, as in Europe, to the nourishment of animals, the horses, cattle, sheep, and hogs, of the one continent are as large as those of the other. There are particular instances, well attested, where individuals of this country have imported good breeders from England, and have improved their size by care in the course of some years. To make a fair comparison between the two countries, it will not answer to bring together animals of what might be deemed the middle or ordinary size of their species; because an error in judging of that middle or ordinary size, would vary the result of the comparison. Thus Mons. D'Aubenton[2] considers a horse of 4 feet five inches high and 400lb. weight French, equal to 4 feet 8.6 inches and 436lb. English, as a middle-sized horse. Such a one is deemed a small horse in America. The extremes must therefore

---

[1] The Tapir is the largest of the animals peculiar to America. I collect his weight thus: Monsieur de Buffon says, XXIII. 274, that he is of the size of a Zebu, or a small cow. He gives us the measures of a Zebu, ib. 4, as taken by himself, *viz.* five feet seven inches from the muzzle to the root of the tail, and five feet one inch circumference behind the fore-legs. A bull, measuring in the same way six feet nine inches and five feet two inches, weighed six hundred pounds, VIII. 153. The Zebu then, and of course the Tapir, would weigh about five hundred pounds. But one individual of every species of European peculiars would probably weigh less than four hundred pounds. These are French measures and weights.—T. J.

[2] VII. 432.—T. J.

be resorted to. The same anatomist[1] dissected a horse of 5 feet 9 inches height, French measure, equal to 6 feet 1.7 English. This is near 6 inches higher than any horse I have seen; and could it be supposed that I had seen the largest horses in America, the conclusion would be, that ours have diminished, or that we have bred from a smaller stock. In Connecticut and Rhode Island, where the climate is favorable to the production of grass, bullocks have been slaughtered which weighed 2,500, 2,200, and 2,100 lbs. nett; and those of 1,800 lbs. have been frequent. I have seen a hog[2] weigh 1,050 lbs. after the blood, bowels, and hair had been taken from him. Before he was killed, an attempt was made to weigh him with a pair of steel yards, graduated to 1,200 lbs., but he weighed more. Yet this hog was probably not within fifty generations of the European stock. I am well informed of another which weighed 1,100 lbs. gross. Asses have been still more neglected than any other domestic animal in America. They are neither fed or housed in the most rigorous season of the year. Yet they are larger than those measured by Mons. D'Aubenton,[3] of 3 feet 7¼ inches, 3 feet 4 inches, and 3 feet 2½ inches, the latter weighing only 215.8 lbs. These sizes, I suppose, have been produced by the same negligence in Europe, which has produced a like diminution here. Where care has been taken of them on that side of the water, they have been raised to a size bordering on that of the horse; not by the *heat* and *dryness* of the climate, but by good food and shelter. Goats have been also much neglected in America. Yet they are very prolific here, bearing twice or three times a year, and from one to five kids at a birth. Mons. de Buffon has been sensible of a difference in this circumstance in favor of America.[4] But what are their greatest weights, I cannot say. A large sheep here weighs 100 lbs. I observe Mons. D'Aubenton calls a ram of 62 lbs. one of the middle size.[5] But to say what are the extremes of growth in these and the other domestic animals of America, would require information of which no one individual is possessed. The weights actually known and stated in the third table preceding will suffice to show, that we may conclude on probable grounds, that, with equal food and care, the climate of America will preserve the races of domestic animals as large as the European stock from which they are derived; and, consequently, that the third member of Mons. de Buffon's assertion that the domestic animals are subject to degeneration from the climate of America, is as probably wrong as the first and second were certainly so.

That the last part of it is erroneous, which affirms that the species of American quadrupeds are comparatively few, is evident from the tables taken together. By these it appears that there are an hundred species aboriginal in America. Mons. de Buffon supposes about double that number existing on the whole earth.[6] Of these Europe, Asia, and Africa, furnish suppose one hundred and twenty-six; that is, the twenty-six common to Europe and America, and about one hundred which are not in America at all. The American species, then, are to those of the rest of the earth, as one hundred to one hundred and

---

[1] VII. 474.—T. J.   [2] In Williamsburg, April, 1769.—T. J.   [3] VIII. 48, 55, 66.—T. J.
[4] XVIII. 96.—T. J.   [5] IX. 41.—T. J.   [6] XXX. 219.—T. J.

twenty-six, or four to five. But the residue of the earth being double the extent of America, the exact proportion would have been but as four to eight.

Hitherto I have considered this hypothesis as applied to brute animals only, and not in its extension to the man of America, whether aboriginal or transplanted. It is the opinion of Mons. de Buffon that the former furnishes no exception to it.[1]

Although the savage of the new world is almost of the same height as the man of our world, that is not sufficient to make him an exception to the general rule of the diminution of human nature in this whole continent; the savage is weak and small in his reproductive organs; he has neither hair nor beard, and no passion for his female. Although lighter than the European, because he is more accustomed to running, he is nevertheless much less strong physically; he is also much less sensitive, and yet more fearful and cowardly; he has no vivacity, no spiritual activity; his physical activity is less a voluntary movement than a compulsion to act caused by necessity; take away his hunger and thirst and you destroy thereby the active principle of all his movements; he will remain stupidly still, standing or lying for whole days at a time. One need not seek further for the cause of the scattered life of the savages and their antipathy for society; the most precious spark of nature has been refused them; they are lacking in ardor for their female, and consequently, in love for their fellow-beings; not knowing this most vital and tender attachment, their other feelings of this nature are cold and sluggish; their love for their parents and children is weak; with them, therefore, the most intimate society of all, that of the immediate family, has only the weakest ties; relationships between families have no ties at all; as a result, no unity, no republic, no social state. Their practice of love dictates their ethical morale; their heart is frozen, their society and authority harsh. They look upon their women only as maids-of-all-work or as pack animals on whom they carelessly unload the burdens of the hunt, and force them, without pity or recognition to do work which is often beyond their strength; they have few children; they give them little care; this is all the result of their original defect; they are indifferent because they are weak, and that indifference towards sex is the initial blemish which wilts nature, prevents it from blooming, and by destroying the seeds of life, cuts off the roots of society. By refusing him the power of sex, nature has mistreated and humbled him more than any of the animals.[2]

An afflicting picture, indeed, which for the honor of human nature, I am glad to believe has no original. Of the Indian of South America I know nothing; for I would not honor with the appellation of knowledge, what I derive from the fables published of them. These I believe to be just as true as the fables of Æsop. This belief is founded on what I have seen of man, white, red, and black, and what has been written of him by authors, enlightened themselves, and writing among an enlightened people. The Indian of North America being more within our reach, I can speak of him somewhat from my own knowledge, but more from the information of others better acquainted with him, and on

---

[1] XVIII. 146.—T. J.   [2] Original was written in French.

whose truth and judgment I can rely. From these sources I am able to say, in contradiction to this representation, that he is neither more defective in ardor, nor more impotent with his female, than the white reduced to the same diet and exercise; that he is brave, when an enterprise depends on bravery; education with him making the point of honor consist in the destruction of an enemy by stratagem, and in the preservation of his own person free from injury; or, perhaps, this is nature, while it is education which teaches us to [1] honor force more than finesse; that he will defend himself against a host of enemies, always choosing to be killed, rather than to surrender,[2] though it be to the whites, who he knows will treat him well; that in other situations, also, he meets death with more deliberation, and endures tortures with a firmness unknown almost to religious enthusiasm with us; that he is affectionate to his children, careful of them, and indulgent in the extreme; that his affections comprehend his other connections, weakening, as with us, from circle to circle, as they recede from the centre; that his friendships are strong and faithful to the uttermost [3] extrem-

[1] *Sol Rodomonte sprezza di venire*
Se non, dove la via meno è ficura (ARISTO, 14, 117.)—T. J.

[2] In so judicious an author as Don Ulloa, and one to whom we are indebted for the most precise information we have of South America, I did not expect to find such assertions as the following: "*Los Indios vencidos son los mas cobardes y pusilanimes que se pueden vér: Se hacen inöcentes, le humillan hasta el desprecio, disculpan su inconsiderado arrojo, y con las suplicas y los ruegos dán seguras pruebas de su pusilanimidad. ó lo que resieren las historias de la Conquista, sobre sus grandes acciones, es en un sendito figurado, ó el caracter de estas gentes no es ahora segun era entonces; pero lo que no tiene duda es, que las Naciones de la parte Septentrional subsisten en la misma libertad que siempre han tenido, sin haber sido sojuzgados por algon Principe extrano, y que viven segun su régimen y costumbres de toda la vida, sin que haya habido motivo para que muden de caracter; y en estos se vé lo mismo, que sucede en los Peru, y de toda la América Meridional, reducidos, y que nunca lo han estado.*" Noticias Americanas, Entretenimiento xviii. § 1. Don Ulloa here admits, that the authors who have described the Indians of South America, before they were enslaved, had represented them as a brave people, and therefore seems to have suspected that the cowardice which he had observed in those of the present race might be the effect of subjugation. But, supposing the Indians of North America to be cowards also, he concludes the ancestors of those of South America to have been so too, and, therefore, that those authors have given fictions for truth. He was probably not acquainted himself with the Indians of North America, and had formed his opinion from hear-say. Great numbers of French, of English, and of Americans, are perfectly acquainted with these people. Had he had an opportunity of inquiring of any of these, they would have told him, that there never was an instance known of an Indian begging his life when in the power of his enemies; on the contrary, that he courts death by every possible insult and provocation. His reasoning, then, would have been reversed thus: "Since the present Indian of North America is brave, and authors tell us that the ancestors of those of South America were brave also, it must follow that the cowardice of their descendants is the effect of subjugation and ill treatment." For he observes, lb. §. 27, that "*los obrages los aniquillan por la inhumanidad con que les trata.*"—T. J.

[3] A remarkable instance of this appeared in the case of the late Colonel Byrd, who was sent to the Cherokee nation to transact some business with them. It happened that some of our disorderly people had just killed one or two of that nation. It was therefore proposed in the council of the Cherokees that Colonel Byrd should be put to death, in revenge for the loss of their countrymen. Among them was a chief named Silòuee, who, on some former occasion, had contracted an acquaintance and friendship with Colonel Byrd. He came to him every night in his tent, and told him not to be afraid, they should not kill him. After many days' deliberation, however, the determination was, contrary to Silòuee's expectation, that Byrd should be put to death, and some warriors were despatched as executioners. Silòuee attended them, and when they entered the tent, he threw himself between them and Byrd, and said to the warriors, "This man is my friend; before you get at him, you must kill me." On which they returned, and the council respected the principle so much as to recede from their determination.—T. J.

ity; that his sensibility is keen, even the warriors weeping most bitterly on the loss of their children, though in general they endeavor to appear superior to human events; that his vivacity and activity of mind is equal to ours in the same situation; hence his eagerness for hunting, and for games of chance. The women are submitted to unjust drudgery. This I believe is the case with every barbarous people. With such, force is law. The stronger sex imposes on the weaker. It is civilization alone which replaces women in the enjoyment of their natural equality. That first teaches us to subdue the selfish passions, and to respect those rights in others which we value in ourselves. Were we in equal barbarism, our females would be equal drudges. The man with them is less strong than with us, but their women stronger than ours; and both for the same obvious reason; because our man and their woman is habituated to labor, and formed by it. With both races the sex which is indulged with ease is the least athletic. An Indian man is small in the hand and wrist, for the same reason for which a sailor is large and strong in the arms and shoulders, and a porter in the legs and thighs. They raise fewer children than we do. The causes of this are to be found, not in a difference of nature, but of circumstance. The women very frequently attending the men in their parties of war and of hunting, child-bearing becomes extremely inconvenient to them. It is said, therefore, that they have learned the practice of procuring abortion by the use of some vegetable; and that it even extends to prevent conception for a considerable time after. During these parties they are exposed to numerous hazards, to excessive exertions, to the greatest extremities of hunger. Even at their homes the nation depends for food, through a certain part of every year, on the gleanings of the forest; that is, they experience a famine once in every year. With all animals, if the female be badly fed, or not fed at all, her young perish; and if both male and female be reduced to like want, generation becomes less active, less productive. To the obstacles, then, of want and hazard, which nature has opposed to the multiplication of wild animals, for the purpose of restraining their numbers within certain bounds, those of labor and of voluntary abortion are added with the Indian. No wonder, then, if they multiply less than we do. Where food is regularly supplied, a single farm will show more of cattle, than a whole country of forests can of buffaloes. The same Indian women, when married to white traders, who feed them and their children plentifully and regularly, who exempt them from excessive drudgery, who keep them stationary and unexposed to accident, produce and raise as many children as the white women. Instances are known, under these circumstances, of their rearing a dozen children. An inhuman practice once prevailed in this country, of making slaves of the Indians. It is a fact well known with us, that the Indian women so enslaved produced and raised as numerous families as either the whites or blacks among whom they lived. It has been said that Indians have less hair than the whites, except on the head. But this is a fact of which fair proof can scarcely be had. With them it is disgraceful to be hairy on the body. They say it likens them to hogs. They therefore pluck the hair as fast as it appears. But the traders who marry their women, and prevail on them to discontinue this practice, say, that nature is the same with them as with the whites. Nor, if the fact be true, is the consequence necessary which has been drawn from it. Negroes have notoriously less hair than the whites; yet they are more ardent. But if cold and moisture be the agents of nature for diminishing the races of animals, how comes she all at once to suspend their operations as to the physical man of the new world, whom the Count acknowledges to be "*à peu près de même stature que l'homme de notre monde,*" and to let loose their influence on his moral faculties? How has this "combination of the elements and other physical causes, so contrary to the enlargement of animal nature in this new world, these obstacles to the development and formation of great germs,"[1] been arrested and suspended, so as to permit the human body to acquire its just dimensions, and by what inconceivable process has their action been directed on his mind alone? To judge of the truth of this, to form a just estimate of their genius and mental powers, more facts are wanting, and great allowance to be made for those circumstances of their situation which call for a display of particular talents only. This done, we shall probably find that they are formed in mind as well as in body, on the same module with the[2] "*Homo sapiens Europæus.*" The principles of their society forbidding all compulsion, they are to be led to duty and to enterprise by personal influence and persuasion. Hence eloquence in council, bravery and address in war, become the foundations of all consequence with them. To these acquirements all their faculties are directed. Of their bravery and address in war we have multiplied proofs, because we have been the subjects on which they were exercised. Of their eminence in oratory we have fewer examples, because it is displayed chiefly in their own councils. Some, however, we have, of very superior lustre. I may challenge the whole orations of Demosthenes and Cicero, and of any more eminent orator, if Europe has furnished more eminent, to produce a single passage, superior to the speech of Logan, a Mingo chief, to Lord Dunmore, then governor of this State. And as a testimony of their talents in this line, I beg leave to introduce it, first stating the incidents necessary for understanding it.

In the spring of the year 1774, a robbery was committted by some Indians on certain land-adventurers on the river Ohio. The whites in that quarter, according to their custom, undertook to punish this outrage in a summary way. Captain Michael Cresap, and a certain Daniel Greathouse, leading on these parties, surprised, at different times, travelling and hunting parties of the Indians, having their women and children with them, and murdered many. Among these were unfortunately the family of Logan, a chief celebrated in peace and war, and long distinguished as the friend of the whites. This unworthy return provoked his vengeance. He accordingly signalized himself in the war which ensued. In the autumn of the same year a decisive battle was fought at the mouth of the Great Kanhaway, between the collected forces of the Shawanese, Mingoes and Delawares, and a detachment of the Virginia militia. The Indians were defeated and sued for peace. Logan, however, disdained to be seen among the suppliants. But lest the sincerity of a treaty should be disturbed, from which so distin-

[1] XVIII. 146.—T. J.　　　　　　　　[2] Linn. Syst. Definition of a Man.—T. J.

guished a chief absented himself, he sent, by a messenger, the following speech, to be delivered to Lord Dunmore.

"I appeal to any white man to say, if ever he entered Logan's cabin hungry, and he gave him not meat; if ever he came cold and naked, and he clothed him not. During the course of the last long and bloody war Logan remained idle in his cabin, an advocate for peace. Such was my love for the whites, that my countrymen pointed as they passed, and said, 'Logan is the friend of white man.' I had even thought to have lived with you, but for the injuries of one man. Colonel Cresap, the last spring, in cold blood, and unprovoked, murdered all the relations of Logan, not even sparing my women and children. There runs not a drop of my blood in the veins of any living creature. This called on me for revenge. I have sought it: I have killed many: I have fully glutted my vengeance: for my country I rejoice at the beams of peace. But do not harbor a thought that mine is the joy of fear. Logan never felt fear. He will not turn on his heel to save his life. Who is there to mourn for Logan?—Not one." [1]

Before we condemn the Indians of this continent as wanting genius, we

[1] Philadelphia, December 31, 1797.

DEAR SIR: Mr. Tazewell has communicated to me the inquiries you have been so kind as to make, relative to a passage in the "Notes on Virginia," which has lately excited some newspaper publications. I feel, with great sensibility, the interest you take in this business, and with pleasure, go into explanations with one whose objects I know to be truth and justice alone. Had Mr. Martin thought proper to suggest to me, that doubts might be entertained of the transaction respecting Logan, as stated in the "Notes on Virginia," and to inquire on what grounds that statement was founded, I should have felt myself obliged by the inquiry; have informed him candidly of the grounds, and cordially have co-operated in every means of investigating the fact, and correcting whatsoever in it should be found to have been erroneous. But he chose to step at once into the newspapers, and in his publications there and the letters he wrote to me, adopted a style which forbade the respect of an answer. Sensible, however, that no act of his could absolve me from the justice due to others, as soon as I found that the story of Logan could be doubted, I determined to inquire into it as accurately as the testimony remaining, after a lapse of twenty odd years, would permit, and that the result should be made known, either in the first new edition which should be printed of the "Notes on Virginia," or by publishing an appendix. I thought that so far as that work had contributed to impeach the memory of Cresap, by handing on an erroneous charge, it was proper it should be made the vehicle of retribution. Not that I was at all the author of the injury; I had only concurred, with thousands and thousands of others, in believing a tranaction on authority which merited respect. For the story of Logan is only repeated in the "Notes on Virginia," precisely as it had been current for more than a dozen years before they were published. When Lord Dunmore returned from the expedition against the Indians, in 1774, he and his officers brought the speech of Logan, and related the circumstances of it. These were so affecting, and the speech itself so fine a morsel of eloquence, that it became the theme of every conversation, in Williamsburg particularly, and generally, indeed, wheresoever any of the officers resided or resorted. I learned it in Williamsburg, I believe at Lord Dunmore's; and I find in my pocket-book of that year (1774) an entry of the narrative, as taken from the mouth of some person, whose name, however, is not noted, nor recollected, precisely in the words stated in the "Notes on Virginia." The speech was published in the Virginia Gazette of that time, (I have it myself in the volume of gazettes of that year,) and though it was the translation made by the common interpreter, and in a style by no means elegant, yet it was so admired, that it flew through all the public papers of the continent, and through the magazines and other periodical publications of Great Britain; and those who were boys at that day will now attest, that the speech of Logan used to be given them as a school exercise for repetition. It was not till about thirteen or fourteen years after the newspaper publications, that the "Notes on Virginia" were published in America. Combating, in these, the contumelious theory of certain European writers, whose celebrity gave currency and weight to their opinions, that our country from the combined effects of soil and climate, degenerated animal nature, in the general, and particularly the moral faculties of man, I considered the speech of Logan as an apt proof of the contrary, and used it as such; and I copied, verbatim, must consider that letters have not yet been introduced among them. Were we to compare them in their present state with the Europeans, north of the Alps, when the Roman arms and arts first crossed those mountains, the comparison would be unequal, because, at that time, those parts of Europe were swarming with numbers; because numbers produce emulation, and multiply the chances of improvement, and one improvement begets another. Yet I may safely ask, how many good poets, how many able mathematicians, how many great inventors in arts or sciences, had Europe, north of the Alps, then produced? And it was sixteen centuries after this before a Newton could be formed. I do not mean to deny that there are varieties in the race of man, distinguished by their powers both of body and mind. I believe there are, as I see to be the case in the

the narrative I had taken down in 1774, and the speech as it had been given us in a better translation by Lord Dunmore. I knew nothing of the Cresaps, and could not possibly have a motive to do them an injury with design. I repeated what thousands had done before, on as good authority as we have for most of the facts we learn through life, and such as, to this moment, I have seen no reason to doubt. That any body questioned it, was never suspected by me, till I saw the letter of Mr. Martin in the Baltimore paper. I endeavored then to recollect who among my contemporaries, of the same circle of society, and consequently of the same recollections, might still be alive; three and twenty years of death and dispersion had left very few. I remembered, however, that General Gibson was still living, and knew that he had been the translator of the speech. He, in answer, declares to me, that he was the very person sent by Lord Dunmore to the Indian town; that, after he had delivered his message there, Logan took him out to a neighboring wood; sat down with him, and rehearsing, with tears, the catastrophe of his family, gave him that speech for Lord Dunmore; that he carried it to Lord Dunmore; translated it for him; has turned to it in the Encyclopedia, as taken from the "Notes on Virginia," and finds that it was his translation I had used, with only two or three verbal variations of no importance. These, I suppose, had arisen in the course of successive copies. I cite General Gibson's letter by memory, not having it with me; but I am sure I cite it substantially right. It establishes unquestionably, that the speech of Logan is genuine; and that being established, it is Logan himself who is author of all the important facts. "Colonel Cresap," says he, "in cold blood and unprovoked, murdered all the relations of Logan, not sparing even my women and children; there runs not a drop of my blood in the veins of any living creature." The person and the fact, in all its material circumstances, are here given by Logan himself. General Gibson, indeed, says, that the title was mistaken; that Cresap was a Captain, and not a Colonel. This was Logan's mistake. He also observes, that it was on another water of the Ohio, and not on the Kanhaway, that his family was killed. This is an error which has crept into the traditionary account; but surely of little moment in the moral view of the subject. The material question is, was Logan's family murdered, and by whom? That it was murdered has not, I believe, been denied; that it was by one of the Cresaps, Logan affirms. This is a question which concerns the memories of Logan and Cresap; to the issue of which I am as indifferent as if I had never heard the name of either. I have begun and shall continue to inquire into the evidence additional to Logan's, on which the fact was founded. Little, indeed, can now be heard of, and that little dispersed and distant. If it shall appear on inquiry, that Logan has been wrong in charging Cresap with the murder of his family, I will do justice to the memory of Cresap, as far as I have contributed to the injury, by believing and repeating what others had believed and repeated before me. If, on the other hand, I find that Logan was right in his charge, I will vindicate, as far as my suffrage may go, the truth of a Chief, whose talents and misfortunes have attached to him the respect and commiseration of the world.

I have gone, my dear Sir, into this lengthy detail to satisfy a mind, in the candor and rectitude of which I have the highest confidence. So far as you may incline to use the communication for rectifying the judgments of those who are willing to see things truly as they are, you are free to use it. But I pray that no confidence which you may repose in any one, may induce you to let it go out of your hands, so as to get into a newspaper: against a contest in that field I am entirely decided. I feel extraordinary gratification, indeed, in addressing this letter to you, with whom shades of difference in political sentiment have not prevented the interchange of good opinion, nor cut off the friendly offices of society and good correspondence. This political tolerance is the more valued by me, who consider social harmony as the first of human felicities, and races of other animals. I only mean to suggest a doubt, whether the bulk and faculties of animals depend on the side of the Atlantic on which their food happens to grow, or which furnishes the elements of which they are compounded? Whether nature has enlisted herself as a Cis or Trans-Atlantic partisan? I am induced to suspect there has been more eloquence than sound reasoning displayed in support of this theory; that it is one of those cases where the judgment has been seduced by a glowing pen; and whilst I render every tribute of honor and esteem to the celebrated zoologist, who has added, and is still adding, so many precious things to the treasures of science, I must doubt whether in this instance he has not cherished error also, by lending her for a moment his vivid imagination and bewitching language.

So far the Count de Buffon has carried this new theory of the tendency of nature to belittle her productions on this side the Atlantic. Its application to the race of whites transplanted from Europe, remained for the Abbé Raynal. *"On doit etre etonné* (he says) *que l'Amerique n'ait pas encore produit un bon poëte, un habile mathematicien, un homme de genie dans un seul art, ou seule science."* Hist. Philos. p. 92, ed. Maestricht, 1774. "America has not yet produced one good poet." When we shall have existed as a people as long as the Greeks did before they produced a Homer, the Romans a Virgil, the French a Racine and Voltaire, the English a Shakespeare and Milton, should this reproach be still true, we will inquire from what unfriendly causes it has proceeded, that the other countries of Europe and quarters of the earth shall not have inscribed any name in the roll of poets.[1] But neither has America produced "one able mathematician, one man of genius in a single art or a single science." In war we have produced a Washington, whose memory will be adored while liberty shall have votaries, whose name shall triumph over time, and will in future ages assume its just station among the most celebrated worthies of the world, when that wretched philosophy shall be forgotten which would have arranged him among the degeneracies of nature. In physics we have produced a Franklin, than whom no one of the present age has made more important discoveries, nor has enriched philosophy with more, or more ingenious solutions of the phenomena of nature. We have supposed Mr. Rittenhouse second to no astronomer living; that in genius he must be the first, because he is self-taught. As an artist he has exhibited as great a proof of mechanical genius as the world has ever produced. He has not indeed made a world; but he has by imitation approached nearer its Maker than any man who has lived from the creation to this day.[2] As in philosophy and war, so in government, in oratory, in painting, in the plastic art, we might show that America, though but a child of yester-

---

the happiest moments, those which are given to the effusions of the heart. Accept them sincerely, I pray you, from one who has the honor to be, with sentiments of high respect and attachment, dear Sir, your most obedient, and most humble servant.—T. J.

[1] Has the world as yet produced more than two poets, acknowledged to be such by all nations? An Englishman only reads Milton with delight, an Italian, Tasso, a Frenchman the Henriade; a Portuguese, Camoens; but Homer and Virgil have been the rapture of every age and nation; they are read with enthusiasm in their originals by those who can read the originals, and in translations by those who cannot.—T. J.

[2] There are various ways of keeping truth out of sight. Mr. Rittenhouse's model of the planetary system has the plagiary application of an Orrery; and the quadrant invented by Godfrey, an

day, has already given hopeful proofs of genius, as well as of the nobler kinds, which arouse the best feelings of man, which call him into action, which substantiate his freedom, and conduct him to happiness, as of the subordinate, which serve to amuse him only. We therefore suppose, that this reproach is as unjust as it is unkind: and that, of the geniuses which adorn the present age, America contributes its full share. For comparing it with those countries where genius is most cultivated, where are the most excellent models for art, and scaffoldings for the attainment of science, as France and England for instance, we calculate thus: The United States contains three millions of inhabitants; France twenty millions; and the British islands ten. We produce a Washington, a Franklin, a Rittenhouse. France then should have half a dozen in each of these lines, and Great Britain half that number, equally eminent. It may be true that France has; we are but just becoming acquainted with her, and our acquaintance so far gives us high ideas of the genius of her inhabitants. It would be injuring too many of them to name particularly a Voltaire, a Buffon, the constellation of Encyclopedists, the Abbé Raynal himself, &c. &c. We, therefore, have reason to believe she can produce her full quota of genius. The present war having so long cut off all communication with Great Britain, we are not able to make a fair estimate of the state of science in that country. The spirit in which she wages war, is the only sample before our eyes, and that does not seem the legitimate offspring either of science or of civilization. The sun of her glory is fast descending to the horizon. Her philosophy has crossed the channel, her freedom the Atlantic, and herself seems passing to that awful dissolution whose issue is not given human foresight to scan.[1]

Having given a sketch of our minerals, vegetables, and quadrupeds, and being led by a proud theory to make a comparison of the latter with those of Europe, and to extend it to the man of America, both aboriginal and emigrant, I will proceed to the remaining articles comprehended under the present query.

Between ninety and a hundred of our birds have been described by Catesby. His drawings are better as to form and attitude than coloring, which is generally too high. They are the following:

American also, and with the aid of which the European nations traverse the globe, is called Hadley's quadrant.—т. j.

[1] In a later edition of the Abbé Raynal's work, he has withdrawn his censure from that part of the new world inhabited by the Federo-Americans; but has left it still on the other parts. North America has always been more accessible to strangers than South. If he was mistaken then as to the former, he may be so as to the latter. The glimmerings which reach us from South America enable us to see that its inhabitants are held under the accumulated pressure of slavery, superstition and ignorance. Whenever they shall be able to rise under this weight, and to show themselves to the rest of the world, they will probably show they are like the rest of the world. We have not yet sufficient evidence that there are more lakes and fogs in South America than in other parts of the earth. As little do we know what would be their operation on the mind of man. That country has been visited by Spaniards and Portuguese chiefly, and almost exclusively. These, going from a country of the old world remarkably dry in its soil and climate, fancied there were more lakes and fogs in South America than in Europe. An inhabitant of Ireland, Sweden, or Finland would have formed the contrary opinion. Had South America then been discovered and settled by a people from a fenny country, it would probably have been represented as much drier than the old world. A patient pursuit of facts, and cautious combination and comparison of them, is the drudgery to which man is subjected by his Maker, if he wishes to attain sure knowledge.—т. j.

BIRDS OF VIRGINIA

LINNÆAN DESIGNATION	CATESBY'S DESIGNATION		POPULAR NAMES	BUFFON OISEAUX
Lanius tyrannus	Muscicapa coronâ rubrâ	1.55	Tyrant. Field martin	8.398
Vultur aura	Buteo specie Gallo-pavonis	1.6	Turkey buzzard	1.246
Falco leucocephalus	Aquila capite albo	1.1	Bald eagle	1.138
Falco sparverius	Accipiter minor	1.5	Little hawk. Sparrow hawk	
Falco columbarious	Accipiter palumbarius	1.3	Pigeon hawk	1.338
Falco furcatus	Accipiter caudâ furcatâ	1.4	Forked tail hawk	1.286,312
	Accipiter piscatorius	1.2	Fishing hawk	1.199
Strix asio	Noctua aurita minor	1.7	Little owl	1.141
Psittacus Caroliniensis	Psittacus Caroliniensis	1.11	Parrot of Carolina. Parroquet	11.383
Corvus cristatus	Pica glandaria, cærulea, cristata	1.15	Blue jay	5.164
Oriolus Baltimore	Icterus ex aureo nigroque varius	1.48	Baltimore bird	5.318
Oriolus spurius	Icterus minor	1.49	Bastard Baltimore	5.321
Gracula quiscula	Monedula purpurea	1.12	Purple jackdaw. Crow blackbird	5.134
Cuculus Americanus	Cuculus Caroliniensis	1.9	Carolina cuckow	12.62
Picus principalis	Picus maximus rostro albo	1.16	White bill woodpecker	13.69
Picus pileatus	Picus niger maximus, capite rubro	1.17	Larger red-crested woodpecker	13.72
Picus erythrocephalus	Picus capite toto rubro	1.20	Red headed woodpecker	13.83
Picus ouratus	Picus major alis aureis	1.18	Gold winged woodpecker. Yucker	13.59
Picus Carolinus	Picus ventre rubro	1.19	Red-bellied woodpecker	13.105
Picus pubescens	Picus varius minimus	1.21	Smallest spotted woodpecker	13.113
Picus villosus	Picus medius quasi-villosus	1.19	Hairy woodpecker. Spec. woodpecker	13.111
Picus varius	Picus varius minor ventre luteo	1.21	Yellow-bellied woodpecker	13.115
Sitta Europæa	{ Sitta capite nigro	1.22	Nuthatch	10.213
	{ Sitta capite fusco	1.22	Small Nuthatch	10.214
Alcedo alcyon	Ispida	1.69	Kingfisher	13.310
Certhia pinus	Parus Americanus lutescens	1.61	Pine-Creeper	9.433
Trochilus colubris	Mellivora avis Caroliniensis	1.65	Humming bird	11.16
Anas Canadensis	Anser Canadensis	1.92	Wild goose	17.122
Anas bucephala	Anas minor purpureo capite	1.95	Buffel's-head duck	17.356

Scientific name	Latin descriptive name	No.	Common name	Index
Anas rustica	Anas minor ex albo & fusco vario	1.98	Little brown duck	17.413
Anas discors. ♂	Querquedula Americana variegata	1.10	White face teal	17.403
Anas discors. ♂	Querquedula Americana fusca	1.99	Blue wing teal	17.405
Anas sponsa	Anas Americanus cristatus elegans	1.97	Summer duck	17.351
	Anas Americanus lato rostro	1.96	Blue wing shoveler	17.275
Mergus cucullatus	Anas cristatus	1.94	Round crested duck	15.437
Columbus podiceps	Prodicipes minor rostro vario	1.91	Pied bill dopchick	15.383
Ardea Herodias	Ardea cristata maxima Americana	3.10	Largest crested heron	14.113
Ardea violacea	Ardea stellaris cristata Americana	1.79	Crested bittern	14.134
Ardea caerulea	Ardea caerulea	1.76	Blue heron. Crane	14.131
Ardea virescens	Ardea stellaris minima	1.80	Small bittern	14.142
Ardea æquinoctialis	Ardea alba minor Caroliniensis	1.77	Little white heron	14.136
	Ardea stellaris Americana	1.78	Brown bittern. Indian hen	14.175
Tantalus loculator	Pelicanus Americanus	1.81	Wood pelican	13.403
Tantalus alber	Numenius albus	1.82	White curlew	15.62
Tantalus fuscus	Numenius fuscus	1.83	Brown curlew	15.64
Charadrius vociferus	Pluvialis vociferus	1.71	Chattering plover. Kildee	15.151
Hæmatopus ostralegus	Hæmatopus	1.85	Oyster-catcher	15.185
Rallus Virginianus	Gallinula Americana	1.70	Soree. Ral-bird	15.256
Meleagris Gallopavo	Gallopava Sylvestris	xliv.	Wild Turkey	3,187.229
Tetrao Virginianus	Perdix Sylvestris Virginiana	3.12	American partridge. American quail	4.237
	Urgallus minor, or kind of Lagopus	3.1	Pheasant. Mountain partridge	3.499
Columba passerina	Turtur minimus guttatus	1.26	Ground dove	4.404
Columba migratorio	Palumbus migratorius	1.23	Pigeon of passage. Wild pigeon	4.351
Columba Caroliniensis	Turtur Caroliniensis	1.24	Turtle. Turtle dove	4.401
Alauda alpestris	Alauda gutture flavo	1.32	Lark. Sky lark	9.79
Alauda magna	Alauda magna	1.33	Field lark. Large lark	6.59
	Sturnus niger allis superné rubentibus	1.13	Red wing. Starling. Marsh blackbird	5.293 / 5.426
Tardus migratorius	Turdus pilaris migratorius	1.29	Fieldfare of Carolina. Robin redbreast	9.257
Tardus rufus	Turdus rufus	1.28	Fox colored thrush. Thrush	5.449
Tardus polyglottos	Turdus minor cinereo albus non maculatus	1.27	Mocking bird	5.451
	Turdus minimus	1.31	Little thrush	5.400
Ampelis garrulus. ♂	Garrulus Caroliniensis	1.46	Chatterer	6.162
Loxia Cardinalis	Coccothranstes rubra	1.38	Red bird. Virginia nightingale	6.185

LINNÆAN DESIGNATION	CATESBY'S DESIGNATION	POPULAR NAMES	BUFFON OISEAUX
Loxia Cærulea	Coccothranstes cærulea	1.39	Blue gross beak	8.125
Emberiza hyemalis	Passer nivalis	1.36	Snow bird	8.47
Emberiza Oryzivora	Hortulanus Caroliniensis	1.14	Rice bird	8.49
Emberiza Ciris	Fringilla tricolor	1.44	Painted finch	7.247
Tanagra cyanea	Linaria cærulea	1.45	Blue linnet	7.122
	Passerculus	1.35	Little sparrow	7.120
	Passer fuscus	1.34	Cowpen bird	7.196
Fringilla erythrophthalma	Passer niger oculis rubris	1.34	Towne bird	7.201
Fringilla tristis	Carduelis Americanus	1.43	American goldfinch. Lettuce bird	7.297
	Fringilla purpurea	1.41	Purple finch	8.129
Muscicapa crinita	Muscicapa cristata ventre luteo	1.52	Crested flycatcher	8.379
Muscicapa rubra	Muscicapa rubra	1.56	Summer red bird	8.410
Muscicapa ruticilla	Ruticilla Americana	1.67	Red start	8.349 9.259
Muscicapa Caroliniensis	Muscicapa vertice nigro	1.66	Cat bird	8.372
	Muscicapa nigrescens	1.53	Black cap flycatcher	8.341
	Muscicapa fusca	1.54	Little brown flycatcher	8.344
	Muscicapa oculis rubris	1.54	Red-eyed flycatcher	8.337
Motacilla Sialis	Rubicula Americana cærulea	1.47	Blue bird	9.308
Motacilla regulus	Regulus cristatus	3.13	Wren	10.58
Motacilla trochilus. δ	Oenanthe Americana pectore luteo	1.50	Yellow breasted chat	6.96
Parus bicolor	Parus cristatus	1.57	Crested titmouse	10.181
Parus Americanus	Parus fringillaris	1.64	Finch creeper	9.442
Parus Virginianus	Parus uropygeo luteo	1.58	Yellow rump	10.184
	Parus cucullo nigro	1.60	Hooded titmouse	10.183
	Parus Americanus gutture luteo	1.62	Yellow throated creeper	
	Parus Caroliniensis	1.63	Yellow titmouse	
Hirundo Pelasgia	Hirundo cauda aculeata Americana	3. 8	American swallow	9.431
Hirundo purpurea	Hirundo purpurea	1.51	Purple marten. House marten	12.478
Caprimulgus Europæus. α	Caprimulgus	1.'8	Goatsucker. Great bat	12.445
Caprimulgus Europæus. δ	Caprimulgus minor Americanus	3.16	Whip poor Will	12.243 12.246

Besides these, we have,

The Royston crow. Corvus cornix.
  Crane. Ardea Canadensis.
  House swallow. Hirundo rustica.
  Ground swallow. Hirundo riparia.
  Greatest gray eagle.
  Smaller turkey buzzard, with a feathered head.
  Greatest owl, or night hawk.
  Wet hawk, which feeds flying.
  Raven.
  Water Pelican of the Mississippi, whose pouch hold a peck.
  Swan.
  Loon.
  Cormorant.
  Duck and mallard.
  Widgeon.
  Sheldrach, or Canvas back.

The Black head.
  Ballcoot.
  Sprigtail.
  Didapper, or dopchick.
  Spoon-billed duck.
  Water-witch.
  Water-pheasant.
  Mow-bird.
  Blue Peter.
  Water Wagtail.
  Yellow-legged Snipe.
  Squatting Snipe.
  Small Plover.
  Whistling Plover.
  Woodcock.
  Red bird, with black head, wings and tail.

And doubtless many others which have not yet been described and classed.

To this catalogue of our indigenous animals, I will add a short account of an anomaly of nature, taking place sometimes in the race of negroes brought from Africa, who, though black themselves, have, in rare instances, white children, called Albinos. I have known four of these myself, and have faithful accounts of three others. The circumstances in which all the individuals agree are these. They are of a pallid cadaverous white, untinged with red, without any colored spots or seams; their hair of the same kinnd of white, short, coarsse, and curled as is that of the negro; all of them well formed, strong, healthy, perfect in their senses, except that of sight, and born of parents who had no mixture of white blood. Three of these Albinos were sisters, having two other full sisters, who were black. The youngest of the three was killed by lightning, at twelve years of age. The eldest died at about 27 years of age, in child-bed, with her second child. The middle one is now alive, in health, and has issue, as the eldest had, by a black man, which issue was black. They are uncommonly shrewd, quick in their apprehensions and in reply. Their eyes are in a perpetual tremulous vibration, very weak, and much affected by the sun; but they see much better in the night than we do. They are of the property of Colonel Skipwith, of Cumberland. The fourth is a negro woman, whose parents came from Guinea, and had three other children, who were of their own color. She is freckled, her eye-sight so weak that she is obliged to wear a bonnet in the summer; but it is better in the night than day. She had an Albino child by a black man. It died at the age of a few weeks. These were the property of Col. Carter, of Albemarle. A sixth instance is a woman the property of a Mr. Butler, near Petersburg. She is stout and robust, has issue a daughter, jet black, by a black man. I am not informed as to her eye-sight. The seventh instance is of a male belonging to a Mr. Lee of Cumberland. His eyes are tremulous and weak. He is tall of stature, and now advanced in years. He is the only male of the Albinos which have come within my information. Whatever be the cause of the disease in the skin, or in its coloring matter, which produces this change, it seems more incident to the female than male sex. To these I may add the mention of a negro man within my own knowledge, born black, and of black parents; on whose chin, when a boy, a white spot appeared. This continued to increase till he became a man, by which time it had extended over his chin, lips, one cheek, the under jaw, and neck on that side. It is of the Albino white, without any mixture of red, and has for several years been stationary. He is robust and healthy, and the change of color was not accompanied with any sensible disease, either general or topical.

Of our fish and insects there has been nothing like a full description or collection. More of them are described in Catesby than in any other work. Many also are to be found in Sir Hans Sloane's Jamaica, as being common to that and this country. The honey-bee is not a native of our continent. Marcgrave, indeed, mentions a species of honey-bee in Brazil. But this has no sting, and is therefore different from the one we have, which resembles perfectly that of Europe. The Indians concur with us in the tradition that it was brought from Europe; but when, and by whom, we know not. The bees have generally extended themselves into the country, a little in advance of the white settlers. The Indians, therefore, call them the white man's fly, and consider their approach as indicating the approach of the settlements of the whites. A question here occurs, How far northwardly have these insects been found? That they are unknown in Lapland, I infer from Scheffer's information, that the Laplanders eat the pine bark, prepared in a certain way, instead of those things sweetened with sugar. *"Hoc comedunt pro rebus saccharo conditis."* Scheff. Lapp. c. 18. Certainly if they had honey, it would be a better substitute for sugar than any preparation of the pine bark. Kalm tell us [1] the honey-bee cannot live through the winter in Canada. They furnish then an additional fact first observed by the Count de Buffon, and which has thrown such a blaze of light on the field of natural history, that no animals are found in both continents, but those which are able to bear the cold of those regions where they probably join.

QUERY VII

A notice of all that can increase the progress of Human Knowledge

Under the latitude of this query, I will presume it not improper nor unacceptable to furnish some data for estimating the climate of Virginia. Journals of observations on the quantity of rain, and degree of heat, being lengthy, confused, and too minute to produce general and distinct ideas, I have taken five years' observations, to wit, from 1772 to 1777, made in Williamsburg and its

[1] I. 126.—T. J.

neighborhood, have reduced them to an average for every month in the year, and stated those averages in the following table, adding an analytical view of the winds during the same period.

The rains of every month, (as of January, for instance,) through the whole period of years, were added separately, and an average drawn from them. The coolest and warmest point of the same day in each year of the period, were added separately, and an average of the greatest cold and greatest heat of that day was formed. From the averages of every day in the month, a general average was formed. The point from which the wind blew, was observed two or three times in every day. These observations, in the month of January, for instance, through the whole period, amounted to three hundred and thirty-seven. At seventy-three of these, the wind was from the north; forty-seven from the north-east, &c. So that it will be easy to see in what proportion each wind usually prevails in each month; or, taking the whole year, the total of observations through the whole period having been three thousand six hundred and ninety-eight, it will be observed that six hundred and eleven of them were from the north, five hundred and fifty-eight from the north-east, &c.

	FALL OF RAIN, ETC., IN INCHES	LEAST AND GREATEST DAILY HEAT, BY FAHRENHEIT'S THERMOMETER	WINDS								
			N.	N.E.	E.	S.E.	S.	S.W.	W.	N.W.	TOTAL
Jan.	3.192	38½ to 44	73	47	32	10	11	78	40	46	337
Feb.	2.049	41 .. 47½	61	52	24	11	4	63	30	31	276
March	3.95	48 .. 54½	49	44	38	28	14	83	29	33	318
April	3.68	56 .. 62½	35	44	54	19	9	58	18	20	257
May	2.871	63 .. 70½	27	36	62	23	7	74	32	20	281
June	3.751	71½ .. 78¼	22	34	43	24	13	81	25	25	267
July	4.497	77 .. 82½	41	44	75	15	7	95	32	19	328
August	9.153	76¼ .. 81	43	52	40	30	9	103	27	30	334
Sept.	4.761	69½ .. 74¼	70	60	51	18	10	81	18	37	345
Oct.	3.633	61¼ .. 66½	52	77	64	15	6	56	23	34	327
Nov.	2.617	47¾ .. 53½	74	21	20	14	9	63	35	58	294
Dec.	2.877	43 .. 48¾	64	37	18	16	10	91	42	56	334
Total	47.038	8 A.M. to 4 P.M.	611	548	521	223	109	926	351	409	3,698

Though by this table it appears we have on an average forty-seven inches of rain annually, which is considerably more than usually falls in Europe, yet from the information I have collected, I suppose we have a much greater proportion of sunshine here than there. Perhaps it will be found, there are twice as many cloudy days in the middle parts of Europe, as in the United States of America. I mention the middle parts of Europe, because my information does not extend to its northern or southern parts.

In an extensive country, it will of course be expected that the climate is not the same in all its parts. It is remarkable, that proceeding on the same parallel of latitude westwardly, the climate becomes colder in like manner as when you proceed northwardly. This continues to be the case till you attain the summit of the Alleghany, which is the highest land between the ocean and the Mississippi. From thence, descending in the same latitude to the Mississippi, the change reverses; and, if we may believe travellers, it becomes warmer there than it is in the same latitude on the sea-side. Their testimony is strengthened by the vegetables and animals which subsist and multiply there naturally, and do not on the sea-coast. Thus Catalpas grow spontaneously on the Mississippi, as far as the latitude of 37°, and reeds as far as 38°. Parroquets even winter on the Scioto, in the 39th degree of latitude. In the summer of 1779, when the thermometer was at 90° at Monticello, and 96° at Williamsburg, it was 110° at Kaskaskia. Perhaps the mountain, which overhangs this village on the north side, may, by its reflection, have contributed somewhat to produce this heat. The difference of temperature of the air at the sea-coast, or on the Chesapeake bay, and at the Alleghany, has not been ascertained; but contemporary observations, made at Williamsburg, or in its neighborhood, and at Monticello, which is on the most eastern ridge of the mountains, called the South-West, where they are intersected by the Rivanna, have furnished a ratio by which that difference may in some degree be conjectured. These observations make the difference between Williamsburg and the nearest mountains, at the position before mentioned, to be on an average 6⅓° of Fahrenheit's thermometer. Some allowance, however, is to be made for the difference of latitude between these two places, the latter being 38° 8′ 17″, which is 52′ 22″ north of the former. By contemporary observations of between five and six weeks, the averaged and almost unvaried difference of the height of mercury in the barometer, at those two places, was .784 of an inch, the atmosphere at Monticello being so much the lightest, that is to say, about one-thirty-seventh of its whole weight. It should be observed, however, that the hill of Monticello is of five hundred feet perpendicular height above the river which washes its base. This position being nearly central between our northern and southern boundaries, and between the bay and Alleghany, may be considered as furnishing the best average of the temperature of our climate. Williamsburg is much too near the south-eastern corner to give a fair idea of our general temperature.

But a more remarkable difference is in the winds which prevail in the different parts of the country. The following table exhibits a comparative view of the winds prevailing at Williamsburg, and at Monticello. It is formed by reducing nine months' observations at Monticello to four principal points, to wit, the north-east, south-east, south-west, and north-west; these points being perpendicular to, or parallel with our coast, mountains, and rivers; and by reducing in like manner, an equal number of observations, to wit, four hundred and twenty-one from the preceding table of winds at Williamsburg, taking them proportionably from every point:

	N.E.	S.E.	S.W.	N.W.	TOTAL
Williamsburg	127	61	132	101	421
Monticello	32	91	126	172	421

By this it may be seen that the south-west wind prevails equally at both places; that the north-east is, next to this, the principal wind towards the sea-coast, and the north-west is the predominant wind at the mountains. The difference between these two winds to sensation, and in fact, is very great. The north-east is loaded with vapor, insomuch, that the salt-makers have found that their crystals would not shoot while that blows; it brings a distressing chill, and is heavy and oppressive to the spirits. The north-west is dry, cooling, elastic, and animating. The eastern and south-eastern breezes come on generally in the afternoon. They have advanced into the country very sensibly within the memory of people now living. They formerly did not penetrate far above Williamsburg. They are now frequent at Richmond, and every now and then reach the mountains. They deposit most of their moisture, however, before they get that far. As the lands become more cleared, it is probable they will extend still further westward.

Going out into the open air, in the temperate, and warm months of the year, we often meet with bodies of warm air, which passing by us in two or three seconds, do not afford time to the most sensible thermometer to seize their temperature. Judging from my feelings only, I think they approach the ordinary heat of the human body. Some of them, perhaps, go a little beyond it. They are of about twenty to thirty feet diameter horizontally. Of their height we have no experience, but probably they are globular volumes wafted or rolled along with the wind. But whence taken, where found, or how generated? They are not to be ascribed to volcanoes, because we have none. They do not happen in the winter when the farmers kindle large fires in clearing up their grounds. They are not confined to the spring season, when we have fires which traverse whole counties, consuming the leaves which have fallen from the trees. And they are too frequent and general to be ascribed to accidental fires. I am persuaded their cause must be sought for in the atmosphere itself, to aid us in which I know but of these constant circumstances: a dry air; a temperature as warm, at least, as that of the spring or autumn; and a moderate current of wind. They are most frequent about sun-set; rare in the middle parts of the day; and I do not recollect having ever met with them in the morning.

The variation in the weight of our atmosphere, as indicated by the barometer, is not equal to two inches of mercury. During twelve months' observation at Williamsburg, the extremes 29 and 30.86 inches, the difference being 1.86 of an inch; and in nine months, during which the height of the mercury was noted at Monticello, the extremes were 28.48 and 29.69 inches, the variation being 1.21 of an inch. A gentleman, who has observed his barometer many years, assures me it has never varied two inches. Contemporary observations made at Monticello and Williamsburg, proved the variations in the weight of air to be simultaneous and corresponding in these two places.

Our changes from heat to cold, and cold to heat, are very sudden and great. The mercury in Fahrenheit's thermometer has been known to descend from 92° to 47° in thirteen hours.

It was taken for granted, that the preceding table of average heat will not give a false idea on this subject, as it proposes to state only the ordinary heat and cold of each month, and not those which are extraordinary. At Williamsburg, in August 1766, the mercury in Fahrenheit's thermometer was at 98°ᶜ corresponding with 29⅓ of Reaumur. At the same place in January 1780, it was 6°, corresponding with 11½ below zero of Reaumur. I believe[1] these may be considered to be nearly the extremes of heat and cold in that part of the country. The latter may most certainly, as that time York river, at York-town, was frozen over, so that people walked across it; a circumstance which proves it to have been colder than the winter of 1740, 1741, usually called the cold winter, when York river did not freeze over at that place. In the same season of 1780, Chesapeake bay was solid, from its head to the mouth of Po-tomac. At Annapolis, where it is 5¼ miles over between the nearest points of land, the ice was from five to seven inches thick quite across, so that loaded carriages went over on it. Those, our extremes of heat and cold, of 6° and 98°, were indeed very distressing to us, and were thought to put the extent of the human constitution to considerable trial. Yet a Siberian would have considered them as scarcely a sensible variation. At Jenniseitz in that country, in latitude 58° 27', we are told that the cold in 1735 sunk the mercury by Fahrenheit's scale to 126° below nothing; and the inhabitants of the same country use stove rooms two or three times a week, in which they stay two hours at a time, the atmosphere of which raises the mercury to 135° above nothing. Late ex-periments show that the human body will exist in rooms heated to 140° of Reaumur, equal to 347° of Fahrenheit's, and 135° above boiling water. The hottest point of the twenty-four hours is about four o'clock, P. M., and the dawn of day the coldest.

The access of frost in autumn, and its recess the spring, do not seem to de-pend merely on the degree of cold; much less on the air's being at the freezing point. White frosts are frequent when the thermometer is at 47°, have killed young plants of Indian corn at 48°, and have been known at 54°. Black frost, and even ice, have been produced at 38½°, which is 6½ degrees above the freezing point. That other circumstances must be combined with this cold to produce frost, is evident from this also, on the higher parts of mountains, where it is absolutely colder than in the plains on which they stand, frosts do not appear so early by a considerable space of time in autumn, and go off sooner in the spring, than in the plains. I have known frosts so severe as to kill the hickory trees round about Monticello, and yet not injure the tender fruit blossoms then in bloom on the top and higher parts of the mountain; and in the course of forty years, during which it had been settled, there have been but two instances of a general loss of fruit on it; while in the circum-jacent country, the fruit has escaped but twice in the last seven years. The plants of tobacco, which grow from the roots of those which have been cut off in the summer, are frequently green here at Christmas. This privilege against the frost is undoubtedly combined with the want of dew on the mountains. That the dew is very rare on their higher parts, I say say with certainty, from

[1] At Paris, in 1753, the mercury in Reaumur's thermometer was at 30½ above zero, and in 1776, it was at 16 below zero. The extremities of heat and cold therefore at Paris, are greater than at Williamsburg, which is in the hottest part of Virginia.—T. J.

twelve years' observations, having scarcely ever, during that time, seen an un-equivocal proof of its existence on them at all during summer. Severe frosts in the depth of winter prove that the region of dews extends higher in that season than the tops of the mountains; but certainly, in the summer season, the vapors, by the time they attain that height, are so attenuated as not to sub-side and form a dew when the sun retires.

The weavil has not yet ascended the high mountains.

A more satisfactory estimate of our climate to some, may perhaps be formed, by noting the plants which grow here, subject, however, to be killed by our severest colds. These are the fig, pomegranate, artichoke, and European walnut. In mild winters, lettuce and endive require no shelter; but, generally, they need a slight covering. I do not know that the want of long moss, reed, myrtle, swamp laurel, holly, and cypress, in the upper country proceeds from a greater degree of cold, nor that they were ever killed with any degree of cold, nor that they were ever killed with any degree of cold in the lower country. The aloe lived in Williamsburg, in the open air, through the severe winter of 1779, 1780.

A change in our climate, however, is taking place very sensibly. Both heats and colds are become much more moderate within the memory even of the middle-aged. Snows are less frequent and less deep. They do not often lie, below the mountains, more than one, two, or three days, and very rarely a week. They are remembered to have been formerly frequent, deep, and of long con-tinuance. The elderly inform me, the earth used to be covered with snow about three months in every year. The rivers, which then seldom failed to freeze over in the course of the winter, scarcely ever do so now. This change has produced an unfortunate fluctuation between heat and cold, in the spring of the year, which is very fatal to fruits. From the year 1741 to 1769, an interval of twenty-eight years, there was no instance of fruit killed by the frost in the neighbor-hood of Monticello. An intense cold, produced by constant snows, kept the buds locked up till the sun could obtain, in the spring of the year, so fixed an ascend-ency as to dissolve those snows, and protect the buds, during their development, from every danger of returning cold. The accumulated snows of the winter re-maining to be dissolved all together in the spring, produced those overflowings of our rivers, so frequent then, and so rare now.

Having had occasion to mention the particular situation of Monticello for other purposes, I will just take notice that its elevation affords an opportunity of seeing a phenomenon which is rare at land, though frequent at sea. The sea-men call is *looming*. Philosophy is as yet in the rear of the seamen, for so far from having accounted for it, she has not given it a name. Its principal effect is to make distant objects appear larger, in opposition to the general law of vision, by which they are diminished. I knew an instance, at Yorktown, from whence the water prospect eastwardly is without termination, wherein a canoe with three men, at a great distance was taken for a ship with its three masts. I am little acquainted with the phenomenon as it shows itself at sea; but at Monti-cello it is familiar. There is a solitary mountain about forty miles off in the South, whose natural shape, as presented to view there, is a regular cone; but by the effect of looming, it sometimes subsides almost totally in the horizon; sometimes it rises more acute and more elevated; sometimes it is hemispherical; and sometimes its sides are perpendicular, its top flat, and as broad as its base. In short, it assumes at times the most whimsical shapes, and all these perhaps successively in the same morning. The blue ridge of mountains comes into view, in the north-east, at about one hundred miles distance, and approaching in a direct line, passes by within twenty miles, and goes off to the south-west. This phenomenon begins to show itself on these mountains, at about fifty miles distance, and continues beyond that as far as they are seen. I remark no particular state, either in the weight, moisture, or heat of the atmosphere, necessary to produce this. The only constant circumstances are its appearance in the morning only, and on objects at least forty or fifty miles distant. In this latter circumstance, if not in both, it differs from the looming on the water. Refraction will not account for the metamorphosis. That only changes the proportions of length and breadth, base and altitude, preserving the general outlines. Thus it may make a circle appear elliptical, raise or depress a cone, but by none of its laws, as yet developed, will it make a circle appear a square, or a cone a sphere.

QUERY VIII

The number of its inhabitants

The table on page 107 shows the number of persons imported for the establishment of our colony in its infant state, and the census of inhabitants at different periods, extracted from our historians and public records, as particularly as I have had opportunities and leisure to examine them. Successive lines in the same year show successive periods of time in that year. I have stated the census in two different columns, the whole inhabitants having been sometimes numbered, and sometimes the *tythes* only. This term, with us, includes the free males above sixteen years of age, and slaves above that age of both sexes. A further examination of our records would render this history of our population much more satisfactory and perfect, by furnishing a greater number of intermediate terms. These, however, which are here stated will enable us to calculate, with a considerable degree of precision, the rate at which we have increased. During the infancy of the colony, while numbers were small, wars, importations, and other accidental circumstances render the progression fluctuating and irregular. By the year 1654, however, it becomes tolerably uniform, importations having in a great measure ceased from the dissolution of the company, and the inhabitants become too numerous to be sensibly affected by Indian wars. Beginning at that period, therefore, we find that from thence to the year 1772, our tythes had increased from 7,209 to 153,000. The whole term being of one hundred and eighteen years, yields a duplication once in every twenty-seven and a quarter years. The intermediate enumerations taken in 1700, 1748, and 1759, furnish proofs of the uniformity of this progression. Should this rate of increase continue, we shall have between six and seven millions of inhabitants within ninety-five years. If we suppose our country to be bounded, at some future day, by the meridian of the mouth of the Great Kanhaway, (within which it has been before conjectured, are 64,461 square miles) there will then be one hundred inhabitants for every square mile, which is nearly the state of population in the British Islands.

YEARS	SETTLERS IMPORTED	CENSUS OF INHABITANTS	CENSUS OF TYTHES
1607	100	....	....
..	....	40	....
..	120	....	....
1608	....	130	....
..	70	....	....
1609	....	490	....
..	16	....	....
..	....	60	....
1610	150	....	....
..	....	200	....
1611	3 ship loads.	....	....
..	300	....	....
1612	80	....	....
1617	....	400	....
1618	200	....	....
..	40	....	....
..	....	600	....
1619	1,216	....	....
1621	1,300	....	....
1622	....	3,800	....
..	....	2,500	....
1628	....	3,000	....
1632	....	....	2,000
1644	....	....	4,822
1645	....	....	5,000
1652	....	....	7,000
1654	....	....	7,209
1700	....	....	22,000
1748	....	....	82,100
1759	....	....	105,000
1772	....	....	153,000
1782	....	567,614	....

Here I will beg leave to propose a doubt. The present desire of America is to produce rapid population by as great importations of foreigners as possible. But is this founded in good policy? The advantage proposed is the multiplication of numbers. Now let us suppose (for example only) that, in this state, we could double our numbers in one year by the importation of foreigners; and this is a greater accession than the most sanguine advocate for emigration has a right to expect. Then I say, beginning with a double stock, we shall attain any given degree of population only twenty-seven years, and three months sooner than if we proceed on our single stock. If we propose four millions and a half as a competent population for this State, we should be fifty-four and a half years attaining it, could we at once double our numbers; and eighty-one and three quarter years, if we rely on natural propagation, as may be seen by the following table:

	PROCEEDING ON OUR PRESENT STOCK	PROCEEDING ON A DOUBLE STOCK
1781	567,614	1,135,228
1808¼	1,135,228	2,270,456
1835½	2,270,456	4,540,912
1862¾	4,540,912	

In the first column are stated periods of twenty-seven and a quarter years; in the second are our numbers at each period, as they will be if we proceed on our actual stock; and in the third are what they would be, at the same periods, were we to set out from the double of our present stock. I have taken the term of four million and a half of inhabitants for example's sake only. Yet I am persuaded it is a greater number than the country spoken of, considering how much inarable land it contains, can clothe and feed without a material change in the quality of their diet. But are there no inconveniences to be thrown into the scale against the advantage expected from a multiplication of numbers by the importation of foreigners? It is for the happiness of those united in society to harmonize as much as possible in matters which they must of necessity transact together. Civil government being the sole object of forming societies, its administration must be conducted by common consent. Every species of government has its specific principles. Ours perhaps are more peculiar than those of any other in the universe. It is a composition of the freest principles of the English constitution, with others derived from natural right and natural reason. To these nothing can be more opposed than the maxims of absolute monarchies. Yet from such we are to expect the greatest number of emigrants. They will bring with them the principles of the governments they leave, imbibed in their early youth; or, if able to throw them off, it will be in exchange for an unbounded licentiousness, passing, as is usual, from one extreme to another. It would be a miracle were they to stop precisely at the point of temperate liberty. These principles, with their language, they will transmit to their children. In proportion to their numbers, they will share with us the legislation. They will infuse into it their spirit, warp and bias its directions, and render it a heterogenious, incoherent, distracted mass. I may appeal to experience, during the present contest, for a verification of these conjectures. But, if they be not certain in event, are they not possible, are they not probable? Is it not safer to wait with patience twenty-seven years and three months longer, for the attainment of any degree of population desired or expected? May not our government be more homogeneous, more peaceable, more durable? Suppose twenty millions of republican Americans thrown all of a sudden into France, what would be the condition of that kingdom? If it would be more turbulent, less happy, less strong, we may believe that the addition of half a million of foreigners to our present numbers would produce a similar effect here. If they come of themselves they are entitled to all the rights of citizenship; but I doubt the expediency of inviting them by extraordinary encouragements. I mean not that these doubts should be extended to the importation of useful artificers. The policy of that measure depends on very different considerations. Spare no expense in obtaining them. They will after a while go to the plough and the hoe; but, in the mean time, they will teach us something we do not know. It is not so in agriculture. The indifferent state of that among us does not proceed from a want of knowledge merely; it is from our having such quantities of land to waste as we please. In Europe the object is to make the most of their land, labor being abundant; here it is to make the most of our labor, land being abundant.

It will be proper to explain how the numbers for the year 1782 have been obtained; as it was not from a perfect census of the inhabitants. It will at the same time develope the proportion between the free inhabitants and slaves. The following return of taxable articles for that year was given in.

53,289 free males above twenty-one years of age.

211,698 slaves of all ages and sexes.

23,766 not distinguished in the returns, but said to be tytheable slaves.

195,439 horses.

609,734 cattle.

5,126 wheels of riding-carriages.

191 taverns.

There were no returns from the eight counties of Lincoln, Jefferson, Fayette, Monongahela, Yohogania, Ohio, Northampton, and York. To find the number of slaves which should have been returned instead of the 23,766 tytheables, we must mention that some observations on a former census had given reason to believe that the numbers above and below sixteen years of age were equal. The double of this number, therefore, to wit, 47,532 must be added to 211,698, which will give us 259,230 slaves of all ages and sexes. To find the number of free inhabitants we must repeat the observation that those above and below sixteen are nearly equal. But as the number 53,289 omits the males below sixteen and twenty-one we must supply them from conjecture. On a former experiment it had appeared that about one-third of our militia, that is, of the males between sixteen and fifty, were unmarried. Knowing how early marriage takes place here, we shall not be far wrong in supposing that the unmarried part of our militia are those between sixteen and twenty-one. If there be young men who do not marry till after twenty-one, there are many who marry before that age. But as men above fifty were not included in the militia, we will suppose the unmarried, or those between sixteen and twenty-one, to be one-fourth of the whole number above sixteen, then we have the following calculation:

53,289 free males above twenty-one years of age.

17,763 free males between sixteen and twenty-one.

17,052 free males under sixteen.

142,104 free males of all ages.

284,208 free inhabitants of all ages.

259,230 slaves of all ages.

543,438 inhabitants, exclusive of the eight counties from which were no returns. In these eight counties in the years 1779 and 1780, were 3,161 militia. Say then,

3,161 free males above the age of sixteen.

3,161 free males under sixteen.

6,322 free females.

12,644 free inhabitants in these eight counties. To find the number of slaves, say, as 284,208 to 259,230, so is 12,644 to 11,532. Adding the third of these numbers to the first, and the fourth to the second, we have,

296,852 free inhabitants.

270,762 slaves.

567,614 inhabitants of every age, sex and condition. But 296,852, the number of free inhabitants, are to 270,762, the number of slaves, nearly as 11 to 10. Under the mild treatment our slaves experience, and their wholesome, though coarse food, this blot in our country increases as fast, or faster than the whites. During the regal government we had at one time obtained a law which imposed such a duty on the importation of slaves as amounted nearly to a prohibition, when one inconsiderate assembly, placed under a peculiarity of circumstance, repealed the law. This repeal met a joyful sanction from the then reigning sovereign, and no devices, no expedients, which could ever be attempted by subsequent assemblies, and they seldom met without attempting them, could succeed in getting the royal assent to a renewal of the duty. In the very first session held under the republican government, the assembly passed a law for the perpetual prohibition of the importation of slaves. This will in some measure stop the increase of this great political and moral evil, while the minds of our citizens may be ripening for a complete emancipation of human nature.

QUERY IX

The number and condition of the Militia and Regular Troops, and their Pay

The following is a state of the militia, taken from returns of 1780 and 1781, except in those counties marked with an asterisk, the returns from which are somewhat older.

Every able-bodied freeman, between the ages of sixteen and fifty, is enrolled

in the militia. Those of every county are formed into companies, and these
again into one or more battalions, according to the numbers in the county.
They are commanded by colonels, and other subordinate officers, as in the
regular service. In every county is a county-lieutenant, who commands the whole
militia of his county, but ranks only as a colonel in the field. We have no

SITUATION	COUNTIES	MILITIA
Westward of the Alleghany. 4,458	Lincoln	600
	Jefferson	300
	Fayette	156
	Ohio	..
	Monongalia	* 1,000
	Washington	* 829
	Montgomery	1,071
	Greenbriar	502
Between the Alleghany and Blue Ridge. 7,673	Hampshire	930
	Berkeley	* 1,100
	Frederick	1,143
	Shenando	* 925
	Rockingham	875
	Augusta	1,375
	Rockbridge	* 625
	Boutetourt	* 700
Between the Blue Ridge and Tide Waters. 18.828	Loudoun	1,746
	Faquier	1,078
	Culpepper	1,513
	Spotsylanvia	480
	Orange	* 600
	Louisa	603
	Goochland	* 550
	Fluvanna	* 296
	Albemarle	873
	Amherst	896
	Buckingham	* 625
	Bedford	1,300
	Henry	1,004
	Pittsylvania	* 725
	Halifax	* 1,139
	Charlotte	612
	Prince Edward	589
	Cumberland	408
	Powhatan	330
	Amelia	* 1,125
	Lunenburg	677
	Mecklenburg	1,100
	Brunswick	559

general officers always existing. These are appointed occasionally, when an invasion or insurrection happens, and their commission determines with the occasion. The governor is head of the military, as well as civil power. The law requires every militia-man to provide himself with the arms usual in the regular service. But this injunction was always indifferently complied with, and the

SITUATION		COUNTIES	MILITIA
On the Tide Waters, and in that Parallel. 19,012	Between James River and Carolina. 6,959	Greensville	500
		Dinwiddie	* 750
		Chesterfield	665
		Prince George	328
		Surrey	380
		Sussex	* 700
		Southampton	874
		Isle of White	* 600
		Nansemond	* 644
		Norfolk	* 880
		Prince Anne	* 594
	Between James & York rivers. 3,009	Henrico	619
		Hanover	706
		New Kent	* 418
		Charles City	286
		James City	235
		Williamsburgh	129
		York	* 244
		Warwick	* 100
		Elizabeth City	182
	Bet. York & Rappahannock. 3,269	Caroline	805
		King William	436
		King and Queen	500
		Essex	468
		Middlesex	* 210
		Gloucester	850
	Betw'n Rappahannock and Powtomac. 4,137	Fairfax	652
		Prince William	614
		Stafford	* 500
		King George	483
		Richmond	412
		Westmoreland	544
		Northumberland	630
		Lancaster	332
	East'n shore. 1,638	Accomac	* 1,208
		Northampton	* 430
	Whole Militia of the State		49,971

arms they had, have been so frequently called for to arm the regulars, that in the lower parts of the country they are entirely disarmed. In the middle country a fourth or fifth part of them may have such firelocks as they had provided to destroy the noxious animals which infest their farms; and on the western side of the Blue ridge they are generally armed with rifles. The pay of our militia, as well as of our regulars, is that of the continental regulars. The condition of our regulars, of whom we have none but continentals, and part of a battalion of state troops, is so constantly on the change, that a state of it at this day would not be its state a month hence. It is much the same with the condition of the other continental troops, which is well enough known.

QUERY X

The Marine

Before the present invasion of this State by the British, under the command of General Phillips, we had three vessels of sixteen guns, one of fourteen, five small gallies, and two or three armed boats. They were generally so badly manned as seldom to be in a condition for service. Since the perfect possession of our rivers assumed by the enemy, I believe we are left with a single armed boat only.

QUERY XI

A description of the Indians established in that State

When the first effectual settlement of our colony was made, which was in 1607, the country from the sea-coast to the mountains, and from the Potomac to the most southern waters of James' river, was occupied by upwards of forty different tribes of Indians. Of these the *Powhatans*, the *Mannahoacs*, and *Monacans*, were the most powerful. Those between the seacoast and falls of the rivers, were in amity with one another, and attached to the *Powhatans* as their link of union. Those between the falls of the rivers and the mountains, were divided into two confederacies; the tribes inhabiting the head waters of Potomac and Rappahannock, being attached to the *Mannahoacs;* and those on the upper parts of James' river to the *Monacans*. But the *Monacans* and their friends were in amity with the *Mannahoacs* and their friends, and waged joint and perpetual war against the *Powhatans*. We are told that the *Powhatans, Mannahoacs,* and *Monacans,* spoke languages so radically different, that interpreters were necessary when they transacted business. Hence we may conjecture, that this was not the case between all the tribes, and, probably, that each spoke the language of the nation to which it was attached; which we know to have been the case in many particular instances. Very possibly there may have been anciently three different stocks, each of which multiplying in a long course of time, had separated into so many little societies. This practice results from the circumstance of their having never submitted themselves to any laws, any coercive power, any shadow of government. Their only controls are their manners, and that moral sense of right and wrong, which, like the sense of tasting and feeling in every man, makes a part of his nature. An offence against these is punished by contempt, by exclusion from society, or, where the case is serious, as that of murder, by the individuals whom it concerns. Imperfect as this species of coercion may seem, crimes are very rare among them; insomuch that were it made a question, whether no law, as among the savage Americans, or too much law, as among the civilized Europeans, submits man to the greatest evil, one who has seen both conditions of existence would pronounce it to be the last; and that the sheep are happier of themselves, than under care of the wolves. It will be said, that great societies cannot exist without government. The savages, therefore, break them into small ones.

The territories of the *Powhatan* confederacy, south of the Potomac, comprehended about eight thousand square miles, thirty tribes, and two thousand four hundred warriors. Captain Smith tells us, that within sixty miles of Jamestown were five thousand people, of whom one thousand five hundred were warriors. From this we find the proportion of their warriors to their whole inhabitants, was as three to ten. The *Powhatan* confederacy, then, would consist of about eight thousand inhabitants, which was one for every square mile; being about the twentieth part of our present population in the same territory, and the hundredth of that of the British islands.

Besides these were the *Nottoways,* living on Nottoway river, the *Meherrins* and *Tuteloes* on Meherrin river, who were connected with the Indians of Carolina, probably with the Chowanocs.

The preceding table contains a state of these several tribes, according to their confederacies and geographical situation, with their numbers when we first became acquainted with them, where these numbers are known. The numbers of some of them are again stated as they were in the year 1669, when an attempt was made by assembly to enumerate them. Probably the enumeration is imperfect, and in some measure conjectural, and that a farther search into the records would furnish many more particulars. What would be the melancholy sequel of their history, may, however, be argued from the census of 1669; by which we discover that the tribes therein enumerated were, in the space of sixty-two years, reduced to about one-third of their former numbers. Spirituous liquors, the small-pox, war, and an abridgement of territory to a people who lived principally on the spontaneous productions of nature, had committed terrible havoc among them, which gencration, under the obstacles opposed to it among them, was not likely to make good. That the lands of this country were taken from them by conquest, is not so general a truth as is supposed. I find in our historians and records, repeated proofs of purchase, which cover a considerable part of the lower country; and many more would doubtless be found on further search. The upper country, we know, has been acquired altogether by purchases made in the most unexceptional form.

Westward of all these tribes, beyond the mountains, and extending to the

NORTH

MANNAHOACS

	TRIBES	COUNTRY	CF. TOWNS	WARRIORS 1669
Between Patowmac and Rappahannoc.	Whonkenties.	Fauquier.		
	Teginaties.	Culpepper.		
	Ontponies.	Orange.		
	Tauxitanians.	Fauquier.		
	Hassinungaes.	Culpepper.		
Bet. Rappahannoc & York.	Stegarakies.	Orange.		
	Shackakonies.	Spotsylvania.		
	Manahoacs.	Stafford. Spotsylvania.		

MONACANS

	TRIBES	COUNTRY	CF. TOWNS	WARRIORS 1669
Between York and James.	Monacans.	James river, above the falls.	Fork of James river.	30
	Monasicapanoes.	Louisa. Fluvanna.		
Between James & Carolina.	Monahassanoes.	Bedford.		
	Massinacacs.	Buckingham.		
	Mohemenchoes.	Cumberland. Powhatan.		

POWHATANS

	TRIBES	COUNTRY	CHIEF TOWNS	WARRIORS 1607	WARRIORS 1669	
Between Patowmac and Rappahannoc.	Tauxenents.	Fairfax.	About Gen. Washing-	40		
	Patówomekes.	Stafford.	Pawtomac cr. [ton's.	200	60	By the name of Matchotics, U. Matchodic, Nanzaticos, Nanzatico, Appomatox, Matox.
	Cuttatawomans.	King George.	About Lamb creek.	20		
	Pissasecs.	King George.	Above Leeds Town.	..	60	
Bet. Rappahannoc & York.	Onaumanients.	Westmoreland.	Nomony river.	100		
	Rappahanocs.	Richmond co.	Rappahanoc creek.	100	30	
	Moáughtacunds.	Richmond.	Moratico river.	80	40	
	Secacaconies.	Northumberland.	Coan river.	30		By the name of Totuskeys
	Wighcocomicoes.	Northumberland.	Wicocomico river.	130	70	
	Cuttatawomans.	Lancaster.	Corotoman.	30		
	Nantaughtacunds.	Essex. Caroline.	Port Tobacco creek.	150	60	
	Mattapoments.	King William.		30	20	
	Pamúnkies.	Gloucester.	Romuncock.	300	50	
	Wérowocómicoes.	Piankatank river.	About Rosewell. [by.	40		
	Payankatonks.	Pamunkey river.	Turk's Ferry. Grimes-	55		
	Youghtanunds.			60		
Between York and James.	Chickahóminies.	Chickahominy r.		250	60	
	Powhatans.	Henrico.	Orapaks.	40	10	
	Arrowhatocs.	Henrico.	Powhatan. Mayo's.	30		
	Wéanocs.	Charles city.	Arrohatocs.	100	15	
	Paspahéghes.	Charles city.	Weynoke.	40		
		James city.	Sandy-Point.			
Between James & Carolina.	Chiskiacs.	York.	Chiskiae.	45	15	
	Kecoughtans.	Elizabeth city.	Roscows.	20		
	Appamáttocs.	Chesterfield.	Bermuda Hundred.	60	50 3 Pohics	
	Quiocohánoes.	Surry.	About Upp. Chipoak.	25		
	Warrasqueaks.	Isle of Wight.	Warrasqueoc.	..	45	
	Nasamónds.	Nansamond.	A't mouth W. branch.	200		
	Chésapeaks.	Princess Anne.	About Lynhaven riv.	100		
Eastern shore.	Accohanocs.	Accom. Northampton.	Accohanoc river.	40		
	Accomácks.	Northampton.	About Cheriton's.	80		

	1699
Nottoways.	..
Meherrics.	90
Tuteloes.	50

SOUTH

WEST

EAST

great lakes, were the *Maſſawomees,* a most powerful confederacy, who harassed unremittingly the *Powhatans* and *Manahoacs.* These were probably the ancestors of tribes known at present by the name of the *Six Nations.*

Very little can now be discovered of the subsequent history of these tribes severally. The *Chickahominies* removed about the year 1661, to Mattapony river. Their chief, with one from each of the Pamunkies and Mattaponies, attended the treaty of Albany in 1685. This seems to have been the last chapter in their history. They retained, however, their separate name so late as 1705, and were at length blended with the Pamunkies and Mattaponies, and exist at present only under their names. There remain of the *Mattaponies* three or four men only, and have more negro than Indian blood in them. They have lost their language, have reduced themselves, by voluntary sales, to about fifty acres of land, which lie on the river of their own name, and have from time to time, been joining the Pamunkies, from whom they are distant but ten miles. The *Pamunkies* are reduced to about ten or twelve men, tolerably pure from mixture with other colors. The older ones among them preserve their language in a small degree, which are the last vestiges on earth, as far as we know, of the Powhatan language. They have about three hundred acres of very fertile land, on Pamunkey river, so encompassed by water that a gate shuts in the whole. Of the *Nottoways,* not a male is left. A few women constitute the remains of that tribe. They are seated on Nottoway river, in Southampton country, on very fertile lands. At a very early period, certain lands were marked out and appropriated to these tribes, and were kept from encroachment by the authority of the laws. They have usually had trustees appointed, whose duty was to watch over their interests, and guard them from insult and injury.

The *Monacans* and their friends, better known latterly by the name of *Tuscaroras,* were probably connected with the Massawomecs, or Five Nations. For though we are[1] told their languages were so different that the intervention of interpreters was necessary between them, yet do we also[2] learn that the Erigas, a nation formerly inhabiting on the Ohio, were of the same original stock with the Five Nations, and that they partook also of the Tuscarora language. Their dialects might, by long separation, have become so unlike as to be unintelligible to one another. We know that in 1712, the Five Nations received the Tuscaroras into their confederacy, and made them the Sixth Nation. They received the Meherrins and Tuteloes also into their protection; and it is most probable, that the remains of many other of the tribes, of whom we find no particular account, retired westwardly in like manner, and were incorporated with one or the other of the western tribes. (5).

I know of no such thing existing as an Indan monument; for I would not honor with that name arrow points, stone hatchets, stone pipes, and half-shapen images. Of labor on the large scale, I think there is no remain as respectable as would be a common ditch for the draining of lands; unless indeed it would be the barrows, of which many are to be found all over this country. These are of different sizes, some of them constructed of earth, and some of loose stones.

[1] Smith.—T. J.   [2] Evans.—T. J.

That they were repositories of the dead, has been obvious to all; but on what particular occasion constructed, was a matter of doubt. Some have thought they covered the bones of those who have fallen in battles fought on the spot of interment. Some ascribed them to the custom, said to prevail among the Indians, of collecting, at certain periods, the bones of all their dead, wheresoever deposited at the time of death. Others again supposed them the general sepulchres for towns, conjectured to have been on or near these grounds; and this opinion was supported by the quality of the lands in which they are found, (those constructed of earth being generally in the softest and most fertile meadow-grounds on river sides,) and by a tradition, said to be handed down from the aboriginal Indians, that, when they settled in a town, the first person who died was placed erect, and earth put about him, so as to cover and support him; that when another died, a narrow passage was dug to the first, the second reclined against him, and the cover of earth replaced, and so on. There being one of these in my neighborhood, I wished to satisfy myself whether any, and which of these opinions were just. For this purpose I determined to open and examine it thoroughly. It was situated on the low grounds of the Rivanna, about two miles above its principal fork, and opposite to some hills, on which had been an Indian town. It was of a spheroidical form, of about forty feet diameter at the base, and had been of about twelve feet altitude, though now reduced by the plough to seven and a half, having been under cultivation about a dozen years. Before this it was covered with trees of twelve inches diameter, and round the base was an excavation of five feet depth and width, from whence the earth had been taken of which the hillock was formed. I first dug superficially in several parts of it, and came to collections of human bones, at different depths, from six inches to three feet below the surface. These were lying in the utmost confusion, some vertical, some oblique, some horizontal, and directed to every point of the compass, entangled and held together in clusters by the earth. Bones of the most distant parts were found together, as, for instance, the small bones of the foot in the hollow of a scull; many sculls would sometimes be in contact, lying on the face, on the side, on the back, top or bottom, so as, on the whole, to give the idea of bones emptied promiscuously from a bag or a basket, and covered over with earth, without any attention to their order. The bones of which the greater numbers remained, were sculls, jawbones, teeth, the bones of the arms, thighs, legs, feet and hands. A few ribs remained, some vertebræ of the neck and spine, without their processes, and one instance only of the [1] bone which serves as a base to the vertebral column. The sculls were so tender, that they generally fell to pieces on being touched. The other bones were stronger. There were some teeth which were judged to be smaller than those of an adult; a scull, which on a slight view, appeared to be that of an infant, but it fell to pieces on being taken out, so as to prevent satisfactory examination; a rib, and a fragment of the under-jaw of a person about half grown; another rib of an infant; and a part of the jaw of a child, which had not cut its teeth. This last furnishing the most decisive proof of the

[1] The *os sacrum.*—T. J.

burial of children here, I was particular in my attention to it. It was part of the right half of the under-jaw. The processes, by which it was attenuated to the temporal bones, were entire, and the bone itself firm to where it had been broken off, which, as nearly as I could judge, was about the place of the eyetooth. Its upper edge, wherein would have been the sockets of the teeth, was perfectly smooth. Measuring it with that of an adult, by placing their hinder processes together, its broken end extended to the penultimate grinder of the adult. This bone was white, all the others of a sand color. The bones of infants being soft, they probably decay sooner, which might be the cause so few were found here. I proceeded then to make a perpendicular cut through the body of the barrow, that I might examine its internal structure. This passed about three feet from its centre, was opened to the former surface of the earth, and was wide enough for a man to walk through and examine its sides. At the bottom, that is, on the level of the circumjacent plain, I found bones; above these a few stones, brought from a cliff a quarter of a mile off, and from the river one-eighth of a mile off; then a large interval of earth, then a stratum of bones, and so on. At one end of the section were four strata of bones plainly distinguishable; at the other, three; the strata in one part not ranging with those in another. The bones nearest the surface were least decayed. No holes were discovered in any of them, as if made with bullets, arrows, or other weapons. I conjectured that in this barrow might have been a thousand skeletons. Everyone will readily seize the circumstances above related, which militate against the opinion, that it covered the bones only of persons fallen in battle; and against the tradition also, which would make it the common sepulchre of a town, in which the bodies were placed upright, and touching each other. Appearances certainly indicate that it has derived both origin and growth from the accustomary collection of bones, and deposition of them together; that the first collection had been deposited on the common surface of the earth, a few stones put over it, and then a covering of earth, that the second had been laid on this, had covered more or less of it in proportion to the number of bones, and was then also covered with earth; and so on. The following are the particular circumstances which give it this aspect. 1. The number of bones. 2. Their confused position. 3. Their being in different strata. 4. The strata in one part having no correspondence with those in another. 5. The different states of decay in these strata, which seem to indicate a difference in the time of inhumation. 6. The existence of infant bones among them.

But on whatever occasion they may have been made, they are of considerable notoriety among the Indians; for a party passing, about thirty years ago, through the part of the country where this barrow is, went through the woods directly to it, without any instructions or inquiry, and having staid about it for some time, with expressions which were construed to be those of sorrow, they returned to the high road, which they had left about half a dozen miles to pay this visit, and pursued their journey. There is another barrow much resembling this, in the low grounds of the south branch of Shenandoah, where it is crossed by the road leading from the Rockfish gap to Staunton. Both of these have, within these dozen years, been cleared of their trees and put under cultivation, are much reduced in their height, and spread in width, by the plough, and will probably disappear in time. There is another on a hill in the Blue Ridge of mountains, a few miles north of Wood's gap, which is made up of small stones thrown together. This has been opened and found to contain human bones, as the others do. There are also many others in other parts of the country.

Great question has arisen from whence came those aboriginals of America? Discoveries, long ago made, were sufficient to show that the passage from Europe to America was always practicable, even to the imperfect navigation of ancient times. In going from Norway to Iceland, from Iceland to Greenland, from Greenland to Labrador, the first traject is the widest; and this having been practised from the earliest times of which we have any account of that part of the earth, it is not difficult to suppose that the subsequent trajects may have been sometimes passed. Again, the late discoveries of Captain Cook, coasting from Kamschatka to California, have proved that if the two continents of Asia and America be separated at all, it is only by a narrow strait. So that from this side also, inhabitants may have passed into America; and the resemblance between the Indians of America and the eastern inhabitants of Asia, would induce us to conjecture, that the former are the descendants of the latter, or the latter of the former; excepting indeed the Esquimaux, who, from the same circumstance of resemblance, and from identity of language must be derived from the Greenlanders, and these probably from some of the northern parts of the old continent. A knowledge of their several languages would be the most certain evidence of their derivation which could be produced. In fact, it is the best proof of the affinity of nations which ever can be referred to. How many ages have elapsed since the English, the Dutch, the Germans, the Swiss, the Norwegians, Danes and Swedes have separated from their common stock? Yet how many more must elapse before the proofs of their common origin, which exist in their several languages, will disappear? It is to be lamented then, very much to be lamented, that we have suffered so many of the Indians tribes already to extinguish, without our having previously collected and deposited in the records of literature, the general rudiments at least of the languages they spoke. Were vocabularies formed of all the languages spoken in North and South America, preserving their appellations of the most common objects in nature, of those which must be present to every nation barbarous or civilized, with the inflections of their nouns and verbs, their principles of regimen and concord, and these deposited in all the public libraries, it would furnish opportunities to those skilled in the languages of the old world to compare them with these, now, or at any future time, and hence to construct the best evidence of the derivation of this part of the human race.

But imperfect as is our knowledge of the tongues spoken in America, it suffices to discover the following remarkable fact: Arranging them under the radical ones to which they may be palpably traced, and doing the same by those of the red men of Asia, there will be found probably twenty in America, for one

INDIAN TRIBES

TRIBES	CROGHAN 1759	BOUQUET 1764	HUTCHINS 1768	WHERE THEY RESIDE
Oswegatchies	....	....	100	At Swagatchy, on the river St. Laurence.
Connasedagoes	....	200 ⎱	300	Near Montreal.
Cohunnewagoes	....	⎰	....	
Orondocs	....	....	100	Near Trois Rivieres.
Abenakies	....	350	150	Near Trois Rivieres.
Little Alkonkins	....	....	100	Near Trois Rivieres.
Michmacs	....	700	....	River St. Laurence.
Amelistes	....	550	....	River St. Laurence.
Chalas	....	130	....	River St. Laurence.
Nipissins	....	400	....	Towards the heads of the Ottawas river.
Algonquins	....	300	....	Towards the heads of the Ottawas river.
Round Heads	....	2,500	....	Riviere aux Tetes boules, on the east side of Lake Superior.
Messasagues	....	2,000	....	Lakes Huron and Superior.
Christianaux—Kris	....	3,000	....	Lake Christianaux.
Assinaboes	....	1,500	....	Lake Assinaboes.
Blancs, or Barbus	....	1,500	....	
Sioux of the Meadows	....	2,500 ⎱	....	
Sioux of the Woods	....	1,800 ⎰	....	On the heads of the Mississippi and westward of that river.
Sioux	10,000	....	10,000	
Ajoues	....	1,100	....	North of the Padoucas.
Panis—White	....	2,000	....	South of the Missouri.
Panis—Freckled	....	1,709	....	South of the Missouri.
Padoucas	....	500	....	South of the Missouri.
Grandes-Eaux	....	1,000	....	
Canses	....	1,600	....	South of the Missouri.
Osages	....	600	....	South of the Missouri.
Missouris	400	3,000	....	On the river Missouri.
Arkansas	....	2,000	....	On the River Arkansas.
Caouitas	....	700	....	East of the Alibamous.

Northward and Westward of the United States

in Asia, of those radical languages, so called because if they were ever the same they have lost all resemblance to one another. A separation into dialects may be the work of a few ages only, but for two dialects to recede from one another till they have lost all vestiges of their common origin, must require an immense course of time; perhaps not less than many people give to the age of the earth. A greater number of those radical changes of language having taken place among the red men of America, proves them of greater antiquity than those of Asia.

I will now proceed to state the nations and numbers of the Aborigines which still exist in a respectable and independent form. And as their undefined boundaries would render it difficult to specify those only which may be within any certain limits, and it may not be unacceptable to present a more general view of them, I will reduce within the form of a catalogue all those within, and circumjacent to, the United States, whose names and numbers have come to my notice. These are taken from four different lists, the first of which was given in the year 1759 to General Stanwix by George Croghan, deputy agent for Indian affairs under Sir William Johnson; the second was drawn up by a French trader of considerable note, resident among the Indians many years, and annexed to Colonel Bouquet's printed account of his expedition in 1764. The third was made out by Captain Hutchins, who visited most of the tribes, by order, for the purpose of learning their numbers, in 1768; and the fourth by John Dodge, an Indian trader, in 1779, except the numbers marked *, which are from other information. [See table on pages 122-123.]

The following tribes are also mentioned:

Croghan's Catal.
- Lezar 400 } From the mouth of Ohio to the mouth of Wabash
- Webings 200 On the Mississippi below the Shakies
- Ousasoys } 4,000 On White Creek, a branch of the Mississippi
- Grand Tuc }
- Linways 1,000 On the Mississippi

Bouquet's
- Les Puans 700 Near Puans Bay
- Folle Avoine 350 Near Puans Bay
- Ouanakina 300 }
- Chiakanessou 350 } Conjectured to be tribes of the Creeks
- Machecous 800 }
- Souikilas 200 }

Dodge's
- Minneamis 2,000 } North-west of Lake Michigan, to the heads of Mississippi, and up to Lake Superior
- Piankishas }
- Mascoutins 800 } On and near the Wabash toward the Illinois
- Vermillions }

But apprehending these might be different appellations for some of the tribes already enumerated, I have not inserted them in the table, but state them sep-

TRIBES	CROGHAN 1759	BOUQUET 1764	HUTCHINS 1768	DODGE 1779	WHERE THEY RESIDE
Mohocks	....	....	160	100	Mohocks river.
Onèidas	....	....	} 300	400	East side of Oneida Lake and head branches of Susquehanna.
Tuscorôras	....	} 1,550	200	....	Between the Oneidas and Onondagoes.
Onondàgoes	....	....	260	230	Near Onondago Lake.
Cayùgas	....	....	200	220	On the Cayuga Lake, near the north branch of Susquehanna.
Senecas	....	....	1,000	650	On the waters of Susquehanna, of Ontario, and the heads of the Ohio.
Aughquàgahs	....	....	150	....	East branch of Susquehanna, and on Aughquagah.
Nànticoes	....	....	100	....	Utsanango, Chaghnet, and Owegy, on the east branch of Susquehanna.
Mohiccons	....	....	100	....	In the same parts.
Conòies	....	....	30	....	In the same parts.
Sapòonies	....	....	30	....	At Diahago and other villages up the north branch of Susquehanna.
Mùnsies	....	....	150	*150	At Diahago and other villages up the north branch of Susquehanna.
Delawares, or Linnelinopies	600	....	150	....	At Diahago and other villages up the north branch of Susquehanna.
Delawares, or Linnelinopies	....	600	600	*500	Between Ohio and Lake Erie and the branches of Beaver creek, Cayahoga and Muskingum.
Shàwanees	500	400	300	300	Sioto and the branches of Muskingum.
Mingoes	....	....	....	60	On a branch of Sioto.
Mohiccons	....	} 300	....	*60	
Cohunnewagos	} 300	300	300	....	Near Sandusky.
Wyandots	....	....	} 250	180	Near Fort St. Joseph's and Detroit.
Wyandots	300	....	250	....	Miami river near Fort Miami.
Twightwees	300	....	....	....	Miami river, about Fort St. Joseph.
Miamis	....	350	....	300	On the banks of the Wabash, near Fort Ouiatonon.
Ouiàtonons	200	400	300	*400	On the banks of the Wabash, near Fort Ouiatonon.
Piànkishas	300	250	300	**400	On the banks of the Wabash, near Fort Ouiatonon.
Shàkirs	....	....	200	....	On the banks of the Wabash, near Fort Ouiatonon.

Within the limits of the United States

Within the limits of the United States	Kaskaskias	....		300	....	Near Kaskaskia.
	Illinois	400	600	300	....	Near Cahokia. Query, If not the same with the Mitchigamis?
	Piorias	....	800	....	....	On the Illinois river, called Pianrias, but supposed to mean Piorias.
	Ponteòtamies	....	350	300	450	Near Fort St. Joseph's and Fort Detroit.
	Ottawas	....	....	550	*300	Near Fort St. Joseph's and Fort Detroit.
	Chippawas	....	....	200	....	On Saguinam bay of Lake Huron.
	Ottawas	....	....		....	On Saguinam bay of Lake Huron.
	Chippawas	....	....	400	....	Near Michillimackinac.
	Ottawas	2,000	5,900	250	5,450	Near Michillimackinac.
	Chippawas	....		400	....	Near Fort St. Mary's on Lake Superior. Several other villages along the banks of Lake Superior. Numbers unknown.
	Chippawas	....	....	....	....	Near Puans bay on Lake Michigan.
	Shakies	200	400	550	....	Near Puans bay on Lake Michigan.
	Mynonàmies	....	....	....	....	Near Puans bay on Lake Michigan.
	Ouisconsings	....	550	....	....	Ouisconsing river.
	Kickapous	600	300	....	250	
	Otogamies—Foxes	....	....	....	....	
	Màscoutens	....	500		....	On Lake Michigan, and between that and the Mississippi.
	Miscòthins	....	....	4,000	....	
	Outimacs	....	....	....	....	
	Musquakies	200	250	....	250	
	Sioux. Eastern	....	....	....	500	On the eastern heads of the Mississippi, and the islands of Lake Superior.
				GALPHIN 1678		
	Cherokees	1,500	2,500	3,000	....	Western parts of North Carolina.
	Chickasaws	....	750	500	....	Western parts of Georgia.
	Catawbas	....	150	....	....	On the Catawba river in South Carolina.
	Chacktaws	2,000	4,500	6,000	....	Western parts of Georgia.
	Upper Creeks	....	....	3,000	....	Western parts of Georgia.
	Lower Creeks	....	1,180		....	
	Natchez	....	150	....	....	
	Alibamous	....	600	....	....	Alabama river, in the western parts of Georgia.

arately as worthy of further inquiry. The variations observable in numbering the same tribe may sometimes be ascribed to imperfect information, and sometimes to a greater or less comprehension of settlements under the same name. (7)

QUERY XII

A notice of the counties, cities, townships, and villages

The counties have been enumerated under Query IX. They are seventy-four in number, of very unequal size and population. Of these thirty-five are on the tide waters, or in that parallel; twenty-three are in the midlands, between the tide waters and Blue Ridge of mountains, eight between the Blue Ridge and Alleghany; and eight westward of the Alleghany.

The State, by another division, is formed into parishes, many of which are commensurate with the counties; but sometimes a county comprehends more than one parish, and sometimes a parish more than one county. This division had relation to the religion of the State, a portion of the Anglican church, with a fixed salary, having been heretofore established in each parish. The care of the poor was another object of the parochial division.

We have no townships. Our country being much intersected with navigable waters, and trade brought generally to our doors, instead of our being obliged to go in quest of it, has probably been one of the causes why we have no towns of any consequence. Williamsburg, which, till the year 1780, was the seat of our government, never contained above 1,800 inhabitants; and Norfolk, the most populous town we ever had, contained but 6,000. Our towns, but more properly our villages and hamlets, are as follows:

On *James River* and its waters, Norfolk, Portsmouth, Hampton, Suffolk, Smithfield, Williamsburg, Petersburg, Richmond, the seat of our government, Manchester, Charlottesville, New London.

On *York River* and its waters, York, Newcastle, Hanover.

On *Rappahannock*, Urbanna, Port-Royal, Fredericksburg, Falmouth.

On *Potomac* and its waters, Dumfries, Colchester, Alexandria, Winchester, Staunton.

On *Ohio*, Louisville.

There are other places at which, like some of the foregoing, the *laws* have said there shall be towns; but *nature* has said there shall not, and they remain unworthy of enumeration. *Norfolk* will probably be the emporium for all the trade of the Chesapeake bay and its waters; and a canal of eight or ten miles will bring to it all that of Albemarle sound and its waters. Secondary to this place, are the towns at the head of the tide waters, to wit, Petersburg on Appomattox; Richmond on James river; Newcastle on York river; Alexandria on Potomac, and Baltimore on Patapsco. From these the distribution will be to subordinate situations in the country. Accidental circumstances, however, may control the indications of nature, and in no instance do they do it more frequently than in the rise and fall of towns.

QUERY XIII

The constitution of the State and its several charters

Queen Elizabeth by her letters patent, bearing date March 25, 1584, licensed Sir Walter Raleigh to search for remote heathen lands, not inhabited by Christian people, and granted to him in fee simple, all the soil within two hundred leagues of the places where his people should, within six years, make their dwellings or abidings; reserving only to herself and her successors, their allegiance and one-fifth part of all the gold and silver ore they should obtain. Sir Walter immediately sent out two ships, which visited Wococon island in North Carolina, and the next year despatched seven with one hundred and seven men, who settled in Roanoke island, about latitude 35° 50'. Here Okisko, king of the Weopomeiocs, in a full council of his people is said to have acknowledged himself the homager of the Queen of England, and, after her, of Sir Walter Raleigh. A supply of fifty men were sent in 1586, and one hundred and fifty in 1587. With these last Sir Walter sent a governor, appointed him twelve assistants, gave them a charter of incorporation, and instructed them to settle on Chesapeake bay. They landed, however, at Hatorask. In 1588, when a fleet was ready to sail with a new supply of colonists and necessaries, they were detained by the Queen to assist against the Spanish armada. Sir Walter having now expended £40,000 in these enterprises, obstructed occasionally by the crown without a shilling of aid from it, was under a necessity of engaging others to adventure their money. He, therefore, by deed bearing date the 7th of March, 1589, by the name of Sir Walter Raleigh, Chief Governor of Assamàcomòc, (probably Acomàc,) alias Wingadacoia, alias Virginia, granted to Thomas Smith and others, in consideration of their adventuring certain sums of money, liberty to trade to this new country free from all customs and taxes for seven years, excepting the fifth part of the gold and silver ore to be obtained; and stipulated with them and the other assistants, then in Virginia, that he would confirm the deed of incorporation which he had given in 1587, with all the prerogatives, jurisdictions, royalties and privileges granted to him by the Queen. Sir Walter, at different times, sent five other adventurers hither, the last of which was in 1602; for in 1603 he was attainted and put into close imprisonment, which put an end to his cares over his infant colony. What was the particular fate of the colonists he had before sent and seated, has never been known; whether they were murdered, or incorporated with the savages.

Some gentlemen and merchants, supposing that by the attainder of Sir Walter Raleigh the grant to him was forfeited, not inquiring over carefully whether the sentence of an English court could affect lands not within the jurisdiction of that court, petitioned king James for a new grant of Virginia to them. He accordingly executed a grant to Sir Thomas Gates and others, bearing date the 9th of March, 1607, under which, in the same year, a settlement was effected at Jamestown, and ever after maintained. Of this grant, however, no particular notice need be taken, as it was superseded by letters patent of the same king, of May 23, 1609, to the Earl of Salisbury and others, incorporating them by the name of "The Treasurer and company of Adventurers and Planters of the City of London for the first colony in Virginia," granting to them and their successors all the lands in Virginia from Point Comfort along the sea-coast, to the northward two hundred miles, and from the same point along the sea-coast to the southward two hundred miles, and all the space from this precinct on the sea-coast up into the land, west and north-west, from sea to sea, and the islands within one hundred miles of it, with all the communities, jurisdictions, royalties, privileges, franchises, and pre-eminencies, within the same, and thereto and thereabouts, by sea and land, appertaining in as ample manner as had before been granted to any adventurer; to be held of the king and his successors, in common soccage, yielding one-fifth part of the gold and silver ore to be therein found, for all manner of services; establishing a counsel in England for the direction of the enterprise, the members of which were to be chosen and displaced by the voice of the majority of the company and adventurers, and were to have the nomination and revocation of governors, officers, and ministers, which by them should be thought needful for the colony, the power of establishing laws and forms of government and magistracy, obligatory not only within the colony, but also on the seas in going and coming to and from it; authorizing them to carry thither any persons who should consent to go, freeing them forever from all taxes and impositions on any goods or merchandise on importations into the colony, or exportation out of it, except the five per cent due for custom on all goods imported into the British dominions, according to the ancient trade of merchants; which five per cent only being paid they might, within thirteen months, re-export the same goods into foreign parts, without any custom, tax, or other duty, to the king or any of his officers, or deputies; with powers of waging war against those who should annoy them; giving to the inhabitants of the colony all the rights of natural subjects, as if born and abiding in England; and declaring that these letters should be construed, in all doubtful parts, in such manner as should be most for the benefit of the grantees.

Afterwards on the 12th of March, 1612, by other letters patent, the king added to his former grants, all islands in any part of the ocean between the 30th and 41st degrees of latitude, and within three hundred leagues of any of the parts before granted to the treasurer and company, not being possessed or inhabited by any other Christian prince or state, nor within the limits of the northern colony.

In pursuance of the authorities given to the company by these charters, and more especially of that part in the charter of 1609, which authorized them to establish a form of government, they on the 24th of July, 1621, by charter under their common seal, declared that from thenceforward there should be two supreme councils in Virginia, the one to be called the council of state, to be placed and displaced by the treasurer, council in England, and company from time to time, whose office was to be that of assisting and advising the governor; the other to be called the general assembly, to be convened by the governor once yearly or oftener, which was to consist of the council of state, and two burgesses out of every town, hundred, or plantation, to be respectively chosen by the inhabitants. In this all matters were to be decided by the greater part of the votes present; reserving to the governor a negative voice; and they were to have power to treat, consult, and conclude all emergent occasions concerning the public weal, and to make laws for the behoof and government of the colony, imitating and following the laws and policy of England as nearly as might be; providing that these laws should have no force till ratified in a general court of the company in England, and returned under their common seal; and declaring that, after the government of the colony should be well framed and settled, no orders of the council in England should bind the colony unless ratified in the said general assembly. The king and company quarrelled, and by a mixture of law and force, the latter were ousted of all their rights without retribution, after having expended one hundred thousand pounds in establishing the colony, without the smallest aid from government. King James suspended their powers by proclamation of July 15, 1624, and Charles I. took the government into his own hands. Both sides had their partisans in the colony, but, in truth, the people of the colony in general thought themselves little concerned in the dispute. There being three parties interested in these several charters, what passed between the first and second, it was thought could not affect the third. If the king seized on the powers of the company, they only passed into other hands, without increase or diminution, while the rights of the people remained as they were. But they did not remain so long. The northern parts of their country were granted away to the lords Baltimore and Fairfax; the first of these obtaining also the rights of separate jurisdiction and government. And in 1650 the parliament, considering itself as standing in the place of their deposed king, and as having succeeded to all his powers, without as well as within the realm, began to assume a right over the colonies, passing an act for inhibiting their trade with foreign nations. This succession to the exercise of kingly authority gave the first color for parliamentary interference with the colonies, and produced that fatal precedent which they continued to follow, after they had retired, in other respects, within their proper functions. When this colony, therefore, which still maintained its opposition to Cromwell and the parliament, was induced in 1651 to lay down their arms, they previously secured their most essential rights by a solemn convention, which, having never seen in print, I will here insert literally from the records.

"ARTICLES agreed on and concluded at James Cittie in Virginia for the surrendering and settling of that plantation under the obedience and government of the commonwealth of England by the commissioners of the Councill of State by authoritie of the parliamt of England, and by the Grand assembly of the Governour, Councill, and Burgesses of that countrey.

"First it is agreed and consted that the plantation of Virginia, and all the inhabitants thereof, shall be and remain in due obedience and subjection to the Commonwealth of England, according to the laws there established, and that this submission and subscription bee acknowledged a voluntary act not forced nor constrained by a conquest upon the countrey, and that they shall have and enjoy such freedoms and priviledges as belong to the free borne people of England, and that the former government by the Commissions and Instructions be void and null.

"2ly. That the Grand assembly as formerly shall convene and transact the affairs of Virginia, wherein nothing is to be acted or done contrairie to the government of the Commonwealth of England and the lawes there established.

"3ly. That there shall be a full and totall remission and indempnitie of all acts, words, or writeings done or spoken against the parliament of England in relation to the same.

"4ly. That Virginia shall have and enjoy the antient bounds and lymitts granted by the charters of the former kings, and that we shall seek a new charter from the parliament to that purpose against any that have intrencht upon the rights thereof.

"5ly. That all the pattents of land granted under the colony seal by any of the precedent governours shall be and remaine in their full force and strength.

"6ly. That the priviledge of haveing ffiftie acres of land for every person transported in that collonie shall continue as formerly granted.

"7ly. That the people of Virginia have free trade as the people of England do enjoy to all places and with all nations according to the lawes of that commonwealth, and that Virginia shall enjoy all priviledges equall with any English plantations in America.

"8ly. That Virginia shall be free from all taxes, customs and impositions whatsoever, and none to be imposed on them without consent of the Grand assembly; and soe that neither fforts nor castle bee erected or garrisons maintained without their consent.

"9ly. That noe charge shall be required from this country in respect of this present ffleet.

"10ly. That for the future settlement of the countrey in their due obedience, the engagement shall be tendred to all the inhabitants according to act of parliament made to that purpose, that all persons who shall refuse to subscribe the said engagement, shall have a yeare's time if they please to remove themselves and their estates out of Virginia, and in the meantime during the said yeare to have equall justice as formerly.

"11ly. That the use of the booke of common prayer shall be permitted for one yeare ensueinge with referrence to the consent of the major part of the parishes provided that those which relate to kingshipp or that government be not used publiquely, and the continuance of ministers in their places, they not misdemeaning themselves, and the payment of their accustomed dues and agreements made with them respectively shall be left as they now stand dureing this ensueing yeare.

"12ly. That no man's cattell shall be questioned as the companies, unless such as have been entrusted with them or have disposed of them without order.

"13ly. That all ammunition, powder and armes, other than for private use, shall be delivered up, securitie being given to make satisfaction for it.

"14ly. That all goods allreadie brought hither by the Dutch or others which are now on shoar shall be free from surprizall.

"15ly. That the quittrents granted unto us by the late kinge for seaven yeares bee confirmed.

"16ly. That the commissioners for the parliament subscribeing these articles engage themselves and the honour of parliament for the full performance thereof;
and that the present governour, and the councill, and the burgesses do likewise
subscribe and engage the whole collony on their parts.

RICHARD BENNETT.—Seale.

WILLIAM CLAIBORNE.—Seale.

EDMOND CURTIS.—Seale.

"Theise articles were signed and sealed by the Commissioners of the Councill of
state for the Commonwealth of England the twelveth day of March 1651."

Then follow the articles stipulated by the governor and council, which relate merely to their own persons and property, and then the ensuing instrument:

"An act of indempnitie made att the surrender of the countrey.
"Whereas, by the authoritie of the parliament wee the commissioners appointed
by the councill of state authorized thereto, having brought a ffleet and force before
James cittie in Virginia to reduce that collonie under the obedience of the commonwealth of England, and finding force raised by the Governour and countrey
to make opposition against the said ffleet, whereby assured danger appearinge of
the ruine and destruction of the plantation, for prevention whereof the burgesses
of all the severall plantations being called to advise and assist therein, uppon long
and serious debate, and in sad contemplation of the great miseries and certain destruction which were soe neerely hovering over the whole countrey; Wee the said
Commissioners have thought fitt and condescending and granted to signe and con-
firme under our hands, seales and by our oath, Articles bearinge date with theise
presents, and do further declare that by the authoritie of the parliament and commonwealth of England derived unto us their commissioners, that according to the
articles in generall wee have granted an act of indempnitie and oblivion to all the
inhabitants of this collonie from all words, actions, or writings that have been
spoken, acted or writt against the parliament or commonwealth of England or any
other person from the beginning of the world to this daye. And this we have done
that all the inhabitants of the collonie may live quietly and securely under the
commonwealth of England. And we do promise that the parliament and commonwealth of England shall confirm and make good all those transactions of ours.
Witness our hands and seales this 12th of March 1651.

RICHARD BENNETT.—Seale.

WILLIAM CLAIBORNE.—Seale.

EDMOND CURTIS.—Seale.

The colony supposed, that, by this solemn convention, entered into with
arms in their hands, they had secured the ancient limits[1] of their country,
its free trade,[2] its exemption from taxation[3] but by their own assembly, and
exclusion of military force[4] from among them. Yet in every of these points
was this convention violated by subsequent kings and parliaments, and other
infractions of their constitution, equally dangerous committed. Their general
assembly, which was composed of the council of state and burgesses, sitting to-

[1] Art. 4.—T. J.
[2] Art. 7.—T. J.
[3] Art. 8.—T. J.
[4] Art. 8.—T. J.

gether and deciding by plurality of voices, was split into two houses, by which the council obtained a separate negative on their laws. Appeals from their supreme court, which had been fixed by law in their general assembly, were arbitrarily revoked to England, to be there heard before the king and council. Instead of four hundred miles on the seacoast, they were reduced, in the space of thirty years, to about one hundred miles. Their trade with foreigners was totally suppressed, and when carried to Great Britain, was there loaded with imposts. It is unnecessary, however, to glean up the several instances of injury, as scattered through American and British history, and the more especially as, by passing on to the accession of the present king, we shall find specimens of them all, aggravated, multiplied and crowded within a small compass of time, so as to evince a fixed design of considering our rights natural, conventional and chartered as mere nullities. The following is an epitome of the first sixteen years of his reign: The colonies were taxed internally and externally; their essential interests sacrificed to individuals in Great Britain; their legislatures suspended; charters annulled; trials by juries taken away; their persons subjected to transportation across the Atlantic, and to trial before foreign judicatories; their supplications for redress thought beneath answer; themselves published as cowards in the councils of their mother country and courts of Europe; armed troops sent among them to enforce submission to these violences; and actual hostilities commenced against them. No alternative was presented but resistance, or unconditional submission. Between these could be no hesitation. They closed in the appeal to arms. They declared themselves independent states. They confederated together into one great republic; thus securing to every State the benefit of an union of their whole force. In each State separately a new form of government was established. Of ours particularly the following are the outlines: The executive powers are lodged in the hands of a governor, chosen annually, and incapable of acting more then three years in seven. He is assisted by a council of eight members. The judiciary powers are divided among several courts, as will be hereafter explained. Legislation is exercised by two houses of assembly, the one called the house of Delegates, composed of two members from each county, chosen annually by the citizens, possessing an estate for life in one hundred acres of uninhabited land, or twenty-five acres with a house on it, or in a house or lot in some town: the other called the Senate, consisting of twenty-four members, chosen quadrennially by the same electors, who for this purpose are distributed into twenty-four districts. The concurrence of both houses is necessary to the passage of a law. They have the appointment of the governor and council, the judges of the superior courts, auditors, attorney-general, treasurer, register of the land office, and delegates to Congress. As the dismemberment of the State had never had its confirmation, but, on the contrary, had always been the subject of protestation and complaint, that it might never be in our own power to raise scruples on that subject, or to disturb the harmony of our new confederacy, the grants to Maryland, Pennsylvania, and the two Carolinas, were ratified.

This constitution was formed when we were new and unexperienced in the science of government. It was the first, too, which was formed in the whole United States. No wonder then that time and trial have discovered very capital defects in it.

1. The majority of the men in the State, who pay and fight for its support, are unrepresented in the legislature, the roll of freeholders entitled to vote not including generally the half of those on the roll of the militia, or of the tax-gatherers.

2. Among those who share the representation, the shares are very unequal. Thus the county of Warwick, with only one hundred fighting men, has an equal representation with the county of Loudon, which has one thousand seven hundred and forty-six. So that every man in Warwick has as much influence in the government as seventeen men in Loudon. But lest it should be thought that an equal interspersion of small among large counties, through the whole State, may prevent any danger of injury to particular parts of it, we will divide it into districts, and show the proportions of land, of fighting men, and of representation in each:

	SQUARE MILES	FIGHTING MEN	DELE-GATES	SENATORS
Between the sea-coast and falls of the rivers	[1] 11,205	19,012	71	12
Between the falls of the rivers and the Blue Ridge mountains	18,759	18,828	46	8
Between the Blue Ridge and the Alleghany	11,911	7,673	16	2
Between the Alleghany and Ohio	[2] 79,650	4,458	16	2
Total	121,525	49,971	149	24

An inspection of this table will supply the place of commentaries on it. It will appear at once that nineteen thousand men, living below the falls of the rivers, possess half the senate, and want four members only of possessing a majority of the house of delegates; a want more than supplied by the vicinity of their situation to the seat of government, and of course the greater degree of convenience and punctuality with which their members may and will attend in the legislature. These nineteen thousand, therefore, living in one part of the country, give law to upwards of thirty thousand living in another, and appoint all their chief officers, executive and judiciary. From the difference of their situation and circumstances, their interests will often be very different.

3. The senate is, by its constitution, too homogenous with the house of delegates. Being chosen by the same electors, at the same time, and out of the same subjects, the choice falls of course on men of the same description. The purpose of establishing different houses of legislation is to introduce the influence of different interests or different principles. Thus in Great Britain it is said their constitution relies on the house of commons for honesty, and the

[1] Of these 542 are on the eastern shore.—T. J.
[2] Of these, 22,616 are eastward of the meridian of the north of the Great Kanhaway.—T. J.

lords for wisdom; which would be a rational reliance, if honesty were to be bought with money, and if wisdom were hereditary. In some of the American States, the delegates and senators are so chosen, as that the first represent the persons, and the second property of the State. But with us, wealth and wisdom have equal chance for admission into both houses. We do not, therefore, derive from the separation of our legislature into two houses, those benefits which a proper complication of principles are capable of producing, and those which alone can compensate the evils which may be produced by their dissensions.

4. All the powers of government, legislative, executive, and judiciary, result to the legislative body. The concentrating these in the same hands is precisely the definition of despotic government. It will be no alleviation that these powers will be exercised by a plurality of hands, and not by a single one. One hundred and seventy-three despots would surely be as oppressive as one. Let those who doubt it turn their eyes on the republic of Venice. As little will it avail us that they are chosen by ourselves. An *elective despotism* was not the government we fought for, but one which should not only be founded on free principles, but in which the powers of government should be so divided and balanced among several bodies of magistracy, as that no one could transcend their legal limits, without being effectually checked and restrained by the others. For this reason that convention which passed the ordinance of government, laid its foundation on this basis, that the legislative, executive, and judiciary departments should be separate and distinct, so that no person should exercise the powers of more than one of them at the same time. But no barrier was provided between these several powers. The judiciary and executive members were left dependent on the legislative, for this subsistence in office, and some of them for their continuance in it. If, therefore, the legislature assumes executive and judiciary powers, no opposition is likely to be made; nor, if made, can it be effectual; because in that case they may put their proceedings into the form of an act of assembly, which will render them obligatory on the other branches. They have, accordingly, in many instances, decided rights which should have been left to judiciary controversy; and the direction of the executive, during the whole time of their session, is becoming habitual and familiar. And this is done with no ill intention. The views of the present members are perfectly upright. When they are led out of their regular province, it is by art in others, and inadvertence in themselves. And this will probably be the case for some time to come. But it will not be a very long time. Mankind soon learn to make interested uses of every right and power which they possess, or may assume. The public money and public liberty, intended to have been deposited with three branches of magistracy, but found inadvertently to be in the hands of one only, will soon be discovered to be sources of wealth and dominion to those who hold them; distinguished, too, by this tempting circumstance, that they are the instrument, as well as the object of acquisition. With money we will get men, said Cæsar, and with men we will get money. Nor should our assembly be deluded by the integrity of their own purposes, and conclude that

these unlimited powers will never be abused, because themselves are not disposed to abuse them. They should look forward to a time, and that not a distant one, when a corruption in this, as in the country from which we derive our origin, will have seized the heads of government, and be spread by them through the body of the people; when they will purchase the voices of the people, and make them pay the price. Human nature is the same on every side of the Atlantic, and will be alike influenced by the same causes. The time to guard against corruption and tyranny, is before they shall have gotten hold of us. It is better to keep the wolf out of the fold, than to trust to drawing his teeth and talons after he shall have entered. To render these considerations the more cogent, we must observe in addition:

5. That the ordinary legislature may alter the constitution itself. On the discontinuance of assemblies, it became necessary to substitute in their place some other body, competent to the ordinary business of government, and to the calling forth the powers of the State for the maintenance of our opposition to Great Britain. Conventions were therefore introduced, consisting of two delegates from each county, meeting together and forming one house, on the plan of the former house of burgesses, to whose places they succeeded. These were at first chosen anew for every particular session. But in March 1775, they recommended to the people to choose a convention, which should continue in office a year. This was done, accordingly, in April 1775, and in the July following that convention passed an ordinance for the election of delegates in the month of April annually. It is well known, that in July 1775, a separation from Great Britain and establishment of republican government, had never yet entered into any person's mind. A convention, therefore, chosen under that ordinance, cannot be said to have been chosen for the purposes which certainly did not exist in the minds of those who passed it. Under this ordinance, at the annual election in April 1776, a convention for the year was chosen. Independence, and the establishment of a new form of government, were not even yet the objects of the people at large. One extract from the pamphlet called Common Sense had appeared in the Virginia papers in February, and copies of the pamphlet itself had got in a few hands. But the idea had not been opened to the mass of the people in April, much less can it be said that they had made up their minds in its favor.

So that the electors of April 1776, no more than the legislators of July 1775, not thinking of independence and a permanent republic, could not mean to vest in these delegates powers of establishing them, or any authorities other than those of the ordinary legislature. So far as a temporary organization of government was necessary to render our opposition energetic, so far their organization was valid. But they received in their creation no power but what were given to every legislature before and since. They could not, therefore, pass an act transcendent to the powers of other legislatures. If the present assembly pass an act, and declare it shall be irrevocable by subsequent assemblies, the declaration is merely void, and the act repealable, as other acts are. So far, and no farther authorized, they organized the government by the ordinance entitled a constitution or form of government. It pretends to no higher authority than the other ordinances of the same session; it does not say that it shall be perpetual; that it shall be unalterable by other legislatures; that it shall be transcendent above the powers of those who they knew would have equal power with themselves. Not only the silence of the instrument is a proof they thought it would be alterable, but their own practice also; for this very convention, meeting as a house of delegates in general assembly with the Senate in the autumn of that year, passed acts of assembly in contradiction to their ordinance of government; and every assembly from that time to this has done the same. I am safe, therefore, in the position that the constitution itself is alterable by the ordinary legislature. Though this opinion seems founded on the first elements of common sense, yet is the contrary maintained by some persons. 1. Because, say they, the conventions were vested with every power necessary to make effectual opposition to Great Britain. But to complete this argument, they must go on, and say further, that effectual opposition could not be made to Great Britain without establishing a form of government perpetual and unalterable by the legislature; which is not true. An opposition which at some time or other was to come to an end, could not need a perpetual institution to carry it on; and a government amendable as its defects should be discovered, was as likely to make effectual resistance, as one that should be unalterably wrong. Besides, the assemblies were as much vested with all powers requisite for resistance as the conventions were. If, therefore, these powers included that of modelling the form of government in the one case, they did so in the other. The assemblies then as well as the conventions may model the government; that is, they may alter the ordinance of government. 2. They urge, that if the convention had meant that this instrument should be alterable, as their other ordinances were, they would have called it an ordinance; but they have called it a *constitution*, which, ex vi termini, means "an act above the power of the ordinary legislature." I answer that *constitutio, constitutium, statutum, lex,* are convertible terms. "*Constitutio* dicitur jus quod a principe conditure." "*Constitutium,* quod ab imperatoribus rescriptum statutumve est." "*Statutum,* idem quod lex." Calvini Lexicon juridicum. *Constitution* and *statute* were originally terms of the [1] civil law, and from thence introduced by ecclesiastics into the English law. Thus in the statute 25 Hen. VIII. c. 19, §. 1, "*Constitutions* and *ordinances*" are used as synonymous. The term *constitution* has many other significations in physics and politics; but in jurisprudence, whenever it is applied to any act of the legislature, it invariably means a statute, law, or ordinance, which is the present case. No inference then of a different meaning can be drawn from the adoption of this title; on the contrary, we might conclude that, by their affixing to it a term synonymous with ordinance or statute. But of what consequence is their meaning, where their power is denied? If they meant to do more than they had power to do, did this give them power? It is not the name, but the authority that renders an act obligatory. Lord

---

[1] To bid, to set, was the ancient legislative word of the English. Ll. Hlotharri and Eadrici. Ll. Inæ. Ll. Eadwerdi. Ll. Aathelstani.—T. J.

Coke says, "an article of the statute, 11 R. II. c. 5, that no person should attempt to revoke any ordinance then made, is repealed, for that such restraint is against the jurisdiction and power of the parliament." 4. Inst. 42. And again, "though divers parliaments have attempted to restrain subsequent parliaments, yet could they never effect it; for the latter parliament hath ever power to abrogate, suspend, qualify, explain, or make void the former in the whole or in any part thereof, notwithstanding any words of restraint, prohibition, or penalty, in the former; for it is a maxim in the laws of the parliament, *quod leges posteriores priores contrarias abrogant.*" 4. Inst. 43. To get rid of the magic supposed to be in the word *constitution,* let us translate it into its definition as given by those who think it above the power of the law; and let us suppose the convention, instead of saying, "We the ordinary legislature, establish a *constitution,*" had said, "We the ordinary legislature, establish an act *above the power of the ordinary legislature.*" Does not this expose the absurdity of the attempt? 3. But, say they, the people have acquiesced, and this has given it an authority superior to the laws. It is true that the people did not rebel against it; and was that a time for the people to rise in rebellion? Should a prudent acquiescence, at a critical time, be construed into a confirmation of every illegal thing done during that period? Besides, why should they rebel? At an annual election they had chosen delegates for the year, to exercise the ordinary powers of legislation, and to manage the great contest in which they were engaged. These delegates thought the contest would be best managed by an organized government. They therefore, among others, passed an ordinance of government. They did not presume to call it perpetual and unalterable. They well knew they had no power to make it so; that our choice of them had been for no such purpose, and at a time when we could have no such purpose in contemplation. Had an unalterable form of government been meditated, perhaps we should have chosen a different set of people. There was no cause then for the people to rise in rebellion. But to what dangerous lengths will this argument lead? Did the acquiescence of the colonies under the various acts of power exercised by Great Britain in our infant State, confirm these acts, and so far invest them with the authority of the people as to render them unalterable, and our present resistance wrong? On every unauthoritative exercise of power by the legislature must the people rise in rebellion, or their silence be construed into a surrender of that power to them? If so, how many rebellions should we have had already? One certainly for every session of assembly. The other States in the union have been of opinion that to render a form of government unalterable by ordinary acts of assembly, the people must delegate persons with special powers. They have accordingly chosen special conventions to form and fix their governments. The individuals then who maintain the contrary opinion in this country, should have the modesty to suppose it possible that they may be wrong, and the rest of America right. But if there be only a possibility of their being wrong, if only a plausible doubt remains of the validity of the ordinance of government, is it not better to remove that doubt by placing it on a bottom which none will dispute? If they be right we shall only have the unnecessary trouble of meeting once in convention. If they be wrong, they expose us to the hazard of having no fundamental rights at all. True it is, this is no time for deliberating on forms of government. While an enemy is within our bowels, the first object is to expel him. But when this shall be done, when peace shall be established, and leisure given us for intrenching within good forms, the rights for which we have bled, let no man be found indolent enough to decline a little more trouble for placing them beyond the reach of question. If anything more be requisite to produce a conviction of the expediency of calling a convention at a proper season to fix our form of government, let is be the reflection:

6. That the assembly exercises a power of determining the quorum of their own body which may legislate for us. After the establishment of the new form they adhered to the *Lex majoris partis,* founded in[1] common law as well as common right. It is the[2] natural law of every assembly of men, whose numbers are not fixed by any other law. They continued for some time to require the presence of a majority of their whole number, to pass an act. But the British parliament fixes its own quorum; our former assemblies fixed their own quorum; and one precedent in favor of power is stronger than an hundred against it. The house of delegates, therefore, have[3] lately voted that, during the present dangerous invasion, forty members shall be a house to proceed to business. They have been moved to this by the fear of not being able to collect a house. But this danger could not authorize them to call that a house which was none; and if they may fix it at one number, they may at another, till it loses its fundamental character of being a representative body. As this vote expires with the present invasion, it is probable the former rule will be permitted to revive; because at present no ill is meant. The power, however, of fixing their own quorum has been avowed, and a precedent set. From forty it may be reduced to four, and from four to one; from a house to a committee, from a committee to a chairman or speaker, and thus an oligarchy or monarchy be substituted under forms supposed to be regular. *"Omnia mala exempla ex bonis orta sunt; sed ubi imperium ad ignaros aut minus bonos pervenit, novum illud exemplum ab dignis et idoneis adindignos et non idoneos fertur."* When, therefore, it is considered, that there is no legal obstacle to the assumption by the assembly of all the powers legislative, executive, and judiciary, and that these may come to the hands of the smallest rag of delegation, surely the people will say, and their representatives, while yet they have honest representatives, will advise them to say, that they will not acknowledge as laws any acts not considered and assented to by the major part of their delegates.

In enumerating the defects of the constitution, it would be wrong to count among them what is only the error of particular persons. In December 1776, our circumstances being much distressed, it was proposed in the house of delegates to create a *dictator,* invested with every power legislative, executive, and judiciary, civil and military, of life and of death, over our persons and over

[1] Bro. abr. Corporations, 31, 34. Hakewell, 93.—T. J.
[2] Puff. Off. hom. I. 2, c. 6, §. 12.—T. J.   [3] June 4, 1781.—T. J.

our properties; and in June 1781, again under calamity, the same proposition was repeated, and wanted a few votes only of being passed. One who entered into this contest from a pure love of liberty, and a sense of injured rights, who determined to make every sacrifice, and to meet every danger, for the re-establishment of those rights on a firm basis, who did not mean to expend his blood and substance for the wretched purpose of changing this matter for that, but to place the powers of governing him in a plurality of hands of his own choice, so that the corrupt will of no one man might in future oppress him, must stand confounded and dismayed when he is told, that a considerable portion of that plurality had mediated the surrender of them into a single hand, and, in lieu of a limited monarchy, to deliver him over to a despotic one! How must we find his efforts and sacrifices abused and baffled, if he may still, by a single vote, be laid prostrate at the feet of one man! In God's name, from whence have they derived this power? Is it from our ancient laws? None such can be produced. Is it from any principle in our new constitution expressed or implied? Every lineament expressed or implied, is in full opposition to it. Its fundamental principle is, that the State shall be governed as a commonwealth. It provides a republican organization, proscribes under the name of *prerogative* the exercise of all powers undefined by the laws; places on this basis the whole system of our laws; and by consolidating them together, chooses that they should be left to stand or fall together, never providing for any circumstances, nor admitting that such could arise, wherein either should be suspended; no, not for a moment. Our ancient laws expressly declare, that those who are but delegates themselves shall not delegate to others powers which require judgment and integrity in their exercise. Or was this proposition moved on a supposed right in the movers, of abandoning their posts in a moment of distress? The same laws forbid the abandonment of that post, even on ordinary occasions; and much more a transfer of their powers into other hands and other forms, without consulting the people. They never admit the idea that these, like sheep or cattle, may be given from hand to hand without an appeal to their own will. Was it from the necessity of the case? Necessities which dissolve a government, do not convey its authority to an oligarchy or a monarchy. They throw back, into the hands of the people, the powers they had delegated, and leaves them as individuals to shift for themselves. A leader may offer, but not impose himself, nor be imposed on them. Much less can their necks be submitted to his sword, their breath to be held at his will or caprice. The necessity which should operate these tremendous effects should at least be palpable and irresistible. Yet in both instances, where it was feared, or pretended with us, it was belied by the event. It was belied, too, by the preceding experience of our sister States, several of whom had grappled through greater difficulties without abandoning their forms of government. When the proposition was first made, Massachusetts had found even the government of committees sufficient to carry them through an invasion. But we at the time of that proposition, were under no invasion. When the second was made, there had been added to this example those of Rhode Island, New York, New Jersey, and Pennsylvania, in all of which the republican form had been found equal to the task of carrying them through the severest trials. In this State alone did there exist so little virtue, that fear was to be fixed in the hearts of the people, and to become the motive of their exertions, and principle of their government? The very thought alone was treason against the people; was treason against mankind in general; as rivetting forever the chains which bow down their necks, by giving to their oppressors a proof, which they would have trumpeted through the universe, of the imbecility of republican government, in times of pressing danger, to shield them from harm. Those who assume the right of giving away the reins of government in any case, must be sure that the herd, whom they hand on to the rods and hatchet of the dictator, will lay their necks on the block when he shall nod to them. But if our assemblies supposed such a recognition in the people, I hope they mistook their character. I am of opinion, that the government, instead of being braced and invigorated for greater exertions under their difficulties, would have been thrown back upon the bungling machinery of county committees for administration, till a convention could have been called, and its wheels again set into regular motion. What a cruel moment was this for creating such an embarrassment, for putting to the proof the attachment of our countrymen to republican government! Those who meant well, of the advocates of this measure, (and most of them meant well, for I know them personally, had been their fellow-laborer in the common cause, and had often proved the purity of their principles,) had been seduced in their judgment by the example of an ancient republic, whose constitution and circumstances were fundamentally different. They had sought this precedent in the history of Rome, where alone it was to be found, and where at length, too, it had proved fatal. They had taken it from a republic rent by the most bitter factions and tumults, where the government was of a heavy-handed unfeeling aristocracy, over a people ferocious, and rendered desperate by poverty and wretchedness; tumults which could not be allayed under the most trying circumstances, but by the omnipotent hand of a single despot. Their constitution, therefore, allowed a temporary tyrant to be erected, under the name of a dictator; and that temporary tyrant, after a few examples, became perpetual. They misapplied this precedent to a people mild in their dispositions, patient under their trial, united for the public liberty, and affectionate to their leaders. But if from the constitution of the Roman government there resulted to their senate a power of submitting all their rights to the will of one man, does it follow that the assembly of Virginia have the same authority? What clause in our constitution has substituted that of Rome, by way of residuary provision, for all cases not otherwise provided for? Or if they may step *ad libitum* into any other form of government for precedents to rule us by, for what oppression may not a precedent be found in this world of the *ballum omnium in omnia?* Searching for the foundations of this proposition, I can find none which may pretend a color of right or reason, but the defect before developed, that there being no barrier between the legislative, executive, and judiciary departments, the legislature may seize the whole; that having seized it, and possessing a right to fix their own quorum, they may reduce that quorum to one, whom they may call a chairman, speaker, dictator, or by any other name they please. Our situation is indeed perilous, and I hope my countrymen will be sensible of it, and will apply, at a proper season, the proper remedy; which is a convention to fix the constitution, to amend its defects, to bind up the several branches of government by certain laws, which, when they transgress, their acts shall become nullities; to render unnecessary an appeal to the people, or in other words a rebellion, on every infraction of their rights, on the peril that their acquiescence shall be construed into an intention to surrender those rights.

QUERY XIV

The administration of justice and the descrpition of the laws

The state is divided into counties. In every county are appointed magistrates, called justices of the peace, usually from eight to thirty or forty in number, in proportion to the size of the county, of the most discreet and honest inhabitants. They are nominated by their fellows, but commissioned by the governor, and act without reward. These magistrates have jurisdiction both criminal and civil. If the question before them be a question of law only, they decide on it themselves; but if it be a fact, or a fact and law combined, it must be referred to a jury. In the latter case, of a combination of law and fact, it is usual for the jurors to decide the fact, and to refer the law arising on it to the decision of the judges. But this division of the subject lies with their discretion only. And if the question relate to any point of public liberty, or if it be one of those in which the judges may be suspected of bias, the jury undertake to decide both law and fact. If they be mistaken, a decision against right, which is casual only, is less dangerous to the state, and less afflicting to the loser, than one which makes part of a regular and uniform system. In truth, it is better to toss up cross and pile in a cause, than to refer it to a judge whose mind is warped by any motive whatever, in that particular case. But the common sense of twelve honest men gives still a better chance of just decision, than the hazard of cross and pile. These judges execute their process by the sheriff or coroner of the county, or by constables of their own appointment. If any free person commit an offence against the commonwealth, if it be below the degree of felony, he is bound by a justice to appear before their court, to answer it on indictment or information. If it amount to felony, he is committed to jail; a court of these justices is called; if they on examination think him guilty, they send him to the jail of the general court, before which court he is to be tried first by a grand jury of 24, of whom 13 must concur in opinion; if they find him guilty, he is then tried by a jury of 12 men of the county where the offence was committed, and by their verdict, which must be unanimous, he is acquitted or condemned without appeal. If the criminal be a slave, the trial by the county court is final. In every case, however, except that of high treason, there resides in the governor a power of pardon. In high treason the pardon can only flow from the general assembly. In civil matters these justices have jurisdiction in all cases of whatever value, not appertaining to the department of the admiralty. This jurisdiction is two fold. If the matter in dispute be of less value than 4⅙ dollars, a single member may try it at any time and place within his county, and may award execution on the goods of the party cast. If it be of that or greater value, it is determinable before the county court, which consists of four at the least of those justices and assembles at the court-house of the county on a certain day in every month. From their determination, if the matter be of the value of ten pounds sterling, or concern the title or bounds of lands, an appeal lies to one of the superior courts.

There are three superior courts, to wit, the high court of chancery, the general court, and court of admiralty. The first and second of these receive appeals from the county courts, and also have original jurisdiction, where the subject of controversy is of the value of ten pounds sterling, or where it concerns the title or bounds of lands. The jurisdiction of the admiralty is original altogether. The high court of chancery is composed of three judges, the general court of five, and the court of admiralty of three. The two first hold their sessions at Richmond at stated times, the chancery twice in the year, and the general court twice for business civil and criminal, and twice more for criminal only. The court of admiralty sits at Williamsburg whenever a controversy arises.

There is one supreme court, called the court of appeals, composed of the judges of the three superior courts, assembling twice a year at stated times at Richmond. This court receives appeals in all civil cases from each of the superior courts, and determines them finally. But it has no original jurisdiction.

If a controversy arise between two foreigners of a nation in alliance with the United States, it is decided by the Consul for their State, or, if both parties chuse it, by the ordinary courts of justice. If one of the parties only be such a foreigner, it is triable before the courts of justice of the country. But if it shall have been instituted in a county court, the foreigner may remove it into the general court, or court of chancery, who are to determine it at their first sessions, as they must also do if it be originally commenced before them. In cases of life and death, such foreigners have a right to be tried by a jury, the one-half foreigners, the other natives.

All public accounts are settled with a board of auditors, consisting of three members appointed by the general assembly, any two of whom may act. But an individual, dissatisfied with the determination of that board, may carry his case into the proper superior court.

A description of the laws.

The general assembly was constituted, as has been already shown, by letters-patent of March the 9th, 1607, in the 4th year of the reign of James the first. The laws of England seem to have been adopted by consent of the settlers, which might easily enough be done whilst they were few and living all together. Of such adoption, however, we have no other proof than their practice till the year 1661, when they were expressly adopted by an act of the assembly, except so far as "a difference of condition' rendered them inapplicable. Under this adoption, the rule, in our courts of judicature was, that the common law of England, and the general statutes previous to the 4th of James, were in force here; but that no subsequent statutes were, *unless we were named in them,* said the judges and other partisans of the crown, but *named or not named,* said those who reflected freely. It will be unnecessary to attempt a description of the laws of England, as that may be found in English publications. To those which were established here, by the adoption of the legislature, have been since added a number of acts of assembly passed during the monarchy, and ordinances of convention and acts of assembly enacted since the establishment of the republic. The following variations from the British model are perhaps worthy of being specified:

Debtors unable to pay their debts, and making faithful delivery of their whole effects, are released from confinement, and their persons forever discharged from restraint for such previous debts: but any property they may afterwards acquire will be subject to their creditors.

The poor, unable to support themselves, are maintained by an assessment on the titheable persons in their parish. This assessment is levied and administered by twelve persons in each parish, called vestrymen, originally chosen by the housekeepers of the parish, but afterwards filling vacancies in their own body by their own choice. These are usually the most discreet farmers, so distributed through their parish, that every part of it may be under the immediate eye of some one of them. They are well acquainted with the details and œconomy of private life, and they find sufficient inducements to execute their charge well, in their philanthropy, in the approbation of their neighbors, and the distinction which that gives them. The poor who have neither property, friends, nor strength to labour, are boarded in the houses of good farmers, to whom a stipulated sum is annually paid. To those who are able to help themselves a little, or have friends from whom they derive some succours, inadequate however to their full maintenance, supplementary aids are given which enable them to live comfortably in their own houses, or in the houses of their friends. Vagabonds without visible property or vocation, are placed in work houses, where they are well clothed, fed, lodged, and made to labour. Nearly the same methods of providing for the poor prevails through all our states; and from Savannah to Portsmouth you will seldom meet a beggar. In the larger towns, indeed, they sometimes present themselves. These are usually foreigners, who have never obtained a settlement in any parish. I never yet saw a native American begging in the street or highways. A subsistence is easily gained here: and if, by misfortunes, they are thrown on the charities of the world, those provided by their own country are so comfortable and so certain, that they never think of relinquishing them to become strolling beggars. Their situation too, when sick, in the family of a good farmer, where every member is emulous to do them kind offices, where they are visited by all the neighbors, who bring them the little rarities which their sickly appetites may crave, and who take by rotation the nightly watch over them, when their condition requires it, is without comparison better than in a general hospital, where the sick, the dying and the dead are crammed together in the same rooms, and often in the same beds. The disadvantages, inseparable from general hospitals, are such as can never be counterpoised by all the regularities of medicine and regimen. Nature and kind nursing save a much greater proportion in our plain way, at a smaller expense, and with less abuse. One branch only of hospital institution is wanting with us; that is a general establishment for those laboring under difficult cases of chirurgery. The aids of this art are not equivocal. But an able chirurgeon cannot be had in every parish. Such a receptacle should therefore be provided for those patients: but no others should be admitted.

Marriages must be solemnized either on special licence, granted by the first magistrate of the county, on proof of the consent of the parent or guardian of either party under age, or after solemn publication, on three several sundays, at some place of religious worship, in the parishes where the parties reside. The act of solemnization may be by the minister of any society of christians, who shall have been previously licensed for this purpose by the court of the county. Quakers and Menonists however are exempted from all these conditions, and marriage among them is to be solemnized by the society itself.

A foreigner of any nation, not in open war with us, becomes naturalized by removing to the state to reside, and taking an oath of fidelity: and thereupon acquires every right of a native citizen: and citizens may divest themselves of that character, by declaring, by solemn deed, or in open court, that they mean to expatriate themselves, and no longer to be citizens of this state.

Conveyances of land must be registered in the court of the county wherein they lie, or in the general court, or they are void, as to creditors, and subsequent purchasers.

Slaves pass by descent and dower as lands do. Where the descent is from a parent, the heir is bound to pay an equal share of their value in money to each of his brothers and sisters.

Slaves, as well as lands, were entailable during the monarchy; but, by an act of the first republican assembly, all donees in tail, present and future, were vested with the absolute dominion of the entailed subject.

Bills of exchange, being protested, carry 10 per cent. interest from their date.

No person is allowed, in any other case, to take more than five per centum per annum simple interest for the loan of moneys.

Gaming debts are made void, and monies actually paid to discharge such debts (if they exceed 40 shillings) may be recovered by the payer within three months, or by any other person afterwards.

Tobacco, flour, beef, pork, tar, pitch, and turpentine must be inspected by persons publicely appointed before they can be exported.

The erecting iron-works and mills is encouraged by many privileges; with necessary cautions however to prevent their dams from obstructing the navigation of the water courses. The general assembly have on several occasions shewn a great desire to encourage the opening the great falls of James and Patowmac rivers. As yet, however, neither of these have been effected.

The laws have also descended to the preservation and improvement of the races of useful animals, such as horses, cattle, deer; to the extirpation of those which are noxious, as wolves, squirrels, crows, blackbirds; and to the guarding our citizens against infectious disorders, by obliging suspected vessels coming into the state, to perform quarantine, and by regulating the conduct of persons having such disorders within the state.

The mode of acquiring lands, in the earliest times of our settlement, was by petition to the general assembly. If the lands prayed for were already cleared of the Indian title, and the assembly thought the prayer reasonable, they passed the property by their vote to the petitioner. But if they had not yet been ceded by the Indians, it was necessary that the petitioner should previously purchase their right. This purchase the assembly verified, by enquries of the Indian proprietors; and being satisfied of its reality and fairness, proceeded further to examine the reasonableness of the petition, and its consistence with policy; and according to the result either granted or rejected the petition. The company also sometimes, though very rarely, granted lands, independently of the general assembly. As the colony increased, and individual applications for land multiplied, it was found to give too much occupation to the general assembly to inquire into and execute the grant in every special case. They therefore thought it better to establish general rules, according to which all grants should be made, and to leave to the governor the execution of them, under these rules. This they did by what have been usually called the land laws, amending them from time to time, as their defects were developed. According to these laws, when an individual wished a portion of unappropriated land, he was to locate and survey it by a public officer, appointed for that purpose: its breadth was to bear a certain proportion to its length: the grant was to be executed by the governor: and the lands were to be improved in a certain manner, within a given time. From these regulations there resulted to the state a sole and exclusive power of taking conveyances of the Indian right of soil; since, according to them an Indian conveyance alone could give no right to an individual, which the laws would acknowledge. The state, or the crown, thereafter, made general purchases of the Indians from time to time, and the governor parcelled them out by special grants, conformed to the rules before described, which it was not in his power, or in that of the crown, to dispense with. Grants, unaccompanied by their proper legal circumstances, were set aside regularly by *scire facias,* or by bill in Chancery. Since the establishment of our new government, this order of things is but little changed. An individual, wishing to appropriate to himself lands still unappropriated by any other, pays to the public treasurer a sum of money proportioned to the quantity he wants. He carries the treasurer's receipt to the auditors of public accompts, who thereupon debit the treasurer with the sum, and order the register of the land-office to give the party a warrant for his land. With this warrant from the register, he goes to the surveyor of the county where the land lies on which he has cast his eye. The Surveyor lays it off for him, gives him its exact description, in the form of a certificate, which certificate he returns to the land-office, where a grant is made out, and is signed by the governor. This vests in him a perfect dominion in his lands, transmissible to whom he pleases by deed or will, or by descent to his heirs, if he die intestate.

Many of the laws which were in force during the monarchy being relative merely to that form of government, or inculcating principles inconsistent with republicanism, the first assembly which met after the establishment of the commonwealth, appointed a committee to revise the whole code, to reduce it into proper form and volume, and report it to the assembly. This work has been executed by three gentlemen, and reported; but probably will not be taken up till a restoration of peace shall leave to the legislature leisure to go through such a work.

The plan of the revisal was this. The common law of England, by which is meant that part of the English law which was anterior to the date of the oldest statutes extant, is made the basis of the work. It was thought dangerous to attempt to reduce it to a text: it was therefore left to be collected from the usual monuments of it. Necessary alterations in that, and so much of the whole body of the British statutes, and of acts of assembly, as were thought proper to be retained, were digested into 126 new acts, in which simplicity of style was aimed at, as far as was safe. The following are the most remarkable alterations proposed:

To change the rules of descent, so as that the lands of any person dying intestate shall be divisible equally among all his children, or other representatives, in equal degree.

To make slaves distributable among the next of kin, as other movables.

To have all public expences, whether of the general treasury, or of a parish or county, (as for the maintenance of the poor, building bridges, courthouses, &c.,) supplied by assessments on the citizens, in proportion to their property.

To hire undertakers for keeping the public roads in repair, and indemnify individuals through whose lands new roads shall be opened.

To define with precision the rules whereby aliens should become citizens, and citizens make themselves aliens.

To establish religious freedom on the broadest bottom.

To emancipate all slaves born after passing the act. The bill reported by the revisers does not itself contain this proposition; but an amendment containing it was prepared, to be offered to the legislature whenever the bill should be taken up, and further directing, that they should continue with their parents to a certain age, then be brought up, at the public expence, to tillage, arts, or sciences, according to their geniusses, till the females should be eighteen, and the males twenty-one years of age, when they should be colonized to such place as the circumstances of the time should render most proper, sending them out with arms, implements of household and of the handicraft arts, seeds, pairs of the useful domestic animals, &c. to declare them a free and independant people, and extend to them our alliance and protection, till they shall have acquired strength; and to send vessels at the same time to other parts of the world for an equal number of white inhabitants; to induce whom to migrate hither, proper encouragements were to be proposed. It will probably be asked, Why not retain and incorporate the blacks into the state, and thus save the expence of supplying by importation of white settlers, the vacancies they will leave? Deep rooted prejudices entertained by the whites; ten thousand recollections, by the blacks, of the injuries they have sustained; new provocations; the real distinctions which nature has made; and many other circumstances will divide us into parties, and produce convulsions, which will probably never end but in the extermination of the one or the other race.—To these objections, which are political, may be added others, which are physical and moral. The first difference which strikes us is that of colour. Whether the black of the negro resides in the reticular membrane between the skin and scarfskin, or in the scarfskin itself; whether it proceeds from the colour of the blood, the colour of the bile, or from that of some other secretion, the difference is fixed in nature, and is as real as if its seat and cause were better known to us. And is this difference of no importance? Is it not the foundation of a greater or less share of beauty in the two races? Are not the fine mixtures of red and white, the expressions of every passion by greater or less suffusions of colour in the one, preferable to that eternal montony, which reigns in the countenances, that immovable veil of black which covers all the emotions of the other race? Add to these, flowing hair, a more elegant symmetry of form, their own judgment in favour of the whites, declared by their preference of them as uniformly as is the preference of the Oran ootan for the black woman over those of his own species. The circumstance of superior beauty, is thought worthy attention in the propagation of our horses, dogs, and other domestic animals; why not in that of man? Besides those of colour, figure, and hair, there are other physical distinctions proving a difference of race. They have less hair on the face and body. They secrete less by the kidnies, and more by the glands of the skin, which gives them a very strong and disagreeable odour. This greater degree of transpiration, renders them more tolerant of heat, and less so of cold than the whites. Perhaps too a difference of structure in the pulmonary apparatus, which a late ingenious [1] experimentalist has discovered to be the principal regulator of animal heat, may have disabled them from extricating, in the act of inspiration, so much of that fluid from the outer air, or obliged them in expiration, to part with more of it. They seem to require less sleep. A black after hard labour through the day, will be induced by the slightest amusements to sit up till midnight or later, though knowing he must be out with the first dawn of the morning. They are at least as brave, and more adventuresome. But this may perhaps proceed from a want of forethought, which prevents their seeing a danger till it be present. When present, they do not go through it with more coolness or steadiness than the whites. They are more ardent after their female; but love seems with them to be more an eager desire, than a tender delicate mixture of sentiment and sensation. Their griefs are transient. Those numberless afflictions, which render it doubtful whether heaven has given life to us in mercy or in wrath, are less felt, and sooner forgotten with them. In general, their existence appears to participate more of sensation than reflection. To this must be ascribed their disposition to sleep when abstracted from their diversions, and unemployed in labour. An animal whose body is at rest, and who does not reflect, must be disposed to sleep of course. Comparing them by their faculties of memory, reason, and imagination, it appears to me that in memory they are equal to the whites; in reason much inferior, as I think one could scarcely be found capable of tracing and comprehending the investigations of Euclid: and that in imagination they are dull, tasteless, and anomalous. It would be unfair to

[1] Crawford.—T. J.

follow them to Africa for this investigation. We will consider them here, on the same stage with the whites, and where the facts are not apochryphal on which a judgment is to be formed. It will be right to make great allowances for the difference of condition, of education, of conversation, of the sphere in which they move. Many millions of them have been brought to, and born in America. Most of them, indeed, have been confined to tillage, to their own homes, and their own society: yet many have been so situated, that they might have availed themselves of the conversation of their masters; many have been brought up to the handicraft arts, and from that circumstance have always been associated with the whites. Some have been liberally educated, and all have lived in countries where the arts and sciences are cultivated to a considerable degree, and have had before their eyes samples of the best works from abroad. The Indians, with no advantages of this kind, will often carve figures on their pipes not destitute of design and merit. They will crayon out an animal, a plant, or a country, so as to prove the existence of a germ in their minds which only wants cultivation. They astonish you with strokes of the most sublime oratory; such as prove their reason and sentiment strong, their imagination glowing and elevated. But never yet could I find that a black had uttered a thought above the level of plain narration; never seen even an elementary trait of painting or sculpture. In music they are more generally gifted than the whites, with accurate ears for tune and time, and they have been found capable of imagining a small catch.[1] Whether they will be equal to the composition of a more extensive run of melody, or of complicated harmony, is yet to be proved. Misery is often the parent of the most affecting touches in poetry.—Among the blacks is misery enough, God knows, but no poetry. Love is the peculiar œstrum of the poet. Their love is ardent, but it kindles the senses only, not the imagination. Religion, indeed, has produced a Phyllis Whately; but it could not produce a poet. The compositions published under her name are below the dignity of criticism. The heroes of the Dunciad are to her, as Hercules to the author of that poem. Ignatius Sancho has approached nearer to merit in composition; yet his letters do more honour to the heart than the head. They breathe the purest effusions of friendship and general philanthropy, and show how great a degree of the latter may be compounded with strong religious zeal. He is often happy in the turn of his compliments, and his style is easy and familiar, except when he affects a Shandean fabrication of words. But his imagination is wild and extravagant, escapes incessantly from every restraint of reason and taste, and, in the course of its vagaries, leaves a tract of thought as incoherent and eccentric, as is the course of a meteor through the sky. His subjects should often have led him to a process of sober reasoning; yet we find him always substituting sentiment for demonstration. Upon the whole, though we admit him to the first place among those of his own color who have presented themselves to the public judgment, yet when we compare him with the writers of the race among whom he lived and particularly with the epistolary class in which he has

---

[1] The instrument proper to them is the Banjar, which they brought hither from Africa, and which is the original of the guitar, its chords being precisely the four lower chords of the guitar. —T. J.

taken his own stand, we are compelled to enrol him at the bottom of the column. This criticism supposes the letters published under his name to be genuine, and to have received amendment from no other hand; points which would not be of easy investigation. The improvement of the blacks in body and mind, in the first instance of their mixture with the whites, has been observed by every one, and proves that their inferiority is not the effect merely of their condition of life. We know that among the Romans, about the Augustan age especially, the condition of their slaves was much more deplorable than that of the blacks on the continent of America. The two sexes were confined in separate apartments, because to raise a child cost the master more than to buy one. Cato, for a very restricted indulgence to his slaves in this particular,[1] took from them a certain price. But in this country the slaves multiply as fast as the free inhabitants. Their situation and manners place the commerce between the two sexes almost without restraint. The same Cato, on a principle of economy, always sold his sick and superannuated slaves. He gives it as a standing precept to a master visiting his farm, to sell his old oxen, old waggons, old tools, old and diseased servants, and everything else become useless. 'Vendat boves vetulos, plaustrum vetus, feramenta vetera, servum senem, servum morbosum, si quid aliud supersit vendat.' Cato de re rusticâ, c. 2. The American slaves cannot enumerate this among the injuries and insults they receive. It was the common practice to expose in the island Æsculapius, in the Tyber, diseased slaves whose cure was like to become tedious.[2] The Emperor Claudius, by an edict, gave freedom to such of them as should recover, and first declared that if any person chose to kill rather than to expose them, it should be deemed homicide. The exposing them is a crime of which no instance has existed with us; and were it to be followed by death, it would be punished capitally. We are told of a certain Vedius Pollio, who, in the presence of Augustus, would have given a slave as food to his fish, for having broken a glass. With the Romans, the regular method of taking the evidence of their slaves was under torture. Here it has been thought better never to resort to their evidence. When a master was murdered, all his slaves, in the same house, or within hearing, were condemned to death. Here punishment falls on the guilty only, and as precise proof is required against him as against a freeman. Yet notwithstanding these and other discouraging circumstances among the Romans, their slaves were often their rarest artists. They excelled too in science, insomuch as to be usually employed as tutors to their master's children. Epictetus, Terence, and Phædrus, were slaves. But they were of the race of whites. It is not their condition then, but nature, which has produced the distinction.—Whether further observation will or will not verify the conjecture, that nature has been less bountiful to them in the endowments of the head, I believe that in those of the heart she will be found to have done them justice. That disposition to theft with which they have been branded, must be ascribed to their situation, and not to any depravity of the moral sense. The man in whose favour no laws of property exist, probably feels himself less bound to respect those made in favour of others. When arguing for ourselves, we lay it

---

[1] *Tous doulous etaxen örusmenou nomesmatous homilein tais therapenan.* (Plutarch. Cato)—T. J. [2] Suet. Claud. 25.—T. J.

down as a fundamental, that laws, to be just, must give a reciprocation of right: that, without this, they are mere arbitrary rules of conduct, founded in force, and not in conscience; and it is a problem which I give to the master to solve, whether the religious precepts against the violation of property were not framed for him as well as his slave? And whether the slave may not as justifiably take a little from one who has taken all from him, as he may slay one who would slay him? That a change in the relations in which a man is placed should change his ideas of moral right and wrong, is neither new, nor peculiar to the colour of the blacks. Homer tells us it was so 2600 years ago.

> "Emisu, ger t'aretes apoainutai euruopa Zeus
> Haneros, eut' an min Kata doulion ema elisin"
> —Od. 17, 323.

> Jove fix'd it certain, that whatever day
> Makes man a slave, takes half his worth away.

But the slaves of which Homer speaks were whites. Notwithstanding these considerations which must weaken their respect for the laws of property, we find among them numerous instances of the most rigid integrity, and as many as among their better instructed masters, of benevolence, gratitude, and unshaken fidelity. The opinion that they are inferior in the faculties of reason and imagination, must be hazarded with great diffidence. To justify a general conclusion, requires many observations, even where the subject may be submitted to the Anatomical knife, to Optical glasses, to analysis by fire or by solvents. How much more then where it is a faculty, not a substance, we are examining; where it eludes the research of all the senses; where the conditions of its existence are various and variously combined; where the effects of those which are present or absent bid defiance to calculation; let me add too, as a circumstance of great tenderness, where our conclusion would degrade a whole race of men from the rank in the scale of beings which their Creator may perhaps have given them. To our reproach it must be said, that though for a century and a half we have had under our eyes the races of black and of red men, they have never yet been viewed by us as subjects of natural history. I advance it, therefore, as a suspicion only, that the blacks, whether originally a distinct race, or made distinct by time and circumstances, are inferior to the whites in the endowments both of body and mind. It is not against experience to suppose that different species of the same genus, or varieties of the same species, may possess different qualifications. Will not a lover of natural history then, one who views the gradations in all the races of animals with the eye of philosophy, excuse an effort to keep those in the department of man as distinct as nature has formed them? This unfortunate difference of colour, and perhaps of faculty, is a powerful obstacle to the emancipation of these people. Many of their advocates, while they wish to vindicate the liberty of human nature, are anxious also to preserve its dignity and beauty. Some of these, embarrassed by the question, 'What further is to be done with them?' join themselves in opposition with those who are actuated by sordid avarice only. Among the Romans emancipation required but one effort. The slave, when made free, might mix with, without staining the blood of his master. But with us a second is necessary, unknown to history. When freed, he is to be removed beyond the reach of mixture.

The revised code further proposes to proportion crimes and punishments. This is attempted in the following scale.

I. Crimes whose punishment extends to *Life*.
    1. High treason. Death by hanging.
                      Forfeiture of lands and goods to the commonwealth.
    2. Petty treason. Death by hanging. Dissection.
                      Forfeiture of half the lands and goods to the representatives of the party slain.
    3. Murder. 1. By poison. Death by poison.
                        Forfeiture of one-half, as before.
            2. In duel.   Death by hanging. Gibbeting, if the challenger.
                      Forfeiture of one-half as before, unless it be the party challenged, then the forfeiture is to the commonwealth.
            3. In any other way. Death by hanging.
                      Forfeiture of one-half as before.
    4. Manslaughter. The second offence is murder.

II. Crimes whose punishment goes to *Limb*.
    1. Rape ....⎫
    2. Sodomy .....⎭ Dismemberment.
    3. Maiming ....⎫ Retaliation, and the forfeiture of half of the lands and
    4. Disfiguring ..⎭   goods to the sufferer.

III. Crimes punishable by *Labour*.

1. Manslaughter, 1st offence.	Labor VII. years for the public.	Forfeiture of half, as in murder.	
2. Counterfeiting money.	Labor VI. years.	Forfeiture of lands and goods to the commonwealth.	
3. Arson. 4. Asportation of vessels.	Labor V. years.	Reparation threefold.	
5. Robbery. 6. Burglary.	Labor IV. years.	Reparation double.	
7. House-breaking. 8. Horse-stealing.	Labor III. years.	Reparation.	
9. Grand larceny.	Labor II. years.	Reparation. Pillory.	
10. Petty larceny.	Labor I. year.	Reparation. Pillory.	
11. Pretensions to witchcraft, &c.	Ducking.		Stripes.
12. Excusable homicide. 13. Suicide. 14. Apostacy. Heresy.	To be pitied, not punished.		

Pardon and privilege of clergy are proposed to be abolished; but if the verdict be against the defendant, the court in their discretion may allow a new trial. No attainder to cause a corruption of blood, or forfeiture of dower. Slaves guilty of offences punishable in others by labour, to be transported to Africa, or elsewhere, as the circumstances of the time admit, there to be continued in slavery. A rigorous regimen proposed for those condemned to labour.

Another object of the revisal is, to diffuse knowledge more generally through the mass of the people. This bill proposes to lay off every country into small districts of five or six miles square, called hundreds and in each of them to establish a school for teaching, reading, writing, and arithmetic. The tutor to be supported by the hundred, and every person in it entitled to send their children three years gratis, and as much longer as they please, paying for it. These schools to be under a visitor who is annually to chuse the boy of best genius in the school, of those whose parents are too poor to give them further education, and to send him forward to one of the grammar schools, of which twenty are proposed to be erected in different parts of the country, for teaching Greek, Latin, geography, and the higher branches of numerical arithmetic. Of the boys thus sent in any one year, trial is to be made at the grammar schools one or two years, and the best genius of the whole selected, and continued six years, and the residue dismissed. By this means twenty of the best geniuses will be raked from the rubbish annually, and be instructed, at the public expence, so far as the grammar schools go. At the end of six years instruction, one half are to be discontinued (from among whom the grammar schools will probably be supplied with future masters); and the other half, who are to be chosen for the superiority of their parts and disposition, are to be sent and continued three years in the study of such sciences as they shall chuse, at William and Mary college, the plan of which is proposed to be enlarged, as will be hereafter explained, and extended to all the useful sciences. The ultimate result of the whole scheme of education would be the teaching all the children of the State reading, writing, and common arithmetic; turning out ten annually, of superior genius, well taught in Greek, Latin, geography, and the higher branches of arithmetic; turning out ten others annually, of still superior parts, who, to those branches of learning, shall have added such of the sciences as their genius shall have them led to; the furnishing to the wealthier part of the people convenient schools at which their children may be educated at their own expence.—The general objects of this law are to provide an education adapted to the years, to the capacity, and the condition of every one, and directed to their freedom and happiness. Specific details were not proper for the law. These must be the business of the visitors entrusted with its execution. The first stage of this education being the schools of the hundreds, wherein the great mass of the people will receive their instruction, the principal foundations of future order will be laid here. Instead, therefore, of putting the Bible and Testament into the hands of the children at an age when their judgments are not sufficiently matured for religious inquiries, their memories may here be stored with the most useful facts from Grecian, Roman, European, and American history. The first elements of morality too may be instilled into their minds; such as, when further developed as their judgments advance in strength, may teach them how to work out their own greatest happiness, by shewing them that it does not depend on the condition of life in which chance has placed them, but is always the result of a good conscience, good health, occupation, and freedom in all just pursuits.—Those whom either the wealth of their parents or the adoption of the state shall destine to higher degrees of learning, will go on to the grammar schools, which constitute the next stage, there to be instructed in the languages. The learning Greek and Latin, I am told, is going into disuse in Europe. I know not what their manners and occupations may call for: but it would be very ill-judged in us to follow their example in this instance. There is a certain period of life, say from eight to fifteen or sixteen years of age, when the mind like the body is not yet firm enough for laborious and close operations. If applied to such, it falls an early victim to premature exertion; exhibiting, indeed, at first, in these young and tender subjects, the flattering appearance of their being men while they are yet children, but ending in reducing them to be children when they should be men. The memory is then most susceptible and tenacious of impressions; and the learning of languages being chiefly a work of memory, it seems precisely fitted to the powers of this period, which is long enough too for acquiring the most useful languages, antient and modern. I do not pretend that language is science. It is only an instruments for the attainment of science. But that time is not lost which is employed in providing tools for future operation: more especially as in this case the books put into the hands of the youth for this purpose may be such as will at the same time impress their minds with useful facts and good principles. If this period be suffered to pass in idleness, the mind becomes lethargic and impotent, as would the body it inhabits if unexercised during the same time. The sympathy between body and mind during their rise, progress and decline, is too strict and obvious to endanger our being misled while we reason from the one to the other.—As soon as they are of sufficient age, it is supposed they will be sent on from the grammar schools to the university, which constitutes our third and last stage, there to study those sciences which may be adapted to their views.—By that part of our plan which prescribes the selection of the youths of genius from among the classes of the poor, we hope to avail the state of those talents which nature has shown as liberally among the poor as the rich, but which perish without use, if not sought for and cultivated.—But of all the views of this law none is more important, none more legitimate, than that of rendering the people the safe, as they are the ultimate, guardians of their own liberty. For this purpose the reading in the first stage, where *they* will receive their whole education, is proposed, as has been said, to be chiefly historical. History, by apprising them of the past, will enable them to judge of the future; it will avail them of the experience of other times and other nations; it will qualify them as judges of the actions and designs of men; it will enable them to know ambition under every disguise it may assume; and knowing it, to defeat its views. In every government on earth is some trace of human weakness, some germ of corruption and degeneracy, which cunning will discover, and wickedness insensibly open, cultivate and improve. Every government degenerates when trusted to the rulers of the people alone. The people themselves therefore are its only safe depositories. And to render even them safe, their minds must be improved to a certain degree. This indeed is not all that is necessary, though it be essentially necessary. An amendment of our constitution must here come in aid of the public education. The influence over government must be shared among all the people. If every individual which composes their mass participates of the ultimate authority, the government will be safe; because the corrupting the whole mass will exceed any private resources of wealth; and public ones cannot be provided but by levies on the people. In this case every man would have to pay his own price. The government of Great Britain has been corrupted, because but one man in ten has a right to vote for members of parliament. The sellers of the government, therefore, get nine-tenths of their price clear. It has been thought that corruption is restrained by confining the right of suffrage to a few of the wealthier of the people: but it would be more effectually restrained by an extension of that right to such members as would bid defiance to the means of corruption.

Lastly, it is proposed, by a bill in this revisal, to begin a public library and gallery, by laying out a certain sum annually in books, paintings, and statues.

QUERY XV

The colleges and public establishments, the roads, buildings, &c.

The college of William and Mary is the only public seminary of learning in this State. It was founded in the time of king William and queen Mary, who granted to it 20,000 acres of land, and a penny a pound duty on certain tobaccoes exported from Virginia and Maryland, which had been levied by the statute of 25 Car. II. The assembly also gave it, by temporary laws, a duty on liquors imported, and skins and furs exported. From these resources it received upwards of 3000l communibus annis. The buildings are of brick, sufficient for an indifferent accommodation of perhaps an hundred students. By its charter it was to be under the government of twenty visitors, who were to be its legislators, and to have a president and six professors, who were incorporated. It was allowed a representative in the general assembly. Under this charter, a professorship of the Greek and Latin languages, a professorship of mathematics, one of moral philosophy, and two of divinity were established. To these were annexed, for a sixth professorship, a considerable donation by Mr. Boyle, of England, for the instruction of the Indians, and their conversion to Christianity. This was called the professorship of Brafferton, from an estate of that name in England, purchased with the monies given. The admission of the learners of Latin and Greek filled the college with children. This rendering it disagreeable and degrading to young gentlemen already prepared for entering on the sciences, they were discouraged from resorting to it, and thus the schools for mathematics and moral philosophy, which might have been of some service, became of very little. The revenues, too, were exhausted in accommodating those who came only to acquire the rudiments of science. After the present revolution, the visitors, having no power to change those circumstances in the constitution of the college which were fixed by the charter, and being therefore confined in the number of professorships, undertook to change the objects of the professorships. They excluded the two schools for divinity, and that for the Greek and Latin languages, and substituted others; so that at present they stand thus:

A professorship for Law and Police:
    Anatomy and Medicine:
    Natural Philosophy and Mathematics:
    Moral Philosophy, the Law of Nature and Nations, the Fine Arts:
    Modern Languages:
    For the Brafferton.

And it is proposed, so soon as the legislature shall have leisure to take up this subject, to desire authority from them to increase the number of professorships, as well for the purpose of subdividing those already instituted, as of adding others for other branches of science. To the professorships usually established in the universities of Europe, it would seem proper to add one for the ancient languages and literature of the North, on account of their connection with our own language, laws, customs, and history. The purposes of the Brafferton institution would be better answered by maintaining a perpetual mission among the Indian tribes, the object of which, besides instructing them in the principles of Christianity, as the founder requires, should be to collect their traditions, laws, customs, languages, and other circumstances which might lead to a discovery of their relation with one another, or descent from other nations. When these objects are accomplished with one tribe, the missionary might pass on to another.

The roads are under the government of the county courts, subject to be controuled by the general court. They order new roads to be opened wherever they think them necessary. The inhabitants of the county are by them laid off into precincts, to each of which they allot a convenient portion of the public roads to be kept in repair. Such bridges as may be built without the assistance of artificers, they are to build. If the stream be such as to require a bridge of regular workmanship, the court employs workmen to build it at the expence of the whole county. If it be too great for the county, application is made to the general assembly, who authorize individuals to build it, and to take a fixed toll from all passengers, or give sanction to such other proposition as to them appears reasonable.

Ferries are admitted only at such places as are particularly pointed out by law, and the rates of ferriage are fixed.

Taverns are licensed by the courts, who fix their rates from time to time.

The private buildings are very rarely constructed of stone or brick, much the greatest proportion being of scantling and boards, plaistered with lime. It is impossible to devise things more ugly, uncomfortable, and happily more perishable. There are two or three plans, on one of which, according to its size, most of the houses in the state are built. The poorest people build huts of logs, laid horizontally in pens, stopping the interstices with mud. These are warmer in winter, and cooler in summer, than the more expensive constructions of scantling and plank. The wealthy are attentive to the raising of vegetables, but very little so to fruits. The poorer people attend to neither, living principally on milk and animal diet. This is the more inexcusable, as the climate requires indispensably a free use of vegetable food, for health as well as comfort, and is very friendly to the raising of fruits.—The only public buildings worthy mention are the Capitol, the Palace, the College, and the Hospital for Lunatics, all of them in Williamsburg, heretofore the seat of our government. The Capitol is a light and airy structure, with a portico in front of two orders, the lower of which, being Doric, is tolerably just in its proportions and ornaments, save only that the intercolonnations are too large. The upper is Ionic, much too small for that on which it is mounted, its ornaments not proper to the order, nor proportioned within themselves. It is crowned with a pediment, which is too high for its span. Yet, on the whole, it is the most pleasing piece of architecture we have. The Palace is not handsome without, but it is spacious and commodious within, is prettily situated, and with the grounds annexed to it, is capable of being made an elegant seat. The College and Hospital are rude, mis-shapen piles, which, but that they have roofs, would be taken for brick-kilns. There are no other public buildings but churches and court-houses, in which no attempts are made at elegance. Indeed, it would not be easy to execute such an attempt, as a workman could scarcely be found here capable of drawing an order. The genius of architecture seems to have shed its maledictions over this land. Buildings are often erected, by individuals, of considerable expence. To give these symmetry and taste, would not increase their cost. It would only change the arrangement of the materials, the form and combination of the members. This would often cost less than the burthen of barbarous ornaments with which these buildings are sometimes charged. But the first principles of the art are unknown, and there exists scarcely a model among us sufficiently chaste to give an idea of them. Architecture being one of the fine arts, and as such within the department of a professor of the college, according to the new arrangement, perhaps a spark may fall on some young subjects of natural taste, kindle up their genius, and produce a reformation in this elegant and useful art. But all we shall do in this way will produce no permanent improvement to our country, while the unhappy prejudice prevails that houses of brick or stone are less wholesome than those of wood. A dew is often observed on the walls of the former in rainy weather, and the most obvious solution is, that the rain has penetrated through these walls. The following facts, however, are sufficient to prove the error of this solution. 1. This dew on the walls appears when there is no rain, if the state of the atmosphere be moist. 2. It appears on the partition as well as the exterior walls. 3. So, also, on pavements of brick or stone. 4. It is more copious in proportion as the walls are thicker; the reverse of which ought to be the case, if this hypothesis were just. If cold water be poured into a vessel of stone, or glass, a dew forms instantly on the outside: but if it be poured into a vessel of wood, there is no such appearance. It is not supposed, in the first case, that the water has exuded through the glass, but that it is precipitated from the circumambient air; as the humid particles of vapour, passing from the boiler of an alembic through its refrigerant, are precipitated from the air, in which they were suspended, on the internal surface of the refrigerant. Walls of brick or stone act as the refrigerant in this instance. They are sufficiently cold to condense and precipitate the moisture suspended in the air of the room, when it is heavily charged therewith. But walls of wood are not so. The question then is, whether air in which this moisture is left floating, or that which is deprived of it, be most wholesome? In both cases, the remedy is easy. A little fire kindled in the room, whenever the air is damp, prevents the precipitation on the walls: and this practice, found healthy in the warmest as well as coldest seasons, is as necessary in a wooden as in a stone or a brick house. I do not mean to say, that the rain never penetrates through walls of brick. On the contrary, I have seen instances of it. But with us it is only through the northern and eastern walls of the house, after north-easterly storm, these being the only ones which continue long enough to force through the walls. This, however, happens too rarely to give a just character of unwholesomeness to such houses. In a house, the walls of which are of well-burnt brick and good mortar, I have seen the rain penetrate through but twice in a dozen or fifteen years. The inhabitants of Europe, who dwell chiefly in houses of stone or brick, are surely as healthy as those of Virginia. These houses have the advantage, too, of being warmer in winter and cooler in summer than those of wood; of being cheaper in their first construction, where lime is convenient, and infinitely more durable. The latter consideration renders it of great importance to eradicate this prejudice from the minds of our countrymen. A country whose buildings are of wood, can never increase in its improvements to any considerable degree. Their duration is highly estimated at 50 years. Every half century then our country becomes a tabula rasa, whereon we have to set out anew, as in the first moment of seating it. Whereas when buildings are of durable materials, every new edifice is an actual and permanent acquisition to the State, adding to its value as well as to its ornament.

QUERY XVI

The measures taken with regard of the estates and possessions of the rebels, commonly called Tories

A tory has been properly defined to be a traitor in thought, but not in deed. The only description, by which the laws have endeavoured to come at them, was that of non-jurors, or persons refusing to take the oath of fidelity to the state. Persons of this description were at one time subjected to double taxation, at another treble, and lastly were allowed retribution, and placed on a level with good citizens. It may be mentioned as a proof, both of the lenity of our government, and unanimity of its inhabitants, that though this war has now raged near seven years not a single execution for treason has taken place.

Under this query I will state the measures which have been adopted as to British property, the owners of which stand on a much fairer footing than the Tories. By our laws, the same as the English as in this respect, no alien can hold lands, nor alien enemy maintain an action for money, or other movable thing. Lands acquired or held by aliens become forfeited to the state; and, on an action by an alien enemy to recover money, or other movable property, the defendant may plead that he is an alien enemy. This extinguishes his right in the hands of the debtor or holder of his movable property. By our separation from Great Britain,

British subjects became aliens, and being at war, they were alien enemies. Their lands were of course forfeited, and their debts irrecoverable. The assembly, however, passed laws at various times, for saving their property. They first sequestered their lands, slaves, and other property on their farms in the hands of commissioners, who were mostly the confidential friends or agents of the owners, and directed their clear profits to be paid into the treasury: and they gave leave to all persons owing debts to British subjects to pay them also into the treasury. The monies so to be brought in were declared to remain the property of the British subject, and, if used by the state, were to be repaid, unless an improper conduct in Great-Britain should render a detention of it reasonable. Depreciation had at that time, though unacknowledged and unperceived by the Whigs begun in some small degree. Great sums of money were paid in by debtors. At a later period, the assembly, adhering to the political principles which forbid an alien to hold lands in the state, ordered all British property to be sold: and, become sensible of the real progress of depreciation, and of the losses which would thence occur, if not guarded against, they ordered that the proceeds of the sales should be converted into their then worth in tobacco, subject to the future direction of the legislature. This act has left the question of retribution more problematical. In May 1780 another act took away the permission to pay into the public treasury debts due to British subjects.

QUERY XVII

The different religions received into that State

The first settlers in this country were emigrants from England, of the English Church, just at a point of time when it was flushed with complete victory over the religious of all other persuasions. Possessed, as they became, of the powers of making, administering, and executing the laws, they showed equal intolerance in this country with their Presbyterian brethren, who had emigrated to the northern government. The poor Quakers were flying from persecution in England. They cast their eyes on these new countries as asylums of civil and religious freedom; but they found them free only for the reigning sect. Several acts of the Virginia assembly of 1659, 1662, and 1693, had made it penal in parents to refuse to have their children baptized; had prohibited the unlawful assembling of Quakers; had made it penal for any master of a vessel to bring a Quaker into the State; had ordered those already here, and such as should come thereafter, to be imprisoned till they should abjure the country; provided a milder punishment for their first and second return, but death for their third; had inhibited all persons from suffering their meetings in or near their houses, entertaining them individually, or disposing of books which supported their tenets. If no execution took place here, as did in New England, it was not owing to the moderation of the church, or spirit of the legislature, as may be inferred from the law itself; but to historical circumstances which have not been handed down to us. The Anglicans retained full possession of the country about a century. Other opinions began then to creep in, and the great care of the government to support their own church, having begotten an equal degree of indolence in its clergy, two-thirds of the people had become dissenters at the commencement of the present revolution. The laws, indeed, were still oppressive on them, but the spirit of the one party had subsided into moderation, and of the other had risen to a degree of determination which commanded respect.

The present state of our laws on the subject of religion is this. The convention of May 1776, in their declaration of rights, declared it to be a truth, and a natural right, that the exercise of religion should be free; but when they proceeded to form on that declaration the ordinance of government, instead of taking up every principle declared in the bill of rights, and guarding it by legislative sanction, they passed over that which asserted our religious rights, leaving them as they found them. The same convention, however, when they met as a member of the general assembly in October, 1776, repealed all *acts of Parliament* which had rendered criminal the maintaining any opinions in matters of religion, the forbearing to repair to church, and the exercising any mode of worship; and suspended the laws giving salaries to the clergy, which suspension was made perpetual in October, 1779. Statutory oppressions in religion being thus wiped away, we remain at present under those only imposed by the common law, or by our own acts of assembly. At the common law, *heresy* was a capital offence, punishable by burning. Its definition was left to the ecclesiastical judges, before whom the conviction was, till the statute of the 1 El. c. 1 circumscribed it, by declaring, that nothing should be deemed heresy, but what had been so determined by authority of the canonical scriptures, or by one of the four first general councils, or by other council, having for the grounds of their declaration the express and plain words of the scriptures. Heresy, thus circumscribed, being an offence against the common law, our act of assembly of October 1777, c. 17, gives cognizance of it to the general court, by declaring that the jurisdiction of that court shall be general in all matters at the common law. The execution is by the writ *De haeretico comburendo*. By our own act of assembly of 1705, c. 30, if a person brought up in the Christian religion denies the being of a God, or the Trinity, or asserts there are more gods than one, or denies the Christian religion to be true, or the scriptures to be of divine authority, he is punishable on the first offence by incapacity to hold any office or employment ecclesiastical, civil, or military; on the second by disability to sue, to take any gift or legacy, to be guardian, executor, or administrator, and by three years' imprisonment without bail. A father's right to the custody of his own children being founded in law on his right of guardianship, this being taken away, they may of course be severed from him, and put by the authority of a court into more orthodox hands. This is a summary view of that religious slavery under which a people have been willing to remain, who have lavished their lives and fortunes for the establishment of their civil freedom.[1] The error seems not sufficiently eradicated, that the operations of the mind, as well as the acts of the body, are subject to the coercion of the laws. But our rulers can have no authority over such natural rights, only as we have submitted to them.

[1] *Furneaux passim.*—T. J.

The rights of conscience we never submitted, we could not submit. We are answerable for them to our God. The legitimate powers of government extend to such acts only as are injurious to others. But it does me no injury for my neighbor to say there are twenty gods, or no God. It neither picks my pocket nor breaks my leg. If it be said, his testimony in a court of justice cannot be relied on, reject it then, and be the stigma on him. Constraint may make him worse by making him a hypocrite, but it will never make him a truer man. It may fix him obstinately in his errors, but will not cure them. Reason and free inquiry are the only effectual agents against error. Give a loose to them, they will support the true religion by bringing every false one to their tribunal, to the test of their investigation. They are the natural enemies of error, and of error only. Had not the Roman government permitted free inquiry, Christianity could never have been introduced. Had not free inquiry been indulged at the era of the reformation, the corruptions of Christianity could not have been purged away. If it be restrained now, the present corruptions will be protected, and new ones encouraged. Was the government to prescribe to us our medicine and diet, our bodies would be in such keeping as our souls are now. Thus in France the emetic was once forbidden as a medicine, and the potato as an article of food. Government is just as infallible, too, when it fixes systems in physics. Galileo was sent to the Inquisition for affirming that the earth was a sphere; the government had declared it to be as flat as a trencher, and Galileo was obliged to abjure his error. This error, however, at length prevailed, the earth became a globe, and Descartes declared it was whirled round its axis by a vortex. The government in which he lived was wise enough to see that this was no question of civil jurisdiction, or we should all have been involved by authority in vortices. In fact, the vortices have been exploded, and the Newtonian principle of gravitation is now more firmly established, on the basis of reason, than it would be were the government to step in, and to make it an article of necessary faith. Reason and experiment have been indulged, and error has fled before them. It is error alone which needs the support of government. Truth can stand by itself. Subject opinion to coercion: whom will you make your inquisitors? Fallible men; men governed by bad passions, by private as well as public reasons. And why subject it to coercion? To produce uniformity. But is uniformity of opinion desirable? No more than of face and stature. Introduce the bed of Procrustes then, and as there is danger that the large men may beat the small, make us all of a size, by lopping the former and stretching the latter. Difference of opinion is advantageous in religion. The several sects perform the office of a *censor morum* over such other. Is uniformity attainable? Millions of innocent men, women, and children, since the introduction of Christianity, have been burnt, tortured, fined, imprisoned; yet we have not advanced one inch towards uniformity. What has been the effect of coercion? To make one half the world fools, and the other half hypocrites. To support roguery and error all over the earth. Let us reflect that it is inhabited by a thousand millions of people. That these profess probably a thousand different systems of religion. That ours is but one of that thousand. That if there be but one right, and ours that one, we should wish to see the nine hundred and ninety-nine wandering sects gathered into the fold of truth. But against such a majority we cannot effect this by force. Reason and persuasion are the only practicable instruments. To make way for these, free inquiry must be indulged; and how can we wish others to indulge it while we refuse it ourselves. But every State, says an inquisitor, has established some religion. No two, say I, have established the same. Is this a proof of the infallibility of establishments? Our sister States of Pennsylvania and New York, however, have long subsisted without any establishment at all. The experiment was new and doubtful when they made it. It has answered beyond conception. They flourish infinitely. Religion is well supported; of various kinds, indeed, but all good enough; all sufficient to preserve peace and order; or if a sect arises, whose tenets would subvert morals, good sense has fair play, and reasons and laughs it out of doors, without suffering the State to be troubled with it. They do not hang more malefactors than we do. They are not more disturbed with religious dissensions. On the contrary, their harmony is unparalleled, and can be ascribed to nothing but their unbounded tolerance, because there is no other circumstance in which they differ from every nation on earth. They have made the happy discovery, that the way to silence religious disputes, is to take no notice of them. Let us too give this experiment fair play, and get rid, while we may, of those tyrannical laws. It is true, we are as yet secured against them by the spirit of the times. I doubt whether the people of this country would suffer an execution for heresy, or a three years' imprisonment for not comprehending the mysteries of the Trinity. But is the spirit of the people an infallible, a permanent reliance? Is it government? Is this the kind of protection we receive in return for the rights we give up? Besides, the spirit of the times may alter, will alter. Our rulers will become corrupt, our people careless. A single zealot may commence persecutor, and better men be his victims. It can never be too often repeated, that the time for fixing every essential right on a legal basis is while our rulers are honest, and ourselves united. From the conclusion of this war we shall be going down hill. It will not then be necessary to resort every moment to the people for support. They will be forgotten, therefore, and their rights disregarded. They will forget themselves, but in the sole faculty of making money, and will never think of uniting to effect a due respect for their rights. The shackles, therefore, which shall not be knocked off at the conclusion of this war, will remain on us long, will be made heavier and heavier, till our rights shall revive or expire in a convulsion.

QUERY XVIII

The particular customs and manners that may happen to be received in that State

It is difficult to determine on the standard by which the manners of a nation may be tried, whether *catholic* or *particular*. It is more difficult for a native to bring to that standard the manners of his own nation, familiarized to him by habit. There must doubtless be an unhappy influence on the manners of our people produced by the existence of slavery among us. The whole commerce between master and slave is a perpetual exercise of the most boisterous passions, the most unremitting despotism on the one part, and degrading submissions on the other. Our children see this, and learn to imitate it; for man is an imitative animal. This quality is the germ of all education in him. From his cradle to his grave he is learning to do what he sees others do. If a parent could find no motive either in his philanthropy or his self-love, for restraining the intemperance of passion towards his slave, it should always be a sufficient one that his child is present. But generally it is not sufficient. The parent storms, the child looks on, catches the lineaments of wrath, puts on the same airs in the circle of smaller slaves, gives a loose to the worst of passions, and thus nursed, educated, and daily exercised in tyranny, cannot but be stamped by it with odious peculiarities. The man must be a prodigy who can retain his manners and morals undepraved by such circumstances. And with what execration should the statesman be loaded, who, permitting one half the citizens thus to trample on the rights of the other, transforms those into depots, and these into enemies, destroys the morals of the one part, and the *armor patriae* of the other. For if a slave can have a country in this world, it must be any other in preference to that in which he is born to live and labor for another; in which he must lock up the faculties of his nature, contribute as far as depends on his individual endeavors to the evanishment of the human race, or entail his own miserable condition on the endless generations proceeding from him. With the morals of the people, their industry also is destroyed. For in a warm climate, no man will labor for himself who can make another labor for him. This is so true, that of the proprietors of slaves a very small proportion indeed are ever seen to labor. And can the liberties of a nation be thought secure when we have removed their only firm basis, a conviction in the minds of the people that these liberties are of the gift of God? That they are not to be violated but with his wrath? Indeed I tremble for my country when I reflect that God is just; that his justice cannot sleep forever; that considering numbers, nature and natural means only, a revolution of the wheel of fortune, an exchange of situation is among possible events; that is may become probable by supernatural interference! The Almighty has no attribute which can take side with us in such a contest. But it is impossible to be temperate and to pursue this subject through the various considerations of policy, of morals, of history natural and civil. We must be contented to hope they will force their way into everyone's mind. I think a change already perceptible, since the origin of the present revolution. The spirit of the master is abating, that of the slave rising from the dust, his condition mollifying, the way I hope preparing, under the auspices of heaven, for a total emancipation, and that this is disposed, in the order of events, to be with the consent of the masters, rather than by their extirpation.

QUERY XIX

The present state of manufactures, commerce, interior and exterior trade

We never had an interior trade of any importance. Our exterior commerce has suffered very much from the beginning of the present contest. During this time we have manufactured within our families the most necessary articles of clothing. Those of cotton will bear some comparison with the same kinds of manufacture in Europe; but those of wool, flax and hemp are very coarse, unsightly, and unpleasant; and such is our attachment to agriculture, and such our preference for foreign manufactures, that be it wise or unwise, our people will certainly return as soon as they can, to the raising raw materials, and exchanging them for finer manufactures than they are able to execute themselves.

The political economists of Europe have established it as a principle, that every State should endeavor to manufacture for itself; and this principle, like many others, we transfer to America, without calculating the difference of circumstance which should often produce a difference of result. In Europe the lands are either cultivated, or locked up against the cultivator. Manufacture must therefore be resorted to of necessity not of choice, to support the surplus of their people. But we have an immensity of land courting the industry of the husbandman. Is it best then that all our citizens should be employed in its improvement, or that one half should be called off from that to exercise manufactures and handicraft arts for the other? Those who labor in the earth are the chosen people of God, if ever He had a chosen people, whose breasts He has made His peculiar deposit for substantial and genuine virtue. It is the focus in which he keeps alive that sacred fire, which otherwise might escape from the face of the earth. Corruption of morals in the mass of cultivators is a phenomenon of which no age nor nation has furnished an example. It is the mark set on those, who, not looking up to heaven, to their own soil and industry, as does the husbandman, for their subsistence, depend for it on casualties and caprice of customers. Dependence begets subservience and venality, suffocates the germ of virtue, and prepares fit tools for the designs of ambition. This, the natural progress and consequence of the arts, has sometimes perhaps been retarded by accidental circumstances; but, generally speaking, the proportion which the aggregate of the other classes of citizens bears in any State to that of its husbandmen, is the proportion of its unsound to its healthy parts, and is a good enough barometer whereby to measure its degree of corruption. While we have land to labor then, let us never wish to see our citizens occupied at a work-bench, or twirling a distaff. Carpenters, masons, smiths, are wanting in husbandry; but, for the general operations of manufacture, let our workshops remain in Europe. It is better to carry provisions and materials to workmen there, than bring them to the provisions and materials, and with them their manners and principles. The loss by the transportation of commodities across the Atlantic will be made up in happiness and permanence of government. The mobs of great cities add just so much to the support of pure government, as sores do to the strength of the human body. It is the manners and spirit of a people which preserve a republic in vigor. A degeneracy in these is a canker which soon eats to the heart of its laws and constitution.

QUERY XX

A notice of the commercial productions particular to the State, and of those objects which the inhabitants are obliged to get from Europe and from other parts of the world

Before the present war we exported, *communibus annis,* according to the best information I can get, nearly as follows:

ARTICLES	QUANTITY	PRICE IN DOLLARS	AMOUNT IN DOLLARS
Tobacco	55,000 hhds. of 1,000 lbs.	at 30d. per hhd.	$1,650,000
Wheat	800,000 bushels.	at 5-6d. per bush.	666,666⅔
Indian corn	600,000 "	at ⅓d. per bush.	200,000
Shipping	. . . .	. . . . . .	100,000
Masts, planks, scantling, shingles, staves }	. . . .	. . . . . .	66,666⅔
Tar, pitch, turpentine	30,000 barrels.	at 1⅓d. per bbl.	40,000
Peltry, *viz.*, skins of deer, beavers, otters, musk rats, raccoons, foxes }	180 hhds. of 600 lbs.	at 5-12d. per lb.	42,000
Pork	4,000 barrels.	at 10d. per bbl.	40,000
Flax-seed, hemp, cotton	. . . .	. . . . . .	8,000
Pit coal, pig iron	. . . .	. . . . . .	6,666⅔
Peas	5,000 bushels.	at ⅔d. per bush.	3,333⅓
Beef	1,000 barrels.	at 3⅓d. per bbl.	3,333⅓
Sturgeon, white shad, herring	. . . .	. . . . . .	3,333⅓
Brandy from peaches and apples, and whiskey }	. . . .	. . . . . .	1,666⅔
Horses	. . . .	. . . . . .	1,666⅔
	. . . .	. . . . . .	[1] $2,833,333⅓

[1]This sum is equal to £850,000; Virginia money, 607,142 guineas.—T. J.

In the year 1758 we exported seventy thousand hogsheads of tobacco, which was the greatest quantity ever produced in this country in one year. But its culture was fast declining at the commencement of this war and that of wheat taken its place; and it must continue to decline on the return of peace. I suspect that the change in the temperature of our climate has become sensible to that plant, which to be good, requires an extraordinary degree of heat. But it

requires still more indispensably an uncommon fertility of soil; and the price
which it commands at market will not enable the planter to produce this by
manure. Was the supply still to depend on Virginia and Maryland alone as
its culture becomes more difficult, the price would rise so as to enable the
planter to surmount those difficulties and to live. But the western country on
the Mississippi, and the midlands of Georgia, having fresh and fertile lands
in abundance, and a hotter sun, will be able to undersell these two States, and
will oblige them to abandon the raising of tobacco altogether. And a happy
obligation for them it will be. It is a culture productive of infinite wretchedness. Those employed in it are in a continual state of exertion beyond the
power of nature to support. Little food of any kind is raised by them; so that
the men and animals on these farms are badly fed, and the earth is rapidly im-
poverished. The cultivation of wheat is the reverse in every circumstance. Besides clothing the earth with herbage, and preserving its fertility, it feeds the
laborers plentifully, requires from them only a moderate toil, except in the
season of harvest, raises great numbers of animals for food and service, and dif-
fuses plenty and happiness among the whole. We find it easier to make an
hundred bushels of wheat than a thousand weight of tobacco, and they are worth
more when made. The weavil indeed is a formidable obstacle to the cultivation
of this grain with us. But principles are already known which must lead to a
remedy. Thus a certain degree of heat, to wit, that of the common air in summer, is necessary to hatch the eggs. If subterranean granaries, or others, therefore, can be contrived below that temperature, the evil will be cured by cold.
A degree of heat beyond that which hatches the egg we know will kill it. But
in aiming at this we easily run into that which produced putrefaction. To produce putrefaction, however, three agents are requisite, heat, moisture, and the
external air. If the absence of any one of these be secured, the other two may
safely be admitted. Heat is the one we want. Moisture then, or external air,
must be excluded. The former has been done by exposing the grain in kilns
to the action of fire, which produces heat, and extracts moisture at the same
time; the latter, by putting the grain into hogsheads, covering it with a coating
of lime, and heading it up. In this situation its bulk produced a heat sufficient
to kill the eggs; the moisture is suffered to remain indeed, but the external air
is excluded. A nicer operation yet has been attempted; that is, to produce an
intermediate temperature of heat between that which kills the egg, and that
which produces putrefaction. The threshing the grain as soon as it is cut, and
laying it in its chaff in large heaps, has been found very nearly to hit this
temperature, though not perfectly, nor always. The heap generates heat sufficient to kill most of the eggs, whilst the chaff commonly restrains it from
rising into putrefaction. But all these methods abridge too much the quantity
which the farmer can manage, and enable other countries to undersell him,
which are not infested with this insect. There is still a desideratum then to
give with us decisive triumph to this branch of agriculture over that of tobacco. The culture of wheat by enlarging our pasture, will render the Arabian
horse an article of very considerable profit. Experience has shown that ours is

the particular climate of America where he may be raised without degeneracy. Southwardly the heat of the sun occasions a deficiency of pasture, and northwardly the winters are too cold for the short and fine hair, the particular sensibility and constitution of that race. Animals transplanted into unfriendly climates, either change their nature and acquire new senses against the new difficulties in which they are placed, or they multiply poorly and become extinct. A good foundation is laid for their propagation here by our possessing already great numbers of horses of that blood, and by a decided taste and preference for them established among the people. Their patience of heat without injury, their superior wind, fit them better in this and the more southern climates even for the drudgeries of the plough and wagon. Northwardly they will become an object only to persons of taste and fortune, for the saddle and light carriages. To those, and for these uses, their fleetness and beauty will recommend them. Besides these there will be other valuable substitutes when the cultivation of tobacco shall be discontinued such as cotton in the eastern parts of the State, and hemp and flax in the western.

It is not easy to say what are the articles either of necessity, comfort, or luxury, which we cannot raise, and which we therefore shall be under a necessity of importing from abroad, as everything hardier than the olive, and as hardy as the fig, may be raised here in the open air. Sugar, coffee and tea, indeed, are not between these limits; and habit having placed them among the necessaries of life with the wealthy part of our citizens, as long as these habits remain we must go for them to those countries which are able to furnish them.

QUERY XXI

The weights, measures and the currency of the hard money. Some details relating to exchange with Europe

Our weights and measures are the same which are fixed by acts of parliament in England. How it has happened that in this as well as the other American States the nominal value of coin was made to differ from what it was in the country we had left, and to differ among ourselves too, I am not able to say with certainty. I find that in 1631 our house of burgesses desired of the privy council in England, a coin debased to twenty-five per cent; that in 1645 they forbid dealing by barter for tobacco, and established the Spanish piece of eight at six shillings, as the standard of their currency; that in 1655 they changed it to five shillings sterling. In 1680 they sent an address to the king, in consequence of which, by proclamation in 1683, he fixed the value of French crowns, rix dollars, and pieces of eight, at six shillings, and the coin of New England at one shilling. That in 1710, 1714, 1727, and 1762, other regulations were made, which will be better presented to the eye stated in the form of the table on page 165.

The first symptom of the depreciation of our present paper money, was that of silver dollars selling at six shillings, which had before been worth but five shilling and ninepence. The assembly thereupon raised them by law to six shillings. As the dollar is now likely to become the money-unit of American, as it passes at this rate in some of our sister States, and as it facilitates their computation in pounds and shillings, &c., converso, this seems to be more convenient than its former denomination. But as this particular coin now stands higher

	1710	1714	1727	1762
Guineas	....	26s.		
British gold coin not milled, gold coin of Spain and France, chequins, Arabian gold. moidores of Portugal	....	5s. dwt.		
Coined gold of the empire	....	5s. dwt.	....	4s. 3d. dwt.
English milled silver money, in proportion to the crown, at	....	5s. 10d.	6s. 3d.	
Pieces of eight of Mexico, Seville & Pillar, ducatoons of Flanders, French ecus, or silver Louis, crusados of Portugal	3¾d. dwt.	....	4d. dwt.	
Peru pieces, cross dollars, and old rix dollars of the empire	3½d. dwt.	....	3¾d. dwt.	
Old British silver coin not milled	....	3¾d. dwt.		

than any other in the proportion of one hundred and thirty-three and a half to one hundred and twenty-five, or sixteen to fifteen, it will be necessary to raise the others in proportion.

QUERY XXII

The public Income and expenses

The nominal amount of these varying constantly and rapidly, with the constant and rapid depreciation of our paper money, it becomes impracticable to say what they are. We find ourselves cheated in every essay by the depreciation intervening between the declaration of the tax and its actual receipt. It will therefore be more satisfactory to consider what our income may be when we shall find means of collecting what our people may spare. I should estimate the whole taxable property of this State at an hundred millions of dollars, or thirty millions of pounds, our money. One per cent on this, compared with anything we ever yet paid, would be deemed a very heavy tax. Yet I think that those who manage well, and use reasonable economy, could pay one and a half per cent, and maintain their household comfortably in the meantime, without aliening any part of their principal, and that the people would submit to this willingly for the purpose of supporting their present contest. We may say, then, that we could raise, from one million to one million and a half of dollars annually, that is from three hundred to four hundred and fifty thousand pounds, Virginia money.

Of our expenses it is equally difficult to give an exact state, and for the same reason. They are mostly stated in paper money, which varying continually, the legislature endeavors at every session, by new corrections, to adapt the nominal sums to the value it is wished they would bear. I will state them, therefore, in real coin, at the point at which they endeavor to keep them:

	DOLLARS
The annual expenses of the general assembly are about	20,000
The governor	3,333⅓
The council of state	10,666⅔
Their clerks	1,166⅔
Eleven judges	11,000
The clerk of the chancery	666⅔
The attorney general	1,000
Three auditors and a solicitor	5,333⅓
Their clerks	2,000
The treasurer	2,000
His clerks	2,000
The keeper of the public jail	1,000
The public printer	1,666⅔
Clerks of the inferior courts	43,333⅓
Public levy; this is chiefly for the expenses of criminal justice	40,000
County levy, for bridges, court-houses, prisons, &c.	40,000
Members of Congress	7,000
Quota of the federal civil list, supposed one-sixth of about $78,000	13,000
Expenses of collecting, six per cent on the above	12,310
The clergy receive only voluntary contributions; suppose them on an average one-eighth of a dollar a tythe on 200,000 tythes	25,000
Contingencies, to make round numbers not far from truth	7,523⅓
	$250,000

or 53,571 guineas. This estimate is exclusive of the military expense. That varies with the force actually employed, and in time of peace will probably be little or nothing. It is exclusive also of the public debts, which are growing while I am writing, and cannot therefore be now fixed. So it is of the maintenance of the poor, which being merely a matter of charity cannot be deemed expended in the administration of government. And if we strike out the $25,000 for the services of the clergy, which neither makes part of that administration, more than what is paid to physicians, or lawyers, and being voluntary, is either much or nothing as everyone pleases, it leaves $225,000, equal to 48,208 guineas, the real cost of the apparatus of government with us. This divided among the actual inhabitants of our country, comes to about two-fifths of a dollar, twenty-one pence sterling, or forty-two sols, the price which each pays annually for the protection of the residue of his property, and the other advantages of a free government. The public revenues of Great Britain divided in like manner on its inhabitants would be sixteen times greater. Deducting even the double of the expenses of government, as before estimated, from the million and a half of dollars which we before supposed might be annually paid without distress, we may conclude that this State can contribute one million of dollars annually towards supporting the federal army, paying the federal debt, building a federal navy, or opening roads, clearing rivers, forming safe ports, and other useful works.

To this estimate of our abilities, let me add a word as to the application of them. If, when cleared of the present contest, and of the debts with which that will charge us, we come to measure force hereafter with any European power. Such events are devoutly to be deprecated. Young as we are, and with such a country before us to fill with people and with happiness, we should point in that direction the whole generative force of nature, wasting none of it in efforts of mutual destruction. It should be our endeavor to cultivate the peace and friendship of every nation, even of that which has injured us most, when we shall have carried our point against her. Our interest will be to throw open the doors of commerce, and to knock off all its shackles, giving perfect freedom to all persons for the vent of whatever they may chuse to bring into our ports, and asking the same in theirs. Never was so much false arithmetic employed on any subject, as that which has been employed to persuade nations that it is their interest to go to war. Were the money which it has cost to gain, at the close of a long war, a little town, or a little territory, the right to cut wood here, or to catch fish there, expended in improving what they already possess, in making roads, opening rivers, building ports, improving the arts, and finding employment for their idle poor, it would render them much stronger, much wealthier and happier. This I hope will be our wisdom. And, perhaps, to remove as much as possible the occasions of making war, it might be better for us to abandon the ocean altogether, that being the element whereon we shall be principally exposed to jostle with other nations; to leave to others to bring what we shall want, and to carry what we can spare. This would make us invulnerable to Europe, by offering none of our property to their prize, and would turn all our citizens to the cultivation of the earth; and, I repeat it again, cultivators of the earth are the most virtuous and independent citizens. It might be time enough to seek employment for them at sea, when the land no longer offers it. But the actual habits of our countrymen attach them to commerce. They will exercise it for themselves. Wars then must sometimes be our lot; and all the wise can do, will be to avoid that half of them which would be produced by our own follies and our own acts of injustice; and to make for the other half the best preparations we can. Of what nature should these be? A land army would be useless for offence, and not the best nor safest instrument of defence. For either of these purposes, the sea is the field on which we should meet an European enemy. On that element it is necessary we should possess some power. To aim at such a navy as the greater nations of Europe possess, would be a foolish and wicked waste of the energies of our countrymen. It would be to pull on our own heads that load of military expense which makes the European laborer go supperless to bed, and moistens his bread with the sweat of his brows. It will be enough if we enable ourselves to prevent insults from those nations of Europe which are weak on the sea, because circumstances exist, which render even the stronger ones weak as to us. Providence has placed their rich-

est and most defenceless possessions at our door; has obliged their most precious commerce to pass, as it were, in review before us. To protect this, or to
assail, a small part only of their naval force will ever be risked across the Atlantic. The dangers to which the elements expose them here are too well known,
and the greater dangers to which they would be exposed at home were any general calamity to involve their whole fleet. They can attack us by detachment
only; and it will suffice to make ourselves equal to what they may detach. Even
a smaller force than they may detach will be rendered equal or superior by
the quickness with which any check may be repaired with us, while losses
with them will be irreparable till too late. A small naval force then is sufficient
for us, and a small one is necessary. What this should be, I will not undertake
to say. I will only say, it should by no means be so great as we are able to
make it. Suppose the million of dollars, or three hundred thousand pounds,
which Virginia could annually spare without distress, to be applied to the
creating a navy. A single year's contribution would build, equip, man, and send
to sea a force which should carry three hundred guns. The rest of the confederacy, exerting themselves in the same proportion, would equip in the same time
fifteen hundred guns more. So that one year's contributions would set up a
navy of eighteen hundred guns. The British ships of the line average seventy-
six guns; their frigates thirty-eight. Eighteen hundred guns then would form a
fleet of thirty ships, eighteen of which might be of the line, and twelve frigates.
Allowing eight men, the British average, for every gun, their annual expense,
including subsistence, clothing, pay, and ordinary repairs, would be about $1,280
for every gun, or $2,304,000 for the whole. I state this only as one year's pos-
sible exertion, without deciding whether more or less than a year's exertion
should be thus applied.

The value of our lands and slaves, taken conjunctly, doubles in about twenty
years. This arises from the multiplication of our slaves, from the extension of
culture, and increased demand for lands. The amount of what may be raised
will of course rise in the same proportion.

QUERY XXIII

*The histories of the State, the memorials published in its name in the time of
its being a colony, and the pamphlets relating to its interior or exterior affairs
present or ancient*

Captain Smith, who next to Sir Walter Raleigh may be considered as the
founder of our colony, has written its history, from the first adventures to it,
till the year 1624. He was a member of the council, and afterwards president
of the colony; and to his efforts principally may be ascribed its support against
the opposition of the natives. He was honest, sensible, and well informed; but
his style is barbarous and uncouth. His history, however, is almost the only
source from which we derive any knowledge of the infancy of our State.

The reverend William Stith, a native of Virginia, and president of its college, has also written the history of the same period, in a large octavo volume of small print. He was a man of classical learning, and very exact, but of no taste in style. He is inelegant, therefore, and his details often too minute to be tolerable, even to a native of the country, whose history he writes.

Beverley, a native also, has run into the other extreme, he has comprised our history from the first propositions of Sir Walter Raleigh to the year 1700, in the hundredth part of the space which Stith employs for the fourth part of the period.

Sir Walter Keith has taken it up at its earliest period, and continued it to the year 1725. He is agreeable enough in style, and passes over events of little importance. Of course he is short and would be preferred by a foreigner.

During the regal government, some contest arose on the exaction of an illegal fee by governor Dinwiddie, and doubtless there were others on other occasions not at present recollected. It is supposed that these are not sufficiently interesting to a foreigner to merit a detail.

The petition of the council and burgesses of Virginia to the king, their memorials to the lords, and remonstrance to the commons in the year 1764, began the present contest; and these having proved ineffectual to prevent the passage of the stamp-act, the resolutions of the house of burgesses of 1765 were passed declaring the independence of the people of Virginia of the parliament of Great Britain, in matters of taxation. From that time till the declaration of independence by Congress in 1776, their journals are filled with assertions of the public rights.

The pamphlets published in this State on the controverted question, were:

1766, An Inquiry into the rights of the British Colonies, by Richard Bland.

1769, The Monitors Letters, by Dr. Arthur Lee.

1774, A summary View of the rights of British America.[1]

1774, Considerations, &c., by Robert Carter Nicholas.

Since the declaration of independence this State has had no controversy with any other, except with that of Pennsylvania, on their common boundary. Some papers on this subject passed between the executive and legislative bodies of the two States, the result of which was a happy accommodation of their rights.

To this account of our historians, memorials, and pamphlets, it may not be unuseful to add a chronological catalogue of American state-papers, as far as I have been able to collect their titles. It is far from being either complete or correct. Where the title alone, and not the paper itself, has come under my observation, I cannot answer for the exactness of the date. Sometimes I have not been able to find any date at all, and sometimes have not been satisfied that such a paper exists. An extensive collection of papers of this description has been for some time in a course of preparation by a gentleman[2] fully equal to the task, and from whom, therefore, we may hope ere long to receive it. In the meantime accept this as the result of my labors, and as closing the tedious detail which you have so undesignedly drawn upon yourself.

[1] By the author of these notes.—T. J.   [2] Mr. Hazard.—T. J.

1496, Mar. 5   Pro Johanne Caboto et filiis suis super terra incognita investiganda.
11. H. 7   12. Ry. 595. 3. Hakl. 4. 2. Mem. A. 409.

1498, Feb. 3   Billa signata anno 13. Henrici septimi. 3. Hakluyt's voiages 5.
13. H. 7

1502, Dec. 19   De potestatibus ad terras incognitas investigandum. 13. Rymer. 37.
18. H. 7

1540, Oct. 17   Commission de François I. à Jacques Catier pour l'establissement
                du Canada. L'Escarbot. 397. 2. Mem. Am. 416.

1548, 2. E. 6   An act against the exaction of money, or any other thing, by any
                officer for license to traffique into Iseland and New-foundland,
                made in An. 2. Edwardi sexti. 3. Hakl. 131.

1578, June 11   The letters-patent granted by her Majestie to Sir Humphrey Gil-
20. El   bert, knight, for the inhabiting and planting of our people in
                America. 3. Hakl. 135.

1583, Feb. 6   Letters-patent of Queen Elizabeth to Adrian Gilbert and others, to
                discover the northwest passage to China. 3. Hakl. 96.

1584, Mar. 25   The letters-patent granted by the Queen's majestie to M. Walter
26 El   Raleigh, now knight, for the discovering and planting of new
                lands and countries, to continue the space of six years and no
                more. 3. Hakl. 243.

Mar. 7, 31. El An assignment by Sir Walter Raleigh for continuing the action of
                inhabiting and planting his people in Virginia. Hakl. 1st ed.
                publ. in 1589. p. 815.

1603, Nov. 8   Lettres de Lieutenant General de l'Acadie et pays circonvoisins
                pour le Sieur de Monts. L'Escarbot. 417.

1606, Apr. 10   Letters-patent to Sir Thomas Gates, Sir George Somers and others
4. Jac. 1   of America. Stith. Apend. No. 1.

1607, Mar. 9   An ordinance and constitution enlarging the council of the two
4. Jac. 1   colonies in Virginia and America, and augmenting their author-
                ity, M. S.

1609, May 23   The second charter to the treasurer and company for Virginia,
7. Jac. 1   erecting them into a body politick. Stith. Ap. 2.

1610, Apr. 10   Letters-patents to the E. of Northampton, granting part of the is-
Jac. 1   land of Newfoundland. 1. Harris. 861.

1611, Mar. 12   A third charter to the treasurer and company for Virginia. Stith.
9. Jac. 1   Ap. 3.

1617, Jac. 1   A commission to Sir Walter Raleigh, Qu.

1620, Apr. 7   Commissio specialis concernens le garbling herbæ Nocotianæ. 17.
18. Jac. 1   Rym. 190.

1620, June 29   A proclamation for restraint of the disordered trading of tobacco.
18. Jac. 1   17. Rym. 233.

1620, Nov. 3   A grant of New-England to the council of Plymouth.
Jac. 1

1621, July 24   An ordinance and constitution of the treasurer, council and com-
Jac. 1   pany in England, for a council of state and general assembly in
                Virginia. Stith. Ap. 4.

1621, Sep. 10   A grant of Nova Scotia to Sir William Alexander. 2. Mem. de
20 Jac. 1   l'Amerique. 193.

1622, Nov. 6   A proclamation prohibiting interloping and disorderly trading to
20 Jac. 1   New England in America. 17. Rym. 416.

De commissione speciali Willelmo Jones militi directa. 17. Rym. 490.   1623, May 9
21 Jac. 1

A grant to Sir Edmund Ployden, of New Albion. Mentioned in Smith's examination. 82.   1623

De commissione Henrico vicecomiti Mandevill et aliis. 17. Rym. 609.   1624, July 15
22. Jac. 1

De commissione speciali concernenti gubernationem in Virginia. 17. Rym. 618.   1624, Aug. 26
22 Jac. 1

A proclamation concerning tobacco. 17. Rym. 621.   1624, Sep. 29
22 Jac. 1

De concessione demiss, Edwardo Ditchfield et aliis. 17. Rym. 633.   1624, Nov. 9
22 Jac. 1

A proclamation for the utter prohibiting the importation and use of all tobacco which is not of the proper growth of the colony of Virginia and the Somer islands, or one of them. 17. Rym. 668.   1625, Mar. 2
22 Jac. 1

De commissione directa Georgio Yardeley militi et aliis. 18. Rym. 311.   1625, Mar. 4
1 Car. 1

Proclamatio de herba Nicotianâ. 18. Rym. 19.   1625, Apr. 9
1 Car. 1

A proclamation for settlinge the plantation of Virginia. 18. Rym. 72.   1625, May 13
1 Car. 1

A grant of the soil, barony, and domains of Nova Scotia to Sir Wm. Alexander of Minstrie. 2. Mem. Am. 226.   1625, July 12

Commissio directa a Johanni Wolstenholme militi et aliis. 18. Rym. 831.   1626, Jan. 31
2 Car. 1

A proclamation touching tobacco. Rym. 848.   1626, Feb. 17
2 Car. 1

A grant of Massachusetts bay by the council of Plymouth to Sir Henry Roswell and others.   1627, Mar. 19
qu? 2 Car. 1

De concessione commissionis specialis proconcilio in Virginia. 18. Rym. 980.   1627, Mar. 26
3 Car. 1

De proclamatione de signatione de tobacco. 18. Rym. 886.   1627, Mar. 30
3 Car. 1

De proclamatione pro ordinatione de tobacco. 18. Rym. 920.   1627, Aug. 9
3 Car. 1

A confirmation of the grant of Massachusetts bay by the crown.   1628, Mar. 4
3 Car. 1

The capitulation of Quebec. Champlain pert. 2. 216. 2. Mem. Am. 489.   1629, Aug. 19

A proclamation concerning tobacco. 19. Rym. 235.   1630, Jan. 6
5 Car. 1

Conveyance of Nova Scotia (Port-royal excepted) by Sir William Alexander to Sir Claude St. Etienne Lord of la Tour and of Uarre and to his son Sir Charles de St. Etienne Lord of St. Denniscourt, on condition that they continue subjects to the king of Scotland under the great seal of Scotland.   1630, Apr. 30

A proclamation forbidding the disorderly trading with the savages in New England in America, especially the furnishing the natives in those and other parts of America by the English with weapons and habiliments of warre. 19. Ry. 210. 3. Rushw. 82.   1630-31, Nov. 24. 6 Car. 1

1630, Dec. 5 6 Car. 1	A proclamation prohibiting the selling arms, &c. to the savages in America. Mentioned 3. Rushw. 75.
1630, Car. 1	A grant of Connecticut by the council of Plymouth to the E. of Warwick.
1630, Car. 1	A confirmation by the crown of the grant of Connecticut [said to be in the petty-bag office in England.]
1631, Mar. 19 6 Car. 1	A conveiance of Connecticut by the E. of Warwick to Lord Say, and Seal, and others. Smith's examination, Appendix No. 1.
1631, June 27 7 Car. 1	A special commission to Edward, Earle of Dorsett, and others, for the better plantation of the colony of Virginia. 19. Ry. 301.
1632, June 29 7 Car. 1	Litere continentes promissionem regis ad tradenum castrum et habitationem de Kebec in Canada ad regem Francorum. 19. Ry. 303.
1632, Mar. 29 8 Car. 1	Traité entre le roy Louis XIII. et Charles roi d'Angleterre pour la restitution de la nouvelle France, la Cadie et Canada et des navires et merchandises pris de part et d'autrie. Fait a St. Germain. 19. Ry. 361. 2. Mem. Am. 5.
1632, June 20 8 Car. 1	A grant of Maryland to Cæcilius Calvert, baron of Baltimore in Ireland.
1633, July 3 9 Car. 1	A petition of the planters of Virginia against the grant to lord Baltimore.
1633, July 3	Order of council upon the dispute between the Virginia planters and lord Baltimore. Votes of repres. Pennsylvania. V.
1633, Aug. 13 9 Car. 1	A proclamation to prevent abuses growing by the unordered retailing of tobacco. Mentioned 3. Rushw. 191.
1633, Sept. 23 9 Car. 1	A special commission to Thomas Young to search, discover and find out what ports are not yet inhabited in Virginia and America and other parts thereunto adjoining. 19. Ry. 472.
1633, Oct. 13 9 Car. 1	A proclamation for preventing of the abuses growing by the unordered retailing of tobacco. 19. Ry. 474.
1633, Mar. 13 Cer. 1	A proclamation restraining the abusive venting of tobacco. 19. Rym. 522.
1634, May 19 10 Car. 1	A proclamation concerning the landing of tobacco, and also forbidding the planting thereof in the king's dominions. 19. Ry. 553.
1634, Car. 1	A commission to the Archbishop of Canterbury and 11 others, for governing the American colonies.
1634, June 19 10 Car. 1	A commission concerning tobacco. M. S.
1635, July 18 11 Car. 1	A commission from Lord Say, and Seal, and others, to John Winthrop to be governor of Connecticut. Smith's App.
1635, Car. 1	A grant to Duke Hamilton.
1636, Apr. 2 12 Car. 1	De commissione speciali Johanni Harvey militi to pro meliori regemine coloniae in Virginia. 20. Ry. 3.
1637, Mar. 14 Car. 1	A proclamation concerning tobacco. Title in 3. Rush. 617.
1636-7, Mar. 16. 12 Car. 1	De commissione speciali Georgio domino Goring et aliis concessâ concernente venditionem de tobacco absque licentiâ regiâ. 20. Ry. 116.

A proclamation against disorderly transporting his Majesty's subjects to the plantations within the parts of America. 20. Ry. 143. 3. Rush. 409. — 1637, Apr. 30 13 Car. 1

An order of the privy council to stay 8 ships now in the Thames from going to New England. 3. Rush. 409. — 1637, May 1 13 Car. 1

A warrant of the Lord Admiral to stop unconformable ministers from going beyond the sea. 3. Rush. 410. — 1637, Car. 1

Order of council upon Claiborne's petition against Lord Baltimore. Votes of representatives of Pennsylvania. vi. — 1638, Apr. 4 Car. 1

An order of the king and council that the attorney general draw up a proclamation to prohibit transportation of passengers to New England without license. 3. Rush. 718. — 1638, Apr. 6 14 Car. 1

A proclamation to restrain the transporting of passengers and provisions to New England without license. 20. Ry. 223. — 1638, May 1 14 Car. 1

A proclamation concerning tobacco. Title 4. Rush. 1060. — 1639, Mar. 25 Car. 1

A proclamation declaring his majesty's pleasure to continue his commission and letters patents for licensing retailers of tobacco. 20. Ry. 348. — 1639, Aug. 19 15 Car. 1

De commissione speciali Henrico Ashton armigero ét aliis ad amovendum Henricum Hawley gubernatorem de Barbadoes. 20. Rym. 357. — 1639, Dec. 16 15 Car. 1

A proclamation concerning retailers of tobacco. 4. Rush. 966. — 1639, Car. 1

De constitutione gubernatoris et concilii pro Virginia. 20. Ry. 484. — 1641, Aug. 9 17 Car. 1

Articles of union and confederacy entered into by Massachusetts, Plymouth, Connecticut and New-haven. 1. Neale. 223. — 1643, Car. 1

Deed from George Fenwick to the old Connecticut jurisdiction. — 1644, Car. 1

An ordinance of the lords and commons assembled in parliament, for exempting from custom and imposition all commodities exported for, or imported from New England, which has been very prosperous and without any public charge to this State, and is likely to prove very happy for the propagation of the gospel in those parts. Tit. in Amer. library 90.5. No date. But seems by the neighbouring articles to have been in 1644.

An act for charging of tobacco brought from New England with custom and excise. Title in American library. 99. 8. — 1644, June 20 Car. 2

An act for the advancing and regulating the trade of this commonwealth. Tit. in Amer. libr. 99. 9. — 1644, Aug. 1 Car. 2

Grant of the Northern neck of Virginia to Lord Hopton, Lord Jermyn, Lord Culpepper, Sir John Berkley, Sir William Moreton, Sir Dudley Wyatt, and Thomas Culpepper. — Sep. 18 1 Car. 2

An act prohibiting trade with the Barbadoes, Virginia, Bermudas and Antego Scobell's Acts. 1027. — 1650, Oct. 3 2 Car. 2

A declaration of Lord Willoughby, governor of Barbadoes, and of his council, against an act of parliament of 3d of October, 1650. 4. Polit. register. 2. cited from 4 Neal. hist. of the Puritans. App. No. 12 but not there. — 1650, Car. 2

A final settlement of boundaries between the Dutch New Netherlands and Connecticut. — 1650, Car. 2

1651, Sept. 26 3 Car. 2	Instructions for Captain Robert Dennis, Mr. Richard Bennet, Mr. Thomas Stagge, and Captain William Claibourn, appointed commissioners for the reducing of Virginia and the inhabitants thereof to their due obedience to the commonwealth of England. 1 Thurloe's state papers, 197.
1651, Oct. 9 8 Car. 2	An act for increase of shipping and encouragement of the navigation of this nation. Scobell's acts, 1449.
1651-2, Mar. 12. 4 Car. 2	Articles agreed on and concluded at James citie in Virginia for the surrendering and settling of that plantation under the obedience and government of the commonwealth of England, by the commissioners of the council of state, by authoritie of the parliament of England, and by the grand assembly of the governor, council, and burgesse of that state. M. S. [Ante. p. 206.]
1651-2, Mar. 12. 4 Car. 1	An act of indempnitie made at the surrender of the country [of Virginia.] [Ante p. 206.]
1654, Aug. 16	Capitulation de Port Royal. Mem. Am. 507.
1655, Car. 2	A proclamation of the protector relating to Jamaica. 3 Thurl. 75.
1655, Sep. 26 7 Car. 2	The protector to the commissioners of Maryland. A letter. 4 Thurl. 55.
1655, Oct. 8 7 Car. 2	An instrument made at the council of Jamaica, Oct. 8, 1655, for the better carrying on of affairs there. 4 Thurl. 17.
1655, Nov. 3	Treaty of Westminster between France and England. 6. corps diplom. part 2. p. 121. 2 Mem. Am. 10.
1656, Mar. 27 8 Car. 2	The assembly at Barbadoes to the protector. 4 Thurl. 651.
1656, Aug. 9	A grant by Cromwell to Sir Charles de Saint Etienne, a baron of Scotland, Crowne and Temple. A French translation of it. 2 Mem. Am. 511.
1656, Car. 2	A paper concerning the advancement of trade, 5 Thurl. 80.
1656, Car. 2	A brief narration of the English rights to the Northern parts of America. 5 Thurl. 81.
1656, Oct. 10 8 Car. 2	Mr. R. Bennet and Mr. S. Matthew to Secretary Thurlow. 5 Thurl. 482.
1656, Oct. 10 8 Car. 2	Objections against the Lord Baltimore's patent, and reasons why the government of Maryland should not be put into his hands. 5 Thurl. 482.
1656, Oct. 10 8 Car. 2	A paper relating to Maryland. 5 Thurl. 483.
1656, Oct. 10 8 Car. 2	A breviet of the proceedings of the lord Baltimore and his officers and compliers in Maryland, against the authority of the parliament of the commonwealth of England and against his highness the lord protector's authority, laws and government. 5 Thurl. 486.
1656, Oct. 15 8 Car. 2	The assembly of Virginia to secretary Thurlow. 5 Thurl. 497.
1657, Apr. 4 9 Car. 2	The governor of Barbadoes to the protector. 6 Thurl. 69.
1661, Car. 2	Petition of the general court at Hartford upon Connecticut for charter. Smith's exam. App. 4.

Charter of the colony of Connecticut. Smith's exam. App. 6.　　　1662, Apr. 23
　　　　　　　　　　　　　　　　　　　　　　　　　　　　　　14 Car. 2

The first charter granted by Charles II. to the proprietaries of　1662-2, Mar.
Carolina, to wit, to the Earl of Clarendon, Duke of Albemarle,　24
Lord Craven, Lord Berkeley, Lord Ashley, Sir George Carteret,　Apr. 4. 15 C.
Sir William Berkeley, and Sir John Colleton. 4 Mem. Am. 554.　2

The concessions and agreement of the lords proprietors of the　1664, Feb. 10
provinces of New Cæsarea, or New Jersey, to and with all and
every of the adventurers and all such as shall settle or plant
there. Smith's New Jersey. App. 1.

A grant of the colony of New York to the Duke of York.　　　1664, Mar. 12
　　　　　　　　　　　　　　　　　　　　　　　　　　　　　　20 Car. 2

A commission to Colonel Nichols and others to settle disputes in　1664, Apr. 26
New England. Hutch. Hist. Mass. Bay, App. 537.　　　　　　16 Car. 2

The commission to Sir Robert Carre and others to put the Duke of　1664, Apr. 26
York in possession of New York, New Jersey, and all other
lands thereunto appertaining.

Sir Robert Carre and others proclamation to the inhabitants of
New York, New Jersey, &c. Smith's N. J. 36.

Deeds of lease and release of New Jersey by the Duke of York to　1664, June 23
Lord Berkeley and Sir George Carteret.　　　　　　　　　24. 16 Car. 2

A conveïance of the Delaware counties to William Penn.

Letters between Stuyvesant and Colonel Nichols on the English　⌠ 1664, Aug.
right. Smith's N. J. 37—42.　　　　　　　　　　　　　　⎰ 19-29, 20-
　　　　　　　　　　　　　　　　　　　　　　　　　　　　⎱ 30, 24
　　　　　　　　　　　　　　　　　　　　　　　　　　　　　Aug. 25.
　　　　　　　　　　　　　　　　　　　　　　　　　　　　⌞ Sept. 4.

Treaty between the English and Dutch for the surrender of the　1664, Aug. 27
New Netherlands. Sm. N. J. 42.

Nicoll's commission to Sir. Robert Carre to reduce the Dutch on　Sept. 3
Delaware bay. Sm. N. J. 47.

Instructions to Sir Robert Carre for reducing of Delaware bay and
settling the people there under his majesty's obedience. Sm.
N. J. 47.

Articles of capitulation between Sir Robert Carre and the Dutch　1664, Oct. 1
and Swedes on Delaware bay and Delaware river. Sm. N. J. 49.

The determination of the commissioners of the boundary between　1664, Dec. 1
the Duke of York and Connecticut. Sm. Ex. Ap. 9.　　　　16 Car. 2

The New Haven case. Smith's Ex. Ap. 20.　　　　　　　　1664

The second charter granted by Charles II. to the same proprietors　1665, June 13
of Carolina. 4. Mem. Am. 586.　　　　　　　　　　　　24. 17 Car. 2

Declaration de guerre par la France contre l'Angleterre. 3. Mem.　1666, Jan. 26
Am. 123.

Declaration of war by the king of England against the king of　1666, Feb. 9
France.　　　　　　　　　　　　　　　　　　　　　　　17 Car. 2

The treaty of peace between France and England made at Breda. 7　1667, July 31
Corps, Dipl. part 1. p. 51. 2. Mem. Am. 32.

The treaty of peace and alliance between England and the United　1667, July 31
Provinces made at Breda. 7 Cor. Dip. p. 1. d. 44. 2. Mem. Am.
40.

1667-8, Feb. 17	Acte de las cession de l'Acadie au roi de France. 2. Mem. Am. 40.
1668, April 21	Directions from the governor and council of New York for a better settlement of the government on Delaware. Sm. N. J. 51.
1668	Lovelace's order for customs at the Hoarkills. Sm. N. J. 55.
16- May 8 21 Car. 2	A confirmation of the grant of the northern neck of Virginia to the Earl of St. Albans, Lord Berkeley, Sir William Moreton and John Tretheway.
1672	Incorporation of the town of Newcastle or Amstell.
1673, Feb. 25 25 Car. 2	A demise of the colony of Virginia to the Earl of Arlington and Lord Culpepper for 31 years. M S.
1673-4	Treaty at London between king Charles II. and the Dutch. Article VI.
	Remonstrance against the two grants of Charles II. of Northern and Southern Virginia. Ment[d]. Beverley 65.
1674, July 13	Sir George Carteret's instructions to Governor Carteret.
1674, Nov. 9	Governor Andros's proclamation on taking possession of Newcastle for the Duke of York. Sm. N. J. 78.
1675, Oct. 1 27 Car. 2	A proclamation for prohibiting the importation of commodities of Europe into any of his majesty's plantations in Africa, Asia, or America, which were not laden in England; and for putting all other laws relating to the trade of the plantations in effectual execution.
1676, Mar. 3	The concessions and agreements of the proprietors, freeholders and inhabitants of the province of West New Jersey in America. Sm. N. J. App. 2.
1676, July 1	A deed quintipartite for the division of New Jersey.
1676, Aug. 18	Letter from the proprietors of New Jersey to Richard Hartshorne. Sm. N. J. 80.
	Proprietors instructions to James Wasse and Richard Hartshorne. Sm. N. J. 83.
1676, Oct. 10 28 Car. 2	The charter of king Charles II. to his subjects of Virginia. M S.
1676	Cautionary epistle from the trustees of Byllinge's part of New Jersey. Sm. N. J. 84.
1677, Sept. 10	Indian deed for the lands between Rankokos creek and Timber creek, in New Jersey.
1677, Sept. 27	Indian deed for lands from Oldman's creek to Timber creek, in New Jersey.
1677, Oct. 10	Indian deed for the lands from Rankokos creek to Assunpink creek, in New Jersey.
1678, Dec. 5	The will of Sir George Carteret, sole proprietor of East Jersey ordering the same to be sold.
1680, Feb. 16	An order of the king in council for the better encouragement of all his majesty's subjects in their trade to his majesty's plantations, and for the better information of all his majesty's loving subjects in these matters—Lond. Gaz. No. 1596. Title in Amer. library. 134. 6.
1680	Arguments against the customs demanded in West New Jersey by the governor of New York, addressed to the Duke's commissioners. Sm. N. J. 117.

Extracts of proceedings of the committee of trade and plantations; copies of letters, reports, &c., between the board of trade, Mr. Penn, Lord Baltimore and Sir John Werden, in the behalf of the Duke of York and the settlement of the Pennsylvania boundaries by the L. C. J. North. Votes of Repr. Pennsyl. vii-xiii.

> 1680, June 14. 23. 25 Oct. 16. Nov. 4. 8 11. 18. 20 23. Dec. 16. 1680-1, Jan. 15. 22. Feb. 24.

A grant of Pennsylvania to William Penn. Votes of Represen. Pennsyl. xviii. — 1631, Mar. 4 Car. 2

The king's declaration to the inhabitants and planters of the province of Pennsylvania. Vo. Repr. Penn. xxiv. — 1681, Apr. 2

Certain conditions or concessions agreed upon by William Penn, proprietary and governor of Pennsylvania, and those who are the adventurers and purchasers in the same province. Votes of Rep. Pennsyl. xxiv. — 1681, July 11

Fundamental laws of the province of West New Jersey. Sm. N. J. 126. — 1681, Nov. 9

The methods of the commissioners for settling and regulation of lands in New Jersey. Sm. N. J. 130. — 1681-2, Jan. 14

Indentures of lease and release by the executors of Sir George Carteret to William Penn and 11 others, conveying East Jersey. — 1681-2, F. 1 2

The Duke of York's fresh grant of East New Jersey to the 24 proprietors. — 1682, Mar. 14

The frame of the government of the province of Pennsylvania, in America. Votes of Repr. Penn. xxvii. — 1682, Apr. 25

The Duke of York's deed for Pennsylvania. Vo. Repr. Penn. xxxv. — 1682, Aug. 21

The Duke of York's deed for the feoffment of Newcastle and twelve miles circle to William Penn. Vo. Repr. Penn. — 1682, Aug. 24

The Duke of York's deed of feoffment of a tract of land 12 miles south from Newcastle to the Whorekills, to William Penn. Vo. Repr. Penn. xxxvii. — 1682, Aug. 24

A commission to Thomas Lord Culpepper to be lieutenant and governor-general of Virginia. M. S. — 1682, Nov. 27 34 Car. 2

An act of union for annexing and uniting of the counties of Newcastle, Jones's and Whorekill's, alias Deal, to the province of Pennsylvania, and of naturalization of all foreigners in the province and counties aforesaid. — 1682, 10th mon. 6th day

An act of settlement. — 1682, Dec. 6

The frame of the government of the province of Pennsylvania and territories thereunto annexed in America. — 1683, Apr. 2

Proceedings of the committee of trade and Plantations in the dispute between Lord Baltimore and Mr. Penn. Vo. R. P. xiii-xviii.
{ 1683, Apr. 17. 27 May 30. June 12.
1684, Feb. 12. July 2, 16, 23, Sept. 30. Dec. 9.
1685, Mar. 17 Aug. 18, 26 Sept. 2 Oct. 8, 17, 31 Nov. 7

A commission by the proprietors of East New Jersey to Robert Barclay to be governor. Sm. N. J. 166. — 1683, July 17

An order of council for issuing a quo warranto against the charter of the colony of the Massachusetts bay in New England, with — 1683, July 26 35 Car. 2

his majesty's declaration that in case the said corporation of Massachusetts bay shall before prosecution had upon the same quo warranto make a full submission and entire resignation to his royal pleasure, he will then regulate their charter in such a manner as shall be for his service and the good of that colony. Title in American library. 139, 6.

1683, Sept. 28   A commission to Lord Howard of Effingham to be lieutenant and
35 Car. 2   governor general of Virginia. M S.

1684, May 3   The humble address of the chief governor, council and representa-
                  tives of the island of Nevis, in the West Indies, presented to his
                  majesty by Colonel Netheway and Captain Jefferson, at Windsor,
                  May 3, 1684. Title in Amer. libr. 142. 3. cites Lond. Gaz. No.
                  1927.

1684, Aug. 2   A treaty with the Indians at Albany.

1686, Nov. 16   A treaty of neutrality for America between France and England. 7
                  Corps Dipl. part 2, p. 44. 2. Mem. Am. 40.

1687, Jan. 20   By the king, a proclamation for the more effectual reducing and
                  suppressing of pirates and privateers in America, as well on the
                  sea as on the land in great numbers, committing frequent rob-
                  beries and piracies, whith hath occasioned a great prejudice and
                  obstruction to trade and commerce, and given a great scandal
                  and disturbance to our government in those parts. Title Amer.
                  libr. 147. 2. cites Lond. Gaz. No. 2315.

1687, Feb. 12   Constitution of the council of proprietors of West Jersey. Smith's
                  N. Jersey. 199.

1687, qu. Sept.   A confirmation of the grant of the Northern neck of Virginia to
27. 4. Jac. 2   Lord Culpepper.

1687, Sept. 5   Governor Coxe's declaration to the council of proprietors of West
                  Jersey. Sm. N. J. 190.

1687, Dec. 16   Provisional treaty of Whitehall concerning America between
                  France and England. 2 Mem. de l'Am. 89.

1687   Governor Coxe's narrative relating to the division line, directed to
                  the council of proprietors of West Jersey. Sm. App. No. 4.

1687   The representation of the council of proprietors of West Jersey to
                  Governor Burnet. Smith. App. No. 5.

                  The remonstrance and petition of the inhabitants of East New
                  Jersey to the king. Sm. App. No. 8.

                  The memorial of the proprietors of East New Jersey to the Lords
                  of trade. Sm. App. No. 9.

1778, Sept. 5   Agreement of the line of partition between East and West New
                  Jersey. Smith's N. J. 196.

1691   Conveyance of the government of West Jersey and territories, by
                  Dr. Coxe, to the West Jersey society.

1691, Oct. 7   A charter granted by King William and Queen Mary to the in-
                  habitants of the province of Massachusetts bay, in New England.
                  2 Mem. de l'Am. 593.

1696, Nov. 7   The frame of government of the province of Pennsylvania and
                  the territories thereunto belonging, passed by Gov. Markham.
                  Nov. 7, 1696.

The treaty of peace between France and England, made at Rys-   1697, Sept. 20
wick. 7 Corps Dipl. part 2. p. 399. 2 Mem. Am. 89.

The opinion and answer of the Lords of trade to the memorial of   1699, July 5
the proprietors of East N. Jersey. Sm. App. No. 10.

The memorial of the proprietors of East New Jersey to the Lords   1700, Jan. 15
of trade. Sm. App. No. 11.

The petition of the proprietors of East and West New Jersey to the
Lords justices of England. Sm. App. No. 12.

A confirmation of the boundary between the colonies of New York   1700, W. 3
and Connecticut, by the crown.

The memorial of the proprietors of East and West New Jersey to   1701, Aug. 12
the king. Sm. App. No. 14.

Representation of the Lords of trade to the Lords justices. Sm.   1701, Oct. 2
App. No. 18.

A treaty with the Indians.   1701

Report of Lords of trade to king William, of draughts of a com-   1701-2, Jan. 6
mission and instructions for a governor of N. Jersey. Sm. N. J.
262.

Surrender from the proprietors of E. and W. N. Jersey, of their   1702, Apr. 15
pretended right of government to her majesty Queen Anne. Sm.
N. J. 211.

The Queen's acceptance of the surrender of government of East   1702, Apr. 17
and West Jersey. Sm. N. J. 219.

Instructions to lord Cornbury. Sm. N. J. 230.   1702, Nov. 16

A commission from Queen Anne to Lord Cornbury, to be captain   1702, Dec. 5
general and governor in chief of New Jersey. Sm. N. J. 220.

Recognition by the council of proprietors of the true boundary of   1703, June 27
the deeds of Sept. 10, and Oct. 10, 1677, (New Jersey.) Sm. N. J.
96.

Indian deeds for the lands above the falls of the Delaware in West   1703
Jersey.

Indian deed for the lands at the head of Rankokus river, in West
Jersey.

A proclamation by Queen Anne, for settling and ascertaining the   1704, June 18
current rates of foreign coins in America. Sm. N. J. 281.

Additional instructions to Lord Cornbury. Sm. N. S. 235.   1705, May 3
Additional instructions to Lord Cornbury. Sm. N. J. 258.   1707, May 3
Additional instructions to Lord Cornbury. Sm. N. J. 259.   1707, Nov. 20

An answer by the council of proprietors for the western division of   1707
N. Jersey, to questions proposed to them by Lord Cornbury. Sm.
N. J. 285.

Instructions to Colonel Vetch in his negotiations with the gov-   1708-9, Feb.
ernors of America. Sm. N. J. 364.   28

Instructions to the governor of New Jersey and New York. Sm. J.   1708-9, Feb.
361.   28

Earl of Dartmouth's letter to governor Hunter.   1710, Aug.

Premiers propositions de la France. 6. Lamberty. 669, 2 Mem. Am.   1711, Apr. 22
341.

Réponses de la France aux demandes préliminaries de la Grande   1711, Oct. 8
Bretagne. 6 Lamb. 681. 2 Mem. Amer. 344.

Sept. 27 1711, —— Oct. 8	Demandes préliminaries plus particulieres de la Grande-Bretagne, avec les réponses. 2 Mem. de l'Am. 346.
Sept. 27 1711, —— Oct. 8	L'acceptation de la part de la Grande-Bretagne. 2 Mem. Am. 356.
1711, Dec. 23	The Queen's instructions to the Bishop of Bristol and Earl of Stafford, her plenipotentiaries, to treat for a general peace. 6 Lamberty, 744. 2. Mem. Am. 358.
May 24 1712, —— June 10	A memorial of Mr. St. John to the Marquis de Torci, with regard to North America, to commerce, and to the suspension of arms. 7. Recueil de Lamberty 161, 2 Mem. de l'Amer. 376.
1712, June 10	Réponse du roi de France au memoire de Londres. 7. Lamberty, p. 163. 2. Mem. Am. 380.
1712, Aug. 19	Traité pour une suspension d'armes entre Louis XIV. roi de France, and Anne, reign de la Grande-Bretagne, fait à Paris. 8. Corps Diplom. part 1. p. 308. 2. Mem. d'Am. 104.
1712, Sept. 10	Offers of France to England, demands of England, and the answers of France. 7. Rec. de Lamb. 461. 2 Mem. Am. 390.
Mar. 31 1713, —— April 11	Traité de paix et d'amitié entre Louis XIV. roi de France, et Anne, reine de la Grande-Bretagne, fait à Utrecht. 15 Corps Diplomatique de Dumont, 339. id. Latin. 2 Actes et memoires de la pais d'Utrecht, 457. id. Lat. Fr. 2. Mem. Am. 113.
Mar. 31 1713, —— April 11	Traité de navigation et de commerce entre Louis XIV. roi de France, et Anne, reine de la Grande-Bretagne. Fait à Utrecht. 8 Corps Dipl. part 1. p. 345. 2 Mem. de l'Am. 137.
1726	A treaty with the Indians.
1728. Jan.	The petition of the representatives of the province of New Jersey, to have a distinct governor. Sm. N. J. 421.
1732, G. 2.	Deed of release by the government of Connecticut to that of New York.
1732, June 9 20. 5 Geo. 2	The charter granted by George II. for Georgia. 4. Mem. de l'Am. 617.
1733	Petition of Lord Fairfax, that a commission might issue for running and marking the dividing line between his district and the province of Virginia.
1733, Nov. 29	Order of the king in council for commissioners to survey and settle the said dividing line between the proprietary and royal territory.
1736, Aug. 5	Report of the Lords of trade relating to the separating the government of the province of New Jersey from New York. Sm. N. J. 423.
1737, Aug. 10	Survey and report of the commissioners appointed on the part of the crown to settle the line between the crown and Lord Fairfax.
1737, Aug. 11	Survey and report of the commissioners appointed on the part of Lord Fairfax to settle the line between the crown and him.
1738, Dec. 21	Order of reference of the surveys between the crown and Lord Fairfax to the council for plantation affairs.
1744, June	Treaty with the Indians of the six nations at Lancaster.
1745, Apr. 6	Report of the council for plantation affairs, fixing the head springs

of Rappahanoc and Potomac, and a commission to extend the line.

Order of the king in council confirming the said report of the council for plantation affairs. — 1745, Apr. 11

Articles préliminaries pour parvenir à la paix, signés à Aix-la-Chapelle entre les ministres de France, de la Grande-Bretagne, et des Province-Unies des Pays-Bas. 2 Mem de l'Am. 159. — 1748, Apr. 3●

Declaration des ministres de France, de la Grande-Bretagne, et des Provinces-Unies des Pays-Bas, pour rectifier les articles I. et II. des préliminaries. 2. Mem. Am. 165. — 1748, May 21

The general and definitive treaty of peace concluded at Aix-la-Chapelle, Lon. Mag. 1748. 503. French 2. Mem. Am. 169. — 1748, Oct. 7-18. 22. G. 2

A treaty with the Indians. — 1754

A conference between governor Bernard and Indian nations at Burlington. Sm. N. J. 449. — 1758, Aug. 7

A conference between governor Denny, governor Bernard, and others, and Indian nations at Easton. Sm. N. J. 455. — 1758, Oct. 8

The capitulation of Niagara. — 1759, July 25 33. G. 2

The king's proclamation promising lands to soldiers. — 175-

The definitive treaty concluded at Paris. Lon. Mag. 1763. 149. — 1763, Feb. 10 3. G. 3

A proclamation for regulating the cessions made by the last treaty of peace. Guth. Georgr. Gram. 623. — 1763, Oct. 7 G. 3

The king's proclamation against settling on any lands on the waters westward of the Alleghany. — 1763

Deed from the six nations of Indians to William Trent, and others, for lands betwixt the Ohio and Monongahela. View of the title to Indiana. Phil. Steiner and Cist. 1776. — 1768, Nov. 3

Deed from the six nations of Indians to the crown for certain lands and settling a boundary. M S. — 1768, Nov. 5

DRAFT OF A CONSTITUTION FOR VIRGINIA [1]
June, 1783

To the citizens of the commonwealth of Virginia, and all others whom it may concern, the delegates for the said commonwealth in Convention assembled, send greeting:

It is known to you and to the world, that the government of Great Britain, with which the American States were not long since connected, assumed over them an authority unwarrantable and oppressive; that they endeavored to enforce this authority by arms, and that the States of New Hampshire, Massachusetts, Rhode Island, Connecticut, New York, New Jersey, Pennsylvania, Delaware, Maryland, Virginia, North Carolina, South Carolina, and Georgia, considering resistance, with all its train of horrors, as a lesser evil than abject submission, closed in the appeal to arms. It hath pleased the Sovereign Disposer of all human events to give to this appeal an issue favorable to the rights of the States; to enable them to reject forever all dependence on a government which had shown itself so capable of abusing the trusts reposed in it; and to obtain from that government a solemn and explicit acknowledgment that they are free, sovereign, and independent States. During the progress of that war, through which we had to labor for the establishment of our rights, the legislature of the commonwealth of Virginia found it necessary to make a temporary organization of government for preventing anarchy, and pointing our efforts to the two important objects of war against our invaders, and peace and happiness among ourselves. But this, like all other acts of legislation, being subject to change by subsequent legislatures, possessing equal powers with themselves; it has been thought expedient, that it should receive those amendments which time and trial have suggested, and be rendered permanent by a power superior to that of the ordinary legislature. The general assembly therefore of this State recommend it to the good people thereof, to choose delegates to meet in general convention, with powers to form a constitution of government for them, and to declare those fundamentals to which all our laws present and future shall be subordinate; and, in compliance with this recommendation, they have thought proper to make choice of us, and to vest us with powers for this purpose.

---

[1] Jefferson was so proud of this draft, as "reaching all the great objects of public liberty," that he published it in pamphlet form in 1786, while in Paris. It bore the title: *Draught of a Fundamental Constitution for the Commonwealth of Virginia* (8 vo, 14 pp.). Jefferson had it bound with his *Notes on Virginia* as an Appendix.

We, therefore, the delegates, chosen by the said good people of this State for the purpose aforesaid, and now assembled in general convention, do in execution of the authority with which we are invested, establish the following constitution and fundamentals of government for the said State of Virginia:

The said State shall forever hereafter be governed as a commonwealth.

The powers of government shall be divided into three distinct departments, each of them to be confided to a separate body of magistracy; to wit, those which are legislative to one, those which are judiciary to another, and those which are executive to another. No person, collection of persons, being of one of these departments, shall exercise any power properly belonging to either of the others, except in the instances hereinafter expressly permitted.

The legislature shall consist of two branches, the one to be called the House of Delegates, the other the Senate, and both together the General Assembly. The concurrence of both of these, expressed on three several readings, shall be necessary to the passage of a law.

Delegates for the general assembly shall be chosen on the last Monday of November in every year. But if an election cannot be concluded on that day, it may be adjourned from day to day till it can be concluded.

The number of delegates which each county may send shall be in proportion to the number of its qualified electors; and the whole number of delegates for the State shall be so proportioned to the whole number of qualified electors in it, that they shall never exceed three hundred, nor be fewer than one hundred. Whenever such excess or deficiency shall take place, the House of Delegates so deficient or excessive shall, notwithstanding this, continue in being during its legal term; but they shall, during that term, re-adjust the proportion, so as to bring their number within the limits before mentioned at the ensuing election. If any county be reduced in its qualified electors below the number authorized to send one delegate, let it be annexed to some adjoining county.

For the election of senators, let the several counties be allotted by the senate, from time to time, into such and so many districts as they shall find best; and let each county at the time of electing its delegates, choose senatorial electors, qualified as themselves are, and four in number for each delegate their county is entitled to send, who shall convene, and conduct themselves, in such manner as the legislature shall direct, with the senatorial electors from the other counties of their district, and then choose, by ballot, one senator for every six delegates which their district is entitled to choose. Let the senatorial districts be divided into two classes, and let the members elected for one of them be dissolved at the first ensuing general election of delegates, the other at the next, and so on alternately forever.

All free male citizens, of full age, and sane mind, who for one year before shall have been resident in the county, or shall through the whole of that time have possessed therein real property of the value of ——; or shall for the same time have been enrolled in the militia, and no others, shall have a right to vote for delegates for the said county, and for senatorial electors for the district. They shall give their votes personally, and *viva voce*.

The general assembly shall meet at the place to which the last adjournment was, on the forty-second day after the day of election of delegates, and thenceforward at any other time or place on their own adjournment, till their office expires, which shall be on the day preceding that appointed for the meeting of the next general assembly. But if they shall at any time adjourn for more than one year, it shall be as if they had adjourned for one year precisely. Neither house, without the concurrence of the other, shall adjourn for more than one week, nor to any other place than the one at which they are sitting. The governor shall also have power, with the advice of the council of State, to call them at any other time to the same place, or to a different one, if that shall have become, since the last adjournment, dangerous from an enemy, or from infection.

A majority of either house shall be a quorum, and shall be requisite for doing business; but any smaller proportion which from time to time shall be thought expedient by the respective houses, shall be sufficient to call for, and to punish, their non-attending members, and to adjourn themselves for any time not exceeding one week.

The members, during their attendance on the general assembly, and for so long a time before and after as shall be necessary for travelling to and from the same, shall be privileged from all personal restraint and assault, and shall have no other privilege whatsoever. They shall receive during the same time, daily wages in gold or silver, equal to the value of two bushels of wheat. This value shall be deemed one dollar by the bushel till the year 1790, in which, and in every tenth year thereafter, the general court, at their first sessions in the year, shall cause a special jury, of the most respectable merchants and farmers, to be summoned, to declare what shall have been the averaged value of wheat during the last ten years; which averaged value shall be the measure of wages for the ten subsequent years.

Of this general assembly, the treasurer, attorney general, register, ministers of the gospel, officers of the regular armies of this State, or of the United States, persons receiving salaries or emoluments from any power foreign to our confederacy, those who are not resident in the county for which they are chosen delegates, or districts for which they are chosen senators,

those who are not qualified as electors, persons who shall have committed treason, felony, or such other crime as would subject them to infamous punishment, or who shall have been convicted by due course of law of bribery or corruption, in endeavoring to procure an election to the said assembly, shall be incapable of being members. All others, not herein elsewhere excluded, who may elect, shall be capable of being elected thereto.

Any member of the said assembly accepting any office of profit under this State, or the United States, or any of them, shall thereby vacate his seat, but shall be capable of being re-elected.

Vacancies occasioned by such disqualifications, by death, or otherwise, shall be supplied by the electors, on a writ from the speaker of the respective house.

The general assembly shall not have power to infringe this constitution; to abridge the civil rights of any person on account of his religious belief; to restrain him from professing and supporting that belief, or to compel him to contributions, other than those he shall have personally stipulated for the support of that or any other; to ordain death for any crime but treason or murder, or military offences; to pardon, or give a power of pardoning persons duly convicted of treason or felony, but instead thereof they may substitute one or two new trials, and no more; to pass laws for punishing actions done before the existence of such laws; to pass any bill of attainder of treason or felony; to prescribe torture in any case whatever; nor to permit the introduction of any more slaves to reside in this State, or the continuance of slavery beyond the generation which shall be living on the thirty-first day of December, one thousand eight hundred; all persons born after that day being hereby declared free.

The general assembly shall have power to sever from this State all or any parts of its territory westward of the Ohio, or of the meridian of the mouth of the Great Kanhaway, and to cede to Congress one hundred square miles of territory in any other part of this State, exempted from the jurisdiction and government of this State so long as Congress shall hold their sessions therein, or in any territory adjacent thereto, which may be tendered to them by any other State.

They shall have power to appoint the speakers of their respective houses, treasurer, auditors, attorney general, register, all general officers of the military, their own clerks and serjeants, and no other officers, except where, in other parts of this constitution, such appointment is expressly given them.

The executive powers shall be exercised by a *Governor,* who shall be chosen by joint ballot of both houses of assembly, and when chosen shall remain in office five years, and be ineligible a second time. During his term he shall hold no other office or emolument under this State, or any other

State or power whatsoever. By executive powers, we mean no reference to those powers exercised under our former government by the crown as of its prerogative, nor that these shall be the standard of what may or may not be deemed the rightful powers of the governor. We give him those powers only, which are necessary to execute the laws (and administer the government), and which are not in their nature either legislative or judiciary. The application of this idea must be left to reason. We do however expressly deny him the prerogative powers of erecting courts, offices, boroughs, corporations, fairs, markets, ports, beacons, light-houses, and sea-marks; of laying embargoes, of establishing precedence, of retaining within the State, or recalling to it any citizen thereof, and of making denizens, except so far as he may be authorized from time to time by the legislature to exercise any of those powers. The power of declaring war and concluding peace, of contracting alliances, of issuing letters of marque and reprisal, of raising and introducing armed forces, of building armed vessels, forts, or strongholds, of coining money or regulating its value, of regulating weights and measures, we leave to be exercised under the authority of the confederation; but in all cases respecting them which are out of the said confederation, they shall be exercised by the governor, under the regulation of such laws as the legislature may think it expedient to pass.

The whole military of the State, whether regular, or of militia, shall be subject to his directions; but he shall leave the execution of those directions to the general officers appointed by the legislature.

His salary shall be fixed by the legislature at the session of the assembly in which he shall be appointed, and before such appointment be made; or if it be not then fixed, it shall be the same which his next predecessor in office was entitled to. In either case he may demand it quarterly out of any money which shall be in the public treasury; and it shall not be in the power of the legislature to give him less or more, either during his continuance in office, or after he shall have gone out of it. The lands, houses, and other things appropriated to the use of the governor, shall remain to his use during his continuance in office.

A *Council of State* shall be chosen by joint ballot of both houses of assembly, who shall hold their offices seven years, and be ineligible a second time. and who, while they shall be of the said council, shall hold no other office or emolument under this State, or any other State or power whatsoever. Their duty shall be to attend and advise the governor when called on by him, and their advice in any case shall be a sanction to him. They shall also have power, and it shall be their duty, to meet at their own will, and to give their advice, though not required by the governor, in cases where they shall think the public good calls for it. Their advice and proceedings shall be entered in books to be kept for that purpose, and shall be signed as approved or disapproved by the members present. These books shall be laid before either house of assembly when called for by them. The said council shall consist of eight members for the present; but their numbers may be increased or reduced by the legislature, whenever they shall think it necessary; provided such reduction be made only as the appointments become vacant by death, resignation, disqualification, or regular deprivation. A majority of their actual number, and not fewer, shall be a quorum. They shall be allowed for the present —— each by the year, payable quarterly out of any money which shall be in the public treasury. Their salary, however, may be increased or abated from time to time, at the discretion of the legislature; provided such increase or abatement shall not, by any ways or means, be made to affect either then, or at any future time, any one of those then actually in office. At the end of each quarter their salary shall be divided into equal portions by the number of days on which, during that quarter, a council has been held, or required by the governor, or by their own adjournment, and one of those portions shall be withheld from each member for every of the said days which, without cause allowed good by the board, he failed to attend, or departed before adjournment without their leave. If no board should have been held during that quarter, there shall be no deduction.

They shall annually choose a *President,* who shall preside in council in the absence of the governor, and who, in case of his office becoming vacant by death or otherwise, shall have authority to exercise all his functions, till a new appointment be made, as he shall also in any interval during which the governor shall declare himself unable to attend to the duties of his office.

The *Judiciary* powers shall be exercised by county courts and such other inferior courts as the legislature shall think proper to continue or to erect, by three superior courts, to wit, a Court of Admiralty, a general Court of Common Law, and a High Court of Chancery; and by one Supreme Court, to be called the Court of Appeals.

The judges of the high court of chancery, general court, and court of admiralty, shall be four in number each, to be appointed by joint ballot of both houses of assembly, and to hold their offices during good behavior. While they continue judges, they shall hold no other office or emolument, under this State, or any other State or power whatsoever, except that they may be delegated to Congress, receiving no additional allowance.

These judges, assembled together, shall constitute the Court of Appeals, whose business shall be to receive and determine appeals from the three superior courts, but to receive no original causes, except in the cases expressly permitted herein.

A majority of the members of either of these courts, and not fewer, shall be a quorum. But in the Court of Appeals nine members shall be necessary to do business. Any smaller numbers however may be authorized by the legislature to adjourn their respective courts.

They shall be allowed for the present —— each by the year, payable quarterly out of any money which shall be in the public treasury. Their salaries, however, may be increased or abated, from time to time, at the discretion of the legislature, provided such increase or abatement shall not by any ways or means, be made to affect, either then, or at any future time, any one of those then actually in office. At the end of each quarter their salary shall be divided into equal portions by the number of days on which, during that quarter, their respective courts sat, or should have sat, and one of these portions shall be withheld from each member for every of the said days which, without cause allowed good by his court, he failed to attend, or departed before adjournment without their leave. If no court should have been held during the quarter, there shall be no deduction.

There shall, moreover, be a *Court of Impeachments,* to consist of three members of the Council of State, one of each of the superior courts of Chancery, Common Law, and Admiralty, two members of the house of delegates and one of the Senate, to be chosen by the body respectively of which they are. Before this court any member of the three branches of government, that is to say, the governor, any member of the council, of the two houses of legislature, or of the superior courts, may be impeached by the governor, the council, or either of the said houses or courts, and by no other, for such misbehavior in office as would be sufficient to remove him therefrom; and the only sentence they shall have authority to pass shall be that of deprivation and future incapacity of office. Seven members shall be requisite to make a court, and two-thirds of those present must concur in the sentence. The offences cognizable by this court shall be cognizable by no other, and they shall be triers of the fact as well as judges of the law.

The justices or judges of the inferior courts already erected, or hereafter to be erected, shall be appointed by the governor, on advice of the council of State, and shall hold their offices during good behavior, or the existence of their courts. For breach of good behavior, they shall be tried according to the laws of the land, before the Court of Appeals, who shall be judges of the fact as well as of the law. The only sentence they shall have authority to pass shall be that of deprivation and future incapacity of office, and two-thirds of the members present must concur in this sentence.

All courts shall appoint their own clerks, who shall hold their offices during good behavior, or the existence of their court; they shall also appoint all other attending officers to continue during their pleasure. Clerks appointed by the supreme or superior courts shall be removable by their respective courts. Those to be appointed by other courts shall have been previously examined, and certified to be duly qualified, by some two members of the general court, and shall be removable for breach of the good behavior by the Court of Appeals only, who shall be judges of the fact as well as of the law. Two-thirds of the members present must concur in the sentence.

The justices or judges of the inferior courts may be members of the legislature.

The judgment of no inferior court shall be final, in any civil case, of greater value than fifty bushels of wheat, as last rated in the general court for setting the allowance to the members of the general assembly, nor in any case of treason, felony, or other crime which should subject the party to infamous punishment.

In all causes depending before any court, other than those of impeachments, of appeals, and military courts, facts put in issue shall be tried by jury, and in all courts whatever witnesses shall give testimony *viva voce* in open court, wherever their attendance can be procured; and all parties shall be allowed counsel and compulsory process for their witnesses.

Fines, amercements, and terms of imprisonment left indefinite by the law, other than for contempts, shall be fixed by the jury, triers of the offence.

The governor, two councillors of State, and a judge from each of the superior Courts of Chancery, Common Law, and Admiralty, shall be a council to revise all bills which shall have passed both houses of assembly, in which council the governor, when present, shall preside. Every bill, before it becomes a law, shall be represented to this council, who shall have a right to advise its rejection, returning the bill, with their advice and reasons in writing, to the house in which it originated, who shall proceed to reconsider the said bill. But if after such reconsideration, two-thirds of the house shall be of opinion that the bill should pass finally, they shall pass and send it, with the advice and written reasons of the said Council of Revision, to the other house, wherein if two-thirds also shall be of opinion it should pass finally, it shall thereupon become law; otherwise it shall not.

If any bill, presented to the said council, be not, within one week (exclusive of the day of presenting it) returned by them, with their advice of rejection and reasons, to the house wherein it originated, or to the clerk of the said house, in case of its adjournment over the expiration of the week, it shall be law from the expiration of the week, and shall then be demandable by the clerk of the House of Delegates, to be filed of record in his office.

The bills which they approve shall become law from the time of such approbation, and shall then be returned to, or demandable by, the clerk of the House of Delegates, to be filed of record in his office.

A bill rejected on advice of the Council of Revision may again be proposed, during the same session of assembly, with such alterations as will render it conformable to their advice.

The members of the said Council of Revision shall be appointed from time to time by the board or court of which they respectively are. Two of the executive and two of the judiciary members shall be requisite to do business; and to prevent the evils of non-attendance, the board and courts may at any time name all, or so many as they will, of their members, in the particular order in which they would choose the duty of attendance to devolve from preceding to subsequent members, the preceding failing to attend. They shall have additionally for their services in this council the same allowance as members of assembly have.

The confederation is made a part of this constitution, subject to such future alterations as shall be agreed to by the legislature of this State, and by all the other confederating States.

The delegates to Congress shall be five in number; any three of whom, and no fewer, may be a representation. They shall be appointed by joint ballot of both houses of assembly for any term not exceeding one year, subject to be recalled, within the term, by joint vote of both the said houses. They may at the same time be members of the legislative or judiciary departments, but not of the executive.

The benefits of the writ of Habeas Corpus shall be extended, by the legislature, to every person within this State, and without fee, and shall be so facilitated that no person may be detained in prison more than ten days after he shall have demanded and been refused such writ by the judge appointed by law, or if none be appointed, then by any judge of a superior court, nor more than ten days after such writ shall have been served on the person detaining him, and no order given, on due examination, for his remandment or discharge.

The military shall be subordinate to the civil power.

Printing presses shall be subject to no other restraint than liableness to legal prosecution for false facts printed and published.

Any two of the three branches of government concurring in opinion, each by the voice of two-thirds of their whole existing number, that a convention is necessary for altering this constitution, or correcting breaches of it, they shall be authorized to issue writs to every county for the election of so many delegates as they are authorized to send to the general assembly, which elections shall be held, and writs returned, as the laws shall have provided in the case of elections of delegates of assembly, *mutatis mutandis,* and the said delegates shall meet at the usual place of holding assemblies, three months after date of such writs, and shall be acknowledged to have equal powers with this present convention. The said writs shall be signed by all the members approving the same.

To introduce this government, the following special and temporary provision is made.

This convention being authorized only to amend those laws which constituted the form of government, no general dissolution of the whole system of laws can be supposed to have taken place; but all laws in force at the meeting of this convention, and not inconsistent with this constitution, remain in full force, subject to alterations by the ordinary legislature.

The present general assembly shall continue till the forty-second day after the last Monday of November in this present year. On the said last Monday of November in this present year, the several counties shall by their electors qualified as provided by this constitution, elect delegates, which for the present shall be, in number, one for every —— militia of the said county, according to the latest returns in possession of the governor, and shall also choose senatorial electors in proportion thereto, which senatorial electors shall meet on the fourteenth day after the day of their election, at the court house of that county of their present district which would stand first in an alphabetical arrangement of their counties, and shall choose senators in the proportion fixed by this constitution. The elections and returns shall be conducted, in all circumstances not hereby particularly prescribed, by the same persons and under the same forms as prescribed by the present laws in elections of senators and delegates of assembly. The said senators and delegates shall constitute the first general assembly of the new government, and shall specially apply themselves to the procuring an exact return from every county of the number of its qualified electors, and to the settlement of the number of delegates to be elected for the ensuing general assembly.

The present governor shall continue in office to the end of the term for which he was elected.

All other officers of every kind shall continue in office as they would have done had their appointment been under this constitution, and new ones, where new are hereby called for, shall be appointed by the authority to which such appointment is referred. One of the present judges of the general court, he consenting thereto, shall by joint ballot of both houses of assembly, at their first meeting, be transferred to the High Court of Chancery.

GOVERNMENT FOR THE WESTERN TERRITORY [1]

March 22, 1784

The Committee to whom was recommitted the report of a plan for a temporary government of the Western territory have agreed to the following resolutions.

Resolved, that so much of the territory ceded or to be ceded by individual states to the United States as is already purchased or shall be purchased of the Indian inhabitants and offered for sale by Congress, shall be divided into distinct states, in the following manner, as nearly as such cessions will admit; that is to say, by parallels of latitude, so that each state shall comprehend from South to North two degrees of latitude beginning to count from the completion of thirty-one degrees North of the Equator; and by meridians of longitude, one of which shall pass through the lowest point of the rapids of Ohio, and the other through the Western Cape of the mouth of the Great Kanhaway, but the territory Eastward of this last meridian, between the Ohio, Lake Erie, and Pennsylvania shall be one state, whatsoever may be its comprehension of latitude. That which may lie beyond the completion of the 45th degree between the said meridians shall make part of the state adjoining it on the South, and that part of the Ohio which is between the same meridians coinciding nearly with the parallel of 39° shall be substituted so far in lieu of that parallel as a boundary line.

That the settlers on any territory so purchased and offered for sale shall, either on their own petition, or on the order of Congress, receive authority from them with appointments of time and place for their free males of full age, within the limits of their state to meet together for the purpose of establishing a temporary government, to adopt the constitution and laws of any one of the original states, so that such laws nevertheless shall be subject to alteration by their ordinary legislature; and to erect, subject to a like alteration, counties or townships for the election of members for their legislature.

That such temporary government shall only continue in force in any state until it shall have acquired 20,000 free inhabitants, when giving due proof thereof to Congress, they shall receive from them authority with appointment of time and place to call a convention of representatives to establish a permanent Constitution and Government for themselves. Provided that both the temporary and permanent governments be established on these

[1] This document was adopted, after amendment, by Congress on April 23, 1784. Three years later it was replaced by the Northwest Ordinance, but most of the ideas set forth by Jefferson were incorporated in the Ordinance.

principles as their basis. 1. That they shall forever remain a part of this confederacy of the United States of America. 2. That in their persons, property and territory they shall be subject to the Government of the United States in Congress assembled, and to the articles of Confederation in all those cases in which the original states shall be so subject. 3. That they shall be subject to pay a part of the federal debts contracted or to be contracted, to be apportioned on them by Congress, according to the same common rule and measure, by which apportionments thereof shall be made on the other states. 4. That their respective Governments shall be in republican forms and shall admit no person to be a citizen who holds any hereditary title. 5. That after the year 1800 of the Christian era, there shall be neither slavery nor involuntary servitude in any of the said states, otherwise than in punishment of crimes whereof the party shall have been convicted to have been personally guilty.

That whensoever any of the said states shall have, of free inhabitants, as many as shall then be in any one the least numerous, of the thirteen original states, such state shall be admitted by its delegates into the Congress of the United States on an equal footing with the said original states: provided nine States agree to such admission according to the reservation of the 11th of the articles of Confederation, and in order to adopt the said articles of Confederation to the state of Congress when its numbers shall be thus increased, it shall be proposed to the legislatures of the states originally parties thereto, to require the assent of two thirds of the United States in Congress assembled in all those cases wherein by the said articles the assent of nine states is now required; which being agreed to by them shall be binding on the new states. Until such admission by their delegates into Congress, any of the said states after the establishment of their temporary government shall have authority to keep a sitting member in Congress, with a right of debating, but not of voting.

That the preceding articles shall be formed into a charter of compact, shall be duly executed by the president of the United States in Congress assembled, under his hand and the seal of the United States, shall be promulgated and shall stand as fundamental constitutions between the thirteen original states and each of the several states now newly described, unalterable but by the joint consent of the United States in Congress assembled, and of the particular state within which such alteration is proposed to be made.

That measures not inconsistent with the principles of the Confederation and necessary for the preservation of peace and good order among the settlers in any of the said new states until they shall assume a temporary Government as aforesaid, may from time to time be taken by the United States in Congress assembled.

NOTES ON THE ESTABLISHMENT OF A MONEY UNIT, AND OF A COINAGE FOR THE UNITED STATES [1]

April, 1784

In fixing the Unit of Money, these circumstances are of principal importance.

I. That it be of *convenient size* to be applied as a measure to the common money transactions of life.

II. That its parts and multiples be in an *easy proportion* to each other, so as to facilitate the money arithmetic.

III. That the Unit and its parts, or divisions, *be so nearly of the value of some of the known coins,* as that they may be of easy adoption for the people.

The Spanish Dollar seems to fulfil all these conditions.

I. Taking into our view all money transactions, great and small, I question if a common measure of more *convenient size* than the Dollar could be proposed. The value of 100, 1000, 10,000 dollars is well estimated by the mind; so is that of the tenth or the hundredth of a dollar. Few transactions are above or below these limits. The expediency of attending to the size of the money Unit will be evident, to anyone who will consider how inconvenient it would be to a manufacturer or merchant, if, instead of the yard for measuring cloth, either the inch or the mile had been made the Unit of Measure.

II. The most *easy ratio* of multiplication and division, is that by ten. Everyone knows the facility of Decimal Arithmetic. Everyone remembers, that, when learning Money-Arithmetic, he used to be puzzled with adding the farthings, taking out the fours and carrying them on; adding the pence, taking out the twelves and carrying them on; adding the shillings, taking out the twenties and carrying them on; but when he came to the pounds, where he had only tens to carry forward, it was easy and free from error. The bulk of mankind are school-boys through life. These little perplexities are always great to them. And even mathematical heads feel the relief of an easier, substituted for a more difficult process. Foreigners, too, who trade and travel among us, will find a great facility in understanding our coins and accounts from this ratio of subdivision. Those who have had occasion

[1] This document paved the way for the adoption of the dollar unit system in the United States.

194

to convert the livres, sols, and deniers of the French; the gilders, stivers, and frenings of the Dutch; the pounds, shillings, pence, and farthings of these several States, into each other, can judge how much they would have been aided, had their several subdivisions been in a decimal ratio. Certainly, in all cases, where we are free to choose between easy and difficult modes of operation, it is most rational to choose the easy. The Financier, therefore, in his report, well proposes that our Coins should be in decimal proportions to one another. If we adopt the Dollar for our Unit, we should strike four coins, one of gold, two of silver, and one of copper, *viz.:*

1. A golden piece, equal in value to ten dollars:
2. The Unit or Dollar itself, of silver:
3. The tenth of a Dollar, of silver also:
4. The hundredth of a Dollar, of copper.

Compare the arithmetical operations, on the same sum of money expressed in this form, and expressed in the pound sterling and its division.

	£	S.	D.	QRS.	DOLLARS			£	S.	D.	QRS.	DOLLARS
Addition.	8	13	11	1-2 =	38.65	Subtraction.		8	13	11	1-2 =	38.65
	4	12	8	3-4 =	20.61			4	12	8	3-4 =	20.61
	13	6	8	1-4 =	59.26			4	1	2	3-4 =	18.04

Multiplication by 8.

£	S.	D.	QRS.	DOLLARS
8	13	11	1-2 =	38.65
20				8
173				$309.20
12				
2087				
4				
8350				
8				

4 ⌐ 66.800
12 ⌐ 16.700
20 ⌐ 1391 8
£69 11 8

Division by 8.

£	S.	D.	QRS.	DOLLARS
8	13	11	1-2 =	8 ⌐ 38.65
20				4.83
173				
12				
2087				
4				

8 ⌐ 8350
4 ⌐ 1043
12 ⌐ 260 3-4
20 ⌐ 21 8 3-4
£1 1 8 3-4

A bare inspection of the above operations will evince the labor which is occasioned by subdividing the Unit into 20ths, 240ths, and 960ths, as the English do, and as we have done; and the ease of subdivision in a decimal ratio. The same difference arises in making payment. An Englishman, to pay, £8, 13s. 1d. 1-2 qrs., must find, by calculation, what combination of the coins of his country will pay this sum; but an American, having the same sum to pay, thus expressed $38.65, will know, by inspection only, that three golden pieces, eight units or dollars, six tenths, and five coppers, pay it precisely.

III. The third condition required is, that the Unit, its multiples, and subdivisions, coincide in value with some of the known coins so nearly, that the people may, by a quick reference in the mind, estimate their value. If this be not attended to, they will be very long in adopting the innovation, if ever they adopt it. Let us examine, in this point of view, each of the four coins proposed.

1. The golden piece will be 1-5 more than a half joe, and 1-15 more than a double guinea. It will be readily estimated, then, by reference to either of them; but more readily and accurately as equal to ten dollars.

2. The Unit, or Dollar, is a known coin, and the most familiar of all, to the minds of the people. It is already adopted from South to North; has identified our currency, and therefore happily offers itself as a Unit already introduced. Our public debt, our requisitions, and their appointments, have given it actual and long possession of the place of Unit. The course of our commerce, too, will bring us more of this than of any other foreign coin, and therefore renders it more worthy of attention. I know of no Unit which can be proposed in competition with the Dollar, but the Pound. But what is the Pound? 1547 grains of fine silver in Georgia; 1289 grains in Virginia, Connecticut, Rhode Island, Massachusetts, and New Hampshire; 1031 1-4 grains in Maryland, Delaware, Pennsylvania, and New Jersey; 966 3-4 grains in North Carolina and New York. Which of these shall we adopt? To which State give that pre-eminence of which all are so jealous? And on which impose the difficulties of a new estimate of their corn, their cattle, and other commodities? Or shall we hang the pound sterling, as a common badge, about all their necks? This contains 1718 3-4 grains of pure silver. It is difficult to familiarize a new coin to the people; it is more difficult to familiarize them to a new coin with an old name. Happily, the dollar is familiar to them all, and is already as much referred to for a measure of value, as their respective provincial pounds.

3. The tenth will be precisely the Spanish bit, or half pistereen. This is a coin perfectly familiar to us all. When we shall make a new coin, then, equal in value to this, it will be of ready estimate with the people.

4. The hundredth, or copper, will differ little from the copper of the four Eastern States, which is 1-108 of a dollar; still less from the penny of New York and North Carolina, which is 1-96 of a dollar; and somewhat more from the penny or copper of Jersey, Pennsylvania, Delaware, and Maryland, which is 1-90 of a dollar. It will be about the medium between the old and the new coppers of these States, and will therefore soon be substituted for

them both. In Virginia, coppers have never been in use. It will be as easy, therefore, to introduce them there of one value as of another. The copper coin proposed will be nearly equal to three-fourths of their penny, which is the same with the penny lawful of the Eastern States.

A great deal of small change is useful in a State, and tends to reduce the price of small articles. Perhaps it would not be amiss to coin three more pieces of silver, one of the value of five-tenths, or half a dollar, one of the value of two-tenths, which would be equal to the Spanish pistereen, and one of the value of five coppers, which would be equal to the Spanish half-bit. We should then have five silver coins, *viz.*:

1. The Unit or Dollar:
2. The half dollar or five-tenths:
3. The double tenth, equal to 2, or one-fifth of a dollar, or to the pistereen:
4. The tenth, equal to a Spanish bit:
5. The five copper piece, equal to .5, or one-twentieth of a dollar, or the half-bit.

The plan reported by the Financier is worthy of his sound judgment. It admits, however, of objection, in the size of the Unit. He proposes that this shall be the 1440th part of a dollar: so that it will require 1440 of his units to make the one before proposed. He was led to adopt this by a mathematical attention to our old currencies, all of which this Unit will measure without leaving a fraction. But as our object is to get rid of those currencies, the advantage derived from this coincidence will soon be past, whereas the inconveniences of this Unit will forever remain, if they do not altogether prevent its introduction. It is defective in two of the three requisites of a Money Unit. 1. It is inconvenient in its application to the ordinary money transactions. 10.000 dollars will require eight figures to express them, to wit 14,400,000 units. A horse or bullock of eighty dollars value, will require a notation of six figures, to wit, 115,200 units. As a money of account, this will be laborious, even when facilitated by the aid of decimal arithmetic: as a common measure of the value of property, it will be too minute to be comprehended by the people. The French are subjected to very laborious calculations, the Livre being their ordinary money of account, and this but between 1-5th and 1-6th of a dollar; but what will be our labors, should our money of account be 1-1440th of a dollar? 2. It is neither equal, nor near to any of the known coins in value.

If we determine that a Dollar shall be our Unit, we must then say with precision what a Dollar is. This coin, struck at different times, of different weights and fineness, is of different values. Sir Isaac Newton's assay and representation to the Lords of the Treasury, in 1717, of those which he examined, make their values as follows:

	DWTS. GRS.	
The Seville piece of eight	17—12 containing	387 grains of pure silver
The Mexico piece of eight	17—10 5-9 "	385 1-2
The Pillar piece of eight	17—9 "	385 3-4
The new Seville piece of eight	14— "	308 7-10

The Financier states the old Dollar as containing 376 grains of fine silver, and the new 365 grains. If the Dollars circulating among us be of every date equally, we should examine the quantity of pure metal in each, and from them form an average for our Unit. This is a work proper to be committed to mathematicians as well as merchants, and which should be decided on actual and accurate experiment.

The quantum of alloy is also to be decided. Some is necessary, to prevent the coin from wearing too fast; too much, fills our pockets with copper, instead of silver. The silver coin assayed by Sir Isaac Newton, varied from 1 1-2 to 76 pennyweights alloy, in the pound troy of mixed metal. The British standard has 18 dwt.; the Spanish coins assayed by Sir Isaac Newton, have from 18 to 19 1-2 dwt.; the new French crown has in fact 19 1-2, though by edict, it should have 20 dwt., that is 1-12.

The taste of our countrymen will require, that their furniture plate should be as good as the British standard. Taste cannot be controlled by law. Let it then give the law, in a point which is indifferent to a certain degree. Let the Legislature fix the alloy of furniture plate at 18 dwt., the British standard, and Congress that of their coin at one ounce in the pound, the French standard. This proportion has been found convenient for the alloy of gold coin, and it will simplify the system of our mint to alloy both metals in the same degree. The coin, too, being the least pure, will be the less easily melted into plate. These reasons are light, indeed, and, of course, will only weigh, if no heavier ones can be opposed to them.

The proportion between the values of gold and silver is a mercantile problem altogether. It would be inaccurate to fix it by the popular exchanges of a half Joe for eight dollars, a Louis for four French crowns, or five Louis for twenty-three dollars. The first of these, would be to adopt the Spanish proportion between gold and silver; the second, the French; the third, a mere popular barter, wherein convenience is consulted more than accuracy. The legal proportion in Spain is 16 for 1; in England, 15 1-2 for 1; in France, 15 for 1. The Spaniards and English are found, in experience, to retain an over-proportion of gold coins, and to lose their silver. The French have a greater proportion of silver. The difference at market has been on the decrease. The Financier states it at present, as at 14 1-2 for one. Just principles will lead us to disregard legal proportions altogether; to enquire into the market price of gold, in the several countries with which we shall principally be connected in commerce, and to take an average from them. Perhaps we might, with safety, lean to a proportion somewhat above par for gold, considering our neighborhood, and commerce with the sources of the coins, and the tendency which the high price of gold in Spain has, to draw thither all that of their mines, leaving silver principally for our and other markets. It is not impossible that 15 for 1, may be found an eligible proportion. I state it, however, as a conjecture only.

As to the alloy for gold coin, the British is an ounce in the pound; the French, Spanish, and Portuguese differ from that, only from a quarter of a grain, to a grain and a half. I should, therefore, prefer the British, merely because its fraction stands in a more simple form, and facilitates the calculations into which it enters.

Should the Unit be fixed at 365 grains of pure silver, gold at 15 for 1, and the alloy of both be one-twelfth, the weight of the coins will be as follows:

	GRAINS		GRAINS		DWT. GRAINS
The Golden piece containing	242⅓	of pure metal,	22.12	of alloy, will weigh	11— 1.45
The Unit or Dollar	365	"	33.18	"	16—14.18
The half dollar, or five tenths	182½	"	16.59	"	8— 7.09
The fifth, or Pistereen	73	"	6.63	"	3— 7.63
The tenth, or Bit	36½	"	3.318	"	1—15.818
The twentieth, or half Bit	18¼	"	1.659	"	19.9

The quantity of fine silver which shall constitute the Unit, being settled, and the proportion of the value of gold to that of silver; a table should be formed from the assay before suggested, classing the several foreign coins according to their fineness, declaring the worth of a pennyweight or grain in each class, and that they shall be lawful tenders at those rates, if not clipped or otherwise diminished; and, where diminished, offering their value for them at the mint, deducting the expense of re-coinage. Here the Legislatures should co-operate with Congress, in providing that no money be received or paid at their treasuries, or by any of their officers, or any bank, but on actual weight; in making it criminal, in a high degree, to diminish their own coins, and, in some smaller degree, to offer them in payment when diminished.

That this subject may be properly prepared, and in readiness for Congress to take up at their meeting in November, something must now be done. The present session drawing to a close, they probably would not choose to enter far into this undertaking themselves. The Committee of the States, however, during the recess, will have time to digest it thoroughly, if Congress will fix some general principles for their government. Suppose they be instructed,

To appoint proper persons to assay and examine, with the utmost accuracy practicable, the Spanish milled dollars of different dates, in circulation with us.

To assay and examine, in like manner, the fineness of all the other coins which may be found in circulation within these States.

To report to the Committee the result of these assays, by them to be laid before Congress.

To appoint, also, proper persons to enquire what are the proportions between the values of fine gold, and fine silver, at the markets of the several countries with which we are, or probably may be, connected in commerce; and what would be a proper proportion here, having regard to the average of their values at those markets, and to other circumstances, and to report the same to the Committee, by them to be laid before Congress.

To prepare an Ordinance for establishing the Unit of Money within these States; for subdividing it; and for striking coins of gold, silver, and copper, on the following principles:

That the Money Unit of these States shall be equal in value to a Spanish milled dollar containing so much fine silver as the assay, before directed, shall show to be contained, on an average, in dollars of the several dates in circulation with us.

That this Unit shall be divided into tenths and hundredths; that there shall be a coin of silver of the value of a Unit; one other of the same metal, of the value of one-tenth of a Unit; one other of copper, of the value of the hundredth of a Unit.

That there shall be a coin of gold of the value of ten Units, according to the report before directed, and the judgment of the Committee thereon.

That the alloy of the said coins of gold and silver, shall be equal in weight to one-eleventh part of the fine metal.

That there be proper devices for these coins.

That measures be proposed for preventing their diminution, and also their currency, and that of any others, when diminished.

That the several foreign coins be described and classed in the said Ordinance, the fineness of each class stated, and its value by weight estimated in Units and decimal parts of Units.

And that the said draught of an Ordinance be reported to Congress at their next meeting, for their consideration and determination.

The preceding notes having been submitted to the consideration of the Financier, he favored me with his opinion and observations on them, which render necessary the following supplementary explanations.

I observed, in the preceding notes, that the true proportion of value between gold and silver was a mercantile problem altogether, and that, perhaps, fifteen for one, might be found an eligible proportion. The Financier is so good as to inform me, that this would be higher than the market would justify. Confident of his better information on this subject, I recede from that idea.[1]

He also informs me, that the several coins, in circulation among us, have been already assayed with accuracy, and the result published in a work on that subject. The assay of Sir Isaac Newton had superseded, in my mind, the necessity of this operation as to the older coins, which were the subject of his examination. This later work, with equal reason, may be considered as saving the same trouble as to the latter coins.

So far, then, I accede to the opinions of the Financier. On the other hand, he seems to concur with me, in thinking his smallest fractional division too minute for a Unit, and, therefore, proposes to transfer that denomination to his largest silver coin, containing 1000 of the units first proposed, and worth about 4s. 2d. lawful, or 25-36 of a Dollar. The only question then remaining between us is, whether the Dollar, or this coin, be best for the Unit. We both agree that *the ease of adoption with the people,* is the thing to be aimed at.

1. As to the Dollar, events have overtaken and superseded the question. It is no longer a doubt whether the people can adopt it with ease; they have adopted it, and will have to be turned out of that, into another tract of calculation, if another Unit be assumed. They have now two Units, which they use with equal facility, *viz.,* the Pound of their respective State, and the Dollar. The first of these is peculiar to each State: the second, happily, common to all. In each State, the people have an easy rule of converting the pound of their State into dollars, or dollars into pounds; and this is enough for them, without knowing how this may be done in every State of the Union. Such of them as live near enough the borders of their State to have dealings with their neighbors, learn also the rule of their neighbors: thus, in Virginia and the Eastern States, where the dollar is 6s. or 3-10 of a pound, to turn pounds into dollars, they multiply by 10 and divide by 3. To turn dollars into pounds, they multiply by 3, and divide by 10. Those in Virginia who live near to Carolina, where the dollar is 8s. or 4-10 of a pound, learn the operation of that State, which is a multiplication by 4, and division by 10, *et e converso.* Those who live near Maryland, where the dollar is 7s. 6d. or 3-8 of a pound, multiply by 3, and divide by 8, *et e converso.* All

---

[1] In a newspaper, which frequently gives good details in political economy, I find, under the Hamburgh head, that the present market price of Gold and Silver is, in England, 15.5 for 1: in Russia, 15: in Holland, 14.75: in Savoy, 14.6: in France, 14.42: in Spain, 14.3: in Germany, 14.155: the average of which is 14.675 or 14 5-8. I would still incline to give a little more than the market price for gold, because of its superior convenience in transportation.—T. J.

these operations are easy, and have been found, by experience, not too much for the arithmetic of the people, when they have occasion to convert their old Unit into dollars, or the reverse.

2. As to the Unit of the Financier; in the States where the dollars is 3-10 of a pound, this Unit will be 5-24. Its conversion into the pound then, will be by a multiplication of 5, and a division by 24. In the States where the dollar is 3-8 of a pound, this Unit will be 25-96 of a pound, and the operation must be to multiply by 25, and divide by 96, *et e converso.* Where the dollar is 4-10 of a pound, this Unit will be 5-18. The simplicity of the fraction, and of course the facility of conversion and reconversion, is therefore against this Unit, and in favor of the dollar, in every instance. The only advantage it has over the dollar, is, that it will in every case express our farthing without a remainder; whereas, though the dollar and its decimals will do this in many cases, it will not in all. But, even in these, by extending your notation one figure further, to wit, to thousands, you approximate to perfect accuracy within less than the two-thousandth part of a dollar; an atom in money which everyone would neglect. Against this single inconvenience, the other advantages of the dollar are more than sufficient to preponderate. This Unit will present to the people a new coin, and whether they endeavor to estimate its value by comparing it with a Pound, or with a Dollar, the Units they now possess, they will find the fraction very compound, and of course less accommodated to their comprehension and habits than the dollar. Indeed the probability is, that they could never be led to compute in it generally.

The Financier supposes that the 1-100 part of a dollar is not sufficiently small, where the poor are purchasers or vendors. If it is not, make a smaller coin. But I suspect that it is small enough. Let us examine facts, in countries where we are acquainted with them. In Virginia, where our towns are few, small, and of course their demand for necessaries very limited, we have never yet been able to introduce a copper coin at all. The smallest coin which anybody will receive there, is the half-bit, or 1-20 of a dollar. In those States where the towns are larger and more populous, a more habitual barter of small wants, has called for a copper coin of 1-90, 1-96, or 1-108 of a dollar. In England, where the towns are many and populous, and where ages of experience have matured the conveniences of intercourse, they have found that some wants may be supplied for a farthing, or 1-208 of a dollar, and they have accommodated a coin to this want. This business is evidently progressive. In Virginia, we are far behind. In some other States, they are further advanced, to wit, to the appreciation of 1-90, 1-96, 1-108 of a dollar. To this most advanced state, then, I accommodated my smallest coin in the decimal arrangement, as *a money of payment,* corresponding with the *money of account.* I have no doubt the time will come when a smaller coin will be called for. When that comes, let it be made. It will probably be the half of the copper I suppose, that is to say, 5-1000 or .005 of a dollar, this being very nearly the farthing of England. But it will be time enough to make it, when the people shall be ready to receive it.

My proposition then, is, that our notation of money shall be decimal, descending *ad libitum* of the person noting; that the Unit of this notation shall be a Dollar; that coins shall be accommodated to it from ten dollars to the hundredth of dollar; and that, to set this on foot, the resolutions be adopted which were proposed in the notes, only substituting *an enquiry into the fineness of the coins* in lieu of *an assay of them.*

ANSWERS TO QUESTIONS PROPOUNDED BY M. DE MEUSNIER [1]

January 24, 1786

1. On the original establishment of the several States, the civil code of England, from whence they had emigrated, was adopted. This of course could extend only to general laws, and not to those which were particular to certain places in England only. The circumstances of the new States obliged them to add some new laws, which their special situation required, and even to change some of the general laws of England in cases which did not suit their circumstances or ways of thinking. The law of descents, for instance, was changed in several States. On the late revolution, the changes which under their new form of government rendered necessary were easily made. It was only necessary to say that the powers of legislation, the judiciary, and the executive powers, heretofore exercised by persons of such and such description, shall henceforth be exercised by persons to be appointed in such and such manners. This was what their constitution did. Virginia thought it might be necessary to examine the whole code of law, to reform such parts of it as had been calculated to produce a devotion to monarchy, and to reduce into smaller volume such useful parts as had become too diffuse. A committee was appointed to execute this work; they did it; and the Assembly began in October, 1785, the examination of it, in order to change such parts of the report as might not meet their approbation, and to establish what they should approve. We may expect to hear the result of their deliberations about the last of February next.

I have heard that Connecticut undertook a like work; but I am not sure of this, nor do I know whether any other of the States have or have not done the same.

2. The constitution of New Hampshire, established in 1776, having been expressly made to continue only during the contest with Great Britain, they proceeded, after the close of that, to form and establish a permanent one, which they did. The Convention of Virginia which organized their new government, had been chosen before a separation from Great Britain had been thought of in their State. They had, therefore, none but the ordinary powers of legislation. This leaves their act for organizing the government

---

[1] Jefferson was asked by De Meusnier, who was preparing several sections of the *Encyclopédie Politique,* to furnish him with information on the United States.

subject to be altered by every legislative assembly; and though no general change in it has been made, yet its effect has been controlled in several special cases. It is therefore thought that that State will appoint a convention for the special purpose of forming a stable constitution. I think no change has been made in any other of the States.

3. The following is a rough estimate of the particular debts of some of the States as they existed in the year 1784:

New Hampshire	$ 500,000	United States' principal of foreign debt nearly	$ 7,000,000
Rhode Island	5,000,000		
Massachusetts	430,000	The principal of the domestic debt is somewhere between 27½ millions and 35½ millions, call it therefore	
Connecticut	3,439,086⅔		
Virginia	2,300,000		31,300,000

$38,300,000

The other States not named here, are probably indebted in the same proportion to their abilities. If so, and we estimate their abilities by the rule of quotaing them, those eight States will owe about fourteen millions, and consequently the particular debts of all the States will amount to twenty-five or twenty-six millions of dollars.

5. A particular answer to this question would lead to very minute details: one general idea, however, may be applied to all the States. Each having their separate debt, and a determinate proportion of the Federal debt, they endeavor to lay taxes sufficient to pay the interest of both of these, and to support their own and the Federal Government. These taxes are generally about one or one and a-half per cent on the value of property; and from two and a-half to five per cent on foreign merchandise imported. But the payment of this interest regularly, is not accomplished in many of the States. The peoples are as yet not recovered from the depredations of the war. When that ended their houses were in ruin, their farms waste, themselves distressed for clothing and necessaries for their households. They cannot as yet, therefore, bear heavy taxes. For the payment of the principal no final measures are yet taken. Some States will have land for sale, the produce of which may pay the principal debt. Some will endeavor to have an exceeding of their taxes to be applied as a sinking fund; and all of them look forward to the increase of population, and of course an increase of productions in their present taxes, to enable them to be sinking their debt. This is a general view. Some of the States have not yet made even just efforts for satisfying either the principal or interest of their public debt.

6. By the close of the year 1785 there had probably passed over about 50,000

emigrants. Most of these were Irish. The greatest number of the residue were Germans. Philadelphia receives most of them, and next to that, Baltimore and New York.

7. Nothing is decided as to Vermont. The four northernmost States wish it to be received into the Union. The Middle and Southern States are rather opposed to it. But the great difficulty arises with New York, which claims that territory. In the beginning every individual revolted at the idea of giving them up. Congress therefore only interfered from time to time, to prevent the two parties from coming to an open rupture. In the meanwhile the minds of the New Yorkers have been familiarizing to the idea of a separation, and I think it will not be long before they will consent to it. In that case, the Southern and Middle States will doubtless acquiesce, and Vermont will be received into the Union.

8. LeMaine, a part of the government of Massachusetts, but detached from it (the State of New Hampshire lying between), begins to desire to be separated. They are very weak in numbers as yet: but whenever they shall attain a certain degree of population, there are circumstances which render it highly probable they will be allowed to become a separate member of the Union.

9. It is believed that the State of Virginia has by this time made a second cession of lands to Congress, comprehending all those between the meridian of the mouth of the Great Kanhaway, the Ohio, Mississippi, and Carolina boundary. Within this lies Kentucky. I believe that their numbers are sufficient already to entitle them to come into Congress. And their reception there will only increase the delay necessary for taking the consent of the several Assemblies. There is no other new State as yet approaching the time of its reception.

10. The number of Royalists which left New York, South Carolina and Georgia, when they were evacuated by the British army was considerable, but I am absolutely unable to conjecture their numbers. From all the other States, I suppose perhaps two thousand may have gone.

11. The Confederation is a wonderfully perfect instrument, considering the circumstances under which it was formed. There are, however, some alterations which experience proves to be wanting. These are principally three. 1. To establish a general rule for the admission of new States into the Union. By the confederation no new States, except Canada, can be permitted to have a vote in Congress without first obtaining the consent of all the thirteen legislatures. It becomes necessary to agree what districts may be established into separate States, and at what period of their population they may come into Congress. The act of Congress of April 23, 1784, has pointed out what ought to be agreed on, to say also what number of votes must concur when the number of voters shall be thus enlarged. 2. The Confed-

eration, in its eighth article, decides that the quota of money to be contributed by the several States shall be proportioned to the value of the landed property in the State. Experience has shown it impracticable to come at this value. Congress have therefore recommended to the States to agree that their quotas shall be in proportion to the number of their inhabitants, counting five slaves, however, but as equal to three free inhabitants. I believe all the States have agreed to this alteration except Rhode Island. 3. The Confederation forbids the States individually to enter into treaties of commerce, or of any other nature, with foreign nations: and it authorizes Congress to establish such treaties, with two reservations however, *viz.,* that they shall agree to no treaty which would, 1. restrain the legislatures from imposing such duties on foreigners as natives are subject to; or 2., from prohibiting the exportation or importation of any species of commodities. Congress may therefore be said to have a power to regulate commerce so far as it can be effected by conventions with other nations, and by conventions which do not infringe the two fundamental reservations before mentioned. But this is too imperfect. Because, till a convention be made with any particular nation, the commerce of any one of our States with that nation may be regulated by the State itself, and even when a convention is made, the regulation of the commerce is taken out of the hands of the several States only so far as it is covered or provided for by that convention or treaty. But treaties are made in such general terms, that the greater part of the regulations would still result to the legislatures. Let us illustrate these observations by observing how far the commerce of France and England can be affected by the State Legislatures. As to England, any one of the legislatures may impose on her goods double the duties which are paid other nations; may prohibit their goods altogether; may refuse them the usual facilities for recovering their debts or withdrawing their property; may refuse to receive their Consuls or to give those Consuls any jurisdiction. But with France, whose commerce is protected by a treaty, no State can give any molestation to that commerce which is defended by the treaty. Thus, though a State may exclude the importation of all wines (because one of the reservations aforesaid is that they may prohibit the importation of any species of commodities), yet they cannot prohibit the importation of French wines, particularly while they allow wines to be brought in from other countries. They cannot impose heavier duties on French commodities than on those of other nations. They cannot throw peculiar obstacles in the way of their recovery of debts due to them, &c., &c., because those things are provided for by treaty. Treaties, however, are very imperfect machines for regulating commerce in the detail. The principal objects in the regulation of our commerce would be: 1. to lay such duties, restrictions, or prohibitions on the goods of any particular nation, as might oblige that nation to concur in just and equal arrangements of commerce. 2. To lay such uniform duties on the articles of commerce throughout all the States, as may avail them of that fund for assisting to bear the burthen of public expenses. Now, this cannot be done by the States separately, because they will not separately pursue the same plan. New Hampshire cannot lay a given duty on a particular article unless Massachusetts will do the same, because it will turn the importation of that article from her ports into those of Massachusetts, from whence they will be smuggled into New Hampshire by land. But though Massachusetts were willing to concur with New Hampshire in laying the same duty, yet she cannot do it for the same reason, unless Rhode Island will also, nor can Rhode Island without Connecticut, nor Connecticut without New York, nor New York without New Jersey, and so on quite to Georgia. It is visible, therefore, that the commerce of the States cannot be regulated to the best advantage but by a single body, and no body so proper as Congress. Many of the States have agreed to add an article to the Confederation for allowing to Congress the regulation of their commerce, only providing that the revenues to be raised on it shall belong to the States in which they are levied. Yet it is believed that Rhode Island will prevent this also. An everlasting recurrence to this same obstacle will occasion a question to be asked. How happens it that Rhode Island is opposed to every useful proposition? Her geography accounts for it, with the aid of one or two observations. The cultivators of the earth are the most virtuous citizens, and possess most of the amor patriæ. Merchants are the least virtuous, and possess the least of the amor patriæ. The latter reside principally in the seaport towns, the former in the interior country. Now, it happened that of the territory constituting Rhode Island and Connecticut, the part containing the seaports was erected into a State by itself, called Rhode Island, and that containing the interior country was erected into another State called Connecticut. For though it has a little seacoast, there are no good ports in it. Hence it happens that there is scarcely one merchant in the whole State of Connecticut, while there is not a single man in Rhode Island who is not a merchant of some sort. Their whole territory is but a thousand square miles, and what of that is in use is laid out in grass farms almost entirely. Hence they have scarcely any body employed in agriculture. All exercise some species of commerce. This circumstance has decided the characters of these two States. The remedies to this evil are hazardous. One would be to consolidate the two States into one. Another would be to banish Rhode Island from the Union. A third, to compel her submission to the will of the other twelve. A fourth, for the other twelve to govern themselves according to the new propositions, and to let Rhode

Island go on by herself according to the ancient articles. But the dangers and difficulties attending all these remedies are obvious.

These are the only alterations proposed to the Confederation, and the last of them is the only additional power which Congress is thought to need.

12. Congress have not yet ultimately decided at what rates they will redeem the paper money in the hands of the holders. But a resolution of 1784 has established the principle, so that there can be little doubt but that the holders of paper money will receive as much real money as the paper was actually worth at the time they received it, and an interest of six per cent from the time they received it. Its worth will be found in the depreciation table of the State wherein it was received; these deprecation tables having been formed according to the market price of the paper money at different epochs.

13. Those who talk of the bankruptcy of the United States, are of two descriptions: 1. Strangers who do not understand the nature and history of our paper money. 2. Holders of that paper money who do not wish that the world should understand it. Thus, when in March, 1780, the paper money being so far depreciated that forty dollars of it would purchase only one silver dollar, Congress endeavored to correct the progress of that depreciation by declaring they would emit no more, and would redeem what was in circulation at the rate of one dollar of silver for forty of paper; this was called by the brokers in paper money, a bankruptcy. Yet these very people who had only given one dollar's worth of provisions, of manufactures, or perhaps of silver, for their forty dollars, were displeased that they could not in a moment multiply their silver into forty. If it were decided that the United States should pay a silver dollar for every paper dollar they emitted, I am of opinion (conjecturing from loose data of my memory only as to the amount and true worth of the sums emitted by Congress and by the several States) that a debt, which in its just amount is not more, perhaps, than six millions of dollars, would amount up to four hundred millions, and instead of assessing every inhabitant with a debt of about two dollars, would fix on him thirty guineas, which is considerably more than the national debt of England affixes on each of its inhabitants, and would make a bankruptcy where there is none. The real just debts of the United States, which were stated under the third query, will be easily paid by the sale of their lands, which were ceded on the fundamental condition of being applied as a sinking fund for this purpose.

14. The whole army of the United States was disbanded at the close of the war. A few guards only were engaged for their magazines. Lately they have enlisted some two or three regiments to garrison the posts along the Northern boundary of the United States.

16. The United States do not own, at present, a single vessel of war; nor has Congress entered into any resolution on that subject.

17. I conjecture there are six hundred and fifty thousand Negroes in the five southernmost States, and not fifty thousand in the rest. In most of these latter, effectual measures have been taken for their future emancipation. In the former, nothing is done towards that. The disposition to emancipate them is strongest in Virginia. Those who desire it, form, as yet, the minority of the whole State, but it bears a respectable portion to the whole in numbers and weight of character, and it is continually recruiting by the addition of nearly the whole of the young men as fas as they come into public life. I flatter myself it will take place there at some period of time not very distant. In Maryland and North Carolina a very few are disposed to emancipate. In South Carolina and Georgia, not the smallest symptom of it, but, on the contrary, these two States, and North Carolina, continue importations of Negroes. These have been long prohibited in all the other States.

18. In Virginia, where a great proportion of the legislature consider the constitution but as other acts of legislation, laws have been frequently passed which controlled its effects. I have not heard that in the other States they have ever infringed their constitution, and I suppose they have not done it, as the Judges would consider any law as void which was contrary to the constitution. Pennsylvania is divided into two parties very nearly equal, the one desiring to change the constitution, the other opposing a change. In Virginia there is a part of the State which considers the act for organizing their government as a constitution, and are content to let it remain; there is another part which considers it only as an ordinary act of the legislature, who, therefore, wish to form a real constitution, correcting some defects which have been observed in the act now in force. Most of the young people as they come into office arrange themselves on this side, and I think they will prevail ere long. But there are no heats on this account. I do not know that any of the other States propose to change their constitution.

19. I have heard of no malversations in office which have been of any consequence, unless we consider as such some factious transactions in the Pennsylvania Assembly; or some acts of the Virginia Assembly which have been contrary to their constitution. The causes of these were explained in the preceding article.

20. Broils among the States may happen in the following ways: 1. A State may be embroiled with the other twelve by not complying with the lawful requisitions of Congress. 2. Two States may differ about their boundaries. But the method of settling these is fixed by the Confederation, and most of the States which have any differences of this kind, are submitting them to this mode of determination, and there is no danger of opposition to the de-

cree by any State. The individuals interested may complain, but this can produce no difficulty. 3. Other contestations may arise between two States, such as pecuniary demands, affrays among their citizens, and whatever else may arise between any two nations, with respect to these, there are two opinions. One that they are to be decided according to the ninth article of he Confederation, which says that Congress shall be the last resort in all differences between two or more States, concerning boundary jurisdiction, *or any other cause whatever;* and prescribes the mode of decision, and the weight of reason is undoubtedly in favor of this opinion, yet there are some who question it.

It has been often said that the decisions of Congress are impotent because the Confederation provides no compulsory power. But when two or more nations enter into compact, it is not usual for them to say what shall be done to the party who infringes it. Decency forbids this, and it is as unnecessary as indecent, because the right of compulsion naturally results to the party injured by the breach. When any one State in the American Union refuses obedience to the Confederation by which they have bound themselves, the rest have a natural right to compel them to obedience. Congress would probably exercise long patience before they would recur to force; but if the case ultimately required it, they would use that recurrence. Should this case ever arise, they will probably coerce by a naval force, as being more easy, less dangerous to liberty, and less likely to produce much bloodshed.

It has been said, too, that our governments, both federal and particular, want energy; that it is difficult to restrain both individuals and States from committing wrong. This is true, and it is an inconvenience. On the other hand, that energy which absolute governments derive from an armed force, which is the effect of the bayonet constantly held at the breast of every citizen, and which resembles very much the stillness of the grave, must be admitted also to have its inconveniences. We weigh the two together, and like best to submit to the former. Compare the number of wrongs committed with impunity by citizens among us with those committed by the sovereign in other countries, and the last will be found most numerous, most oppressive on the mind, and most degrading of the dignity of man.

22. The States differed very much in their proceedings as to British property, and I am unable to give the details. In Virginia, the sums sequestered in the treasury remain precisely as they did at the conclusion of the peace. The British having refused to make satisfaction for the slaves they carried away, contrary to the treaty of peace, and to deliver up the ports within our limits, the execution of that treaty is in some degree suspended. Individuals, however, are paying off their debts to British subjects, and the laws even permit the latter to recover them judicially. But as the amount of these debts

are twenty or thirty times the amount of all the money in circulation in that State, the same laws permit the debtor to pay his debts in seven equal and annual payments.

ADDITIONAL QUESTIONS OF M. DE MEUSNIER, AND ANSWERS

1. What has led Congress to determine, that the concurrence of seven votes is requisite in questions which, by the Confederation, are submitted to the decision of a majority of the United States in Congress assembled?

The ninth article of Confederation, section six, evidently establishes three orders of questions in Congress. 1. The greater ones, which relate to making peace or war, alliances, coinage, requisitions for money, raising military force, or appointing its commander-in-chief. 2. The lesser ones, which comprehend all other matters submitted by the Confederation to the federal head. 3. The single question of adjourning from day to day. This gradation of questions is distinctly characterized by the article.

In proportion to the magnitude of these questions, a greater concurrence of the voices composing the Union was thought necessary. Three degrees of concurrence, well distinguished by substantial circumstances, offered themselves to notice. 1. A concurrence of a *majority of the people* of the Union. It was thought that this would be insured, by requiring the voices of nine States; because, according to the loose estimates which had been made of the inhabitants, and the proportion of them which were free, it was believed that even the nine smallest would include a majority of the free citizens of the Union. The voices, therefore, of nine States were required in the greater questions. 2. A concurrence of the *majority of the States*. Seven constitute that majority. This number, therefore, was required in the lesser questions. 3. A concurrence of the *majority of Congress,* that is to say, of the States actually present in it. As there is no Congress, when there are not seven States present, this concurrence could never be of less than four States. But these might happen to be the four smallest, which would not include one-ninth part of the free citizens of the Union. This kind of majority, therefore, was entrusted with nothing but the power of adjourning themselves from day to day.

Here then are three kind of majorities. 1. Of the people. 2. Of the States. 3. Of the Congress: each of which is entrusted to a certain length.

Though the paragraph in question be clumsily expressed, yet it strictly announces its own intentions. It defines with precision, the *greater* questions, for which nine votes shall be requisite. In the *lesser* questions, it then re-

quires a *majority of the United States in Congress assembled:* a term which
will apply either to the number seven, as being a *majority of the States,* or
to the number four as being a *majority of Congress.* Which of the two kinds
of majority, was meant? Clearly, that which would leave a still smaller kind,
for the decision of the question of adjournment. The contrary construction
would be absurd.

This paragraph, therefore, should be understood, as if it had been expressed
in the following terms: "The United States, in Congress assembled, shall
never engage in war, &c., but with the consent of nine States: nor determine
any other question, but with the consent of a majority of the whole States,
except the question of adjournment from day to day, which may be determined by a majority of the States actually present in Congress."

2. How far is it permitted, to bring on the reconsideration of a question
which Congress has once determined?

The first Congress which met, being composed mostly of persons who had
been members of the legislatures of their respective States, it was natural for
them to adopt those rules in their proceedings, to which they had been accustomed in their legislative houses; and the more so, as these happened to be
nearly the same, as having been copied from the same original, those of the
British parliament. One of those rules of proceeding was, that "a question
once determined, cannot be proposed, a second time, in the same session."
Congress, during their first session, in the autumn of 1774, observed this rule
strictly. But before their meeting in the spring of the following year, the war
had broken out. They found themselves at the head of that war, in an executive as well as legislative capacity. They found that a rule, wise and necessary for a legislative body, did not suit an executive one, which, being governed by events, must change their purposes as those change. Besides, their
session was then to become of equal duration with the war; and a rule,
which should render their legislation immutable, during all that period,
could not be submitted to. They, therefore, renounced it in practice, and
have ever since continued to reconsider their questions freely. The only restraint as yet provided against the abuse of this permission to reconsider, is,
that when a question has been decided, it cannot be proposed for reconsideration, but by someone who voted in favor of the former decision, and declares
that he has since changed his opinion. I do not recollect accurately enough,
whether it be necessary that his vote should have decided that of his State,
and the vote of his State have decided that of Congress.

Perhaps it might have been better, when they were forming the federal
constitution, to have assimilated it, as much as possible, to the particular constitutions of the States. All of these have distributed the legislative, executive
and judiciary powers, into different departments. In the federal constitution,

the judiciary powers are separated from the others; but the legislative and executive are both exercised by Congress. A means of amending this defect has been thought of. Congress having a power to establish what committees of their own body they please, and to arrange among them the distribution of their business, they might, on the first day of their annual meeting, appoint an executive committee, consisting of a member from each State, and refer to them all executive business which should occur during their session; confining themselves to what is of a legislative nature, that is to say, to the heads described in the ninth article, as of the competence of nine States only, and to such other questions as should lead to the establishment of general rules. The journal of this committee, of the preceding day, might be read the next morning in Congress, and considered as approved, unless a vote was demanded on a particular article, and that article changed. The sessions of Congress would then be short, and when they separated, the Confederation authorizes the appointment of a committee of the States, which would naturally succeed to the business of the executive committee. The legislative business would be better done, because the attention of the members would not be interrupted by the details of execution; and the executive business would be better done, because, business of this nature is better adapted to small, than great bodies. A monarchical head should confide the execution of its will to departments, consisting, each, of a plurality of hands, who would warp that will, as much as possible, towards wisdom and moderation, the two qualities it generally wants. But, a republican head, founding its decrees, originally, in these two qualities, should commit them to a single hand for execution, giving them, thereby, a promptitude which republican proceedings generally want. Congress could not, indeed, confide their executive business to a smaller number than a committee consisting of a member from each State. This is necessary to insure the confidence of the Union. But it would be gaining a great deal, to reduce the executive head to thirteen, and to relieve themselves of those details. This, however, has as yet been the subject of private conversations only.

3. A succinct account of paper money in America?

Previous to the Revolution, most of the States were in the habit, whenever they had occasion for more money than could be raised immediately by taxes, to issue paper notes or bills, in the name of the State, wherein they promised to pay to the bearer the sum named in the note or bill. In some of the States no time of payment was fixed, nor tax laid to enable payment. In these, the bills depreciated. But others of the States named in the bill the day when it should be paid, laid taxes to bring in money enough for that purpose, and paid the bills punctually, on or before the day named. In these States, paper money was in as high estimation as gold and silver. On the commencement of the late Revolution, Congress had no money. The external commerce of the States being suppressed, the farmer could not sell his produce, and, of course, could not pay a tax. Congress had no resource then but in paper money. Not being able to lay a tax for its redemption, they could only promise that taxes should be laid for that purpose, so as to redeem the bills by a certain day. They did not foresee the long continuance of the war, the almost total suppression of their exports, and other events, which rendered the performance of their engagement impossible. The paper money continued for a twelvemonth equal to gold and silver. But the quantities which they were obliged to emit for the purpose of the war, exceeded what had been the usual quantity of the circulating medium. It began, therefore, to become cheaper, or, as we expressed it, it depreciated, as gold and silver would have done, had they been thrown into circulation in equal quantities. But not having, like them, an intrinsic value, its depreciation was more rapid and greater than could ever have happened with them. In two years, it had fallen to two dollars of paper money for one of silver; in three years, to four for one; in nine months more, it fell to ten for one; and in the six months following, that is to say, by September, 1779, it had fallen to twenty for one.

Congress, alarmed at the consequences which were to be apprehended, should they lose this resource altogether, thought it necessary to make a vigorous effort to stop its further depreciation. They therefore determined, in the first place, that their emissions should not exceed two hundred millions of dollars, to which term they were then nearly arrived; and though they knew that twenty dollars of what they were then issuing, would buy no more for their army than one silver dollar would buy, yet they thought it would be worth while to submit to the sacrifice of nineteen out of twenty dollars, if they could thereby stop further depreciation. They, therefore, published an address to their constituents, in which they renewed their original declarations, that this paper money should be redeemed at dollar for dollar. They proved the ability of the States to do this, and that their liberty would be cheaply bought at that price. The declaration was ineffectual. No man received the money at a better rate; on the contrary, in six months more, that is, by March, 1780, it had fallen to forty for one. Congress then tried an experiment of a different kind. Considering their former offers to redeem this money at par, as relinquished by the general refusal to take it, but in progressive depreciation, they required the whole to be brought in, declared it should be redeemed at its present value, of forty for one, and that they would give to the holders new bills, reduced in their denomination to the sum of gold or silver, which was actually to be paid for them. This would reduce the nominal sum of the mass in circulation to the present worth of that mass, which was five millions; a sum not too great for the circulation of the States, and which, they therefore hoped, would not depreciate further, as they continued firm in their purpose of emitting no more. This effort was as unavailing as the former. Very little of the money was brought in. It continued to circulate and to depreciate, till the end of 1780, when it had fallen to seventy-five for one, and the money circulated from the French army, being, by that time, sensible in all the States north of the Potomac, the paper ceased its circulation altogether in those States. In Virginia and North Carolina it continued a year longer, within which time it fell to one thousand for one, and then expired, as it had done in the other States, without a single groan. Not a murmur was heard on this occasion, among the people. On the contrary, universal congratulations took place on their seeing this gigantic mass, whose dissolution had threatened convulsions which should shake their infant confederacy to its centre, quietly interred in its grave. Foreigners, indeed, who do not, like the natives, feel indulgence for its memory, as of a being which has vindicated their liberties, and fallen in the moment of victory, have been loud, and still are loud in their complaints. A few of them have reason; but the most noisy are not the best of them. They are persons who have become bankrupt by unskilful attempts at commerce with America. That they may have some pretext to offer to their creditors, they have bought up great masses of this dead money in America, where it is to be had at five thousand for one, and they show the certificates of their paper possessions, as if they had all died in their hands, and had been the cause of their bankruptcy. Justice will be done to all, by paying to all persons what this money actually cost them, with an interest of six per cent from the time they received it. If difficulties present themselves in the ascertaining the epoch of the receipt, it has been thought better that the State should lose, by admitting easy proofs, than that individuals, and especially foreigners, should, by being held to such as would be difficult, perhaps impossible.

4. Virginia certainly owed two millions sterling to Great Britain at the conclusion of the war. Some have conjectured the debt as high as three millions. I think that State owed near as much as all the rest put together. This is to be ascribed to peculiarities in the tobacco trade. The advantages made by the British merchants, on the tobaccos consigned to them, were so enormous, that they spared no means of increasing those consignments. A powerful engine for this purpose, was the giving good prices and credit to the planter, till they got him more immersed in debt than he could pay, without selling his lands or slaves. They then reduced the prices given for his tobacco, so that let his shipments be ever so great, and his demand of necessaries ever so economical, they never permitted him to clear off his debt.

These debts had become hereditary from father to son, for many generations, so that the planters were a species of property, annexed to certain mercantile houses in London.

5. The members of Congress are differently paid by different States. Some are on fixed allowances, from four to eight dollars a day. Others have their expenses paid, and a surplus for their time. This surplus is of two, three, or four dollars a day.

6. I do not believe there has ever been a moment, when a single Whig, in any one State, would not have shuddered at the very idea of a separation of their State from the confederacy. The Tories would, at all times, have been glad to see the confederacy dissolved, even by particles at a time, in hopes of their attaching themselves again to Great Britain.

7. The 11th article of Confederation admits Canada to accede to the Confederation at its own will, but adds, "no other colony shall be admitted to the same, unless such admission be agreed to by nine States." When the plan of April, 1784, for establishing new States was on the carpet, the committee who framed the report of that plan, had inserted this clause, "provided nine States agree to such admission, according to the reservation of the 11th of the articles of Confederation." It was objected, 1. That the words of the confederation, "no other colony," could refer only to the residuary possessions of Great Britain, as the two Floridas, Nova Scotia, &c., not being already parts of the Union; that the law for "admitting" a new member into the Union, could not be applied to a territory which was already in the Union, as making part of a State which was a member of it. 2. That it would be improper to allow "nine" States to receive a new member, because the same reasons which rendered that number proper now, would render a greater one proper, when the number composing the Union should be increased. They therefore struck out this paragraph and inserted a proviso, that "the consent of so many States, in Congress, shall first be obtained, as may, at the time, be competent"; thus leaving the question, whether the 11th article applies to the admission of new States, to be decided when that admission shall be asked. See the Journal of Congress of April 20, 1784. Another doubt was started in this debate, *viz.:* whether the agreement of the nine States, required by the Confederation, was to be made by their legislatures, or by their delegates in Congress? The expression adopted, *viz.:* "so many States, in Congress, is first obtained," show what was their sense of this matter. If it be agreed that the 11th article of the Confederation is not to be applied to the admission of these new States, then it is contended that their admission comes within the 13th article, which forbids "any alteration, unless agreed to in a Congress of the United States, and afterwards confirmed by the legislatures of every State." The independence of the new States of Ken-

tucky and Franklin, will soon bring on the ultimate decesion of all these questions.

8. Particular instances whereby the General Assembly of Virginia have shown that they considered the ordinance called their constitution, as every other ordinance, or act of the legislature, subject to be altered by the legislature for the time being.

1. The convention which formed that constitution, declared themselves to be the House of Delegates, during the term for which they were originally elected, and in the autumn of the year met the Senate, elected under the new constitution, and did legislative business with them. At this time, there were malefactors in the public jail, and there was as yet no court established for their trial. They passed a law, appointing certain members by name, who were then members of the Executive Council, to be a court for the trial of these malefactors, though the constitution had said, in express words, that no person should exercise the powers of more than one of the three departments, legislative, executive and judiciary at the same time. This proves that the very men who had made that constitution understood that it would be alterable by the General Assembly. This court was only for that occasion. When the next General Assembly met, after the election of the ensuing year, there was a new set of malefactors in the jail, and no court to try them. This Assembly passed a similar law to the former, appointing certain members of the Executive Council to be an occasional court for this particular case. Not having the journals of Assembly by me, I am unable to say whether this measure was repealed afterwards. However, they are instances of *executive* and *judiciary* powers exercised by the same persons, under the authority of a law, made in contradiction to the constitution.

2. There was a process depending in the ordinary courts of justice, between two individuals of the names of Robinson and Fauntleroy, who were relations, of different descriptions, to one Robinson, a British subject, lately dead. Each party claimed a right to inherit the lands of the decedent according to the laws. Their right should by the constitution have been decided by the judiciary courts; and it was actually depending before them. One of the parties petitioned the Assembly (I think it was in the year 1782), who passed a law deciding the right in his favor. In the following year, a Frenchman, master of a vessel, entered into port without complying with the laws established in such cases, whereby he incurred the forfeitures of the law to any person who would sue for them. An individual instituted a legal process to recover these forfeitures according to the law of the land. The Frenchman petitioned the Assembly, who passed a law deciding the question of forfeiture in his favor. These acts are occasional repeals of that part of the con-

stitution which forbids the same persons to exercise *legislative* and *judiciary* powers at the same time.

The Assembly is in the habitual exercise, during their sessions, of directing the Executive what to do. There are few pages of their journals which do not show proofs of this, and consequently instances of the *legislative* and *executive* powers exercised by the same persons at the same time. These things prove that it has been the uninterrupted opinion of every Assembly, from that which passed the ordinance called the constitution down to the present day, that their acts may control that ordinance, and, of course, that the State of Virginia has no fixed constitution at all.

[The following observations were made by Jefferson on an article entitled "États Unis," prepared for the Encyclopédie Méthodique, June 22, 1786. The article was submitted to him before publication.]

Page 8. The malefactors sent to America were not sufficient in number to merit enumeration, as one class out of three which peopled America. It was at a late period of their history that this practice began. I have no book by me which enables me to point out the date of its commencement. But I do not think the whole number sent would amount to two thousand, and being principally men, eaten up with disease, they married seldom and propagated little. I do not suppose that themselves and their descendants are at present four thousand, which is little more than one thousandth part of the whole inhabitants.

Indented servants formed a considerable supply. These were poor Europeans, who went to America to settle themselves. If they could pay their passage, it was well. If not, they must find means of paying it. They were at liberty, therefore, to make an agreement with any person they chose, to serve him such a length of time as they agreed on, upon condition that he would repay to the master of the vessel the expenses of their passage. If, being foreigners, unable to speak the language, they did not know how to make a bargain for themselves, the captain of the vessel contracted for them with such persons as he could. This contract was by deed indented, which occasioned them to be called indented servants. Sometimes they were called redemptioners, because by their agreement with the master of the vessel, they could *redeem* themselves from his power by paying their passage, which they frequently effected by hiring themselves on their arrival, as is before mentioned. In some States I know that these people had a right of marrying themselves without their master's leave, and I did suppose they had that right everywhere. I did not know that in any of the States they demanded so much as a week for every day's absence without leave. I suspect this must have been at a very early period, while the governments were in the hands of the first emigrants, who, being mostly laborers, were narrow-minded and severe. I know that in Virginia the laws allowed their servitude to be protracted only two days for every one they were absent without leave. So mild was this kind of servitude, that it was very frequent for foreigners, who carried to America money enough not only to pay their passage, but to buy themselves a farm, to indent themselves to a master for three years for a certain sum of money, with a view to learn the husbandry of the country. I will here make a general observation. So desirous are the poor of Europe to get to America, where they may better their condition, that being unable to pay their passage, they will agree to serve two or three years on their arrival here, rather than not go. During the time of that service, they are better fed, better clothed, and have lighter labor, than while in Europe. Continuing to work for hire a few years longer, they buy a farm, marry, and enjoy all the sweets of a domestic society of their own. The American governments are censured for permitting this species of servitude, which lays the foundation of the happiness of these people. But what should these governments do? Pay the passage of all those who choose to go into their country? They are not able; nor were they able, do they think the purchase worth the price? Should they exclude these people from their shores? Those who know their situations in Europe and America, would not say that this is the alternative which humanity dictates. It is said that these people are deceived by those who carry them over. But this is done in Europe. How can the American governments prevent it? Should they punish the deceiver? It seems more incumbent on the European government, where the act is done, and where a public injury is sustained from it. However, it is only in Europe that this deception is heard of. The individuals are generally satisfied in America with their adventure, and very few of them wish not to have made it. I must add that the Congress have nothing to do with this matter. It belongs to the legislatures of the several States.

Page 26. *"Une puissance, en effet,"* &c. The account of the settlement of the colonies, which precedes this paragraph, shows that that settlement was not made by public authority, or at the public expense of England; but by the exertions, and at the expense of individuals. Hence it happened, that their constitutions were not formed systematically, but according to the circumstances which happened to exist in each. Hence, too, the principles of the political connection between the old and new countries, were never settled. That it would have been advantageous to have settled them, is certain; and, particularly, to have provided a body which should decide, in the last resort, all cases wherein both parties were interested. But it is not certain that that right would have been given, or ought to have been given to the Parliament; much less, that it resulted to the Parliament, without having been given to it expressly. Why was it necessary that there should have been a body to decide in the last resort? Because, it would have been for the good of both parties. But this reason shows it ought not to have been the Parliament, since that would have exercised it for the good of one party only.

Page 105. As to the change of the 8th article of Confederation, for quoting requisitions of money on the States.

By a report of the Secretary of Congress, dated January the 4th, 1786, eight States had then acceded to the proposition; to wit, Massachusetts, Connecticut, New York, New Jersey, Pennsylvania, Maryland, Virginia, and North Carolina.

Congress, on the 18th of April, 1783, recommended to the States to invest them with a power, for twenty-five years, to levy an impost of five per cent on all articles imported from abroad. New Hampshire, Massachusetts, Connecticut, New Jersey, Pennsylvania, Delaware, Virginia, North Carolina, and South Carolina, had complied with this, before the 4th of January, 1786. Maryland had passed an act for the same purpose; but, by a mistake in referring to the date of the recommendation of Congress, the act failed of its effect. This was therefore to be rectified. Since the 4th of January, the public papers tell us that Rhode Island has complied fully with this recommendation. It remains still for New York and Georgia to do it. The exportations of America, which are tolerably well known, are the best measure for estimating the importations. These are probably worth about twenty millions of dollars, annually. Of course, this impost will pay the interest of a debt to that amount. If confined to the foreign debt, it will pay the whole interest of that, and sink half a million of the capital, annually. The expenses of collecting this impost, will probably be six per cent on its amount, this being the usual expense of collection in the United States. This will be sixty thousand dollars.

On the 30th of April, 1784, Congress recommended to the States, to invest them with a power, for fifteen years, to exclude from their ports the vessels of all nations, not having a treaty of commerce with them; and to pass, as to all nations, an act on the principles of the British navigation act. Not that they were disposed to carry these powers into execution, with such as would meet them in fair and equal arrangements of commerce; but that they might be able to do it against those who should not. On the 4th of January, 1786, New Hampshire, Massachusetts, Rhode Island, Connecticut, New York, Pennsylvania, Maryland, Virginia, and North Carolina, had done it. It remained for New Jersey, Delaware, South Carolina, and Georgia, to do the same.

In the meantime, the general idea has advanced before the demands of Congress, and several States have passed acts, for vesting Congress with the whole regulation of their commerce, reserving the revenue arising from these regulations, to the disposal of the State in which it is levied. The States which, according to the public papers, have passed such acts, are New Hampshire, Massachusetts, Rhode Island, New Jersey, Delaware, and Virginia; but the Assembly of Virginia, apprehensive that this disjointed method of proceeding may fail in its effect, or be much retarded, passed a resolution on the 21st of January, 1786, appointing commissioners to meet others from the other States, who they invite into the same measure, to digest the form of an act, for investing Congress with such powers over their commerce, as shall be thought expedient, which act is to be reported to their several Assemblies, for their adoption. This was the state of the several propositions relative to the impost, and regulation of commerce, at the date of our latest advices from America.

Page 125. The General Assembly of Virginia, at their session in 1785, passed an act, declaring that the district, called Kentucky, shall be a separate and independent State, on these conditions. 1. That the people of that district shall consent to it. 2. That Congress shall consent to it, and shall receive them into the federal Union. 3. That they shall take on themselves a proportionable part of the public debt of Virginia. 4. That they shall confirm all titles to lands within their district, made by the State of Virginia, before their separation.

Page 139. It was in 1783, and not in 1781, that Congress quitted Philadelphia.

Page 140. *"Le Congrès qui se trouvoit à la portée des rebelles fut effrayé."* I was not present on this occasion, but I have had relations of the transaction from several who were. The conduct of Congress was marked with indignation and firmness. They received no propositions from the mutineers. They came to the resolutions, whch may be seen in the journals of June the 21st, 1783, then adjourned regularly, and went through the body of the mutineers to their respective lodgings. The measures taken by Dickinson, the President of Pennsylvania, for punishing this insult, not being satisfactory to Congress, they assembled, nine days after, at Princeton, in Jersey. The people of Pennsylvania sent petitions declaring their indignation at what had passed, their devotion to the federal head, and their dispositions to protect it, and praying them to return; the legislature, as soon as assembled, did the same thing; the Executive, whose irresolution had been so exceptionable, made apologies. But Congress were now removed; and, to the opinion that this example was proper, other causes were now added, sufficient to *prevent* their return to Philadelphia.

Page 155. 1. 2. Omit *"La dette actuelle,"* &c.

And also, *"Les détails,"* &c., &c., to the end of the paragraph, *"celles des*

États Unis"; page 156. The reason is, that these passages seem to suppose, that the several sums emitted by Congress, at different times, amounting nominally to two hundred millions of dollars, had been actually worth that at the time of emission, and, of course, that the soldiers and others had received that sum from Congress. But nothing is further from the truth. The soldier, victualler, or other persons who receives forty dollars for a service, at the close of the year 1779, received, in fact, no more than he who received one dollar for the same service, in the year 1775, or 1776; because, in those years, the

EMISSION	SUM EMITTED	DEPRE-CIATION	WORTH OF THE SUM EMITTED, IN SILVER DOLLARS
1775. June 23	2,000,000	....	2,000,000
" November 29	3,000,000	....	3,000,000
1776. Feb. 17	4,000,000	....	4,000,000
" August 13	5,000,000	....	5,000,000
1777. May 20	5,000,000	$2\frac{2}{3}$	1,877,273
" August 15	1,000,000	3	333,333$\frac{1}{3}$
" Nov. 7	1,000,000	4	250,000
" Dec. 3	1,000,000	4	250,000
1778. January 8	1,000,000	4	250,000
" January 22	2,000,000	4	500,000
" February 16	2,000,000	5	400,000
" March 5	2,000,000	5	400,000
" April 4	1,000,000	6	166,666$\frac{2}{3}$
" April 11	5,000,000	6	833,333$\frac{1}{3}$
" April 18	500,000	6	83,333$\frac{1}{3}$
" May 22	5,000,000	5	1,000,000
" June 20	5,000,000	4	1,250,000
" July 30	5,000,000	$4\frac{1}{2}$	1,111,111
" September 5	5,000,000	5	1,000,000
" September 26	10,000,100	5	2,000,020
" November 4	10,000,100	6	1,666,683$\frac{1}{3}$
" December 14	10,000,100	6	1,666,683$\frac{1}{3}$
1779. January 14	24,447,620	8	3,055,952$\frac{1}{2}$
" February 3	5,000,160	10	500,016
" February 12	5,000,160	10	500,016
" April 2	5,000,160	17	294,127
" May 5	10,000,100	24	416,670$\frac{5}{6}$
" June 4	10,000,100	20	500,005
" July 17	15,000,280	20	750,014
" September 17	15,000,260	24	625,010$\frac{5}{6}$
" October 14	5,000,180	30	166,672$\frac{2}{3}$
" November 17	10,050,540	$38\frac{1}{2}$	261,053
" November 29	10,000,140	$38\frac{1}{2}$	259,743
	200,000,000		36,367,719$\frac{5}{6}$

paper money was at par with silver; whereas, by the close of 1779, forty paper dollars were worth but one of silver, and would buy no more of the necessaries of life. To know what the monies emitted by Congress were worth to the people, at the time they received them, we will state the date and amount of every several emission, the depreciation of paper money at the time, and the real worth of the emission in silver or gold.

Thus, it appears, that the two hundred millions of dollars, emitted by Congress, were worth, to those who received them, but about thirty-six millions of silver dollars. If we estimate at the same value, the like sum of two hundred millions, supposed to have been emitted by the States, and reckon the Federal debt, foreign and domestic, at about forty-three millions, and the State debts, at about twenty-five millions, it will form an amount of one hundred and forty millions of dollars, or seven hundred and thirty-five millions of livres, Tournois, the total sum which the war has cost the inhabitants of the United States. It continued eight years, from the battle of Lexington to the cessation of hostilities in America. The annual expense, then, was about seventeen millions and five hundred thousand dollars, while that of our enemies was a greater number of guineas.

It will be asked, how will the two masses of Continental and of State money have cost the people of the United States seventy-two millions of dollars, when they are to be redeemed, now, with about six millions? I answer, that the difference, being sixty-six millions, has been lost on the paper bills, separately, by the successive holders of them. Everyone, through whose hands a bill passed, lost on that bill what it lost in value, during the time it was in his hands. This was a real tax on him; and, in this way, the people of the United States actually contributed those sixty-six millions of dollars, during the war, and by a mode of taxation the most oppressive of all, because the most unequal of all.

Page 166; bottom line. Leave out *"Et c'est une autre économie,"* &c. The reason of this, is, that in 1784, purchases of lands were to be made of the Indians, which were accordingly made. But in 1785, they did not propose to make any purchase. The money desired in 1785, five thousand dollars, was probably to pay agents residing among the Indians, or balances of the purchases of 1784. These purchases will not be made every year; but only at distant intervals, as our settlements are extended; and it may be regarded as certain, that not a foot of land will ever be taken from the Indians, without their own consent. The sacredness of their rights, is felt by all thinking persons in America, as much as in Europe.

Page 170. Virginia was quotaed the highest of any State in the Union. But during the war, several States appear to have paid more, because they were free from the enemy, whilst Virginia was cruelly ravaged. The requisition of 1784, was so quotaed on the several States, as to bring up their arrearages; so that when they should have paid the sums then demanded, all would be on an equal footing. It is necessary to give a further explanation of this requisition. The requisitions of one million and two hundred thousand dollars, of eight millions, and two millions, had been made during the war, as an experiment, to see whether, in that situation, the States could furnish the necessary supplies. It was found they could not. The money was thereupon obtained by loans in Europe; and Congress meant, by their requisition of 1784, to abandon the requisitions of one million and two hundred thousand dollars, and of two millions, and also one-half of the eight millions. But as all the States, almost, had made some payments in part of that requisition, they were obliged to retain such a proportion of it, as would enable them to call for equal contributions from all the others.

Page 170. I cannot say how it has happened, that the debt of Connecticut is greater than that of Virginia. The latter is the richest in productions, and, perhaps, made greater exertions to pay for her supplies in the course of the war.

Page 172. *"Les Américains serant après une banqueroute,"* &c. The objections made to the United States, being here condensed together in a short compass, perhaps, it would not be improper to condense the answers in as small a compass, in some such form as follows. That is, after the words *"aucun espoir,"* add, "But to these charges it may be justly answered, that those are no bankrupts who acknowledge the sacredness of their debts, in their just and real amount, who are able, within a reasonable time, to pay them, and who are actually proceeding in that payment; that they furnish, in fact, the supplies necessary for the support of their government; that their officers and soldiers are satisfied, as the interest of their debt is paid regularly, and the principal is in a course of payment; that the question, whether they fought ill, should be asked of those who met them at Bunker's hill, Bennington, Stillwater, King's mountain, the Cowpens, Guilford, and the Eutaw. And that the charges of ingratitude, madness, infidelity and corruption, are easily made by those to whom falsehoods cost nothing; but that no instances, in support of them, have been produced, or can be produced."

Page 187. *"Les officiers et les soldats ont eté payés,"* &c. The balances due to the officers and soldiers have been ascertained, and a certificate of the sum given to each; on these, the interest is regularly paid; and every occasion is seized of paying the principal, by receiving these certificates as money, whenever public property is sold, till a more regular and effectual method can be taken, for paying the whole.

Page 191. *"Quoique la loi dont nous parlons, ne s'observe plus en Angleterre."* "An alien born may purchase lands or other estates, but not for his own use; for the King is thereupon entitled to them." "Yet an alien may acquire a property in goods, money and other personal estate, or may hire a house for his habitation. For this is necessary for the advancement of trade." "Also, an alien may bring an action concerning personal property, and may make a will, and dispose of his personal estate." "When I mention these rights of an alien, I must be understood of alien *friends* only, or such whose countries are in peace with ours; for alien *enemies* have no rights, no privileges, unless by the King's special favor, during the time of war." Blackstone, B. 1. c. 10, page 372. "An alien *friend* may have personal actions, but not real; an alien *enemy* shall have neither real, personal, or mixed actions. The reason why an alien *friend* is allowed to maintain a personal action, is, because he would otherwise be incapacitated to merchandise, which may be as much to our prejudice as his." Cunningham's law dict. title, Aliens. The above is the clear law of England, practiced from the earliest ages to this day, and never denied. The passage quoted by M. de Meusnier from 2 Blackstone, c. 26, is from his chapter, "Of title to things *personal by occupancy.*" The word "personal," shows, that nothing in this chapter relates to lands, which are *real* estate; and, therefore, this passage does not contract the one before quoted from the same author, (1 Bl. c. 10.) which says, that the lands of an alien belong to the King. The words, "of title by *occupancy,*" show, that it does not relate to *debts,* which, being a moral existence only, cannot be the subject of *occupancy.* Blackstone, in this passage, (B. 2. c. 26.) speaks only of personal goods of an alien, which another may find, and seize as prime occupant.

Page 193. *"Le remboursement présentera des difficultés des sommes considérables,"* &c. There is no difficulty nor doubts on this subject. Everyone is sensible how this is to be ultimately settled. Neither the British creditor, nor the State, will be permitted to lose by these payments. The debtor will be credited for what he paid, according to what it was really worth at the time he paid it, and he must pay the balance. Nor does he lose by this; for if a man who owed one thousand dollars to a British merchant, paid eight hundred paper dollars into the treasury, when the depreciation was at eight for one, it is clear he paid but one hundred real dollars, and must now pay nine hundred. It is probable, he received those eight hundred dollars for one hundred bushels of wheat, which were never worth more than one hundred silver dollars. He is credited, therefore, the full worth of his wheat. The equivoque is in the use of the word "dollar."

Page 226. *"Qu' on abolisse les privilèges du clergé."* This privilege, originally allowed to the clergy, is now extended to every man, and even to women. It is a right of exemption from capital punishment, for the first offence, in most cases. It is, then, a pardon by the law. In other cases, the Executive gives the pardon. But when laws are made as mild as they should be, both those pardons are absurd. The principle of Beccaria is sound. Let the legislators be merciful, but the executors of the law inexorable. As the term *"privilèges du clergé"* may be understood by foreigners, perhaps, it will be better to strike it out here, and substitute the word "pardon."

Page 239. *"Les commissaires veulent,"* &c. Manslaughter is the killing a man with design, but in a sudden gust of passion, and where the killer has not had time to cool. The first offence is not punished capitally, but the second is. This is the law of England and of all the American States; and is not now a new proposition. Those laws have supposed that a man, whose passions have so much dominion over him, as to lead him to repeated acts of murder, is unsafe to society: that it is better he should be put to death by the law, than others, more innocent than himself, on the movements of his impetuous passions.

Ibid. *"Mal-aisé d' indiquer la nuance précise,"* &c. In forming a scale of crimes and punishments, two considerations have principal weight. 1. The atrocity of the crime. 2. The peculiar circumstances of a country, which furnish greater temptations to commit it, or greater facilities for escaping detetection. The punishment must be heavier to counterbalance this. Were the first the only consideration, all nations would form the same scale. But, as the circumstances of a country have influence on the punishment, and no two countries exist precisely under the same circumstances, no two countries will form the same scale of crimes and punishments. For example; in America, the inhabitants let their horses go at large, in the uninclosed lands, which are so extensive, as to maintain them altogether. It is easy, therefore, to steal them, and easy to escape. Therefore, the laws are obliged to oppose these temptations with a heavier degree of punishment. For this reason, the stealing of a horse in America, is punished more severely, than stealing the same value in any other form. In Europe, where horses are confined so securely, that it is impossible to steal them, that species of theft need not be punished more severely than any other. In some countries of Europe, stealing fruit from trees is punished capitally. The reason is, that it being impossible to lock fruit trees up in coffers, as we do our money, it is impossible to oppose physical bars to this species of theft. Moral ones are, therefore, opposed by the laws. This, to an unreflecting American, appears the most enormous of all the abuses of power; because, he has been used to see fruits hanging in such quantities, that, if not taken by men, they would rot: he has been used to consider them, therefore, as of no value, and as not furnishing materials for the commission of a crime. This must serve as an apology for the arrangements of crimes and punishments, in the scale under our consideration. A different one would be formed here; and still different ones in Italy, Turkey, China, &c.

Page 240. *"Les officiers Américains,"* &c., to page 264, *"qui le méritoient."* I would propose to new model this section, in the following manner. 1. Give a succinct history of the origin and establishment of the Cincinnati. 2. Examine whether, in its present form, it threatens any dangers to the State. 3. Propose the most practicable method of preventing them.

Having been in America, during the period in which this institution was formed, and being then in a situation which gave me opportunities of seeing it, in all its stages, I may venture to give M. de Meusnier materials for the first branch of the preceding distribution of the subject. The second and third, he will best execute himself. I should write its history in the following form:

When, on the close of that war, which established the independence of America, its army was about to be disbanded, the officers, who, during the course of it, had gone through the most trying scenes together, who, by mutual aids and good offices, had become dear to one another, felt with great oppression of mind, the approach of that moment which was to separate them, never, perhaps, to meet again. They were from different States, and from distant parts of the same State. Hazard alone could, therefore, give them but rare and partial occasions of seeing each other. They were, of course, to abandon altogether the hope of ever meeting again, or to devise some occasion which might bring them together. And why not come together on purpose, at stated times? Would not the trouble of such a journey be greatly overpaid, by the pleasure of seeing each other again, by the sweetest of all consolations, the talking over the scenes of difficulty and of endearment they had gone through? This, too, would enable them to know who of them should succeed in the world, who should be unsuccessful, and to open the purses of all to every laboring brother. This idea was too soothing, not to be cherished in conversation. It was improved into that of a regular association, with an organized administration, with periodical meetings, general and particular, fixed contributions for those who should be in distress, and a badge, by which, not only those who had not had occasion to become personally known, should be able to recognize one another, but which should be worn by their descendants, to perpetuate among them the friendships which had bound their ancestors together.

General Washington was, at that moment, oppressed with the operation of disbanding an army which was not paid, and the difficulty of this operation was increased, by some two or three States having expressed sentiments, which did not indicate a sufficient attention to their payment. He was sometimes present, when his officers were fashioning in their conversations, their newly proposed society. He saw, the innocence of its origin, and foresaw no effects less innocent. He was, at that time, writing his valedictory letter to the States, which has been so deservedly applauded by the world. Far from thinking it a moment to multiply the causes of irritation, by thwarting a proposition which had absolutely no other basis but that of benevolence and friendship, he was rather satisfied to find himself aided in his difficulties by this new incident, which occupied, and, at the same time, soothed the minds of the officers. He thought, too, that this institution would be one instrument the more for strengthening the federal bond, and for promoting federal ideas. The institution was formed. They incorporated into it the officers of the French army and navy, by whose sides they had fought, and with whose aid they had finally prevailed, extending it to such grades as they were told might be permitted to enter into it. They sent an officer to France, to make the proposition to them, and to procure the badges which they had devised for their order. The moment of disbanding the army having come, before they could have a full meeting to appoint their President, the General was prayed to act in that office till their first general meeting, which was to be held at Philadelphia, in the month of May following.

The laws of the society were published. Men who read them in their closets, unwarmed by those sentiments of friendship which had produced them, inattentive to those pains which an approaching separation had excited in the minds of the institutors, politicians, who see in everything only the dangers with which it threatens civil society, in fine, the laboring people, who, shielded by equal laws, had never seen any difference between man and man, but had read of terrible oppressions, which people of their description experience in other countries, from those who are distinguished by titles and badges, began to be alarmed at this new institution. A remarkable silence, however, was observed. Their solicitiudes were long confined within the circles of private conversation. At length, however, a Mr. Burke, Chief Justice of South Carolina, broke that silence. He wrote against the new institution, foreboding its dangers, very imperfectly indeed, because he had nothing but his imagination to aid him. An American could do no more; for to detail the real evils of aristocracy, they must be seen in Europe. Burke's fears were thought exaggerations in America; while in Europe, it is known that even Mirabeau has but faintly sketched the curses of hereditary aristocracy as they are experienced here, and as they would have followed in America, had this institution remained. The epigraph of Burke's pamphlet, was, "Blow ye the trumpet in Zion." Its effect corresponded with its epigraph. This institution became, first, the subject of general conversation. Next, it was made the subject of deliberation in the legislative Assemblies of some of the States. The Governor of South Carolina censured it, in an address to the

Assembly of that State. The Assemblies of Massachusetts, Rhode Island, and Pennsylvania, condemned its principles. No circumstance, indeed, brought the consideration of it expressly before Congress; yet it had sunk deep into their minds. An offer having been made to them, on the part of the Polish order of Divine Providence, to receive some of their distinguished citizens into that order, they made that an occasion to declare, that these distinctions were contrary to the principles of their Confederation.

The uneasiness excited by this institution, had very early caught the notice of General Washington. Still recollecting all the purity of the motives which gave it birth, he became sensible that it might produce political evils, which the warmth of those motives had masked. Add to this, that it was disapproved by the mass of citizens of the Union. This, alone, was reason strong enough, in a country where the will of the majority is the law, and ought to be the law. He saw that the objects of the institution were too light, to be opposed to considerations as serious as these; and that it was become necessary to annihilate it absolutely. On this, therefore, he was decided. The first annual meeting at Philadelphia was now at hand; he went to that, determined to exert all his influence for its suppression. He proposed it to his fellow officers, and urged it with all his powers. It met an opposition which was observed to cloud his face with an anxiety, that the most distressful scenes of the war had scarcely ever produced. It was canvassed for several days, and, at length, it was no more a doubt what would be its ultimate fate. The order was on the point of receiving its annihilation, by the vote of a great majority of its members. In this moment, their envoy arrived from France, charged with letters from the French officers, accepting with cordiality the proposed badges of union, with solicitations from others to be received into the order, and with notice that their respectable Sovereign had been pleased to recognize it, and permit his officers to wear its badges. The prospect now changed. The question assumed a new form. After the offer made by them, and accepted by their friends, in what words could they clothe a proposition to retract it, which would not cover themselves with the reproaches of levity and ingratitude? which would not appear an insult to those whom they loved? Federal principles, popular discontent, were considerations whose weight was known and felt by themselves. But would foreigners know and feel them equally? Would they so far acknowledge their cogency, as to permit without any indignation, the eagle and ribbon to be torn from their breasts, by the very hands which had placed them there? The idea revolted the whole society. They found it necessary, then, to preserve so much of their institution as might continue to support this foreign branch, while they should prune off every other, which would give offence to their fellow citizens: thus sacrificing, on each hand, to their friends and to their country.

The society was to retain its existence, its name, its meetings, and its charitable funds: but these last were to be deposited with their respective legislatures. The order was to be no longer hereditary, a reformation, which had been pressed even from this side the Atlantic; it was to be communicated to no new members; the general meetings, instead of annual, were to be triennial only. The eagle and ribbon, indeed, were retained; because they were worn, and they wished them to be worn by their friends who were in a country where they would not be objects of offence; but themselves never wore them. They laid them up in their bureaus with the medals of American Independence, with those of the trophies they had taken, and the battles they had won. But through all the United States, no officer is seen to offend the public eye, with the display of this badge. These changes have tranquillized the American States. Their citizens feel too much interest in the reputation of their officers, and value too much, whatever may serve to recall to the memory of their allies, the moments wherein they formed but one people, not to do justice to the circumstance which prevented a total annihilation of the order. Though they are obliged by a prudent foresight, to keep out everything from among themselves, which might pretend to divide them into orders, and to degrade one description of men below another, yet they hear with pleasure, that their allies, whom circumstances have already placed under these distinctions, are willing to consider it as one, to have aided them in the establishment of their liberties, and to wear a badge which may recall them to their remembrance; and it would be an extreme affliction to them, if the domestic reformation which has been found necessary, if the censures of individual writers, or if any other circumstance should discourage the wearing their badge or lessen its reputation.

This short but true history of the order of the Cincinnati, taken from the mouths of persons on the spot, who were privy to its origin and progress, and who knew its present state, is the best apology which can be made for an insinuation, which appeared to be, and was really, so heterogeneous to the governments in which it was erected.

It should be further considered, that in America no other distinction between man and man had ever been known, but that of persons in office, exercising powers by authority of the laws, and private individuals. Among these last, the poorest laborer stood on equal ground with the wealthiest millionnaire, and generally on a more favored one, whenever their rights seemed to jar. It has been seen that a shoemaker or other artisan, removed by the voice of his country from his work bench into a chair of office, has instantly commanded all the respect and obedience which the laws ascribe to his office.

But of distinction by birth or badge, they had no more idea than they had of the mode of existence in the moon or planets. They had heard only that there were such, and knew that they must be wrong. A due horror of the evils which flow from these distinctions, could be excited in Europe only, where the dignity of man is lost in arbitrary distinctions, where the human species is classed into several stages of degradation, where the many are crushed under the weight of the few, and where the order established, can present to the contemplation of a thinking being, no other picture than that of God Almighty and his angels, trampling under foot the host of the damned. No wonder, then, that the institution of the Cincinnati should be innocently conceived by one order of American citizens, should raise in the other orders, only a slow, temperate, and rational opposition, and should be viewed in Europe as a detestable parricide.

The second and third branches of this subject, no body can better execute than M. de Meusnier. Perhaps it may be curious to him to see how they strike an American mind at present. He shall, therefore, have the ideas of one who was an enemy to the institution from the first moment of its conception, but who was always sensible that the officers neither foresaw nor intended the injury they were doing to their country.

As to the question, then, whether any evil can proceed from the institution as it stands at present, I am of opinion there may. 1. From the meetings. These will keep the officers formed into a body; will continue a distinction between the civil and military, which it would be for the good of the whole to obliterate, as soon as possible; and the military assemblies will not only keep alive the jealousies and fears of the civil government, but give ground for these fears and jealousies. For when men meet together, they will make business if they have none; they will collate their grievances, some real, some imaginary, all highly painted; they will communicate to each other the sparks of discontent; and these may engender a flame which will consume their particular, as well as the general happiness. 2. The charitable part of the institution is still more likely to do mischief, as it perpetuates the dangers apprehended in the preceding clause. For here is a fund provided of permanent existence. To whom will it belong? To the descendants of American officers of a certain description. These descendants, then, will form a body, having sufficient interest to keep up an attention to their description, to continue meetings, and perhaps, in some moment, when the political eye shall be slumbering, or the firmness of their fellow citizens relaxed, to replace the insignia of the order and revive all its pretensions. What good can the officers propose which may weigh against these possible evils? The securing their descendants against want? Why afraid to trust them to the same fertile soil, and the same genial climate, which will secure from want the descendants of their other fellow citizens? Are they afraid they will be reduced to labor the earth for their sustenance? They will be rendered thereby both more honest and happy. An industrious farmer occupies a more dignified place in the scale of beings, whether moral or political, than a lazy lounger, valuing himself on his family, too proud to work, and drawing out a miserable existence, by eating on that surplus of other men's labor, which is the sacred fund of the helpless poor. A pitiful annuity will only prevent them from exerting that industry and those talents which would soon lead them to better fortune.

How are these evils to be prevented? 1. At their first general meeting, let them distribute the funds on hand to the existing objects of their destination, and discontinue all further contributions. 2. Let them declare, at the same time, that their meetings, general and particular, shall thenceforth cease. 3. Let them melt up their eagles and add the mass to the distributable fund, that their descendants may have no temptation to hang them in their button holes.

These reflections are not proposed as worthy the notice of M. de Meusnier. He will be so good as to treat the subject in his own way, and no body has a better. I will only pray him to avail us of his forcible manner, to evince that there is evil to be apprehended, even from the ashes of this institution, and to exhort the society in America to make their reformation complete; bearing in mind, that we must keep the passions of men on our side, even when we are persuading them to do what they ought to do.

Page 268. *"Et en effet la population,"* &c. Page 270. *"Plus de confiance."*

To this we answer that no such census of the numbers was ever given out by Congress, nor ever presented to them: and further, that Congress never have, at any time, declared by their vote, the number of inhabitants in their respective States. On the 22d of June, 1775, they first resolved to emit paper money. The sum resolved on was two millions of dollars. They declared, then, that the twelve confederate colonies (for Georgia had not yet joined them) should be pledged for the redemption of these bills. To ascertain in what proportion each State should be bound, the members from each were desired to say, as nearly as they could, what was the number of the inhabitants of their respective States. They were very much unprepared for such a declaration. They guessed, however, as well as they could. The following are the numbers, as they conjectured them, and the consequent apportionment of the two millions of dollars.

	INHABITANTS	DOLLARS
New Hampshire	100,000	82,713
Massachusetts	350,000	289,496
Rhode Island	58,000	47,973
Connecticut	200,000	165,426
New York	200,000	165,426
New Jersey	130,000	107,527
Pennsylvania	300,000	248,139
Delaware	30,000	24,813
Maryland	250,000	206,783
Virginia	400,000	330,852
North Carolina	200,000	165,426
South Carolina	200,000	165,426
	2,418,000	2,000,000

Georgia having not yet acceded to the measures of the other States, was not quotaed; but her numbers were generally estimated at about thirty thousand, and so would have made the whole two million four hundred and forty-eight thousand persons, of every condition. But it is to be observed, that though Congress made this census the basis of their apportionment, yet they did not even give it a place on their journals; much less publish it to the world with their sanction. The way it got abroad was this: As the members declared from their seats the number of inhabitants which they conjectured to be in their State, the secretary of Congress wrote them on a piece of paper, calculated the portion of two millions of dollars to be paid by each, and entered the sum only in the journals. The members, however, for their own satisfaction, and the information of their States, took copies of this enumeration and sent them to their States. From thence they got into the public papers: and when the English news writers found it answer their purpose to compare this with the enumeration of 1783, as their principle is "to lie boldly that they may not be suspected of lying," they made it amount to three millions one hundred and thirty-seven thousand eight hundred and nine, and ascribed its publication to Congress itself.

In April, 1785, Congress being to call on the States to raise a million and a half of dollars annually for twenty-five years, it was necessary to apportion this among them. The States had never furnished them with their exact numbers. It was agreed, too, that in this apportionment five slaves should be counted as three freemen only. The preparation of this business was in the hands of a committee; they applied to the members for the best information they could give them of the number of their States. Some of the States had taken pains to discover their numbers. Others had done nothing in that way, and, of course, were now where they were in 1775, when their numbers were first called on to declare their numbers. Under these circumstances, and on the principle of counting three-fifths only of the slaves, the committee apportioned the money among the States, and reported their work to Congress. In this they had assessed South Carolina as having one hundred and seventy thousand inhabitants. The delegate for that State, however, prevailed on Congress to assess them on the footing of one hundred and fifty thousand only, in consideration of the state of total devastation in which the enemy had left their country. The difference was then laid on the other States, and the following was the result:

	INHABITANTS	DOLLARS
New Hampshire	82,200	52,708
Massachusetts	350,000	224,427
Rhode Island	50,400	32,318
Connecticut	206,000	132,091
New York	200,000	128,243
New Jersey	130,000	83,358
Pennsylvania	320,000	205,189
Delaware	35,000	22,443
Maryland	220,700	141,517
Virginia	400,000	256,487
North Carolina	170,000	109,006
South Carolina	150,000	96,183
Georgia	25,000	16,030
	2,339,300	1,500,000

Still, however, Congress refused to give the enumeration the sanction of a place on their journals, because it was not formed on such evidence as a strict attention to accuracy and truth required. They used it from necessity, because they could get no better rule, and they entered on their journals only the apportionment of money. The members, however, as before, took copies of the enumeration, which was the groundwork of the apportionment, sent them to their States, and thus this second enumeration got into the public papers, and was by the English ascribed to Congress as their declaration of their present numbers. To get at the real numbers which this enumeration supposes, we must add twenty thousand to the number on which South Carolina was quoted; we must consider that seven hundred thousand slaves are counted but as four hundred and twenty thousand persons, and add, on that account, two hundred and eighty thousand. This will give us a total of two millions six hundred and thirty-nine thousand three hundred inhabitants of every condition in the thirteen States, being two hundred and twenty-one thousand three hundred more than the enumeration of 1775, instead of seven hundred and ninety-eight thousand five hundred and nine less, which the English papers asserted to be the diminution of numbers in the United States, according to the confession of Congress themselves.

Page 272. "*Comportera peut-être une population de trente millions.*"

The territory of the United States contains about a million of square miles, English. There is, in them, a greater proportion of fertile lands than in the British dominions in Europe. Suppose the territory of the United States, then, to attain an equal degree of population with the British European dominions, they will have an hundred millions of inhabitants. Let us extend our views to what may be the population of the two continents of North and South America, supposing them divided at the narrowest part of the isthmus of Panama. Between this line and that of 50 ° of north latitude, the northern continent contains about five millions of square miles, and south of this line of division the southern continent contains about seven millions of square miles. I do not pass the 50th degree of northern latituude in my reckoning, because we must draw a line somewhere, and considering the soil and climate beyond that, I would only avail my calculation of it, as a make weight, to make good what the colder regions within that line may be supposed to fall short in their future population. Here are twelve millions of square miles, then, which, at the rate of population before assumed, will nourish twelve hundred millions of inhabitants, a number greater than the present population of the whole globe is supposed to amount to. If those who propose medals for the resolution of questions, about which nobody makes any question, those who have invited discussion on the pretended problem, Whether the discovery of America was for the good of mankind? if they, I say, would have viewed it only as doubling the numbers of mankind, and, of course, the quantum of existence and happiness, they might have saved the money and the reputation which their proposition has cost them. The present population of the inhabited parts of the United States is of about ten to the square mile; and experience has shown us, that wherever we reach that, the inhabitants become uneasy, as too much compressed, and go off in great numbers to search for vacant country. Within forty years their whole territory will be peopled at that rate. We may fix that, then, as the term beyond which the people of those States will not be restrained within their present limits; we may fix that population, too, as the limit which they will not exceed till the whole of those two continents are filled up to that mark, that is to say, till they shall contain one hundred and twenty millions of inhabitants. The soil of the country on the western side of the Mississippi, its climate, and its vicinity to the United States, point it out as the first which will receive population from that nest. The present occupiers will just have force enough to repress and restrain the emigrations to a certain degree of consistence. We have seen lately a single person go and decide on a settlement in Kentucky, many hundred miles from any white inhabitant, remove thither with his family and a few neighbors; and though perpetually harassed by the Indians, that settlement in the course of ten years has acquired thirty thousand inhabitants. Its numbers are increasing while we are writing, and the State, of which it formerly made a part, has offered it independence.

Page 280, line five. *"Huit des onze États,"* &c. Say, "There were ten States present; six voted unanimously for it, three against it, and one was divided; and seven votes being requisite to decide the proposition affirmatively, it was lost. The voice of a single individual of the State which was divided, or of one of those which were of the negative, would have prevented this abominable crime from spreading itself over the new country. Thus we see the fate of millions unborn hanging on the tongue of one man, and heaven was silent in that awful moment! But it is to be hoped it will not always be silent, and that the friends of the rights of human nature will in the end prevail.

"On the 16th of March, 1785, it was moved in Congress that the same proposition should be referred to a committee, and it was referred by the votes of eight States against three. We do not hear that anything further is yet done on it."

Page 286. *"L'autorité du Congrès étoit nécessaire."* The substance of the passage alluded to in the journal of Congress, May the 26th, 1784, is, "That the authority of Congress to make *requisitions* of troops during peace is questioned; that such an authority would be dangerous, combined with the acknowledged one of emitting or borrowing money; and that a few troops only being wanted to guard magazines and garrison the frontier posts, it would be more proper at present to *recommend* than to require."

Mr. Jefferson presents his compliments to M. de Meusnier, and sends him copies of the thirteenth, twenty-third, and twenty-fourth articles of treaty between the King of Prussia and the United States.

If M. de Meusnier proposed to mention the facts of cruelty of which he and Mr. Jefferson spoke yesterday, the twenty-fourth article will introduce them properly, because they produced a sense of the necessity of that article. These facts are, 1. The death of upwards of eleven thousand American prisoners in one prison ship (the Jersey), and in the space of three years. 2. General Howe's permitting our prisoners, taken at the battle of Germantown, and placed under a guard in the yard of the State-house of Philadelphia, to be so long without any food furnished them that many perished with hunger. Where the bodies laid, it was seen that they had eaten all the grass around them within their reach, after they had lost the power of rising, or moving from their place. 3. The second fact was the act of a commanding officer; the first, of several commanding officers, and for so long a time as must suppose the approbation of government. But the following was the act of government itself. During the periods that our affairs seemed unfavorable, and theirs successful, that is to say, after the evacuation of New York, and again, after the taking of Charleston, in South Carolina, they regularly sent our prisoners, taken on the seas and carried to England, to the East Indies. This is so certain, that in the month of November or December, 1785, Mr. Adams having officially demanded a delivery of the American prisoners sent to the East Indies, Lord Cærmarthen answered, officially, "That orders were immediately issued for their discharge." M. de Meusnier is at liberty to quote this fact. 4. A fact to be ascribed not only to the government, but to the parliament, who passed an act for that purpose in the beginning of the war, was the obliging our prisoners taken at sea, to join them, and fight against their countrymen. This they effected by starving and whipping them. The insult on Captain Stanhope, which happened at Boston last year, was a consequence of this. Two persons, Dunbar and Lowthorp, whom Stanhope had treated in this manner (having particularly inflicted twenty-four lashes on Dunbar), meeting him at Boston, attempted to beat him. But the people interposed and saved him. The fact is referred to in that paragraph of the Declaration of Independence, which says, "He has constrained our fellow-citizens, taken captive on the high seas, to bear arms against their country, to become the executioners of their friends and brethren, or to fall themselves by their hands." This was the most afflicting to our prisoners of all the cruelties exercised on them. The others affected the body only, but this the mind; they were haunted by the horror of having, perhaps, themselves shot the ball by which a father or a brother fell. Some of them had constancy enough to hold out against half allowance of food and repeated whippings. These were generally sent to England, and from thence to the East Indies. One of them escaped from the East Indies, and got back to Paris, where he gave an account of his sufferings to Mr. Adams, who happened to be then at Paris.

M. de Meusnier, where he mentions that the slave law has been passed in Virginia, without the clause of emancipation, is pleased to mention, that neither Mr. Wythe, nor Mr. Jefferson was present, to make the proposition they had meditated; from which, people, who do not give themselves the trouble to reflect or inquire, might conclude hastily, that their absence was the cause why the proposition was not made; and, of course, that there were not in the Asseembly, persons of virtue and firmness enough to propose the clause for emancipation. This supposition would not be true. There were persons there, who wanted neither the virtue to propose, nor talents to enforce the proposition, had they seen that the disposition of the legislature was ripe for it. These worthy characters would feel themselves wounded, degraded, and discouraged by this idea. Mr. Jefferson would therefore be obliged to M. de Meusnier, to mention it in some such manner as this. "Of the two commissioners, who had concerted the amendatory clause for the gradual emancipation of slaves, Mr. Wythe could not be present, he being a member of the judiciary department, and Mr. Jefferson was absent on the legation to France. But there were not wanting in that Assembly, men of virtue enough to propose, and talents to vindicate this clause. But they saw, that the moment of doing it with success was not yet arrived, and that an unsuccessful effort, as too often happens, would only rivet still closer the chains of bondage, and retard the moment of delivery to this oppressed description of men. What a stupendous, what an incomprehensible machine is man! who can endure toil, famine, stripes, imprisonment, and death itself, in vindication of his own liberty, and, the next moment be deaf to all those motives whose power supported him through his trial, and inflict on his fellow men a bondage, one hour of which is fraught with more misery, than ages of that which he rose in rebellion to oppose. But we must await, with patience, the workings of an overruling Providence, and hope that this is preparing the deliverance of these, our suffering brethren. When the measure of their tears shall be full, when their groans shall have involved heaven itself in darkness, doubtless, a God of justice will awaken to their distress, and by diffusing light and liberality among their oppressors, or, at length, by his exterminating thunder, manifest his attention to the things of this world, and that they are not left to the guidance of a blind fatality."

MEMORANDA TAKEN ON A JOURNEY FROM PARIS INTO THE SOUTHERN PARTS OF FRANCE, AND NORTHERN OF ITALY, IN THE YEAR 1787

March 3-June 10, 1787

CHAMPAGNE. March 3. *Sens* to *Vermanton*. The face of the country is in large hills, not too steep for the plough, somewhat resembling the Elk hill, and Beaver-dam hills of Virginia. The soil is generally a rich mulatto loam, with a mixture of coarse sand and some loose stone. The plains of the Yonne are of the same color. The plains are in corn, the hills in vineyard, but the wine not good. There are a few apple trees, but none of any other kind, and no inclosures. No cattle, sheep, or swine; fine mules.

Few châteaux; no farm-houses, all the people being gathered in villages. Are they thus collected by that dogma of their religion, which makes them believe, that to keep the Creator in good humor with his own works, they must mumble a mass every day? Certain it is, that they are less happy and less virtuous in villages, than they would be insulated with their families on the grounds they cultivate. The people are illy clothed. Perhaps they have put on their worst clothes at this moment, as it is raining. But I observe women and children carrying heavy burthens, and laboring with the hoe. This is an unequivocal indication of extreme poverty. Men, in a civilized country, never expose their wives and children to labor above their force and sex, as long as their own labor can protect them from it. I see few beggars. Probably this is the effect of a police.

BURGUNDY. March 4. *Lucy le bois. Cussy les forges. Rouvray. Maison-neuve. Vitteaux. La Chaleure. Pont de Panis. Dijon.* The hills are higher and more abrupt. The soil, a good red loam and sand, mixed with more or less grit, small stone, and sometimes rock. All in corn. Some forest wood here and there, broom, whins and holly, and a few inclosures of quick hedge. Now and then a flock of sheep.

The people are well clothed, but it is Sunday. They have the appearance of being well fed. The Château de Sevigny, near Cussy les forges, is a charming situation. Between Maison-neuve and Vitteaux the road leads through an avenue of trees, eight American miles long, in a right line. It is impossible to paint the ennui of this avenue. On the summits of the hills which border the valley in which Vitteaux is, there is a parapet of rock, twenty, thirty, or forty feet perpendicular, which crowns the hills. The tops are nearly level, and appear to be covered with earth. Very singular. Great masses of rock in the hills between la Chaleure and Pont de Panis, and a conical hill in the approach to the last place.

Dijon. The tavern price of a bottle of the best wine (*e.g.,* of Vaune) is four livres. The best round potatoes here I ever saw. They have begun a canal thirty feet wide, which is to lead into the Saone at ——. It is fed by springs. They are not allowed to take any water out of the riviere d'Ouche, which runs through this place, on account of the mills on that river. They talk of making a canal to the Seine, the nearest navigable part of which at present is fifteen leagues from hence. They have very light wagons here for the transportation of their wine. They are long and narrow; the fore wheels as high as the hind. Two pieces of wine are drawn by one horse in one of these wagons. The road in this part of the country is divided into portions of forty or fifty feet by stones, numbered, which mark the task of the laborers.

March 7 and 8. From *la Baraque* to *Chagny.* On the left are plains which extend to the Saone, on the right the ridge of mountains called the Cote. The plains are of a reddish-brown, rich loam, mixed with much small stone. The Cote has for its basis a solid rock, on which is about a foot of soil and small stone, in equal quantities, the soil red and of middling quality. The plains are in corn; the Cote in vines. The former have no inclosures, the latter is in small ones of dry stone wall. There is a good deal of forest. Some small herds of small cattle and sheep. Fine mules, which come from Provence, and cost twenty louis. They break them at two years old, and they last to thirty.

The corn lands here rent for about fifteen livres the arpent. They are now planting, pruning, and sticking their vines. When a new vineyard is made, they plant the vines in gutters about four feet apart. As the vines advance, they lay them down. They put out new shoots, and fill all the intermediate space, till all trace of order is lost. They have ultimately about one foot square to each vine. They begin to yield good profit at five or six years old, and last one hundred, or one hundred and fifty years. A vigneron at Voulenay carried me into his vineyard, which was of about ten arpents. He told me that some years it produced him sixty pieces of wine, and some, not more than three pieces. The latter is the most advantageous produce, because the wine is better in quality, and higher in price in proportion as less is made, and the expenses at the same time diminsh in the same proportion. Whereas, when much is made, the expenses are increased, while the price and quality become less. In very plentiful years, they often give one half the wine for casks to contain the other half. The cask for two hundred and fifty bottles, costs six livres in scarce years, and ten in plentiful. The Feuillette is of one hundred and twenty-five bottles, the Piece of two hundred and fifty, and the Queue or Botte, of five hundred. An arpent rents at from twenty to sixty livres. A farmer of ten arpents has about three laborers engaged by the year. He pays four louis to a man, and half as much to a woman, and feeds them. He kills one hog, and salts it, which is all the meat used in the family during the year.

Their ordinary food is bread and vegetables. At Pommard and Voulenay, I observed them eating good wheat bread; at Meursault, rye. I asked the reason of this difference. They told me that the white wines fail in quality much oftener than the red, and remain on hand. The farmer, therefore, cannot afford to feed his laborers so well. At Meursault, only white wines are made, because there is too much stone for the red. On such slight circumstances depends the condition of man! The wines which have given such celebrity to Burgundy, grow only on the Cote, an extent of about five leagues long, and half a league wide. They begin at Chambertin, and go through Vougeau, Romanie, Veanue, Nuys, Beaune, Pommard, Voulenay, Meursault, and end at Monrachet. Those of the two last are white, the others red. Chambertin, Vougeau and Veaune are strongest, and will bear transportation and keeping. They sell, therefore, on the spot for twelve hundred livres the queue, which is forty-eight sous the bottle. Voulenay is the best of the other reds, equal in flavor to Chambertin, etc., but being lighter, will not keep, and therefore sells for not more than three hundred livres the queue, which is twelve sous the bottle. It ripens sooner than they do, and consequently is better for those who wish to broach at a year old. In like manner of the white wines, and for the same reason, Monrachet sells for twelve hundred livres the queue (forty-eight sous the bottle), and Meursault of the best quality, viz., the Goutte d'or, at only one hundred and fifty livres (six sous the bottle). It is remarkable, that the best of each kind, that is, of the red and white, is made at the extremities of the line, to wit, at Chambertin and Monrachet. It is pretended that the adjoining vineyards produce the same qualities, but that belonging to obscure individuals, they have not obtained a name, and therefore sell as other wines. The aspect of the Cote is a little south of east. The western side is also covered with vines, and is apparently of the same soil, yet the wines are of the coarsest kinds. Such, too, are those which are produced in the plains; but there the soil is richer and less strong. Vougeau is the property of the monks of Citeaux, and produces about two hundred pieces. Monrachet contains about fifty arpents, and produces, one year with another, about one hundred and twenty pieces. It belongs to two proprietors only, Monsieur de Clarmont, who leases to some wine merchants, and the Marquis de Sarsnet, of Dijon, whose part is farmed to a Monsieur de la Tour, whose family for many generations have had the farm. The best wines are carried to Paris by land. The transportation costs thirty-six livres the piece. The more indifferent go by water. Bottles cost four and a half sous each.

March 9. *Chalons. Sennecy. Tournus. St. Albin. Macon.* On the left are fine plains of the Saone; on the right, high lands, rather waving than hilly, sometimes sloping gently to the plains, sometimes dropping down in precipices, and occasionally broken into beautiful valleys by the streams which run into the Saone. The plains are a dark rich loam, in pasture and corn; the heights more or less red or reddish, always gritty, of middling quality only, their sides in vines, and their summits in corn. The vineyards are inclosed with dry stone walls, and there are some quick hedges in the corn grounds. The cattle are few and indifferent. There are some good oxen, however. They draw by the head. Few sheep, and small. A good deal of wood lands.

I passed three times the canal called le Charollois, which they are opening from Chalons on the Saone to Dijon on the Loire. It passes near Chagny, and will be twenty-three leagues long. They have worked on it three years, and will finish it in four more. It will reanimate the languishing commerce of Champagne and Burgundy, by furnishing a water transportation for their wines to Nantes, which also will receive new consequence by becoming the emporium of that commerce. At some distance on the right are high mountains, which probably form the separation between the waters of the Saone and Loire. Met a malefactor in the hands of one of the Marechausée; perhaps a dove in the talons of the hawk. The people begin now to be in separate establishments, and not in villages. Houses are mostly covered with tile.

BEAUJOLOIS. *Maison blanche. St. George, Château de Laye-Epinaye.* The face of the country is like that from Chalons to Macon. The plains are a dark rich loam, the hills a red loam of middling quality, mixed generally with more or less coarse sand and grit, and a great deal of small stone. Very little forest. The vineyards are mostly inclosed with dry stone wall. A few small cattle and sheep. Here, as in Burgundy, the cattle are all white.

This is the richest country I ever beheld. It is about ten or twelve leagues in length, and three, four, or five in breadth; at least, that part of it which is under the eye of the traveller. It extends from the top of a ridge of mountains, running parallel with the Saone, and sloping down to the plains of that river, scarcely anywhere too steep for the plough. The whole is thick set with farm-houses, chauteaux, and the Bastides of the inhabitants of Lyons. The people live separately, and not in villages. The hillsides are in vine and corn; the plains in corn and pasture. The lands are farmed either for money, or on half-stocks. The rents of the corn lands, farmed for money, are about ten or twelve livres the arpent. A farmer takes, perhaps, about one hundred and fifty arpents, for three, six, or nine years. The first year they are in corn; the second in other small grain, with which he sows red clover. The third is for the clover. The spontaneous pasturage is of green sward, which they call fromenteau. When lands are rented on half-stocks, the cattle, sheep, etc., are furnished by the landlord. They are valued, and must be left of equal value. The increase of these, as well as the produce of the farm, is divided equally. These leases are only from year to year. They have a method of mixing beautifully the culture of vines, trees, and corn. Rows of fruit trees are planted about twenty feet apart. Between the trees, in the row, they plant vines four feet apart, and espalier them. The intervals are sowed alternately in corn, so as to be one year in corn, the next in pasture, the third in corn, the fourth in pasture, etc. One hundred toises of vines in length, yield generally about four pieces of wine. In Dauphiné, I am told, they plant vines only at the roots of the trees, and let them cover the whole trees. But this spoils both the wine and the fruit. Their wine when distilled, yields but one-third its quantity in brandy. The wages of a laboring man here, are five louis; of a woman, one half. The women do not work with the hoe; they only weed the vines, the corn, etc., and spin. They speak a patois very difficult to understand. I passed some time at the Chateau de Laye-Epinaye. Monsieur de Laye has a seignory of about fifteen thousand arpents, in pasture, corn, vines, and wood. He has over this, as is usual, a certain jurisdiction, both criminal and civil. But this extends only to the first crude examination, which is before his judges. The subject is referred for final examination and decision, to the regular judicatures of the country. The Seigneur is keeper of the peace of his domains. He is therefore subject to the expenses of maintaining it. A criminal prosecuted to sentence and execution, costs M. de Laye about five thousand livres. This is so burdensome to the Seigneurs, that they are slack in criminal prosecutions. A good effect from a bad cause. Through all Champagne, Burgundy, and the Beaujolois, the husbandry seems good, except that they manure too little. This proceeds from the shortness of their leases. The people of Burgundy and Beaujolois are well clothed, and have the appearance of being well fed. But they experience all the oppressions which result from the nature of the general government, and from that of their particular tenures, and of the seignorial government to which they are subject. What a cruel reflection, that a rich country cannot long be a free one. M. de Laye has a Diana and Endymion, a very superior morsel of sculpture by Michael Angelo Slodtz, done in 1740. The wild gooseberry is in leaf; the wild pear and sweet briar in bud.

Lyons. There are some feeble remains here, of an amphitheatre of two hundred feet diameter, and of an aqueduct in brick. The Pont d'Ainay has nine arches of forty feet from centre to centre. The piers are of six feet. The almond is in bloom.

DAUPHINÉ. From *St. Fond* to *Mornas.* March 15, 16, 17, 18. The Rhone makes extensive plains, which lie chiefly on the eastern side, and are often in two stages. Those of Montelimart are three or four miles wide, and rather good. Sometimes, as in the neighborhood of Vienne, the hills come in precipices to the river, resembling then very much our Susquehanna and its hills, except that the Susquehanna is ten times as wide as the Rhone. The highlands are often very level. The soil, both of hill and plain, where there is soil, is generally tinged, more or less, with red. The hills are sometimes mere masses of rock, sometimes a mixture of loose stone and earth. The plains are always stony, and, as often as otherwise, covered perfectly with a coat of round stones, of the size of the fist, so as to resemble the remains of inundations, from which all the soil has been carried away. Sometimes they are middling good, sometimes barren. In the neighborhood of Lyons, there is more corn than wine. Towards Tains, more wine than corn. From thence, the plains, where best, are in corn, clover, almonds, mulberries, walnuts; where there is still some earth, they are in corn, almonds, and oaks. The hills are in vines. There is a good deal of forest-wood near Lyons, but not much afterwards. Scarcely any inclosures. There are a few small sheep before we reach Tains; there the number increases.

Nature never formed a country of more savage aspect, than that on both sides the Rhone. A huge torrent rushes like an arrow between high precipices, often of massive rock, at other times of loose stone, with but little earth. Yet has the hand of man subdued this savage scene, by planting corn where there is a little fertility, trees where there is still less, and vines where there is none. On the whole, it assumes a romantic, picturesque, and pleasing air. The hills on the opposite side of the river, being high, steep, and laid up in terraces, are of a singular appearance. Where the hills are quite in waste, they are covered with broom, whins, box, and some clusters of small pines. The high mountains of Dauphiné and Languedoc are now covered with snow. The almond is in general bloom, and the willow putting out its leaf. There were formerly olives at Pains; but a great cold, some years ago, killed them, and they have not been replanted. I am told at Montelimart, that an almond tree yields about three livres profit a year. Supposing them three toises apart, there will be one hundred to the arpent, which gives three hundred livres a year, besides the corn growing on the same ground. A league below Vienne, on the opposite side of the river, is Cote Rotie. It is a string of broken hills, extending a league on the river, from the village of Ampuys to the towns of Condrieux. The soil is white, tinged a little, sometimes, with yellow, sometimes with red, stony, poor, and laid up in terraces. Those parts of the hills only, which look to the sun at midday, or the earlier hours of the afternoon, produce wines of the first quality. Seven hundred vines, three feet apart, yield a feuillette, which is about two and a half pieces, to the arpent. The best red wine is produced at the upper end, in the neighborhood of Ampuys; the best white, next to Condrieux. They sell of the first quality and last vintage, at one hundred and fifty livres the piece, equal to twelve sous the bottle. Transportation to Paris is sixty livres, and the bottle four sous; so it may be delivered at Paris in bottles, at twenty sous. When old, it costs ten or eleven louis the piece. There is a quality which keeps well, bears transportation, and cannot be drunk under four years. Another must be drunk at a year old. They are equal in flavor and price.

The wine called Hermitage is made on the hills impending over the village of Tains; on one of which is the hermitage, which gives name to the hills for about two miles, and to the wine made on them. There are but three of those hills which produce wine of the first quality, and of these, the middle regions only. They are about three hundred feet perpendicular height, three-quarters of a mile in length, and have a southern aspect. The soil is scarcely tinged red, consists of small rotten stone, and is, where the best wine is made, without any perceptible mixture of earth. It is in sloping terraces. They use a little dung. An homme de vignes, which consists of seven hundred plants, three feet apart, yields generally about three quarters of a piece, which is nearly four pieces to the arpent. When new, the piece is sold at about two hundred and twenty-five livres; when old, at three hundred. It cannot be drunk under four years, and improves fastest in a hot situation. There is so little white made in proportion to the red, that it is difficult to buy it separate. They make the white sell the red. If bought separately, it is from fifteen to sixteen louis the piece, new, and three livres the bottle, old. To give quality to the red, they mix one eight of white grapes. Portage to Paris is seventy-two livres the piece, weighing six hundred pounds. There are but about one thousand pieces of both red and white, of the first quality, made annually. Vineyards are never rented here, nor are laborers in the vineyard hired by the year. They leave buds proportioned to the strength of the vine; sometimes as much as fifteen inches. The last hermit died in 1751.

In the neighborhood of Montelimart, and below that, they plant vines in rows, six, eight, or ten feet apart, and two feet asunder in the row, filling the intervals with corn. Sometimes the vines are in double rows, two feet apart. I saw single asses in ploughs proportioned to their strength. There are few chateaux in this province. The people, too, are mostly gathered into villages. There are, however, some scattering farm-houses. These are made either of mud, or of round stone and mud. They make inclosures also, in both those ways. Day laborers receive sixteen or eighteen sous the day, and feed themselves. Those by the year receive, men three louis, women half that, and are fed. They rarely eat meat; a single hog salted, being the year's stock for a family. But they have plenty of cheese, eggs, potatoes and other vegetables, and walnut oil with their salad. It is a trade here, to gather dung along the road for their vines. This proves they have few cattle. I have seen neither hares nor partridges since I left Paris, nor wild fowl on any of the rivers. The roads from Lyons to St. Rambert, are neither paved nor gravelled. After that, they are coated with broken flint. The ferry boats on the Rhone and the Isere, are moved by the stream, and very rapidly. On each side of the river is a movable stage, one end of which is on an axle and two wheels, which, according to the tide, can be advanced or withdrawn, so as to apply to the gunwale of the boat. The Prætorian palace at Vienne is forty-four feet wide, of the Corinthian order, four columns in front, and four in flank. It was begun in the year 400, and finished by Charlemagne. The Sepulchral pyramid, a little way out of the town, has an order for its basement, the pedestal of which, from point to point of its cap, is twenty-four feet one inch. At each angle, is a column, engaged one fourth in the wall. The circumference of the three fourths disengaged, is four feet four inches; consequently, the diameter is twenty-three inches. The base of the column indicates it to be Ionic, but the capitals are not formed. The cornice, too, is a bastard Ionic, without modillions or dentils. Between the columns, on each side, is an arch of eight feet four inches, opening with a pilaster on each side of it. On the top of the basement is a zocle, in the plane of the frieze below. On that is the pyramid, its base in the plane of the collarins of the pilaster below. The pyramid is a little truncated on its top. This monument is inedited.

March 18th. *Principality of Orange.* The plains on the Rhone here are two or three leagues wide, reddish, good, in corn, clover, almonds, olives. No forests. Here begins the country of olives, there being very few till we enter this principality. They are the only tree which I see planted among vines. Thyme grows wild here on the hills. Asses, very small, sell here for two or three louis. The high hills in Dapuhiné are covered with snow. The remains of the Roman aqueduct are of brick: a fine piece of Mosaic, still on its bed, forming the floor of a cellar. Twenty feet of it still visible. They are taking down the circular wall of the amphitheatre to pave a road.

March 19th to 23d. LANGUEDOC. *Pont St. Esprit. Bagnols, Connault. Valignieres. Remoulins. St. Gervasy, Nismes, Pont d'Arles.* To Remoulins, there is a mixture of hill and dale. Thence to Nismes, hills on the right, on the left, plains extending to the Rhone and the sea. The hills are rocky. Where there is soil, it is reddish and poor. The plains, generally reddish and good, but stony. When you approach the Rhone, going to Arles, the soil becomes a dark gray loam with some sand, and very good. The culture is corn, clover, St. foin, olives, vines, mulberries, willow, and some almonds. There is no forest. The hills are inclosed in dry stone wall. Many sheep.

From the summit of the first hill, after leaving Pont St. Esprit, there is a beautiful view of the bridge at about two miles distance, and a fine landscape of the country both ways. From thence, an excellent road, judiciously conducted, through very romantic scenes. In one part, descending the face of a hill, it is laid out in serpentine, and not zigzag, to ease the descent. In others, it passes through a winding meadow, from fifty to one hundred yards, walled, as it were, on both sides, by hills of rock; and at length issues into plain country. The waste hills are covered with thyme, box, and chenevert. Where the body of the mountains has a surface of soil, the summit has sometimes a crown of rock, as observed in Champagne. At Nismes, the earth is full of limestone. The horses are shorn. They are now pruning the olive. A very good tree produces sixty pounds of olives, which yield fifteen pounds of oil; the best quality sells at twelve sous the pound retail, and ten sous, wholesale.. The high hills of Languedoc still covered with snow. The horse chestnut and mulberry are leafing; apple trees and peas blossoming. The first butterfly I have seen. After the vernal equinox, they are often six or eight months without rain. Many separate farm-houses, numbers of people in rags, and abundance of beggars. The mine of wheat, weighing thirty pounds, costs four livres and ten sous. Wheat bread, three sous the pound. Vin ordinaire, good, and of a strong body, two or three sous the bottle. Oranges, one sou apiece. They are nearly finishing at Nismes, a great mill, worked by a steam engine, which pumps water from a lower into an upper cistern, from whence two overshot wheels are supplied, each of which turns two pair of stones. The upper cistern being once filled with water, it passes through the wheels into the lower one, from whence it is returned to the upper by the pumps. A stream of water of one quarter or one half inch diameter, supplies the waste of evaporation, absorption, etc. This is furnished from a well by a horse. The arches of the Pont St. Esprit are of eighty-eight feet. Wild figs, very flourishing, grow out of the joints of the Pont du Gard. The fountain of Nismes is so deep, that a stone was thirteen seconds descending from the surface to the bottom.

March 24th. From *Nismes* to *Arles*. The plains extending from Nismes to the Rhone, in the direction of Arles, are broken in one place by a skirt of low hills. They are red and stony at first, but as you approach the Rhone, they are of a dark gray mould, with a little sand, and very good. They are in corn and clover, vines, olives, almonds, mulberries, and willow. There are some sheep, no wood, no inclosures.

The high hills of Languedoc are covered with snow. At an ancient church, in the suburbs of Arles, are some hundreds of ancient stone coffins, along the roadside. The ground is thence called les champs elysées. In a vault in a church, are some curiously wrought, and in a back yard are many ancient statues, inscriptions, etc. Within the town, are a part of two Corinthian columns, and of the pediment with which they were crowned, very rich, having belonged to the ancient capitol of the place. But the principal monument here, is an amphitheatre, the external portico of which is tolerably complete. How many porticoes there were, cannot be seen: but at one of the principal gates, there are still five, measuring, from out to in, seventy-eight feet ten inches, the vault diminishing inwards. There are sixty-four arches, each of which is, from centre to centre, twenty feet six inches. Of course, the diameter is of four hundred and thirty-eight feet; or of four hundred and fifty feet, if we suppose the four principal arches a little larger than the rest. The ground-floor is supported on innumerable vaults. The first story, externally, has a tall pedestal, like a pilaster, between every two arches: the upper story, a column, the base of which would indicate it Corinthian. Every column is truncated as low as the impost of the arch, but the arches are all entire. The whole of the upper entablature is gone, and of the Attic, if there was one. Not a single seat of the internal is visible. The whole of the inside, and nearly the whole of the outside, is masked by buildings. It is supposed there are one thousand inhabitants within the amphitheatre. The walls are more entire and firm than those of the amphitheatre at Nismes. I suspect its plan and distribution to have been very different from that.

Terrasson. The plains of the Rhone from Arles to this place, are a league or two wide: the mould is of a dark gray, good, in corn and lucerne. Neither wood, nor inclosures. Many sheep.

St. Remis. From Terrasson to St. Remis, is a plain of a league or two wide, bordered by broken hills of massive rock. It is gray and stony, mostly in olives. Some almonds, mulberries, willows, vines, corn, and lucerne. Many sheep. No forest, nor inclosures.

A laboring man's wages here, are one hundred and fifty livres, a woman's half, and fed. Two hundred and eighty pounds of wheat sell for forty-two livres. They make no butter here. It costs, when brought, fifteen sous the pound. Oil is ten sous the pound. Tolerably good olive trees yield, one with another, about twenty pounds of oil. An olive tree must be twenty years old before it has paid its own expenses. It lasts forever. In 1765, it was so cold that the Rhone was frozen over at Arles for two months. In 1767, there was a cold spell of a week, which killed all the olive trees. From being fine weather, in one hour there was ice hard enough to bear a horse. It killed people on the road. The old roots of the olive trees put out again. Olive grounds sell for twenty-four livres a tree, and lease at twenty-four sous the tree. The trees are fifteen pieds apart. But lucerne is a more profitable culture. An arpent yields one hundred quintals of hay a year, worth three livres the quintal. It is cut four or five times a year. It is sowed in the broadcast, and lasts five or six years. An arpent of ground for corn, rents at from thirty to thirty-six livres. Their leases are for six or nine years. They plant willow for fire-wood, and for hoops to their casks. It seldom rains here in summer. There are some chateaux, many separate farm-houses, good, and ornamented in the small way, so as to show that the tenant's whole time is not occupied in procuring physical necessaries.

March 25th. *Orgon. Pontroyal. St. Cannat.* From Orgon to Pontroyal, after quitting the plains of the Rhone, the country seems still to be a plain, cut into compartments by chains of mountains of massive rock, running through it in various directions. From Pontroyal to St. Cannat, the land lies rather in basins. The soil is very various, gray and clay, gray and stony, red and stony; sometimes good, sometimes middling, often barren. We find some golden willows. Towards Pontroyal, the hills begin to be in vines, and afterwards, in some pasture of green sward and clover. About Orgon are some inclosures of quick set, others of conical yews planted close. Towards St. Cannat, they begin to be of stone.

The high mountains are covered with snow. Some separate farm-houses of mud. Near Pontroyal is a canal for watering the country; one branch goes to Terrasson, the other to Arles.

March 25th, 26th, 27th, 28th. *Aix.* The country is waving, in vines, pasture of green sward and clover, much inclosed with stone, and abounding with sheep.

On approaching Aix, the valley which opens from thence towards the mouth of the Rhone and the sea, is rich and beautiful; a perfect grove of olive trees, mixed among which, are corn, lucerne, and vines. The waste grounds throw out thyme and lavender. Wheat bread is three sous the pound. Cow's milk sixteen sous the quart, sheep's milk six sous, butter of sheep's milk twenty sous the pound. Oil, of the best quality, is twelve sous the pound, and sixteen sous if it be virgin oil. This is what runs from the olive when put into the press, spontaneously; afterwards they are forced by the press and by hot water. Dung costs ten sous the one hundred pounds. Their fire-wood is chene-vert and willow. The latter is lopped every three years. An ass sells for from one to three louis; the best mules for thirty louis. The best asses will carry two hundred pounds; the best horses three hundred pounds; the best mules six hundred pounds. The temperature of the mineral waters of Aix, is 90 ° of Fahrenheit's thermometer, at the spout. A mule eats half as much as a horse. The allowance to an ass for the day, is a handful of bran mixed with straw. The price of mutton and beef, about six and a half sous the pound. The beef comes from Auvergne, and is poor and bad. The mutton is small, but of excellent flavor. The wages of a laboring man are one hundred and fifty livres the year, a woman's sixty to sixty-six livres, and fed. Their bread is half wheat, half rye, made once in three or four weeks, to prevent too great a consumption. In the morning, they eat bread with an anchovy, or an onion. Their dinner in the middle of the day, is bread, soup, and vegetables. Their supper the same. With their vegetables, they have

always oil and vinegar. The oil costs about eight sous the pound. They drink what is called piquette. This is made after the grapes are pressed, by pouring hot water on the pumice. On Sunday they have meat and wine. Their wood for building comes mostly from the Alps, down the Durance and Rhone. A stick of pine, fifty feet long, girting six feet and three inches at one end, and three feet three inches at the other, costs, delivered here, from fifty-four to sixty livres. Sixty pounds of wheat cost seven livres. One of their little asses will travel with his burden about five or six leagues a day, and day by day; a mule from six to eight leagues.[1]

March 29. *Marseilles.* The country is hilly, intersected by chains of hills and mountains of massive rock. The soil is reddish, stony, and indifferent where best. Wherever there is any soil, it is covered with olives. Among these are corn, vines, some lucerne, mulberry, some almonds and willow. Neither inclosures, nor forest. A very few sheep.

On the road I saw one of those little whirlwinds which we have in Virginia, also some gullied hillsides. The people are in separate establishments. Ten morning observations of the thermometer, from the 20th to the 31st of March inclusive, made at Nismes, St. Remis, Aix and Marseilles, give me an average of 52½°, and 46° and 61° for the greatest and least morning heats. Nine afternoon observations, yield an average of 62⅔°, and 57° and 66° the greatest and least. The longest day here, from sunrise to sunset, is fifteen hours and fourteen minutes; the shortest is eight hours and forty-six minutes; the latitude being ———. There are no tides in the Mediterranean. It is observed to me, that the olive tree grows nowhere more than thirty leagues distant from that sea. I suppose, however, that both Spain and Portugal furnish proofs to the contrary, and doubt its truth as to Asia, Africa, and America. They are six or eight months at a time, here, without rain. The most delicate figs known in Europe, are those growing about this place, called figues Marcelloises, or les veritables Marcelloises, to distinguish them from others of inferior quality growing here. These keep any length of time. All others exude a sugar in the spring of the year, and become sour. The only process for preserving them, is drying them in the sun, without putting anything to them whatever. They sell at fifteen sous the pound, while there are others as cheap as five sous the pound. I meet here a small dried grape from Smyrna without a seed. There are few of the plants growing in this neighborhood. The best grape for drying known here, is called des Panses. They are very large, with a thick skin and much juice. They are best against a wall of southern aspect, as their abundance of juice requires a great deal of sun to dry it. Pretty good fig trees are about the size of the

[1] It is twenty American miles from Aix to Marseilles, and they call it five leagues. Their league, then, is of four American miles.—T. J.

apricot tree, and yield about twenty pounds of figs when dry, each. But the largest will yield the value of a louis. They are sometimes fifteen inches in diameter. It is said the Marseilles fig degenerates when transported into any other part of the country. The leaves of the mulberry tree will sell for about three livres, the purchaser gathering them. The caper is a creeping plant. It is killed to the roots every winter. In the spring it puts out branches, which creep to the distance of three feet from the centre. The fruit forms on the stem as that extends itself, and must be gathered every day as it forms. This is the work of women. The pistache grows in this neighborhood also, but not very good. They eat them in their milky state. Monsieur de Bergasse has a wine cellar two hundred and forty pieds long, in which are one hundred and twenty tuns, of from fifty to one hundred pieces each. These tuns are twelve pieds diameter; the staves four inches thick, the heading two and a half pouces thick. The temperature of his cellar is of $9\frac{1}{2}°$ of Reaumur. The best method of packing wine, when bottled, is to lay the bottles on their side, and cover them with sand. The 2d of April, the young figs are formed; the 4th we have Windsor beans. They have had asparagus ever since the middle of March. The 5th, I see strawberries and the Guelder rose in blossom. To preserve the raisin, it is first dipped into ley and then dried in the sun. The aloe grows in the open ground. I measured a mule, not the largest, five feet and two inches high. Marseilles is in an amphitheatre, at the mouth of the Vaune, surrounded by high mountains of naked rock, distant two or three leagues. The country within that amphitheatre is a mixture of small hills, valleys, and plains. The latter are naturally rich. The hills and valleys are forced into production. Looking from the Chateau de Notre Dame de la Garde, it would seem as if there was a Bastide for every arpent. The plain land sells for one hundred louis the caterelle, which is less than an acre. The ground of the arsenal in Marseilles, sold for from fifteen to forty louis the square verge, being nearly the square yard English. In the fields open to the sea, they are obliged to plant rows of canes, every here and there, to break the force of the wind. Saw at the Chateau Borelli, pumps worked by the wind.

April 6. From *Marseilles* to *Aubagne*. A valley on the Vaune, bordered on each side by high mountains of massive rock, on which are only some small pines. The interjacent valley is of small hills, valleys and plains, reddish, gravelly, and originally poor, but fertilized by art, and covered with corn, vines, olives, figs, almonds, mulberries, lucerne and clover. The river is twelve or fifteen feet wide, one or two feet deep, and rapid.

From *Aubagne* to *Cuges, Beausset, Toulon*. The road quitting the Vaune and its wealthy valley, a little after Aubagne, enters those mountains of rock, and is engaged with them about a dozen miles. Then it passes six or eight

miles through a country still very hilly and stony, but laid up in terraces, covered with olives, vines and corn. It then follows for two or three miles a hollow between two of those high mountains, which has been found or made by a small stream. The mountains then, reclining a little from their perpendicular, and presenting a coat of soil, reddish and tolerably good, have given place to the little village of Olioules, in the gardens of which are oranges in the open ground. It continues hilly till we enter the plain of Toulon. On different parts of this road there are figs in the open fields. At Cuges, is a plain of about three-fourths of a mile in diameter, surrounded by high mountains of rock. In this, the caper is principally cultivated. The soil is mulatto, gravelly, and of middling quality, or rather indifferent. The plants are set in quincunx, about eight feet apart. They have been covered during winter by a hill of earth a foot high. They are now inclosing, pruning and ploughing them.

Toulon. From Olioules to Toulon, the figs are in the open fields. Some of them have stems of fifteen inches diameter. They generally fork near the ground, but sometimes have a single stem of five feet long. They are as large as apricot trees. The olive trees of this day's journey are about the size of large apple trees. The people are in separate establishments. Toulon is in a valley at the mouth of the Goutier, a little river of the size of the Vaune; surrounded by high mountains of naked rock, leaving some space between them and the sea. This space is hilly, reddish, gravelly, and of middling quality, in olives, vines, corn, almonds, figs and capers. The capers are planted eight feet apart. A bush yields, one year with one another, two pounds, worth twelve sous the pound. Every plant then, yields twenty-four sous, equal to one shilling sterling. An acre containing six hundred and seventy-six plants, would yield thirty-three pounds sixteen shillings sterling. The fruit is gathered by women, who can gather about twelve pounds a day. They begin to gather about the last of June, and end about the middle of October. Each plant must be picked every day. These plants grow equally well in the best or worst soil, or even in the walls where there is no soil. They will last the life of a man or longer. The heat is so great at Toulon in summer, as to occasion very great cracks in the earth. Where the caper is in a soil that will admit it, they plough it. They have peas here through the winter, sheltering them occasionally; and they have had them ever since the 25th of March without shelter.

April 6. *Hieres.* This is a plain of two or three miles diameter, bounded by the sea on one side, and mountains of rock on the other. The soil is reddish, gravelly, tolerably good and well watered. It is in olives, mulberries, vines, figs, corn, and some flax. There are also some cherry trees. From Hieres to the sea, which is two or three miles, is a grove of orange trees, olives, and mulberries. The largest orange tree is of two feet diameter one way, and one foot the other, (for the section of all the larger ones would be an oval, not a round,) and about twenty feet high. Such a tree will yield about six thousand oranges a year. The garden of M. Fille, has fifteen thousand six hundred orange trees. Some years they yield forty thousand livres, some only ten thousand; but generally about twenty-five thousand. The trees are from eight to ten feet apart. They are blossoming and bearing all the year, flowers and fruit in every stage, at the same time. But the best fruit is that which is gathered in April and May. Hieres is a village of about five thousand inhabitants, at the foot of a mountain which covers it from the north, and from which extends a plain of two or three miles to the sea-shore. It has no port. Here are palm trees twenty or thirty feet high, but they bear no fruit. There is also a botanical garden kept by the King. Considerable salt ponds here. Hieres is six miles from the public road. It is built on a narrow spur of the mountain. The streets in every direction are steep, in steps of stairs, and about eight feet wide. No carriage of any kind can enter it. The wealthiest inhabitants use *chaises a porteurs.* But there are few wealthy, the bulk of the inhabitants being laborers of the earth. At a league's distance in the sea, is an island on which is the Chateau de Geans, belonging to the Marquis de Pontoives; there is a causeway leading to it. The cold of the last November killed the leaves of a great number of the orange trees, and some of the trees themselves.

From Hieres to *Cuers, Pignans, Luc,* is mostly a plain, with mountains on each hand, at a mile or two distance. The soil is generally reddish, and the latter part very red and good. The growth is, olives, figs, vines, mulberries, corn, clover, and lucerne. The olive trees are from three to four feet in diameter. There are hedges of pomegranates, sweetbriar, and broom. A great deal of thyme growing wild. There are some inclosures of stone; some sheep and goats.

April 9th. From Luc to *Vidauban, Muy, Frejus,* the road leads through valleys, and crosses occasionally the mountains which separate them. The valleys are tolerably good, always red and stony, gravelly or gritty. Their produce as before. The mountains are barren.

Lesterelle, Napoule. Eighteen miles of ascent and descent, of a very high mountain. Its growth, where capable of any, two-leaved pine, very small, and some chene-vert.

Antibes, Nice. From Napoule, the road is generally near the sea, passing over little hills or strings of valleys, the soil stony, and much below mediocrity in its quality. Here and there, is a good plain.

There is snow on the high mountains. The first frogs I have heard, are of this day (the 9th). At Antibes are oranges in the open ground, but in small inclosures; palm trees also. From thence to the Var, are the largest fig trees and olive trees I have seen. The fig trees are eighteen inches in diameter, and six feet stem; the olives, sometimes six feet in diameter, and as large heads as the largest low-ground apple trees. This tree was but a shrub where I first fell in with it, and has become larger and larger to this place. The people are mostly in villages. The several provinces, and even cantons are distinguished by the form of the women's hats, so that one may know of what canton a woman is, by her hat.

Nice. The pine bur is used here for kindling fires. The people are in separate establishments. With respect to the orange, there seems to be no climate on this side of the Alps, sufficiently mild in itself to preserve it without shelter. At Olioules, they are between two high mountains; at Hieres, covered on the north by a very high mountain; at Antibes and Nice, covered by mountains, and also within small high enclosures. Quere. To trace the true line from east to west, which forms the northern and natural limit of that fruit? Saw an elder tree (sambucus) near Nice, fifteen inches in diameter, and eight feet stem. The wine made in this neighborhood is good, though not of the first quality. There are one thousand mules, loaded with merchandise, which pass every week between Nice and Turin, counting those coming as well as going.

April 13th. *Scarena. Sospello.* There are no orange trees after we leave the environs of Nice. We lose the olive after rising a little above the village of Scarena, on Mount Braus, and find it again on the other side, a little before we get down to Sospello. But wherever there is soil enough, it is terraced, and in corn. The waste parts are either in two-leaved pine and thyme, or of absolutely naked rock. Sospello is on a little torrent, called Bevera, which runs into the river Roia, at the mouth of which is Ventimiglia. The olive trees on the mountain, are now loaded with fruit; while some at Sospello are in blossom. Firewood here and at Scarena, costs fifteen cous the quintal.

April 14th. *Ciandola. Tende.* In crossing Mount Brois, we lose the olive tree after getting to a certain height, and find it again on the other side at the village of Breglio. Here we come to the river Roia, which, after receiving the branch on which is Sospello, leads to the sea at Ventimiglia. The Roia is about twelve yards wide, and abounds with speckled trout. Were a road made from Breglio, along the side of the Roia, to Ventimiglia, it might turn the commerce of Turin to this last place instead of Nice; because it would avoid the mountains of Braus and Brois, leaving only that of Tende; that is to say, it would avoid more than half the difficulties of the passage. Further on, we come to the Chateau di Saorgio, where a scene is presented, the most singular and picturesque I ever saw. The

castle and village seem hanging to a cloud in front. On the right, is a
mountain cloven through, to let pass a gurgling stream; on the left, a
river, over which is thrown a magnificent bridge. The whole forms a
basin, the sides of which are shagged with rocks, olive trees, vines, herds,
etc. Near here, I saw a tub wheel without a ream; the trunk descended
from the top of the waterfall to the wheel, in a direct line, but with the
usual inclination. The produce along this passage, is most generally olives,
except on the heights as before observed; also corn, vines, mulberries,
figs, cherries, and walnuts. They have cows, goats, and sheep. In passing
on towards Tende, olives fail us ultimately at the village of Fontan, and
there the chestnut trees begin in good quantity. Ciandola consists of only
two houses, both taverns. Tende is a very inconsiderable village, in which
they have not yet the luxury of glass windows; nor in any of the villages
on this passage, have they yet the fashion of powdering the hair. Common
stone and limestone are so abundant, that the apartments of every story
are vaulted with stone, to save wood.

April 15th. *Limone. Coni.* I see abundance of limestone as far as the
earth is uncovered with snow; *i. e.,* within half or three-quarters of an
hour's walk of the top. The snows descend much lower on the eastern
than the western side. Wherever there is soil, there is corn quite to the
commencement of the snows, and I suppose under them also. The waste
parts are in two-leaved pine, lavender and thyme. From the foot of the
mountain to Coni, the road follows a branch of the Po, the plains of which
being narrow, and widen at length into a general plain country, bounded
on one side by the Alps. They are good, dark colored, sometimes tinged
with red, and in pasture, corn, mulberries, and some almonds. The hillsides bordering these plains, are reddish, and where they admit of it, are
in corn; but this is seldom. They are mostly in chestnut, and often absolutely barren. The whole of the plains are plentifully watered from the
river, as is much of the hillside. A great deal of golden willow all along
the rivers, on the whole of this passage through the Alps. The southern
parts of France, but still more the passage through the Alps, enable one
to form a scale of the tenderer plants, arranging them according to their
several powers of resisting cold. Ascending three different mountains, Braus,
Brois, and Tende, they disappear one after another; and descending on
the other side, they show themselves again one after another. This is their
order, from the tenderest to the hardiest. Caper, orange, palm, aloe, olive,
pomegranate, walnut, fig, almond. But this must be understood of the
plant; for as to the fruit, the order is somewhat different. The caper, for
example, is the tenderest plant, yet being so easily protected, it is the most
certain in its fruit. The almond, the hardiest plant, loses its fruit the

oftenest, on account of its forwardness. The palm, hardier than the caper and the orange, never produces perfect fruit in these parts. Coni is a considerable town, and pretty well built. It is walled.

April 16th. *Centale. Savigliano. Racconigi. Poerino. Turin.* The Alps, as far as they are in view from north to south, show the gradation of climate, by the line which terminates the snows lying on them. This line begins at their foot northwardly, and rises, as they pass on to the south, so as to be half way up their sides on the most southern undulations of the mountain, now in view. From the mountains to Turin, we see no tree tenderer than the walnut. Of these, as well as of almonds and mulberries, there are a few; somewhat more of vines, but most generally, willows and poplars. Corn is sowed with all these. They mix with them also clover and small grass. The country is a general plain; the soil dark, and sometimes, though rarely, reddish. It is rich, and much infested with wild onions. At Racconigi, I see the tops and shocks of maize, which prove it is cultivated here; but it can be in small quantities only, because I observe very little ground, but what has already something else in it. Here and there, are small patches prepared, I suppose, for maize. They have a method of planting the vine, which I have not seen before. At intervals of about eight feet, they plant from two to six plants of vine in a cluster. At each cluster they fix a forked staff, the plane of the prongs of the fork at a right angle with the row of vines. Athwart these prongs they lash another staff, like a handspike, about eight feet long, horizontally, seven or eight feet from the ground. Of course, it crosses the rows at right angles. The vines are brought from the foot of the fork up to this cross piece, turned over it, and conducted along over the next, the next, and so on, as far as they will extend, the whole forming an arbor eight feet wide and high, and of the whole length of the row, little interrupted by the stems of the vines, which being close around the fork, pass up through hoops, so as to occupy a space only of smaller diameter. All the buildings in this country are of brick, sometimes covered with plaster, sometimes not. There is a very large and handsome bridge of seven arches over the torrent of Sangone. We cross the Po, in swinging batteaux. Two are placed side by side, and kept together by a plank floor, common to both and lying on the gunwales. The carriage drives on this, without taking out any of the horses. About one hundred and fifty yards up the river, is a fixed stake, and a rope tied to it, the other end of which is made fast to one side of the batteaux, so as to throw them oblique to the current. The stream then acting on them, as on an inclined plane, forces them across the current in the portion of a circle of which the rope is the radius. To support the rope in its whole length, there are two intermediate canoes, about fifty yards apart, in the heads of which are short masts. To the top of these, the rope is lashed, the canoes being free otherwise to concur with the general vibration, in their smaller arcs of circles. The Po is there, about fifty yards wide, and about one hundred in the neighborhood of Turin.

April 17th, 18th. *Turin*. The first nightingale I have heard this year, is to-day (18th). There is a red wine of Nebiule made in the neighborhood, which is very singular. It is about as sweet as the silky Madeira, as astringent on the palate as Bordeaux, and as brisk as Champagne. It is a pleasing wine. At Moncaglieri, about six miles from Turin, on the right side of the Po, begins a ridge of mountains, which, following the Po by Turin, after some distance, spreads wide, and forms the duchy of Montferrat. The soil is mostly red, and in vines, affording a wine called Montferrat, which is thick and strong.

April 19th. *Settimo. Chivasco. Ciliano. S. Germano. Vercelli*. The country continues plain and rich, the soil black. The culture, corn, pasture, maize, vines, mulberries, walnuts, some willow and poplar. The maize bears a very small proportion to the small grain. The earth is formed into ridges from three to four feet wide, and the maize sowed in the broadcast on the higher parts of the ridge, so as to cover a third or half of the whole surface. It is sowed late in May. This country is plentifully and beautifully watered at present. Much of it is by torrents which are dry in summer. These torrents make a great deal of waste ground, covering it with sand and stones. These wastes are sometimes planted in trees, sometimes quite unemployed. They make hedges of willows, by setting the plants from one to three feet apart. When they are grown to the height of eight or ten feet, they bend them down, and interlace them one with another. I do not see any of these, however, which are become old. Probably, therefore, they soon die. The women here smite on the anvil, and work with the maul and spade. The people of this country are ill dressed in comparison with those of France, and there are more spots of uncultivated ground. The plough here is made with a single handle, which is a beam twelve feet long, six inches in diameter below, and tapered to about two inches at the upper end. They use goads for the oxen, not whips. The first swallows I have seen, are to-day. There is a wine called Gatina, made in the neighborhood of Vercelli, both red and white. The latter resembles Calcavallo. There is also a red wine of Salusola which is esteemed. It is very light. In the neighborhood of Vercelli begin the rice fields. The water with which they are watered is very dear. They do not permit rice to be sown within two miles of the cities on account of the insalubrity. Notwithstanding this, when the water is drawn off the fields in August, the whole country is subject to agues and fevers. They estimate that the same measure of ground yields three times as much rice as wheat, and with half the labor. They are now sowing. As soon as sowed, they let on the water, two or three inches deep. After six weeks, or two months, they draw it off to weed; then let it on again, and it remains till August, when it is drawn off, about three or four weeks before the grain is ripe. In September they cut it. It is first threshed, then beaten in the mortar to separate the husk, then by different siftings it is separated into three qualities. Twelve rupes, equal to three hundred pounds of twelve ounces each, sell for sixteen livres, money of Piedmont, where the livre is exactly the shilling of England. Twelve rupes of maize sell for nine livres. The machine for separating the husk is thus made. In the axis of a water-wheel are a number of arms inserted, which, as they revolve, catches each the cog of a pestle, lifts it to a certain height, and lets it fall again. These pestles are five and a quarter inches square, ten feet long, and at their lower end formed into a truncated cone of three inches diameter, where cut off. The conical part is covered with iron. The pestles are ten and a half inches apart in the clear. They pass through two horizontal beams, which string them, as it were, together, and while the mortises in the beams are loose, as to let the pestles work vertically, it restrains them to that motion. There is a mortar of wood, twelve or fifteen inches deeps, under each pestle, covered with a board, the hole of which is only large enough to let the pestle pass freely. There are two arms in the axis for every pestle, so that the pestle gives two strokes for every revolution of the wheel. Poggio, a muleteer, who passes every week between Vercelli and Genoa, will smuggle a sack of rough rice for me to Genoa; it being death to export it in that form. They have good cattle, and in good number, mostly cream-colored; and some middle-sized sheep. The streams furnish speckled trout.

April 20th. *Novara. Buffalora. Sedriano. Milan.* From Vercelli to Novara the fields are all in rice, and now mostly under water. The dams separating the several water-plats, or ponds, are set in willow. At Novara there are some figs in the gardens, in situations well protected. From Novara to the Ticino, it is mostly stony and waste, grown up in broom. From Ticino to Milan, it is all in corn. Among the corn are willows, principally a good many mulberries, some walnuts, and here and there an almond. The country still a plain, the soil black and rich, except between Novara and the Ticino, as before mentioned. There is very fine pasture round Vercelli and Novara to the distance of two miles, within which rice is not permitted. We cross the Sisto on the same kind of vibrating or pendulum boat as on the Po. The river is eighty or ninety yards wide;

the rope fastened to an island two hundred yards above, and supported by five intermediate canoes. It is about one and a half inches in diameter. On these rivers they use a short oar of twelve feet long, the flat end of which is hooped with iron, shooting out a prong at each corner, so that it may be used occasionally as a setting pole. There is snow on the Apennines, near Genoa. They have still another method here of planting the vine. Along rows of trees, they lash poles from tree to tree. Between the trees are set vines, which, passing over the pole, are carried on to the pole of the next tree, whose vines are in like manner brought to this, and twined together, thus forming the intervals between rows of trees alternately into arbors and open space. They have another method also of making quick-set hedges. Willows are planted from one to two feet apart, and interlaced, so that every one is crossed by three or four others.

April 21st, 22d. *Milan.* Figs and pomegranates grow here unsheltered, as I am told. I saw none, and therefore suppose them rare. They had formerly olives; but a great cold in 1709 killed them, and they have not been replanted. Among a great many houses painted *al fresco*, the Casa Roma and Casa Candiani, by Appiani, and Casa Belgioiosa, by Martin, are superior. In the second is a small cabinet, the ceiling of which is in small hexagons, within which are cameos and heads painted alternately, no two the same. The salon of the Casa Belgioiosa is superior to anything I have ever seen. The mixture called Scaiola, of which they make their walls and floors, is so like the finest marble as to be scarcely distinguishable from it. The nights of the 20th and 21st instant the rice ponds froze half an inch thick. Drouths of two or three months are not uncommon here in summer. About five years ago, there was such a hail as to kill cats. The Count del Verme tells me of a penlulum odometer for the wheel of a carriage. Leases here are mostly for nine years. Wheat costs a louis d'or the one hundred and forty pounds. A laboring man receives sixty livres, and is fed and lodged. The trade of this country is principally rice, raw silk, and cheese.

April 23d. *Casino,* five miles from Milan. I examined another rice-beater of six-pestles. They are eight feet nine inches long. Their ends, instead of being a truncated cone, have nine teeth of irou, bound closely together. Each tooth is a double pyramid, joined at the base. When put together, they stand with the upper ends placed in contact, so as to form them into one great cone, and the lower ends diverging. The upper are socketed into the end of the pestle, and the lower, when a little blunted by use, are not unlike the jaw teeth of the mammoth, with their studs. They say here, that pestles armed with these teeth, clean the rice faster, and break it less. The mortar, too, is of stone, which is supposed as good as wood, and more durable. One half of these pestles are always up. They rise about twenty-one inches, and each makes thirty-eight strokes in a minute; one hundred pounds of rough rice is put into the six mortars, and beaten somewhat less than a quarter of an hour. It is then taken out, put into a sifter of four feet diameter, suspended horizontally; sifted there; shifted into another of the same size; sifted there; returned to the mortars; beaten little more than a quarter of an hour; sifted again; and it is finished. The six pestles will clear four thousand pounds in twenty-four hours. The pound here is twenty-eight ounces; the ounce equal to that of Paris. The best rice requires half an hour's boiling; a more indifferent kind, somewhat less. To sow the rice, they first plough the ground, then level it with a drag harrow, and let on the water; when the earth has become soft, they smooth it with a shovel under the water, and then sow the rice in the water.

Rozzano. Parmesan cheese. It is supposed this was formerly made at Parma, and took its name thence, but none is made there now. It is made through all the country extending from Milan for one hundred and fifty miles. The most is made about Lodi. The making of butter being connected with that of making cheese, both must be described together. There are, in the stables I saw, eighty-five cows, fed on hay and grass, not on grain. They are milked twice in twenty-four hours, ten cows yielding at the two milkings a *brenta* of milk, which is twenty-four of our gallons. The night's milk is scummed in the morning at daybreak, when the cows are milked again, and the new milk mixed with the old. In three hours, the whole mass is scummed a second time, the milk remaining in a kettle for cheese, and the cream being put into a cylindrical churn, shaped like a grindstone, eighteen inches radius, and fourteen inches thick. In this churn there are three staves pointing inwardlly, endwise, to break the current of the milk. Through its centre passes an iron axis, with a handle at each end. It is turned about an hour and a half by two men till the butter is produced. Then they pour off the buttermilk, and put in some water which they agitate backwards and forwards about a minute, and pour it off. They take out the butter, press it with their hands into loaves, and stamp it. It has no other washing. Sixteen American gallons of milk yield fifteen pounds of butter, which sell at twenty-four sous the pound.

The milk, which, after being scummed as before, had been put into a copper kettle, receives its due quantity of rennet, and is gently warmed, if the season requires it. In about four hours it becomes a slip. Then the whey begins to separate. A little of it is taken out. The curd is then thoroughly broken by a machine like a chocolate mill. A quarter of an ounce of saffron is put to seven brenta of milk, to give color to the cheese. The kettle is then moved over the hearth, and heated by a quick fire till the curd is hard enough, being broken into small lumps by continued stirring. It is moved off the fire, most of the whey taken out, the curd compressed into a globe by the hand, a linen cloth slipped under it, and it is drawn out in that. A loose hoop is then laid on a bench, and the curd, as wrapped in the linen, is put into the hoop; it is a little pressed by the hand, the hoop drawn tight and made fast. A board two inches thick is laid on it, and a stone on that of about twenty pounds weight. In an hour, the whey is run off, and the cheese finished. They sprinkle a little salt on it every other day in summer, and every day in winter, for six weeks. Seven brentas of milk make a cheese of fifty pounds, which requires six months to ripen, and is then dried to forty-five pounds. It sells on the spot for eighty-eight livres the one hundred pounds. There are now one hundred and fifty cheeses in this dairy. They are nineteen inches diameter, and six inches thick. They make a cheese a day in summer, and two in three days, or one in two days, in winter.

The whey is put back into the kettle, the buttermilk poured into it, and of this, they make a poor cheese for the country people. The whey of this is given to the hogs. Eight men suffice to keep the cows, and to do all the business of this dairy. Mascarponi, a kind of curd, is made by pouring some buttermilk into cream, which is thereby curdled, and is then pressed into a linen cloth.

The ice-houses at Rozzano are dug about fifteen feet deep, and twenty feet diameter, and poles are driven down all round. A conical thatched roof is then put over them, fifteen feet high, and pieces of wood are laid at the bottom, to keep the ice out of the water which drips from it, and goes off by a sink. Straw is laid on this wood, and then the house filled with ice, always putting straw between the ice and the walls, and covering ultimately with straw. About a third is lost by melting. Snow gives the most delicate flavor to creams; but ice is the most powerful congealer, and lasts longest. A tuft of trees surrounds these ice-houses.

Round Milan, to the distance of five miles, are corn, pasture, gardens, mulberries, willows, and vines. For in this State, rice ponds are not permitted within five miles of the cities.

Binasco. Pavia. Near Cassino the rice ponds begin, and continue to within five miles of Pavia, the whole ground being in rice, pasture, and willows. The pasture is in the rice grounds which are resting. In the neighborhood of Pavia, again, are corn, pasture, etc., as round Milan. They gave me green peas at Pavia.

April 24th. *Voghera. Tortona. Novi.* From Pavia to Novi, corn, pasture, vines, mulberries, willows; but no rice. The country continues plain, except that the Apennines are approaching on the left. The soil, always good, is dark till we approach Novi, and then red. We cross the Po where it is three hundred yards wide, in a pendulum boat. The rope is fastened on one side of the river, three hundred yards above, and supported by eight intermediate canoes, with little masts in them to give a greater elevation to the rope. We pass in eleven minutes. Women, girls, and boys are working with the hoe, and breaking the clods with mauls.

April 25th. *Voltaggio. Campo-Marone. Genoa.* At Novi, the Apennines begin to rise. Their growth of timber is oak, tall, small and knotty, and chestnut. We soon lose the walnut, ascending, and find it again, about one-fourth of the way down, on the south side. About half way down, we find figs and vines, which continue fine and in great abundance. The Apennines are mostly covered with soil, and are in corn, pasture, mulberries, and figs, in the parts before indicated. About half way from their foot to Genoa, at Campo-Marone, we find again the olive tree. Hence the produce becomes mixed, of all the kinds before mentioned. The method of sowing the Indian corn at Campo-Marone, is as follows: With a hoe shaped like the blade of a trowel, two feet long, and six inches broad at its upper end, pointed below, and a little curved, they make a trench. In that, they drop the grains six inches apart. Then two feet from that, they make another trench, throwing the earth they take out of that on the grain of the last one, with a singular sleight and quickness; and so through the whole piece. The last trench is filled with the earth adjoining.

April 26th. *Genoa.* Strawberries at Genoa. Scaffold poles for the upper parts of a wall, as for the third story, rest on the window sills of the story below. Slate is used here for paving, for steps, for stairs, (the rise as well as tread) and for fixed Venetian blinds. At the Palazzo Marcello Durazzo, benches with straight legs, and bottoms of cane. At the Palazzo del prencipe Lomellino, at Sestri, a phaeton with a canopy. At the former, tables folding into one plane. At Nervi they have peas, strawberries, etc., all the year round. The gardens of the Count Durazzo at Nervi exhibit as rich a mixture of the *utile dulci,* as I ever saw. All the environs in Genoa, are in olives, figs, oranges, mulberries, corn, and garden stuff. Aloes in many places, but they never flower.

April 28th. *Noli.* The Apennine and Alps appear to me, to be one and the same continued ridge of mountains, separating everywhere the waters of the Adriatic Gulf from those of the Mediterranean. Where it forms an elbow, touching the Mediterranean, as a smaller circle touches a larger, within which it is inscribed, in the manner of a tangent, the name changes from Alps to Apennine. It is the beginning of the Apennine which constitutes the State of Genoa, the mountains there generally falling down in barren naked precipices into the sea. Wherever there is soil on the lower parts, it is principally in olives and figs, in vines also, mulberries and corn. Where there are hollows well protected, there are oranges. This is the case at Golfo de Laspeze, Sestri, Bugiasco, Nervi, Genoa, Pegli, Savona, Finale, Oneglia, (where there are abundance,) St. Remo, Ventimiglia, Mantone, and Monaco. Noli, into which I was obliged to put, by a change of wind, is forty miles from Genoa. There are twelve hundred inhabitants in the village, and many separate houses round about. One of the precipices hanging over the sea is covered with aloes. But neither here, nor anywhere else I have been, could I procure satisfactory information that they ever flower. The current of testimony is to the contrary. Noli furnishes many fishermen. Paths penetrate up into the mountains in several directions, about three-fourths of a mile; but these are practicable only for asses and mules. I saw no cattle nor sheep in the settlement. The wine they make, is white and indifferent. A curious cruet for oil and vinegar in one piece, I saw here. A bishop resides here, whose revenue is two thousand livres, equal to sixty-six guineas. I heard a nightingale here.

April 29th. *Albenga.* In walking along the shore from Louano to this place, I saw no appearance of shells. The tops of the mountains are covered with snow, while there are olive trees, etc., on the lower parts. I do not remember to have seen assigned anywhere, the cause of the apparent color of the sea. Its water is generally clear and colorless, if taken up and viewed in a glass. That of the Mediterranean is remarkably so. Yet in the mass, it assumes, *by reflection,* the color of the sky or atmosphere, black, green, blue, according to the state of the weather. If any person wished to retire from his acquaintance, to live absolutely unknown, and yet in the midst of physical enjoyments, it should be in some of the little villages of this coast, where air, water and earth concur to offer what each has most precious. Here are nightingales, baccaficas, ortolans, pheasants, partridges, quails, a superb climate, and the power of changing it from summer to winter at any moment, by ascending the mountains. The earth furnishes wine, oil, figs, oranges, and every production of the garden, in every season. The sea yields lobsters, crabs, oysters, thunny, sardines, anchovies, etc. Ortolans sell at this time, at thirty sous, equal to one shilling sterling, the dozen. At this season, they must be fattened. Through the whole of my route from Marseilles, I observe they plant a great deal of cane or reed, which is convenient while growing, as a cover from the cold and boisterous winds, and when cut, it serves for espaliers to vines, peas, etc. Through Piedmont, Lombardy, the Milanese, and Genoese, the garden bean is a great article of culture; almost as much so as corn. At Albenga, is a rich plain opening from between two ridges of mountains, triangularly, to the sea, and of several miles extent. Its growth is olives, figs, mulberries, vines, corn and

beans. There is some pasture. A bishop resides here, whose revenue is forty thousand livres. This place is said to be rendered unhealthy in summer, by the river which passes through the valley.

April 30th. *Oneglia.* The wind continuing contrary. I took mules at Albenga for Oneglia. Along this tract are many of the tree called carroubier, being a species of locust. It is the ceratonia siliqua of Linnæus. Its pods furnish food for horses, and also for the poor, in time of scarcity. It abounds in Naples and Spain. Oneglia and Port Maurice, which are within a mile of each other, are considerable places, and in a rich country. At St. Remo, are abundance of oranges and lemons, and some palm trees.

May 1st. *Ventimiglia. Menton. Monaco. Nice.* At Bordighera, between Ventimiglia and Menton, are extensive plantations of palms, on the hill as well in the plain. They bring fruit, but it does not ripen. Something is made of the midrib, which is in great demand at Rome, on the Palm Sunday, and which renders this tree profitable here. From Menton to Monaco, there is more good land, and extensive groves of oranges and lemons. Orange water sells here at forty sous, equal to sixteen pence sterling, the American quart. The distances on this coast, are, from Laspeze, at the eastern end of the territories of Genoa, to Genoa, fifty-five miles geometrical; to Savona, thirty; Albenga, thirty; Oneglia, twenty; Ventimiglia, twenty-five; Monaco, ten; Nice, ten; in the whole, one hundred and eighty miles. A superb road might be made along the margin of the sea from Laspeze, where the champaign country of Italy opens, to Nice, where the Alps go off northwardly, and the post roads of France begin; and it might even follow the margin of the sea quite to Cette. By this road, travellers would enter Italy without crossing the Alps, and all the little insulated villages of the Genoese would communicate together, and in time form one continued village along that road.

May 3d. *Luc. Brignolles. Tourves. Pourcieux. La Galiniere.* Long, small mountains, very rocky, the soil reddish, from bad to middling; in olives, grapes, mulberries, vines and corn. Brignolles is in an extensive plain, between two ridges of mountains, and along a water-course which continues to Tourves. Thence to Pourcieux we cross a mountain, low and easy. The country is rocky and poor. To La Galiniere are waving grounds, bounded by mountains of rock at a little distance. There are some inclosures of dry wall from Luc to la Galiniere; also, sheep and hogs. There is snow on the high mountains. I see no plums in the vicinities of Brignolles; which makes me conjecture that the celebrated plum of that name, is not derived from this place.

May 8. *Orgon. Avignon. Vaucluse.* Orgon is on the Durance. From thence, its plain opens till it becomes common with that of the Rhone;

so that from Orgon to Avignon is entirely a plain of rich dark loam, which is in willows, mulberries, vines, corn and pasture. A very few figs. I see no olives in this plain. Probably the cold winds have too much power here. From the Bac de Nova (where we cross the Durance) to Avignon, is about nine American miles; and from the same Bac to Vaucluse, eleven miles. In the valley of Vaucluse, and on the hills impending over it, are olive trees. The stream issuing from the fountain of Vaucluse is about twenty yards wide, four or five feet deep, and of such rapidity that it could not be stemmed by a canoe. They are now mowing hay, and gathering mulberry leaves. The high mountains just back of Vaucluse are covered with snow. Fine trout in the stream of Vaucluse, and the valley abounds peculiarly with nightingales. The vin blanc de M. de Rocheque of Avignon, resembles dry Lisbon. He sells it at six years old for twenty-two sous the bottle, the price of the bottle, etc., included.

Avignon. Remoulins. Some good plains, but generally hills, stony and poor. In olives, mulberries, vines and corn. Where it is waste, the growth is chene-vert, box, furze, thyme, and rosemary.

May 10. *Nismes. Lunel.* Hills on the right, plains on the left. The soil reddish, a little stony, and of middling quality. The produce, olives, mulberries, vines, corn, St. foin. No wood and few inclosures. Lunel is famous for its vin de muscat blanc, thence called Lunel, or vin muscat de Lunel. It is made from the raisin muscat, without fermentating the grain in the hopper. When fermented it makes a red muscat, taking the tinge from the disolution of the skin of the grape, which injures the quality. When a red muscat is required, they prefer coloring it with a little Alicant wine. But the white is best. The piece of two hundred and forty bottles, after being properly drawn off from its lees, and ready for bottling, costs from one hundred and twenty to two hundred livres, the first quality and last vintage. It cannot be bought old, the demand being sufficient to take it all the first year. They are not more than from fifty to one hundred pieces a year, made of this first quality. A *setterie* yields about one piece, and my informer supposes there are about two setteries in an arpent. Portage to Paris by land is fifteen livres the quintal. The best *recoltes* are those of M. Bouquet and M. Tremoulet. The vines are in rows four feet apart, every way.

May 11. *Montpelier.* Snow on the Cevennes, still visible from here. With respect to the muscat grape, of which the wine is made, there are two kinds, the red and the white. The first has a red skin, but a white juice. If it be fermented in the *cuve,* the coloring matter which resides in the skin is imparted to the wine. If not fermented in the cuve, the wine is white. Of the white grape, only a white wine can be made. The species of

St. foin cultivated here by the name of sparsette, is the hedysarum ono-bryches. They cultivate a great deal of madder (garance) rubia tinctorum here, which is said to be immensely profitable. Monsieur de Gouan tells me that the pine, of which they use the burs for fuel, is the pinus sativus, being two leaved. They use for an edging to the borders of their gardens, the santolina, which they call garderobe. I find the yellow clover here, in a garden; and the large pigeon succeeding well, confined in a house.

May 12. *Frontignan.* Some tolerably good plains in olives, vines, corn, St. foin, and lucerne. A great proportion of the hills are waste. There are some inclosures of stone, and some sheep. The first four years of madder are unproductive; the fifth and sixth yield the whole value of the land. Then it must be renewed. The sparsette is the common or true St. foin. It lasts about five years; in the best land it is cut twice, in May and September, and yields three thousand pounds of dry hay to the setterie the first cutting, and five hundred pounds the second. The setterie is of seventy-five *dextres en tout sens,* supposed about two arpents. Lucerne is the best of all forage; it is sowed here in the broadcast, and lasts about twelve or fourteen years. It is cut four times a year, and yields six thousand pounds of dry hay at the four cuttings, to the setterie. The territory in which the vin muscat de Frontignan is made, is about a league of three thousand toises long, and one-fourth of a league broad. The soil is reddish and stony, often as much stone as soil. On the left, it is a plain; on the right, hills. There are made about one thousand pieces (of two hundred and fifty bottles each) annually, of which six hundred are of the first quality, made on the *coteaux.* Of these, Madame Soubeinan makes two hundred, Monsieur Reboulle, ninety, Monsieur Lambert, médicin de la faculté de Montpelier, sixty, Monsieur Thomas, notaire, fifty, Monsieur Argilliers, fifty, Monsieur Audibert, forty; equal to four hundred and ninety; and there are some small proprietors who make small quantities. The first quality is sold, *brut,* for one hundred and twenty livres the piece; but it is then thick, and must have a winter and the *fouet* to render it potable and brilliant. The fouet is like a chocolate mill, the handle of iron, the brush of stiff hair. In bottles, this wine costs twenty-four sous, the bottles, etc., included. It is potable the April after it is made, is best that year, and after ten years begins to have a pitchy taste, resembling it to Malaga. It is not permitted to ferment more than half a day, because it would not be so liquorish. The best color, and its natural one, is the amber. By force of whipping, it is made white, but loses flavor. There are but two or three pieces a year of red muscat made; there being but one vineyard of the red grape, which belongs to a baker called Pascal. This sells in bottles at thirty sous, the bottle included. Rondelle, negociant en vin, Porte St. Bernard, fauxbourg St. Germains,

Paris, buys three hundred pieces of the first quality every year. The coteaux yield about half a piece to the setterie, the plains a whole piece. The inferior quality is not at all esteemed. It is bought by the merchants of Cette, as is also the wine of Bezieres, and sold by them for Frontignan of the first quality. They sell thirty thousand pieces a year under that name. The town of Frontignan marks its casks with a hot iron: an individual of that place having two casks emptied, was offered forty livres for the empty cask by a merchant of Cette. The town of Frontignan contains about two thousand inhabitants; it is almost on the level of the ocean. Transportation to Paris is fifteen livres the quintal, and takes fifteen days. The price of packages is about eight livres eight sous the one hundred bottles. A setterie of good vineyard sells for from three hundred and fifty to five hundred livres, and rents for fifty livres. A laboring man hires at one hundred and fifty livres the year, and is fed and lodged; a woman at half as much. Wheat sells at ten livres the settier, which weighs one hundred pounds, poids de table. They make some Indian corn here, which is eaten by the poor. The olives do not extend northward of this into the country, above twelve or fifteen leagues. In general, the olive country in Languedoc is about fifteen leagues broad. More of the waste lands between Frontignan and Mirval are capable of culture; but it is a marshy country, very subject to fever and ague, and generally unhealthy. Thence arises, as is said, a want of hands.

Cette. There are in this town about ten thousand inhabitants. Its principal commerce is wine; it furnishes great quantities of grape pomice for making verdigrise. They have a very growing commerce; but it is kept under by the privileges of Marseilles.

May 13. *Agde.* On the right of the Etang de Tau, are plains of some width, then hills, in olives, vines, mulberry, corn and pasture. On the left, a narrow sand-bar separating the Etang from the sea, along which it is proposed to make a road from Cette to Agde. In this case, the post would lead from Montpelier, by Cette and Agde, to Bezieres, being leveller, and an hour, or an hour and a half nearer. Agde contains six or eight thousand inhabitants.

May 14. *Bezieres.* Rich plains in corn, St. foin and pasture; hills at a little distance to the right, in olives; the soil both of hill and plain is red, going from Agde to Bezieres. But at Bezieres the country becomes hilly, and is in olives, St. foin, pasture, some vines and mulberries.

May 15. *Bezieres. Argilies. Le Saumal.* From Argilies to Saumal are considerable plantations of vines. Those on the red hills to the right, are said to produce good wine. No wood, no inclosures. There are sheep and good cattle. The Pyrenees are covered with snow. I am told they are so in certain parts all the year. The canal of Languedoc, along which I now travel, is six toises wide at bottom, and ten toises at the surface of the water, which is one toise deep. The barks which navigate it are seventy and eighty feet long, and seventeen or eighteen feet wide. They are drawn by one horse, and worked by two hands, one of which is generally a woman. The locks are mostly kept by women, but the necessary operations are much too laborious for them. The encroachments by the men, on the offices proper for the women, is a great derangement in the order of things. Men are shoemakers, tailors, upholsterers, stay-makers, mantua-makers, cooks, housekeepers, house-cleaners, bed-makers; they *coiffe* the ladies, and bring them to bed: the women, therefore, to live, are obliged to undertake the offices which they abandon. They become porters, carters, reapers, sailors, lock-keepers, smiters on the anvil, cultivators of the earth, etc. Can we wonder, if such of them as have a little beauty, prefer easier courses to get their livelihood, as long as that beauty lasts? Ladies who employ men in the offices which should be reserved for their sex, are they not bawds in effect? For every man whom they thus employ, some girl, whose place he has thus taken, is driven to whoredom. The passage of the eight locks at Bezieres, that is, from the opening of the first to the last gate, took one hour and thirty-three minutes. The bark in which I go, is about thirty-five feet long, drawn by one horse, and goes from two to three geographical miles an hour. The canal yields abundance of carp and eel. I see also small fish resembling our perch and chub. Some plants of white clover and some of yellow, on the banks of the canal near Capestan; santolina also, and a great deal of yellow iris. Met a raft of about three hundred and fifty beams, forty feet long, and twelve or thirteen inches in diameter, formed into fourteen rafts, tacked together. The extensive and numerous fields of St. foin in general bloom, are beautiful.

May 16th. *Le Saumal. Marseillette.* May 17th. *Marseillette. Carcassonne.* From Saumal to Carcassonne, we have always the river Aube close on our left. This river runs in the valley between the Cevennes and Pyrenees, serving as the common receptacle for both their waters. It is from fifty to one hundred and fifty yards wide, always rapid, rocky, and insusceptible of navigation. The canal passes in the side of hills made by that river, overlooks the river itself, and its plains, and has its prospect ultimately terminated, on one side, by mountains of rock overtopped by the Pyrenees, on the other, by small mountains, sometimes of rock, sometimes of soil, overtopped by the Cevennes. Marseillette is on a ridge, which separates the river Aube from the Etang de Marseillette. The canal, in its approach to this village, passes the ridge and rides along the front, overlooking the Etang, and the plains on its border; and having passed the village, re-crosses the ridge, and resumes its general ground in front of the Aube. The land is in corn, St. foin, pasture, vines, mulberries, willows, and olives.

May 18th. *Carcassonne. Castelnaudari.* Opposite to Carcassonne, the canal receives the river Fresquel, about thirty yards wide, which is its substantial supply of water from hence to Bezieres. From Bezieres to Agde, the river Orb furnishes it, and the Eraut, from Agde to the Etang de Thau. By means of *ecluse ronde* at Agde, the waters of the Eraut can be thrown towards Bezieres, to aid those of the Orb, as far as the ecluse de Porcaraigne, nine geometrical miles. Where the Fresquel enters the canal, there is, on the opposite side, a waste, to let off the superfluous waters. The horseway is continued over this waste, by a bridge of stone of eighteen arches. I observe them fishing in the canal, with a skimming net of about fifteen feet diameter, with which they tell me they catch carp. Flax in blossom. Neither strawberries nor peas yet at Carcassonne. The Windsor bean just come to table. From the ecluse de la Lande we see the last olive trees near a metairée, or farm house, called la Lande. On a review of what I have seen and heard of this tree, the following seem to be its northern limits. Beginning on the Atlantic, at the Pyrenees, and along them to the meridian of la Lande, or of Carcassonne; up that meridian to the Cevennes, as they begin just there to raise themselves high enough to afford it shelter. Along the Cevennes, to the parallel of forty-five degrees of latitude, and along that parallel (crossing the Rhone near the mouth of the Isere) to the Alps; thence along the Alps and Apennines, to what parallel of latitude I know not. Yet here the tracing of the line becomes the most interesting. For from the Atlantic, so far, we see this production the effect of shelter and latitude combined. But where does it venture to launch forth unprotected by shelter, and by the mere force of latitude alone? Where for instance does its northern limits cross the Adriatic? I learn that the olive tree resists cold to eight degrees of Reaumur below the freezing point, which corresponds to fourteen above zero of Fahrenheit; and that the orange resists to four degrees below freezing of Reaumur, which is twenty-three degrees above zero of Fahrenheit.

May 19th. *Castelnaudari. St. Feriol. Escamaze. Lampy.* Some sheep and cattle. No inclosures. St. Feriol, Escamaze, and Lampy are in the *montagnes noires.* The country almost entirely waste. Some of it in shrubbery. The *voute* d'Escamaze is of one hundred and thirty-five yards. Round about Castelnaudari, the country is hilly, as it has been constantly from Bezieres; it is very rich. Where it is plain, or nearly plain, the soil is black; in general, however, it is hilly and reddish, and in corn. They cultivate a great deal of Indian corn here, which they call millet; it is planted but not yet up.

May 20th. *Castelnaudari. Naurouze. Villefranche. Baziege.* At Naurouze, is the highest ground which the canal had to pass, between the two seas. It became necessary then to find water still higher to bring it here. The river Fresquell heading by its two principal branches in the *montagnes nories,* a considerable distance off to the eastward, the springs of the most western one were brought together, and conducted to Naurouze, where its waters are divided, part furnishing the canal towards the ocean, the rest towards the Mediterranean, as far as the ecluse de Fresquel, where as has been before noted, the Lampy branch, and the Alzau, under the name of the Fresquel, enter.

May 20th. They have found that a lock of six pieds is best; however, eight pieds is well enough. Beyond this, it is bad. Monsieur Pin tells me of a lock of thirty pieds, made in Sweden, of which it is impossible to open the gates. They therefore divided it into four locks. The small gates of the locks of this canal, have six square pieds of surface. They tried the machinery of the jack for opening them. They were more easily opened, but very subject to be deranged, however strongly made. They returned therefore to the original wooden screw, which is excessively slow and laborious. I calculated that five minutes are lost at every basin by the screw, which, on the whole number of basis, is one eighth of the time necessary to navigate the canal; and of course, if a method of lifting the gate at one stroke could be found, it would reduce the passage from eight to seven days, and the freight equally. I suggested to Monsieur Pin and others, a quadrantal gate, turning on a pivot, and lifted by a lever like a pump handle, aided by a windlass and cord, if necessary. He will try it, and inform me of the success. The price of transportation from Cette to Bourdeaux, through the canal and Garonne is —— the quintal; round by the straits of Gibraltar is ——. Two hundred and forty barks, the largest of twenty-two hundred quintals (or say, in general, of one hundred tons) suffice to perform the business of this canal, which is stationary, having neither increased nor diminished for many years. When pressed, they can pass and repass between Toulouse and Bezieres in fourteen days; but sixteen is the common period. The canal is navigated ten and a half months of the year; the other month and a half being necessary to lay it dry, cleanse it and repair the works. This is done in July and August, when there would perhaps, be a want of water.

May 21st. *Baziege. Toulouse.* The country continues hilly, but very rich. It is in mulberries, willows, some vines, corn, maize, pasture, beans, flax. A great number of chateaux and good houses, in the neighborhood of the canal. The people partly in farm houses, partly in villages. I suspect the farm houses are occupied by the farmers, while the laborers (who are mostly by the day) reside in the villages. Neither strawberries nor peas yet at Baziege or Toulouse. Near the latter, are some fields of yellow clover.

At Toulouse the canal ends. It has four communications with the Mediterranean. 1. Through the ponds at Thau, Frontignan, Palavas, Maguelone, and Manjo, the Canal de la Radela Aiguesmortes, le Canal des Salines de Pecair, and the arm of the Rhone called Bras de Fer, which ends at Fourgues, opposite to Arles, and thence down to Rhone. 2. At Cette, by a canal of a few hundred toises, leading out of the Etang de Thau into the sea. The vessels pass the Etang, through a length of nine thousand toises, with sails. 3. At Agde, by the river Eraut, twenty-five hundred toises. It has but five or six pieds of water at its mouth. It is joined to the canal at the upper part of this communication, by a branch of a canal two hundred and seventy toises long. 4. At Narbonne, by a canal they are now opening, which leads from the great canal near the aqueduct of the river Cesse, twenty-six hundred toises, into the Aude. This new canal will have five lock-basins of about twelve pieds fall, each. Then you are to cross the Aude very obliquely, and descend a branch of it six thousand toises, through four lock-basins to Narbonne, and from Narbonne down the same branch, twelve hundred toises into the Etang de Sigen, across that Etang four thousand toises, issuing at an inlet, called Grau de la Nouvelle, into the Gulf of Lyons. But only vessels of thirty or forty tons can enter this inlet. Of these four communications, that of Cette only, leads to a deep sea-port, because the exit is there by a canal, and not a river. Those by the Rhone, Eraut, and Aude, are blocked up by bars at the mouth of those rivers. It is remarkable that all the rivers running into the Mediterranean, are obstructed at their entrance by bars and shallows, which often change their position. This is the case with the Nile, Tyber, the Po, the Lez, le Lyoron, the Orbe, the Gly, the Tech, the Tet, etc. Indeed, the formation of these bars seems not confined to the mouths of the rivers, though it takes place at them, more certainly. Along almost the whole of the coast, from Marseilles towards the Pyrenees, banks of sand are thrown up, parallel with the coast, which have insulated portions of the sea, that is, formed them into etangs, ponds, or sounds, through which here and there, narrow and shallow inlets only, are preserved by the currents of the rivers. These sounds fill up in time, with the mud and sand deposited in them by the rivers. Thus the Etang de Vendres, navigated formerly by vessels of sixty tons, is now nearly filled up by the mud and sand of the Aude. The Vistre and Vidourle which formerly emptied themselves into the Gulf of Lyons, are now received by the Etangs de Manjo and Aiguesmortes, that is to say, the part of the Gulf of Lyons which formerly received, and still receives those rivers, is now cut off from the sea by a bar of sand, which has been thrown up in it, and has formed it into sounds. Other proofs that the land gains there on the sea, are, that the towns of St. Gilles and Notre Dame d'Aspots, formerly seaports, are now far from the sea, and that Aiguesmortes, where are still to be seen the iron rings to which vessels were formerly moored, and where St. Louis embarked for Palestine, has now in its vicinities, only ponds which cannot be navigated, and communicates with the sea by an inlet, called Grau du Roy, through which only fishing barks can pass. It is pretty well established, that all the Delta of Egypt has been formed by the depositions of the Nile, and the alluvions of the sea, and it is probable that that operation is still going on. Has this peculiarity of the Mediterranean any connection with the scantiness of its tides, which even at the equinoxes, are of two or three feet only?

The communication from the western end of the canal to the ocean is by the river Garonne. This is navigated by flat boats of eight hundred quintals, when the water is well; but when it is scanty, these boats carry only two hundred quintals till they get to the mouth of the Tarn. It has been proposed to open a canal that far, from Toulouse, along the right side of the river.

May 22d. *Toulouse.* 23d. *Agen.* 24th. *Castres. Bordeaux.* The Garonne and rivers emptying into it, make extensive and rich plains, which are in mulberries, willows, corn, maize, pasture, beans and flax. The hills are in corn, maize, beans, and a considerable proportion of vines. There seems to be as much maize as corn in this country. Of the latter, there is more rye than wheat. The maize is now up, and about three inches high. It is sowed in rows two feet, or two and a half feet apart, and is pretty thick in the row. Doubtless they mean to thin it. There is a great deal of forage they call farouche. It is a species of red trefoil, with few leaves, a very coarse stalk, and a cylindrical blossom of two inches in length, and three quarters of an inch in diameter, consisting of floscules, exactly as does that of the red clover. It seems to be a coarse food, but very plentiful. They say it is for their oxen. These are very fine, large, and cream-colored. The services of the farm, and of transportation, are performed chiefly by them. There are a few horses and asses, but no mules. Even in the city of Bordeaux, we see scarcely any beasts of draught but oxen. When we cross the Garonne at Langon, we find the plains entirely of sand and gravel, and they continue so to Bordeaux. Where they are capable of anything, they are in vines, which are in rows, four, five, or six feet apart, and sometimes more. Near Langon is Saulerne, where the best white wines of Bordeaux are made. The waste lands are in fern, furze, shrubbery, and dwarf trees. The farmers live on their farms. At Agen, Castres, Bordeaux, strawberries and peas are now brought to table, so that the country on the canal of Languedoc seems to have later seasons than that east and west of it. What can be the cause? To the eastward, the protection of the Cevennes makes the warm season advance sooner. Does the neighborhood of the Mediterranean co-operate? And does that of the ocean mollify and advance the season to the westward? There are ortolans at Agen, but none at Bordeaux. The buildings on the canal and the Garonne are mostly of brick, the size of the bricks the same with that of the ancient Roman brick, as seen in the remains of their buildings in this country. In those of a circus at Bordeaux, considerable portions of which are standing, I measured the bricks, and found them nineteen or twenty inches long, eleven or twelve inches wide, and from one and a half to two inches thick; their texture as fine, compact, and solid as that of porcelain. The bricks now made, though of the same dimensions, are not so fine. They are burnt in a kind of furnace, and make excellent work. The elm tree shows itself at Bordeaux, peculiarly proper for being spread flat for arbors. Many are done in this way on the quay des Charterons. Strawberries, peas, and cherries at Bordeaux.

May 24th, 25th, 26th, 27th, 28th. *Bordeaux.* The cantons in which the most celebrated wines of Bordeaux are made, are Medoc down the river, Grave adjoining the city, and the parishes next above; all on the same side of the river. In the first is made red wine principally, in the two last, white. In Medoc, they plant the vines in cross rows of three and a half pieds. They keep them so low, that poles extended along the rows one way, horizontally, about fifteen or eighteen inches above the ground, serve to tie the vines to, and leave the cross row open to the plough. In Grave, they set the plants in quincunx, *i. e.* in equilateral triangles of three and a half pieds every side; and they stick a pole of six or eight feet high to every vine, separately. The vine stock is sometimes three or four feet high. They find these two methods equal in culture, duration, quantity and quality. The former however, admits the alternative of tending by hand or with the plough. The grafting of the vine, though a critical operation, is practised with success. When the graft has taken, they bend it into the earth, and let it take root above the scar. They begin to yield an indifferent wine at three years old, but not a good one till twenty-five years, nor after eighty, when they begin to yield less, and worse, and must be renewed. They give three or four workings in the year, each worth seventy, or seventy-five livres the *journal,* which is of eight hundred and forty square toises and contains about three thousand plants. They dung a little in Medoc and Grave, because of the poverty of the soil; but very little, as more would effect the wine. The journal yields, *communibus annis,* about three pieces (of two hundred and forty or two hundred and fifty bottles each). The vineyards of first quality are all worked by their proprietors. Those of the second rent for three hundred livres the journal, those of the third at two hundred livres. They employ a kind of overseer at four or five hundred livres the year, finding him lodging and drink; but he feeds himself. He superintends and directs, though he is expected to work but little. If the proprietor has a garden, the overseer tends that. They never hire laborers by the year. The day wages for a man are thirty sous, a woman's fifteen sous, feeding themselves. The women make the bundles of sarment, weed, pull off the snails, tie the vines, and gather the grapes. During the vintage they are paid high and fed well.

Of red wines, there are four vineyards of the first quality, viz., 1. Châuteau Margau, belonging to the Marquis d'Agicourt, who makes about one hundred and fifty tons, of one thousand bottles each. He has engaged to Jernon, a merchant. 2. La Tour de Segur, en Saint Lambert, belonging to Monsieur Miresmenil, who makes one hundred and twenty-five tons. 3. Hautbrion, belonging two-thirds to M. le Comte de Femelle, who has engaged to Barton, a merchant; the other third to the Comte de Toulouse, at Toulouse. The whole is seventy-five tuns. 4. Château de la Fite, belonging to the President Pichard, at Bordeaux, who makes one hundred and seventy-five tuns. The wines of the three first are not in perfection till four years old; those of De la Fite, being somewhat lighter, are good at three years, that is, the crop of 1786 is good in the spring of 1789. These growths of the year 1783 sell now at two thousand livres the tun; those of 1784, on account of the superior quality of that vintage, sell at twenty-four hundred livres; those of 1785, at eighteen hundred livres; those of 1786, at eighteen hundred livres, though they had sold at first for only fifteen hundred livres. Red wines of the second quality, are Rozan, Dabbadie or Lionville, la Rose, Quirouen, Durfort; in all eight hundred tuns, which sell at one thousand livres, new. The third class are, Calons, Mouton, Gassie, Arboete, Pontette, de Ferme, Candale; in all two thousand tuns, at eight or nine hundred livres. After these, they are reckoned common wines, and sell from five hundred livres down to one hundred and twenty livres the tun. All red wines decline after a certain age, losing color, flavor, and body. Those of Bordeaux begin to decline at about seven years old.

Of white wines, those made in the canton of Grave are most esteemed at Bordeaux. The best crops are, 1. Pontac, which formerly belonged to M. de Pontac, but now to M. de Lamont. He makes forty tuns, which sell at four hundred livres, new. 2. St. Brise, belonging to M. de Pontac, thirty tuns, at three hundred and fifty livres. 3. De Carbonius, belonging to the Benedictine monks, who make fifty tuns, and never selling till three or four years old, get eight hundred livres the tun. Those made in the three parishes next above Grave, and more esteemed at Paris, are, 1. Sauterne. The best crop belonging to M. Diquem at Bordeaux, or M. de Salus, his son-in-law; one hundred and fifty tuns, at three hundred livres, new, and six hundred livres, old. The next best crop is M. de Filotte's; one hundred tuns, sold at the same price. 2. Prignac. The best is the President du Roy's, at Bordeaux. He makes one hundred and seventy-five tuns, which sell at three hundred livres, new, and six hundred livres, old. Those of 1784, for their extraordinary quality, sell at eight hundred livres. 3. Barsac. The best belongs to the President Pichard, who makes one hundred and fifty tuns, at two hundred and eight livres, new, and six hundred livres, old. Sauterne is the pleasantest; next Prignac, and lastly Barsac; but Barsac is the strongest; next Prignac, and lastly Sauterne; and all stronger than Grave. There are other good crops made in the same parishes of Sauterne, Prignac, and Barsac; but none as good as these. There is a virgin wine, which, though made of a red grape, is of a light rose color, because, being made without pressure, the coloring matter of the skin does not mix with the juice. There are other white wines, from the preceding prices down to seventy-five livres. In general, the white wines keep longest. They will be in perfection till fifteen or twenty years of age. The best vintage now to be bought, is of 1784; both of red and white. There has been no other good year since 1779.

The celebrated vineyards before mentioned are plains, as is generally the canton of Medoc, and that of the Grave. The soil of Hautbrion, particularly, which I examined, is a sand, in which is near as much round gravel or small stone, and very little loam; and this is the general soil of Medoc. That of Pontac, which I examined also, is a little different. It is clayey, with a fourth or fifth of fine rotten stone; and at two feet depth it becomes all a rotten stone. M. de Lamont tells me he has a kind of grape without seeds, which I did not formerly suppose to exist; but I saw at Marseilles dried raisins from Smyrna without seeds. I saw in his farm at Pontac some plants of white clover, and a good deal of yellow; also some small peach trees in the open ground. The principal English wine merchants at Bordeaux are, Jemon, Barton, Johnston, Foster, Skinner, Copinger and McCartey; the chief French wine merchants are Feger, Nerac, Bruneau, Jauge, and du Verget. Desgrands, a wine broker, tells me they never mix the wines of first quality; but they mix the inferior ones to improve them. The smallest wines make the best brandy. They yield about a fifth or sixth.

May 28th, 29th. From Bordeaux to Blaye, the country near the river is hilly, chiefly in vines, some corn, some pasture; further out, are plains, boggy and waste. The soil, in both cases, clay and grit. Some sheep on the waste. To Etauliere, we have sometimes boggy plains, sometimes waving grounds and sandy, always poor, generally waste, in fern and furze, with some corn however, interspersed. To Mirambeau and St. Genis, it is hilly, poor, and mostly waste. There are some corn and maize however, and better trees than usual. Towards Pons, it becomes a little red, mostly rotten stone. There are vines, corn, and maize, which is up. At Pons we approach the Clarenton; the country becomes better, a blackish mould mixed with a rotten chalky stone; a great many vines, corn, maize, and farouche. From Lajart to Saintes and Rochefort, the soil is reddish, its foundation a chalky rock, at about a foot depth; in vines, corn, maize, clover, lucerne, and pasture. There are more and better trees than I have seen in all my journey; a great many apple and cherry trees; fine cattle and many sheep. May 30th. From Rochefort to le Rochex, it is sometimes hilly and red, with a chalky foundation middling good; in corn, pasture, and some waste; sometimes it is reclaimed marsh, in clover and corn except the parts accessible to the tide, which are in wild grass. About Rochelle, it is a low plain. Towards Usseau, and half way to Marans, level highlands, red, mixed with an equal quantity of broken chalk; mostly in vines, some corn and pasture; then to Marans and half way to St. Hermines, it is reclaimed marsh, dark, tolerably good, and all in pasture; there we rise to plains a little higher, red, with a chalky foundation, boundless to the eye, and altogether in corn and maize. May 31st. At St. Hermines, the country becomes very hilly, a red clay mixed with chalky stone, generally waste, in furze and broom, with some patches of corn and maize; and so it continues to Chantenay, and St. Fulgent. Through the whole of this road from Bordeaux are frequent hedge rows, and small patches of forest wood, not good, yet better than I had seen in the preceding part of my journey. Towards Montaigu, the soil mends a little; the cultivated parts in corn and pasture, the uncultivated in broom. It is in very small inclosures of ditch and quickset. On approaching the Loire to Nantes, the country is leveller; the soil from Rochelle to this place may be said to have been sometimes red, but oftener grey, and always on a chalky foundation. The last census, of about 1770, made one hundred and twenty thousand inhabitants at Nantes. They conjecture there are now one hundred and fifty thousand, which equals it to Bordeaux. June 1st, 2d. The country from Nantes to L'Orient is very hilly, and poor, the soil grey; nearly half is waste, in furze and broom, among which is some poor grass. The cultivated parts are in corn, some maize, a good many apple trees; no vines. All is in small inclosures of quick hedge and ditch. There are patches and hedge-rows of forest wood, not quite deserving the name of timber. The people are mostly in villages; they eat rye bread, and are ragged. The villages announce a general poverty, as does every other appearance. Women smite on the anvil, and work with the hoe, and cows are yoked to labor. There are great numbers of cattle, insomuch that butter is their staple. Neither asses nor mules; yet it is said that the fine mules I have met with on my journey, are raised in Poictou. There are but few chateaux here. I observe mill-ponds, and hoes with long handles. Have they not, in common with us, derived these from England, of which Bretagne is probably a colony? L'Orient is supposed to contain twenty-five thousand inhabitants. They tell me here, that to make a reasonable profit on potash and pearl ash, as bought in America, the former should sell at thirty livres, the latter thirty-six livres the quintal. Of turpentine they make no use in their vessels. Bayonne furnishes pitch enough; but tar is in demand, and ours sells well. The tower of L'Orient is sixty-five pieds above the level of the sea, one hundred and twenty pieds high, twenty-five pieds in diameter; the stairs four feet radius, and cost thirty thousand livres, besides the materials of the old tower.

June 3d, 4th, 5th. The country and productions from L'Orient to Rennes, and from Rennes to Nantes, are precisely similar to those from Nantes to L'Orient. About Rennes, it is somewhat leveller, perhaps less poor, and almost entirely in pasture. The soil always grey. Some small separate houses which seem to be the residence of laborers, or very small farmers; the walls frequently of mud, and the roofs generally covered with slate. Great plantations of walnut, and frequently of pine. Some apple trees and sweet briar still in bloom, and broom generally so. I have heard no nightingale since the last day of May. There are gates in this country made in such a manner, that the top rail of the gate overshoots backwards the hind post, so as to counterpoise the gate, and prevent its swagging.

Nantes. Vessels of eight feet draught only can come to Nantes. Those which are larger lie at Point Boeuf, ten leagues below Nantes, and five leagues above the mouth of the river. There is a continued navigation from Nantes to Paris, through the Loire, the Canal de Briare and the Seine. Carolina rice is preferred to that of Lombardy for the Guinea trade, because it requires less water to boil it.

June 6th, 7th, 8th. *Nantes. Ancenis. Angers. Tours.* Ascending the Loire from Nantes, the road as far as Angers, leads over the hills, which are grey, oftener below than above mediocrity, and in corn, pasture, vines, some maize, flax, and hemp. There are no waste lands. About the limits of Bretagne and Anjou, which are between Loriottiere and St. George, the lands change for the better. Here and there, we get views of the plains on the Loire, of some extent, and good appearance, in corn and pasture. After passing Angers, the road is raised out of the reach of inundations, so as at the same time, to ward them off from the interior plains. It passes generally along the river side; but sometimes leads through the plains, which, after we pass Angers, become extensive and good, in corn, pasture, some maize, hemp, flax, peas, and beans; many willows, also poplars and walnuts. The flax is near ripe. Sweet briar in general bloom. Some broom here still, on which the cattle and sheep browse in winter and spring, when they have no other green food; and the hogs eat the blossoms and pods, in spring and summer. This blossom, though disagreeable when smelt in a small quantity, is of delicious fragrance when there is a whole field of it. There are some considerable vineyards in the river plains, just before we reach Les trois volées, (which is at the one hundred and thirty-sixth milestone) and after that, where the hills on the left come into view, they are mostly in vines. Their soil is clayey and stony, a little reddish, and of southern aspect. The hills on the other side of the river, looking to the north, are not in vines. There is very good wine made on these hills; not equal indeed to the Bordeaux of best quality, but to that of good quality, and like it. It is a great article of exportation from Anjou and Touraine, and probably is sold abroad, under the name of Bordeaux. They are now mowing the first crop of hay. All along both hills of the Loire, is a mass of white stone, not durable, growing black with time, and so soft that the people cut their houses out of the solid, with all the partitions, chimneys, doors, etc. The hillsides resemble cony burrows, full of inhabitants. The borders of the Loire, are almost a continued village. There are many chateaux; many cattle, sheep, and horses; some asses.

Tours is at the one hundred and nineteenth milestone. Being desirous of inquiring here into a fact stated by Voltaire, in his Questions Encyclopédiques, article Coquilles, relative to the growth of shells unconnected with animal bodies, at the Chateau of Monsieur de la Sauvagiere, near Tours, I called on Monsieur Gentil, premier secretaire de l'Intendance, to whom the Intendant had written on my behalf, at the request of the Marquis de Chastellux. I stated to him the fact as advanced by Voltaire, and found he was, of all men, the best to whom I could have addressed myself. He told me he had been in correspondence with Voltaire on that very subject, and was perfectly acquainted with Monsieur de la Sauvagiere, and the Faluniere where the fact is said to have taken place. It is at the Chateau de Grillemont, six leagues from Tours, on the road to Bordeaux, belonging now to Monsieur d'Orcai. He says, that de la Sauvagiere was a man of truth, and might be relied on for whatever facts he stated as of his own observations; but that he was overcharged with imagination, which, in matters of opinion and theory, often led him beyond his facts; that this feature in his character had appeared principally in what he wrote on the antiquities of Touraine; but that, as to the fact in question, he believed him. That he himself, indeed, had not watched the same identical shells, as Sauvagiere had done, growing from small to great; but that he had often seen such masses of those shells of all sizes, from a point to a full size, as to carry conviction to his mind that they were in the act of growing; that he had once made a collection of shells for the Emperor's cabinet, reserving duplicates of them for himself; and that these afforded proofs of the same fact; that he afterwards gave those duplicates to a Monsieur du Verget, a physician of Tours, of great science and candor, who was collecting on a larger scale, and who was perfectly in sentiment with Monsieur de la Sauvagiere, that not only the Faluniere, but many other places about Tours, would convince any unbiased observer, that shells are a fruit of the earth, spontaneously produced; and he gave me a copy of de la Sauvagiere's Recueil de Dissertations, presented by the author, wherein is one Sur la vegetation spontanée des coquilles du Chateau des Places. So far, I repeat from him. What are we to conclude? That we have not materials enough yet, to form any conclusion. The fact stated by Sauvagiere is not against any law of nature, and is therefore possible; but it is so little analogous to her habitual processes, that, if true, it would be extraordinary; that to command our belief, therefore, there should be such a suite of observations, as that their untruth would be more extraordinary than the existence of the fact they affirm. The bark of trees, the skin of fruits and animals, the feathers of birds, receive their growth and nutriment from the internal circulation of a juice through the vessels of the individual they cover. We conclude from analogy, then, that the shells of the testaceous tribe, receive also their growth from a like internal circulation. If it be urged, that this does not exclude the possibility of a like shell being produced by the passage of a fluid through the pores of the circumjacent body, whether of earth, stone, or water; I answer, that it is not within the usual economy of nature, to use two processes for one species of production. While I withhold my assent, however, from this hypothesis, I must deny it to every other I have even seen, by which their authors pretend to account for the origin of shells in high places. Some of these are against the laws of nature, and therefore impossible; and others are built on positions more difficult to assent to, than that of de la Sauvagiere. They all suppose the shells to have covered submarine animals, and have then to answer the question. How came they fifteen thousand feet above the level of the sea? And they answer it, by demanding what cannot be conceded. One, therefore, who had rather have no opinion than a false one, will suppose this question one of those beyond the investigation of human sagacity; or wait till further and fuller observations enable him to decide it.

Chanteloup. I heard a nightingale to-day at Chanteloup. The gardener says, it is the male who alone sings, while the female sits; and that when the young are hatched, he also ceases. In the border at Chanteloup, is an ingenious contrivance to hide the projecting steps of a stair-case. Three steps were of necessity to project into the boudoir: they are therefore made triangular steps; and instead of being rested on the floor, as usual, they are made fast at their broad end to the stair door, swinging out and in, with that. When it shuts, it runs them under the other steps; when open, it brings them out to their proper place. In the kitchen garden, are three pumps, worked by one horse. The pumps are placed in an equilateral triangle, each side of which is of about thirty-five feet. In the centre is a post, ten or twelve feet high, and one foot in diameter. In the top of this, enters the bent end of a lever, of about twelve or fifteen feet long, with a swingletree at the other end. About three feet from the bent end, it receives on a pin, three horizontal bars of iron, which at their other end lay hold of one corner of a quadrantal crank (like a bell crank) moving in a vertical plane, to the other corner of which is hooked the vertical handle of the pump. The crank turns on its point as a centre, by a pin or pivot passing through it. The horse moving the lever horizontally in a circle, every point of the lever describes a horizontal circle. That which receives the three bars, describes a circle of six feet in diameter. It gives a stroke then of six feet to the handle of each pump, at each revolution.

Blois. Orleans. June 9, 10. At Blois, the road leaves the river, and traverses the hills, which are mostly reddish, sometimes grey, good enough, in vines, corn, St. foin. From Orleans to the river Juines, at Estampes, it is a continued plain of corn and St. foin, tolerably good, sometimes grey, sometimes red. From Estampes to Estrechy, the country is mountainous and rocky, resembling that of Fontainebleau. Quere. If it may not be the same vein?

A TOUR TO SOME OF THE GARDENS OF ENGLAND
March-April, 1786

[Memorandums made on a tour to some of the gardens in England, described by Whateley in his book on gardening.] While his descriptions, in point of style, are models of perfect elegance and classical correctness, they are as remarkable for their exactness. I always walked over the gardens with his book in my hand, examined with attention the particular spots he described, found them so justly characterized by him as to be easily recognized, and saw with wonder, that his fine imagination had never been able to seduce him from the truth. My inquiries were directed chiefly to such practical things as might enable me to estimate the expense of making and maintaining a garden in that style. My journey was in the months of March and April, 1786.

Chiswick.—Belongs to Duke of Devonshire. A garden about six acres;— the octagonal dome has an ill effect, both within and without: the garden shows still too much of art. An obelisk of very ill effect; another in the middle of a pond useless.

Hampton-Court.—Old fashioned. Clipt yews grown wild.

Twickenham.—Pope's original garden, three and a half acres. Sir Wm. Stanhope added one and a half acres. This is a long narrow slip, grass and trees in the middle, walk all round. Now Sir Wellbore Ellis's. Obelisk at bottom of Pope's garden, as monument to his mother. Inscription, "Ah! Editha, matrum optima, mulierum amantissima, Vale." The house about thirty yards from the Thames: the ground shelves gently to the water side; on the back of the house passes the street, and beyond that the garden. The grotto is under the street, and goes out level to the water. In the centre of the garden a mound with a spiral walk round it. A rookery.

Esher-Place.—The house in a bottom near the river; on the other side the ground rises pretty much. The road by which we come to the house forms a dividing line in the middle of the front; on the right are heights, rising one beyond and above another, with clumps of trees; on the farthest a temple. A hollow filled up with a clump of trees, the tallest in the bottom, so that the top is quite flat. On the left the ground descends. Clumps of trees, the clumps on each hand balance finely—a most lovely mixture of concave and convex. The garden is of about forty-five acres, besides the park which joins. Belongs to Lady Frances Pelham.

Claremont.—Lord Clive's. Nothing remarkable.

Paynshill.—Mr. Hopkins. Three hundred and twenty-three acres, garden and park all in one. Well described by Whateley. Grotto said to have cost £7,000. Whateley says one of the bridges is of stone, but both now are of wood, the lower sixty feet high: there is too much evergreen. The dwelling-house built by Hopkins, ill-situated: he has not been there in five years. He lived there four years while building the present house. It is not finished; its architecture is incorrect. A Doric temple, beautiful.

Woburn.—Belongs to Lord Peters. Lord Loughborough is the present tenant for two lives. Four people to the farm, four to the pleasure garden, four to the kitchen garden. All are intermixed, the pleasure garden being merely a highly-ornamented walk through and round the divisions of the farm and kitchen garden.

Caversham.—Sold by Lord Cadogan to Major Marsac. Twenty-five acres of garden, four hundred acres of park, six acres of kitchen garden. A large lawn, separated by a sunk fence from the garden, appears to be part of it. A straight, broad gravel walk passes before the front and parallel to it, terminated on the right by a Doric temple, and opening at the other end on a fine prospect. This straight walk has an ill effect. The lawn in front, which is pasture, well disposed with clumps of trees.

Wotton.—Now belonging to the Marquis of Buckingham, son of George Grenville. The lake covers fifty acres, the river five acres, the basin fifteen acres, the little river two acres—equal to seventy-two acres of water. The lake and great river are on a level; they fall into the basin five feet below, and that again into the little river five feet lower. These waters lie in form of an **⌊∴** the house is in middle of open side, fronting the angle. A walk goes round the whole, three miles in circumference, and containing within it about three hundred acres: sometimes it passes close to the water, sometimes so far off as to leave large pasture grounds between it and the water. But two hands to keep the pleasure ground in order; much neglected. The water affords two thousand brace of carp a year. There is a Palladian bridge, of which, I think, Whateley does not speak.

Stowe.—Belongs to the Marquis of Buckingham, son of George Grenville, and who takes it from Lord Temple. Fifteen men and eighteen boys employed in keeping pleasure grounds. Within the walk are considerable portions separated by inclosures and used for pasture. The Egyptian pyramid is almost entirely taken down by the late Lord Temple, to erect a building there, in commemoration of Mr. Pitt, but he died before beginning it, and nothing is done to it yet. The grotto and two rotundas are taken away. There are four levels of water, receiving it one from the other. The basin contains seven acres, the lake below that ten acres. Kent's building is called the temple of Venus. The inclosure is entirely by ha-ha. At each end of the front line there is a recess like the bastion of a fort. In one of these is the temple of Friendship, in the other the temple of Venus. They are seen the one from the other, the line of sight passing, not through the garden, but through the country parallel to the line of the garden. This has a good effect. In the approach to Stowe, you are brought a mile through a straight avenue, pointing to the Corinthian arch and to the house, till you get to the arch, then you turn short to the right. The straight approach is very ill. The Corinthian arch has a very useless appearance, inasmuch as it has no pretension to any destination. Instead of being an object from the house, it is an obstacle to a very pleasing distant prospect. The Grecian valley being clear of trees, while the hill on each side is covered with them, is much deepened to appearance.

Leasowes, in Shropshire.—Now the property of Mr. Horne by purchase. One hundred and fifty acres within the walk. The waters small. This is not even an ornamented farm—it is only a grazing farm with a path round it, here and there a seat of board, rarely anything better. Architecture has contributed nothing. The obelisk is of brick. Shenstone had but three hundred pounds a year, and ruined himself by what he did to this farm. It is said that he died of the heart-aches which his debts occasioned him. The part next the road is of red earth, that on the further part grey. The first and second cascades are beautiful. The landscape at number eighteen, and prospect at thirty-two, are fine. The walk through the wood is umbrageous and pleasing. The whole arch of prospect may be of ninety degrees. Many of the inscriptions are lost.

Hagley, now Lord Wescot's.—One thousand acres: no distinction between park and garden—both blended, but more of the character of garden. Eight or nine laborers keep it in order. Between two and three hundred deer in it, some of them red deer. They breed sometimes with the fallow. This garden occupying a descending hollow between the Clent and Witchbury hills, with the spurs from those hills, there is no level in it for a spacious water. There are, therefore, only some small ponds. From one of these there is a fine cascade; but it can only be occasionally, by opening the sluice. This is in a small, dark, deep hollow, with recesses of stone in the banks on every side. In one of these is a Venus predique, turned half round as if inviting you with her into the recess. There is another cascade seen from the portico on the bridge. The castle is triangular, with a round tower at each angle, one only entire; it seems to be between forty and fifty feet high. The ponds yield a great deal of trout. The walks are scarcely gravelled.

Blenheim.—Twenty-five hundred acres, of which two hundred is garden, one hundred and fifty water, twelve kitchen garden, and the rest park. Two hundred people employed to keep it in order, and to make alterations and additions. About fifty of these employed in pleasure grounds. The turf is mowed once in ten days. In summer, about two thousand fallow deer in the park, and two or three thousand sheep. The palace of Henry II. was remaining till taken down by Sarah, widow of the first Duke of Marlborough. It was on a round spot levelled by art, near what is now water, and but a little above it. The island was a part of the high road leading to the palace. Rosamond's bower was near where is now a little grove, about two hundred yards from the palace. The well is near where the bower was. The water here is very beautiful, and very grand. The cascade from the lake, a fine one; except this the garden has no great beauties. It is not laid out in fine lawns and woods, but the trees are scattered thinly over the ground, and every here and there small thickets of shrubs, in oval raised beds, cultivated, and flowers among the shrubs. The gravelled walks are broad—art appears too much. There are but a few seats in it, and nothing of architecture more dignified. There is no one striking position in it. There has been a great addition to the length of the river since Whateley wrote.

Enfield Chase.—One of the four lodges. Garden about sixty acres. Originally by Lord Chatham, now in the tenure of Dr. Beaver, who married the daughter of Mr. Sharpe. The lease lately renewed—not in good repair. The water very fine; would admit of great improvement by extending walks, etc., to the principal water at the bottom of the lawn.

Moor Park.—The lawn about thirty acres. A piece of ground up the hill of six acres. A small lake. Clumps of spruce firs. Surrounded by walk—separately inclosed—destroys unity. The property of Mr. Rous, who bought of Sir Thomas Dundas. The building superb; the principal front a Corinthian portico of four columns; in front of the wings a colonnade, Ionic, subordinate. Back front a terrace, four Corinthian pilasters. Pulling down wings of building; removing deer; wants water.

Kew.—Archimedes' screw for raising water. A horizontal shaft made to turn the oblique one of the screw by a patent machinery of this form:

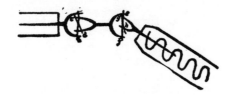

THE PIECES SEPARATE

A is driven by its shank into the horizontal axis of the wheel which turns the machine.

B is an intermediate iron to connect the motion of A and C.

C is driven by its shank into the axis of the screw.

D is a cross axis, the ends, *a* and *b,* going into the corresponding holes *a* and *b* of the iron A, and the ends, *c* and *d,* going into the corresponding holes *c* and *d* of the iron B.

E is another cross axis, the ends, *e* and *f,* going into the corresponding holes *e* and *f* of the iron B, and the ends, *g* and *h,* going into the corresponding holes *g* and *h* of the iron C.

MEMORANDUMS ON A TOUR FROM PARIS TO AMSTERDAM, STRASBURG, AND BACK TO PARIS

March 3-April 23, 1788

Amsterdam.—Joists of houses placed, not with their sides horizontally and perpendicularly, but diamond wise, thus: first, for greater strength; second, to arch between with brick,

thus: Windows opening so that they admit air and not rain. The upper sash opens on a horizontal axis, or pins in the centre of the sides, the lower sash slides up.

Windows

Manner of fixing a flag staff on the mast of a vessel: *a* is the bolt on which it turns; *b* a bolt which is taken in and out to fasten it or to let it down. When taken out, the lower end of the staff is shoved out of its case, and the upper end being heaviest brings itself down: a rope must have been previously fastened to the butt end, to pull it down again when you want to raise the flag end. Dining tables letting down with single or double leaves, so as to take the room of their thickness only with a single leaf when open,

thus: or thus: double-leaves open:

shut, thus: or thus: shut:

Peat costs about one doit each, or twelve and a half stivers the hundred. One hundred make seven cubic feet, and to keep a tolerably comfortable fire for a study or chamber, takes about six every hour and a half.

A machine for drawing light *empty* boats over a dam at Amsterdam. It is an axis in peritrochio fixed on the dam. From the dam each way is a sloping stage, the boat is presented to this, the rope of the axis made fast to it, and it is drawn up. The water on one side of the dam is about four feet higher than on the other.

The camels used for lightening ships over the Pampus will raise the ships eight feet. There are beams passing through the ship's sides, projecting to the off side of the camel and resting on it; of course that alone would keep the camel close to the ship. Besides this, there are a great number of windlasses on the camels, the ropes of which are made fast to the gunwale of the ship. The camel is shaped to the ship on the near side, and straight on the off one. When placed along side, water is let into it so as nearly to sink it; in this state it receives the beams, etc., of the ship, and then the water is pumped out.

Wind saw-mills. See the plans detailed in the moolen book which I bought. A circular foundation of brick is raised about three or four feet high, and covered with a curb or sill of wood, and has little rollers under its sill which make it turn easily on the curb. A hanging bridge projects at each end about fifteen or twenty feet beyond the circular area, thus:

horizontally, and thus: in the profile to increase the play of the timbers on the frame. The wings are at one side, as at *a;* there is a shelter over the hanging bridges, but of plank with scarce any frame, very light.

A bridge across a canal formed by two scows, which open each to the opposite shore and let boats pass.

A lantern over the street door, which gives light equally into the ante-chamber and the street. It is a hexagon, and occupies the place of the middle pane of glass in the circular top of the street door.

A bridge on a canal, turning on a swivel, by which means it is arranged along the side of the canal so as not to be in the way of boats when not in use. When used, it is turned across the canal. It is, of course, a little more than double the width of the canal.

Hedges of beech, which, not losing the old leaf till the new bud pushes it off, has the effect of an evergreen as to cover.

Mr. Ameshoff, merchant at Amsterdam. The distribution of his aviary is worthy of notice. Each kind of the large birds has its coop eight feet wide and four feet deep; the middle of the front is occupied by a broad glass window, on one side of which is a door for the keeper to enter at, and on the other a little trap-door for the birds to pass in and out. The floor strewed with clean hay. Before each coop is a court of eight by sixteen feet, with wire in front and netting above, if the fowls be able to fly. For such as require it, there are bushes of evergreen growing in their court for them to lay their eggs under. The coops are frequently divided into two stories: the upper for those birds which perch, such as pigeons, etc., the lower for those which feed on the ground, as pheasants, partridges, etc. The court is in common for both stories, because the birds do no injury to each other. For the water-fowl there is a pond of water passing through the courts, with a movable separation. While they are breeding they must be separate, afterwards they may come together. The small birds are some of them in a common aviary, and some in cages.

The Dutch wheelbarrow is in this form: which is very convenient for loading and unloading.

Mr. Herman Hend Damen, merchant-broker of Amsterdam, tells me that the emigrants to America come from the Palatinate down the Rhine, and take shipping from Amsterdam. Their passage is ten guineas if paid here, and eleven if paid in America. He says they might be had in any number to go to America, and settle lands as tenants on half stocks or metairies. Perhaps they would serve their employer one year as an indemnification for the passage, and then be bound to remain on his lands seven years. They would come to Amsterdam at their own expense. He thinks they would employ more than fifty acres each; but *quære,* especially if they have fifty acres for their wife also?

Hodson.—The best house. Stadhonderian, his son, in the government. Friendly, but old and very infirm.

Hope.—The first house in Amsterdam. His first object England; but it is supposed he would like to have the American business also, yet he would probably make our affairs subordinate to those of England.

Vollenhoven.—An excellent old house; connected with no party.

Sapportus.—A brother, very honest and ingenuous, well-disposed; acts for Hope, but will say with truth what he can do for us. The best person to consult with as to the best house to undertake a piece of business. He has brothers in London in business. Jacob Van Staphorst tells me there are about fourteen millions of florins, new money, placed in loans in Holland every year, being the savings of individuals out of their annual revenue, etc. Besides this, there are every year reimbursements of old loans from some quarter or other to be replaced at interest in some new loan.

1788. March 16th. Baron Steuben has been generally suspected of having suggested the first idea of the self-styled Order of Cincinnati. But Mr. Adams tells me, that in the year 1776 he had called at a tavern in the State of New York, to dine, just at the moment when the British army was landing at Frog's Neck. Generals Washington, Lee, Knox, and Parsons, came to the same tavern. He got into conversation with Knox. They talked of ancient history—of Fabius, who used to raise the Romans from the dust; of the present contest, etc.; and General Knox, in the course of the conversation, said he should wish for some ribbon to wear in his hat, or in his buttonhole, to be transmitted to his descendants as a badge and a proof that he had fought in defence of their liberties. He spoke of it in such precise terms, as showed he had revolved it in his mind before. Mr. Adams says he and Knox were standing together in the door of the tavern, and does not recollect whether General Washington and the others were near enough to hear the conversation, or were even in the room at that moment. Baron Steuben did not arrive in America till above a year after that. Mr. Adams is now fifty-three years old, *i. e.* nine years more than I am.

It is said this house will cost four tons of silver, or forty thousand pounds sterling. The separation between the middle building and wings in the upper

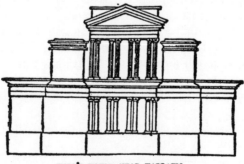

HOPE'S HOUSE, NEAR HARLAEM.

story has a capricious appearance, yet a pleasing one. The right wing of the house (which is the left in the plan) extends back to a great length, so as to make the ground plan in the form of an L. The parapet has a panel of wall, and a panel of balusters alternately, which lighten it. There is no portico, the columns being backed against the wall of the front.

March 30th, 31st. *Amsterdam. Utrecht. Nimeguen.* The lower parts of the low countries seem partly to have been gained from the sea, and partly to be made up of the plains of the Yssel, the Rhine, the Maese and the Schelde united. To Utrecht nothing but plains are seen, a rich black mould, wet, lower than the level of the waters which intersect it; almost entirely in grass; few or no farm-houses, as the business of grazing requires few laborers. The canal is lined with country houses, which bespeak the wealth and cleanliness of the country; but generally in an uncouth state, and exhibiting no regular architecture. After passing Utrecht, the hills northeast of the Rhine come into view, and gather in towards the river, till at Wyck Dursted they are within three or four miles, and at Amelengen they join the river. The plains, after passing Utrecht, become more sandy; the hills are very poor and sandy, generally waste in broom, sometimes a little corn. The plains are in corn, grass, and willow. The plantations of the latter are immense, and give it the air of an uncultivated country. There are new few chateaux; farmhouses abound, built generally of brick, and covered with tile or thatch. There are some apple trees, but no forest; a few inclosures of willow wattling. In the gardens are hedges of beech, one foot apart, which, not losing its old leaves till they are pushed off in the spring by the young ones, gives the shelter of evergreens. The Rhine is here about three hundred yards wide, and the road to Nimeguen passing it a little below Wattelingen, leaves Hetern in sight on the left. On this side, the plains of the Rhine, the Ling, and the Waal unite. The Rhine and Waal are crossed on vibrating boats, the rope supported by a line of seven little barks. The platform by which you go on to the ferry-boat is supported by boats. The view from the hill at Cress is sublime. It commands the Waal, and extends far up the Rhine. That also up and down the Waal from the Bellevue of Nimeguen, is very fine. The chateau here is pretended to have lodged Julius Cæsar. This is giving it an antiquity of at least eighteen centuries, which must be apocryphal. Some few sheep to-day, which were feeding in turnip patches.

April 1st. *Cranenburg. Cleves. Santen. Reynberg. Hoogstaat.* The transition from ease and opulence to extreme poverty is remarkable on crossing the line between the Dutch and Prussian territories. The soil and climate are the same; the governments alone differ. With the poverty, the fear also of slaves is visible in the faces of the Prussian subjects. There is an improvement, however, in the physigonomy, especially could it be a little brightened up. The road leads generally over the hills, but sometimes through skirts of the plains of the Rhine. These are always extensive and good. They want manure, being visibly worn down. The hills are almost always sandy, barren, uncultivated, and insusceptible of culture, covered with broom and moss; here and there a little indifferent forest, which is sometimes of beech. The plains are principally in corn; some grass and willow.. There are no chateaux, nor houses that bespeak the existence even of a middle class. Universal and equal poverty overspreads the whole. In the villages, too, which seem to be falling down, the over-proportion of women is evident. The cultivators seem to live on their farms. The farm-houses are of mud, the better sort of brick; all covered over with thatch. Cleves is little more than a village. If there are shops or magazines of merchandise in it, they show little. Here and there at a window some small articles are hung up within the glass. The gooseberry beginning to leaf.

April 2d. Passed the Rhine at *Essenberg*. It is there about a quarter of a mile wide, or five hundred yards. It is crossed in a scow with sails. The wind being on the quarter, we were eight or ten minutes only in the passage. Duysberg is but a village in fact, walled in; the buildings mostly of brick. No new ones, which indicate a thriving state. I had understood that near that were remains of the encampment of Varus, in which he and his legions fell by the arms of Arminius (in the time of Tiberius I think it was), but there was not a person to be found in Duysberg who could understand either English, French, Italian, or Latin. So I could make no inquiry.

From *Duysberg* to *Dusseldorf* the road leads sometimes over the hills, sometimes through the plains of the Rhine, the quality of which is as before described. On the hills, however, are considerable groves of oak, of spontaneous growth, which seem to be of more than a century; but the soil being barren, the trees, though high, are crooked and knotty. The undergrowth is broom and moss. In the plains is corn entirely. As they are become rather sandy for grass, there are no inclosures on the Rhine at all. The houses are poor and ruinous, mostly of brick, and scantling mixed. A good deal of grape cultivated.

Dusseldorf.—The gallery of paintings is sublime, particularly the room of Vanderwerff. The plains from Dusseldorf to Cologne are much more extensive, and go off in barren downs at some distance from the river. These downs extend far, according to appearance. They are manuring the plains with lime. A gate at the Elector's chateau on this road in this form. We cross at Cologne on a pendulum boat. I observe the hog of this country (Westphalia), of which the celebrated ham is made, is tall, gaunt, and with heavy lop ears. Fatted at a year old would weigh one hundred or one hundred and twenty pounds. At two years old, two hundred pounds. Their principal food is acorns. The pork, fresh, sells at two and a half pence sterling the pound. The hams, ready made, at eight and a half pence sterling the pound. One hundred and six pounds of this country are equal to one hundred pounds of Holland. About four pounds of fine Holland salt are put on one hundred pounds of pork. It is smoked in a room which has no chimney. Well-informed people here tell me there is no other part of the world where the bacon is smoked. They do not know that we do it. Cologne is the principal market of exportation. They find that the small hog makes the sweetest meat.

Cologne is a sovereign city, having no territory out of its walls. It contains about sixty thousand inhabitants; appears to have much commerce, and to abound with poor. Its commerce is principally in the hands of Protestants, of whom there are about sixty houses in the city. They are extremely restricted in their operations, and otherwise oppressed in every form by the government, which is Catholic, and excessively intolerant. Their Senate, some time ago, by a majority of twenty-two to eighteen, allowed them to have a church; but it is believed this privilege will be revoked. There are about two hundred and fifty Catholic churches in the city. The Rhine is here about four hundred yards wide. This city is in 51° latitude, wanting about 6'. Here the vines begin, and it is the most northern spot on the earth on which wine is made. Their first grapes came from Orleans, since that from Alsace, Champagne, etc. It is thirty-two years only since the first vines were sent from Cassel, near Mayence, to the Cape of Good Hope, of which the Cape wine is now made. Afterwards new supplies were sent from the same quarter. That I suppose is the most southern spot on the globe where wine is made, and it is singular that the same vine should have furnished two wines as much opposed to each other in quality as in situation. I was addressed here by Mr. Damen, of Amsterdam, to Mr. Jean Jaques Peuchen, of this place, merchant.

April 4th. *Cologne. Bonne. Andernach. Coblentz.* I saw many walnut trees to-day in the open fields. It would seem as if this tree and wine required the same climate. The soil begins now to be reddish, both on the hills and in the plains. Those from Cologne to Bonne extend about three miles from the river on each side; but a little above Bonne they become contracted, and continue from thence to be from one mile to nothing, comprehending both sides of the river. They are in corn, some clover and rape, and many vines. These are planted in rows three feet apart both ways. The vine is left about six or eight feet high, and stuck with poles ten or twelve feet high. To these poles they are tied in two places, at the height of about two and four feet. They are now performing this operation. The hills are generally excessively steep, a great proportion of them barren; the rest in vines principally, sometimes small patches of corn. In the plains, though rich, I observed they dung their vines plentifully; and it is observed here, as elsewhere, that the plains yield much wine, but bad. The good is furnished from the hills. The walnut, willow, and apple tree beginning to leaf.

Andernach is the port on the Rhine to which the famous mill-stones of Cologne are brought; the quarry, as some say, being at Mendich, three or four leagues from thence. I suppose they have been called Cologne mill-stones, because the merchants of that place having the most extensive correspondence, have usually sent them to all parts of the world. I observed great collections of them at Cologne. This is one account.

April 5th. *Coblentz. Nassau.* Another account is, that these stones are cut at Triers and brought down the Moselle. I could not learn the price of them at the quarry; but I was shown a grind-stone of the same stone, five feet diameter, which cost at Triers six florins. It was of but half the thickness of a mill-stone. I supposed, therefore, that two mill-stones would cost about as much as three of these grind-stones, *i. e.,* about a guinea and a half. This country abounds with slate.

The best Moselle wines are made about fifteen leagues from hence, in an excessively mountainous country. The first quality (without any comparison) is that made on the mountain of Brownberg, adjoining to the village of Dusmond; and the best crop is that of the Baron Breidbach Burrhesheim, grand Chambellan et grand Baillif de Coblentz. His Receveur, of the name of Mayer, lives at Dusmond. The last fine year was 1783, which sells now at fifty louis the foudre, which contains six aumes of one hundred and seventy bottles each, equal to about one thousand one hundred and ten bottles. This is about twenty-two sous Tournois the bottle. In general, the Baron Burrhesheim's crops will sell as soon as made, say at the vintage, for one hundred and thirty, one hundred and forty, and one hundred and fifty ecus the foudre (the ecu is one and a half florins of Holland), say two hundred. 2. Vialen is the second quality, and sells new at one hundred and twenty ecus the foudre. 3. Crach-Bispost is the third, and sells for about one hundred and five ecus. I compared Crach of 1783 with Baron Burrheisheim's of the same year. The latter is quite clear of acid, stronger, and very sensibly the best. 4. Selting, which sells at one hundred ecus. 5. Kous-Berncastle, the fifth quality, sells at eighty or ninety. After this there is a gradation of qualities down to thirty ecus. These wines must be five or six years old before they are quite ripe for drinking. One thousand plants yield a foudre of wine a year in the most plentiful vineyards. In other vineyards, it will take two thousand or two thousand and five hundred plants to yield a foudre. The culture of one thousand plants costs about one louis a year. A day's labor of a man is paid in winter twenty kreitzers (*i. e.,* one-third of a florin), in summer twenty-six; a woman's is half that. The red wines of this country are very indifferent, and will not keep. The Moselle is here from one hundred to two hundred yards wide; the Rhine three hundred to four hundred. A jessamine in the Count de Moustier's garden in leaf.

In the Elector of Treves' palace at Coblentz, are large rooms very well warmed by warm air conveyed from an oven below, through tubes which

open into the rooms. An oil and vinegar cruet in this form. At Coblentz we pass the river on a pendulum boat, and the road to Nassau is over tremendous hills, on which is here and there a little corn, more vines, but mostly barren. In some of these barrens are forests of beech and oak, tolerably large, but crooked and knotty; the undergrowth beech brush, broom, and moss. The soil of the plains, and of the hills where they are cultivable, is reddish. Nassau is a village the whole rents of which should not amount to more than a hundred or two guineas. Yet it gives the title of Prince to the house of Orange to which it belongs.

April 6th. *Nassau. Schwelbach. Wisbaden. Hocheim. Frankfort.* The road from Nassau to Schwelbach is over hills, or rather mountains, both high and steep; always poor, and above half of them barren in beech and oak. At Schwelbach there is some chestnut. The other parts are either in winter grain, or preparing for that of the spring. Between Schwelbach and Wisbaden we come in sight of the plains of the Rhine, which are very extensive. From hence the lands, both high and low, are very fine, in corn, vines, and fruit trees. The country has the appearance of wealth, especially in the approach to Frankfort.

April 7th. *Frankfort.* Among the poultry, I have seen no turkeys in Germany till I arrive at this place. The stork, or crane, is very commonly tame here. It is a miserable, dirty, ill-looking bird. The Lutheran is the reigning religion here, and is equally intolerant to the Catholic and Calvinist, excluding them from the free corps.

April 8th. *Frankfort. Hanau.* The road goes through the plains of the Maine, which are mulatto, and very fine. They are well cultivated till you pass the line between the republic and the landgraviate of Hesse, when you immediately see the effect of the difference of government, notwithstanding the tendency which the neighborhood of such a commercial town as Frankfort has to counteract the effects of tyranny in its vicinities, and to animate them in spite of oppression. In Frankfort all is life, bustle, and motion; in Hanau the silence and quiet of the mansions of the dead. Nobody is seen moving in the streets; every door is shut; no sound of the saw, the hammer, or other utensil of industry. The drum and fife are all that is heard. The streets are cleaner than a German floor, because nobody passes them. At Williamsbath, near Hanau, is a country seat of the Landgrave. There is a ruin which is clever. It presents the remains of an old castle. The ground plan is in this form: The upper story in this: A circular room of thirty-one and a half feet diameter within. The four little square towers at the corners finish at the floor of the upper story, so as to be only platforms to walk out on. Over the circular room is a platform also, which is covered by the broken parapet which once crowned the top, but is now fallen off some parts, whilst the other parts remain. I like better, however, the form of the ruin at Hagley, in England, which was thus a sentry box here, covered over with bark, so as to look exactly like the trunk of an old

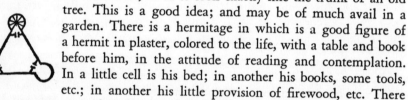

tree. This is a good idea; and may be of much avail in a garden. There is a hermitage in which is a good figure of a hermit in plaster, colored to the life, with a table and book before him, in the attitude of reading and contemplation. In a little cell is his bed; in another his books, some tools, etc.; in another his little provision of firewood, etc. There is a monument erected to the son of the present landgrave, in the form of a pyramid, the base of which is eighteen and a half feet. The side declines from the perpendicular about twenty-one and a half degrees. An arch is carried through it both ways so as to present a door in each side. In the middle of this, at the crossing of the two arches, is a marble monument with this inscription: "ante tempus." He died at twelve years of age. Between Hanau and Frankfort, in sight of the road, is the village of Bergen, where was fought the battle of Bergen in the war before last. Things worth noting here are: 1. A folding ladder. 2. Manner of packing china cups and saucers, the former in a circle within the latter. 3. The marks of different manufactures of china, to wit: Dresden with two swords. Hecks with a wheel with **W**, Frankendaal with ⚵ (for Charles Theodore), and a 👑 over it. Berlin with 4. The top rail of a wagon supported by the washers on the ends of the axle-trees.

April 10th. *Frankfort. Hocheim. Mayence.* The little tyrants round about having disarmed their people, and made it very criminal to kill game, one knows when they quit the territory of Frankfort by the quantity of game which is seen. In the Republic, everybody being allowed to be armed, and to hunt on their own lands, there is very little game left in its territory. The hog hereabouts resembles extremely the little hog of Virginia. Round like that, a small head, and short upright ears. This makes the ham of Mayence so much esteemed at Paris.

We cross the Rhine at Mayence on a bridge one thousand eight hundred and forty feet long, supported by forty-seven boats. It is not in a direct line, but curved up against the stream; which may strengthen it if the difference between the upper and lower curve be sensible, if the planks of the floor be thick, well jointed together, and forming sectors of circles, so as to act on the whole as the stones of an arch. But it has by no means this appearance. Near one end, one of the boats has an axis in peritrochio, and a chain, by which it may be let drop down stream some distance, with the portion of the floor belonging to it, so as to let a vessel through. Then it is wound up again into place, and to consolidate it the more with the adjoining parts, the loose section is a little higher, and has at each end a folding stage, which folds back on it when it moves down, and when brought up again into place, these stages are folded over on the bridge. This whole operation takes but four or five minutes. In the winter the bridge is taken away entirely, on account of the ice. And then everything passes on the ice, through the whole winter.

April 11th. *Mayence. Rudesheim. Johansberg. Marke-bronn.* The women do everything here. They dig the earth, plough, saw, cut and split wood, row, tow the bat-teaux, etc. In a small but dull kind of batteau, with two hands rowing with a kind of large paddle, and a square sail, but scarcely a breath of wind, we went down the river at the rate of five miles an hour, making it three and a half hours to Rudesheim. The floats of wood which go with the current only, go one mile and a half an hour. They go night and day. There are five boat-mills abreast here. Their floats seem to be about eight feet broad. The Rhine yields salmon, carp, pike, and perch, and the little rivers running into it yield speckled trout. The plains from Maintz to Rudesheim are good and in corn; the

A TOWER AT RUDESHEIM.

hills mostly in vines. The banks of the river are so low that, standing up in the batteau, I could generally see what was in the plains. Yet they are seldom overflowed.

Though they begin to make wine, as has been said, at Cologne, and continue it up the river indefinitely; yet it is only from Rudesheim to Hocheim that wines of the very first quality are made. The river happens there to run due east and west, so as to give its hills on that side a southern aspect. And even in this canton, it is only Hocheim, Johansberg, and Rudesheim, that are considered as of the very first quality. Johansberg is a little mountain (berg signifies mountain), whereon is a religious house, about fifteen miles below Mayence, and near the village of Vingel. It has a southern aspect, the soil a barren mulatto clay, mixed with a good deal of stone, and some slate. This wine used to be but on a par with Hocheim and Rudesheim; but the place having come to the Bishop of Fulda, he improved its culture so as to render it stronger; and since the year 1775, it sells at double the price of the other two. It has none of the acid of the Hocheim and other Rhenish wines. There are about sixty tuns made in a good year, which sell, as soon as of a drinkable age, at one thousand franks each. The tun here contains seven and a half aumes of one hundred and seventy bottles each. Rudesheim is a village of about eighteen or twenty miles below Mayence. Its fine wines are made on the hills about a mile below the village, which look to the south, and on the middle and lower parts of them. They are terraced. The soil is grey, about one-half of slate and rotten stone, the other half of barren clay, excessively steep. Just behind the village also is a little spot, called Hinder House, belonging to the Counts of Sicken and Oschstein, whereon each makes about a tun of wine of the very first quality. This spot extends from the bottom to the top of the hill. The vignerons of Rudesheim dung their wines about once in five or six years, putting a one-horse tumbrel load of dung on every twelve feet square. One thousand plants yield about four aumes in a good year. The best crops are,

The Chanoines of Mayence, who make	15	pieces of 7½	aumes.
Le Comte de Sicken	6	"	"
Le Comte d'Oschstein	9	"	"
L'Electeur de Mayence	6	"	"
Le Comte de Meternisch	6	"	"
Monsieur de Boze	5	"	"
M. Ackerman, baliff et aubergiste des Trois Couronnes	8	"	"
M. Ackerman le fils, aubergiste à la couronne	5	"	"
M. Lynn, aubergiste de l'ange	5	"	"
Baron de Wetzel	7	"	"
Convent de Mariahousen, des religieuses Benedictines.	7	"	"
M. Johan Yung	8	"	"
M. de Rieden	5	"	"

92

These wines begin to be drinkable at about five years old. The proprietors sell them old or young, according to the prices offered, and according to their own want of money. There is always a little difference between different casks, and therefore when you choose and buy a single cask, you pay three, four, five or six hundred florins for it. They are not at all acid, and to my taste much preferable to Hocheim, though but of the same price. Hocheim is a village about three miles above Mayence, on the Maine, where it

empties into the Rhine. The spot whereon the good wine is made is the hillside from the church down to the plain, a gentle slope of about a quarter of a mile wide, and extending half a mile towards Mayence. It is of south-western aspect, very poor, sometimes grey, sometimes mulatto, with a moderate mixture of small broken stone. The vines are planted three feet apart, and stuck with sticks about six feet high. The vine, too, is cut at that height. They are dunged once in three or four years. One thousand plants yield from one to two aumes a year: they begin to yield a little at three years old, and continue to one hundred years, unless sooner killed by a cold winter. Dick, keeper of the Rothen-house tavern at Frankfort, a great wine merchant, who has between three and four hundred tuns of wine in his cellars, tells me that Hocheim of the year 1783, sold, as soon as it was made, at ninety florins the aume, Rudesheim of the same year, as soon as made, at one hundred and fifteen florins, and Markebronn seventy florins. But a peasant of Hocheim tells me that the best crops of Hocheim in the good years, when sold new, sell but for about thirty-two or thirty-three florins the aume; but that it is only the poorer proprietors who sell new. The fine crops are,

Count Ingleheim about	10 tuns.	
Baron d'Alberg	8 "	All of these keep till about fifteen years old, before they sell, unless they are offered a very good price sooner.
Count Schimbon	14 "	
The Chanoines of Mayence	18 "	
Counsellor Schik de Vetsler	15 "	
Convent of Jacobsberg	8 "	
The Chanoine of Fechbach	10 "	
The Carmelites of Frankfort	8 "	Who only sell by the bottle in their own tavern in Frankfort.
The Bailiff of Hocheim	11 "	Who sells at three or four years old.
Zimmerman, a bourgeois	4 "	These being poor, sell new.
Feldman, a carpenter	2 "	

Markebronn (bronn signifies a spring, and is probably of affinity with the Scotch word, burn) is a little canton in the same range of hills, adjoining to the village of Hagenheim, about three miles above Johansberg, subject to the elector of Mayence. It is a sloping hillside of southern aspect, mulatto, poor, and mixed with some stone. This yields wine of the second quality.

April 12th. *Mayence. Oppenheim. Dorms. Manheim.* On the road between Mayence and Oppenheim are three cantons, which are also esteemed as yielding wines of the second quality. These are Laudenheim, Bodenheim, and Nierstein. Laudenheim is a village about four or five miles from Mayence. Its wines are made on a steep hillside, the soil of which is grey, poor and mixed with some stone. The river there happens to make a short turn to the southwest, so as to present its hills to the southeast. Bodenheim is a village nine miles, and Nierstein another about ten or eleven miles from Mayence. Here, too, the river is northeast and soutwest, so as to give the hills between these villages a southeast aspect; and at Thierstein, a valley making off, brings the face of the hill round to the south. The hills between these villages are almost perpendicular, of a vermilion red, very poor, and having as much rotten stone as earth. It is to be observed that these are the only cantons on the south side of the river which yield good wine, the hills on this side being generally exposed to the cold winds, and turned from the sun. The annexed bill of prices current, will give an idea of the estimation of these wines respectively.

With respect to the grapes in this country, there are three kinds in use for making white wine, (for I take no notice of the red wines, as being absolutely worthless). 1. The Klemperien, of which the inferior qualities of Rhenish wines are made, and is cultivated because of its hardness. The wines of this grape descend as low as one hundred florins the tun of eight aumes. 2. The Rhysslin grape, which grows only from Hocheim down to Rudesheim. This is small and delicate, and therefore succeeds only in this chosen spot. Even at Rudesheim it yields a fine wine only in the little spot called Hinder House, before mentioned; the mass of good wines made at Rudesheim, below the village, being of the third kind of grape, which is called the Orleans grape.

To Oppenheim the plains of the Rhine and Maine are united. From that place we see the commencement of the Berg-strasse, or mountains which separate at first the plains of the Rhine and Maine, then cross the Neckar at Heidelberg, and from thence forms the separation between the plains of the Neckar and Rhine, leaving those of the Rhine about ten or twelve miles wide. These plains are sometimes black, sometimes mulatto, always rich. They are in corn, potatoes, and some willow. On the other side again, that is, on the west side, the hills keep at first close to the river. They are about one hundred and fifty or two hundred feet high, sloping, red, good, and mostly in vines. Above Oppenheim they begin to go off till they join the mountains of Lorraine and Alsace, which separate the waters of the Moselle and Rhine, leaving to the whole valley of the Rhine about twenty or twenty-five miles breadth. About Worms these plains are sandy, poor, and often covered only with small pine.

April 13th. *Manheim.* There is a bridge over the Rhine, here, supported on thirty-nine boats, and one over the Neckar on eleven boats. The bridge over the Rhine is twenty-one and a half feet wide from rail to rail. The

The elector placed, in 1768, two males and five females of the Angora goat at Dossenheim, which is at the foot of the Bergstrasse mountains. He sold twenty-five last year, and has now seventy. They are removed into the mountains four leagues beyond Dossenheim. Heidelberg is on the Neckar just where it issues from the Bergstrasse mountains, occupying the first skirt of plain which it forms. The château is up the hill a considerable height. The gardens lie above the château, climbing up the mountain in terraces. This château is the most noble ruin I have ever seen, having been reduced to that state by the French in the time of Louis XIV., 1693. Nothing remains under cover but the chapel. The situation is romantic and pleasing beyond expression. It is on a great scale much like the situation of Petrarch's château, at Vaucluse, on a small one. The climate, too, is like that of Italy. The apple, the pear, cherry, peach, apricot, and almond, are all in bloom. There is a station in the garden to which the château re-echoes distinctly four syllables. The famous tun of Heidelberg was new built in 1751, and made to contain thirty foudres more than the ancient one. It is said to contain two hundred and thirty-six foudres of one thousand two hundred bottles each. I measured it, and found its length external to be twenty-eight feet ten inches; its diameter at the end twenty feet three inches; the thickness of the staves seven and a half inches; thickness of the hoops seven and a half inches; besides a great deal of external framing. There is no wine in it now. The gardens at Schwetzinger show how much money may be laid out to make an ugly thing. What is called the English quarter, however, relieves the eye from the straight rows of trees, round and square basins, which constitute the great mass of the garden. There are some tolerable morsels of Grecian architecture, and a good ruin. The Aviary, too, is clever. It consists of cells of about eight feet wide, arranged round, and looking into a circular area of about forty or fifty feet diameter. The cells have doors both of wire and glass, and have small shrubs in them. The plains of the Rhine on this side are twelve miles wide, bounded by the Bergstrasse mountains. These appear to be eight hundred or a thousand feet high; the lower part in vines, from which

 is made what is called the vin de Nichar; the upper in chestnut. There are some cultivated spots however, quite to the top. The plains are generally mulatto, in corn principally; they are planting potatoes in some parts, and leaving others open for maize and tobacco. Many peach and other fruit tres on the lower part of the mountain. The path on some parts of these mountains are somewhat in the style represented in the margin.

Manheim. Kaeferthal. Manheim. Just beyond Kaeferthal is an extensive, sandy waste, planted in pine, in which the elector has about two hundred sangliers, tamed. I saw about fifty; the heaviest I am told, would weigh

boats are four feet deep, fifty-two feet long, and nine feet eight inches broad. The space between boat and boat is eighteen feet ten inches. From these data the length of the bridge should be 9ft. 8in. + 18ft. 10in. × 40 = 1140 feet. In order to let vessels pass through, two boats well framed together, with their flooring, are made to fall down stream together. Here, too, they make good ham. It is fattened on round potatoes and Indian corn. The farmers smoke what is for their own use in their chimneys. When it is made for sale, and in greater quantities than the chimney will hold, they make the smoke of the chimney pass into an adjoining loft, or apartment, from which it has no issue; and here they hang their hams.

An economical curtain bedstead. The bedstead is seven feet by four feet two inches. From each leg there goes up an iron rod three-eights of an inch in diameter. Those from the legs at the foot of the bed meet-ing at top as in the margin, and those from the head meeting in like manner, so that the two at the foot form one point, and the two at the head another. On these points lays an oval iron rod, whose long diameter is five feet, and short one three feet one inch. There is a hole through this rod at each end, by which it goes on firm on the point of the upright rods. Then a nut screws it down firmly. Ten breadths of stuff two feet ten inches wide, and eight feet six inches long, form the curtains. There in no top nor vallons. The rings are fastened within two and a half or three inches of the top on the inside, which two and a half or three inches stand up, and are an orna-ment somewhat like a ruffle.

I have observed all along the Rhine that they make the oxen draw by the horns. A pair of very handsome chariot horses, large, bay, and seven, years old, sell for fifty louis. One pound of beef sells for eight kreitzers, (i. e. eight sixtieths of a florin;) one pounds of mutton or veal, six kreitzers; one pound of pork, seven and a half kreitzers; one pound of ham, twelve kreitzers; one pound of fine, wheat bread, two kreitzers; one pound of but-ter, twenty kreitzers; one hundred and sixty pounds of wheat, six francs; one hundred and sixty pounds of maize, five francs; one hundred and sixty pounds of potatoes, one franc; one hundred pounds of hay, one franc; a cord of wood (which is 4 4 and 6 feet), seven francs; a laborer by the day receives twenty-four kreitzers, and feeds himself. A journee or arpent of land (which is eight by two hundred steps), such as the middling plains of the Rhine, will sell for two hundred francs. There are more soldiers here than other inhabitants, to wit: six thousand soldiers and four thousand males of full age of the citizens, the whole number of whom is reckoned at twenty thousand.

April 14th. *Manheim. Dossenheim. Heidelberg. Schwetzingen Manheim.*

about three hundred pounds. They are fed on round potatoes, and range in the forest of pines. At the village of Kaeferthal is a plantation of rhubarb, begun in 1769, by a private company. It contains twenty arpens or jourries, and its culture costs about four or five hundred francs a year; it some times employs forty or fifty laborers at a time. The best age to sell the rhubarb at is the fifth or sixth year, but the sale being dull, they keep it sometimes to the tenth year; they find it best to let it remain in the ground. They sell about two hundred kentals a year at two or three francs a pound, and could sell double that quantity from the ground if they could find a market. The apothecaries of Frankfort and of England are the principal buyers. It is in beds, resembling lettuce-beds; the plants four, five or six feet apart. When dug, a thread is passed through every piece of root, and it is hung separate in a kind of rack; when dry it is rasped; what comes off is given to the cattle.

April 15. *Manheim. Spire. Carlsruhe.* The valley preserves its width, extending on each side of the river about ten or twelve miles, but the soil loses much in its quality, becoming sandy and lean, often barren and overgrown with pine thicket. At Spire is nothing remarkable. Between that and Carlsruhe we pass the Rhine in a common scow with oars, where it is between three and four hundred yards wide. Carlsruhe is the residence of the Margrave of Baden, a sovereign prince. His château is built in the midst of a natural forest of several leagues diameter, and of the best trees I have seen in these countries: they are mostly oak, and would be deemed but indifferent in America. A great deal of money has been spent to do more harm than good to the ground—cutting a number of straight alleys through the forest. He has a pheasantry of the gold and silver kind, the latter very tame, but the former excessively shy. A little inclosure of stone, two and a half feet high and thirty feet diameter, in which are two tamed beavers. There is a pond of fifteen feet diameter in the centre, and at each end a little cell for them to retire into, which is stowed with boughs and twigs with leaves on them, which is their principal food. They eat bread also;—twice a week the water is changed. They cannot get over this wall. Some cerfs of a peculiar kind, spotted like fawns, the horns remarkably long, small and sharp, with few points. I am not sure there were more than two to each main beam, and if I saw distinctly, there came out a separate and subordinate beam from the root of each. Eight Angora goats—beautiful animals—all white. This town is only an appendage of the château, and but a moderate one. It is a league from Durlach, half way between that and the river. I observe they twist the flues of their stoves in any form for ornament merely, without smoking, as thus, *e. g.*

April 16. *Carlsruhe. Rastadt. Scholhoven. Bischofheim. Kehl. Strasburg.* The valley of the Rhine still preserves its breadth, but varies in quality; sometimes a rich mulatto loam, sometimes a poor sand, covered with small pine. The culture is generally corn. It is to be noted, that through the whole of my route through the Netherlands and the valley of the Rhine, there is a little red clover every here and there, and a great deal of grape cultivated. The seed of this is sold to be made into oil. The grape is now in blossom. No inclosures. The fruit trees are generally blossoming through the whole valley. The high mountains of the Bergstrasse, as also of Alsace, are covered with snow. Within this day or two, the every-day dress of the country women here is black. Rastadt is a seat also of the Margrave of Baden. Scholhoven and Kehl are in his territory, but not Bischofheim. I see no beggars since I entered his government, nor is the traveller obliged to ransom himself every moment by a chausiee gold. The roads are excellent, and made so, I presume, out of the coffers of the prince. From Cleves till I enter the Margravate of Baden, the roads have been strung with beggars—in Hesse the most, and the road tax very heavy. We pay it cheerfully, however, through the territory of Frankfort and thence up the Rhine, because fine gravelled roads are kept up; but through the Prussian, and other parts of the road below Frankfort, the roads are only as made by the carriages, there not appearing to have been ever a day's work employed on them. At Strasburg we pass the Rhine on a wooden bridge.

At *Brussels* and *Antwerp,* the fuel is pit-coal, dug in Brabant. Through all Holland it is turf. From Cleves to Cologne it is pit-coal brought from England. They burn it in open stoves. From thence it is wood, burnt in close stoves, till you get to Strasburg, where the open chimney comes again into use.

April 16th, 17th, 18th. *Strasburg.* The vin de paille is made in the neighborhood of Colmar, in Alsace, about ——— from this place. It takes its name from the circumstance of spreading the grapes on straw, where they are preserved till spring, and then made into wine. The little juice then remaining in them makes a rich sweet wine, but the dearest in the world, without being the best by any means. They charge nine florins the bottle for it in the taverns of Strasburg. It is the caprice of wealth alone which continues so losing an operation. This wine is sought because dear; while the better wine of Frontignan is rarely seen at a good table because it is cheap.

Strasburg. Saverne. Phalsbourg. As far as Saverne the country is in waving hills and hollows; red, rich enough; mostly in small grain, but some vines; a little stone. From Saverne to Phalsbourg we cross a considerable mountain, which takes an hour to rise it.

April 19th. *Phalsbourg. Fenestrange. Moyenvic. Nancy.* Asparagus to-day

at Moyenvic. The country is always either mountainous or hilly; red, tolerably good, and in small grain. On the hills about Fenestrange, Moyenvic,
and Nancy, are some small vineyards where a bad wine is made. No inclosures. Some good sheep, indifferent cattle, and small horses. The most
forest I have seen in France, principally of beech, pretty large. The houses,
as in Germany, are of scantling, filled in with wicker and mortar, and covered either with thatch or tiles. The people, too, here as there, are gathered
in villages. Oxen plough here with collars and hames. The awkward figure
of their mould-board leads one to consider what should be its form. The
offices of the mould-board are to receive the sod after the share has cut
under it, to raise it gradually, and to reverse it. The fore-end of it, then,
should be horizontal to enter under the sod, and the hind end perpendicular
to throw it over; the intermediate surface changing gradually from the horizontal to the perpendicular. It should be as wide as the furrow, and of a
length suited to the construction of the plough. The following would seem
a good method of making it: Take a block, whose length, breadth and
thickness, are that of your intended mould-board, suppose two and a half
feet long and eight inches broad and thick. Draw the

FIG. I. FIG. 2.

lines *a d* and *c d*, figure 1, with a saw, the toothed edge
of which is straight, enter at *a* and cut on, guiding the
hind part of the saw on the line *a b*, and the fore part
on the line *a d*, till the saw reaches the points *c* and *d*,
then enter it at *c* and cut on, guiding it by the lines *c b* and
c d till it reaches the points *b* and *d*. The quarter, *a b c d*,
will then be completely cut out, and the diagonal from *d* to *b* laid bare.
The piece may now be represented as in figure 2. Then saw in transversely
at every two inches till the saw reaches the line *c e*, and the diagonal *b d*,
and cut out the pieces with an adze. The upper surface will thus be formed.
With a gauge opened to eight inches, and guided by the lines *c e*, scribe
the upper edge of the board from *d b*, cut that edge perpendicular to the
face of the board, and scribe it of the proper thickness. Then form the
underside by the upper, by cutting transversely with the saw and taking
out the piece with an adze. As the upper edge of the wing of the share
rises a little, the fore end of the board, *b c*, will rise as much from a strict
horizontal position, and will throw the hind end, *e d*, exactly as much
beyond the perpendicular, so as to promote the reversing of the sod. The
women here, as in Germany, do all sorts of work. While one considers
them as useful and rational companions, one cannot forget that they are
objects of our pleasures; nor can they ever forget it. While employed in
dirt and drudgery, some tag of a ribbon, some ring, or bit of bracelet,
earbob or necklace, or something of that kind, will show that the desire of

pleasing is never suspended in them. It is an honorable circumstance for man, that the first moment he is at his ease, he allots the internal employments to his female partner, and takes the external on himself. And this circumstance, or its reverse, is a pretty good indication that a people are, or are not at their ease. Among the Indians, this indication fails from a particular cause: every Indian man is a soldier or warrior, and the whole body of warriors constitute a standing army, always employed in war or hunting. To support that army, there remain no laborers but the women. Here, then, is so heavy a military establishment, that the civil part of the nation is reduced to women only. But this is a barbarous perversion of the natural destination of the two sexes. Women are formed by nature for attentions, not for hard labor. A woman never forgets one of the numerous train of little offices which belong to her. A man forgets often.

April 20th. *Nancy. Toule. Void. Ligny en Barrois. Bar le Duc. St. Dizier.* Nancy itself is a neat little town, and its environs very agreeable. The valley of the little branch of the Moselle, on which it is, is about a mile wide: the road then crossing the head-waters of the Moselle, the Maese, and the Marne, the country is very hilly, and perhaps a third of it poor and in forests of beech: the other two-thirds from poor up to middling, red, and stony. Almost entirely in corn, now and then only some vines on the hills. The Moselle at Toule is thirty or forty yards wide: the Maese near Void about half that: the Marne at St. Dizier about forty yards. They all make good plains of from a quarter of a mile to a mile wide. The hills of the Maese abound with chalk. The rocks coming down from the tops of the hills, on all the road of this day, at regular intervals like the ribs of an animal, have a very irregular appearance. Considerable flocks of sheep and asses, and, in the approach to St. Dizier, great plantations of apple and cherry trees; here and there a peach tree, all in general bloom. The roads through Lorraine are strung with beggars.

April 21st. *St. Dizier. Vitry le Francais. Chalons sur Marne. Epernay.* The plains of the Marne and Sault uniting, appear boundless to the eye till we approach their confluence at Vitry, where the hills come in on the right; after that the plains are generally about a mile, mulatto, of middling quality, sometimes stony. Sometimes the ground goes off from the river so sloping, that one does not know whether to call it high or low land. The hills are mulatto also, but whitish, occasioned by the quantity of chalk which seems to constitute their universal base. They are poor, and principally in vines. The streams of water are of the color of milk, occasioned by the chalk also. No inclosures, some flocks of sheep; children gathering dung in the roads. Here and there a chateau; but none considerable.

April 22d. *Epernay.* The hills abound with chalk. Of this they make lime,

not so strong as stone lime, and therefore to be used in greater proportion.
They cut the blocks into regular forms also, like stone, and build houses of
it. The common earth, too, well impregnated with this, is made into mortar,
moulded in the form of brick, dried in the sun, and houses built of them
which last one hundred or two hundred years. The plains here a mile wide,
red, good, in corn, clover, lucerne, St. foin. The hills are in vines, and this
being precisely the canton where the most celebrated wines of Champagne
are made, details must be entered into. Remember, however, that they will
always relate to the white wines, unless where the red are expressly mentioned. The reason is that their red wines, though much esteemed on the
spot, are by no means esteemed elsewhere equally with their white; nor do
they merit equal esteem.

A topographical sketch of the position of the wine villages, the course of
the hills, and consequently the aspect of the vineyards.

Soil, meagre, mulatto clay, mixed with small broken stone, and a little hue
of chalk. Very dry.

Aspect, may be better seen by the annexed diagram. The wine of Aij
is made from *a* to *b,* those of Dizij from *b* to *c,* Auvillij *d* to *e,* Cumieres

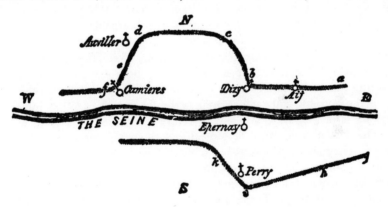

e to *f,* Epernay *g* to *h,* Perij *i* to *k.* The hills are generally about two hundred and fifty feet high. The good wine is made only in the middle region.
The lower region, however, is better than the upper; because this last is
exposed to cold winds, and a colder atmosphere.

Culture. The vines are planted two feet apart. Afterwards they are multiplied (provignés). When a stock puts out two shoots they lay them down,
spread them open and cover them with earth, so as to have in the end
about a plant for every square foot. For performing this operation they

have a hook, of this shape, ⊤ and nine inches long, which, being stuck in the ground, holds down the main stock, while the laborer separates and covers the new shoot. They leave two buds above the ground. When the vine has shot up high enough, they stick it with split sticks of oak, from an inch to an inch and a half square, and four feet long, and tie the vine to its stick with straw. These sticks cost two florins the hundred, and will last forty years. An arpent, one year with another, in the fine vineyards, gives twelve pieces, and in the inferior vineyards twenty-five pieces, of two hundred bottles each. An arpent of the first quality sells for three thousand florins, and there have been instances of seven thousand two hundred florins. The arpent contains one hundred verges, of twenty-two pieds square. The arpent of inferior quality sells at one thousand florins. They plant the vines in a hole about a foot deep, and fill that hole with good mould, to make the plant take. Otherwise it would perish. Afterwards, if ever they put dung, it is very little. During wheat harvest there is a month or six weeks that nothing is done in the vineyard, that is to say, from the 1st of August to the beginning of vintage. The vintage commences early in September, and lasts a month. A day's work of a laborer in the busiest season is twenty sous, and he feeds himself: in the least busy season it is fifteen sous. Corn lands are rented from four florins to twenty-four; but vine lands are never rented. The three façons (or workings) of an arpent cost fifteen florins. The whole year's expense of an arpent is worth one hundred florins.

Grapes.—The bulk of their grapes are purple, which they prefer for making even white wine. They press them very lightly, without treading or permitting them to ferment at all, for about an hour; so that it is the beginning of the running only which makes the bright wine. What follows the beginning is of a straw color, and therefore not placed on a level with the first. The last part of the juice, produced by strong pressure, is red and ordinary. They choose the bunches with as much care, to make wine of the very first quality, as if to eat. Not above one-eighth of the whole grapes will do for this purpose. The white grape, though not so fine for wine as the red, when the red can be produced, and more liable to rot in a moist season, yet grows better if the soil be excessively poor, and therefore in such a soil is preferred, or rather, is used of necessity, because there the red would not grow at all.

Wine.—The white wines are either mousseux, sparkling, or non-mousseux, still. The sparkling are little drunk in France, but are almost alone known and drunk in foreign countries. This makes so great a demand, and so certain a one, that it is the dearest by about an eighth, and therefore they endeavor to make all sparkling if they can. This is done by bottling in the spring, from the beginning of March till June. If it succeeds, they lose abundance of bottles, from one-tenth to one-third. This is another cause for increasing the price. To make the still wine, they bottle in September. This is only done when they know from some circumstance that the wine will not be sparkling. So if the spring bottling fails to make a sparkling wine, they decant it into other bottles in the fall, and it then makes the very best still wine. In this operation, it loses from one-tenth to one-twentieth by sediment. They let it stand in the bottles in this case forty-eight hours, with only a napkin spread over their mouths, but no cork. The best sparkling wine, decanted in this manner, makes the best still wine, and which will keep much longer than that originally made still by being bottled in September. The sparkling wines lose their briskness the older they are, but they gain in quality with age to a certain length. These wines are in perfection from two to ten years old, and will even be very good to fifteen. 1766 was the best year ever known. 1775 and 1776 next to that. 1783 is the last good year, and that not to be compared with those. These wines stand icing very well.

Aij. M. Dorsay makes one thousand and one hundred pieces, which sell, as soon as made, at three hundred florins, and in good years four hundred florins, in the cask. I paid in his cellar, to M. Louis, his homme d'affaires, for the remains of the year 1783, three florins ten sous the bottle. Sparkling Champagne, of the same degree of excellence, would have cost four florins, (the piece and demiqueue are the same; the feuillette is one hundred bottles). M. le Duc makes four hundred to five hundred pieces. M. de Villermont, three hundred pieces. M. Janson, two hundred and fifty pieces. All of the first quality, red and white in equal quantities.

Auvillaij. The Benedictine monks make one thousand pieces, red and white, but three-fourths red, both of the first quality. The king's table is supplied by them. This enables them to sell at five hundred and fifty florins the piece. Though their white is hardly as good as Dorsay's, their red is the best. L'Abbatiale, belonging to the bishop of the place, makes one thousand to twelve hundred pieces, red and white, three-fourths red, at four hundred to five hundred and fifty florins, because neighbors to the monks.

Cumieres is all of the second quality, both red and white, at one hundred and fifty to two hundred florins the piece.

Epernay. Madame Jermont makes two hundred pieces at three hundred florins. M. Patelaine, one hundred and fifty pieces. M. Mare, two hundred pieces. M. Chertems, sixty pieces. M. Lauchay, fifty pieces. M. Cousin (Aubergiste de l'hôtel de Rohan à Epernay), one hundred pieces. M. Pierrot, one hundred pieces. Les Chanoines regulieres d'Epernay, two hundred pieces. Mesdames les Ursulines religieuses, one hundred pieces. M. Gilette, two hundred pieces. All of the first quality; red and white in equal quantities.

Pierrij. M. Casotte makes five hundred pieces. M. de la Motte, three hundred pieces. M. de Failli, three hundred pieces. I tasted his wine of

1779, one of the good years. It was fine, though not equal to that of M. Dorsay, of 1783. He sells it at two florins ten sous to merchants, and three florins to individuals. Les Seminaristes, one hundred and fifty pieces. M. Hoquart, two hundred pieces. All of the first quality; white and red in equal quantities.

At Cramont, also, there are some wines of the first quality made. At Avisi also, and Aucy, Le Meni, Mareuil, Verzis-Verzenni. This last place belongs to the Marquis de Sillery. The wines are carried to Sillery, and there stored, whence they are called Vins de Sillery, though not made at Sillery.

All these wines of Epernay and Pierrij sell almost as dear as M. Dorsay's, their quality being nearly the same. There are many small proprietors who might make wine of the first quality, if they would cull their grapes, but they are too poor for this. Therefore, the proprietors before named, whose names are established, buy of the poorer ones the right to cull their vineyards, by which means they increase their quantity, as they find about one-third of the grapes will make wines of the first quality.

The lowest-priced wines of all are thirty florins the piece, red or white. They make brandy of the pumice. In very bad years, when their wines become vinegar, they are sold for six florins the piece, and made into brandy. They yield one-tenth brandy.

White Champagne is deemed good in proportion as it is silky and still. Many circumstances derange the scale of wines. The proprietor of the best vineyard, in the best year, having bad weather come upon him while he is gathering his grapes, makes a bad wine, while his neighbor, holding a more indifferent vineyard, which happens to be ingathering while the weather is good, makes a better. The M. de Casotte at Pierrij formerly was the first house. His successors, by some imperceptible change of culture, have degraded the quality of their wines. Their cellars are admirably made, being about six, eight or ten feet wide, vaulted, and extending into the ground, in a kind of labyrinth, to a prodigious distance, with an air-hole of two feet diameter every fifty feet. From the top of the vault to the surface of the earth, is from fifteen to thirty feet. I have nowhere seen cellars comparable to these. In packing their bottles, they lay on their side; then cross them at each end, they lay laths, and on these another row of bottles, heads and points; and so on. By this means, they can take out a bottle from the top, or where they will.

April 23d. *Épernay. Château Thieray. St. Jean. Meaux. Vergalant. Paris.* From Épernay to St. Jean the road leads over hills, which in the beginning are indifferent, but get better towards the last. The plains, wherever seen, are inconsiderable. After passing St. Jean, the hills become good, and the plains increase. The country about Vergalant is pretty. A skirt of a low ridge which runs in on the extensive plains of the Marne and Seine, is very picturesque. The general bloom of fruit trees proves there are more of them than I had imagined from travelling in other seasons, when they are less distinguishable at a distance from the forest trees.

TRAVELLING NOTES FOR MR. RUTLEDGE AND MR. SHIPPEN
June 3, 1788

General Observations.—On arriving at a town, the first thing is to buy the plan of the town, and the book noting its curiosities. Walk round the ramparts when there are any, go to the top of a steeple to have a view of the town and its environs.

When you are doubting whether a thing is worth the trouble of going to see, recollect that you will never again be so near it, that you may repent the not having seen it, but can never repent having seen it. But there is an opposite extreme too, that is, the seeing too much. A judicious selection is to be aimed at, taking care that the indolence of the moment have no influence in the decision. Take care particularly not to let the porters of churches, cabinets, etc., lead you through all the little details of their profession, which will load the memory with trifles, fatigue the attention, and waste that and your time. It is difficult to confine these people to the few objects worth seeing and remembering. They wish for your money, and suppose you give it the more willingly the more they detail to you.

When one calls in the taverns for the *vin du pays,* they give what is natural and unadulterated and cheap: when *vin etrangere* is called for, it only gives a pretext for charging an extravagant price for an unwholesome stuff, very often of their own brewery. The people you will naturally see the most of will be tavern keepers, *valets de place,* and postilions. These are the hackneyed rascals of every country. Of course they must never be considered when we calculate the national character.

Objects of attention for an American.—1. Agriculture. Everything belonging to this art, and whatever has a near relation to it. Useful or agreeable animals which might be transported to America. Species of plants for the farmer's garden, according to the climate of the different States.

2. Mechanical arts, so far as they respect things necessary in America, and inconvenient to be transported thither ready-made, such as forges, stone quarries, boats, bridges, (very especially,) etc., etc.

3. Lighter mechanical arts, and manufactures. Some of these will be worth a superficial view; but circumstances rendering it impossible that America

should become a manufacturing country during the time of any man now living, it would be a waste of attention to examine these minutely.

4. Gardens peculiarly worth the attention of an American, because it is the country of all others where the noblest gardens may be made without expense. We have only to cut out the superabundant plants.

5. Architecture worth great attention. As we double our numbers every twenty years, we must double our houses. Besides, we build of such perishable materials, that one half of our houses must be rebuilt in every space of twenty years, so that in that time, houses are to be built for three-fourths of our inhabitants. It is, then, among the most important arts; and it is desirable to introduce taste into an art which shows so much.

6. Painting. Statuary. Too expensive for the state of wealth among us. It would be useless, therefore, and preposterous, for us to make ourselves connoisseurs in those arts. They are worth seeing, but not studying.

7. Politics of each country, well worth studying so far as respects internal affairs. Examine their influence on the happiness of the people. Take every possible occasion for entering into the houses of the laborers, and especially at the moments of their repast; see what they eat, how they are clothed, whether they are obliged to work too hard; whether the government or their landlord takes from them an unjust proportion of their labor; on what footing stands the property they call their own, their personal liberty, etc., etc.

8. Courts. To be seen as you would see the tower of London or menagerie of Versailles with their lions, tigers, hyenas, and other beast of prey, standing in the same relation to their fellows. A slight acquaintance with them will suffice to show you that, under the most imposing exterior, they are the weakest and worst part of mankind. Their manners, could you ape them, would not make you beloved in your own country, nor would they improve it could you introduce them there to the exclusion of that honest simplicity now prevailing in America, and worthy of being cherished.

OPINION AGAINST THE CONSTITUTIONALITY OF A
NATIONAL BANK
February 15, 1791

The bill for establishing a National Bank undertakes among other things:

1. To form the subscribers into a corporation.

2. To enable them in their corporate capacities to receive grants of land; and so far is against the laws of *mortmain*.[1]

3. To make alien subscribers capable of holding lands; and so far is against the laws of *alienage*.

4. To transmit these lands, on the death of a proprietor, to a certain line of successors; and so far changes the course of *descents*.

5. To put the lands out of the reach of forfeiture or escheat; and so far is against the laws of *forfeituure and escheat*.

6. To transmit personal chattels to successors in a certain line; and so far is against the laws of *distributiuon*.

7. To give them the sole and exclusive right of banking under the national authority; and so far is against the laws of *monopoly*.

8. To communicate to them a power to make laws paramount to the laws of the States; for so they must be construed, to protect the institution from the control of the State legislatures; and so, probably, they will be construed.

I consider the foundation of the Constitution as laid on this ground: That "all powers not delegated to the United States, by the Constitution, nor prohibited by it to the States, are reserved to the States or to the people." [XIIth amendment.] To take a single step beyond the boundaries thus specially drawn around the powers of Congress, is to take possession of a boundless field of power, no longer susceptible of any definition.

The incorporation of a bank, and the powers assumed by this bill, have not, in my opinion, been delegated to the United States, by the Constitution.

I. They are not among the powers specially enumerated: for these are:

1st. A power to lay taxes for the purpose of paying the debts of the United States; but no debt is paid by this bill, nor any tax laid. Were it a bill to raise money, its origination in the Senate would condemn it by the Constitution.

---

[1] Though the Constitution controls the laws of mortmain so far as to permit Congress itself to hold land for certain purposes, yet not so far as to permit them to communicate a similar right to other corporate bodies.—T. J.

311

2d. "To borrow money." But this bill neither borrows money nor ensures the borrowing it. The proprietors of the bank will be just as free as any other money holders, to lend or not to lend their money to the public. The operation proposed in the bill, first, to lend them two millions, and then to borrow them back again, cannot change the nature of the latter act, which will still be a payment, and not a loan, call it by what name you please.

3. To "regulate commerce with foreign nations, and among the States, and with the Indian tribes." To erect a bank, and to regulate commerce, are very different acts. He who erects a bank, creates a subject of commerce in its bills; so does he who makes a bushel of wheat, or digs a dollar out of the mines; yet neither of these persons regulates commerce thereby. To make a thing which may be bought and sold, is not to prescribe regulations for buying and selling. Besides, if this was an exercise of the power of regulating commerce, it would be void, as extending as much to the internal commerce of every State, as to its external. For the power given to Congress by the Constitution does not extend to the internal regulation of the commerce of a State (that is to say of the commerce between citizen and citizen), which remain exclusively with its own legislature; but to its external commerce only, that is to say, its commerce with another State, or with foreign nations, or with the Indian tribes. Accordingly the bill does not propose the measure as a regulation of trade, but as "productive of considerable advantages to trade." Still less are these powers covered by any other of the special enumerations.

II. Nor are they within either of the general phrases, which are the two following:

1. To lay taxes to provide for the general welfare of the United States, that is to say, "to lay taxes for *the purpose* of providing for the general welfare." For the laying of taxes is the *power,* and the general welfare the *purpose* for which the power is to be exercised. They are not to lay taxes *ad libitum for any purpose they please;* but only *to pay the debts or provide for the welfare of the Union*. In like manner, they are not *to do anything they please* to provide for the general welfare, but only to *lay taxes* for that purpose. To consider the latter phrase, not as describing the purpose of the first, but as giving a distinct and independent power to do any act they please, which might be for the good of the Union, would render all the preceding and subsequent enumerations of power completely useless.

It would reduce the whole instrument to a single phrase, that of instituting a Congress with power to do whatever would be for the good of the United States; and, as they would be the sole judges of the good or evil, it would be also a power to do whatever evil they please.

It is an established rule of construction where a phrase will bear either of two meanings, to give it that which will allow some meaning to the other parts of the instrument, and not that which would render all the others useless. Certainly no such universal power was meant to be given them. It was intended to lace them up straitly within the enumerated powers, and those without which, as means, these powers could not be carried into effect. It is known that the very power now proposed *as a means* was rejected as *an end* by the Convention which formed the Constitution. A proposition was made to them to authorize Congress to open canals, and an amendatory one to empower them to incorporate. But the whole was rejected, and one of the reasons for rejection urged in debate was, that then they would have a power to erect a bank, which would render the great cities, where there were prejudices and jealousies on the subject, adverse to the reception of the Constitution.

2. The second general phrase is, "to make all laws *necessary* and proper for carrying into execution the enumerated powers." But they can all be carried into execution without a bank. A bank therefore is not *necessary,* and consequently not authorized by this phrase.

It has been urged that a bank will give great facility or convenience in the collection of taxes. Suppose this were true: yet the Constitution allows only the means which are *"necessary,"* not those which are merely "convenient" for effecting the enumerated powers. If such a latitude of construction be allowed to this phrase as to give any non-enumerated power, it will go to everyone, for there is not one which ingenuity may not torture into a *convenience* in some instance *or other,* to *someone* of so long a list of enumerated powers. It would swallow up all the delegated powers, and reduce the whole to one power, as before observed. Therefore it was that the Constitution restrained them to the *necessary* means, that is to say, to those means without which the grant of power would be nugatory.

But let us examine this convenience and see what it is. The report on this subject, page 3, states the only *general* convenience to be, the preventing the transportation and re-transportation of money between the States and the treasury, (for I pass over the increase of circulating medium, ascribed to it as a want, and which, according to my ideas of paper money, is clearly a demerit.) Every State will have to pay a sum of tax money into the treasury; and the treasury will have to pay, in every State, a part of the interest on the public debt, and salaries to the officers of government resident in that State. In most of the States there will still be a surplus of tax money to come up to the seat of government for the officers residing there. The payments of interest and salary in each State may be made by treasury orders on the State collector. This will take up the great export of the money he has collected in his State, and consequently prevent the great mass of it from being drawn out of the State. If there be a balance of commerce in favor of that State against the one in which the government resides, the surplus of taxes will be remitted by the bills of exchange drawn for that commercial balance. And so it must be if there was a bank. But if there be no balance of commerce, either direct or circuitous, all the banks in the world could not bring up the surplus of taxes, but in the form of money. Treasury orders then, and bills of exchange may prevent the displacement of the main mass of the money collected, without the aid of any bank; and where these fail, it cannot be prevented even with that aid.

Perhaps, indeed, bank bills may be a more *convenient* vehicle than treasury orders. But a little *difference* in the degree of *convenience,* cannot constitute the necessity which the constitution makes the ground for assuming any non-enumerated power.

Besides, the existing banks will, without a doubt, enter into arrangements for lending their agency, and the more favorable, as there will be a competition among them for it; whereas the bill delivers us up bound to the National Bank, who are free to refuse all arrangement, but on their own terms, and the public not free, on such refusal, to employ any other bank. That of Philadelphia, I believe, now does this business, by their post-notes, which, by an arrangement with the treasury, are paid by any State collector to whom they are presented. This expedient alone suffices to prevent the existence of that *necessity* which may justify the assumption of a non-enumerated power as a means for carrying into effect an enumerated one. The thing may be done, and has been done, and well done, without this assumption; therefore, it does not stand on that degree of *necessity* which can honestly justify it.

It may be said that a bank whose bills would have a currency all over the States, would be more convenient than one whose currency is limited to a single State. So it would be still more convenient that there should be a bank, whose bills should have a currency all over the world. But it does not follow from this superior conveniency, that there exists anywhere a power to establish such a bank; or that the world may not go on very well without it.

Can it be thought that the Constitution intended that for a shade or two of *convenience,* more or less, Congress should be authorized to break down the most ancient and fundamental laws of the several States; such as those against mortmain, the laws of alienage, the rules of descent, the acts of distribution, the laws of escheat and forfeiture, the laws of monopoly? Nothing but a necessity invincible by any other means, can justify such a prostitution of laws, which constitute the pillars of our whole system of jurisprudence. Will Congress be too straight-laced to carry the Constitution into honest effect, unless they may pass over the foundation-laws of the State government for the slightest convenience of theirs?

The negative of the President is the shield provided by the Constitution to protect against the invasions of the legislature: 1. The right of the Executive. 2. Of the Judiciary. 3. Of the States and State legislatures. The present is the case of a right remaining exclusively with the States, and consequently one of those intended by the Constitution to be placed under its protection.

It must be added, however, that unless the President's mind on a view of everything which is urged for and against this bill, is tolerably clear that it is unauthorised by the Constitution; if the pro and the con hang so even as to balance his judgment, a just respect for the wisdom of the legislature would naturally decide the balance in favor of their opinion. It is chiefly for cases where they are clearly misled by error, ambition, or interest, that the Constitution has placed a check in the negative of the President.

OPINION ON THE QUESTION WHETHER THE UNITED STATES HAVE A RIGHT TO RENOUNCE THEIR TREATIES WITH FRANCE, OR TO HOLD THEM SUSPENDED TILL THE GOVERNMENT OF THAT COUNTRY SHALL BE ESTABLISHED

April 28, 1793

I proceed in compliance with the requisition of the President to give an opinion in writing on the general question, whether the United States have a right to renounce their treaties with France, or to hold them suspended till the government of that country shall be established?

In the consultation at the President's on the 19th inst., the Secretary of the Treasury took the following positions and consequences. France was a monarchy when we entered into treaties with it; but it has declared itself a republic, and is preparing a republican form of government. As it may issue in a republic or a military despotism, or something else which may possibly render our alliance with it dangerous to ourselves, we have a right of election to renounce the treaty altogether, or to declare it suspended till their government shall be settled in the form it is ultimately to take; and then we may judge whether we will call the treaties into operation again, or declare them forever null. Having that right of election, now, if we receive their minister without any qualifications, it will amount to an act of election to continue the treaties; and if the change they are undergoing should issue in a form which should bring danger on us, we shall not be then free to renounce them. To elect to continue them is equivalent to the making a new treaty, at this time, in the same form, that is to say, with a clause of guarantee; but to make a treaty with a clause of guarantee, during a war, is a departure from neutrality, and would make us associates in the war. To renounce or suspend the treaties, therefore, is a necessary act of neutrality.

If I do not subscribe to the soundness of this reasoning, I do most fully to its ingenuity. I shall now lay down the principles which, according to my understanding, govern the case.

I consider the people who constitute a society or nation as the source of all authority in that nation; as free to transact their common concerns by any agents they think proper; to change these agents individually, or the organization of them in form or function whenever they please; that all the

316

acts done by these agents under the authority of the nation, are the acts of the nation, are obligatory to them and enure to their use, and can in no wise be annulled or affected by any change in the form of the government, or of the persons administering it, consequently the treaties between the United States and France, were not treaties between the United States and Louis Capet, but between the two nations of America and France; and the nations remaining in existence, though both of them have since changed their forms of government, the treaties are not annulled by these changes. The law of nations, by which this question is to be determined, is composed of three branches. 1. The moral law of our nature. 2. The usages of nations. 3. Their special conventions. The first of these only concerns this question, that is to say the moral law to which man has been subjected by his creator, and of which his feelings or conscience, as it is sometimes called, are the evidence with which his creator has furnished him. The moral duties which exist between individual and individual in a state of nature, accompany them into a state of society, and the aggregate of the duties of all the individuals composing the society constitutes the duties of that society towards any other; so that between society and society the same moral duties exist as did between the individuals composing them, while in an unassociated state, and their maker not having released them from those duties on their forming themselves into a nation. Compacts then, between nation and nation, are obligatory on them by the same moral law which obliges individuals to observe their compacts. There are circumstances, however, which sometimes excuse the non-performance of contracts between man and man; so are there also between nation and nation. When performance, for instance, becomes *impossible,* non-performance is not immoral; so if performance becomes *self-destructive* to the party, the law of self-preservation overrules the laws of obligation in others. For the reality of these principles I appeal to the true fountains of evidence, the head and heart of every rational and honest man. It is there nature has written her moral laws, and where every man may read them for himself. He will never read there the permission to annul his obligations for a time, or forever, whenever they become dangerous, useless, or disagreeable; certainly not when merely useless or disagreeable, as seems to be said in an authority which has been quoted, (Vattel, p. 2, 197) and though he may, under certain degrees of danger, yet the danger must be imminent, and the degree great. Of these, it is true, that nations are to be judges for themselves; since no one nation has a right to sit in judgment over another, but the tribunal of our consciences remains, and that also of the opinion of the world. These will revise the sentence we pass in our own case, and as we respect these, we must see that in judging ourselves we have honestly done the part of impartial and rigorous judges.

But reason which gives this right of self-liberation from a contract in certain cases, has subjected it to certain just limitations.

I. The danger which absolves us must be great, inevitable and imminent. Is such the character of that now apprehended from our treaties with France? What is that danger? 1st. Is it that if their government issues in a military despotism, an alliance with them may taint us with despotic principles? But their government when we allied ourselves to it, was perfect despotism, civil, and military, yet the treaties were made in that very state of things, and, therefore, that danger can furnish no just cause.

2d. Is it that their government may issue in a republic, and too much strengthen our republican principles? But this is the hope of the great mass of our constituents, and not their dread. They do not look with longing to the happy mean of a limited monarchy.

3d. But, says the doctrine I am combatting, the change the French are undergoing, may possibly end in something we know not what, and may bring on us danger we know not whence. In short, it may end in a Raw-head and bloody bones in the dark. Very well—let Raw-head and bloody bones come. We shall be justified in making our peace with him by renouncing our ancient friends and his enemies; for observe, it is not the *possibility of danger* which absolves a party from his contract, for that possibility always exists, and in every case. It existed in the present one, at the moment of making the contract. If *possibilities* would void contracts, there never could be a valid contract, for possibilities hang over everything. Obligation is not suspended till the danger is become real, and the moment of it so imminent, that we can no longer avoid decision without forever losing the opportunity to do it. But can a danger which has not yet taken its shape, which does not yet exist, and never may exist which cannot therefore be defined—can such a danger, I ask, be so imminent that if we fail to pronounce on it in this moment, we can never have another opportunity of doing it?

4. As to the danger apprehended, Is it that (the treaties remaining valid) the clause guaranteeing their West Indian lands will engage us in the war? But does the guarantee engage us to enter into the war on any event? Are we to enter into it before we are called on by our allies?

Have we been called on by them? Shall we ever be called on?

Is it their interest to call on us?

Can they call on us before their islands are invaded, or immediately threatened?

If they can save themselves, have they a right to call on us?

Are we obliged to go to war at once, without trying peaceable negotiations with their enemy?

If all these questions are against us, there are still others left behind.

Are we in a condition to go to war?

Can we be expected to begin before we are in condition?

Will the islands be lost if we do not save them?

Have we the means of saving them?

If we cannot save them, are we bound to go to war for a desperate object?

Many, if not most of these questions offer grounds of doubt whether the clause of guarantee will draw us into the war. Consequently, if this be danger apprehended, it is not yet certain enough to authorize us in sound morality to declare, at this moment, the treaties null.

5. Is danger apprehended from the 17th article of the treaty of commerce, which admits French ships of war and privateers to come and go freely, with prizes made on their enemies, while their enemies are not to have the same privilege with prizes made on the French? But Holland and Prussia have approved of this article in our treaty with France, by subscribing to an express salvo of it in our treaties with them. (Dutch treaty 22, convention 6. Prussian treaty 19.) And England, in her last treaty with France (Art. 40), has entered into the same stipulation verbatim, and placed us in her ports on the same footing in which she is in ours, in case of a war of either of us with France. If we are engaged in such a war, England must receive prizes made on us by the French, and exclude those made on the French by us. Nay, further; in this very article of her treaty with France, is a salvo of any similar article in any anterior treaty of either party; and ours with France being anterior, this salvo confirms it expressly. Neither of these three powers, then, have a right to complain of this article in our treaty.

6. Is the danger apprehended from the 22d article of our treaty of commerce, which prohibits the enemies of France from fitting our privateers in our posts, or selling their prizes here; but we are free to refuse the same thing to France, there being no stipulation to the contrary; and we ought to refuse it on principles of fair neutrality.

7. But the reception of a minister from the republic of France, without qualifications, it is thought, will bring us into danger; because this, it is said, will determine the continuance of the treaty, and take from us the right of self-liberation, when at any time hereafter our safety would require us to use it. The reception of the minister at all (in favor of which Colonel Hamilton has given his opinion, though reluctantly, as he confessed), is an acknowledgment of the legitimacy of their government; and if the qualifications meditated are to deny that legitimacy, it will be a curious compound which is to admit and to deny the same thing. But I deny that the reception of a minister has anything to do with the treaties. There is not a word in either of them about sending ministers. This has been done between us under the

common usage of nations, and can have no effect either to continue or annul the treaties.

But how can any act of election have the effect to continue a treaty which is acknowledged to be going on still?—for it was not pretended the treaty was void, but only voidable if we choose to declare it so. To make it void, would require an act of election, but to let it go on, requires only that we should do nothing; and doing nothing can hardly be an infraction of peace or neutrality.

But I go further and deny that the most explicit declaration made at this moment that we acknowledge the obligation of the treaties, could take from us the right of non-compliance at any future time, when compliance would involve us in great and inevitable danger.

I conclude, then, that few of these sources threaten any danger at all; and from none of them is it inevitable; and consequently, none of them give us the right at this moment of releasing ourselves from our treaties.

II. A second limitation on our right of releasing ourselves, is that we are to do it from so much of the treaties only as is bringing great and inevitable danger on us, and not from the residue, allowing the other party a right at the same time, to determine whether on our non-compliance with that part, they will declare the whole void. This right they would have, but we should not. Vattel, 2. 202. The only part of the treaty which can really lead us into danger, is the clause of guarantee. That clause is all that we could suspend in any case, and the residue will remain or not at the will of the other party.

III. A third limitation is that when a party from necessity or danger withholds compliance with part of a treaty, it is bound to make compensation where the nature of the case admits and does not dispense with it. 2 Vattel, 324. Wolf, 270. 443. If actual circumstances excuse us from entering into the war under the clause of guarantee, it will be a question whether they excuse us from compensation. Our weight in the war admits of an estimate; and that estimate would form the measure of compensation.

If, in withholding a compliance with any part of the treaties, we do it without just cause or compensation, we give to France a cause of war, and so become associated in it on the other side. An injured friend is the bitterest of foes, and France has not discovered either timidity, or over-much forbearance on the late occasions. Is this the position we wish to take for our constituents? It is certainly not the one they would take for themselves.

I will proceed now to examine the principal authority which has been relied on for establishing the right of self-liberation; because though just in part, it would lead us far beyond justice, if taken in all the latitude of which his expressions would admit. Questions of natural right are triable by their conformity with the moral sense and reason of man. Those who write treatises of natural law, can only declare what their own moral sense and reason dictate in the several cases they state. Such of them as happen to have feelings and a reason coincident with those of the wise and honest part of mankind, are respected and quoted as witnesses of what is morally right or wrong in particular cases. Grotius, Puffendorf, Wolf, and Vattel are of this number. Where they agree their authority is strong; but where they differ (and they often differ), we must appeal to our own feelings and reason to decide between them. The passages in question shall be traced through all these writers; that we may see wherein they concur, and where that concurrence is wanting. It shall be quoted from them in the order in which they wrote, that is to say, from Grotius first, as being the earliest writer, Puffendorf next, then Wolf, and lastly Vattel, as latest in time.

The doctrine then of Grotius, Puffendorf, and Wolf is, that "treaties remain obligatory, notwithstanding any change in the form of government, except in the single case, where the preservation of that form was the object of the treaty"; there the treaty extinguishes, not by the election or declaration of the party remaining in *status quo,* but independently of that, by the evanishment of the object. Vattel lays down in fact the same doctrine, that treaties continue obligatory, notwithstanding a change of government by the will of the other party;—that to oppose that will would be a wrong; and that the ally remains an ally, notwithstanding the change. So far he concurs with all the previous writers:—but he then adds what they had not said nor could say; but if this change renders the alliance *useless, dangerous* or *disagreeable* to it, it is free to renounce it. It was unnecessary for him to have specified the exception of *danger* in this particular case, because the exception exists in all cases, and its extent has been considered; but when he adds that, because a contract is become merely *useless* or *disagreeable* we are free to renounce it,—he is in opposition to Grotius, Puffendorf, and Wolf, who admit no such license against the obligation of treaties, and he is in opposition to the morality of every honest man to whom we may safely appeal to decide whether he feels himself free to renounce a contract the moment it becomes *merely useless* or *disagreeable* to him. We may appeal to Vattel himself in those parts of his book where he cannot be misunderstood, and to his known character, as one of the most zealous and constant advocates for the preservation of good faith in all our dealings. Let us hear him on other occasions; and first where he shows what degree of danger or injury will authorize self-liberation from a treaty: "If simple lesion," (lesion—the loss sustained by selling a thing for less than half value, which degree of loss renders the sale void by the Roman law,) "if simple lesion," says he, "or some degree of disadvantage in a treaty does not suffice to render it invalid, it is not so as to inconvenience which would go to the *ruin* of the nation. As every treaty

GROTIUS 2. 16. 16.	PUFFENDORF 8. 9. 6.	WOLF 1146.	VATTEL, 2. 197.

Hither must be referred the common question concerning personal and real treaties. If indeed it be with a free people, there can be no doubt but that the engagement is in its nature real, because the subject is a permanent thing, and even though the government of the State be changed into a kingdom, the treaty remains; because the same body remains though the head is changed; and as it was before now, the government which is exercised by a king does not cease to be the government of the people. There is an exception when the object seems peculiar to the government, as if free cities contract a league for the defence of their freedom.

It is certain that every alliance made with a republic is real in its nature, and continues consequently to the term agreed on by the treaty, although the magistrates who concluded it be dead before, so that the form of government is changed even from a democracy to a monarchy; for in this case the people do not cease to be the same, and the king, in the case supposed, being established by the consent of the people who abolished the republican government, is understood to accept the crown with all the engagements which the people confessing it had contracted as being free and governing themselves. There must nevertheless be an exception of the alliances contracted with a view to preserve the present government; as if two republics league for mutual defence against those who would undertake to invade their liberty; for if one of these two people consent afterwards voluntarily to change the form of the government, the alliance end of itself, because the reason on which it was founded no longer subsists.

The alliance which is made with a free people, or with a popular government, is a real alliance; and as when the form of government changes, the people remain the same (for it is the association which forms the people, and not the manner of administering the government). This alliance subsists, though the form of government changes, unless, as is evident, the reason of the alliance was particular to the popular state.

The same question presents itself in real alliances, and in general on every alliance made with a State, and not in particular with a king for the defence of his person. We ought, without doubt, to defend our ally against all invasion, against all foreign violence, and even against rebel subjects. We ought, in like manner, to defend a republic against the enterprises of an oppressor of the public liberty. But we ought to recollect that we are the ally of the state or of the nation, and not its judge. If the nation has deposed its king in form; if the people of a republic have driven away its magistrates, and have established themselves free, or if they have acknowledged the authority of an usurper, whether expressly or tacitly, to oppose these domestic arrangements —to contest their justice or validity— would be to meddle with the government of the nation, and to do it an injury. The ally remains the ally of the state, notwithstanding the change which has taken place; but if this change renders the alliance useless, dangerous, or disagreeable to it, it is free to renounce it; for it may say with truth, that it would not have allied itself with this nation, if it had been under the present form of its government.

ought to be made by sufficient power, a treaty pernicious to the State is null, and not at all obligatory: No governor of a nation having power to engage things capable of *destroying* the State, for the safety of which the empire entrusts to him, the nation itself, bound necessarily to whatever its preservation and safety require, cannot enter into engagements contrary to its indispensable obligations." Here then we find that the degree of injury or danger which he deems sufficient to liberate us from a treaty, is that which would go to the absolute ruin or destruction of the State;—not simply the lesion of the Roman law, not merely the being disadvantageous or dangerous; for as he himself says, Section 158, "lesion cannot render a treaty invalid. It is his duty who enters into engagements, to weigh well all things before he concludes. He may do with his property what he pleases. He may relinquish his rights or renounce his advantages, as he judges proper. The acceptance is not obliged to inform himself of his motives nor to weigh their just value. If we could free ourselves from a compact because we find ourselves injured by it, there would be nothing firm in the contracts of nations. Civil laws may set limits to lesion, and determine the degree capable of producing a nullity of the contract; but sovereigns acknowledge no judge. How establish lesion among them? Who will determine the degree sufficient to invalidate a treaty? The happiness and peace of nations require manifestly that their treaties should not depend on a means of nullity so vague and so dangerous."

Let us hear him again on the general subject of the observation of treaties, Section 163: "It is demonstrated in natural law that he who promises another, confers on him a perfect right to require the thing promised, and that consequently, not to observe a perfect promise is to violate the right of another; it is as manifest injustice as to plunder anyone of their right. All the tranquillity, the happiness and security of mankind, rest on justice or the obligation to respect the rights of others. The respect of others for our right of domain and property is the security of our actual possessions. The faith of promises is the security for the things which cannot be delivered or executed on the spot. No more security, no more commerce among men, if they think themselves not bound to preserve faith, to keep their word. This obligation, then, is as necessary as it is natural and indubitable among nations who live together in a state of nature, and who acknowledge no superior on earth. To maintain order and peace in their society, nations and their governors then ought to observe inviolably their promises and their treaties. This is a great truth, although too often neglected in practice, is generally acknowledged by all nations, the reproach of perfidy is a bitter affront among sovereigns. Now he who does not observe a treaty is assuredly perfidious, since he violates his faith. On the contrary, nothing is so glorious to a prince and his nation as the reputation of inviolable fidelity to his word." Again, Section

219, "Who will doubt that treaties are of the things sacred among nations? They decide matters the most important; they impose rules on the pretensions of sovereigns, they cause the rights of nations to be acknowledged; they assume their most precious interests. Among political bodies, sovereigns, who acknowledge no superior on earth, treaties are the only means of adjusting their different pretensions; of establishing a rule, to know on what to count, on what to depend. But treaties are but vain words, if nations do not consider them as respectable engagements, as rules inviolable for sovereigns, and sacred through the whole earth." Section 220: "The faith of treaties, that firm and sincere will, that invincible constancy in fulfilling engagements, of which a declaration is made in a treaty, is then holy and sacred among nations, whose safety and repose it ensures; and if nations will not be wanting to themselves, they will load with infamy whoever violates his faith."

After evidence so copious and explicit of the respect of this author for the sanctity of treaties, we should hardly have expected that his authority would have been resorted to for a wanton invalidation of them whenever they should become merely *useless or disagreeable*. We should hardly have expected that, rejecting all the rest of his book, this scrap would have been culled and made the hook whereon to hang such a chain of immoral consequences. Had the passage accidentally met our eye, we should have imagined it had fallen from the author's pen under some momentary view, not sufficiently developed to found a conjecture what he meant, and we may certainly affirm that a fragment like this cannot weigh against the authority of all other writers; against the uniform and systematic doctrine of the very work from which it is torn; against the moral feelings and the reason of all honest men. If the terms of the fragment are not misunderstood, they are in full contradiction to all the written and unwritten evidences of morality. If they are misunderstood, they are no longer a foundation for the doctrines which have been built on them.

But even had this doctrine been as true as it is manifestly false, it would have been asked, to whom is it that the treaties with France have become *disagreeable?* How will it be proved that they are *useless?*

The conclusion of the sentence suggests a reflection too strong to be suppressed, "for the party may say with truth that it would not have allied itself with this nation if it had been under the present form of its government." The republic of the United States allied itself with France when under a despotic government. She changes her government, and declares it shall be a republic; prepares a form of republic extremely free, and in the meantime is governing herself as such. And it is proposed that America shall declare the treaties void, because it may say with truth that it would not have allied itself with that nation if it had been under the present form of its government. Who is the American who can say with truth that he would not have allied himself to France if she had been a republic? Or that a republic of any form would be as *disagreeable* as her ancient despotism?

Upon the whole I conclude, that the treaties are still binding, notwithstanding the change of government in France; that no part of them but the clause of guarantee holds up *danger,* even at a distance, and consequently that a liberation from no other part would be prepared in any case; that if that clause may ever bring *danger,* it is neither extreme nor imminent, nor even probable that the authority for renouncing a treaty, when *useless or disagreeable,* is either misunderstood or in opposition to itself, to all other writers, and to every moral feeling; that were it not so, these treaties are in fact neither useless or disagreeable; that the receiving a minister from France at this time is an act of no significance with respect to the treaties, amounting neither to an admission nor denial of them, forasmuch as he comes not under any stipulation in them; that were it an explicit admission, or were it an express declaration of their obligation now to be made, it would not take from us that right which exists at all times, of liberating ourselves when an adherence to the treaties would be *ruinous* or *destructive* to the society; and that the not renouncing the treaties now is so far from being a breach of neutrality, that the doing it would be the breach, by giving just cause of war to France.

1. *Resolved,* That the several States composing the United States of America, are not united on the principle of unlimited submission to their general government; but that, by a compact under the style and title of a Constitution for the United States, and of amendments thereto, they constituted a general government for special purposes—delegated to that government certain definite powers, reserving, each State to itself, the residuary mass of right to their own self-government; and that whensoever the general government assumes undelegated powers, its acts are unauthoritative, void, and of no force: that to this compact each State acceded as a State, and is an integral party, its co-States forming, as to itself, the other party: that the government created by this compact was not made the exclusive or final judge of the extent of the powers delegated to itself; since that would have made its discretion, and not the Constitution, the measure of its powers; but that, as in all other cases of compact among powers having no common judge, each party has an equal right to judge for itself, as well of infractions as of the mode and measure of redress.

2. *Resolved,* That the Constitution of the United States, having delegated to Congress a power to punish treason, counterfeiting the securities and current coin of the United States, piracies, and felonies committed on the high seas, and offences against the law of nations, and no other crimes whatsoever; and it being true as a general principle, and one of the amendments to the Constitution having also declared, that "the powers not delegated to the United States by the Constitution, nor prohibited by it to the States, are reserved to the States respectively, or to the people," therefore the act of Congress, passed on the 14th day of July, 1798, and intituled "An Act in addition to the act intituled An Act for the punishment of certain crimes against the United States," as also the act passed by them on the — day of June, 1798, intituled "An Act to punish frauds committed on the bank of the United States," (and all their other acts which assume to create, define, or punish crimes, other than those so enumerated in the Constitution,) are altogether void, and of no force; and that the power to create, define, and punish such

---

[1] The resolutions were a protest against the Alien and Sedition Acts passed by Congress. They were adopted by the Kentucky legislature on November 10, 1798. Jefferson did not make public the fact that he had written the resolutions.

other crimes is reserved, and, of right, appertains solely and exclusively to the respective States, each within its own territory.

3. *Resolved,* That it is true as a general principle, and is also expressly declared by one of the amendments to the Constitution, that "the powers not delegated to the United States by the Constitution, nor prohibited by it to the States, are reserved to the States respectively, or to the people"; and that no power over the freedom of religion, freedom of speech, or freedom of the press being delegated to the United States by the Constitution, nor prohibited by it to the States, all lawful powers respecting the same did of right remain, and were reserved to the States or the people: that thus was manifested their determination to retain to themselves the right of judging how far the licentiousness of speech and of the press may be abridged without lessening their useful freedom, and how far those abuses which cannot be separated from their use should be tolerated, rather than the use be destroyed. And thus also they guarded against all abridgement by the United States of the freedom of religious opinions and exercises, and retained to themselves the right of protecting the same, as this State, by a law passed on the general demand of its citizens, had already protected them from all human restraint or interference. And that in addition to this general principle and express declaration, another and more special provision has been made by one of the amendments to the Constitution, which expressly declares, that "Congress shall make no law respecting an establishment of religion, or prohibiting the free exercise thereof, or abridging the freedom of speech or of the press": thereby guarding in the same sentence, and under the same words, the freedom of religion, of speech, and of the press: insomuch, that whatever violated either, throws down the sanctuary which covers the others, and that libels, falsehood, and defamation, equally with heresy and false religion, are withheld from the cognizance of federal tribunals. That, therefore, the act of Congress of the United States, passed on the 14th day of July, 1798, intituled "An Act in addition to the act intituled An Act for the punishment of certain crimes against the United States," which does abridge the freedom of the press, is not law, but is altogether void, and of no force.

4. *Resolved,* That alien friends are under the jurisdiction and protection of the laws of the State wherein they are: that no power over them has been delegated to the United States, nor prohibited to the individual States, distinct from their power over citizens. And it being true as a general principle, and one of the amendments to the Constitution having also declared, that "the powers not delegated to the United States by the Constitution, nor prohibited by it to the States, are reserved to the States respectively, or to the people," the act of the Congress of the United States, passed on the — day

of July, 1798, intituled "An Act concerning aliens," which assumes powers over alien friends, not delegated by the Constitution, is not law, but is altogether void, and of no force.

5. *Resolved,* That in addition to the general principle, as well as the express declaration, that powers not delegated are reserved, another and more special provision, inserted in the Constitution from abundant caution, has declared that "the migration or importation of such persons as any of the States now existing shall think proper to admit, shall not be prohibited by the Congress prior to the year 1808": that this commonwealth does admit the migration of alien friends, described as the subject of the said act concerning aliens: that a provision against prohibiting their migration, is a provision against all acts equivalent thereto, or it would be nugatory: that to remove them when migrated, is equivalent to a prohibition of their migration, and is, therefore, contrary to the said provision of the Constitution, and void.

6. *Resolved,* That the imprisonment of a person under the protection of the laws of this commonwealth, on his failure to obey the simple *order* of the President to depart out of the United States, as is undertaken by said act intituled "An Act concerning aliens," is contrary to the Constitution, one amendment to which has provided that "no person shall be deprived of liberty without due progress of law"; and that another having provided that "in all criminal prosecutions the accused shall enjoy the right to public trial by an impartial jury, to be informed of the nature and cause of the accusation, to be confronted with the witnesses against him, to have compulsory process for obtaining witnesses in his favor, and to have the assistance of counsel for his defence," the same act, undertaking to authorize the President to remove a person out of the United States, who is under the protection of the law, on his own suspicion, without accusation, without jury, without public trial, without confrontation of the witnesses against him, without hearing witnesses in his favor, without defence, without counsel, is contrary to the provision also of the Constitution, is therefore not law, but utterly void, and of no force: that transferring the power of judging any person, who is under the protection of the laws, from the courts to the President of the United States, as is undertaken by the same act concerning aliens, is against the article of the Constitution which provides that "the judicial power of the United States shall be vested in courts, the judges of which shall hold their offices during good behavior"; and that the said act is void for that reason also. And it is further to be noted, that this transfer of judiciary power is to that magistrate of the general government who already possesses all the Executive, and a negative on all Legislative powers.

7. *Resolved,* That the construction applied by the General Government (as is evidenced by sundry of their proceedings) to those parts of the Consti-

tution of the United States which delegate to Congress a power "to lay and collect taxes, duties, imports, and excises, to pay the debts, and provide for the common defence and general welfare of the United States," and "to make all laws which shall be necessary and proper for carrying into execution the powers vested by the Constitution in the government of the United States, or in any department or officer thereof," goes to the destruction of all limits prescribed to their power by the Constitution: that words meant by the instrument to be subsidiary only to the execution of limited powers, ought not to be so construed as themselves to give unlimited powers, nor a part to be so taken as to destroy the whole residue of that instrument: that the proceedings of the General Government under color of these articles, will be a fit and necessary subject of revisal and correction, at a time of greater tranquillity, while those specified in the preceding resolutions call for immediate redress.

8th. *Resolved,* That a committee of conference and correspondence be appointed, who shall have in charge to communicate the preceding resolutions to the Legislatures of the several States; to assure them that this commonwealth continues in the same esteem of their friendship and union which it has manifested from that moment at which a common danger first suggested a common union: that it considers union, for specified national purposes, and particularly to those specified in their late federal compact, to be friendly to the peace, happiness and prosperity of all the States: that faithful to that compact, according to the plain intent and meaning in which it was understood and acceded to by the several parties, it is sincerely anxious for its preservation: that it does also believe, that to take from the States all the powers of self-government and transfer them to a general and consolidated government, without regard to the special delegations and reservations solemnly agreed to in that compact, is not for the peace, happiness or prosperity of these States; and that therefore this commonwealth is determined, as it doubts not its co-States are, to submit to undelegated, and consequently unlimited powers in no man, or body of men on earth: that in cases of an abuse of the delegated powers, the members of the general government, being chosen by the people, a change by the people would be the constitutional remedy; but, where powers are assumed which have not been delegated, a nullification of the act is the rightful remedy: that every State has a natural right in cases not within the compact, (*casus non fœderis,*) to nullify of their own authority all assumptions of power by others within their limits: that without this right, they would be under the dominion, absolute and unlimited, of whosoever might exercise this right of judgment for them: that nevertheless, this commonwealth, from motives of regard and respect for its co-States, has wished to communicate with them on the subject: that with them alone it is proper to communicate, they alone being parties to the compact, and solely authorized to judge in the last resort of the powers exercised under it, Congress being not a party, but merely the creature of the compact, and subject as to its assumptions of power to the final judgment of those by whom, and for whose use itself and its powers were all created and modified: that if the acts before specified should stand, these conclusions would flow from them; that the general government may place any act they think proper on the list of crimes, and punish it themselves whether enumerated or not enumerated by the constitution as cognizable by them: that they may transfer its cognizance to the President, or any other person, who may himself be the accuser, counsel, judge and jury, whose *suspicions* may be the evidence, his *order* the sentence, his *officer* the executioner, and his breast the sole record of the transaction: that a very numerous and valuable description of the inhabitants of these States being, by this precedent, reduced, as outlaws, to the absolute dominion of one man, and the barrier of the Constitution thus swept away from us all, no rampart now remains against the passions and the powers of a majority in Congress to protect from a like exportation, or other more grievous punishment, the minority of the same body, the legislatures, judges, governors and counsellors of the States, nor their other peaceable inhabitants, who may venture to reclaim the constitutional rights and liberties of the States and people, or who for other causes, good or bad, may be obnoxious to the views, or marked by the suspicions of the President, or be thought dangerous to his or their election, or other interests, public or personal: that the friendless alien has indeed been selected as the safest subject of a first experiment; but the citizen will soon follow, or rather, has already followed, for already has a sedition act marked him as its prey: that these and successive acts of the same character, unless arrested at the threshold, necessarily drive these States into revolution and blood, and will furnish new calumnies against republican government, and new pretexts for those who wish it to be believed that man cannot be governed but by a rod of iron: that it would be a dangerous delusion were a confidence in the men of our choice to silence our fears for the safety of our rights: that confidence is everywhere the parent of despotism—free government is founded in jealousy, and not in confidence; it is jealousy and not confidence which prescribes limited constitutions, to bind down those whom we are obliged to trust with power: that our Constitution has accordingly fixed the limits to which, and no further, our confidence may go; and let the honest advocate of confidence read the Alien and Sedition acts, and say if the Constitution has not been wise in fixing limits to the government it created, and whether we should be wise in destroying those limits. Let him say what the government is, if it be not a tyranny, which the men of our choice have conferred on our President, and the President of our choice has assented to, and accepted over the friendly strangers to whom the mild spirit of our country and its law have pledged hospitality and protection: that the men of our choice have more respected the bare *suspicions* of the President, than the solid right of innocence, the claims of justification, the sacred force of truth, and the forms and substance of law and justice. In questions of power, then, let no more be heard of confidence in man, but bind him down from mischief by the chains of the Constitution. That this commonwealth does therefore call on its co-States for an expression of their sentiments on the acts concerning aliens, and for the punishment of certain crimes herein before specified, plainly declaring whether these acts are or are not authorized by the federal compact. And it doubts not that their sense will be so announced as to prove their attachment unaltered to limited government, whether general or particular. And that the rights and liberties of their co-States will be exposed to no dangers by remaining embarked in a common bottom with their own. That they will concur with this commonwealth in considering the said acts as so palpably against the Constitution as to amount to an undisguised declaration that that compact is not meant to be the measure of the powers of the General Government, but that it will proceed in the exercise over these States, of all powers whatsoever: that they will view this as seizing the rights of the States, and consolidating them in the hands of the General Government, with a power assumed to bind the States (not merely as the cases made federal, *casus fœderis* but), in all cases whatsoever, by laws made, not with their consent, but by others against their consent: that this would be to surrender the form of government we have chosen, and live under one deriving its powers from its own will, and not from our authority; and that the co-States, recurring to their natural right in cases not made federal, will concur in declaring these acts void, and of no force, and will each take measures of its own for providing that neither these acts, nor any others of the General Government not plainly and intentionally authorized by the Constitution, shall be exercised within their respective territories.

9th. *Resolved,* That the said committee be authorized to communicate by writing or personal conferences, at any times or places whatever, with any person or persons who may be appointed by any one or more co-States to correspond or confer with them; and that they lay their proceedings before the next session of Assembly.

FIRST INAUGURAL ADDRESS
March 4, 1801

FRIENDS AND FELLOW CITIZENS: Called upon to undertake the duties of the first executive office of our country, I avail myself of the presence of that portion of my fellow citizens which is here assembled, to express my grateful thanks for the favor with which they have been pleased to look toward me, to declare a sincere consciousness that the task is above my talents, and that I approach it with those anxious and awful presentiments which the greatness of the charge and the weakness of my powers so justly inspire. A rising nation, spread over a wide and fruitful land, traversing all the seas with the rich productions of their industry, engaged in commerce with nations who feel power and forget right, advancing rapidly to destinies beyond the reach of mortal eye—when I contemplate these transcendent objects, and see the honor, the happiness, and the hopes of this beloved country committed to the issue and the auspices of this day, I shrink from the contemplation, and humble myself before the magnitude of the undertaking. Utterly indeed, should I despair, did not the presence of many whom I here see remind me, that in the other high authorities provided by our constitution, I shall find resources of wisdom, of virtue, and of zeal, on which to rely under all difficulties. To you, then, gentlemen, who are charged with the sovereign functions of legislation, and to those associated with you, I look with encouragement for that guidance and support which may enable us to steer with safety the vessel in which we are all embarked amid the conflicting elements of a troubled world.

During the contest of opinion through which we have passed, the animation of discussion and of exertions has sometimes worn an aspect which might impose on strangers unused to think freely and to speak and to write what they think; but this being now decided by the voice of the nation, announced according to the rules of the constitution, all will, of course, arrange themselves under the will of the law, and unite in common efforts for the common good. All, too, will bear in mind this sacred principle, that though the will of the majority is in all cases to prevail, that will, to be rightful, must be reasonable; that the minority possess their equal rights, which equal laws must protect, and to violate which would be oppression. Let us, then, fellow-citizens, unite with one heart and one mind. Let us restore to social intercourse that harmony and affection without which liberty and even life itself are but dreary things. And let us reflect that having banished from our land that religious intolerance under which mankind so long bled and suffered, we have yet gained little if we countenance a political intolerance as despotic, as wicked, and capable of as bitter and bloody persecutions. During the throes and convulsions of the ancient world, during the agonizing spasms of infuriated man, seeking through blood and slaughter his long-lost liberty, it was not wonderful that the agitation of the billows should reach even this distant and peaceful shore; that this should be more felt and feared by some and less by others; that this should divide opinions as to measures of safety. But every difference of opinion is not a difference of principle. We have called by different names brethren of the same principle. We are all republicans—we are federalists. If there be any among us who would wish to dissolve this Union or to change its republican form, let them stand undisturbed as monuments of the safety with which error of opinion may be tolerated where reason is left free to combat it. I know, indeed, that some honest men fear that a republican government cannot be strong; that this government is not strong enough. But would the honest patriot, in the full tide of successful experiment, abandon a government which has so far kept us free and firm, on the theoretic and visionary fear that this government, the world's best hope, may by possibility want energy to preserve itself? I trust not. I believe this, on the contrary, the strongest government on earth. I believe it is the only one where every man, at the call of the laws, would fly to the standard of the law, and would meet invasions of the public order as his own personal concern. Sometimes it is said that man cannot be trusted with the government of himself. Can he, then, be trusted with the government of others? Or have we found angels in the forms of kings to govern him? Let history answer this question.

Let us, then, with courage and confidence pursue our own federal and republican principles, our attachment to our union and representative government. Kindly separated by nature and a wide ocean from the exterminating havoc of one quarter of the globe; too high-minded to endure the degradations of the others; possessing a chosen country, with room enough for our descendants to the hundredth and thousandth generation; entertaining a due sense of our equal right to the use of our own faculties, to the acquisitions of our industry, to honor and confidence from our fellow citizens, resulting not from birth but from our actions and their sense of them; enlightened by a benign religion, professed, indeed, and practiced in various forms, yet all of them including honesty, truth, temperance, gratitude, and the love of man; acknowledging and adoring an overruling Providence, which by all its dispensations proves that it delights in the happiness of man here and his greater happiness hereafter; with all these blessings, what more is necessary to make us a happy and prosperous people? Still one thing more, fellow citizens—a wise and frugal government, which shall restrain men from injuring one another, which shall leave them otherwise free to regulate their own pursuits of industry and improvement, and shall not take from the mouth of labor the bread it has earned. This is the sum of good government, and this is necessary to close the circle of our felicities.

About to enter, fellow citizens, on the exercise of duties which comprehend everything dear and valuable to you, it is proper that you should understand what I deem the essential principles of our government, and consequently those which ought to shape its administration. I will compress them within the narrowest compass they will bear, stating the general principle, but not all its limitations. Equal and exact justice to all men, of whatever state or persuasion, religious or political; peace, commerce, and honest friendship with all nations—entangling alliances with none; the support of the State governments in all their rights, as the most competent administrations for our domestic concerns and the surest bulwarks against anti-republican tendencies; the preservation of the general government in its whole constitutional vigor, as the sheet anchor of our peace at home and safety abroad; a jealous care of the right of election by the people—a mild and safe corrective of abuses which are lopped by the sword of the revolution where peaceable remedies are unprovided; absolute acquiescence in the decisions of the majority—the vital principle of republics, from which there is no appeal but to force, the vital principle and immediate parent of despotism; a well-disciplined militia—our best reliance in peace and for the first moments of war, till regulars may relieve them; the supremacy of the civil over the military authority; economy in the public expense, that labor may be lightly burdened; the honest payment of our debts and sacred preservation of the public faith; encouragement of agriculture, and of commerce as its handmaid; the diffusion of information and the arraignment of all abuses at the bar of public reason; freedom of religion; freedom of the press; freedom of person under the protection of the *habeas corpus;* and trial by juries impartially selected—these principles form the bright constellation which has gone before us, and guided our steps through an age of revolution and reformation. The wisdom of our sages and the blood of our heroes have been devoted to their attainment. They should be the creed of our political faith—the text of civil instruction—the touchstone by which to try the services of those we trust; and should we wander from them in moments of error or alarm, let us hasten to retrace our steps and to regain the road which alone leads to peace, liberty, and safety.

I repair, then, fellow citizens, to the post you have assigned me. With experience enough in subordinate offices to have seen the difficulties of this, the greatest of all, I have learned to expect that it will rarely fall to the lot of imperfect man to retire from this station with the reputation and the favor which bring him into it. Without pretensions to that high confidence reposed in our first and great revolutionary character, whose preëminent services had entitled him to the first place in his country's love, and destined for him the fairest page in the volume of faithful history, I ask so much confidence only as may give firmness and effect to the legal administration of your affairs. I shall often go wrong through defect of judgment. When right, I shall often be thought wrong by those whose positions will not command a view of the whole ground. I ask your indulgence for my own errors, which will never be intentional; and your support against the errors of others, who may condemn what they would not if seen in all its parts. The approbation implied by your suffrage is a consolation to me for the past; and my future solicitude will be to retain the good opinion of those who have bestowed it in advance, to conciliate that of others by doing them all the good in my power, and to be instrumental to the happiness and freedom of all.

Relying, then, on the patronage of your good will, I advance with obedience to the work, ready to retire from it whenever you become sensible how much better choice it is in your power to make. And may that Infinite Power which rules the destinies of the universe, lead our councils to what is best, and give them a favorable issue for your peace and prosperity.

FIRST ANNUAL MESSAGE TO CONGRESS

December 8, 1801

FELLOW CITIZENS OF THE SENATE AND HOUSE OF REPRESENTATIVES: It is a circumstance of sincere gratification to me that on meeting the great council of our nation, I am able to announce to them, on the grounds of reasonable certainty, that the wars and troubles which have for so many years afflicted our sister nations have at length come to an end, and that the communications of peace and commerce are once more opening among them. While we devoutly return thanks to the beneficent Being who has been pleased to breathe into them the spirit of conciliation and forgiveness, we are bound with peculiar gratitude to be thankful to him that our own peace has been preserved through so perilous a season, and ourselves permitted quietly to cultivate the earth and to practice and improve those arts which tend to increase our comforts. The assurances, indeed, of friendly disposition, received from all the powers with whom we have principal relations, had inspired a confidence that our peace with them would not have been disturbed. But a cessation of the irregularities which had affected the commerce of neutral nations, and of the irritations and injuries produced by them, cannot but add to this confidence; and strengthens, at the same time, the hope, that wrongs committed on unoffending friends, under a pressure of circumstances, will now be reviewed with candor, and will be considered as founding just claims of retribution for the past and new assurance for the future.

Among our Indian neighbors, also, a spirit of peace and friendship generally prevails; and I am happy to inform you that the continued efforts to introduce among them the implements and the practice of husbandry, and of the household arts, have not been without success; that they are becoming more and more sensible of the superiority of this dependence for clothing and subsistence over the precarious resources of hunting and fishing; and already we are able to announce, that instead of that constant diminution of their numbers, produced by their wars and their wants, some of them begin to experience an increase of population.

To this state of general peace with which we have been blessed, one only exception exists. Tripoli, the least considerable of the Barbary States, had come forward with demands unfounded either in right or in compact, and had permitted itself to denounce war, on our failure to comply before a given day. The style of the demand admitted but one answer. I sent a small squadron of frigates into the Mediterranean, with assurances to that power of our sincere desire to remain in peace, but with orders to protect our commerce against the threatened attack. The measure was seasonable and salutary. The bey had already declared war in form. His cruisers were out. Two had arrived at Gibraltar. Our commerce in the Mediterranean was blockaded, and that of the Atlantic in peril. The arrival of our squadron dispelled the danger. One of the Tripolitan cruisers having fallen in with, and engaged the small schooner *Enterprise,* commanded by Lieutenant Sterret, which had gone as a tender to our larger vessels, was captured, after a heavy slaughter of her men, without the loss of a single one on our part. The bravery exhibited by our citizens on that element, will, I trust, be a testimony to the world that it is not the want of that virtue which makes us seek their peace, but a conscientious desire to direct the energies of our nation to the multiplication of the human race, and not to its destruction. Unauthorized by the Constitution, without the sanction of Congress, to go beyond the line of defence, the vessel being disabled from committing further hostilities, was liberated with its crew. The legislature will doubtless consider whether, by authorizing measures of offence, also, they will place our force on an equal footing with that of its adversaries. I communicate all material information on this subject, that in the exercise of the important function confided by the Constitution to the legislature exclusively, their judgment may form itself on a knowledge and consideration of every circumstance of weight.

I wish I could say that our situation with all the other Barbary states was entirely satisfactory. Discovering that some delays had taken place in the performance of certain articles stipulated by us, I thought it my duty, by immediate measures for fulfilling them, to vindicate to ourselves the right of considering the effect of departure from stipulation on their side. From the papers which will be laid before you, you will be enabled to judge whether our treaties are regarded by them as fixing at all the measure of their demands, or as guarding from the exercise of force our vessels within their power; and to consider how far it will be safe and expedient to leave our affairs with them in their present posture.

I lay before you the result of the census lately taken of our inhabitants, to a conformity with which we are to reduce the ensuing rates of representation and taxation. You will perceive that the increase of numbers during the last ten years, proceeding in geometrical ratio, promises a duplication in little more than twenty-two years. We contemplate this rapid growth, and the prospect it holds up to us, not with a view to the injuries it may enable us to do to others in some future day, but to the settlement of the extensive country still remaining vacant within our limits, to the multiplications of men susceptible of happiness, educated in the love of order, habituated to self-government, and valuing its blessings above all price.

Other circumstances, combined with the increase of numbers, have produced an augmentation of revenue arising from consumption, in a ratio far beyond that of population alone, and though the changes of foreign relations now taking place so desirably for the world, may for a season affect this branch of revenue, yet, weighing all probabilities of expense, as well as of income, there is reasonable ground of confidence that we may now safely dispense with all the internal taxes, comprehending excises, stamps, auctions, licenses, carriages, and refined sugars, to which the postage on newspapers may be added, to facilitate the progress of information, and that the remaining sources of revenue will be sufficient to provide for the support of government, to pay the interest on the public debts, and to discharge the principals in shorter periods than the laws or the general expectations had contemplated. War, indeed, and untoward events, may change this prospect of things, and call for expenses which the imposts could not meet; but sound principles will not justify our taxing the industry of our fellow citizens to accumulate treasure for wars to happen we know not when, and which might not perhaps happen but from the temptations offered by that treasure.

These views, however, of reducing our burdens, are formed on the expectation that a sensible, and at the same time a salutary reduction, may take place in our habitual expenditures. For this purpose, those of the civil government, the army, and navy, will need revisal.

When we consider that this government is charged with the external and mutual relations only of these states; that the states themselves have principal care of our persons, our property, and our reputation, constituting the great field of human concerns, we may well doubt whether our organization is not too complicated, too expensive; whether offices and officers have not been multiplied unnecessarily, and sometimes injuriously to the service they were meant to promote. I will cause to be laid before you an essay toward a statement of those who, under public employment of various kinds, draw money from the treasury or from our citizens. Time has not permitted a perfect enumeration, the ramifications of office being too multiplied and remote to be completely traced in a first trial. Among those who are dependent on executive discretion, I have begun the reduction of what was deemed necessary. The expenses of diplomatic agency have been considerably diminished. The inspectors of internal revenue who were found to obstruct the accountability of the institution, have been discontinued. Several agencies created by executive authority, on salaries fixed by that also, have been suppressed, and should suggest the expediency of regulating that power by law, so as to subject its exercises to legislative inspection and sanction. Other reformations of the same kind will be pursued with that caution which is requisite in removing useless things, not to injure what is retained. But the great mass of public offices is established by law, and, therefore, by law alone can be abolished. Should the legislature think it expedient to pass this roll in review, and try all its parts by the test of public utility, they may be assured of every aid and light which executive information can yield. Considering the general tendency to multiply offices and dependencies, and to increase expense to the ultimate term of burden which the citizen can bear, it behooves us to avail ourselves of every occasion which presents itself for taking off the surcharge; that it never may be seen here that, after leaving to labor the smallest portion of its earnings on which it can subsist, government shall itself consume the residue of what it was instituted to guard.

In our care, too, of the public contributions intrusted to our direction, it would be prudent to multiply barriers against their dissipation, by appropriating specific sums to every specific purpose susceptible of definition; by disallowing all applications of money varying from the appropriation in object, or transcending it in amount; by reducing the undefined field of contingencies, and thereby circumscribing discretionary powers over money; and by bringing back to a single department all accountabilities for money where the examination may be prompt, efficacious, and uniform.

An account of the receipts and expenditures of the last year, as prepared by the Secretary of the Treasury, will as usual be laid before you. The success which has attended the late sales of the public lands, shows that with attention they may be made an important source of receipt. Among the payments, those made in discharge of the principal and interest of the national debt, will show that the public faith has been exactly maintained. To these will be added an estimate of appropriations necessary for the ensuing year. This last will of course be effected by such modifications of the systems of expense, as you shall think proper to adopt.

A statement has been formed by the Secretary of War, on mature consideration, of all the posts and stations where garrisons will be expedient, and of the number of men requisite for each garrison. The whole amount is considerably short of the present military establishment. For the surplus no particular use can be pointed out. For defence against invasion, their number is as nothing; nor is it conceived needful or safe that a standing army should be kept up in time of peace for that purpose. Uncertain as we must ever be of the particular point in our circumference where an enemy may choose to invade us, the only force which can be ready at every point and competent to oppose them, is the body of neighboring citizens as formed into a militia. On these, collected from the parts most convenient, in numbers proportioned to the invading foe, it is best to rely, not only to meet the first attack, but if it threatens to be permanent, to maintain the defence until regulars may be engaged to relieve them. These considerations render it important that we should at every session continue to amend the defects which from time to time show themselves in the laws for regulating the militia, until they are sufficiently perfect. Nor should we now or at any time separate, until we can say we have done everything for the militia which we could do were an enemy at our door.

The provisions of military stores on hand will be laid before you, that you may judge of the additions still requisite.

With respect to the extent to which our naval preparations should be carried, some difference of opinion may be expected to appear; but just attention to the circumstances of every part of the Union will doubtless reconcile all. A small force will probably continue to be wanted for actual service in the Mediterranean. Whatever annual sum beyond that you may think proper to appropriate to naval preparations, would perhaps be better employed in providing those articles which may be kept without waste or consumption, and be in readiness when any exigence calls them into use. Progress has been made, as will appear by papers now communicated, in providing materials for seventy-four gun ships as directed by law.

How far the authority given by the legislature for procuring and establishing sites for naval purposes has been perfectly understood and pursued in the execution, admits of some doubt. A statement of the expenses already incurred on that subject, shall be laid before you. I have in certain cases sus-pended or slackened these expenditures, that the legislature might deter-mine whether so many yards are necessary as have been contemplated. The works at this place are among those permitted to go on; and five of the seven frigates directed to be laid up, have been brought and laid up here, where, besides the safety of their position, they are under the eye of the executive administration, as well as of its agents, and where yourselves also will be guided by your own view in the legislative provisions respecting them which may from time to time be necessary. They are preserved in such con-dition, as well the vessels as whatever belongs to them, as to be at all times ready for sea on a short warning. Two others are yet to be laid up so soon as they shall have received the repairs requisite to put them also into sound condition. As a superintending officer will be necessary at each yard, his duties and emoluments, hitherto fixed by the executive, will be a more proper subject for legislation. A communication will also be made of our progress in the execution of the law respecting the vessels directed to be sold.

The fortifications of our harbors, more or less advanced, present consid-erations of great difficulty. While some of them are on a scale sufficiently proportioned to the advantages of their position, to the efficacy of their pro-tection, and the importance of the points within it, others are so extensive, will cost so much in their first erection, so much in their maintenance, and require such a force to garrison them, as to make it questionable what is best now to be done. A statement of those commenced or projected, of the expenses already incurred, and estimates of their future cost, so far as can be foreseen, shall be laid before you, that you may be enabled to judge whether any attention is necessary in the laws respecting this subject.

Agriculture, manufactures, commerce, and navigation, the four pillars of our prosperity, are the most thriving when left most free to individual enter-prise. Protection from casual embarrassments, however, may sometimes be seasonably interposed. If in the course of your observations or inquiries they should appear to need any aid within the limits of our constitutional powers, your sense of their importance is a sufficient assurance they will occupy your attention. We cannot, indeed, but all feel an anxious solicitude for the diffi-culties under which our carrying trade will soon be placed. How far it can be relieved, otherwise than by time, is a subject of important consideration.

The judiciary system of the United States, and especially that portion of it recently erected, will of course present itself to the contemplation of Con-gress; and that they may be able to judge of the proportion which the insti-tution bears to the business it has to perform, I have caused to be procured from the several States, and now lay before Congress, an exact statement of all the causes decided since the first establishment of the courts, and of those which were depending when additional courts and judges were brought in to their aid.

And while on the judiciary organization, it will be worthy your consideration, whether the protection of the inestimable institution of juries has been extended to all the cases involving the security of our persons and property. Their impartial selection also being essential to their value, we ought further to consider whether that is sufficiently secured in those States where they are named by a marshal depending on executive will, or designated by the court or by officers dependent on them.

I cannot omit recommending a revisal of the laws on the subject of naturalization. Considering the ordinary chances of human life, a denial of citizenship under a residence of fourteen years is a denial to a great proportion of those who ask it, and controls a policy pursued from their first settlement by many of these States, and still believed of consequence to their prosperity. And shall we refuse the unhappy fugitives from distress that hospitality which the savages of the wilderness extended to our fathers arriving in this land? Shall oppressed humanity find no asylum on this globe? The constitution, indeed, has wisely provided that, for admission to certain offices of important trust, a residence shall be required sufficient to develop character and design. But might not the general character and capabilities of a citizen be safely communicated to everyone manifesting a *bonâ fide* purpose of embarking his life and fortunes permanently with us? with restrictions, perhaps, to guard against the fraudulent usurpation of our flag; an abuse which brings so much embarrassment and loss on the genuine citizen, and so much danger to the nation of being involved in war, that no endeavor should be spared to detect and suppress it.

These, fellow citizens, are the matters respecting the state of the nation, which I have thought of importance to be submitted to your consideration at this time. Some others of less moment, or not yet ready for communication, will be the subject of separate messages. I am happy in this opportunity of committing the arduous affairs of our government to the collected wisdom of the Union. Nothing shall be wanting on my part to inform, as far as in my power, the legislative judgment, nor to carry that judgment into faithful execution. The prudence and temperance of your discussions will promote, within your own walls, that conciliation which so much befriends national conclusion; and by its example will encourage among our constituents that progress of opinion which is tending to unite them in object and in will. That all should be satisfied with any one order of things is not to be expected, but I indulge the pleasing persuasion that the great body of our citizens will cordially concur in honest and disinterested efforts, which have for their object to preserve the general and State governments in their constitutional form and equilibrium; to maintain peace abroad, and order and obedience to the laws at home; to establish principles and practices of administration favorable to the security of liberty and prosperity, and to reduce expenses to what is necessary for the useful purposes of government.

SECOND ANNUAL MESSAGE
December 15, 1802

TO THE SENATE AND HOUSE OF REPRESENTATIVES OF THE UNITED STATES: When we assemble together, fellow citizens, to consider the state of our beloved country, our just attentions are first drawn to those pleasing circumstances which mark the goodness of that Being from whose favor they flow, and the large measure of thankfulness we owe for his bounty. Another year has come around, and finds us still blessed with peace and friendship abroad; law, order, and religion, at home; good affection and harmony with our Indian neighbors; our burdens lightened, yet our income sufficient for the public wants, and the produce of the year great beyond example. These, fellow citizens, are the circumstances under which we meet; and we remark with special satisfaction, those which, under the smiles of Providence, result from the skill, industry and order of our citizens, managing their own affairs in their own way and for their own use, unembarrassed by too much regulations, unoppressed by fiscal exactions.

On the restoration of peace in Europe, that portion of the general carrying trade which had fallen to our share during the war, was abridged by the returning competition of the belligerent powers. This was to be expected, and was just. But in addition we find in some parts of Europe monopolizing discriminations, which, in the form of duties, tend effectually to prohibit the carrying thither our own produce in our own vessels. From existing amities, and a spirit of justice, it is hoped that friendly discussion will produce a fair and adequate reciprocity. But should false calculations of interest defeat our hope, it rests with the legislature to decide whether they will meet inequalities abroad with countervailing inequalities at home, or provide for the evil in any other way.

It is with satisfaction I lay before you an act of the British Parliament anticipating this subject so far as to authorize a mutual abolition of the duties and countervailing duties permitted under the treaty of 1794. It shows on their part a spirit of justice and friendly accommodation which it is our duty and our interest to cultivate with all nations. Whether this would produce a due equality in the navigation between the two countries, is a subject for your consideration.

Another circumstance which claims attention, as directly affecting the very source of our navigation, is the defect or the evasion of the law providing for the return of seamen, and particularly of those belonging to vessels sold abroad. Numbers of them, discharged in foreign ports, have been thrown on the hands of our consuls, who, to rescue them from the dangers into which their distresses might plunge them, and save them to their country, have found it necessary in some cases to return them at the public charge.

The cession of the Spanish province of Louisiana to France, which took place in the course of the late war, will, if carried into effect, make a change in the aspect of our foreign relations which will doubtless have a just weight in any deliberations of the legislature connected with that subject.

There was reason, not long since, to apprehend that the warfare in which we were engaged with Tripoli might be taken up by some others of the Barbary powers. A reinforcement, therefore, was immediately ordered to the vessels already there. Subsequent information, however, has removed these apprehensions for the present. To secure our commerce in that sea with the smallest force competent, we have supposed it best to watch strictly the harbor of Tripoli. Still, however, the shallowness of their coast, and the want of smaller vessels on our part, has permitted some cruisers to escape unobserved; and to one of these an American vessel unfortunately fell a prey. The captain, one American seaman, and two others of color, remain prisoners with them unless exchanged under an agreement formerly made with the bashaw, to whom, on the faith of that, some of his captive subjects had been restored.

The convention with the State of Georgia has been ratified by their legislature, and a repurchase from the Creeks has been consequently made of a part of the Tallahassee county. In this purchase has been also comprehended part of the lands within the fork of Oconee and Oakmulgee rivers. The particulars of the contract will be laid before Congress so soon as they shall be in a state for communication.

In order to remove every ground of difference possible with our Indian neighbors, I have proceeded in the work of settling with them and marking the boundaries between us. That with the Choctaw nation is fixed in one part, and will be through the whole in a short time. The country to which their title had been extinguished before the revolution is sufficient to receive a very respectable population, which Congress will probably see the expediency of encouraging so soon as the limits shall be declared. We are to view this position as an outpost of the United States, surrounded by strong neighbors and distant from its support. And how far that monopoly which prevents population should here be guarded against, and actual habitation made a condition of the continuance of title, will be for your consideration. A prompt settlement, too, of all existing rights and claims within this territory, presents itself as a preliminary operation.

In that part of the Indian territory which includes Vincennes, the lines settled with the neighboring tribes fix the extinction of their title at a breadth of twenty-four leagues from east to west, and about the same length parallel with and including the Wabash. They have also ceded a tract of four miles square, including the salt springs near the mouth of the river.

In the department of finance it is with pleasure I inform you that the receipts of external duties for the last twelve months have exceeded those of any former year, and that the ratio of increase has been also greater than usual. This has enabled us to answer all the regular exigencies of government, to pay from the treasury in one year upward of eight millions of dollars, principal and interest, of the public debt, exclusive of upward of one million paid by the sale of bank stock, and making in the whole a reduction of nearly five millions and a half of principal; and to have now in the treasury four millions and a half of dollars, which are in a course of application to a further discharge of debt and current demands. Experience, too, so far, authorizes us to believe, if no extraordinary event supervenes, and the expenses which will be actually incurred shall not be greater than were contemplated by Congress at their last session, that we shall not be disappointed in the expectations then formed. But nevertheless, as the effect of peace on the amount of duties is not yet fully ascertained, it is the more necessary to practice every useful economy, and to incur no expense which may be avoided without prejudice.

The collection of the internal taxes having been completed in some of the States, the officers employed in it are of course out of commission. In others, they will be so shortly. But in a few, where the arrangement for the direct tax had been retarded, it will still be some time before the system is closed. It has not yet been thought necessary to employ the agent authorized by an act of the last session for transacting business in Europe relative to debts and loans. Nor have we used the power confided by the same act, of prolonging the foreign debts by reloans, and of redeeming, instead thereof, an equal sum of the domestic debt. Should, however, the difficulties of remittances on so large a scale render it necessary at any time, the power shall be executed, and the money thus unemployed abroad shall, in conformity with that law, be faithfully applied here in an equivalent extinction of domestic debt. When effects so salutary result from the plans you have already sanctioned, when merely by avoiding false objects of expense we are able, without a direct tax, without internal taxes, and without borrowing, to make large and effectual payments toward the discharge of our public debt and the emancipation of our posterity from that moral canker, it is an encouragement, fellow citizens, of the highest order, to proceed as we have begun, in substituting economy for taxation, and in pursuing what is useful for a nation placed as we are, rather than what is practiced by others under different circumstances. And whensoever we are destined to meet events which shall call forth all the energies of our countrymen, we have the firmest reliance on those energies, and the comfort of leaving for calls like these the extraordinary resources of loans and internal taxes. In the meantime, by payments of the principal of our debt, we are liberating, annually, portions of the external taxes, and forming from them a growing fund still further to lessen the necessity of recurring to extraordinary resources.

The usual accounts of receipts and expenditures for the last year, with an estimate of the expenses of the ensuing one, will be laid before you by the Secretary of the Treasury.

No change being deemed necessary in our military establishment, an estimate of its expenses for the ensuing year on its present footing, as also of the sums to be employed in fortifications and other objects within that department, has been prepared by the Secretary of War, and will make a part of the general estimates which will be presented to you.

Considering that our regular troops are employed for local purposes, and that the militia is our general reliance for great and sudden emergencies, you will doubtless think this institution worthy of a review, and give it those improvements of which you find it susceptible.

Estimates for the naval department, prepared by the Secretary of the Navy for another year, will in like manner be communicated with the general estimates. A small force in the Mediterranean will still be necessary to restrain the Tripoline cruisers, and the uncertain tenure of peace with some other of the Barbary powers, may eventually require that force to be augmented. The necessity of procuring some smaller vessels for that service will raise the estimate, but the difference in their maintenance will soon make it a measure of economy.

Presuming it will be deemed expedient to expend annually a sum towards providing the naval defence which our situation may require, I cannot but recommend that the first appropriations for that purpose may go to the saving what we already possess. No cares, no attentions, can preserve vessels from rapid decay which lie in water and exposed to the sun. These decays require great and constant repairs, and will consume, if continued, a great portion of the money destined to naval purposes. To avoid this waste of our resources, it is proposed to add to our navy-yard here a dock, within which our vessels may be laid up dry and under cover from the sun. Under these circumstances experience proves that works of wood will remain scarcely at all affected by time. The great abundance of running water which this situation possesses, at heights far above the level of the tide, if employed as is practised for lock navigation, furnishes the means of raising and laying up our vessels on a dry and sheltered bed. And should the measure be found useful here, similar depositories for laying up as well as for building and repairing vessels may hereafter be undertaken at other navy-yards offering the same means. The plans and estimates of the work, prepared by a person of skill and experience, will be presented to you without delay; and from this it will be seen that scarcely more than has been the cost of one vessel is necessary to save the whole, and that the annual sum to be employed toward its completion may be adapted to the views of the legislature as to naval expenditure.

To cultivate peace and maintain commerce and navigation in all their lawful enterprises; to foster our fisheries and nurseries of navigation and for the nurture of man, and protect the manufactures adapted to our circumstances; to preserve the faith of the nation by an exact discharge of its debts and contracts, expend the public money with the same care and economy we would practise with our own, and impose on our citizens no unnecessary burden; to keep in all things within the pale of our constitutional powers, and cherish the federal union as the only rock of safety—these, fellow-citizens, are the landmarks by which we are to guide ourselves in all our proceedings. By continuing to make these our rule of action, we shall endear to our countrymen the true principles of their Constitution, and promote a union of sentiment and of action equally auspicious to their happiness and safety. On my part, you may count on a cordial concurrence in every measure for the public good, and on all the information I possess which may enable you to discharge to advantage the high functions with which you are invested by your country.

SPECIAL MESSAGE RECOMMENDING A WESTERN EXPLORING EXPEDITION

January 18, 1803

GENTLEMEN OF THE SENATE AND OF THE HOUSE OF REPRESENTATIVES: As the continuance of the act for establishing trading-houses with the Indian tribes, will be under the consideration of the legislature at its present session, I think it my duty to communicate the views which have guided me in the

Illinois at least, so that we may present as firm a front on that as on our eastern border. We possess what is below the Yazoo, and can probably acquire a certain breadth from the Illinois and Wabash to the Ohio; but between the Ohio and Yazoo, the country all belongs to the Chickasaws, the most friendly tribe within our limits, but the most decided against the alienation of lands. The portion of their country most important for us is exactly that which they do not inhabit. Their settlements are not on the Mississippi, but in the interior country. They have lately shown a desire to become agricultural, and this leads to the desire of buying implements and comforts. In the strengthening and gratifying of these wants, I see the only prospect of planting on the Mississippi itself, the means of its own safety. Duty has required me to submit these views to the judgment of the legislature; but as their disclosure might embarrass and defeat their effect, they are committed to the special confidence of the two houses.

While the extension of the public commerce among the Indian tribes, may deprive of that source of profit such of our citizens as are engaged in it, it might be worthy the attention of Congress, in their care of individual as well as of the general interest, to point in another direction the enterprise of these citizens, as profitably for themselves, and more usefully for the public. The river Missouri, and the Indians inhabiting it, are not as well known as is rendered desirable by their connection with the Mississippi, and consequently with us. It is, however, understood, that the country on that river is inhabited by numerous tribes, who furnish great supplies of furs and peltry to the trade of another nation, carried on in a high latitude, through an infinite number of portages and lakes, shut up by ice through a long season. The commerce on that line could bear no competition with that of the Missouri, traversing a moderate climate, offering, according to the best accounts, a continued navigation from its source, and possibly with a single portage, from the western ocean, and finding to the Atlantic a choice of channels through the Illinois or Wabash, the lakes and Hudson, through the Ohio and Susquehanna, or Potomac or James rivers, and through the Tennessee and Savannah rivers. An intelligent officer, with ten or twelve chosen men, fit for the enterprise, and willing to undertake it, taken from our posts, where they may be spared without inconvenience, might explore the whole line, even to the western ocean; have conferences with the natives on the subject of commercial intercourse; get admission among them for our traders, as others are admitted; agree on convenient deposits for an interchange of articles; and return with the information acquired, in the course of two summers. Their arms and accoutrements, some instruments of observation, and light and cheap presents for the Indians, would be all the apparatus they could carry, and with an expectation of a soldier's por-

execution of that act, in order that you may decide on the poli
ing it, in the present or any other form, or discontinue it alto
shall, on the whole, seem most for the public good.

The Indian tribes residing within the limits of the United Sta
a considerable time, been growing more and more uneasy at
diminution of the territory they occupy, although effected by the
untary sales; and the policy has long been gaining strength wit
refusing absolutely all further sale, on any conditions; insomuch t
time, it hazards their friendship, and excites dangerous jealousie
turbations in their minds to make any overture for the purcha
smallest portions of their land. A very few tribes only are not yet o
in these dispositions. In order peaceably to counteract this policy
and to provide an extension of territory which the rapid increase
numbers will call for, two measures are deemed expedient. First: to
age them to abandon hunting, to apply to the raising stock, to agr
and domestic manufactures, and thereby prove to themselves that le
and labor will maintain them in this, better than in their former m
living. The extensive forests necessary in the hunting life will then b
useless, and they will see advantage in exchanging them for the mea
improving their farms and of increasing their domestic comforts. Seco
to multiply trading-houses among them, and place within their reach t
things which will contribute more to their domestic comfort than the
session of extensive but uncultivated wilds. Experience and reflection
develop to them the wisdom of exchanging what they can spare and
want, for what we can spare and they want In leading them thus to ag
culture, to manufactures, and civilization; in bringing together their a
our settlements, and in preparing them ultimately to participate in the ben
fits of our government, I trust and believe we are acting for their greates
good. At these trading-houses we have pursued the principles of the act o
Congress, which directs that the commerce shall be carried on liberally, and
requires only that the capital stock shall not be diminished. We consequently
undersell private traders, foreign and domestic; drive them from the competition; and thus, with the good will of the Indians, rid ourselves of a
description of men who are constantly endeavoring to excite in the Indian
mind suspicions, fears, and irritations toward us. A letter now enclosed,
shows the effect of our competition on the operations of the traders, while
the Indians, perceiving the advantage of purchasing from us, are soliciting
generally our establishment of trading-houses among them. In one quarter
this is particularly interesting. The legislature, reflecting on the late occurrences on the Mississippi, must be sensible how desirable it is to possess a
respectable breadth of country on that river, from our southern limit to the

tion of land on their return, would constitute the whole expense. Their pay would be going on, whether here or there. While other civilized nations have encountered great expense to enlarge the boundaries of knowledge, by undertaking voyages of discovery, and for other literary purposes, in various parts and directions, our nation seems to owe to the same object, as well as to its own interests, to explore this, the only line of easy communication across the continent, and so directly traversing our own part of it. The interests of commerce place the principal object within the constitutional powers and care of Congress, and that it should incidentally advance the geographical knowledge of our own continent, can not but be an additional gratification. The nation claiming the territory, regarding this as a literary pursuit, which it is in the habit of permitting within its own dominions, would not be disposed to view it with jealousy, even if the expiring state of its interests there did not render it a matter of indifference. The appropriation of two thousand five hundred dollars, "for the purpose of extending the external commerce of the United States," while understood and considered by the executive as giving the legislative sanction, would cover the undertaking from notice, and prevent the obstructions which interested individuals might otherwise previously prepare in its way.

THIRD ANNUAL MESSAGE
October 17, 1803

TO THE SENATE AND HOUSE OF REPRESENTATIVES OF THE UNITED STATES: In calling you together, fellow citizens, at an earlier day than was contemplated by the act of the last session of Congress, I have not been insensible to the personal inconveniences necessarily resulting from an unexpected change in your arrangements. But matters of great public concernment have rendered this call necessary, and the interest you feel in these will supersede in your minds all private considerations.

Congress witnessed, at their last session, the extraordinary agitation produced in the public mind by the suspension of our right of deposit at the port of New Orleans, no assignment of another place having been made according to treaty. They were sensible that the continuance of that privation would be more injurious to our nation than any consequences which could flow from any mode of redress, but reposing just confidence in the good faith of the government whose officer had committed the wrong, friendly and reasonable representations were resorted to, and the right of deposit was restored.

Previous, however, to this period, we had not been unaware of the danger to which our peace would be perpetually exposed while so important a key to the commerce of the western country remained under foreign power. Difficulties, too, were presenting themselves as to the navigation of other streams, which, arising within our territories, pass through those adjacent. Propositions had, therefore, been authorized for obtaining, on fair conditions, the sovereignty of New Orleans, and of other possessions in that quarter interesting to our quiet, to such extent as was deemed practicable; and the provisional appropriation of two millions of dollars, to be applied and accounted for by the President of the United States, intended as part of the price, was considered as conveying the sanction of Congress to the acquisition proposed. The enlightened government of France saw, with just discernment, the importance to both nations of such liberal arrangements as might best and permanently promote the peace, friendship, and interests of both; and the property and sovereignty of all Louisiana, which had been restored to them, have on certain conditions been transferred to the United States by instruments bearing date the 30th of April last. When these shall have received the constitutional sanction of the Senate, they will without delay be communicated to the Representatives also, for the exercise of their functions, as to those conditions which are within the powers vested by the Constitution in Congress. While the property and sovereignty of the Mississippi and its waters secure an independent outlet for the produce of the western States, and an uncontrolled navigation through their whole course, free from collision with other powers and the dangers to our peace from that source, the fertility of the country, its climate and extent, promise in due season important aids to our treasury, an ample provision for our posterity, and a wide-spread field for the blessings of freedom and equal laws.

With the wisdom of Congress it will rest to take those ulterior measures which may be necessary for the immediate occupation and temporary government of the country; for its incorporation into our Union; for rendering the change of government a blessing to our newly-adopted brethren; for securing to them the rights of conscience and of property; for confirming to the Indian inhabitants their occupancy and self-government, establishing friendly and commercial relations with them, and for ascertaining the geography of the country acquired. Such materials for your information, relative to its affairs in general, as the short space of time has permitted me to collect, will be laid before you when the subject shall be in a state for your consideration.

Another important acquisition of territory has also been made since the last session of Congress. The friendly tribe of Kaskaskia Indians with which we have never had a difference, reduced by the wars and wants of savage life to a few individuals unable to defend themselves against the neighboring tribes, has transferred its country to the United States, reserving only for its members what is sufficient to maintain them in an agricultural way. The considerations stipulated are, that we shall extend to them our patronage and protection, and give them certain annual aids in money, in implements of agriculture, and other articles of their choice. This country, among the most fertile within our limits, extending along the Mississippi from the mouth of the Illinois to and up the Ohio, though not so necessary as a barrier since the acquisition of the other bank, may yet be well worthy of being laid open to immediate settlement, as its inhabitants may descend with rapidity in support of the lower country should future circumstances expose that to foreign enterprise. As the stipulations in this treaty also involve matters within the competence of both houses only, it will be laid before Congress as soon as the Senate shall have advised its ratification.

With many other Indian tribes, improvements in agriculture and household manufacture are advancing, and with all our peace and friendship are established on grounds much firmer than heretofore. The measure adopted of establishing trading-houses among them, and of furnishing them necessaries in exchange for their commodities, at such moderated prices as leave no gain, but cover us from loss, has the most conciliatory and useful effect upon them, and is that which will best secure their peace and good will.

The small vessels authorized by Congress with a view to the Mediterranean service, have been sent into that sea, and will be able more effectually to confine the Tripoline cruisers within their harbors, and supersede the necessity of convoy to our commerce in that quarter. They will sensibly lessen the expenses of that service the ensuing year.

A further knowledge of the ground in the north-eastern and north-western angles of the United States has evinced that the boundaries established by the treaty of Paris, between the British territories and ours in those parts, were too imperfectly described to be susceptible of execution. It has therefore been thought worthy of attention, for preserving and cherishing the harmony and useful intercourse subsisting between the two nations, to remove by timely arrangements what unfavorable incidents might otherwise render a ground of future misunderstanding. A convention has therefore been entered into, which provides for a practicable demarkation of those limits to the satisfaction of both parties.

An account of the receipts and expenditures of the year ending 30th September last, with the estimates for the service of the ensuing year, will be laid before you by the Secretary of the Treasury so soon as the receipts of the last quarter shall be returned from the more distant States. It is already ascertained that the amount paid into the treasury for that year has been between eleven and twelve millions of dollars, and that the revenue accrued during the same term exceeds the sum counted on as sufficient for our current expenses, and to extinguish the public debt within the period heretofore proposed.

The amount of debt paid for the same year is about three millions one hundred thousand dollars, exclusive of interest, and making, with the payment of the preceding year, a discharge of more than eight millions and a half of dollars of the principal of that debt, besides the accruing interest; and there remain in the treasury nearly six millions of dollars. Of these, eight hundred and eighty thousand have been reserved for payment of the first instalment due under the British convention of January 8th, 1802, and two millions are what have been before mentioned as placed by Congress under the power and accountability of the president, toward the price of New Orleans and other territories acquired, which, remaining untouched, are still applicable to that object, and go in diminution of the sum to be funded for it.

Should the acquisition of Louisiana be constitutionally confirmed and carried into effect, a sum of nearly thirteen millions of dollars will then be added to our public debt, most of which is payable after fifteen years; before which term the present existing debts will all be discharged by the established operation of the sinking fund. When we contemplate the ordinary annual augmentation of imposts from increasing population and wealth, the augmentation of the same revenue by its extension to the new acquisition, and the economies which may still be introduced into our public expenditures, I cannot but hope that Congress in reviewing their resources will find means to meet the intermediate interests of this additional debt without recurring to new taxes, and applying to this object only the ordinary progression of our revenue. Its extraordinary increase in times of foreign war will be the proper and sufficient fund for any measures of safety or precaution which that state of things may render necessary in our neutral position.

Remittances for the instalments of our foreign debt having been found practicable without loss, it has not been thought expedient to use the power given by a former act of Congress of continuing them by reloans, and of redeeming instead thereof equal sums of domestic debt, although no difficulty was found in obtaining that accommodation.

The sum of fifty thousand dollars appropriated by Congress for providing gun-boats, remains unexpended. The favorable and peaceful turn of affairs on the Mississippi rendered an immediate execution of that law unnecessary, and time was desirable in order that the institution of that branch of our force might begin on models the most approved by experience. The same issue of events dispensed with a resort to the appropriation of a million and a half of dollars contemplated for purposes which were effected by happier means.

We have seen with sincere concern the flames of war lighted up again in Europe, and nations with which we have the most friendly and useful relations engaged in mutual destruction. While we regret the miseries in which we see others involved let us bow with gratitude to that kind Providence which, inspiring with wisdom and moderation our late legislative councils while placed under the urgency of the greatest wrongs, guarded us from hastily entering into the sanguinary contest, and left us only to look on and to pity its ravages. These will be heaviest on those immediately engaged. Yet the nations pursuing peace will not be exempt from all evil. In the course of this conflict, let it be our endeavor, as it is our interest and desire, to cultivate the friendship of the belligerent nations by every act of justice and of incessant kindness; to receive their armed vessels with hospitality from the distresses of the sea, but to administer the means of annoyance to none; to establish in our harbors such a police as may maintain law and order; to restrain our citizens from embarking individually in a war in which their country takes no part; to punish severely those persons, citizen or alien, who shall usurp the cover of our flag for vessels not entitled to it, infecting thereby with suspicion those of real Americans, and committing us into controversies for the redress of wrongs not our own; to exact from every nation the observance, toward our vessels and citizens, of those principles and practices which all civilized people acknowledge; to merit the character of a just nation, and maintain that of an independent one, preferring every consequence to insult and habitual wrong. Congress will consider whether the existing laws enable us efficaciously to maintain this course with our citizens in all places, and with others while within the limits of our jurisdiction, and will give them the new modifications necessary for these objects. Some contraventions of right have already taken place, both within our jurisdictional limits and on the high seas. The friendly disposition of the governments from whose agents they have proceeded, as well as their wisdom and regard for justice, leave us in reasonable expectation that they will be rectified and prevented in future; and that no act will be countenanced by them which threatens to disturb our friendly intercourse. Separated by a wide ocean from the nations of Europe, and from the political interests which entangle them together, with productions and wants which render our commerce and friendship useful to them and theirs to us, it cannot be the interest of any to assail us, nor ours to disturb them. We should be most unwise, indeed, were we to cast away the singular blessings of the position in which nature has placed us, the opportunity she has endowed us with of pursuing, at a distance from foreign contentions, the paths of industry, peace, and happiness; of cultivating general friendship, and of bringing collisions of interest to the umpirage of reason rather than of force. How desirable then must it be, in a government like ours, to see its citizens adopt individually the views, the interests, and the conduct which their country should pursue, divesting themselves of those passions and partialities which tend to lessen useful friendships, and to embarrass and embroil us in the calamitous scenes of Europe. Confident, fellow citizens, that you will duly estimate the importance of neutral dispositions toward the observance of neutral conduct, that you will be sensible how much it is our duty to look on the bloody arena spread before us with commiseration indeed, but with no other wish than to see it closed, I am persuaded you will cordially cherish these dispositions in all discussions among yourselves, and in all communications with your constituents; and I anticipate with satisfaction the measures of wisdom which the great interests now committed to *you* will give you an opportunity of providing, and *myself* that of approving and carrying into execution with the fidelity I owe to my country.

FOURTH ANNUAL MESSAGE
November 8, 1804

TO THE SENATE AND HOUSE OF REPRESENTATIVES OF THE UNITED STATES: To a people, fellow citizens, who sincerely desire the happiness and prosperity of other nations; to those who justly calculate that their own well-being is advanced by that of the nations with which they have intercourse, it will be a satisfaction to observe that the war which was lighted up in Europe a little before our last meeting has not yet extended its flames to other nations, nor been marked by the calamities which sometimes stain the footsteps of war. The irregularities too on the ocean, which generally harass the commerce of neutral nations, have, in distant parts, disturbed ours less than on former occasions. But in the American seas they have been greater from peculiar causes; and even within our harbors and jurisdiction, infringements on the authority of the laws have been committed which have called for serious attention. The friendly conduct of the governments from whose officers and subjects these acts have proceeded, in other respects and in places more under their observation and control, gives us confidence that our representations on this subject will have been properly regarded.

While noticing the irregularities committed on the ocean by others, those on our own part should not be omitted nor left unprovided for. Complaints have been received that persons residing within the United States have taken on themselves to arm merchant vessels, and to force a commerce into certain ports and countries in defiance of the laws of those countries. That individuals should undertake to wage private war, independently of the authority of their country, cannot be permitted in a well-ordered society. Its tendency to produce aggression on the laws and rights of other nations, and to endanger the peace of our own is so obvious, that I doubt not you will adopt measures for restraining it effectually in future.

Soon after the passage of the act of the last session, authorizing the establishment of a district and port of entry on the waters of the Mobile, we learnt that its object was misunderstood on the part of Spain. Candid explanations were immediately given, and assurances that, reserving our claims in that quarter as a subject of discussion and arrangement with Spain, no act was mediated, in the meantime, inconsistent with the peace and friendship existing between the two nations, and that conformably to these intentions would be the execution of the law. That government had, however, thought proper to suspend the ratification of the convention of 1802. But the explanations which would reach them soon after, and still more, the confirmation of them by the tenor of the instrument establishing the port and district, may reasonably be expected to replace them in the disposition and views of the whole subject which originally dictated the conviction.

I have the satisfaction to inform you that the objections which had been urged by that government against the validity of our title to the country of Louisiana have been withdrawn, its exact limits, however, remaining still to be settled between us. And to this is to be added that, having prepared and delivered the stock created in execution of the convention of Paris, of April 30, 1803, in consideration of the cession of that country, we have received from the government of France an acknowledgment, in due form, of the fulfilment of that stipulation.

With the nations of Europe in general our friendship and intercourse are undisturbed, and from the governments of the belligerent powers especially we continue to receive those friendly manifestations which are justly due to an honest neutrality, and to such good offices consistent with that as we have opportunities of rendering.

The activity and success of the small force employed in the Mediterranean in the early part of the present year, the reinforcement sent into that sea, and the energy of the officers having command in the several vessels, will, I trust, by the sufferings of war, reduce the barbarians of Tripoli to the desire of peace on proper terms. Great injury, however, ensues to ourselves as well as to others interested, from the distance to which prizes must be brought for adjudication, and from the impracticability of bringing hither such as are not seaworthy.

The bey of Tunis having made requisitions unauthorized by our treaty, their rejection has produced from him some expressions of discontent. But to those who expect us to calculate whether a compliance with unjust demands will not cost us less than a war, we must leave as a question of calculation for them, also, whether to retire from unjust demands will not cost them less than a war. We can do to each other very sensible injuries by war, but the mutual advantages of peace make that the best interest of both.

Peace and intercourse with the other powers on the same coast continue on the footing on which they are established by treaty.

In pursuance of the act providing for the temporary government of Louisiana, the necessary officers for the territory of Orleans were appointed in due time, to commence the exercise of their functions on the first day of October. The distance, however, of some of them, and indispensable previous arrangements, may have retarded its commencement in some of its parts; the form of government thus provided having been considered but as temporary, and open to such improvements as further information of the circumstances of our brethren there might suggest, it will of course be subject to your consideration.

In the district of Louisiana, it has been thought best to adopt the division into subordinate districts, which had been established under its former government. These being five in number, a commanding officer has been appointed to each, according to the provision of the law, and so soon as they can be at their station, that district will also be in its due state of organization; in the meantime their places are supplied by the officers before commanding there. The functions of the governor and judges of Indiana have commenced; the government, we presume, is proceeding in its new form. The lead mines in that district offer so rich a supply of that metal, as to merit attention. The report now communicated will inform you of their state, and of the necessity of immediate inquiry into their occupation and titles.

With the Indian tribes established within our newly-acquired limits, I have deemed it necessary to open conferences for the purpose of establishing a good understanding and neighborly relations between us. So far as we have yet learned, we have reason to believe that their dispositions are generally favorable and friendly; and with these dispositions on their part, we have in our own hands means which cannot fail us for preserving their peace and friendship. By pursuing a uniform course of justice toward them, by aiding them in all the improvements which may better their condition, and especially by establishing a commerce on terms which shall be advantageous to them and only not losing to us, and so regulated as that no incendiaries of our own or any other nation may be permitted to disturb the natural effects of our just and friendly offices, we may render ourselves so necessary to their comfort and prosperity, that the protection of our citizens from their disorderly members will become their interest and their voluntary care. Instead, therefore, of an augmentation of military force proportioned to our extension of frontier, I proposed a moderate enlargement of the capital employed in that commerce, as a more effectual, economical, and humane instrument for preserving peace and good neighborhood with them.

On this side the Mississippi an important relinquishment of native title has been received from the Delawares. That tribe, desiring to extinguish in their people the spirit of hunting, and to convert superfluous lands into the means of improving what they retain, have ceded to us all the country between the Wabash and the Ohio, south of, and including the road from the rapids towards Vincennes, for which they are to receive annuities in animals and implements for agriculture, and in other necessaries. This acquisition is important, not only for its extent and fertility, but as fronting three hundred miles on the Ohio, and near half that on the Wabash. The produce of the settled countries descending those rivers, will no longer pass in review of the Indian frontier but in a small portion, and with the cession heretofore made with the Kaskaskias, nearly consolidates our possessions north of the Ohio, in a very respectable breadth, from Lake Erie to the Mississippi. The Piankeshaws having some claim to the country ceded by the Delawares, it has been thought best to quiet that by fair purchase also. So soon as the treaties on this subject shall have received their constitutional sanctions, they shall be laid before both houses.

The act of Congress of February 28th, 1803, for building and employing a number of gun-boats, is now in a course of execution to the extent there provided for. The obstacle to naval enterprise which vessels of this construction offer for our seaport towns; their utility toward supporting within our waters the authority of the laws; the promptness with which they will be manned by the seamen and militia of the place the moment they are wanting; the facility of their assembling from different parts of the coast to any point where they are required in greater force than ordinary; the economy of their maintenance and preservation from decay when not in actual service; and the competence of our finances to this defensive provision, without any new burden, are considerations which will have due weight with Congress in deciding on the expediency of adding to their number from year to year, as experience shall test their utility, until all our important harbors, by these and auxiliary means, shall be insured against insult and opposition to the laws.

No circumstance has arisen since your last session which calls for any augmentation of our regular military force. Should any improvement occur in the militia system, that will be always seasonable.

Accounts of the receipts and expenditures of the last year with estimates for the ensuing one, will as usual be laid before you.

The state of our finances continues, to fulfil our expectations. Eleven millions and a half of dollars, received in the course of the year ending on the 30th of September last, have enabled us, after meeting all the ordinary expenses of the year, to pay upward of $3,600,000 of the public debt, exclusive of interest. This payment, with those of the two preceding years, has extinguished upward of twelve millions of the principal, and a greater sum of interest, within that period; and by a proportional diminution of interest, renders already sensible the effect of the growing sum yearly applicable to the discharge of the principal.

It is also ascertained that the revenue accrued during the last year, exceeds that of the preceding; and the probable receipts of the ensuing year may safely be relied on as sufficient, with the sum already in the treasury, to meet all the current demands of the year, to discharge upward of three millions and a half of the engagements incurred under the British and French conventions, and to advance in the farther redemption of the funded debts as rapidly as had been contemplated. These, fellow citizens, are the principal matters which I have thought it necessary at this time to communicate for your consideration and attention. Some others will be laid before you in the course of the session, but in the discharge of the great duties confided to you by our country, you will take a broader view of the field of legislation. Whether the great interests of agriculture, manufactures, commerce, or navigation, can, within the pale of your constitutional powers, be aided in any of their relations; whether laws are provided in all cases where they are wanting; whether those provided are exactly what they should be; whether any abuses take place in their administration, or in that of the public revenues; whether the organization of the public agents or of the public force is perfect in all its parts; in fine, whether anything can be done to advance the general good, are questions within the limits of your functions which will necessarily occupy your attention. In these and other matters which you in your wisdom may propose for the good of our country, you may count with assurance on my hearty co-operation and faithful execution.

SECOND INAUGURAL ADDRESS
March 4, 1805

Proceeding, fellow citizens, to that qualification which the constitution requires, before my entrance on the charge again conferred upon me, it is my duty to express the deep sense I entertain of this new proof of confidence from my fellow citizens at large, and the zeal with which it inspires me, so to conduct myself as may best satisfy their just expectations.

On taking this station on a former occasion, I declared the principles on which I believed it my duty to administer the affairs of our commonwealth. My conscience tells me that I have, on every occasion, acted up to that declaration, according to its obvious import, and to the understanding of every candid mind.

In the transaction of your foreign affairs, we have endeavored to cultivate the friendship of all nations, and especially of those with which we have the most important relations. We have done them justice on all occasions, favored where favor was lawful, and cherished mutual interests and intercourse on fair and equal terms. We are firmly convinced, and we act on that conviction, that with nations, as with individuals, our interests soundly calculated, will ever be found inseparable from our moral duties; and history bears witness to the fact, that a just nation is taken on its word, when recourse is had to armaments and wars to bridle others.

At home, fellow citizens, you best know whether we have done well or ill. The suppression of unnecessary offices, of useless establishments and expenses, enabled us to discontinue our internal taxes. These covering our land with officers, and opening our doors to their intrusions, had already begun that process of domiciliary vexation which, once entered, is scarcely to be restrained from reaching successively every article of produce and property. If among these taxes some minor ones fell which had not been inconvenient, it was because their amount would not have paid the officers who collected them, and because, if they had any merit, the state authorities might adopt them, instead of others less approved.

The remaining revenue on the consumption of foreign articles, is paid cheerfully by those who can afford to add foreign luxuries to domestic comforts, being collected on our seaboards and frontiers only, and incorporated with the transactions of our mercantile citizens, it may be the pleasure and pride of an American to ask, what farmer, what mechanic, what laborer, ever sees a tax-gatherer of the United States? These contributions enable us to support the current expenses of the government, to fulfil contracts with foreign nations, to extinguish the native right of soil within our limits, to extend those limits, and to apply such a surplus to our public debts, as places at a short day their final redemption, and that redemption once affected, the revenue thereby liberated may, by a just repartition among the states, and a corresponding amendment of the constitution, be applied, *in time of peace,* to rivers, canals, roads, arts, manufactures, education, and other great objects within each state. *In time of war,* if injustice, by ourselves or others, must sometimes produce war, increased as the same revenue will be increased by population and consumption, and aided by other resources reserved for that crisis, it may meet within the year all the expenses of the year, without encroaching on the rights of future generations, by burdening them with the debts of the past. War will then be but a suspension of useful works, and a return to a state of peace, a return to the progress of improvement.

I have said, fellow citizens, that the income reserved had enabled us to extend our limits; but that extension may possibly pay for itself before we are called on, and in the meantime, may keep down the accruing interest; in all events, it will repay the advances we have made. I know that the acquisition of Louisiana has been disapproved by some, from a candid apprehension that the enlargement of our territory would endanger its union. But who can limit the extent to which the federative principle may operate effectively? The larger our association, the less will it be shaken by local passions; and in any view, is it not better that the opposite bank of the Mississippi should be settled by our own brethren and children, than by strangers of another family? With which shall we be most likely to live in harmony and friendly intercourse?

In matters of religion, I have considered that its free exercise is placed by the constitution independent of the powers of the general government. I have therefore undertaken, on no occasion, to prescribe the religious exercises suited to it; but have left them, as the constitution found them, under the direction and discipline of state or church authorities acknowledged by the several religious societies.

The aboriginal inhabitants of these countries I have regarded with the commiseration their history inspires. Endowed with the faculties and the rights of men, breathing an ardent love of liberty and independence, and occupying a country which left them no desire but to be undisturbed, the stream of overflowing population from other regions directed itself on these shores; without power to divert, or habits to contend against, they have been overwhelmed by the current, or driven before it; now reduced within limits too narrow for the hunter's state, humanity enjoins us to teach them agriculture and the domestic arts; to encourage them to that industry which alone can enable them to maintain their place in existence, and to prepare them in time for that state of society, which to bodily comforts adds the improvement of the mind and morals. We have therefore liberally furnished them with the implements of husbandry and household use; we have placed among them instructors in the arts of first necessity; and they are covered with the ægis of the law against aggressors from among ourselves.

But the endeavors to enlighten them on the fate which awaits their present course of life, to induce them to exercise their reason, follow its dictates, and change their pursuits with the change of circumstances, have powerful obstacles to encounter; they are combated by the habits of their bodies, prejudice of their minds, ignorance, pride, and the influence of interested and crafty individuals among them, who feel themselves something in the present order of things, and fear to become nothing in any other. These persons inculcate a sanctimonious reverence for the customs of their ancestors; that whatsoever they did, must be done through all time; that reason is a false guide, and to advance under its counsel, in their physical, moral, or political condition, is perilous innovation; that their duty is to remain as their Creator made them, ignorance being safety, and knowledge full of danger; in short, my friends, among them is seen the action and counteraction of good sense and bigotry; they, too, have their anti-philosophers, who find an interest in keeping things in their present state, who dread reformation, and exert all their faculties to maintain the ascendency of habit over the duty of improving our reason, and obeying its mandates.

In giving these outlines, I do not mean, fellow citizens, to arrogate to myself the merit of the measures; that is due, in the first place, to the reflecting character of our citizens at large, who, by the weight of public opinion, influence and strengthen the public measures; it is due to the sound discretion with which they select from among themselves those to whom they confide the legislative duties; it is due to the zeal and wisdom of the characters thus selected, who lay the foundations of public happiness in wholesome laws, the execution of which alone remains for others; and it is due to the able and faithful auxiliaries, whose patriotism has associated with me in the executive functions.

During this course of administration, and in order to disturb it, the artillery of the press has been levelled against us, charged with whatsoever its licentiousness could devise or dare. These abuses of an institution so important to freedom and science, are deeply to be regretted, inasmuch as they tend to lessen its usefulness, and to sap its safety; they might, indeed, have been corrected by the wholesome punishments reserved and provided by the laws of the several States against falsehood and defamation; but public duties more urgent press on the time of public servants, and the offenders have therefore been left to find their punishment in the public indignation.

Nor was it uninteresting to the world, that an experiment should be fairly and fully made, whether freedom of discussion, unaided by power, is not sufficient for the propagation and protection of truth—whether a government, conducting itself in the true spirit of its constitution, with zeal and purity, and doing no act which it would be unwilling the whole world should witness, can be written down by falsehood and defamation. The experiment has been tried; you have witnessed the scene; our fellow citizens have looked on, cool and collected; they saw the latent source from which these outrages proceeded; they gathered around their public functionaries, and when the constitution called them to the decision by suffrage, they pronounced their verdict, honorable to those who had served them, and consolatory to the friend of man, who believes he may be intrusted with his own affairs.

No inference is here intended, that the laws, provided by the State against false and defamatory publications, should not be enforced; he who has time, renders a service to public morals and public tranquillity, in reforming these abuses by the salutary coercions of the law; but the experiment is noted, to prove that, since truth and reason have maintained their ground against false opinions in league with false facts, the press, confined to truth, needs no other legal restraint; the public judgment will correct false reasonings and opinions, on a full hearing of all parties; and no other definite line can be drawn between the inestimable liberty of the press and its demoralizing licentiousness. If there be still improprieties which this rule would not restrain, its supplement must be sought in the censorship of public opinion.

Contemplating the union of sentiment now manifested so generally, as auguring harmony and happiness to our future course, I offer to our country sincere congratulations. With those, too, not yet rallied to the same point, the disposition to do so is gaining strength; facts are piercing through the veil drawn over them; and our doubting brethren will at length see, that the mass of their fellow citizens, with whom they cannot yet resolve to act, as to principles and measures, think as they think, and desire what they desire; that our wish, as well as theirs, is, that the public efforts may be directed honestly to the public good, that peace be cultivated, civil and religious liberty unassailed, law and order preserved, equality of rights maintained, and that state of property, equal or unequal, which results to every man from his own industry, or that of his fathers. When satisfied of these views, it is not in human nature that they should not approve and support them; in the meantime, let us cherish them with patient affection; let us do them justice, and more than justice, in all competitions of interest; and we need not doubt that truth, reason, and their own interests, will at length prevail, will gather them into the fold of their country, and will complete their entire union of opinion, which gives to a nation the blessing of harmony, and the benefit of all its strength.

I shall now enter on the duties to which my fellow citizens have again called me, and shall proceed in the spirit of those principles which they have approved. I fear not that any motives of interest may lead me astray; I am sensible of no passion which could seduce me knowingly from the path of justice; but the weakness of human nature, and the limits of my own understanding, will produce errors of judgment sometimes injurious to your interests. I shall need, therefore, all the indulgence I have heretofore experienced—the want of it will certainly not lessen with increasing years. I shall need, too, the favor of that Being in whose hands we are, who led our forefathers, as Israel of old, from their native land, and planted them in a country flowing with all the necessaries and comforts of life; who has covered our infancy with his providence, and our riper years with his wisdom and power; and to whose goodness I ask you to join with me in supplications, that he will so enlighten the minds of your servants, guide their councils, and prosper their measures, that whatsoever they do, shall result in your good, and shall secure to you the peace, friendship, and approbation of all nations.

FIFTH ANNUAL MESSAGE
December 3, 1805

TO THE SENATE AND HOUSE OF REPRESENTATIVES OF THE UNITED STATES: At a moment when the nations of Europe are in commotion and arming against each other, and when those with whom we have principal intercourse are engaged in the general contest, and when the countenance of some of them toward our peaceable country threatens that even that may not be unaffected by what is passing on the general theatre, a meeting of the representatives of the nation in both houses of Congress has become more than usually desirable. Coming from every section of our country, they bring with them the sentiments and the information of the whole, and will be enabled to give a direction to the public affairs which the will and wisdom of the whole will approve and support.

In taking a view of the state of our country, we in the first place notice the late affliction of two of our cities under the fatal fever which in latter times has occasionally visited our shores. Providence in his goodness gave it an early termination on this occasion, and lessened the number of victims which have usually fallen before it. In the course of the several visitations by this disease it has appeared that it is strictly local; incident to the cities and on the tide waters only; incommunicable in the country, either by persons under the disease or by goods carried from diseased places; that its access is with the autumn, and that it disappears with the early frosts. These restrictions within narrow limits of time and space give security even to our maritime cities during three-fourths of the year, and to the country always. Although from these facts it appears unnecessary, yet to satisfy the fears of foreign nations, and cautions on their part not to be complained of in a danger whose limits are yet unknown to them, I have strictly enjoined on the officers at the head of the customs to certify with exact truth for every vessel sailing for a foreign port, the state of health respecting this fever which prevails at the place from which she sails. Under every motive from character and duty to certify the truth, I have no doubt they have faithfully executed this injunction. Much real injury has, however, been sustained from a propensity to identify with this epidemic, and to call by the same name, fevers of very different kinds, which have been known at all times and in all countries, and never have been placed among those deemed contagious. As we advance in our knowledge of this disease, as facts develop the sources from which individuals receive it, the state authorities charged with the care of the public health, and Congress with that of the general commerce, will become able to regulate with effect their respective functions in these departments. The burden of quarantines is felt at home as well as abroad; their efficacy merits examination. Although the health laws of the States should be found to need no present revisal by Congress, yet commerce claims that their attention be ever awake to them.

Since our last meeting the aspect of our foreign relations has considerably changed. Our coasts have been infested and our harbors watched by private armed vessels, some of them without commissions, some with illegal commissions, others with those of legal form but committing piratical acts beyond the authority of their commissions. They have captured in the very entrance of our harbors, as well as on the high seas, not only the vessels of our friends coming to trade with us, but our own also. They have carried them off under pretence of legal adjudication, but not daring to approach a court of justice, they have plundered and sunk them by the way, or in obscure places where no evidence could arise against them; maltreated the crews, and abandoned them in boats in the open sea or on desert shores without food or covering. These enormities appearing to be unreached by any control of their sovereigns, I found it necessary to equip a force to cruise within our own seas, to arrest all vessels of these descriptions found hovering on our coast within the limits of the Gulf Stream, and to bring the offenders in for trial as pirates.

The same system of hovering on our coasts and harbors under color of seeking enemies, has been also carried on by public armed ships, to the great annoyance and oppression of our commerce. New principles, too, have been interloped into the law of nations, founded neither in justice nor the usage of acknowledgment of nations. According to these, a belligerent takes to himself a commerce with its own enemy which it denies to a neutral, on the ground of its aiding that enemy in the war. But reason revolts at such an inconsistency, and the neutral having equal right with the belligerent to decide the question, the interest of our constituents and the duty of maintaining the authority of reason, the only umpire between just nations, impose on us the obligation of providing an effectual and determined opposition to a doctrine so injurious to the rights of peaceable nations. Indeed, the confidence we ought to have in the justice of others, still countenances the hope that a sounder view of those rights will of itself induce from every belligerent a more correct observance of them.

With Spain our negotiations for a settlement of differences have not had a satisfactory issue. Spoliations during the former war, for which she had formally acknowledged herself responsible, have been refused to be compensated, but on conditions affecting other claims in nowise connected with them. Yet the same practices are renewed in the present war, and are already of great amount. On the Mobile, our commerce passing through that river continues to be obstructed by arbitrary duties and vexatious searches. Propositions for adjusting amicably the boundaries of Louisiana have not been acceded to. While, however, the right is unsettled, we have avoided changing the state of things by taking new posts or strengthening ourselves in the disputed territories, in the hope that the other power would not, by contrary conduct, oblige us to meet their example, and endanger conflicts of authority the issue of which may not be easily controlled. But in this hope we have now reason to lessen our confidence. Inroads have been recently made into the territories of Orleans and the Mississippi, our citizens have been seized and their property plundered in the very parts of the former which had been actually delivered up by Spain, and this by the regular officers and soldiers of that government. I have therefore found it necessary at length to give orders to our troops on that frontier to be in readiness to protect our citizens, and to repel by arms any similar aggression in future. Other details, necessary for your full information of the state of things between this country and that shall be the subject of another communication.

In reviewing these injuries from some of the belligerent powers, the moderation, the firmness, and the wisdom of the legislature will be all called into action. We ought still to hope that time and a more correct estimate of interest, as well as of character, will produce the justice we are bound to expect. But should any nation deceive itself by false calculations, and disappoint that expectation, we must join in the unprofitable contest of trying which party can do the other the most harm. Some of these injuries may perhaps admit a peaceable remedy. Where that is competent it is always the most desirable. But some of them are of a nature to be met by force only, and all of them may lead to it. I cannot, therefore, but recommend such preparations as circumstances call for. The first object is to place our seaport towns out of the danger of insult. Measures have been already taken for furnishing them with heavy cannon for the service of such land batteries as may make a part of their defence against armed vessels approaching them. In aid of these it is desirable that we should have a competent number of gunboats; and the number, to be competent, must be considerable. If immediately begun, they may be in readiness for service at the opening of the next season. Whether it will be necessary to augment our land forces will be decided by occurrences probably in the course of your session. In the meantime, you will consider whether it would not be expedient, for a state of peace as well as of war, so to organize or class the militia as would enable us, on a sudden emergency, to call for the services of the younger portions, unencumbered with the old and those having families. Upward of three hundred thousand able-bodied men, between the ages of eighteen and twenty-six years, which the last census shows we may now count within our limits, will furnish a competent number for offence or defence in any point where they may be wanted, and will give time for raising regular forces after the necessity of them shall become certain; and the reducing to the early period of life all its active service cannot but be desirable to our younger citizens, of the present as well as future times, inasmuch as its engages to them in more advanced age a quiet and undisturbed repose in the bosom of their families. I cannot, then, but earnestly recommend to your early consideration the expediency of so modifying our militia system as, by a separation of the more active part from that which is less so, we may draw from it, when necessary, an efficient corps fit for real and active service, and to be called to it in regular rotation.

Considerable provision has been made, under former authorities from Congress, of materials for the construction of ships of war of seventy-four guns. These materials are on hand, subject to the further will of the legislature.

An immediate prohibition of the exportation of arms and ammunition is also submitted to your determination.

Turning from these unpleasant views of violence and wrong, I congratulate you on the liberation of our fellow citizens who were stranded on the coast of Tripoli and made prisoners of war. In a government bottomed on the will of all, the life and liberty of every individual citizen become interesting to all. In the treaty, therefore, which has concluded our warfare with that State, an article for the ransom of our citizens has been agreed to. An operation by land, by a small band of our countrymen, and others—engaged for the occasion, in conjunction with the troops of the ex-bashaw of that country, gallantly conducted by our late consul Eaton, and their successful enterprise on the city of Derne, contributed, doubtless, to the impression which produced peace; and the conclusion of this prevented opportunities of which the officers and men of our squadron destined for Tripoli would have availed themselves, to emulate the acts of valor exhibited by their brethren in the attack of the last year. Reflecting with high satisfaction on the distinguished bravery displayed whenever occasion permitted in the Mediterranean service, I think it would be a useful encouragement, as well as a just reward, to make an opening for some present promotion by enlarging our peace establishment of captains and lieutenants.

With Tunis some misunderstandings have arisen, not yet sufficiently explained, but friendly discussions with their ambassador recently arrived, and a mutual disposition to do whatever is just and reasonable, cannot fail of dissipating these; so that we may consider our peace on that coast, generally, to be on as sound a footing as it has been at any preceding time. Still it will not be expedient to withdraw, immediately, the whole of our force from that sea.

The law for providing a naval peace establishment fixes the number of frigates which shall be kept in constant service in time of peace, and prescribes that they shall not be manned by more than two-thirds of their complement of seamen and ordinary seamen. Whether a frigate may be trusted to two-thirds only of her proper complement of men must depend on the nature of the service on which she is ordered; that may sometimes, for her safety, as well as to insure her object, require her fullest complement. In adverting to this subject, Congress will perhaps consider whether the best limitation on the executive discretion in this case would not be by the number of seamen which may be employed in the whole service, rather than by the number of vessels. Occasions oftener arise for the employment of small than of large vessels, and it would lessen risk as well as expense to be authorized to employ them of preference. The limitation suggested by the number of seamen would admit a selection of vessels best adapted to the service.

Our Indian neighbors are advancing, many of them with spirit and others beginning to engage, in the pursuits of agriculture and household manufacture. They are becoming sensible that the earth yields subsistence with less labor and more certainty than the forest, and find it their interest, from time to time, to dispose of parts of their surplus and waste lands for the means of improving those they occupy, and of subsisting their families while they are preparing their farms. Since your last session, the northern tribes have sold to us the lands between the Connecticut reserve and the former Indian boundary; and those on the Ohio, from the same boundary to the rapids, and for a considerable depth inland. The Chickasaws and Cherokees have sold us the country between and adjacent to the two districts of Tennessee, and the Creeks, the residue of their lands in the fork of Ocmulgee, up to the Ulcofauhatche. The three former purchases are important, inasmuch as they consolidate disjointed parts of our settled country, and render their intercourse secure; and the second particularly so, as with the small point on the river which we expect is by this time ceded by the Piankeshaws, it completes our possession of the whole of both banks of the Ohio, from its source to near its mouth, and the navigation of that river is thereby rendered forever safe to our citizens settled and settling on its extensive waters. The purchase from the Creeks too has been for some time particularly interesting to the State of Georgia.

The several treaties which have been mentioned will be submitted to both houses of Congress for the exercise of their respective functions.

Deputations now on their way to the seat of government, from various nations of Indians inhabiting the Missouri and other parts beyond the Mississippi, come charged with the assurances of their satisfaction with the new relations in which they are placed with us, of their disposition to cultivate our peace and friendship, and their desire to enter into commercial intercourse with us. A statement of our progress in exploring the principal rivers of that country, and of the information respecting them hitherto obtained, will be communicated so soon as we shall receive some further relations which we have reason shortly to expect.

The receipts at the treasury during the year ending the 30th day of September last, have exceeded the sum of thirteen millions of dollars, which, with not quite five millions in the treasury at the beginning of the year, have enabled us, after meeting other demands, to pay nearly two millions of the debt contracted under the British treaty and convention, upward of four millions of principal of the public debt, and four millions of interest. These payments, with those which had been made in three years and a half preceding, have extinguished of the funded debt nearly eighteen millions of principal. Congress, by their act of November 10th, 1803, authorized us to borrow one million seven hundred and fifty thousand dollars, toward meeting the claims of our citizens assumed by the convention with France.

We have not, however, made use of this authority, because the sum of four millions and a half, which remained in the treasury on the same 30th day of September last, with the receipts which we may calculate on for the ensuing year, besides paying the annual sum of eight millions of dollars appropriated to the funded debts, and meeting all the current demands which may be expected, will enable us to pay the whole sum of three millions seven hundred and fifty thousand dollars assumed by the French convention, and still leaves a surplus of nearly a million of dollars at our free disposal. Should you concur in the provisions of arms and armed vessels recommended by the circumstances of the times, this surplus will furnish the means of doing so.

On this first occasion of addressing Congress, since, by the choice of my constituents, I have entered on a second term of administration, I embrace the opportunity to give this public assurance, that I will exert my best endeavors to administer faithfully the executive department, and will zealously co-operate with you in every measure which may tend to secure the liberty, property, and personal safety of our fellow citizens, and to consolidate the republican forms and principles of our government.

In the course of your session you shall receive all the aid which I can give for the despatch of the public business, and all the information necessary for your deliberations, of which the interests of our own country and the confidence reposed in us by others will admit a communication.

SIXTH ANNUAL MESSAGE
December 2, 1806

TO THE SENATE AND HOUSE OF REPRESENTATIVES OF THE UNITED STATES IN CONGRESS ASSEMBLED: It would have given me, fellow citizens, great satisfaction to announce in the moment of your meeting that the difficulties in our foreign relations, existing at the time of your last separation, had been amicably and justly terminated. I lost no time in taking those measures which were most likely to bring them to such a termination, by special missions charged with such powers and instructions as in the event of failure could leave no imputation on either our moderation or forbearance. The delays which have since taken place in our negotiations with the British government appears to have proceeded from causes which do not forbid the expectation that during the course of the session I may be enabled to lay before you their final issue. What will be that of the negotiations for settling our differences with Spain, nothing which had taken place at the date of the last despatches enables us to pronounce. On the western side of the Mississippi she advanced in considerable force, and took post at the settlement of Bayou Pierre, on the Red river. This village was originally settled by France, was held by her as long as she held Louisiana, and was delivered to Spain only as a part of Louisiana. Being small, insulated, and distant, it was not observed, at the moment of redelivery to France and the United States, that she continued a guard of half a dozen men which had been stationed there. A proposition, however, having been lately made by our commander-in-chief, to assume the Sabine river as a temporary line of separation between the troops of the two nations until the issue of our negotiation shall be known; this has been referred by the Spanish commandant to his superior, and in the meantime, he has withdrawn his force to the western side of the Sabine river. The correspondence on this subject, now communicated, will exhibit more particularly the present state of things in that quarter.

The nature of that country requires indispensably that an unusual proportion of the force employed there should be cavalry or mounted infantry. In order, therefore, that the commanding officer might be enabled to act with effect, I had authorized him to call on the governors of Orleans and Mississippi for a corps of five hundred volunteer cavalry. The temporary arrangement he has proposed may perhaps render this unnecessary. But I inform you with great pleasure of the promptitude with which the inhabitants of those territories have tendered their services in defence of their country. It has done honor to themselves, entitled them to the confidence of their fellow-citizens in every part of the Union, and must strengthen the general determination to protect them efficaciously under all circumstances which may occur.

Having received information that in another part of the United States a great number of private individuals were combining together, arming and organizing themselves contrary to law, to carry on military expeditions against the territories of Spain, I thought it necessary, by proclamations as well as by special orders, to take measures for preventing and suppressing this enterprise, for seizing the vessels, arms, and other means provided for it, and for arresting and bringing to justice its authors and abettors. It was due to that good faith which ought ever to be the rule of action in public as well as in private transactions; it was due to good order and regular governments, that while the public force was acting strictly on the defensive and merely to protect our citizens from aggression, the criminal attempts of private individuals to decide for their country the question of peace or war, by commencing active and unauthorized hostilities, should be promptly and efficaciously suppressed.

Whether it will be necessary to enlarge our regular force will depend on the result of our negotiation with Spain; but as it is uncertain when that result will be known, the provisional measures requisite for that, and to meet any pressure intervening in that quarter, will be a subject for your early consideration.

The possession of both banks of the Mississippi reducing to a single point the defence of that river, its waters, and the country adjacent, it becomes highly necessary to provide for that point a more adequate security. Some position above its mouth, commanding the passage of the river, should be rendered sufficiently strong to cover the armed vessels which may be stationed there for defence, and in conjunction with them to present an insuperable obstacle to any force attempting to pass. The approaches to the city of New Orleans, from the eastern quarter also, will require to be examined, and more effectually guarded. For the internal support of the country, the encouragement of a strong settlement on the western side of the Mississippi, within reach of New Orleans, will be worthy the consideration of the legislature.

The gun-boats authorized by an act of the last session are so advanced that they will be ready for service in the ensuing spring. Circumstances permitted us to allow the time necessary for their more solid construction. As a much larger number will still be wanting to place our seaport towns and waters in that state of defence to which we are competent and they entitled, a similar appropriation for a further provision for them is recommended for the ensuing year.

A further appropriation will also be necessary for repairing fortifications already established, and the erection of such works as may have real effect in obstructing the approach of an enemy to our seaport towns, or their remaining before them.

In a country whose constitution is derived from the will of the people, directly expressed by their free suffrages; where the principal executive functionaries, and those of the legislature, are renewed by them at short periods; where under the characters of jurors, they exercise in person the greatest portion of the judiciary powers; where the laws are consequently so formed and administered as to bear with equal weight and favor on all, restraining no man in the pursuits of honest industry, and securing to everyone the property which that acquires, it would not be supposed that any safeguards could be needed against insurrection or enterprise on the public peace or authority. The laws, however, aware that these should not be trusted to moral restraints only, have wisely provided punishments for these crimes when committed. But would it not be salutary to give also the means of preventing their commission? Where an enterprise is meditated by private individuals against a foreign nation in amity with the United States, powers of prevention to a certain extent are given by the laws; would they not be as reasonable and useful were the enterprise preparing against the United States? While adverting to this branch of the law, it is proper to observe, that in enterprises meditated against foreign nations, the ordinary process of binding to the observance of the peace and good behavior, could it be extended to acts to be done out of the jurisdiction of the United States, would be effectual in some cases where the offender is able to keep out of sight every indication of his purpose which could draw on him the exercise of the powers now given by law.

The states on the coast of Barbary seem generally disposed at present to respect our peace and friendship; with Tunis alone some uncertainty remains. Persuaded that it is our interest to maintain our peace with them on equal terms, or not at all, I propose to send in due time a reinforcement into the Mediterranean, unless previous information shall show it to be unnecessary.

We continue to receive proofs of the growing attachment of our Indian neighbors, and of their disposition to place all their interests under the patronage of the United States. These dispositions are inspired by their confidence in our justice, and in the sincere concern we feel for their welfare; and as long as we discharge these high and honorable functions with the integrity and good faith which alone can entitle us to their continuance, we may expect to reap the just reward in their peace and friendship.

The expedition of Messrs. Lewis and Clarke, for exploring the river Missouri, and the best communication from that to the Pacific ocean, has had all the success which could have been expected. They have traced the Missouri nearly to its source, descended the Columbia to the Pacific ocean, ascertained with accuracy the geography of that interesting communication across our continent, learned the character of the country, of its commerce, and inhabitants; and it is but justice to say that Messrs. Lewis and Clarke, and their brave companions, have by this arduous service deserved well of their country.

The attempt to explore the Red river, under the direction of Mr. Freeman, though conducted with a zeal and prudence meriting entire approbation, has not been equally successful. After proceeding up it about six hundred miles, nearly as far as the French settlements had extended while the country was in their possession, our geographers were obliged to return without completing their work.

Very useful additions have also been made to our knowledge of the Mississippi by Lieutenant Pike, who has ascended to its source, and whose journal and map, giving the details of the journey, will shortly be ready for communication to both houses of Congress. Those of Messrs. Lewis and Clarke, and Freeman, will require further time to be digested and prepared. These important surveys, in addition to those before possessed, furnish materials for commencing an accurate map of the Mississippi, and its western waters. Some principal rivers, however, remain still to be explored, toward which the authorization of Congress, by moderate appropriations, will be requisite.

I congratulate you, fellow citizens, on the approach of the period at which you may interpose your authority constitutionally, to withdraw the citizens of the United States from all further participation in those violations of human rights which have been so long continued on the unoffending inhabitants of Africa, and which the morality, the reputation, and the best interests of our country, have long been eager to proscribe. Although no law you may pass can take prohibitory effect till the first day of the year one thousand eight hundred and eight, yet the intervening period is not too long to prevent, by timely notice, expeditions which cannot be completed before that day.

The receipts at the treasury during the year ending on the 30th of September last, have amounted to near fifteen millions of dollars, which have enabled us, after meeting the current demands, to pay two millions seven hundred thousand dollars of the American claims, in parts of the price of Louisiana; to pay of the funded debt upward of three millions of principal, and nearly four of interest; and in addition, to reimburse, in the course of the present month, near two millions of five and a half per cent stock. These payments and reimbursements of the funded debt, with those which have been made in four years and a half preceding, will, at the close of the present year, have extinguished upward of twenty-three millions of principal.

The duties composing the Mediterranean fund will cease by law at the end of the present season. Considering, however, that they are levied chiefly on luxuries, and that we have an impost on salt, a necessary of life, the free use of which otherwise is so important, I recommend to your consideration the suppression of the duties on salt, and the continuation of the Mediterranean fund, instead thereof, for a short time, after which that also will become unnecessary for any purpose now within contemplation.

When both of these branches of revenue shall in this way be relinquished, there will still ere long be an accumulation of moneys in the treasury beyond the instalments of public debt which we are permitted by contract to pay. They cannot, then, without a modification assented to by the public creditors, be applied to the extinguishment of this debt, and the complete liberation of our revenues—the most desirable of all objects; nor, if our peace continues, will they be wanting for any other existing purpose. The question, therefore, now comes forward,—to what other objects shall these surpluses be appropriated, and the whole surplus of impost, after the entire discharge of the public debt, and during those intervals when the purposes of war shall not call for them? Shall we suppress the impost and give that advantage to foreign over domestic manufactures? On a few articles of more general and necessary use, the suppression in due season will doubtless be right, but the great mass of the articles on which impost is paid is foreign luxuries, purchased by those only who are rich enough to afford themselves the use of them. Their patriotism would certainly prefer its continuance and application to the great purposes of the public education, roads, rivers, canals, and such other objects of public improvement as it may be thought proper to add to the constitutional enumeration of federal powers. By these operations new channels of communication will be opened between the States; the lines of separation will disappear, their interests will be identified, and their union cemented by new and indissoluble ties. Education is here placed among the articles of public care, not that it would be proposed to take its ordinary branches out of the hands of private enterprise, which manages so much better all the concerns to which it is equal; but a public institution can alone supply those sciences which, though rarely called for, are yet necessary to complete the circle, all the parts of which contribute to the improvement of the country, and some of them to its preservation. The subject is now proposed for the consideration of Congress, because, if approved by the time the State legislatures shall have deliberated on this extension of the federal trusts, and the laws shall be passed, and other arrangements made for their execution, the necessary funds will be on hand and without employment. I suppose an amendment to the constitution, by consent of the States, necessary, because the objects now recommended are not among those enumerated in the constitution, and to which it permits the public moneys to be applied.

The present consideration of a national establishment for education, particularly, is rendered proper by this circumstance also, that if Congress, approving the proposition, shall yet think it more eligible to found it on a donation of lands, they have it now in their power to endow it with those which will be among the earliest to produce the necessary income. This foundation would have the advantage of being independent on war, which may suspend other improvements by requiring for its own purposes the resources destined for them.

This, fellow citizens, is the state of the public interest at the present moment, and according to the information now possessed. But such is the situation of the nations of Europe, and such too the predicament in which we stand with some of them, that we cannot rely with certainty on the present aspect of our affairs that may change from moment to moment, during the course of your session or after you shall have separated. Our duty is, therefore, to act upon things as they are, and to make a reasonable provision for whatever they may be. Were armies to be raised whenever a speck of war is visible in our horizon, we never should have been without them. Our resources would have been exhausted on dangers which have never happened, instead of being reserved for what is really to take place. A steady, perhaps a quickened pace in preparations for the defence of our seaport towns and waters; an early settlement of the most exposed and vulnerable parts of our country; a militia so organized that its effective portions can be called to any point in the Union, or volunteers instead of them to serve a sufficient time, are means which may always be ready yet never preying on our resources until actually called into use. They will maintain the public interests while a more permanent force shall be in course of preparation. But much will depend on the promptitude with which these means can be brought into activity. If war be forced upon us in spite of our long and vain appeals to the justice of nations, rapid and vigorous movements in its outset will go far toward securing us in its course and issue, and toward throwing its burdens on those who render necessary the resort from reason to force.

The result of our negotiations, or such incidents in their course as may enable us to infer their probable issue; such further movements also on our western frontiers as may show whether war is to be pressed there while negotiation is protracted elsewhere, shall be communicated to you from time to time as they become known to me, with whatever other information I possess or may receive, which may aid your deliberations on the great national interests committed to your charge.

SPECIAL MESSAGE

January 22, 1807

TO THE SENATE AND HOUSE OF REPRESENTATIVES OF THE UNITED STATES: Agreeably to the request of the House of Representatives, communicated in their resolution of the sixteenth instant, I proceed to state under the reserve therein expressed, information received touching an illegal combination of private individuals against the peace and safety of the Union, and a military expedition planned by them against the territories of a power in amity with the United States, with the measures I have pursued for suppressing the same.

I had for some time been in the constant expectation of receiving such further information as would have enabled me to lay before the legislature the termination as well as the beginning and progress of this scene of depravity, so far as it has been acted on the Ohio and its waters. From this the state and safety of the lower country might have been estimated on probable grounds, and the delay was indulged the rather, because no circumstance had yet made it necessary to call in the aid of the legislative functions. Information now recently communicated has brought us nearly to the period contemplated. The mass of what I have received, in the course of these transactions, is voluminous, but little has been given under the sanction of an oath, so as to constitute formal and legal evidence. It is chiefly in the form of letters, often containing such a mixture of rumors, conjectures, and suspicions, as render it difficult to sift out the real facts, and unadvisable to hazard more than general outlines, strengthened by concurrent information, or the particular credibility of the relater. In this state of the evidence, delivered sometimes too under the restriction of private confidence, neither safety nor justice will permit the exposing names, except that of the principal actor, whose guilt is placed beyond question.

Some time in the latter part of September, I received intimations that designs were in agitation in the western country, unlawful and unfriendly to the peace of the Union; and that the prime mover in these was Aaron Burr, heretofore distinguished by the favor of his country. The grounds of these intimations being inconclusive, the objects uncertain, and the fidelity of that country known to be firm, the only measure taken was to urge the informants to use their best endeavors to get further insight into the designs and proceedings of the suspected persons, and to communicate them to me.

It was not until the latter part of October, that the objects of the conspiracy began to be perceived, but still so blended and involved in mystery that nothing distinct could be singled out for pursuit. In this state of uncertainty as to the crime contemplated, the acts done, and the legal course to be pursued, I thought it best to send to the scene where these things were principally in transaction, a person, in whose integrity, understanding, and discretion, entire confidence could be reposed, with instructions to investigate the plots going on, to enter into conference (for which he had sufficient credentials) with the governors and all other officers, civil and military, and with their aid to do on the spot whatever should be necessary to discover the designs of the conspirators, arrest their means, bring their persons to punishment, and to call out the force of the country to suppress any unlawful enterprise in which it should be found they were engaged. By this time it was known that many boats were under preparation, stores of provisions collecting, and an unusual number of suspicious characters in motion on the Ohio. and its waters. Besides despatching the confidential agent to that quarter, orders were at the same time sent to the governors of the Orleans and Mississippi territories, and to the commanders of the land and naval forces there, to be on their guard against surprise, and in constant readiness to resist any enterprise which might be attempted on the vessels, posts, or other objects under their care; and on the 8th of November, instructions were forwarded to General Wilkinson to hasten an accommodation with the Spanish commander on the Sabine, and as soon as that was effected, to fall back with his principal force to the hither bank of the Mississippi, for the defence of the intersecting points on that river. By a letter received from that officer on the 25th of November, but dated October 21st, we learn that a confidential agent of Aaron Burr had been deputed to him, with communications partly written in cipher and partly oral, explaining his designs, exaggerating his resources, and making such offers of emolument and command, to engage him and the army in his unlawful enterprise, as he had flattered himself would be successful. The general, with the honor of a soldier and fidelity of a good citizen, immediately despatched a trusty officer to me with information of what had passed, proceeding to establish such an understanding with the Spanish commandant on the Sabine as permitted him to withdraw his force across the Mississippi, and to enter on measures for opposing the projected enterprise.

The general's letter, which came to hand on the 25th of November, as has been mentioned, and some other information received a few days earlier, when brought together, developed Burr's general designs, different parts of which only had been revealed to different informants. It appeared that he contemplated two distinct objects, which might be carried on either jointly or separately, and either the one or the other first, as circumstances should direct. One of these was the severance of the Union of these States by the Alleghany mountains; the other, an attack on Mexico. A third object was provided, merely ostensible, to wit: the settlement of a pretended purchase of a tract of country on the Washita, claimed by a Baron Bastrop. This was to serve as the pretext for all his preparations, an allurement for such followers as really wished to acquire settlements in that country, and a cover under which to retreat in the event of final discomfiture of both branches of his real design.

He found at once that the attachment of the western country to the present Union was not to be shaken; that its dissolution could not be effected with the consent of its inhabitants, and that his resources were inadequate, as yet, to effect it by force. He took his course then at once, determined to seize on New Orleans, plunder the bank there, possess himself of the military and naval stores, and proceed on his expedition to Mexico; and to this object all his means and preparations were now directed. He collected from all the quarters where himself or his agents possessed influence, all the ardent, restless, desperate, and disaffected persons who were ready for any enterprise analogous to their characters. He seduced good and well-meaning citizens, some by assurances that he possessed the confidence of the government and was acting under its secret patronage, a pretence which obtained some credit from the state of our differences with Spain; and others by offers of land in Bastrop's claim on the Washita.

This was the state of my information of his proceedings about the last of November, at which time, therefore, it was first possible to take specific measures to meet them. The proclamation of November 27th, two days after the receipt of General Wilkinson's information, was now issued. Orders were despatched to every intersecting point on the Ohio and Mississippi, from Pittsburg to New Orleans, for the employment of such force either of the regulars or of the militia, and of such proceedings also of the civil authorities, as might enable them to seize on all the boats and stores provided for the enterprise, to arrest the persons concerned, and to suppress effectually the further progress of the enterprise. A little before the receipt of these orders in the State of Ohio, our confidential agent, who had been diligently employed in investigating the conspiracy, had acquired sufficient information to open himself to the governor of that State, and apply for the immediate exertion of the authority and power of the State to crush the combination. Governor Tiffin and the legislature, with a promptitude, an energy, and patriotic zeal, which entitle them to a distinguished place in the affection of their sister States, effected the seizure of all the boats, provisions, and other preparations within their reach, and thus gave a first blow, materially disabling the enterprise in its outset.

In Kentucky, a premature attempt to bring Burr to justice, without sufficient evidence for his conviction, had produced a popular impression in his favor, and a general disbelief of his guilt. This gave him an unfortunate opportunity of hastening his equipments. The arrival of the proclamation and orders, and the application and information of our confidential agent, at length awakened the authorities of that State to the truth, and then produced the same promptitude and energy of which the neighboring State had set the example. Under an act of their legislature of December 23d, militia was instantly ordered to different important points, and measures taken for doing whatever could yet be done. Some boats (accounts vary from five to double or treble that number) and persons (differently estimated from one to three hundred) had in the meantime passed the falls of the Ohio, to rendezvous at the mouth of the Cumberland, with others expected down that river.

Not apprized, till very late, that any boats were building on Cumberland, the effect of the proclamation had been trusted to for some time in the State of Tennessee; but on the 19th of December, similar communications and instructions with those of the neighboring States were despatched by express to the governor and a general officer of the western division of the State, and on the 23d of December our confidential agent left Frankfort for Nashville, to put into activity the means of that State also. But by information received yesterday, I learn that on the 22d of December, Mr. Burr descended the Cumberland with two boats merely of accommodation, carrying with him from that State no quota toward his unlawful enterprise. Whether after the arrival of the proclamation, of the orders, or of our agent, any exertion which could be made by that State, or the orders of the governor of Kentucky for calling out the militia at the mouth of Cumberland, would be in time to arrest these boats, and those from the falls of the Ohio, is still doubtful.

On the whole, the fugitives from Ohio, with their associates from Cumberland, or any other place in that quarter, cannot threaten serious danger to the city of New Orleans.

By the same express of December nineteenth, orders were sent to the governors of New Orleans and Mississippi, supplementary to those which had been given on the twenty-fifth of November, to hold the militia of their territories in readiness to co-operate for their defence, with the regular troops and armed vessels then under command of General Wilkinson. Great alarm, indeed, was excited at New Orleans by the exaggerated accounts of Mr. Burr, disseminated through his emissaries, of the armies and navies he was to assemble there. General Wilkinson had arrived there himself on the 24th of November, and had immediately put into activity the resources of the place for the purpose of its defence; and on the tenth of December he was joined by his troops from the Sabine. Great zeal was shown by the inhabitants generally, the merchants of the place readily agreeing to the most laudable exertions and sacrifices for manning the armed vessels with their seamen, and the other citizens manifesting unequivocal fidelity to the Union, and a spirit of determined resistance to their expected assailants.

Surmises have been hazarded that this enterprise is to receive aid from certain foreign powers. But these surmises are without proof or probability. The wisdom of the measures sanctioned by Congress at its last session had placed us in the paths of peace and justice with the only powers with whom we had any differences, and nothing has happened since which makes it either their interest or ours to pursue another course. No change of measures has taken place on our part; none ought to take place at this time. With the one, friendly arrangement was then proposed, and the law deemed necessary on the failure of that was suspended to give time for a fair trial of the issue. With the same power, negotiation is still preferred, and provisional measures only are necessary to meet the event of rupture. While, therefore, we do not deflect in the slightest degree from the course we then assumed, and are still pursuing, with mutual consent, to restore a good understanding, we are not to impute to them practices as irreconcilable to interest as to good faith, and changing necessarily the relations of peace and justice between us to those of war. These surmises are, therefore, to be imputed to the vauntings of the author of this enterprise, to multiply his partisans by magnifying the belief of his prospects and support.

By letters from General Wilkinson, of the 14th and 18th of September, which came to hand two days after date of the resolution of the House of Representatives, that is to say, on the morning of the 18th instant, I received the important affidavit, a copy of which I now communicate, with extracts of so much of the letters as come within the scope of the resolution. By these it will be seen that of three of the principal emissaries of Mr. Burr, whom the general had caused to be apprehended, one had been liberated by *habeas corpus,* and the two others, being those particularly employed in the endeavor to corrupt the general and army of the United States, have been embarked by him for our ports in the Atlantic States, probably on the consideration that an impartial trial could not be expected during the present agitations of New Orleans, and that that city was not as yet a safe place of confinement. As soon as these persons shall arrive, they will be delivered to the custody of the law, and left to such course of trial, both as to place and process, as its functionaries may direct. The presence of the highest judicial authorities, to be assembled at this place within a few days, the means of pursuing a sounder course of proceedings here than elsewhere, and the aid of the executive means, should the judges have occasion to use them, render it equally desirable for the criminals as for the public, that being already removed from the place where they were first apprehended, the first regular arrest should take place here, and the course of proceedings receive here its proper direction.

SPECIAL MESSAGE
February 10, 1807

TO THE SENATE AND HOUSE OF REPRESENTATIVES OF THE UNITED STATES: In compliance with the request of the House of Representatives, expressed in their resolution of the 5th instant, I proceed to give such information as is possessed, of the effect of gun-boats in the protection and defence of harbors, of the numbers thought necessary, and of the proposed distribution of them among the ports and harbors of the United States.

Under the present circumstances, and governed by the intentions of the legislature, as manifested by their annual appropriations of money for the purposes of defence, it has been concluded to combine—1st, land batteries, furnished with heavy cannon and mortars, and established on all the points around the place favorable for preventing vessels from lying before it; 2d, movable artillery which may be carried, as an occasion may require, to points unprovided with fixed.batteries; 3d, floating batteries; and 4th, gun-boats, which may oppose an enemy at its entrance and co-operate with the batteries for his expulsion.

On this subject professional men were consulted as far as we had opportunity. General Wilkinson, and the late General Gates, gave their opinions in writing, in favor of the system, as will be seen by their letters now communicated. The higher officers of the navy gave the same opinions in separate conferences, as their presence at the seat of government offered occasions of consulting them, and no difference of judgment appeared on the subjects. Those of Commodore Barron and Captain Tingey, now here, are recently furnished in writing, and transmitted herewith to the legislature.

The efficacy of gun-boats for the defence of harbors, and of other smooth and enclosed waters, may be estimated in part from that of galleys, formerly much used, but less powerful, more costly in their construction and maintenance, and requiring more men. But the gun-boat itself is believed to be in use with every modern maritime nation for the purpose of defence. In the Mediterranean, on which are several small powers, whose system like ours is peace and defence, few harbors are without this article of protection. Our own experience there of the effect of gun-boats for harbor service, is recent. Algiers is particularly known to have owed to a great provision of these vessels the safety of its city, since the epoch of their construction. Before that it had been repeatedly insulted and injured. The effect of gun-boats at present in the neighborhood of Gibraltar, is well known, and how much they were used both in the attack and defence of that place during a former war. The extensive resort to them by the two greatest naval powers in the world, on an enterprise of invasion not long since in prospect, shows their confidence in their efficacy for the purposes for which they are suited. By the northern powers of Europe, whose seas are particularly adapted to them, they are still more used. The remarkable action between the Russian flotilla of gun-boats and galleys, and a Turkish fleet of ships-of-the-line and frigates, in the Liman sea, 1788, will be readily recollected. The latter, commanded by their most celebrated admiral, were completely defeated, and several of their ships-of-the-line destroyed.

From the opinions given as to the number of gun-boats necessary for some of the principal seaports, and from a view of all the towns and ports from Orleans to Maine inclusive, entitled to protection, in proportion to their situation and circumstances, it is concluded, that to give them a due measure of protection in time of war, about two hundred gun-boats will be requisite. According to first ideas, the following would be their general distribution, liable to be varied on more mature examination, and as circumstances shall vary, that is to say:

To the Mississippi and its neighboring waters, forty gun-boats.

To Savannah and Charleston, and the harbors on each side, from St. Mary's to Currituck, twenty-five.

To the Chesapeake and its waters, twenty.

To Delaware bay and river, fifteen.

To New York, the Sound, and waters as far as Cape Cod, fifty.

To Boston and the harbors north of Cape Cod, fifty.

The flotilla assigned to these several stations, might each be under the care of a particular commandant, and the vessels composing them would, in ordinary, be distributed among the harbors within the station in proportion to their importance.

Of these boats a proper proportion would be of the larger size, such as those heretofore built, capable of navigating any seas, and of reinforcing occasionally the strength of even the most distant port when menaced with danger. The residue would be confined to their own or the neighboring harbors, would be smaller, less furnished for accommodation, and consequently less costly. Of the number supposed necessary, seventy-three are built or building, and the hundred and twenty-seven still to be provided, would cost from five to six hundred thousand dollars. Having regard to the convenience of the treasury, as well as to the resources of building, it has been thought that one half of these might be built in the present year, and the other year the next. With the legislature, however, it will rest to stop where we are, or at any further point, when they shall be of opinion that the number provided shall be sufficient for the object.

At times when Europe as well as the United States shall be at peace, it would not be proposed that more than six or eight of these vessels should be kept afloat. When Europe is in war, treble that number might be necessary to be distributed among those particular harbors which foreign vessels of war are in the habit of frequenting, for the purpose of preserving order therein.

But they would be manned, in ordinary, with only their complement for navigation, relying on the seamen and militia of the port if called into action on sudden emergency. It would be only when the United States should themselves be at war, that the whole number would be brought into actual service, and would be ready in the first moments of the war to co-operate with other means for covering at once the line of our seaports. At all times, those unemployed would be withdrawn into places not exposed to sudden enterprise, hauled up under sheds from the sun and weather, and kept in preservation with little expense for repairs or maintenance.

It must be superfluous to observe, that this species of naval armament is proposed merely for defensive operation; that it can have but little effect toward protecting our commerce in the open seas even on our coast; and still less can it become an excitement to engage in offensive maritime war, toward which it would furnish no means.

SEVENTH ANNUAL MESSAGE
October 27, 1807

TO THE SENATE AND HOUSE OF REPRESENTATIVES OF THE UNITED STATES: Circumstances, fellow citizens, which seriously threatened the peace of our country, have made it a duty to convene you at an earlier period than usual. The love of peace, so much cherished in the bosoms of our citizens, which has so long guided the proceedings of the public councils, and induced forbearance under so many wrongs, may not insure our continuance in the quiet pursuits of industry. The many injuries and depredations committed on our commerce and navigation upon the high seas for years past, the successive innovations on those principles of public law which have been established by the reason and usage of nations as the rule of their intercourse, and the umpire and security of their rights and peace, and all the circumstances which induced the extraordinary mission to London, are already known to you. The instructions given to our ministers were framed in the sincerest spirit of amity and moderation. They accordingly proceeded, in conformity therewith, to propose arrangements which might embrace and settle all the points in difference between us, which might bring us to a mutual understanding on our neutral and national rights, and provide for a commercial intercourse on conditions of some equality. After long and fruitless endeavors to effect the purposes of their mission, and to obtain arrangements within the limits of their instructions, they concluded to sign such as could be obtained, and to send them for consideration, candidly declaring to the other negotiators, at the same time, that they were acting against their instructions, and that their government, therefore, could not be pledged for ratification. Some of the articles proposed might have been admitted on a principle of compromise, but others were too highly disadvantageous, and no sufficient provision was made against the principal source of the irritations and collisions which were constantly endangering the peace of the two nations. The question, therefore, whether a treaty should be accepted in that form could have admitted but of one decision, even had no declarations of the other party impaired our confidence in it. Still anxious not to close the door against friendly adjustment, new modifications were framed, and further concessions authorized than could before have been supposed necessary; and our ministers were instructed to resume their negotiations on these grounds. On this new reference to amicable discussion, we were reposing in confidence, when on the 22d day of June last, by a formal order from the British admiral, the frigate Chesapeake, leaving her port for distant service, was attacked by one of those vessels which had been lying in our harbors under the indulgences of hospitality, was disabled from proceeding, had several of her crew killed, and four taken away. On this outrage no commentaries are necessary. Its character has been pronounced by the indignant voice of our citizens with an emphasis and unanimity never exceeded. I immediately, by proclamation, interdicted our harbors and waters to all British armed vessels, forbade intercourse with them, and uncertain how far hostilities were intended, and the town of Norfolk, indeed, being threatened with immediate attack, a sufficient force was ordered for the protection of that place, and such other preparations commenced and pursued as the prospect rendered proper. An armed vessel of the United States was despatched with instructions to our ministers at London to call on that government for the satisfaction and security required by the outrage. A very short interval ought now to bring the answer, which shall be communicated to you as soon as received; then also, or as soon after as the public interests shall be found to admit, the unratified treaty, and the proceedings relative to it, shall be made known to you.

The aggression thus begun has been continued on the part of the British commanders, by remaining within our waters, in defiance of the authority of the country, by habitual violations of its jurisdiction, and at length by putting to death one of the persons whom they had forcibly taken from on board the Chesapeake. These aggravations necessarily lead to the policy, either of never admitting an armed vessel into our harbors, or of maintaining in every harbor such an armed force as may constrain obedience to the laws, and protect the lives and property of our citizens, against their armed guests. But the expense of such a standing force, and its inconsistence with our principles, dispense with those courtesies which would necessarily call for it, and leave us equally free to exclude the navy, as we are the army, of a foreign power, from entering our limits.

To former violations of maritime rights, another is now added of very extensive effect. The government of that nation has issued an order interdicting all trade by neutrals between ports not in amity with them; and being now at war with nearly every nation on the Atlantic and Mediterranean seas, our vessels are required to sacrifice their cargoes at the first port they touch, or to return home without the benefit of going to any other market. Under this new law of the ocean, our trade on the Mediterranean has been swept away by seizures and condemnations, and that in other seas is threatened with the same fate.

Our differences with Spain remain still unsettled; no measure having been taken on her part, since my last communication to Congress, to bring them to a close. But under a state of things which may favor a reconsideration, they have been recently pressed, and an expectation is entertained that they may now soon be brought to an issue of some sort. With their subjects on our borders, no new collisions have taken place nor seem immediately to be apprehended. To our former grounds of complaint has been added a very serious one, as you will see by the decree, a copy of which is now communicated. Whether this decree, which professes to be conformable to that of the French government of November 21st, 1806, heretofore communicated to Congress, will also be conformed to that in its construction and application in relation to the United States, had not been ascertained at the date of our last communications. These, however, gave reason to expect such a conformity.

With the other nations of Europe our harmony has been uninterrupted, and commerce and friendly intercourse have been maintained on their usual footing.

Our peace with the several States on the coast of Barbary appears as firm as at any former period, and is as likely to continue as that of any other nation.

Among our Indian neighbors in the north-western quarter, some fermentation was observed soon after the late occurrences, threatening the continuance of our peace. Messages were said to be interchanged, and tokens to be passing, which usually denote a state of restlessness among them, and the character of the agitators pointed to the sources of excitement. Measures were immediately taken for providing against that danger; instructions were given to require explanations, and with assurances of our continued friendship, to admonish the tribes to remain quiet at home, taking no part in quarrels not belonging to them. As far as we are yet informed, the tribes in our vicinity, who are most advanced in the pursuits of industry, are sincerely disposed to adhere to their friendship with us, and to their peace with all others; while those more remote do not present appearances sufficiently quiet to justify the intermission of military precaution on our part.

The great tribes on our south-western quarter, much advanced beyond the others in agriculture and household arts, appear tranquil, and identifying their views with ours, in proportion to their advancement. With the whole of these people, in every quarter, I shall continue to inculcate peace and friendship with all their neighbors, and perseverance in those occupations and pursuits which will best promote their own well-being.

The appropriations of the last session, for the defence of our seaport towns and harbors, were made under expectation that a continuance of our peace would permit us to proceed in that work according to our convenience. It has been thought better to apply the sums then given, toward the defence of New York, Charleston, and New Orleans chiefly, as most open and most likely first to need protection; and to leave places less immediately in danger to the provisions of the present session.

The gun-boats, too, already provided, have on a like principle been chiefly assigned to New York, New Orleans, and the Chesapeake. Whether our movable force on the water, so material in aid of the defensive works on the land, should be augmented in this or any other form, is left to the wisdom of the legislature. For the purpose of manning these vessels in sudden attacks on our harbors, it is a matter for consideration, whether the seamen of the United States may not justly be formed into a special militia, to be called on for tours of duty in defence of the harbors where they shall happen to be; the ordinary militia of the place furnishing that portion which may consist of landsmen.

The moment our peace was threatened, I deemed it indispensable to secure a greater provision of those articles of military stores with which our magazines were not sufficiently furnished. To have awaited a previous and special sanction by law would have lost occasions which might not be retrieved. I did not hesitate, therefore, to authorize engagements for such supplements to our existing stock as would render it adequate to the emergencies threatening us; and I trust that the legislature, feeling the same anxiety for the safety of our country, so materially advanced by this precaution, will approve, when done, what they would have seen so important to be done if then assembled. Expenses, also unprovided for, arose out of the necessity of calling all our gun-boats into actual service for the defence of our harbors; of all which accounts will be laid before you.

Whether a regular army is to be raised, and to what extent, must depend on the information so shortly expected. In the meantime, I have called on the States for quotas of militia, to be in readiness for present defence; and have, moreover, encouraged the acceptance of volunteers; and I am happy to inform you that these have offered themselves with great alacrity in every part of the Union. They are ordered to be organized, and ready at a moment's warning to proceed on any service to which they may be called, and every preparation within the executive powers has been made to insure us the benefit of early exertions.

I informed Congress at their last session of the enterprises against the public peace, which were believed to be in preparation by Aaron Burr and his associates, of the measures taken to defeat them, and to bring the offenders to justice. Their enterprises were happily defeated by the patriotic exertions of the militia wherever called into action, by the fidelity of the army, and energy of the commander-in-chief in promptly arranging the difficulties presenting themselves on the Sabine, repairing to meet those arising on the Mississippi, and dissipating, before their explosion, plots engendering there. I shall think it my duty to lay before you the proceedings and the evidence publicly exhibited on the arraignment of the principal offenders before the circuit court of Virginia. You will be enabled to judge whether the defeat was in the testimony, in the law, or in the administration of the law; and wherever it shall be found, the legislature alone can apply or originate the remedy. The framers of our constitution certainly supposed they had guarded, as well their government against destruction by treason, as their citizens against oppression, under pretence of it; and if these ends are not attained, it is of importance to inquire by what means, more effectual, they may be secured.

The accounts of the receipts of revenue, during the year ending on the thirtieth day of September last, being not yet made up, a correct statement will be hereafter transmitted from the treasury. In the meantime, it is ascertained that the receipts have amounted to near sixteen millions of dollars, which, with the five millions and a half in the treasury at the beginning of the year, have enabled us, after meeting the current demands and interest incurred, to pay more than four millions of the principal of our funded debt. These payments, with those of the preceding five and a half years, have extinguished of the funded debt twenty-five millions and a half of dollars, being the whole which could be paid or purchased within the limits of the law and of our contracts, and have left us in the treasury eight millions and a half of dollars. A portion of this sum may be considered as a commencement of accumulation of the surpluses of revenue, which, after paying the instalments of debts as they shall become payable, will remain without any specific object. It may partly, indeed, be applied toward completing the defence of the exposed points of our country, on such a scale as shall be adapted to our principles and circumstances. This object is doubtless among the first entitled to attention, in such a state of our finances, and it is one which, whether we have peace or war, will provide security where it is due. Whether what shall remain of this, with the future surpluses, may be usefully applied to purposes already authorized, or more usefully to others requiring new authorities, or how otherwise they shall be disposed of, are questions calling for the notice of Congress, unless indeed they shall be superseded by a change in our public relations now awaiting the determination of others. Whatever be that determination, it is a great consolation that it will become known at a moment when the supreme council of the nation is assembled at its post, and ready to give the aids of its wisdom and authority to whatever course the good of our country shall then call us to pursue.

Matters of minor importance will be the subjects of future communications; and nothing shall be wanting on my part which may give information or despatch to the proceedings of the legislature in the exercise of their high duties, and at a moment so interesting to the public welfare.

SPECIAL MESSAGE
January 20, 1808

TO THE HOUSE OF REPRESENTATIVES OF THE UNITED STATES: Some days previous to your resolution of the 13th instant, a court of inquiry had been instituted at the request of General Wilkinson, charged to make the inquiry into his conduct which the first resolution desires, and had commenced their proceedings. To the judge-advocate of that court the papers and information on that subject, transmitted to me by the House of Representatives, have been delivered, to be used according to the rules and powers of that court.

The request of a communication of any information, which may have been received at any time since the establishment of the present government, touching combinations with foreign nations for dismembering the Union, or the corrupt receipt of money by any officer of the United States from the agents of foreign governments, can be complied with but in a partial degree.

It is well understood that, in the first or second year of the presidency of

General Washington, information was given to him relating to certain combinations with the agents of a foreign government for the dismemberment of the Union; which combinations had taken place before the establishment of the present federal government. This information, however, is believed never to have been deposited in any public office, or left in that of the president's secretary, these having been duly examined, but to have been considered as personally confidential, and, therefore, retained among his private papers. A communication from the governor of Virginia to General Washington, is found in the office of the president's secretary, which, although not strictly within the terms of the request of the House of Representatives, is communicated, inasmuch as it may throw some light on the subjects of the correspondence of that time, between certain foreign agents and citizens of the United States.

In the first or second year of the administration of President Adams, Andrew Ellicott, then employed in designating, in conjunction with the Spanish authorities, the boundaries between the territories of the United States and Spain, under the treaty with that nation, communicated to the executive of the Untied States papers and information respecting the subjects of the present inquiry, which were deposited in the office of State. Copies of these are now transmitted to the House of Representatives, except of a single letter and a reference from the said Andrew Ellicott, which being expressly desired to be kept secret, is therefore not communicated, but its contents can be obtained from himself in a more legal form, and directions have been given to summon him to appear as a witness before the court of inquiry.

A paper "on the commerce of Louisiana," bearing date of the 18th of April, 1798, is found in the office of State, supposed to have been communicated by Mr. Daniel Clark, of New Orleans, then a subject of Spain, and now of the House of Representatives of the United States, stating certain commercial transactions of General Wilkinson, in New Orleans; an extract from this is now communicated, because it contains facts which may have some bearing on the questions relating to him.

The destruction of the war-office, by fire, in the close of 1800, involved all information it contained at that date.

The papers already described, therefore, constitute the whole information on the subjects, deposited in the public offices, during the preceding administrations, as far as has yet been found; but it cannot be affirmed that there may be no others, because, the papers of the office being filed, for the most part, alphabetically, unless aided by the suggestion of any particular name which may have given such information, nothing short of a careful examination of the papers in the offices generally, could authorize such affirmation.

About a twelvemonth after I came to the administration of the government, Mr. Clark gave some verbal information to myself, as well as to the Secretary of State, relating to the same combinations for the dismemberment of the Union. He was listened to freely, and he then delivered the letter of Governor Gagoso, addressed to himself, of which a copy is now communicated. After his return to New Orleans, he forwarded to the Secretary of State other papers, with a request that, after perusal, they should be burned. This, however, was not done, and he was so informed by the Secretary of State, and that they would be held subject to his order. These papers have not yet been found in the office. A letter, therefore, has been addressed to the former chief clerk, who may, perhaps, give information respecting them. As far as our memories enable us to say, they related only to the combinations before spoken of, and not at all to the corrupt receipt of money by any officer of the United States; consequently, they respected what was considered as a dead matter, known to the preceding administrations, and offering nothing new to call for investigations, which those nearest the dates of the transactions had not thought proper to institute.

In the course of the communications made to me on the subject of the conspiracy of Aaron Burr, I sometimes received letters, some of them anonymous, some under names true or false, expressing suspicions and insinuations against General Wilkinson. But one only of them, and that anonymous, specified any particular fact, and that fact was one of those which had already been communicated to a former administration.

No other information within the purview of the request of the house is known to have been received by any department of the government from the establishment of the present federal government. That which has recently been communicated to the House of Representatives, and by them to me, is the first direct testimony ever made known to me, charging General Wilkinson with the corrupt receipt of money; and the House of Representatives may be assured that the duties which this information devolves on me shall be exercised with rigorous impartiality. Should any want of power in the court to compel the rendering of testimony, obstruct that full and impartial inquiry, which alone can establish guilt or innocence, and satisfy justice, the legislative authority only will be competent to the remedy.

EIGHTH ANNUAL MESSAGE
November 8, 1808

TO THE SENATE AND HOUSE OF REPRESENTATIVES OF THE UNITED STATES: It would have been a source, fellow citizens, of much gratification, if our last communications from Europe had enabled me to inform you that the belligerent nations, whose disregard of neutral rights has been so destructive to our commerce, had become awakened to the duty and true policy of revoking their unrighteous edicts. That no means might be omitted to produce this salutary effect, I lost no time in availing myself to the act authorizing a suspension, in whole or in part, of the several embargo laws. Our ministers at London and Paris were instructed to explain to the respective governments there, our disposition to exercise the authority in such manner as would withdraw the pretext on which the aggressions were originally founded, and open the way for a renewal of that commercial intercourse which it was alleged on all sides had been reluctantly obstructed. As each of those governments had pledged its readiness to concur in renouncing a measure which reached its adversary through the incontestable rights of neutrals only, and as the measure had been assumed by each as a retaliation for an asserted acquiescence in the aggressions of the other, it was reasonably expected that the occasion would have been seized by both for evincing the sincerity of their profession, and for restoring to the commerce of the United States its legitimate freedom. The instructions to our ministers with respect to the different belligerents were necessarily modified with reference to their different circumstances, and to the condition annexed by law to the executive power of suspension, requiring a degree of security to our commerce which would not result from a repeal of the decrees of France. Instead of a pledge, therefore, of a suspension of the embargo as to her in case of such a repeal, it was presumed that a sufficient inducement might be found in other considerations, and particularly in the change produced by a compliance with our just demands by one belligerent, and a refusal by the other, in the relations between the other and the United States. To Great Britain, whose power on the ocean is so ascendant, it was deemed not inconsistent with that condition to state explicitly, that on her rescinding her orders in relation to the United States their trade would be opened with her, and remain shut to her enemy, in case of his failure to rescind his decrees also. From France no answer has been received, nor any indication that the requisite change in her decrees in contemplated. The favorable reception of the proposition to Great Britain was the less to be doubted, as her orders of council had not only been referred for their vindication to an acquiescence on the part of the United States no longer to be pretended, but as the arrangement proposed, while it resisted the illegal decrees of France, involved, moreover, substantially, the precise advantages professedly aimed at by the British orders. The arrangement has nevertheless been rejected.

This candid and liberal experiment having thus failed, and no other event having occurred on which a suspension of the embargo by the executive was authorized, it necessarily remains in the extent originally given to it. We have the satisfaction, however, to reflect, that in return for the privations by the measure, and which our fellow citizens in general have borne with patriotism, it has had the important effects of saving our mariners and our vast mercantile property, as well as of affording time for prosecuting the defensive and provisional measures called for by the occasion. It has demonstrated to foreign nations the moderation and firmness which govern our councils, and to our citizens the necessity of uniting in support of the laws and the rights of their country, and has thus long frustrated those usurpations and spoliations which, if resisted, involve war; if submitted to, sacrificed a vital principle of our national independence.

Under a continuance of the belligerent measures which, in defiance of laws which consecrate the rights of neutrals, overspread the ocean with danger, it will rest with the wisdom of Congress to decide on the course best adapted to such a state of things; and bringing with them, as they do, from every part of the Union, the sentiments of our constituents, my confidence is strengthened, that in forming this decision they will, with an unerring regard to the essential rights and interests of the nation, weigh and compare the painful alternatives out of which a choice is to be made. Nor should I do justice to the virtues which on other occasions have marked the character of our fellow citizens, if I did not cherish an equal confidence that the alternative chosen, whatever it may be, will be maintained with all the fortitude and patriotism which the crisis ought to inspire.

The documents containing the correspondences on the subject of the foreign edicts against our commerce, with the instructions given to our ministers at London and Paris, are now laid before you.

The communications made to Congress at their last session explained the posture in which the close of the discussion relating to the attack by a British ship of war on the frigate Chesapeake left a subject on which the nation had manifested so honorable a sensibility. Every view of what had passed authorized a belief that immediate steps would be taken by the British government for redressing a wrong, which, the more it was investigated, appeared the more clearly to require what had not been provided for in the special mission. It is found that no steps have been taken for the purpose. On the contrary, it will be seen, in the documents laid before you, that the inadmissible preliminary which obstructed the adjustment is still adhered to; and, moreover, that it is now brought into connection with the distinct and irrelative case of the orders in council. The instructions which had been given to our ministers at London with a view to facilitate, if necessary, the reparation claimed by the United States, are included in the documents communicated.

Our relations with the other powers of Europe have undergone no material changes since your last session. The important negotiations with Spain, which had been alternately suspended and resumed, necessarily experience a pause under the extraordinary and interesting crisis which distinguished her internal situation.

With the Barbary powers we continue in harmony, with the exception of an unjustifiable proceeding of the dey of Algiers toward our consul to that regency. Its character and circumstances are now laid before you, and will enable you to decide how far it may, either now or hereafter, call for any measures not within the limits of the executive authority.

With our Indian neighbors the public peace has been steadily maintained. Some instances of individual wrong have, as at other times, taken place, but in nowise implicating the will of the nation. Beyond the Mississippi, the Iowas, the Sacs, and the Alabamas, have delivered up for trial and punishment individuals from among themselves accused of murdering citizens of the United States. On this side of the Mississippi, the Creeks are exerting themselves to arrest offenders of the same kind; and the Choctaws have manifested their readiness and desire for amicable and just arrangements respecting depradations committed by disorderly persons of their tribe. And, generally, from a conviction that we consider them as part of ourselves, and cherish with sincerity their rights and interests, the attachment of the Indian tribes is gaining strength daily—is extending from the nearer to the more remote, and will amply requite us for the justice and friendship practised towards them. Husbandry and household manufacture are advancing among them, more rapidly with the southern than the northern tribes, from circumstances of soil and climate; and one of the two great divisions of the Cherokee nation have now under consideration to solicit the citizenship of the United States, and to be identified with us in laws and government, in such progressive manner as we shall think best.

In consequence of the appropriations of the last session of Congress for the security of our seaport towns and harbors, such works of defence have been erected as seemed to be called for by the situation of the several places, their relative importance, and the scale of expense indicated by the amount of the appropriation. These works will chiefly be finished in the course of the present season, except at New York and New Orleans, where most was to be done; and although a great proportion of the last appropriation has been expended on the former place, yet some further views will be submitted to Congress for rendering its security entirely adequate against naval enterprise. A view of what has been done at the several places, and of what is proposed to be done, shall be communicated as soon as the several reports are received.

Of the gun-boats authorized by the act of December last, it has been thought necessary to build only one hundred and three in the present year. These, with those before possessed, are sufficient for the harbors and waters exposed, and the residue will require little time for their construction when it is deemed necessary.

Under the act of the last session for raising an additional military force, so many officers were immediately appointed as were necessary for carrying on the business of recruiting, and in proportion as it advanced, others have been added. We have reason to believe their success has been satisfactory, although such returns have not yet been received as enable me to present to you a statement of the numbers engaged.

I have not thought it necessary in the course of the last season to call for any general detachments of militia or volunteers under the law passed for that purpose. For the ensuing season, however, they will require to be in readiness should their services be wanted. Some small and special detachments have been necessary to maintain the laws of embargo on that portion of our northern frontier which offered peculiar facilities for evasion, but these were replaced as soon as it could be done by bodies of new recruits. By the aid of these, and of the armed vessels called into actual service in other quarters, the spirit of disobedience and abuse which manifested itself early, and with sensible effect while we were unprepared to meet it, has been considerably repressed.

Considering the extraordinary character of the times in which we live, our attention should unremittingly be fixed on the safety of our country. For a people who are free, and who mean to remain so, a well-organized and armed militia is their best security. It is, therefore, incumbent on us, at every meeting, to revise the condition of the militia, and to ask ourselves if it is prepared to repel a powerful enemy at every point of our territories exposed to invasion. Some of the States have paid a laudable attention to this object; but every degree of neglect is to be found among others. Congress alone have power to produce a uniform state of preparation in this great organ of defence; the interests which they so deeply feel in their own and their country's security will present this as among the most important objects of their deliberation.

Under the acts of March 11th and April 23d, respecting arms, the difficulty of procuring them from abroad, during the present situation and dispositions of Europe, induced us to direct our whole efforts to the means of internal supply. The public factories have, therefore, been enlarged, additional machineries erected, and in proportion as artificers can be found or formed, their effect, already more than doubled, may be increased so as to keep pace with the yearly increase of the militia. The annual sums appropriated by the latter act, have been directed to the encouragement of private factories of arms, and contracts have been entered into with individual undertakers to nearly the amount of the first year's appropriation.

The suspension of our foreign commerce, produced by the injustice of the belligerent powers, and the consequent losses and sacrifices of our citizens, are subjects of just concern. The situation into which we have thus been forced, has impelled us to apply a portion of our industry and capital to internal manufactures and improvements. The extent of this conversion is daily increasing, and little doubt remains that the establishments formed and forming will—under the auspices of cheaper materials and subsistence, the freedom of labor from taxation with us, and of protecting duties and prohibitions—become permanent. The commerce with the Indians, too, within our own boundaries, is likely to receive abundant aliment from the same internal source, and will secure to them peace and the progress of civilization, undisturbed by practices hostile to both.

The accounts of the receipts and expenditures during the year ending on the 30th day of September last, being not yet made up, a correct statement will hereafter be transmitted from the Treasury. In the meantime, it is ascertained that the receipts have amounted to near eighteen millions of dollars, which, with the eight millions and a half in the treasury at the beginning of the year, have enabled us, after meeting the current demands and interest incurred, to pay two millions three hundred thousand dollars of the principal of our funded debt, and left us in the treasury, on that day, near fourteen millions of dollars. Of these, five millions three hundred and fifty thousand dollars will be necessary to pay what will be due on the first day of January next, which will complete the reimbursement of the eight per cent stock. These payments, with those made in the six years and a half preceding, will have extinguished thirty-three millions five hundred and eighty thousand dollars of the principal of the funded debt, being the whole which could be paid or purchased within the limits of the law and our contracts; and the amount of principal thus discharged will have liberated the revenue from about two millions of dollars of interest, and added that sum annually to the disposable surplus. The probable accumulation of the surpluses of revenue beyond what can be applied to the payment of the public debt, whenever the freedom and safety of our commerce shall be restored, merits the consideration of Congress. Shall it lie unproductive in the public vaults? Shall the revenue be reduced? Or shall it rather be appropriated to the improvements of roads, canals, rivers, education, and other great foundations of prosperity and union, under the powers which Congress may already possess, or such amendment of the constitution as may be approved by the States? While uncertain of the course of things, the time may be advantageously employed in obtaining the powers necessary for a system of improvement, should that be thought best.

Availing myself of this the last occasion which will occur of addressing the two houses of the legislature at their meeting, I cannot omit the expression of my sincere gratitude for the repeated proofs of confidence manifested to me by themselves and their predecessors since my call to the administration, and the many indulgences experienced at their hands. The same grateful acknowledgments are due to my fellow citizens generally, whose support has been my great encouragement under all embarrassments. In the transaction of their business I cannot have escaped error. It is incident to our imperfect nature. But I may say with truth, my errors have been of the understanding, not of intention; and that the advancement of their rights and interests has been the constant motive for every measure. On these considerations I solicit their indulgence. Looking forward with anxiety to their future destinies, I trust that, in their steady character unshaken by difficulties, in their love of liberty, obedience to law, and support of the public authorities, I see a sure guaranty of the permanence of our republic; and retiring from the charge of their affairs, I carry with me the consolation of a firm persuasion that Heaven has in store for our beloved country long ages to come of prosperity and happiness.

SCHEME FOR A SYSTEM OF AGRICULTURAL SOCIETIES
March, 1811

Several persons, farmers and planters of the county of Albemarle, having, during their visits and occasional meetings together, in conversations on the subjects of their agricultural pursuits, received considerable benefits from an intercommunication of their plans and processes in husbandry, they have imagined that these benefits might be usefully extended by enlarging the field of communication so as to embrace the whole dimensions of the State. Were practical and observing husbandmen in each county to form themselves into a society, commit to writing themselves, or state in conversations at their meetings to be written down by others, their practices and observations, their experiences and ideas, selections from these might be made from time to time by every one for his own use, or by the society or a committee of it, for more general purposes. By an interchange of these selections among the societies of the different counties, each might thus become possessed of the useful ideas and processes of the whole; and every one adopt such of them as he should deem suitable to his own situation. Or to abridge the labor of such multiplied correspondences, a central society might be agreed on to which, as a common deposit, all the others should send their communications. The society thus honored by the general confidence, would doubtless feel and fulfil the duty of selecting such papers as should be worthy of entire communication, of extracting and digesting from others whatever might be useful, and of condensing their matter within such compass as might reconcile it to the reading, as well as to the purchase of the great mass of practical men. Many circumstances would recommend, for the central society, that which should be established in the county of the seat of government. The necessary relations of every county with that would afford facilities for all the transmissions which should take place between them. The annual meeting of the legislature at that place, the individuals of which would most frequently be members of their county societies, would give opportunities of informal conferences which might promote a general and useful understanding among all the societies; and presses established there offer conveniences entirely peculiar to that situation.

In a country, of whose interests agriculture forms the basis, wherein the sum of productions is limited by the quantity of the labor it possesses, and not of its lands, a more judicious employment of that labor would be a clear addition of gain to individuals as well as to the nation, now lost to both by a want of skill and information in its direction. Every one must have seen farms otherwise equal, the one producing the double of the other by the superior culture and management of its possessor; and every one must have under his eye numerous examples of persons setting out in life with no other possession than skill in agriculture, and speedily, by its sole exercise, acquire wealth and independence. To promote, therefore, the diffusion of this skill, and thereby to procure, with the same labor now employed, greater means of subsistence and of happiness to our fellow citizens, is the ultimate object of this association; and towards effecting it, we consider the following particulars among those most worthy of the attention of the societies proposed.

1st. And principally the cultivation of our primary staples of wheat, tobacco, and hemp, for market.

2d. All subsidiary articles for the support of the farm, the food, the clothing and the comfort of the household, as Indian corn, rye, oats, barley, buckwheat, millet, the family of peas and beans, the whole family of grasses, turnips, potatoes, Jerusalem artichokes, and other useful roots, cotton and flax, the garden and orchard.

3d. The care and services of useful animals for the saddle or draught, for food or clothing, and the destruction of noxious quadrupeds, fowls, insects, and reptiles.

4th. Rotations of crops, and the circumstances which should govern or vary them, according to the varieties of soil, climate, and markets, of our different counties.

5th. Implements of husbandry and operations with them, among which the plough and all its kindred instruments for dividing the soil, holds the first place, and the threshing machine an important one, the simplification of which is a great desideratum. Successful examples, too, of improvement in the operations of these instruments would be an excitement to correct the slovenly and unproductive practices too generally prevalent.

6th. Farm buildings and conveniences, inclosures, roads, fuel, timber.

7th. Manures, plaster, green-dressings, fallows, and other means of ameliorating the soil.

8th. Calendars of works, showing how a given number of laborers and a draught of animals are to be employed every day in the year so as to perform within themselves, and in their due time, according to the usual course of seasons, all the operations of a farm of given size. This being essential to the proportioning the labor to the size of the farm.

9th. A succinct report of the different practices of husbandry in the county, including the bad as well as the good, that those who follow the former may read and see their own condemnation in the same page which offers better examples for their adoption. It is believed that a judicious execution of this article alone, might nearly supersede every other duty of the society, inasmuch as it would present every good practice which has occurred to the mind of any cultivator of the State for imitation, and every bad one for avoidance. And the choicest processes culled from every farm, would compose a course probably near perfection.

10th. The county communications being first digested in their respective societies, a methodical and compact digest and publication of these would be the duty of the central society; and on the judicious performance of this, would in a great degree depend the utility of the institutions, and extent of improvement flowing from them.

11th. That we may not deter from becoming members, those practical and observing husbandmen whose knowledge is the most valuable, and who are mostly to be found in that portion of citizens with whom the observance of economy is necessary, all duties of every kind should be performed gratis; and to defray the expenses of the central publication alone, each member should pay at the first stated meeting of his society in every year, —— dollars, for which he should be entitled to receive a copy of the publication bound in boards.

12th. The first association of —— persons in any county notifying themselves as constituted to the central society, should be received as the society of the county making a part of the general establishment here proposed; but every county society should be free to adopt associate members, although residents of other counties, and to receive and avail the institution of communications from persons not members, whether in or out of their county.

We are far from presuming to offer this organization and these principles of constitution as complete, and worthy the implicit adoption of other societies. They are suggested only as propositions for consideration and amendment, and we shall readily accede to any others more likely to effect the purposes we have in view. We know that agricultural societies are already established in some counties; but we are not informed of their particular constitutions. We request these to be admitted into their brotherhood, and to make with them parts of one great whole. We have learned that such a society is formed or forming at the seat of our government. We ask their affiliation, and give them our suffrage for the station of central society. We promise to all our zealous co-operation in promoting the objects of the institution, and to contribute our mite in exchange for the more abundant information we shall receive from others.

For these purposes we now constitute ourselves an agricultural society of the county of Albemarle, and adopt as rules for present observance, the principles before stated.

Our further organization shall be a president, secretary and treasurer, to be chosen at the first stated meeting to be held in every year, by a majority of the members present, provided those present be a majority of the existing members, and to continue in office until another election shall be made.

There shall be four stated meetings in every year, to wit: on the first Mondays in January, April, July and October.

The place of meeting, and rules of the society, shall be established, revoked or altered, and new members admitted, at any of the stated meetings, by a majority of the attending members, if they be a majority of those present, not being less than one-fourth of the whole. And, lest the powers given to the greater quorum of a majority of the whole, should at any time remain unexercised from insufficient attendance, the same may be exercised by a resolution of the lesser quorum of one-fourth, passed at a stated meeting: provided it be confirmed at the next stated meeting, by either a greater or lesser quorum, and in the meantime have no force.

Those who for two whole years shall not have attended any stated meetings shall, *ipso facto,* cease to be members. And to ascertain at all times who are the existing members, the names of those attending every meeting shall be regularly entered in the journals of the society.

The president shall preside at all meetings when present, and when absent, a president *pro tempore* may be appointed for that purpose *by those present.*

EXCERPTS FROM THE REPORT TO THE LEGISLATURE OF VIRGINIA RELATIVE TO THE UNIVERSITY OF VIRGINIA [1]

August, 1818

In proceeding to the third and fourth duties prescribed by the Legislature, of reporting "the branches of learning, which should be taught in the University, and the number and description of the professorships they will require," the Commissioners were first to consider at what point it was understood that university education should commence. Certainly not with the alphabet, for reasons of expediency and impractability, as well from the obvious sense of the Legislature, who, in the same act, make other provision for the primary instruction of the poor children, expecting, doubtless, that in other cases it would be provided by the parent, or become, perhaps, subject to future and further attention of the Legislature. The objects of this primary education determine its character and limits. These objects would be,

To give to every citizen the information he needs for the transaction of his own business;

[1] The report was written by Jefferson. It appeared originally in the *Analectic Magazine,* vol. XIII (February, 1819), pp. 104-116.

To enable him to calculate for himself, and to express and preserve his ideas, his contracts and accounts, in writing;

To improve, by reading, his morals and faculties;

To understand his duties to his neighbors and country, and to discharge with competence the functions confided to him by either;

To know his rights; to exercise with order and justice those he retains; to choose with discretion the fiduciary of those he delegates; and to notice their conduct with diligence, with candor, and judgment;

And, in general, to observe with intelligence and faithfulness all the social relations under which he shall be placed.

To instruct the mass of our citizens in these, their rights, interests and duties, as men and citizens, being then the objects of education in the primary schools, whether private or public, in them should be taught reading, writing and numerical arithmetic, the elements of mensuration (useful in so many callings), and the outlines of geography and history. And this brings us to the point at which are to commence the higher branches of education, of which the Legislature require the development; those, for example, which are,

To form the statesmen, legislators and judges, on whom public prosperity and individual happiness are so much to depend;

To expound the principles and structure of government, the laws which regulate the intercourse of nations, those formed municipally for our own government, and a sound spirit of legislation, which, banishing all arbitrary and unnecessary restraint on individual action, shall leave us free to do whatever does not violate the equal rights of another;

To harmonize and promote the interests of agriculture, manufactures and commerce, and by well informed views of political economy to give a free scope to the public industry;

To develop the reasoning faculties of our youth, enlarge their minds, cultivate their morals, and instill into them the precepts of virtue and order;

To enlighten them with mathematical and physical sciences, which advance the arts, and administer to the health, the subsistence, and comforts of human life;

And, generally, to form them to habits of reflection and correct action, rendering them examples of virtue to others, and of happiness within themselves.

These are the objects of that higher grade of education, the benefits and blessings of which the Legislature now propose to provide for the good and ornament of their country, the gratification and happiness of their fellow-citizens, of the parent especially, and his progeny, on which all his affections are concentrated.

In entering on this field, the Commissioners are aware that they have to encounter much difference of opinion as to the extent which it is expedient that this institution should occupy. Some good men, and even of respectable information, consider the learned sciences as useless acquirements; some think they do not better the condition of man; and others that education, like private and individual concerns, should be left to private individual effort; not reflecting that an establishment embracing all the sciences which may be useful and even necessary in the various vocations of life, with the buildings and apparatus belonging to each, are far beyond the reach of individual means, and must either derive existence from public patronage, or not exist at all. This would leave us, then, without those callings which depend on education, or send us to other countries to seek the instruction they require. But the Commissioners are happy in considering the statute under which they are assembled as proof that the Legislature is far from the abandonment of objects so interesting. They are sensible that the advantages of well-directed education, moral, political and economical, are truly above all estimate. Education generates habits of application, of order, and the love of virtue; and controls, by the force of habit, any innate obliquities in our moral organization. We should be far, too, from the discouraging persuasion that man is fixed, by the law of his nature, at a given point; that his improvement is a chimera, and the hope delusive of rendering ourselves wiser, happier or better than our forefathers were. As well might it be urged that the wild and uncultivated tree, hitherto yielding sour and bitter fruit only, can never be made to yield better; yet we know that the grafting art implants a new tree on the savage stock, producing what is most estimable both in kind and degree. Education, in like manner, engrafts a new man on the native stock, and improves what in his nature was vicious and perverse into qualities of virtue and social worth. And it cannot be but that each generation succeeding to the knoweldge acquired by all those who preceded it, adding to it their own acquisitions and discoveries, and handing the mass down for successive and constant accumulation, must advance the knowledge and well-being of mankind, not *infinitely,* as some have said, but *indefinitely,* and to a term which no one can fix and foresee. Indeed, we need look back half a century, to times which many now living remember well, and see the wonderful advances in the sciences and arts which have been made within that period. Some of these have rendered the elements themselves subservient to the purposes of man, have harnessed them to the yoke of his labors, and effected the great blessings of moderating his own, of accompanying what was beyond his feeble force, and extending the comforts of life to a much enlarged circle, to those who had before known its necessaries only. That these are not the vain dreams of sanguine hope, we have before our eyes real and living examples. What, but education, has advanced us beyond the condition of our indigenous neighbors? And what chains them to their present state of barbarism and wretchedness, but a bigoted veneration for the supposed superlative wisdom of their fathers, and the preposterous idea that they are to look backward for better things, and not forward, longing, as it should seem, to return to the days of eating acorns and roots, rather than indulgence in the degeneracies of civilization? And how much more encouraging to the achievement of science and improvement is this, than the desponding view that the condition of man cannot be ameliorated, that what has been must ever be, and that to secure ourselves where we are, we must tread with awful reverence in the footsteps of our fathers. This doctrine is the genuine fruit of the alliance between Church and State; the tenants of which, finding themselves but too well in their present condition, oppose all advances which might unmask their usurpations, and monopolies of honors, wealth, and power, and fear every change, as endangering the comforts they now hold. Nor must we omit to mention, among the benefits of education, the incalculable advantage of training up able counsellors to administer the affairs of our country in all its departments, legislative, executive and judiciary, and to bear their proper share in the councils of our national government; nothing more than education advancing the prosperity, the power, and the happiness of a nation.

Encouraged, therefore, by the sentiments of the Legislature, manifested in this statute, we present the following tabular statement of the branches of learning which we think should be taught in the University, forming them into groups, each of which are within the powers of a single professor:

I. Languages, ancient:
    Latin
    Greek
    Hebrew
II. Languages, modern:
    French
    Spanish
    Italian
    German
    Anglo-Saxon
III. Mathematics, pure:
    Algebra
    Fluxions
    Geometry, Elementary
            Transcendental
    Architecture, Military
            Naval
IV. Physico-Mathematics:
    Mechanics

Statics
Dynamics
Pneumatics
Acoustics
Optics
Astronomy
Geography
V. Physics, or Natural Philosophy:
    Chemistry
    Mineralogy
VI. Botany
    Zoology
VII. Anatomy
    Medicine
VIII. Government
    Political Economy
    Law of Nature and Nations
    History, being interwoven
        with Politics and Law

IX. Law, municipal   Ethics
 X. Idealogy   Rhetoric
        General Grammar   Belles Lettres and the fine arts.

Some of the terms used in this table being subject to a difference of ac-
ceptation, it is proper to define the meaning and comprehension intended
to be given them here:

Geometry, Elementary, is that of straight lines and of the circle.
   Transcendental, is that of all other curves; it includes, of course, *Projectiles,*
      a leading branch of military art.
Military Architecture includes Fortification, another branch of that art.
Statics respect matter generally, in a state of rest, and include Hydrostatics,
      or the laws of fluids particularly, at rest or in equilibrio.
Dynamics, used as a general term, include
   Dynamics proper, or the laws of *solids* in motion; and
   Hydrodynamics, or Hydraulics, those of *fluids* in motion.
Pneumatics teach the theory or air, its weight, motion, condensation, rare-
      faction, &c.
Acoustics, or Phonics, the theory of sound.
Optics, the laws of light and vision.
Physics, or Physiology, in a general sense, mean the doctrine of the physical
      objects of our senses.
Chemistry is meant, with its other usual branches, to comprehend the theory
      of agriculture.
Mineralogy, in addition to its peculiar subjects, is here understood to embrace
      what is real in geology.
Ideology is the doctrine of thought.
General Grammar explains the construction of language.

Some articles in this distribution of sciences will need observation. A
professor is proposed for ancient languages, the Latin, Greek, and Hebrew,
particularly; but these languages being the foundation common to all the
sciences, it is difficult to foresee what may be the extent of this school. At
the same time, no greater obstruction to industrious study could be proposed than the presence, the intrusions and the noisy turbulence of a multitude of small boys; and if they are to be placed here for the rudiments of
the languages, they may be so numerous that its character and value as an
University will be merged in those of a Grammar school. It is, therefore,
greatly to be wished, that preliminary schools, either on private or public
establishment, could be distributed in districts through the State, as preparatory to the entrance of students into the University. The tender age at which
his part of education commences, generally about the tenth year, would
weigh heavily with parents in sending their sons to a school so distant as
the central establishment would be from most of them. Districts of such

extent as that every parent should be within a day's journey of his son at school, would be desirable in cases of sickness, and convenient for supplying their ordinary wants, and might be made to lessen sensibly the expense of this part of their education. And where a sparse population would not, within such a compass, furnish subjects sufficient to maintain a school, a competent enlargement of district must, of necessity, there be submitted to. At these district schools or colleges, boys should be rendered able to read the easier authors, Latin and Greek. This would be useful and sufficient for many not intended for an University education. At these, too, might be taught English grammar, the higher branches of numerical arithmetic, the geometry of straight lines and of the circle, the elements of navigation, and geography to a sufficient degree, and thus afford to greater numbers the means of being qualified for the various vocations of life, needing more instruction than merely menial or praedial labor, and the same advantages to youths whose education may have been neglected until too late to lay a foundation in the learned languages. These institutions, intermediate between the primary schools and University, might then be the passage of entrance for youths into the University, where their classical learning might be critically completed, by a study of the authors of highest degree; and it is at this stage only that they should be received at the University. Giving then a portion of their time to a finished knowledge of the Latin and Greek, the rest might be appropriated to the modern languages, or to the commencement of the course of science for which they should be destined. This would generally be about the fifteenth year of their age, when they might go with more safety and contentment to that distance from their parents. Until this preparatory provision shall be made, either the University will be overwhelmed with the grammar school, or a separate establishment, under one or more ushers, for its lower classes, will be advisable, at a mile or two distant from the general one; where, too, may be exercised the stricter government necessary for young boys, but unsuitable for youths arrived at years of discretion.

The considerations which have governed the specification of languages to be taught by the professor of modern languages were, that the French is the language of general intercourse among nations, and as a depository of human science, is unsurpassed by any other language, living or dead; that the Spanish is highly interesting to us, as the language spoken by so great a portion of the inhabitants of our continents, with whom we shall probably have great intercourse ere long, and is that also in which is written the greater part of the earlier history of America. The Italian abounds with works of very superior order, valuable for their matter, and still more distinguished as models of the finest taste in style and composition. And the German now stands in a line with that of the most learned nations in

richness and erudtion and advance in the sciences. It is too of common
descent with the language of our own country, a branch of the same original
Gothic stock, and furnishes valuable illustrations for us. But in this point
of view, the Anglo-Saxon is of peculiar value. We have placed it among
the modern languages, because it is in fact that which we speak, in the
earliest form in which we have knowledge of it. It has been undergoing,
with time, those gradual changes which all languages, ancient and modern,
have experienced; and even now needs only to be printed in the modern
character and orthography to be intelligible, in a considerable degree, to an
English reader. It has this value, too, above the Greek and Latin, that
while it gives the radix of the mass of our language, they explain its innovations only. Obvious proofs of this have been presented to the modern
reader in the disquisitions of Horn Tooke; and Fortescue Aland has well
explained the great instruction which may be derived from it to a full
understanding of our ancient common law, on which, as a stock, our whole
system of law is engrafted. It will form the first link in the chain of an
historical review of our language through all its successive changes to the
present day, will constitute the foundation of that critical instruction in it
which ought to be found in a seminary of general learning, and thus reward
amply the few weeks of attention which would alone be requisite for its
attainment; a language already fraught with all the eminent science of our
parent country, the future vehicle of whatever we may ourselves achieve,
and destined to occupy so much space on the globe, claims distinguished
attention in American education.

Medicine, where fully taught, is usually subdivided into several professorships, but this cannot well be without the accessory of an hospital, where
the student can have the benefit of attending clinical lectures, and of assisting at operations of surgery. With this accessory, the seat of our University
is not yet prepared, either by its population or by the numbers of poor who
would leave their own houses, and accept of the charities of an hospital.
For the present, therefore, we propose but a single professor for both medicine and anatomy. By him the medical science may be taught, with a history
and explanations of all its successive theories from Hippocrates to the present
day; and anatomy may be fully treated. Vegetable pharmacy will make a
part of the botanical course, and mineral and chemical pharmacy of those
of mineralogy and chemistry. This degree of medical information is such
as the mass of scientific students would wish to possess, as enabling them
in their course through life, to estimate with satisfaction the extent and
limits of the aid to human life and health, which they may understand-
ingly expect from that art; and constitutes such a foundation for those
intended for the profession, that the finishing course of practice at the bed-

sides of the sick, and at the operations of surgery in a hospital, can neither be long nor expensive. To seek this finishing elsewhere, must therefore be submitted to for a while.

In conformity with the principles of our Constitution, which places all sects of religion on an equal footing, with the jealousies of the different sects in guarding that equality from encroachment and surprise, and with the sentiments of the Legislature in favor of freedom of religion, manifested on former occasions, we have proposed no professor of divinity; and the rather as the proofs of the being of a God, the creator, preserver, and supreme ruler of the universe, the author of all the relations of morality, and of the laws and obligations these infer, will be within the province of the professor of ethics; to which adding the developments of these moral obligations, of those in which all sects agree, with a knowledge of the languages, Hebrew, Greek, and Latin, a basis will be formed common to all sects. Proceeding thus far without offence to the Constitution, we have thought it proper at this point to leave every sect to provide, as they think fittest, the means of further instruction in their own peculiar tenets.

We are further of opinion, that after declaring by law that certain sciences shall be taught in the University, fixing the number of professors they require, which we think should, at present, be ten, limiting (except as to the professors who shall be first engaged in each branch) a maximum for their salaries (which should be a certain but moderate subsistence, to be made up by liberal tuition fees, as an excitement to assiduity), it will be best to leave to the discretion of the visitors, the grouping of these sciences together, according to the accidental qualifications of the professors; and the introduction also of other branches of science, when enabled by private donations, or by public provision, and called for by the increase of population, or other change of circumstances; to establish beginnings, in short, to be developed by time, as those who come after us shall find expedient. They will be more advanced than we are in science and in useful arts, and will know best what will suit the circumstances of their day.

We have proposed no formal provision for the gymnastics of the school, although a proper object of attention for every institution of youth. These exercises with ancient nations, constituted the principal part of the education of their youth. Their arms and mode of warfare rendered them severe in the extreme; ours, on the same correct principle, should be adapted to our arms and warfare; and the manual exercise, military manoeuvres, and tactics generally, should be the frequent exercises of the students, in their hours of recreation. It is at that age of aptness, docility, and emulation of the practices of manhood, that such things are soonest learnt and longest remembered. The use of tools too in the manual arts is worthy of encouragement, by facilitating to such as choose it, an admission into the neighboring workshops. To these should be added the arts which embellish life, dancing, music, and drawing; the last more especially, as an important part of military education. These innocent arts furnish amusement and happiness to those who, having time on their hands, might less inoffensively employ it. Needing, at the same time, no regular incorporation with the institution, they may be left to accessory teachers, who will be paid by the individuals employing them, the University only providing proper apartments for their exercise.

The fifth duty prescribed to the Commissioners, is to propose such general provisions as may be properly enacted by the Legislature, for the better organizing and governing the University.

In the education of youth, provision is to be made for, 1, tuition; 2, diet; 3, lodging; 4, government; and 5, honorary excitements. The first of these constitutes the proper functions of the professors; 2, the dieting of the students should be left to private boarding houses of their own choice, and at their own expense; to be regulated by the Visitors from time to time, the house only being provided by the University within its own precincts, and thereby of course subjected to the general regimen, moral or sumptuary, which they shall prescribe. 3. They should be lodged in dormitories, making a part of the general system of buildings. 4. The best mode of government for youth, in large collections, is certainly a desideratum not yet attained with us. It may be well questioned whether *fear* after a certain age, is a motive to which we should have ordinary recourse. The human character is susceptible of other incitements to correct conduct, more worthy of employ, and of better effect. Pride of character, laudable ambition, and moral dispositions are innate correctives of the indiscretions of that lively age; and when strengthened by habitual appeal and exercise, have a happier effect on future character than the degrading motive of fear. Hardening them to disgrace, to corporal punishments, and servile humiliations cannot be the best process for producing erect character. The affectionate deportment between father and son, offers in truth the best example for that of tutor and pupil; and the experience and practice of other [1] countries, in this respect, may be worthy of enquiry and consideration with us. It will then be for the wisdom and discretion of the Visitors to devise and perfect a proper system of government, which, if it be founded in reason and comity, will be more likely to nourish in the minds of our youth the combined spirit of order and self-respect, so congenial with our political institutions, and so important to be woven into the American character.

[1] A police exercised by the students themselves, under proper discretion, has been tried with success in some countries, and the rather as forming them for initiation into the duties and practices of civil life.—T. J.

AUTOBIOGRAPHY
January 6-July 21, 1821

January 6, 1821. At the age of 77, I begin to make some memoranda, and state some recollections of dates and facts concerning myself, for my own more ready reference, and for the information of my family.

The tradition in my father's family was, that their ancestor came to this country from Wales, and from near the mountain of Snowdon, the highest in Great Britain. I noted once a case from Wales, in the law reports, where a person of our name was either plaintiff or defendant; and one of the same name was secretary to the Virginia Company. These are the only instances in which I have met with the name in that country. I have found it in our early records; but the first particular information I have of any ancestor was of my grandfather, who lived at the place in Chesterfield called Ozborne's, and owned the lands afterwards the glebe of the parish. He had three sons; Thomas who died young, Field who settled on the waters of Roanoke and left numerous descendants, and Peter, my father, who settled on the lands I still own, called Shadwell, adjoining my present residence. He was born February 29, 1707-8, and intermarried 1739, with Jane Randolph, of the age of 19, daughter of Isham Randolph, one of the seven sons of that name and family, settled at Dungeness in Goochland. They trace their pedigree far back in England and Scotland, to which let everyone ascribe the faith and merit he chooses.

My father's education had been quite neglected; but being of a strong mind, sound judgment, and eager after information, he read much and improved himself, insomuch that he was chosen, with Joshua Fry, Professor of Mathematics in William and Mary college, to continue the boundary line between Virginia and North Carolina, which had been begun by Colonel Byrd; and was afterwards employed with the same Mr. Fry, to make the first map of Virginia which had ever been made, that of Captain Smith being merely a conjectural sketch. They possessed excellent materials for so much of the country as is below the blue ridge; little being then known beyond that ridge. He was the third or fourth settler, about the year 1737, of the part of the country in which I live. He died, August 17th, 1757, leaving my mother a widow, who lived till 1776, with six daughters and two sons, myself the elder. To my younger brother he left his estate on James River, called Snowden, after the supposed birth-place of the family: to myself, the lands on which I was born and live.

He placed me at the English school at five years of age; and at the Latin at nine, where I continued until his death. My teacher, Mr. Douglas, a clergyman from Scotland, with the rudiments of the Latin and Greek languages, taught me the French; and on the death of my father, I went to the Reverend Mr. Maury, a correct classical scholar, with whom I continued two years; and then, to wit, in the spring of 1760, went to William and Mary college, where I continued two years. It was my great good fortune, and what probably fixed the destinies of my life, that Dr. William Small of Scotland, was then professor of Mathematics, a man profound in most of the useful branches of science, with a happy talent of communication, correct and gentlemanly manners, and an enlarged and liberal mind. He, most happily for me, became soon attached to me, and made me his daily companion when not engaged in the school; and from his conversation I got my first views of the expansion of science, and of the system of things in which we are placed. Fortunately, the philosophical chair became vacant soon after my arrival at college, and he was appointed to fill it *per interim:* and he was the first who ever gave, in that college, regular lectures in Ethics, Rhetoric and Belles lettres. He returned to Europe in 1762, having previously filled up the measure of his goodness to me, by procuring for me, from his most intimate friend, George Wythe, a reception as a student of law, under his direction, and introduced me to the acquaintance and familiar table of Governor Fauquier, the ablest man who had ever filled that office. With him, and at his table, Dr. Small and Mr Wythe, his *amici omnium horarum,* and myself, formed a *partie quarree,* and to the habitual conversations on these occasions I owed much instruction. Mr. Wythe continued to be my faithful and beloved mentor in youth, and my most affectionate friend through life. In 1767, he led me into the practice of the law at the bar of the General court, at which I continued until the Revolution shut up the courts of justice.

In 1769, I became a member of the legislature by the choice of the county in which I live, and so continued until it was closed by the Revolution. I made one effort in that body for the permission of the emancipation of slaves, which was rejected: and indeed, during the regal government, nothing liberal could expect success. Our minds were circumscribed within narrow limits, by an habitual belief that it was our duty to be subordinate to the mother country in all matters of government, to direct all our labors in subservience to her interests, and even to observe a bigoted intolerance for all religions but hers. The difficulties with our representatives were of habit and despair, not of reflection and conviction. Experience soon proved that they could bring their minds to rights, on the first summons of their attention. But the King's Council, which acted as another house of legislature, held their places at will, and were in most humble obedience to that will: the Governor too, who had a negative on our laws, held by the same tenure, and with still greater devotedness to it: and, last of all, the Royal negative closed the last door to every hope of amelioration.

On the 1st of January, 1772, I was married to Martha Skelton, widow of Bathurst Skelton, and daughter of John Wayles then twenty-three years old. Mr. Wayles was a lawyer of much practice, to which he was introduced more by his great industry, punctuality, and practical readiness, than by eminence in the science of his profession. He was a most agreeable companion, full of pleasantry and good humor, and welcomed in every society. He acquired a handsome fortune, and died in May, 1773, leaving three daughters: the portion which came on that event to Mrs. Jefferson, after the debts should be paid, which were very considerable, was about equal to my own patrimony, and consequently doubled the ease of our circumstances.

When the famous Resolutions of 1765, against the Stamp-act, were proposed, I was yet a student of law in Williamsburgh. I attended the debate, however, at the door of the lobby of the House of Burgesses, and heard the splendid display of Mr. Henry's talents as a popular orator. They were great indeed; such as I have never heard from any other man. He appeared to me to speak as Homer wrote. Mr. Johnson, a lawyer, and member from the Northern Neck, seconded the resolutions, and by him the learning and the logic of the case were chiefly maintained. My recollections of these transactions may be seen page 60 of the life of Patrick Henry, by Wirt, to whom I furnished them.

In May, 1769, a meeting of the General Assembly was called by the Governor, Lord Botetourt. I had then become a member; and to that meeting became known the joint resolutions and address of the Lords and Commons, of 1768-9, on the proceedings in Massachusetts. Counter-resolutions, and an address to the King by the House of Burgesses, were agreed to with little opposition, and a spirit manifestly displayed itself of considering the cause of Massachusetts as a common one. The Governor dissolved us: but we met the next day in the Apollo of the Raleign tavern, formed ourselves into a voluntary convention, drew up articles of association against the use of any merchandise imported from Great Britain, signed and recommended them to the people, repaired to our several counties, and were re-elected without any other exception than of the very few who had declined assent to our proceedings.

Nothing of particular excitement occurring for a considerable time, our countrymen seemed to fall into a state of insensibility to our situation; the duty on tea, not yet repealed, and the declaratory act of a right in the British Parliament to bind us by their laws in all cases whatsoever, still suspended over us. But a court of inquiry held in Rhode Island in 1762, with a power to send persons to England to be tried for offences committed here, was considered, at our session of the spring of 1773, as demanding attention. Not thinking our old and leading members up to the point of forwardness and zeal which the times required, Mr. Henry, Richard Henry Lee, Francis L. Lee, Mr. Carr and myself agreed to meet in the evening, in a private room of the Raleigh, to consult on the state of things. There may have been a member or two more whom I do not recollect. We were all sensible that the most urgent of all measures was that of coming to an understanding with all the other colonies, to consider the British claims as a common cause to all, and to produce a unity of action: and, for this purpose, that a committee of correspondence in each colony would be the best instrument for intercommunication: and that their first measure would probably be, to propose a meeting of deputies from every colony, at some central place, who should be charged with the direction of the measures which should be taken by all. We, therefore, drew up the resolutions which may be seen in Wirt, page 87. The consulting members proposed to me to move them, but I urged that it should be done by Mr. Carr, my friend and brother-in-law, then a new member, to whom I wished an opportunity should be given of making known to the house his great worth and talents. It was so agreed; he moved them, they were agreed to *nem. con.,* and a committee of correspondence appointed, of whom Peyton Randolph, the speaker, was chairman. The Governor (then Lord Dunmore) dissolved us, but the committee met the next day, prepared a circular letter to the speakers of the other colonies, inclosing to each a copy of the resolutions, and left it in charge with their chairman to forward them by expresses.

The origination of these committees of correspondence between the colonies has been since claimed for Massachusetts, and Marshall [1] has given into this error, although the very note of his appendix to which he refers, shows that their establishment was confined to their own towns. This matter will be seen clearly stated in a letter of Samuel Adams Wells to me of April 2nd, 1819, and my answer of May 12th. I was corrected by the letter of Mr. Wells in the information I had given Mr. Wirt, as stated in his note, page 87, that the messengers of Massachusetts and Virginia crossed each other on the way, bearing similar propositions; for Mr. Wells shows that Massachusetts did not adopt the measure, but on the receipt of our proposition, delivered at their next session. Their message, therefore, which passed ours, must have related to something else, for I well remember Peyton Randolph's informing me of the crossing of our messengers.

The next event which excited our sympathies for Massachusetts, was the

---

[1] The reference is to John Marshall's *Life of George Washington*, Volume II, p. 151.

Boston port bill, by which that port was to be shut up on the 1st of June, 1774. This arrived while we were in session in the spring of that year. The lead in the House, on these subjects, being no longer left to the old members, Mr. Henry, R. H. Lee, Fr. L. Lee, three or four other members, whom I do not recollect, and myself, agreeing that we must boldly take an unequivocal stand in the line with Massachusetts, determined to meet and consult on the proper measures, in the council-chamber, for the benefit of the library in that room. We were under conviction of the necessity of arousing our people from the lethargy into which they had fallen, as to passing events; and thought that the appointment of a day of general fasting and prayer would be most likely to call up and alarm their attention. No example of such a solemnity had existed since the days of our distresses in the war of '55, since which a new generation had grown up. With the help, therefore, of Rushworth, whom we rummaged over for the revolutionary precedents and forms of the Puritans of that day, preserved by him, we cooked up a resolution, somewhat modernizing their phrases, for appointing the 1st day of June, on which the port bill was to commence, for a day of fasting, humiliation, and prayer, to implore Heaven to avert from us the evils of civil war, to inspire us with firmness in support of our rights, and to turn the hearts of the King and Parliament to moderation and justice. To give greater emphasis to our proposition, we agreed to wait the next morning on Mr. Nicholas, whose grave and religious character was more in unison with the tone of our resolution, and to solicit him to move it. We accordingly went to him in the morning. He moved it the same day; the 1st of June was proposed; and it passed without opposition. The Governor dissolved us, as usual. We retired to the Apollo, as before, agreed to an association, and instructed the committee of correspondence to propose to the corresponding committees of the other colonies, to appoint deputies to meet in Congress at such place, *annually,* as should be convenient, to direct, from time to time, the measures required by the general interest: and we declared that an attack on any one colony, should be considered as an attack on the whole. This was in May. We further recommended to the several counties to elect deputies to meet at Williamsburgh, the 1st of August ensuing, to consider the state of the colony, and particularly to appoint delegates to a general Congress, should that measure be acceded to by the committees of correspondence generally. It was acceded to; Philadelphia was appointed for the place, and the 5th of September for the time of meeting. We returned home, and in our several counties invited the clergy to meet assemblies of the people on the 1st of June, to perform the ceremonies of the day, and to address to them discourses suited to the occasion. The people met generally, with anxiety and alarm in their countenances, and the effect of the day, through the whole colony, was like a shock of electricity, arousing every man, and placing him erect and solidly on his centre. They chose, universally, delegates for the convention. Being elected one for my own county, I prepared a draught of instructions to be given to the delegates whom we should send to the Congress, which I meant to propose at our meeting. In this I took the ground that, from the beginning, I had thought the only one orthodox or tenable, which was, that the relation between Great Britain and these colonies was exactly the same as that of England and Scotland, after the accession of James, and until the union, and the same as her present relations with Hanover, having the same executive chief, but no other necessary political connection; and that our emigration from England to this country gave her no more rights over us, than the emigrations of the Danes and Saxons gave to the present authorities of the mother country, over England. In this doctrine, however, I had never been able to get anyone to agree with me but Mr. Wythe. He concurred in it from the first dawn of the question, What was the political relation between us and England? Our other patriots, Randolph, the Lees, Nicholas, Pendleton, stopped at the half-way house of John Dickinson, who admitted that England had a right to regulate our commerce, and to lay duties on it for the purposes of regulation, but not of raising revenue. But for this ground there was no foundation in compact, in any acknowledged principles of colonization, nor in reason: expatriation being a natural right, and acted on as such, by all nations, in all ages. I set out for Williamsburgh some days before that appointed for our meeting, but was taken ill of a dysentery on the road, and was unable to proceed. I sent on, therefore, to Williamsburgh, two copies of my draught, the one under cover to Peyton Randolph, who I knew would be in the chair of the convention, the other to Patrick Henry. Whether Mr. Henry disapproved the ground taken, or was too lazy to read it (for he was the laziest man in reading I ever knew) I never learned: but he communicated it to nobody. Peyton Randolph informed the convention he had received such a paper from a member, prevented by sickness from offering it in his place, and he laid it on the table for perusal. It was read generally by the members, approved by many, though thought too bold for the present state of things; but they printed it in pamphlet form, under the title of "A Summary View of the Rights of British America." It found its way to England, was taken up by the opposition, interpolated a little by Mr. Burke so as to make it answer opposition purposes, and in that form ran rapidly through several editions. This information I had from Parson Hurt, who happened at the time to be in London, whither he had gone to receive clerical orders; and I was informed afterwards by Peyton Randolph, that it had procured me the honor of having my name inserted in a long list of proscriptions, enrolled in a bill of attainder commenced in one of the Houses of Parliament, but suppressed in embryo by the hasty step of events, which warned them to be a little cautious. Montague, agent of the House of Burgesses in England, made extracts from the bill, copied the names, and sent them to Peyton Randolph. The names, I think, were about twenty, which he repeated to me, but I recollect those only of Hancock, the two Adamses, Peyton Randolph himself, Patrick Henry, and myself. The convention met on the 1st of August, renewed their association, appointed delegates to the Congress, gave them instructions very temperately and properly expressed, both as to style and matter; and they repaired to Philadelphia at the time appointed. The splendid proceedings of that Congress, at their first session, belong to general history, are known to everyone, and need not therefore be noted here. They terminated their session on the 26th of October, to meet again on the 10th of May ensuing. The convention, at their ensuing session of March, '75, approved of the proceedings of Congress, thanked their delegates, and reappointed the same persons to represent the colony at the meeting to be held in May: and foreseeing the probability that Peyton Randolph, their president, and speaker also of the House of Burgesses, might be called off, they added me, in that event, to the delegation.

Mr. Randolph was, according to expectation, obliged to leave the chair of Congress, to attend the General Assembly summoned by Lord Dunmore, to meet on the 1st day of June, 1775. Lord North's conciliatory propositions, as they were called, had been received by the Governor, and furnished the subject for which this assembly was convened. Mr. Randolph accordingly attended, and the tenor of these propositions being generally known, as having been addressed to all the governors, he was anxious that the answer of our Assembly, likely to be the first, should harmonize with what he knew to be the sentiments and wishes of the body he had recently left. He feared that Mr. Nicholas, whose mind was not yet up to the mark of the times, would undertake the answer, and therefore pressed me to prepare it. I did so, and, with his aid, carried it through the House, with long and doubtful scruples from Mr. Nicholas and James Mercer, and a dash of cold water on it here and there, enfeebling it somewhat, but finally with unanimity, or a vote approaching it. This being passed, I repaired immediately to Philadelphia, and conveyed to Congress the first notice they had of it. It was entirely approved there. I took my seat with them on the 21st of June. On the 24th, a committee which had been appointed to prepare a declaration of the causes of taking up arms, brought in their report (drawn I believe by J. Rutledge) which, not being liked, the House recommitted it, on the 26th, and added Mr. Dickinson and myself to the committee. On the rising of the House, the committee having not yet met, I happened to find myself near Governor

W. Livingston, and proposed to him to draw the paper. He excused himself and proposed that I should draw it. On my pressing him with urgency, "we are as yet but new acquaintances, sir," said he, "why are you so earnest for my doing it?" "Because," said I, "I have been informed that you drew the Address to the people of Great Britain, a production, certainly, of the finest pen in America." "On that," says he, "perhaps, sir, you may not have been correctly informed." I had received the information in Virginia from Colonel Harrison on his return from that Congress. Lee, Livingston, and Jay had been the committee for that draught. The first, prepared by Lee, had been disapproved and recommitted. The second was drawn by Jay, but being presented by Governor Livingston, had led Colonel Harrison into the error. The next morning, walking in the hall of Congress, many members being assembled, but the House not yet formed, I observed Mr. Jay speaking to R. H. Lee, and leading him by the button of his coat to me. "I understand, sir," said he to me, "that this gentleman informed you, that Governor Livingston drew the Address to the people of Great Britain." I assured him, at once, that I had not received that information from Mr. Lee, and that not a word had ever passed on the subject between Mr. Lee and myself; and after some explanations the subject was dropped. These gentlemen had had some sparrings in debate before, and continued ever very hostile to each other.

I prepared a draught of the declaration committed to us. It was too strong for Mr. Dickinson. He still retained the hope of reconciliation with the mother country, and was unwilling it should be lessened by offensive statements. He was so honest a man, and so able a one, that he was greatly indulged even by those who could not feel his scruples. We therefore requested him to take the paper, and put it into a form he could approve. He did so, preparing an entire new statement, and preserving of the former only the last four paragraphs and half of the preceding one. We approved and reported it to Congress, who accepted it. Congress gave a signal proof of their indulgence to Mr. Dickinson, and of their great desire not to go too fast for any respectable part of our body, in permitting him to draw their second petition to the King according to his own ideas, and passing it with scarcely any amendment. The disgust against this humility was general; and Mr. Dickinson's delight at its passage was the only circumstance which reconciled them to it. The vote being passed, although further observation on it was out of order, he could not refrain from rising and expressing his satisfaction, and concluded by saying, "there is but one word, Mr. President, in the paper which I disapprove, and that is the word *Congress*"; on which Ben Harrison rose and said, "There is but one word in the paper, Mr. President, of which I approve, and that is the word *Congress.*"

On the 22d of July, Dr. Franklin, Mr. Adams, R. H. Lee, and myself, were appointed a committee to consider and report on Lord North's conciliatory resolution. The answer of the Virginia Assembly on that subject having been approved, I was requested by the committee to prepare this report, which will account for the similarity of feature in the two instruments.

On the 15th of May, 1776, the convention of Virginia instructed their delegates in Congress, to propose to that body to declare the colonies independent of Great Britain, and appointed a committee to prepare a declaration of rights and plan of government.

In Congress, Friday, June 7, 1776. The delegates from Virginia moved, in obedience to instructions from their constituents, that the Congress should declare that these United colonies are, and of right ought to be, free and independent states, that they are absolved from all allegiance to the British crown, and that all political connection between them and the state of Great Britain is, and ought to be, totally dissolved; that measures should be immediately taken for procuring the assistance of foreign powers, and a Confederation be formed to bind the colonies more closely together.

The House being obliged to attend at that time to some other business, the proposition was referred to the next day, when the members were ordered to attend punctually at ten o'clock.

Saturday, June 8. They proceeded to take it into consideration, and referred it to a committee of the whole, into which they immediately resolved themselves, and passed that day and Monday, the 10th, in debating on the subject.

It was argued by Wilson, Robert R. Livingston, E. Rutledge, Dickinson, and others—

That, though they were friends to the measures themselves, and saw the impossibility that we should ever again be united with Great Britain, yet they were against adopting them at this time:

That the conduct we had formerly observed was wise and proper now, of deferring to take any capital step till the voice of the people drove us into it:

That they were our power, and without them our declarations could not be carried into effect:

That the people of the middle colonies (Maryland, Delaware, Pennsylvania, the Jerseys and New York) were not yet ripe for bidding adieu to British connection, but that they were fast ripening, and, in a short time, would join in the general voice of America:

That the resolution, entered into by this House on the 15th of May, for suppressing the exercise of all powers derived from the crown, had shown, by the ferment into which it had thrown these middle colonies, that they had not yet accommodated their minds to a separation from the mother country:

That some of them had expressly forbidden their delegates to consent to such a declaration, and others had given no instructions, and consequently no powers to give such consent:

That if the delegates of any particular colony had no power to declare such colony independent, certain they were, the others could not declare it for them; the colonies being as yet perfectly independent of each other:

That the assembly of Pennsylvania was now sitting above stairs, their convention would sit within a few days, the convention of New York was now sitting, and those of the Jerseys and Delaware counties would meet on the Monday following, and it was probable these bodies would take up the question of Independence, and would declare to their delegates the voice of their state:

That if such a declaration should now be agreed to, these delegates must retire, and possibly their colonies might secede from the Union:

That such a secession would weaken us more than could be compensated by any foreign alliance:

That in the event of such a division, foreign powers would either refuse to join themselves to our fortunes, or, having us so much in their power as that desperate declaration would place us, they would insist on terms proportionately more hard and prejudicial:

That we had little reason to expect an alliance with those to whom alone, as yet, we had cast our eyes:

That France and Spain had reason to be jealous of that rising power, which would one day certainly strip them of all their American possessions:

That it was more likely they should form a connection with the British court, who, if they should find themselves unable otherwise to extricate themselves from their difficulties, would agree to a partition of our territories, restoring Canada to France, and the Floridas to Spain, to accomplish for themselves a recovery of these colonies:

That it would not be long before we should receive certain information of the disposition of the French court, from the agent whom we had sent to Paris for that purpose:

That if this disposition should be favorable, by waiting the event of the present campaign, which we all hoped would be successful, we should have reason to expect an alliance on better terms:

That this would in fact work no delay of any effectual aid from such ally, as, from the advance of the season and distance of our situation, it was impossible we could receive any assistance during this campaign:

That it was prudent to fix among ourselves the terms on which we should form alliance, before we declared we would form one at all events:

And that if these were agreed on, and our Declaration of Independence ready by the time our Ambassador should be prepared to sail, it would be as well as to go into that Declaration at this day.

On the other side, it was urged by J. Adams, Lee, Wythe, and others, that no gentleman had argued against the policy or the right of separation from Britain, nor had supposed it possible we should ever renew our connection; that they had only opposed its being now declared:

That the question was not whether, by a Declaration of Independence, we should make ourselves what we are not; but whether we should declare a fact which already exists:

That, as to the people or parliament of England, we had always been independent of them, their restraints on our trade deriving efficacy from our acquiescence only, and not from any rights they possessed of imposing them, and that so far, our connection had been federal only, and was now dissolved by the commencement of hostilities:

That, as to the King, we had been bound to him by allegiance, but that this bond was now dissolved by his assent to the last act of Parliament, by which he declares us out of his protection, and by his levying war on us, a fact which had long ago proved us out of his protection; it being a certain position in law, that allegiance and protection are reciprocal, the one ceasing when the other is withdrawn:

That James the II never declared the people of England out of his protection, yet his actions proved it, and the Parliament declared it:

No delegates then can be denied, or ever want, a power of declaring an existing truth:

That the delegates from the Delaware counties having declared their constituents ready to join, there are only two colonies, Pennsylvania and Maryland, whose delegates are absolutely tied up, and that these had, by their instructions, only reserved a right of confirming or rejecting the measure:

That the instructions from Pennsylvania might be accounted for from the times in which they were drawn, near a twelvemonth ago, since which the face of affairs has totally changed:

That within that time, it had become apparent that Britain was determined to accept nothing less than a *carte-blanche,* and that the King's answer to the Lord Mayor, Aldermen and Common Council of London, which had come to hand four days ago, must have satisfied everyone of this point:

That the people wait for us to lead the way:

That *they* are in favor of the measure, though the instructions given by some of their *representatives* are not:

That the voice of the representatives is not always consonant with the voice of the people, and that this is remarkably the case in these middle colonies:

That the effect of the resolution of the 15th of May has proved this, which, raising the murmurs of some in the colonies of Pennsylvania and Maryland, called forth the opposing voice of the freer part of the people, and proved them to be the majority even in these colonies:

That the backwardness of these two colonies might be ascribed, partly to the influence of proprietary power and connections, and partly, to their having not yet been attacked by the enemy:

That these causes were not likely to be soon removed, as there seemed no probability that the enemy would make either of these the seat of this summer's war:

That it would be vain to wait either weeks or months for perfect unanimity, since it was impossible that all men should ever become of one sentiment on any question:

That the conduct of some colonies, from the beginning of this contest, had given reason to suspect it was their settled policy to keep in the rear of the confederacy, that their particular prospect might be better, even in the worst event:

That, therefore, it was necessary for those colonies who had thrown themselves forward and hazarded all from the beginning, to come forward now also, and put all again to their own hazard:

That the history of the Dutch Revolution, of whom three states only confederated at first, proved that a secession of some colonies would not be so dangerous as some apprehended:

That a declaration of Independence alone could render it consistent with European delicacy, for European powers to treat with us, or even to receive an Ambassador from us:

That till this, they would not receive our vessels into their ports, nor acknowledge the adjudications of our courts of admiralty to be legitimate, in cases of capture of British vessels:

That though France and Spain may be jealous of our rising power, they must think it will be much more formidable with the addition of Great Britain; and will therefore see it their interest to prevent a coalition; but should they refuse, we shall be but where we are; whereas without trying, we shall never know whether they will aid us or not:

That the present campaign may be unsuccessful, and therefore we had better propose an alliance while our affairs wear a hopeful aspect:

That to wait the event of this campaign will certainly work delay, because, during the summer, France may assist us effectually, by cutting off those supplies of provisions from England and Ireland, on which the enemy's armies here are to depend; or by setting in motion the great power they have collected in the West Indies, and calling our enemy to the defence of the possessions they have there:

That it would be idle to lose time in settling the terms of alliance, till we had first determined we would enter into alliance:

That it is necessary to lose no time in opening a trade for our people, who will want clothes, and will want money too, for the payment of taxes:

And that the only misfortune is, that we did not enter into alliance with France six months sooner, as, besides opening her ports for the vent of our last year's produce, she might have marched an army into Germany, and prevented the petty princes there, from selling their unhappy subjects to subdue us.

It appearing in the course of these debates, that the colonies of New York, New Jersey, Pennsylvania, Delaware, Maryland, and South Carolina were not yet matured for falling from the parent stem, but that they were fast advancing to that state, it was thought most prudent to wait a while for them, and to postpone the final decision to July 1st; but, that this might occasion as little delay as possible, a committee was appointed to prepare a Declaration of Independence. The committee were John Adams, Dr. Franklin, Roger Sherman, Robert R. Livingston, and myself. Committees were also appointed, at the same time, to prepare a plan of confederation for the colonies, and to state the terms proper to be proposed for foreign alliance. The committee for drawing the Declaration of Independence, desired me to do it. It was accordingly done, and being approved by them, I reported it to the House on Friday, the 28th of June, when it was read, and ordered to lie on the table. On Monday, the 1st of July, the House resolved itself into a committee of the whole, and resumed the consideration of the original motion made by the delegates of Virginia, which, being again debated through the day, was carried in the affirmative by the votes of New Hampshire, Connecticut, Massachusetts, Rhode Island, New Jersey, Maryland, Virginia, North Carolina and Georgia. South Carolina and Pennsylvania voted against it. Delaware had but two members present, and they were divided. The delegates from New York declared they were for it themselves, and were assured their constituents were for it; but that their instructions having been drawn near a twelvemonth before, when reconciliation was still the general object, they were enjoined by them to do nothing which should impede that object. They, therefore, thought themselves not justifiable in voting on either side, and asked leave to withdraw from the question; which was given them. The committee rose and reported their resolution to the House. Mr. Edward Rutledge, of South Carolina, then requested the determination might be put off to the next day, as he believed his colleagues, though they disapproved of the resolution, would then join in it for the sake of unanimity. The ultimate question, whether the House would agree to the resolution of the committee, was accordingly postponed to the next day, when it was again moved, and South Carolina concurred in voting for it. In the meantime, a third member had come post from the Delaware counties, and turned the vote of that colony in favor of the resolution. Members of a different sentiment attending that morning from Pennsylvania also, her vote was changed, so that the whole twelve colonies who were authorized to vote at all, gave their voices for it; and, within a few days, the convention of New York approved of it, and thus supplied the void occasioned by the withdrawing of her delegates from the vote.

Congress proceeded the same day to consider the Declaration of Independence, which had been reported and lain on the table the Friday preceding, and on Monday referred to a committee of the whole. The pusillanimous idea that we had friends in England worth keeping terms with, still haunted the minds of many. For this reason, those passages which conveyed censures on the people of England were struck out, lest they should give them offence. The clause too, reprobating the enslaving the inhabitants of Africa, was struck out in complaisance to South Carolina and Georgia, who had never attempted to restrain the importation of slaves, and who, on the contrary, still wished to continue it. Our northern brethren also, I believe, felt a little tender under those censures; for though their people had very few slaves themselves, yet they had been pretty considerable carriers of them to others. The debates, having taken up the greater parts of the 2d, 3d, and 4th days of July, were, on the evening of the last, closed; the Declaration was reported by the committee, agreed to by the House, and signed by every member present, except Mr. Dickinson. As the sentiments of men are known not only by what they receive, but what they reject also, I will state the form of the Declaration as originally reported. The parts struck out by Congress shall be distinguished by a black line drawn under them; [1] and those inserted by them shall be placed in the margin, or in a concurrent column.

The Declaration thus signed on the 4th, on paper, was engrossed on parchment, and signed again on the 2d of August.

[Some erroneous statements of the proceedings on the Declaration of Independence having got before the public in latter times, Mr. Samuel A. Wells asked explanations of me, which are given in my letter to him of May 12, '19, before and now again referred to.[2] I took notes in my place

[1] The Declaration of Independence is printed separately in pp. 21-25.
[2] See pp. 757-761.

while these things were going on, and at their close wrote them out in form and with correctness, and from 1 to 7 of the two preceding sheets, are the originals then written; as the two following are of the earlier debates on the Confederation, which I took in like manner.]

On Friday, July 12, the committee appointed to draw the articles of Confederation reported them, and, on the 22d, the House resolved themselves into a committee to take them into consideration. On the 30th and 31st of that month, and 1st of the ensuing, those articles were debated which determined the proportion, or quota, of money which each state should furnish to the common treasury, and the manner of voting in Congress. The first of these articles was expressed in the original draught in these words: "Art. XI. All charges of war and all other expenses that shall be incurred for the common defence, or general welfare, and allowed by the United States assembled, shall be defrayed out of a common treasury, which shall be supplied by the several colonies in proportion to the number of inhabitants of every age, sex, and quality, except Indians not paying taxes, in each colony, a true account of which, distinguishing the white inhabitants, shall be triennially taken and transmitted to the Assembly of the United States."

Mr. Chase moved that the quotas should be fixed, not by the number of inhabitants of every condition, but by that of the "white inhabitants." He admitted that taxation should be always in proportion to property, that this was, in theory, the true rule; but that, from a variety of difficulties, it was a rule which could never be adopted in practice. The value of the property in every State, could never be estimated justly and equally. Some other measure for the wealth of the State must therefore be devised, some standard referred to, which would be more simple. He considered the number of inhabitants as a tolerably good criterion of property, and that this might always be obtained. He therefore thought it the best mode which we could adopt, with one exception only: he observed that negroes are property, and as such, cannot be distinguished from the lands or personalities held in those States where there are few slaves; that the surplus of profit which a Northern farmer is able to lay by, he invests in cattle, horses, &c., whereas a Southern farmer lays out the same surplus in slaves. There is no more reason, therefore, for taxing the Southern States on the farmer's head, and on his slave's head, than the Northern ones on their farmer's heads and the heads of their cattle; that the method proposed would, therefore, tax the Southern States according to their numbers and their wealth conjunctly, while the Northern would be taxed on numbers only: that negroes, in fact, should not be considered as members of the State, more than cattle, and that they have no more interest in it.

Mr. John Adams observed, that the numbers of people were taken by this article, as an index of the wealth of the State, and not as subjects of taxation; that, as to this matter, it was of no consequence by what name you called your people, whether by that of freemen or of slaves; that in some countries the laboring poor were called freemen, in others they were called slaves; but that the difference as to the state was imaginary only. What matters it whether a landlord, employing ten laborers on his farm, gives them annually as much money as will buy them the necessaries of life, or gives them those necessaries at short hand? The ten laborers add as much wealth annually to the State, increase its exports as much in the one case as the other. Certainly five hundred freemen produce no more profits, no greater surplus for the payment of taxes, than five hundred slaves. Therefore, the State in which are the laborers called freemen, should be taxed no more than that in which are those called slaves. Suppose, by an extraordinary operation of nature or of law, one half the laborers of a State could in the course of one night be transformed into slaves; would the State be made the poorer or the less able to pay taxes? That the condition of the laboring poor in most countries, that of the fishermen particularly of the Northern States, is as abject as that of slaves. It is the number of laborers which produces the surplus for taxation, and numbers, therefore, indiscriminately, are the fair index of wealth; that it is the use of the word "property" here, and its application to some of the people of the State, which produces the fallacy. How does the Southern farmer procure slaves? Either by importation or by purchase from his neighbor. If he imports a slave, he adds one to the number of laborers in his country, and proportionately to its profits and abilities to pay taxes; if he buys from his neighbor, it is only a transfer of a laborer from one farm to another, which does not change the annual produce of the State, and therefore, should not change its tax: that if a Northern farmer works ten laborers on his farm, he can, it is true, invest the surplus of ten men's labor in cattle; but so may the Southern farmer, working ten slaves; that a State of one hundred thousand freemen can maintain no more cattle, than one of one hundred thousand slaves. Therefore, they have no more of that kind of property; that a slave may indeed, from the custom of speech, be more properly called the wealth of his master, than the free laborer might be called the wealth of his employer; but as to the State, both were equally its wealth, and should, therefore, equally add to the quota of its tax.

Mr. Harrison proposed, as a compromise, that two slaves should be counted as one freeman. He affirmed that slaves did not do as much work as freemen, and doubted if two effected more than one; that this was proved by the price of labor; the hire of a laborer in the Southern colonies being from 8 to £12, while in the Northern it was generally £24.

Mr. Wilson said, that if this amendment should take place, the Southern colonies would have all the benefit of slaves, whilst the Northern ones would bear the burthen: that slaves increase the profits of a State, which the Southern States mean to take to themselves; that they also increase the burthen of defence, which would of course fall so much the heavier on the Northern: that slaves occupy the places of freemen, and eat their food. Dismiss your slaves, and freemen will take their places. It is our duty to lay every discouragement on the importation of slaves; but this amendment would give the *jus trium liberorum* to him who would import slaves: that other kinds of property were pretty equally distributed through all the colonies: there were as many cattle, horses and sheep, in the North as the South, and South as the North; but not so as to slaves: that experience has shown that those colonies have been always able to pay most, which have the most inhabitants, whether they be black or white; and the practice of the Southern colonies has always been to make every farmer pay poll taxes upon all his laborers, whether they be black or white. He acknowledges, indeed, that freemen work the most; but they consume the most also. They do not produce a greater surplus for taxation. The slave is neither fed nor clothed so expensively as a freeman. Again, white women are exempted from labor generally, but negro women are not. In this, then, the Southern States have an advantage as the article now stands. It has sometimes been said, that slavery is necessary, because the commodities they raise would be too dear for market if cultivated by freemen; but now it is said that the labor of the slave is the dearest.

Mr. Payne urged the original resolution of Congress, to proportion the quotas of the States to the number of souls.

Dr. Witherspoon was of opinion, that the value of lands and houses was the best estimate of the wealth of a nation, and that it was practicable to obtain such a valuation. This is the true barometer of wealth. The one now proposed is imperfect in itself, and unequal between the States. It has been objected that negroes eat the food of freemen, and, therefore, should be taxed; horses also eat the food of freemen; therefore they also should be taxed. It has been said too, that in carrying slaves into the estimate of the taxes the State is to pay, we do no more than those States themselves do, who always take slaves into the estimate of the taxes the individual is to pay. But the cases are not parallel. In the Southern colonies slaves pervade the whole colony; but they do not pervade the whole continent. That as to the original resolution of Congress, to proportion the quotas according to the souls, it was temporary only, and related to the moneys heretofore emitted: whereas we are now entering into a new compact, and therefore stand on original ground.

August 1. The question being put, the amendment proposed was rejected by the votes of New Hampshire, Massachusetts, Rhode Island, Connecticut, New York, New Jersey, and Pennsylvania, against those of Delaware, Maryland, Virginia, North and South Carolina. Georgia was divided.

The other article was in these words: "Art. XVII. In determining questions, each colony shall have one vote."

JULY 30, 31, AUGUST 1. Present forty-one members. Mr. Chase observed this article was the most likely to divide us, of any one proposed in the draught then under consideration: that the larger colonies had threatened they would not conferedate at all, if their weight in Congress should not be equal to the numbers of people they added to the confederacy; while the smaller ones declared against a union, if they did not retain an equal vote for the protection of their rights. That it was of the utmost consequence to bring the parties together, as, should we sever from each other, either no foreign power will ally with us at all, or the different States will form different alliances, and thus increase the horrors of those scenes of civil war and bloodshed, which in such a state of separation and independence, would render us a miserable people. That our importance, our interests, our peace required that we should confederate, and that mutual sacrifices should be made to effect a compromise of this difficult question. He was of opinion, the smaller colonies would lose their rights, if they were not in some instances allowed an equal vote; and, therefore, that a discrimination should take place among the questions which would come before Congress. That the smaller States should be secured in all questions concerning life or liberty, and the greater ones, in all respecting property. He, therefore, proposed, that in votes relating to money, the voice of each colony should be proportioned to the number of its inhabitants.

Dr. Franklin thought, that the votes should be so proportioned in all cases. He took notice that the Delaware counties had bound up their delegates to disagree to this article. He thought it a very extraordinary language to be held by any State, that they would not confederate with us, unless we would let them dispose of our money. Certainly, if we vote equally, we ought to pay equally; but the smaller States will hardly purchase the privilege at this price. That had he lived in a State where the representation, originally equal, had become unequal by time and accident, he might have submitted rather than disturb government; but that we should be very wrong to set out in this practice, when it is in our power to establish what is right. That at the time of the Union between England and Scotland, the latter had made the objection which the smaller States now do; but experience had proved that no unfairness had ever been shown them: that their advocates had prognosticated that it would again happen, as in times of old, that the whale would swallow Jonas, but he thought the prediction reversed in event, and that Jonas had swallowed the whale; for the Scotch had in fact got possession of the government, and gave laws to the English. He reprobated the original agreement of Congress to vote by colonies, and, therefore, was for their voting, in all cases, according to the number of taxables.

Dr. Witherspoon opposed every alteration of the article. All men admit that a confederacy is necessary. Should the idea get abroad that there is likely to be no union among us, it will damp the minds of the people, diminish the glory of our struggle, and lessen its importance; because it will open to our view future prospects of war and dissension among ourselves. If an equal vote be refused, the smaller States will become vassals to the larger; and all experience has shown that the vassals and subjects of free States are the most enslaved. He instanced the Helots of Sparta, and the provinces of Rome. He observed that foreign powers, discovering this blemish, would make it a handle for disengaging the smaller States from so unequal a confederacy. That the colonies should in fact be considered as individuals; and that, as such, in all disputes, they should have an equal vote; that they are now collected as individuals making a bargain with each other, and, of course, had a right to vote as individuals. That in the East India Company they voted by persons, and not by their proportion of stock. That the Belgic confederacy voted by provinces. That in questions of war the smaller States were as much interested as the larger, and therefore, should vote equally; and indeed, that the larger States were more likely to bring war on the confederacy, in proportion as their frontier was more extensive. He admitted that equality of representation was an excellent principle, but then it must be of things which are co-ordinate; that is, of things similar, and of the same nature: that nothing relating to individuals could ever come before Congress; nothing but what would respect colonies. He distinguished between an incorporating and a federal union. The union of England was an incorporating one; yet Scotland had suffered by that union; for that its inhabitants were drawn from it by the hopes of places and employments: nor was it an instance of equality of representation; because, while Scotland was allowed nearly a thirteenth of representation, they were to pay only one fortieth of the land tax. He expressed his hopes, that in the present enlightened state of men's minds, we might expect a lasting confederacy, if it was founded on fair principles.

John Adams advocated the voting in proportion to numbers. He said that we stand here as the representatives of the people: that in some States the people are many, in others they are few; that therefore, their vote here should be proportioned to the numbers from whom it comes. Reason, justice and equity never had weight enough on the face of the earth, to govern the councils of men. It is interest alone which does it, and it is interest alone which can be trusted: that therefore the interests within doors, should be the mathematical representatives of the interests without doors: that the individuality of the colonies is a mere sound. Does the individuality of a colony increase its wealth or numbers? If it does, pay equally. If it does not add weight in the scale of the confederacy, it cannot add to their rights, nor weight in argument. A. has £50, B. £500, C. £1000 in partnership. Is it just they should equally dispose of the moneys of the partnership? It has been said, we are independent individuals making a bargain together. The question is not what we are now, but what we ought to be when our bargain shall be made. The confederacy is to make us one individual only; it is to form us like separate parcels of metal, into one common mass. We shall no longer retain our separate individuality, but become a single individual as to all questions submitted to the confederacy. Therefore, all those reasons, which prove the justice and expediency of equal representation in other assemblies, hold good here. It has been objected that a proportional vote will endanger the smaller States. We answer that an equal vote will endanger the larger. Virginia, Pennsylvania, and Massachusetts, are the three greater colonies. Consider their distance, their difference of produce, of interests, and of manners, and it is apparent they can never have an interest or inclination to combine for the oppression of the smaller: that the smaller will naturally divide on all questions with the larger. Rhode Island, from its relation, similarity and intercourse, will generally pursue the same objects with Massachusetts; Jersey, Delaware, and Maryland, with Pennsylvania.

Dr. Rush took notice, that the decay of the liberties of the Dutch republic proceeded from three causes. 1. The perfect unanimity requisite on all occasions. 2. Their obligation to consult their constituents. 3. Their voting by provinces. This last destroyed the equality of representation, and the liberties of Great Britain also are sinking from the same defect. That a part of our rights is deposited in the hands of our legislatures. There, it was admitted, there should be an equality of representation. Another part of our rights is deposited in the hands of Congress: why is it not equally necessary there should be an equal representation there? Were it possible to collect the whole body of the people together, they would determine the questions submitted to them by their majority. Why should not the same majority decide when voting here, by their representatives? The larger colonies are so providentially divided in situation, as to render every fear of their combining visionary. Their interests are different, and their circumstances dissimilar. It is more probable they will become rivals, and leave it in the power of the smaller States to give preponderance to any scale they please. The voting by the number of free inhabitants, will have one excellent effect, that of inducing the colonies to discourage slavery, and to encourage the increase of their free inhabitants.

Mr. Hopkins observed, there were four larger, four smaller, and four middle-sized colonies. That the four largest would contain more than half the inhabitants of the confederated States, and therefore, would govern the others as they should please. That history affords no instance of such a thing as equal representation. The Germanic body votes by States. The Helvetic body does the same; and so does the Belgic confederacy. That too little is known of the ancient confederations, to say what was their practice.

Mr. Wilson thought, that taxation should be in proportion to wealth, but that representation should accord with the number of freemen. That government is a collection or result of the wills of all: that if any government could speak the will of all, it would be perfect; and that, so far as it departs from this, it becomes imperfect. It has been said that Congress is a representation of States, not of individuals. I say, that the objects of its care are all the individuals of the States. It is strange that annexing the name of "State" to ten thousand men, should give them an equal right with forty thousand. This must be the effect of magic, not of reason. As to those matters which are referred to Congress, we are not so many States; we are one large State. We lay aside our individuality, whenever we come here. The Germanic body is a burlesque on government; and their practice, on any point, is a sufficient authority and proof that it is wrong. The greatest imperfection in the constitution of the Belgic confederacy is their voting by provinces. The interest of the whole is constantly sacrificed to that of the small States. The history of the war in the reign of Queen Anne sufficiently proves this. It is asked, shall nine colonies put it into the power of four to govern them as they please? I invert the question, and ask, shall two millions of people put it in the power of one million to govern them as they please? It is pretended, too, that the smaller colonies will be in danger from the greater. Speak in honest language and say, the minority will be in danger from the majority. And is there an assembly on earth, where this danger may not be equally pretended? The truth is, that our proceedings will then be consentaneous with the interests of the majority, and so they ought to be. The probability is much greater, that the larger States will disagree, than that they will combine. I defy the wit of man to invent a possible case, or to suggest any one thing on earth, which shall be for the interests of Virginia, Pennsylvania and Massachusetts, and which will not also be for the interest of the other States.

These articles, reported July 12, '76, were debated from day to day, and time to time, for two years, were ratified July 9, '78, by ten States, by New Jersey on the 26th of November of the same year, and by Delaware on the

23d of February following. Maryland alone held off two years more, acceding to them March 1, '81, and thus closing the obligation.

Our delegation had been renewed for the ensuing year, commencing August 11; but the new government was now organized, a meeting of the legislature was to be held in October, and I had been elected a member by my county. I knew that our legislation, under the regal government, had many very vicious points which urgently required reformation, and I thought I could be of more use in forwarding that work. I therefore retired from my seat in Congress on the 2d of September, resigned it, and took my place in the legislature of my State, on the 7th of October.

On the 11th, I moved for leave to bring in a bill for the establishment of courts of justice, the organization of which was of importance. I drew the bill; it was approved by the committee, reported and passed, after going through its due course.

On the 12th, I obtained leave to bring in a bill declaring tenants in tail to hold their lands in fee simple. In the earlier times of the colony, when lands were to be obtained for little or nothing, some provident individuals procured large grants; and, desirous of founding great families for themselves, settled them on their descendants in fee tail. The transmission of this property from generation to generation, in the same name, raised up a distinct set of families, who, being privileged by law in the perpetuation of their wealth, were thus formed into a Patrician order, distinguished by the splendor and luxury of their establishments. From this order, too, the king habitually selected his counsellors of State; the hope of which distinction devoted the whole corps to the interests and will of the crowd. To annul this privilege, and instead of an aristocracy of wealth, of more harm and danger, than benefit, to society, to make an opening for the aristocracy of virtue and talent, which nature has wisely provided for the direction of the interests of society, and scattered with equal hand through all its conditions, was deemed essential to a well-ordered republic. To effect it, no violence was necessary, no deprivation of natural right, but rather an enlargement of it by a repeal of the law. For this would authorize the present holder to divide the property among his children equally, as his affections were divided; and would place them, by natural generation, on the level of their fellow citizens. But this repeal was strongly opposed by Mr. Pendleton, who was zealously attached to ancient establishments; and who, taken all in all, was the ablest man in debate I have ever met with. He had not indeed the poetical fancy of Mr. Henry, his sublime imagination, his lofty and overwhelming diction; but he was cool, smooth and persuasive; his language flowing, chaste and embellished; his conceptions quick, acute and full of resource; never vanquished: for if he lost the main battle, he returned upon you, and regained so much of it as to make it a drawn one, by dexterous manœuvres, skirmishes in detail, and the recovery of small advantages which, little singly, were important all together. You never knew when you were clear of him, but were harassed by his perseverance, until the patience was worn down of all who had less of it than himself. Add to this, that he was one of the most virtuous and benevolent of men, the kindest friend, the most amiable and pleasant of companions, which ensured a favorable reception to whatever came from him. Finding that the general principle of entails could not be maintained, he took his stand on an amendment which he proposed, instead of an absolute abolition, to permit the tenant in tail to convey in fee simple, if he chose it; and he was within a few votes of saving so much of the old law. But the bill passed finally for entire abolition.

In that one of the bills for organizing our judiciary system, which proposed a court of Chancery, I had provided for a trial by jury of all matters of fact, in that as well as in the courts of law. He defeated it by the introduction of four words only, *"if either party choose."* The consequence has been, that as no suitor will say to his judge, "Sir, I distrust you, give me a jury," juries are rarely, I might say, perhaps, never, seen in that court, but when called for by the Chancellor of his own accord.

The first establishment in Virginia which became permanent, was made in 1607. I have found no mention of negroes in the colony until about 1650. The first brought here as slaves were by a Dutch ship; after which the English commenced the trade, and continued it until the revolutionary war. That suspended, *ipso facto,* their further importation for the present, and the business of the war pressing constantly on the legislature, this subject was not acted on finally until the year '78, when I brought in a bill to prevent their further importation. This passed without opposition, and stopped the increase of the evil by importation, leaving to future efforts its final eradication.

The first settlers of this colony were Englishmen, loyal subjects to their king and church, and the grant to Sir Walter Raleigh contained an express proviso that their laws "should not be against the true Christian faith, now professed in the church of England." As soon as the state of the colony admitted, it was divided into parishes, in each of which was established a minister of the Anglican church, endowed with a fixed salary, in tobacco, a glebe house and land with the other necessary appendages. To meet these expenses, all the inhabitants of the parishes were assessed, whether they were or not members of the established church. Towards Quakers who came here, they were most cruelly intolerant, driving them from the colony by the severest penalties. In process of time, however, other sectarisms were introduced, chiefly of the Presbyterian family; and the established clergy, secure for life in their glebes and salaries, adding to these, generally, the emoluments of a classical school, found employment enough, in their farms and school-rooms, for the rest of the week, and devoted Sunday only to the edification of their flock, by service, and a sermon at their parish church. Their other pastoral functions were little attended to. Against this inactivity, the zeal and industry of sectarian preachers had an open and undisputed field; and by the time of the revolution, a majority of the inhabitants had become dissenters from the established church, but were still obliged to pay contribution to support the pastors of the minority. This unrighteous compulsion, to maintain teachers of what they deemed religious errors, was grievously felt during the regal government, and without a hope of relief. But the first republican legislature, which met in '76, was crowded with petitions to abolish this spiritual tyrannny. These brought on the severest contests in which I have ever been engaged. Our great opponents were Mr. Pendleton and Robert Carter Nicholas; honest men, but zealous churchmen. The petitions were referred to the committee of the whole house on the state of the country and, after desperate contests in that committee, almost daily from the 11th of October to the 5th of December, we prevailed so far only, as to repeal the laws which rendered criminal the maintenance of any religious opinions, the forbearance of repairing to church, or the exercise of any mode of worship; and further, to exempt dissenters from contributions to the support of the established church; and to suspend, only until the next session, levies on the members of that church for the salaries of their own incumbents. For although the majority of our citizens were dissenters, as has been observed, a majority of the legislature were churchmen. Among these, however, were some reasonable and liberal men, who enabled us, on some points, to obtain feeble majorities. But our opponents carried, in the general resolutions of the committee of November 19, a declaration that religious assemblies ought to be regulated, and that provision ought to be made for continuing the succession of the clergy, and superintending their conduct. And, in the bill now passed, was inserted an express reservation of the question, Whether a general assessment should not be established by law, on everyone, to the support of the pastor of his choice; or whether all should be left to voluntary contributions; and on this question, debated at every session, from '76 to '79 (some of our dissenting allies, having now secured their particular object, going over to the advocates of a general assessment), we could only obtain a suspension from session to session until '79, when the question against a general assessment was finally carried, and the establishment of the Anglican church entirely put down. In justice to the two honest but zealous opponents who have been named, I must add, that although, from their natural temperaments, they were more disposed generally to acquiesce in things as they are, than to risk innovations, yet whenever the public will had once decided, none were more faithful or exact in their obedience to it.

The seat of our government had originally been fixed in the peninsula of Jamestown, the first settlement of the colonists; and had been afterwards removed a few miles inland to Williamsburg. But this was at a time when our settlements had not extended beyond the tide waters. Now they had crossed the Alleghany; and the centre of population was very far removed from what it had been. Yet Williamsburg was still the depository of our archives, the habitual residence of the Governor and many other of the public functionaries, the established place for the sessions of the legislature, and the magazine of our military stores; and its situation was so exposed that it might be taken at any time in war, and, at this time particularly, an enemy might in the night run up either of the rivers, between which it lies, land a force above, and take possession of the place, without the possibility of saving either persons or things. I had proposed its removal so early as October, '76; but it did not prevail until the session of May, '79.

Early in the session of May, '79, I prepared, and obtained leave to bring in a bill, declaring who should be deemed citizens, asserting the natural right of expatriation, and prescribing the mode of exercising it. This, when I withdrew from the house, on the 1st of June following, I left in the hands of George Mason, and it was passed on the 26th of that month.

In giving this account of the laws of which I was myself the mover and draughtsman, I, by no means, mean to claim to myself the merit of obtaining their passage. I had many occasional and strenuous coadjutors in debate, and one, most steadfast, able and zealous; who was himself a host. This was George Mason, a man of the first order of wisdom among those who acted on the theatre of the revolution, of expansive mind, profound judgment, cogent in argument, learned in the lore of our former constitution, and earnest for the republican change on democratic principles. His elocution was neither flowing nor smooth; but his language was strong, his manner most impressive, and strengthened by a dash of biting cynicism, when provocation made it seasonable.

Mr. Wythe, while speaker in the two sessions of 1777, between his return from Congress and his appointment to the Chancery, was an able and constant associate in whatever was before a committee of the whole. His pure integrity, judgment and reasoning powers, gave him great weight.

Of him, see more in some notes inclosed in my letter of August 31, 1821, to Mr. John Saunderson.[1]

Mr. Madison came into the House in 1776, a new member and young; which circumstances, concurring with his extreme modesty, prevented his venturing himself in debate before his removal to the Council of State, in November, '77. From thence he went to Congress, then consisting of few members. Trained in these successive schools, he acquired a habit of self-possession, which placed at ready command the rich resources of his luminous and discriminating mind, and of his extensive information, and rendered him the first of every assembly afterwards, of which he became a member. Never wandering from his subject into vain declamation, but pursuing it closely, in language pure, classical and copious, soothing always the feelings of his adversaries by civilities and softness of expression, he rose to the eminent station which he held in the great National Convention of 1787; and in that of Virginia which followed, he sustained the new constitution in all its parts, bearing off the palm against the logic of George Mason, and the fervid declamation of Mr. Henry. With these consummate powers, were united a pure and spotless virtue which no calumny has ever attempted to sully. Of the powers and polish of his pen, and of the wisdom of his administration in the highest office of the nation, I need say nothing. They have spoken, and will forever speak for themselves.

So far we were proceeding in the details of reformation only; selecting points of legislation, prominent in character and principle, urgent, and indicative of the strength of the general pulse of reformation. When I left Congress, in '76, it was in the persuasion that our whole code must be reviewed, adapted to our republican form of government; and, now that we had no negatives of Councils, Governors, and Kings to restrain us from doing right, that it should be corrected, in all its parts, with a single eye to reason, and the good of those for whose government it was framed. Early, therefore, in the session of '76, to which I returned, I moved and presented a bill for the revision of the laws, which was passed on the 24th of October; and on the 5th of November, Mr. Pendleton, Mr. Wythe, George Mason, Thomas L. Lee, and myself, were appointed a committee to execute the work. We agreed to meet at Fredericksburg to settle the plan of operation, and to distribute the work. We met there accordingly, on the 13th of January, 1777. The first question was, whether we should propose to abolish the whole existing system of laws, and prepare a new and complete Institute, or preserve the general system, and only modify it to the present state of things. Mr. Pendleton, contrary to his usual disposition in favor of ancient things, was for the former proposition, in which

[1] See pp. 767-768.

he was joined by Mr. Lee. To this it was objected, that to abrogate our whole system would be a bold measure, and probably far beyond the views of the legislature; that they had been in the practice of revising, from time to time, the laws of the colony, omitting the expired, the repealed, and the obsolete, amending only those retained, and probably meant we should now do the same, only including the British statutes as well as our own: that to compose a new Institute, like those of Justinian and Bracton, or that of Blackstone, which was the model proposed by Mr. Pendleton, would be an arduous undertaking, of vast research, of great consideration and judgment; and when reduced to a text, every word of that text, from the imperfection of human language, and its incompetence to express distinctly every shade of idea, would become a subject of question and chicanery, until settled by repeated adjudications; and this would involve us for ages in litigation and render property uncertain, until, like the statutes of old, every word had been tried and settled by numerous decisions, and by new volumes of reports and commentaries; and that no one of us, probably, would undertake such a work, which to be systematical, must be the work of one hand. This last was the opinion of Mr. Wythe, Mr. Mason, and myself. When we proceeded to the distribution of the work, Mr. Mason excused himself, as, being no lawyer, he felt himself unqualified for the work, and he resigned soon after. Mr. Lee excused himself on the same ground, and died, indeed, in a short time. The other two gentlemen, therefore, and myself divided the work among us. The common law and statutes to the 4 James I. (when our separate legislature was established) were assigned to me; the British statutes, from that period to the present day, to Mr. Wythe; and the Virginia laws to Mr. Pendleton. As the law of Descents, and the criminal law fell of course within my portion, I wished the committee to settle the leading principles of these, as a guide for me in framing them; and, with respect to the first, I proposed to abolish the law of primogeniture, and to make real property descendible in parcenary to the next of kin, as personal property is, by the statute of distribution. Mr. Pendleton wished to preserve the right of primogeniture, but seeing at once that that could not prevail, he proposed we should adopt the Hebrew principle, and give a double portion to the elder son. I observed, that if the eldest son could eat twice as much, or do double work, it might be a natural evidence of his right to a double portion; but being on a par in his powers and wants, with his brothers and sisters, he should be on a par also in the partition of the patrimony; and such was the decision of the other members.

On the subject of the Criminal law, all were agreed, that the punishment of death should be abolished, except for treason and murder; and that, for other felonies, should be substituted hard labor in the public works, and in some cases, the *Lex talionis*. How this last revolting principle came to obtain our approbation I do not remember. There remained, indeed, in our laws, a vestige of it in a single case of a slave; it was the English law, in the time of the Anglo-Saxons, copied probably from the Hebrew law of "an eye for an eye, a tooth for a tooth," and it was the law of several ancient people; but the modern mind had left it far in the rear of its advances. These points, however, being settled, we repaired to our respective homes for the preparation of the work.

In the execution of my part, I thought it material not to vary the diction of the ancient statutes by modernizing it, nor to give rise to new questions by new expressions. The text of these statutes had been so fully explained and defined, by numerous adjudications, as scarcely ever now to produce a question in our courts. I thought it would be useful, also, in all new draughts, to reform the style of the later British statutes, and of our own acts of Assembly; which, from their verbosity, their endless tautologies, their involutions of case within case, and parenthesis within parenthesis, and their multiplied efforts at certainty, by *saids* and *aforesaids,* by *ors* and by *ands,* to make them more plain, are really rendered more perplexed and incomprehensible, not only to common readers, but to the lawyers themselves. We were employed in this work from that time to February, 1779, when we met at Williamsburg, that is to say, Mr. Pendleton, Mr. Wythe and myself; and meeting day by day, we examined critically our several parts, sentence by sentence, scrutinizing and amending, until we had agreed on the whole. We then returned home, had fair copies made of our several parts, which were reported to the General Assembly, June 18, 1779, by Mr. Wythe and myself, Mr. Pendleton's residence being distant, and he having authorized us by letter to declare his approbation. We had, in this work, brought so much of the Common law as it was thought necessary to alter, all the British statutes from *Magna Charta* to the present day, and all the laws of Virginia, from the establishment of our legislature, in the 4th Jac. 1. to the present time, which we thought should be retained, within the compass of one hundred and twenty-six bills, making a printed folio of ninety pages only. Some bills were taken out, occasionally, from time to time, and passed; but the main body of the work was not entered on by the legislature until after the general peace, in 1785, when, by the unwearied exertions of Mr. Madison, in opposition to the endless quibbles, chicaneries, perversions, vexations and delays of lawyers and demi-lawyers, most of the bills were passed by the legislature, with little alteration.

The bill for establishing religious freedom, the principles of which had, to a certain degree, been enacted before, I had drawn in all the latitude

of reason and right. It still met with opposition; but, with some mutila-
tions in the preamble, it was finally passed; and a singular proposition
proved that its protection of opinion was meant to be universal. Where
the preamble declares, that coercion is a departure from the plan of the
holy author of our religion, an amendment was proposed, by inserting the
word "Jesus Christ," so that it should read, "a departure from the plan
of Jesus Christ, the holy author of our religion"; the insertion was rejected
by a great majority, in proof that they meant to comprehend, within the
mantle of its protection, the Jew and the Gentile, the Christian and Ma-
hometan, the Hindoo, and Infidel of every denomination.

Beccaria, and other writers on crimes and punishments, had satisfied the
reasonable world of the unrightfulness and inefficacy of the punishment of
crimes by death; and hard labor on roads, canals and other public works,
had been suggested as a proper substitute. The Revisors had adopted these
opinions; but the general idea of our country had not yet advanced to
that point. The bill, therefore, for proportioning crimes and punishments,
was lost in the House of Delegates by a majority of a single vote. I learned
afterwards, that the substitute of hard labor in public, was tried (I believe
it was in Pennsylvania) without success. Exhibited as a public spectacle,
with shaved heads and mean clothing, working on the high roads, produced in the criminals such a prostration of character, such an abandonment of self-respect, as, instead of reforming, plunged them into the most
desperate and hardened depravity of morals and character. To pursue the
subject of this law.—I was written to in 1785 (being then in Paris) by directors appointed to superintend the building of a Capitol in Richmond,
to advise them as to a plan, and to add to it one of a Prison. Thinking it
a favorable opportunity of introducing into the State an example of architecture, in the classic style of antiquity, and the Maison quarrée of Nismes,
an ancient Roman temple, being considered as the most perfect model existing of what may be called Cubic architecture, I applied to M. Clerissault,
who had published drawings of the Antiquities of Nismes, to have me a
model of the building made in stucco, only changing the order from Corinthian to Ionic, on account of the difficulty of the Corinthian capitals. I
yielded, with reluctance, to the taste of Clerissault, in his preference of the
modern capital of Scamozzi to the more noble capital of antiquity. This
was executed by the artist whom Choiseul Gouffier had carried with him
to Constantinople, and employed, while Ambassador there, in making those
beautiful models of the remains of Grecian architecture which are to be
seen at Paris. To adapt the exterior to our use, I drew a plan for the interior, with the apartments necessary for legislative, executive, and judiciary
purposes; and accommodated in their size and distribution to the form and

dimensions of the building. These were forwarded to the Directors, in 1786, and were carried into execution, with some variations, not for the better, the most important of which, however, admit of future correction. With respect to the plan of a Prison, requested at the same time, I had heard of a benevolent society, in England, which had been indulged by the government, in an experiment of the effect of labor, in *solitary confinement,* on some of their criminals; which experiment had succeeded beyond expectation. The same idea had been suggested in France, and an Architect of Lyons had proposed a plan of a well-contrived edifice, on the principle of solitary confinement. I procured a copy, and as it was too large for our purposes, I drew one on a scale less extensive, but susceptible of additions as they should be wanting. This I sent to the Directors, instead of a plan of a common prison, in the hope that it would suggest the idea of labor in solitary confinement, instead of that on the public works, which we had adopted in our Revised Code. Its principle, accordingly, but not its exact form, was adopted by Latrobe in carrying the plan into execution, by the erection of what is now called the Penitentiary, built under his direction. In the meanwhile, the public opinion was ripening, by time, by reflection, and by the example of Pennsylvania, where labor on the highways had been tried, without approbation, from 1786 to '89, and had been followed by their Penitentiary system on the principle of confinement and labor, which was proceeding auspiciously. In 1796, our legislature resumed the subject, and passed the law for amending the Penal laws of the commonwealth. They adopted solitary, instead of public, labor, established a gradation in the duration of the confinement, approximated the style of the law more to the modern usage, and, instead of the settled distinctions of murder and manslaughter, preserved in my bill, they introduced the new terms of murder in the first and second degree. Whether these have produced more or fewer questions of definition, I am not sufficiently informed of our judiciary transactions to say. I will here, however, insert the text of my bill, with the notes I made in the course of my researches into the subject.[1]

The acts of Assembly concerning the College of William and Mary, were properly within Mr. Pendleton's portion of our work; but these related chiefly to its revenue, while its constitution, organization and scope of science, were derived from its charter. We thought that on this subject, a systematical plan of general education should be proposed, and I was requested to undertake it. I accordingly prepared three bills for the Revisal, proposing three distinct grades of education, reaching all classes. 1st. Elementary schools, for all children generally, rich and poor. 2d. Colleges, for

[1] See pp. 29-40.

a middle degree of instruction, calculated for the common purposes of life, and such as would be desirable for all who were in easy circumstances. And, 3d, an ultimate grade for teaching the sciences generally, and in their highest degree. The first bill proposed to lay off every county into Hundreds, or Wards, of a proper size and population for a school, in which reading, writing, and common arithmetic should be taught; and that the whole State should be divided into twenty-four districts, in each of which should be a school for classical learning, grammar, geography, and the higher branches of numerical arithmetic. The second bill proposed to amend the constitution of William and Mary College, to enlarge its sphere of science, and to make it in fact a University. The third was for the establishment of a library. These bills were not acted on until the same year, '96, and then only so much of the first as provided for elementary schools. The College of William and Mary was an establishment purely of the Church of England; the Visitors were required to be all of that Church; the Professors to subscribe its thirty-nine Articles; its Students to learn its Catechism; and one of its fundamental objects was declared to be, to raise up Ministers for that church. The religious jealousies, therefore, of all the dissenters, took alarm lest this might give an ascendancy to the Anglican sect, and refused acting on that bill. Its local eccentricity, too, and unhealthy autumnal climate, lessened the general inclination towards it. And in the Elementary bill, they inserted a provision which completely defeated it; for they left it to the court of each county to determine for itself, when this act should be carried into execution, within their county. One provision of the bill was, that the expenses of these schools should be borne by the inhabitants of the county, every one in proportion to his general tax rate. This would throw on wealth the education of the poor; and the justices, being generally of the more wealthy class, were unwilling to incur that burden, and I believe it was not suffered to commence in a single county. I shall recur again to this subject, towards the close of my story, if I should have life and resolution enough to reach that term; for I am already tired of talking about myself.

The bill on the subject of slaves, was a mere digest of the existing laws respecting them, without any intimation of a plan for a future and general emancipation. It was thought better that this should be kept back, and attempted only by way of amendment, whenever the bill should be brought on. The principles of the amendment, however, were agreed on, that is to say, the freedom of all born after a certain day, and deportation at a proper age. But it was found that the public mind would not yet bear the proposition, nor will it bear it even at this day. Yet the day is not distant when it must bear and adopt it, or worse will follow. Nothing is more certainly written in the book of fate, than that these people are to be free; nor is it less certain that the two races, equally free, cannot live in the same government. Nature, habit, opinion have drawn indelible lines of distinction between them. It is still in our power to direct the process of emancipation and deportation, peaceably, and in such slow degree, as that the evil will wear off insensibly, and their place be, *pari passu,* filled up by free white laborers. If, on the contrary, it is left to force itself on, human nature must shudder at the prospect held up. We should in vain look for an example in the Spanish deportation or deletion of the Moors. This precedent would fall far short of our case.

I considered four of these bills, passed or reported, as forming a system by which every fibre would be eradicated of ancient or future aristocracy; and a foundation laid for a government truly republican. The repeal of the laws of entail would prevent the accumulation and perpetuation of wealth, in select families, and preserve the soil of the country from being daily more and more absorbed in mortmain. The abolition of primogeniture, and equal partition of inheritances, removed the feudal and unnatural distinctions which made one member of every family rich, and all the rest poor, substituting equal partition, the best of all Agrarian laws. The restoration of the rights of conscience relieved the people from taxation for the support of a religion not theirs; for the establishment was truly of the religion of the rich, the dissenting sects being entirely composed of the less wealthy people; and these, by the bill for a general education, would be qualified to understand their rights, to maintain them, and to exercise with intelligence their parts in self-government; and all this would be effected, without the violation of a single natural right of any one individual citizen. To these, too, might be added, as a further security, the introduction of the trial by jury, into the Chancery courts, which have already ingulfed, and continue to ingulf, so great a proportion of the jurisdiction over our property.

On the 1st of June, 1779, I was appointed Governor of the Commonwealth, and retired from the legislature. Being elected, also, one of the Visitors of William and Mary college, a self-electing body, I effected, during my residence in Williamsburg that year, a change in the organization of that institution, by abolishing the Grammar school, and the two professorships of Divinity and Oriental languages, and substituting a professorship of Law and Police, one of Anatomy, Medicine and Chemistry, and one of Modern languages; and the charter confining us to six professorships, we added the Law of Nature and Nations, and the Fine Arts to the duties of the Moral professor, and Natural History to those of the professor of Mathematics and Natural Philosophy.

Being now, as it were, identified with the Commonwealth itself, to write my own history, during the two years of my administration, would be to write the public history of that portion of the revolution within this State. This has been done by others, and particularly by Mr. Girardin, who wrote his Continuation of Burke's History of Virginia, while at Milton, in this neighborhood, had free access to all my papers while composing it, and has given as faithful an account as I could myself. For this portion, therefore, of my own life, I refer altogether to his history. From a belief that, under the pressure of the invasion under which we were then laboring, the public would have more confidence in a Military chief, and that the Military commander, being invested with the Civil power also, both might be wielded with more energy, promptitude and effect for the defence of the State, I resigned the administration at the end of my second year, and General Nelson was appointed to succeed me.

Soon after my leaving Congress, in September, '76, to wit, on the last day of that month, I had been appointed, with Dr. Franklin, to go to France, as a Commissioner, to negotiate treaties of alliance and commerce with that government. Silas Deane, then in France, acting as agent for procuring military stores, was joined with us in commission. But such was the state of my family that I could not leave it, nor could I expose it to the dangers of the sea, and of capture by the British ships, then covering the ocean. I saw, too, that the laboring oar was really at home, where much was to be done, of the most permanent interest, in new modelling our governments, and much to defend our fanes and fire-sides from the desolations of an invading enemy, pressing on our country in every point. I declined, therefore, and Dr. Lee was appointed in my place. On the 15th of June, 1781, I had been appointed, with Mr. Adams, Dr. Franklin, Mr. Jay, and Mr. Laurens, a Minister Plenipotentiary for negotiating peace, then expected to be effected through the mediation of the Empress of Russia. The same reasons obliged me still to decline; and the negotiation was in fact never entered on. But, in the autumn of the next year, 1782, Congress receiving assurances that a general peace would be concluded in the winter and spring, they renewed my appointment on the 13th of November of that year. I had, two months before that, lost the cherished companion of my life, in whose affections, unabated on both sides, I had lived the last ten years in unchequered happiness. With the public interests, the state of my mind concurred in recommending the change of scene proposed; and I accepted the appointment, and left Monticello on the 19th of December, 1782, for Philadelphia, where I arrived on the 27th. The Minister of France, Luzerne, offered me a passage in the Romulus frigate, which I accepted; but she was then lying a few miles below Baltimore, blocked up in the ice. I remained, therefore, a month in Philadelphia, looking over the papers in the office of State, in order to possess myself of the general state of our foreign relations, and then went to Baltimore, to await the liberation of the frigate from the ice. After waiting there nearly a month, we received information that a Provisional treaty of peace had been signed by our Commissioners on the 3d of September, 1782, to become absolute, on the conclusion of peace between France and Great Britain. Considering my proceeding to Europe as now of no utility to the public, I returned immediately to Philadelphia, to take the orders of Congress, and was excused by them from further proceeding. I, therefore, returned home, where I arrived on the 15th of May, 1783.

On the 6th of the following month, I was appointed by the legislature a delegate to Congress, the appointment to take place on the 1st of November ensuing, when that of the existing delegation would expire. I, accordingly, left home on the 16th of October, arrived at Trenton, where Congress was sitting, on the 3d of November, and took my seat on the 4th, on which day Congress adjourned, to meet at Annapolis on the 26th.

Congress had now become a very small body, and the members very remiss in their attendance on its duties, insomuch, that a majority of the States, necessary by the Confederation to constitute a House even for minor business, did not assemble until the 13th of December.

They, as early as January 7, 1782, had turned their attention to the moneys current in the several States, and had directed the Financier, Robert Morris, to report to them a table of rates, at which the foreign coins should be received at the treasury. That officer, or rather his assistant, Gouverneur Morris, answered them on the 15th, in an able and elaborate statement of the denominations of money current in the several States, and of the comparative value of the foreign coins chiefly in circulation with us. He went into the consideration of the necessity of establishing a standard of value with us, and of the adoption of a money Unit. He proposed for that Unit, such a fraction of pure silver as would be a common measure of the penny of every State, without leaving a fraction. This common divisor he found to be 1-1440 of a dollar, or 1-1600 of the crown sterling. The value of a dollar was, therefore, to be expressed by 1,440 units, and of a crown by 1,600; each Unit containing a quarter of a grain of fine silver. Congress turning again their attention to this subject the following year, the Financier, by a letter of April 30, 1783, further explained and urged the Unit he had proposed; but nothing more was done on it until the ensuing year, when it was again taken up, and referred to a committee, of which I was a member. The general views of the Financier were sound, and the principle was ingenious on which he proposed to found his Unit; but it was too minute for ordinary use, too laborious for computation, either by the head or in figures. The price of a loaf of bread, $\frac{1}{20}$ of a dollar, would be 72 units.

A pound of butter, $\frac{1}{5}$ of a dollar, 288 units.

A horse or bullock, of eighty dollars value, would require a notation of six figures, to wit, 115,200, and the public debt, suppose of eighty millions, would require twelve figures, to wit, 115,200,000,000 units. Such a system of money-arithmetic would be entirely unmanageable for the common purposes of society. I proposed, therefore, instead of this, to adopt the Dollar as our Unit of account and payment, and that its divisions and sub-divisions should be in the decimal ratio. I wrote some Notes on the subject, which I submitted to the consideration of the Financier. I received his answer and adherence to his general system, only agreeing to take for his Unit one hundred of those he first proposed, so that a Dollar should be $14^{4}\%_{00}$, and a crown 16 units. I replied to this, and printed my notes and reply on a flying sheet, which I put into the hands of the members of Congress for consideration, and the Committee agreed to report on my principle. This was adopted the ensuing year, and is the system which now prevails. I insert, here, the Notes and Reply, as showing the different views on which the adoption of our money system hung.[1] The divisions into dimes, cents, and mills is now so well understood, that it would be easy of introduction into the kindred branches of weights and measure. I use, when I travel, an Odometer of Clarke's invention, which divides the mile into cents, and I find every one comprehends a distance readily, when stated to him in miles and cents; so he would in feet and cents, pounds and cents, &c.

The remissness of Congress, and their permanent session, began to be a subject of uneasiness; and even some of the legislatures had recommended to them intermissions, and periodical sessions. As the Confederation had made no provision for a visible head of the government, during vacations of Congress, and such a one was necessary to superintend the executive business, to receive and communicate with foreign ministers and nations, and to assemble Congress on sudden and extraordinary emergencies, I proposed, early in April, the appointment of a committee, to be called the "Committee of the States," to consist of a member from each State, who should remain in session during the recess of Congress: that the functions of Congress should be divided into executive and legislative, the latter to be reserved, and the former, by a general resolution, to be delegated to that Committee. This proposition was afterwards agreed to; a Committee appointed, who entered on duty on the subsequent adjournment of Congress, quarrelled very soon, split into two parties, abandoned their post, and left the government without any visible head, until the next meeting in Con-

[1] See pp. 194-203.

gress. We have since seen the same thing take place in the Directory of France; and I believe it will forever take place in any Executive consisting of a plurality. Our plan, best, I believe, combines wisdom and practicability, by providing a plurality of Counsellors, but a single Arbiter for ultimate decision. I was in France when we heard of this schism, and separation of our Committee, and, speaking with Dr. Franklin of this singular disposition of men to quarrel, and divide into parties, he gave his sentiments, as usual, by way of Apologue. He mentioned the Eddystone lighthouse, in the British channel, as being built on a rock, in the mid-channel, totally inaccessible in winter, from the boisterous character of that sea, in that season; that, therefore, for the two keepers employed to keep up the lights, all provisions for the winter were necessarily carried to them in autumn, as they could never be visited again till the return of the milder season; that, on the first practicable day in the spring, a boat put off to them with fresh supplies. The boatmen met at the door one of the keepers, and accosted him with a "How goes it, friend? Very well. How is your companion? I do not know. Don't know? Is not he here? I can't tell. Have not you seen him today? No. When did you see him? Not since last fall. You have killed him? Not I, indeed." They were about to lay hold of him, as having certainly murdered his companion; but he desired them to go up stairs and examine for themselves. They went up, and there found the other keeper. They had quarrelled, it seems, soon after being left there, had divided into two parties, assigned the cares below to one, and those above to the other, and had never spoken to, or seen, one another since.

But to return to our Congress at Annapolis. The definitive treaty of peace which had been signed at Paris on the 3d of September, 1783, and received here, could not be ratified without a House of nine States. On the 23d of December, therefore, we addressed letters to the several Governors, stating the receipt of the definitive treaty; that seven States only were in attendance, while nine were necessary to its ratification; and urging them to press on their delegates the necessity of their immediate attendance. And on the 26th, to save time, I moved that the Agent of Marine (Robert Morris) should be instructed to have ready a vessel at this place, at New York, and at some Eastern port, to carry over the ratification of the treaty when agreed to. It met the general sense of the House, but was opposed by Dr. Lee, on the ground of expense, which it would authorize the Agent to incur for us; and, he said, it would be better to ratify at once, and send on the ratification. Some members had before suggested, that seven States were competent to the ratification. My motion was therefore postponed, and another brought forward by Mr. Read, of South Carolina, for an immediate ratification. This was debated the 26th and 27th. Reed, Lee, Williamson and Jeremiah Chase, urged that ratification was a mere matter of form, that the treaty was conclusive from the moment it was signed by the ministers; that, although the Confederation requires the assent of *nine States* to *enter into* a treaty, yet, that its conclusion could not be called *entrance into it;* that supposing nine States requisite, it would be in the power of five States to keep us always at war; that nine States had virtually authorized the ratification, having ratified the provisional treaty, and instructed their ministers to agree to a definitive one in the same terms, and the present one was, in fact, substantially, and almost verbatim, the same; that there now remain but sixty-seven days for the ratification, for its passage across the Atlantic, and its exchange; that there was no hope of our soon having nine States present; in fact, that this was the ultimate point of time to which we could venture to wait; that if the ratification was not in Paris by the time stipulated, the treaty would become void; that if ratified by seven States, it would go under our seal, without its being known to Great Britain that only seven had concurred; that it was a question of which they had no right to take cognizance, and we were only answerable for it to our constituents; that it was like the ratification which Great Britain had received from the Dutch, by the negotiations of Sir William Temple.

On the contrary, it was argued by Monroe, Gerry, Howel, Ellery and myself, that by the modern usage of Europe, the ratification was considered as the act which gave validity to a treaty, until which, it was not obligatory.[1] That the commission to the ministers reserved the ratification to Congress; that, the treaty itself stipulated that it should be ratified; that it became a second question, who were competent to the ratification? That the Confederation expressly required nine States to enter into any treaty; that, by this, that instrument must have intended, that the assent of nine States should be necessary, as well to the *completion* as to the *commencement* of the treaty, its object having been to guard the rights of the Union in all those important cases where nine States are called for; that by the contrary construction, seven States, containing less than one-third of our whole citizens, might rivet on us a treaty, commenced indeed under commission and instructions from nine States, but formed by the minister in express contradiction to such instructions, and in direct sacrifice of the interests of so great a majority; that the definitive treaty was admitted not to be a verbal copy of the provisional one, and whether the departures from it were of substance, or not, was a question on which nine States alone were competent to decide; that the circumstances of the ratification of the provisional articles by nine States, the instructions to our ministers

[1] Vattel L. 2, § 156. L. 4, § 77. 1. Mably Droit D'Europe, 86.—т. j.

to form a definitive one by them, and their actual agreement in substance, do not render us competent to ratify in the present instance; if these circumstances are in themselves a ratification, nothing further is requisite than to give attested copies of them, in exchange for the British ratification; if they are not, we remain where we were, without a ratification by nine States, and incompetent ourselves to ratify; that it was but four days since the seven States, now present, unanimously concurred in a resolution, to be forwarded to the Governors of the absent States, in which they stated, as a cause for urging on their delegates, that nine States were necessary to ratify the treaty; that in the case of the Dutch ratification, Great Britain had courted it, and therefore was glad to accept it as it was; that they knew our Constitution, and would object to a ratification by seven; that, if that circumstance was kept back, it would be known hereafter, and would give them ground to deny the validity of a ratification, into which they should have been surprised and cheated, and it would be a dishonorable prostitution of our seal; that there is a hope of nine States; that if the treaty would become null, if not ratified in time, it would not be saved by an imperfect ratification; but that, in fact, it would not be null, and would be placed on better ground, going in unexceptionable form, though a few days too late, and rested on the small importance of this circumstance, and the physical impossibilities which had prevented a punctual compliance in point of time; that this would be approved by all nations, and by Great Britain herself, if not determined to renew the war, and if so determined, she would never want excuses, were this out of the way. Mr. Read gave notice, he should call for the yeas and nays; whereon those in opposition, prepared a resolution, expressing pointedly the reasons of their dissent from his motion. It appearing, however, that his proposition could not be carried, it was thought better to make no entry at all. Massachusetts alone would have been for it; Rhode Island, Pennsylvania and Virginia against it, Delaware, Maryland and North Carolina, would have been divided.

Our body was little numerous, but very contentious. Day after day was wasted on the most unimportant questions. A member, one of those afflicted with the morbid rage of debate, of an ardent mind, prompt imagination, and copious flow of words, who heard with impatience any logic which was not his own, sitting near me on some occasion of a trifling but wordy debate, asked me how I could sit in silence, hearing so much false reasoning, which a word should refute? I observed to him, that to refute indeed was easy, but to silence was impossible; that in measures brought forward by myself, I took the laboring oar, as was incumbent on me; but that in general, I was willing to listen; that if every sound argument or objection was used by some one or other of the numerous debaters, it was enough; if not, I thought it sufficient to suggest the omission, without going into a repetition of what had been already said by others: that this was a waste and abuse of the time and patience of the House, which could not be justified. And I believe, that if the members of deliberate bodies were to observe this course generally, they would do in a day, what takes them a week; and it is really more questionable, than may at first be thought, whether Bonaparte's dumb legislature, which said nothing, and did much, may not be preferable to one which talks much, and does nothing. I served with General Washington in the legislature of Virginia, before the revolution, and, during it, with Dr. Franklin in Congress. I never heard either of them speak ten minutes at a time, nor to any but the main point, which was to decide the question. They laid their shoulders to the great points, knowing that the little ones would follow of themselves. If the present Congress errs in too much talking, how can it be otherwise, in a body to which the people send one hundred and fifty lawyers, whose trade it is to question everything, yield nothing, and talk by the hour? That one hundred and fifty lawyers should do business together, ought not to be expected. But to return again to our subject.

Those who thought seven States competent to the ratification, being very restless under the loss of their motion, I proposed, on the third of January, to meet them on middle ground, and therefore moved a resolution, which premised, that there were but seven States present, who were unanimous for the ratification, but that they differed in opinion on the question of competency; that those however in the negative were unwilling that any powers which it might be supposed they possessed, should remain unexercised for the restoration of peace, provided it could be done, saving their good faith, and without importing any opinion of Congress, that seven States were competent, and resolving that the treaty be ratified so far as they had power; that it should be transmitted to our ministers, with instructions to keep it uncommunicated; to endeavor to obtain three months longer for exchange of ratifications; that they should be informed, that so soon as nine States shall be present, a ratification by nine shall be sent them: if this should get to them before the ultimate point of time for exchange, they were to use it, and not the other; if not, they were to offer the act of the seven States in exchange, informing them the treaty had come to hand while Congress was not in session; that but seven States were as yet assembled, and these had unanimously concurred in the ratification. This was debated on the third and fourth; and on the fifth, a vessel being to sail for England, from this port (Annapolis), the House directed the President to write to our ministers accordingly.

January 14. Delegates from Connecticut having attended yesterday, and another from South Carolina coming in this day, the treaty was ratified without a dissenting voice; and three instruments of ratification were ordered to be made out, one of which was sent by Colonel Harmer, another by Colonel Franks, and the third transmitted to the Agent of Marine, to be forwarded by any good opportunity.

Congress soon took up the consideration of their foreign relations. They deemed it necessary to get their commerce placed with every nation, on a footing as favorable as that of other nations; and for this purpose, to propose to each a distinct treaty of commerce. This act too would amount to an acknowledgment, by each, of our independence, and of our reception into the fraternity of nations; which, although as possessing our station of right, and in fact we would not condescend to ask, we were not unwilling to furnish opportunities for receiving their friendly salutations and welcome. With France, the United Netherlands, and Sweden, we had already treaties of commerce; but commissions were given for those countries also, should any amendments be thought necessary. The other States to which treaties were to be proposed, were England, Hamburg, Saxony, Prussia, Denmark, Russia, Austria, Venice, Rome, Naples, Tuscany, Sardinia, Genoa, Spain, Portugal, the Porte, Algiers, Tripoli, Tunis, and Morocco.

On the 7th of May Congress resolved that a Minister Plenipotentiary should be appointed, in addition to Mr. Adams and Dr. Franklin, for negotiating treaties of commerce with foreign nations, and I was elected to that duty. I accordingly left Annapolis on the 11th, took with me my eldest daughter, then at Philadelphia (the two others being too young for the voyage), and proceeded to Boston, in quest of a passage. While passing through the different States, I made a point of informing myself of the state of the commerce of each; went on to New Hampshire with the same view, and returned to Boston. Thence I sailed on the 5th of July, in the Ceres, a merchant ship of Mr. Nathaniel Tracey, bound to Cowes. He was himself a passenger, and, after a pleasant voyage of nineteen days, from land to land, we arrived at Cowes on the 26th. I was detained there a few days by the indisposition of my daughter. On the 30th, we embarked for Havre, arrived there on the 31st, left it on the 3d of August, and arrived at Paris on the 6th. I called immediately on Dr. Franklin, at Passy, communicated to him our charge, and we wrote to Mr. Adams, then at the Hague, to join us at Paris.

Before I had left America, that is to say, in the year 1781, I had received a letter from M. de Marbois, of the French legation in Philadelphia, informing me, he had been instructed by his government to obtain such statistical accounts of the different States of our Union, as might be useful for their information; and addressing to me a number of queries relative to the State of Virginia. I had always made it a practice, whenever an opportunity occurred, of obtaining any information of our country, which might be of use to me in any station, public or private, to commit it to writing. These memoranda were on loose papers, bundled up without order, and difficult of recurrence, when I had occasion for a particular one. I thought this a good occasion to embody their substance, which I did in the order of Mr. Marbois' queries, so as to answer his wish, and to arrange them for my own use. Some friends, to whom they were occasionally communicated, wished for copies; but their volume rendering this too laborious by hand, I proposed to get a few printed, for their gratification. I was asked such a price, however, as exceeded the importance of the object. On my arrival at Paris, I found it could be done for a fourth of what I had been asked here. I therefore corrected and enlarged them, and had two hundred copies printed, under the title of "Notes on Virginia." I gave a very few copies to some particular friends in Europe, and sent the rest to my friends in America. An European copy, by the death of the owner, got into the hands of a bookseller, who engaged its translation, and when ready for the press, communicated his intentions and manuscript to me, suggesting that I should correct it, without asking any other permission for the publication. I never had seen so wretched an attempt at translation. Interverted, abridged, mutilated, and often reversing the sense of the original, I found it a blotch of errors, from beginning to end. I corrected some of the most material, and, in that form, it was printed in French. A London bookseller, on seeing the translation, requested me to permit him to print the English original. I thought it best to do so, to let the world see that it was not really so bad as the French translation had made it appear. And this is the true history of that publication.

Mr. Adams soon joined us at Paris, and our first employment was to prepare a general form, to be proposed to such nations as were disposed to treat with us. During the negotiations for peace with the British Commissioner, David Hartley, our Commissioners had proposed, on the suggestion of Dr. Franklin, to insert an article, exempting from capture by the public or private armed ships, of either belligerent, when at war, all merchant vessels and their cargoes, employed merely in carrying on the commerce between nations. It was refused by England, and unwisely, in my opinion. For, in the case of a war with us, their superior commerce places infinitely more at hazard on the ocean, than ours; and, as hawks abound in proportion to game, so our privateers would swarm, in proportion to the wealth exposed to their prize, while theirs would be few, for want of subjects of capture. We inserted this article in our form, with a provision against the molestation of fishermen, husbandmen, citizens unarmed, and following their occupations in unfortified places, for the humane treatment of prisoners of war, the abolition of contraband of war, which exposes merchant vessels to such vexatious and ruinous detentions and abuses; and for the principle of free bottoms, free goods.

In a conference with the Count de Vergennes, it was thought better to leave to legislative regulation, on both sides, such modifications of our commercial intercourse, as would voluntarily flow from amicable dispositions. Without urging, we sounded the ministers of the several European nations, at the court of Versailles, on their dispositions towards mutual commerce, and the expediency of encouraging it by the protection of a treaty. Old Frederic, of Prussia, met us cordially, and without hesitation, and appointing the Baron de Thulemeyer, his minister at the Hague, to negotiate with us, we communicated to him our Projét, which, with little alteration by the King, was soon concluded. Denmark and Tuscany entered also into negotiations with us. Other powers appearing indifferent, we did not think it proper to press them. They seemed, in fact, to know little about us, but as rebels, who had been successful in throwing off the yoke of the mother country. They were ignorant of our commerce, which had been always monopolized by England, and of the exchange of articles it might offer advantageously to both parties. They were inclined, therefore, to stand aloof, until they could see better what relations might be usefully instituted with us. The negotiations, therefore, begun with Denmark and Tuscany, we protracted designedly, until our powers had expired; and abstained from making new propositions to others having no colonies; because our commerce being an exchange of raw for wrought materials, is a competent price for admission into the colonies of those possessing them; but were we to give it, without price, to others, all would claim it, without price, on the ordinary ground of *gentis amicissimæ*.

Mr. Adams being appointed Minister Plenipotentiary of the United States, to London, left us in June, and in July, 1785, Dr. Franklin returned to America, and I was appointed his successor at Paris. In February, 1786, Mr. Adams wrote to me, pressingly, to join him in London immediately, as he thought he discovered there some symptoms of better disposition towards us. Colonel Smith, his secretary of legation, was the bearer of his urgencies for my immediate attendance. I, accordingly, left Paris on the 1st of March, and, on my arrival in London, we agreed on a very summary form of treaty, proposing an exchange of citizenship for our citizens, our ships, and our productions generally, except as to office. On my presentation, as usual, to the King and Queen, at their levées, it was impossible for anything to be more ungracious, than their notice of Mr. Adams and myself. I saw, at once, that the ulcerations of mind in that quarter, left noth-

ing to be expected on the subject of my attendance; and, on the first conference with the Marquis of Caermarthen, the Minister for foreign affairs,
the distance and disinclination which he betrayed in his conversation, the
vagueness and evasions of his answers to us, confirmed me in the belief of
their aversion to have anything to do with us. We delivered him, however,
our Projét, Mr. Adams not despairing as much as I did, of its effect. We
afterwards, by one or more notes, requested his appointment of an inter-
view and conference, which, without directly declining, he evaded, by pre-
tences of other pressing occupations for the moment. After staying there
seven weeks, till within a few days of the expiration of our commission, I
informed the minister, by note, that my duties at Paris required my return
to that place, and that I should, with pleasure, be the bearer of any commands to his Ambassador there. He answered, that he had none, and,
wishing me a pleasant journey, I left London the 26th, and arrived at
Paris the 30th of April.

While in London, we entered into negotiations with the Chevalier Pinto,
Ambassador of Portugal, at that place. The only article of difficulty between us was, a stipulation that our bread stuff should be received in Portugal, in the form of flour as well as of grain. He approved of it himself, but
observed that several Nobles, of great influence at their court, were the
owners of wind-mills in the neighborhood of Lisbon, which depended
much for their profits on manufacturing our wheat, and that this stipulation would endanger the whole treaty. He signed it, however, and its fate
was what he had candidly portended.

My duties, at Paris, were confined to a few objects; the receipt of our
whale-oils, salted fish, and salted meats, on favorable terms; the admission
of our rice on equal terms with that of Piedmont, Egypt and the Levant;
a mitigation of the monopolies of our tobacco by the Farmers-general, and
a free admission of our productions into their islands, were the principal
commercial objects which required attention; and, on these occasions, I was
powerfully aided by all the influence and the energies of the Marquis de
La Fayette, who proved himself equally zealous for the friendship and
welfare of both nations; and, in justice, I must also say, that I found the
government entirely disposed to befriend us on all occasions, and to yield
us every indulgence, not absolutely injurious to themselves. The Count de
Vergennes had the reputation, with the diplomatic corps, of being wary and
slippery in his diplomatic intercourse; and so he might be with those whom
he knew to be slippery, and double-faced themselves. As he saw that I had
no indirect views, practised no subtleties, meddled in no intrigues, pursued
no concealed object, I found him as frank, as honorable, as easy of access
to reason, as any man with whom I had ever done business; and I must

say the same for his successor, Montmorin, one of the most honest and worthy of human beings.

Our commerce, in the Mediterranean, was placed under early alarm, by the capture of two of our vessels and crews by the Barbary cruisers. I was very unwilling that we should acquiesce in the European humiliation, of paying a tribute to those lawless pirates, and endeavored to form an association of the powers subject to habitual depredations from them. I accordingly prepared, and proposed to their Ministers at Paris, for consultation with their governments, articles of a special confederation, in the following form:

"Proposals for concerted operation among the powers at war with the piratical States of Barbary.

1. "It is proposed, that the several powers at war with the piratical States of Barbary, or any two or more of them who shall be willing, shall enter into a convention to carry on their operations against those States, in concert, beginning with the Algerines.

2. "This convention shall remain open to any other powers, who shall, at any future time, wish to accede to it; the parties reserving the right to prescribe the conditions of such accession, according to the circumstances existing at the time it shall be proposed.

3. "The object of the convention shall be, to compel the piratical States to perpetual peace, without price, and to guarantee that peace to each other.

4. "The operations for obtaining this peace shall be constant cruises on their coast, with a naval force now to be agreed on. It is not proposed that this force shall be so considerable as to be inconvenient to any party. It is believed that half a dozen frigates, with as many Tenders or Xebecs, one half of which shall be in cruise, while the other half is at rest, will suffice.

5. "The force agreed to be necessary, shall be furnished by the parties, in certain quotas, now to be fixed; it being expected, that each will be willing to contribute, in such proportion as circumstances may render reasonable.

6. "As miscarriages often proceed from the want of harmony among officers of different nations, the parties shall now consider and decide, whether it will not be better to contribute their quotas in money, to be employed in fitting out and keeping on duty, a single fleet of the force agreed on.

7. "The difficulties and delays, too, which will attend the management of the operations, if conducted by the parties themselves separately, distant as their courts may be from one another, and incapable of meeting in consultation, suggest a question, whether it will not be better for them to give full powers, for that purpose, to their Ambassadors, or other Ministers resident at some one court of Europe, who shall form a Committee, or Council, for carrying this convention into effect; wherein, the vote of each mem-

ber shall be computed in proportion to the quota of his sovereign, and the majority so computed, shall prevail in all questions within the view of this convention. The court of Versailles is proposed, on account of its neighborhood to the Mediterranean, and because all those powers are represented there, who are likely to become parties to this convention.

8. "To save to that Council the embarrassment of personal solicitations for office, and to assure the parties that their contributions will be applied solely to the object for which they are destined, there shall be no establishment of officers for the said Council, such as Commissioners, Secretaries, or any other kind, with either salaries or perquisites, nor any other lucrative appointments but such whose functions are to be exercised on board the said vessels.

9. "Should war arise between any two of the parties to this convention, it shall not extend to this enterprise, nor interrupt it; but as to this they shall be reputed at peace.

10. "When Algiers shall be reduced to peace, the other piratical States, if they refuse to discontinue their piracies, shall become the objects of this convention, either successively or together, as shall seem best.

11. "Where this convention would interfere with treaties actually existing between any of the parties and the States of Barbary, the treaty shall prevail, and such party shall be allowed to withdraw from the operations against that State."

Spain had just concluded a treaty with Algiers, at the expense of three millions of dollars, and did not like to relinquish the benefit of that, until the other party should fail in their observance of it. Portugal, Naples, the two Sicilies, Venice, Malta, Denmark and Sweden, were favorably disposed to such an association; but their representatives at Paris expressed apprehensions that France would interfere, and, either openly or secretly, support the Barbary powers; and they required, that I should ascertain the dispositions of the Count de Vergennes on the subject. I had before taken occasion to inform him of what we were proposing, and, therefore, did not think it proper to insinuate any doubt of the fair conduct of his government; but, stating our propositions, I mentioned the apprehensions entertained by us, that England would interfere in behalf of those piratical governments. "She dares not do it," said he. I pressed it no further. The other Agents were satisfied with this indication of his sentiments, and nothing was now wanting to bring it into direct and formal consideration, but the assent of our government, and their authority to make the formal proposition. I communicated to them the favorable prospect of protecting our commerce from the Barbary depredations, and for such a continuance of time, as, by an exclusion of them from the sea, to change their habits and characters, from a predatory to an agricultural people: towards which, however, it was expected they would contribute a frigate, and its expenses, to be in constant cruise. But they were in no condition to make any such engagement. Their recommendatory powers for obtaining contributions were so openly neglected by the several States, that they declined an engagement which they were conscious they could not fulfil with punctuality; and so it fell through.

In 1786, while at Paris, I became acquainted with John Ledyard, of Connecticut, a man of genius, of some science, and of fearless courage and enterprise. He had accompanied Captain Cook in his voyage to the Pacific, had distinguished himself on several occasions by an unrivalled intrepidity, and published an account of that voyage, with details unfavorable to Cook's deportment towards the savages, and lessening our regrets at his fate. Ledyard had come to Paris, in the hope of forming a company to engage in the fur trade of the Western coast of America. He was disappointed in this, and, being out of business, and of a roaming, restless character, I suggested to him the enterprise of exploring the Western part of our continent, by passing through St. Petersburg to Kamschatka, and procuring a passage thence in some of the Russian vessels to Nootka Sound, whence he might make his way across the continent to the United States; and I undertook to have the permission of the Empress of Russia solicited. He eagerly embraced the proposition, and M. de Sémoulin, the Russian Ambassador, and more particularly Baron Grimm, the special correspondent of the Empress, solicited her permission for him to pass through her dominions, to the Western coast of America. And here I must correct a material error, which I have committed in another place, to the prejudice of the Empress. In writing some notes of the life of Captain Lewis, prefixed to his "Expedition to the Pacific," I stated that the Empress gave the permission asked, and afterwards retracted it. This idea, after a lapse of twenty-six years, had so insinuated itself into my mind, that I committed it to paper, without the least suspicion of error. Yet I find, on recurring to my letters of that date, that the Empress refused permission at once, considering the enterprise as entirely chimerical. But Ledyard would not relinquish it, persuading himself that, by proceeding to St. Petersburg, he could satisfy the Empress of its practicability, and obtain her permission. He went accordingly, but she was absent on a visit to some distant part of her dominions, and he pursued his course to within two hundred miles of Kamschatka, where he was overtaken by an arrest from the Empress, brought back to Poland, and there dismissed. I must therefore, in justice, acquit the Empress of ever having for a moment countenanced, even by the indulgence of an innocent passage through her territories, this interesting enterprise.

The pecuniary distresses of France produced this year a measure of which there had been no example for near two centuries, and the consequences of which, good and evil, are not yet calculable. For its remote causes, we must go a little back.

Celebrated writers of France and England had already sketched good principles on the subject of government; yet the American Revolution seems first to have awakened the thinking part of the French nation in general, from the sleep of despotism in which they were sunk. The officers too, who had been to America, were mostly young men, less shackled by habit and prejudice, and more ready to assent to the suggestions of common sense, and feeling of common rights, than others. They came back with new ideas and impressions. The press, notwithstanding its shackles, began to disseminate them; conversation assumed new freedoms; Politics became the theme of all societies, male and female, and a very extensive and zealous party was formed, which acquired the appellation of the Patriotic party, who, sensible of the abusive government under which they lived, sighed for occasions of reforming it. This party comprehended all the honesty of the kingdom, sufficiently at leisure to think, the men of letters, the easy Bourgeois, the young nobility, partly from reflection, partly from mode; for these sentiments became matter of mode, and as such, united most of the young women to the party. Happily for the nation, it happened, at the same moment, that the dissipations of the Queen and court, the abuses of the pension-list, and dilapidations in the administration of every branch of the finances, had exhausted the treasures and credit of the nation, insomuch that its most necessary functions were paralyzed. To reform these abuses would have overset the Minister; to impose new taxes by the authority of the King, was known to be impossible, from the determined opposition of the Parliament to their enregistry. No resource remained then, but to appeal to the nation. He advised, therefore, the call of an Assembly of the most distinguished characters of the nation, in the hope that, by promises of various and valuable improvements in the organization and regimen of the government, they would be induced to authorize new taxes, to control the opposition of the Parliament, and to raise the annual revenue to the level of expenditures. An Assembly of Notables, therefore, about one hundred and fifty in number, named by the King, convened on the 22d of February. The Minister (Calonne) stated to them, that the annual excess of expenses beyond the revenue, when Louis XVI came to the throne, was thirty-seven millions of livres; that four hundred and forty millions had been borrowed to re-establish the navy; that the American war had cost them fourteen hundred and forty millions (two hundred and fifty-six millions of dollars), and that the interest of these sums, with other increased expenses, had added forty millions more to the annual deficit. (But a subsequent and more candid estimate made it fifty-six millions). He proffered them an universal redress of grievances, laid open those grievances fully, pointed out sound remedies, and, covering his canvas with objects of this magnitude, the deficit dwindled to a little accessory, scarcely attracting attention. The persons chosen were the most able and independent characters in the kingdom, and their support, if it could be obtained, would be enough for him. They improved the occasion for redressing their grievances, and agreed that the public wants should be relieved; but went into an examination of the causes of them. It was supposed that Colonne was conscious that his accounts could not bear examination; and it was said, and believed, that he asked of the King, to send four members to the Bastile, of whom the Marquis de La Fayette was one, to banish twenty others, and two of his Ministers. The King found it shorter to banish him. His successor went on in full concert with the Assembly. The result was an augmentation of the revenue, a promise of economies in its expenditure, of an annual settlement of the public accounts before a council, which the Comptroller, having been heretofore obliged to settle only with the King in person, of course never settled at all; an acknowledgment that the King could not lay a new tax, a reformation of the Criminal laws, abolition of torture, suppression of corvees, reformation of the gabelles, removal of the interior Custom Houses, free commerce of grain, internal and external, and the establishment of Provincial Assemblies; which, altogether, constituted a great mass of improvement in the condition of the nation. The establishment of the Provincial Assemblies was, in itself, a fundamental improvement. They would be of the choice of the people, one-third renewed every year, in those provinces where there are no States, that is to say, over about three-fourths of the kingdom. They would be partly an Executive themselves, and partly an Executive Council to the Intendant, to whom the Executive power, in his province, had been heretofore entirely delegated. Chosen by the people, they would soften the execution of hard laws, and, having a right of representation to the King, they would censure bad laws, suggest good ones, expose abuses, and their representations, when united, would command respect. To the other advantages, might be added the precedent itself of calling the Assemblée des Notables, which would perhaps grow into habit. The hope was, that the improvements thus promised would be carried into effect; that they would be maintained during the present reign, and that that would be long enough for them to take some root in the constitution, so that they might come to be considered as a part of that, and be protected by time, and the attachment of the nation.

The Count de Vergennes had died a few days before the meeting of the

Assembly, and the Count de Montmorin had been named Minister of Foreign Affairs, in his place. Villedeuil succeeded Calonne, as Comptroller General, and Loménie de Brienne, Archbishop of Toulouse, afterwards of Sens, and ultimately Cardinal Loménie, was named Minister principal, with whom the other Ministers were to transact the business of their departments, heretofore done with the King in person; and the Duke de Nivernois, and M. de Malesherbes, were called to the Council. On the nomination of the Minister principal, the Marshals de Ségur and de Castries retired from the departments of War and Marine, unwilling to act subordinately, or to share the blame of proceedings taken out of their direction. They were succeeded by the Count de Brienne, brother of the Prime Minister, and the Marquis de La Luzerne, brother to him who had been Minister in the United States.

A dislocated wrist, unsuccessfully set, occasioned advice from my surgeon, to try the mineral waters of Aix, in Provence, as a corroborant. I left Paris for that place therefore, on the 28th of February, and proceeded up the Seine, through Champagne and Burgundy, and down the Rhone through the Beaujolais by Lyons, Avignon, Nismes to Aix; where, finding on trial no benefit from the waters, I concluded to visit the rice country of Piedmont, to see if anything might be learned there, to benefit the rivalship of our Carolina rice with that, and thence to make a tour of the seaport towns of France, along its Southern and Western coast, to inform myself, if anything could be done to favor our commerce with them. From Aix, therefore, I took my route by Marseilles, Toulon, Hieres, Nice, across the Col de Tende, by Coni, Turin, Vercelli, Novara, Milan, Pavia, Novi, Genoa. Thence, returning along the coast of Savona, Noli, Albenga, Oneglia, Monaco, Nice, Antibes, Frejus, Aix, Marseilles, Avignon, Nismes, Montpellier, Frontignan, Cette, Agde, and along the canal of Languedoc, by Bezieres, Narbonne, Carcassonne, Castelnaudari, through the Souterrain of St. Feriol, and back by Castelnaudari, to Toulouse; thence to Montauban, and down the Garonne by Langon to Bordeaux. Thence to Rochefort, la Rochelle, Nantes, L'Orient; then back by Rennes to Nantes, and up the Loire by Angers, Tours, Amboise, Blois to Orleans, thence direct to Paris, where I arrived on the 10th of June. Soon after my return from this journey, to wit, about the latter part of July, I received my younger daughter, Maria, from Virginia, by the way of London, the youngest having died some time before.

The treasonable perfidy of the Prince of Orange, Stadtholder and Captain General of the United Netherlands, in the war which England waged against them, for entering into a treaty of commerce with the United States, is known to all. As their Executive officer, charged with the conduct of the war, he contrived to baffle all the measures of the States General, to dislocate all their military plans, and played false into the hands of England against his own country, on every possible occasion, confident in her protection, and in that of the King of Prussia, brother to his Princess. The States General, indignant at this patricidal conduct, applied to France for aid, according to the stipulations of the treaty concluded with her in '85. It was assured to them readily, and in cordial terms, in a letter from the Count de Vergennes, to the Marquis de Verac, Ambassador of France at the Hague, of which the following is an extract:

Extract from the despatch of the Count de Vergennes, to the Marquis de Verac, Ambassador from France, at the Hague, dated March 1, 1786:
"The King will give his aid, as far as may be in his power, towards the success of the affair, and will, on his part, invite the Patriots to communicate to him their views, their plans, and their discontents. You may assure them that the King takes a real interest in themselves as well as their cause, and that they may rely upon his protection. On this they may place the greater dependence, as we do not conceal, that if the Stadtholder resumes his former influence, the English System will soon prevail, and our alliance become a mere affair of the imagination. The Patriots will readily feel, that this position would be incompatible both with the dignity and consideration of his Majesty. But in case the Chief of the Patriots should have to fear a division, they would have time sufficient to reclaim those whom the Anglomaniacs had misled, and to prepare matters in such a manner, that the question when again agitated, might be decided according to their wishes. In such a hypothetical case, the King authorizes you to act in concert with them, to pursue the direction which they may think proper to give you, and to employ every means to augment the number of the partisans of the good cause. It remains for me to speak of the personal security of the Patriots. You may assure them, that under every circumstance, the King will take them under his immediate protection, and you will make known wherever you may judge necessary, that his Majesty will regard as a personal offence every undertaking against their liberty. It is to be presumed that this language, energetically maintained, may have some effect on the audacity of the Anglomaniacs, and that the Prince de Nassau will feel that he runs some risk in provoking the resentment of his Majesty."[1]

This letter was communicated by the Patriots to me, when at Amsterdam, in 1788, and a copy sent by me to Mr. Jay, in my letter to him of March 16, 1788.

The object of the Patriots was, to establish a representative and republican government. The majority of the States General were with them, but the majority of the populace of the towns was with the Prince of Orange; and that populace was played off with great effect, by the triumvirate of . . . Harris, the English Ambassador, afterwards Lord Malmesbury, the Prince

[1] Original was written in French.

of Orange, a stupid man, and the Princess as much a man as either of her colleagues, in audaciousness, in enterprise, and in the thirst of domination. By these, the mobs of the Hague were excited against the members of the States General; their persons were insulted and endangered in the streets; the sanctuary of their houses was violated; and the Prince, whose function and duty it was to repress and punish these violations of order, took no steps for that purpose. The States General, for their own protection, were therefore obliged to place their militia under the command of a Committee. The Prince filled the courts of London and Berlin with complaints at this usurpation of his prerogatives, and, forgetting that he was but the first servant of a Republic, marched his regular troops against the city of Utrecht, where the States were in session. They were repulsed by the militia. His interests now became marshalled with those of the public enemy, and against his own country. The States, therefore, exercising their rights of sovereignty, deprived him of all his powers. The great Frederic had died in August, '86. He had never intended to break with France in support of the Prince of Orange. During the illness of which he died, he had, through the Duke of Brunswick, declared to the Marquis de La Fayette, who was then at Berlin, that he meant not to support the English interest in Holland: that he might assure the government of France, his only wish was, that some honorable place in the Constitution should be reserved for the Stadtholder and his children, and that he would take no part in the quarrel, unless an entire abolition of the Stadtholderate should be attempted. But his place was now occupied by Frederic William, his great-nephew, a man of little understanding, much caprice, and very inconsiderate; and the Princess, his sister, although her husband was in arms against the legitimate authorities of the country, attempting to go to Amsterdam, for the purpose of exciting the mobs of that place, and being refused permission to pass a military post on the way, he put the Duke of Brunswick at the head of twenty thousand men, and made demonstrations of marching on Holland. The King of France hereupon declared, by his Chargé des Affaires in Holland, that if the Prussian troops continued to menace Holland with an invasion, his Majesty, in quality of Ally, was determined to succor that province. In answer to this, Eden gave official information to Count Montmorin, that England must consider as at an end its convention with France relative to giving notice of its naval armaments, and that she was arming generally. War being now imminent, Eden, since Lord Aukland, questioned me on the effect of our treaty with France, in the case of a war, and what might be our dispositions. I told him frankly, and without hesitation, that our dispositions would be neutral, and that I thought it would be the interest of both these powers that we should be so; because, it would relieve both from all anxiety as to feeding their West India islands; that England, too, by suffering us to remain so, would avoid a heavy land war on our Continent, which might very much cripple her proceedings elsewhere; that our treaty, indeed, obliged us to receive into our ports the armed vessels of France, with their prizes, and to refuse admission to the prizes made on her by her enemies: that there was a clause, also, by which we guaranteed to France her American possessions, which might perhaps force us into the war, if these were attacked. "Then it will be war," said he, "for they will assuredly be attacked." Liston, at Madrid, about the same time, made the same inquiries of Carmichael. The Government of France then declared a determination to form a camp of observation at Givet, commenced arming her marine, and named the Bailli de Suffrein their Generalissimo on the Ocean. She secretly engaged, also, in negotiations with Russia, Austria, and Spain, to form a quadruple alliance. The Duke of Brunswick having advanced to the confines of Holland, sent some of his officers to Givet, to reconnoitre the state of things there, and report them to him. He said afterwards, that "if there had been only a few tents at that place, he should not have advanced further, for that the King would not, merely for the interest of his sister, engage in a war with France." But, finding that there was not a single company there, he boldly entered the country, took their towns as fast as he presented himself before them, and advanced on Utrecht. The States had appointed the Rhingrave of Salm their Commander-in-Chief; a Prince without talents, without courage, and without principle. He might have held out in Utrecht for a considerable time, but he surrendered the place without firing a gun, literally ran away and hid himself, so that for months it was not known what had become of him. Amsterdam was then attacked, and capitulated. In the meantime, the negotiations for the quadruple alliance were proceeding favorably; but the secrecy with which they were attempted to be conducted, was penetrated by Fraser, Chargé des Affaires of England at St. Petersburg, who instantly notified his court, and gave the alarm to Prussia. The King saw at once what would be his situation, between the jaws of France, Austria, and Russia. In great dismay, he besought the court of London not to abandon him, sent Alvensleben to Paris to explain and soothe; and England, through the Duke of Dorset and Eden, renewed her conferences for accommodation. The Archbishop, who shuddered at the idea of war, and preferred a peaceful surrender of right to an armed vindication of it, received them with open arms, entered into cordial conferences, and a declaration, and counter-declaration, were cooked up at Versailles, and sent to London for approbation. They were approved there, reached Paris at one o'clock of the 27th, and were signed that night at Versailles. It was said and believed at Paris, that M. de Montmorin, literally *"pleuroit comme un enfant,"* when obliged to sign this counter-declaration; so distressed was he by the dishonor of sacrificing the Patriots, after assurance so solemn of protection, and absolute encouragement to proceed. The Prince of Orange was reinstated in all his powers, now become regal. A great emigration of the Patriots took place; all were deprived of office, many exiled, and their property confiscated. They were received in France, and subsisted, for some time, on her bounty. Thus fell Holland, by the treachery of her Chief, from her honorable independence, to become a province of England; and so, also, her Stadtholder, from the high station of the first citizen of a free Republic, to be the servile Viceroy of a foreign Sovereign. And this was effected by a mere scene of bullying and demonstration; not one of the parties, France, England, or Prussia, having ever really meant to encounter actual war for the interest of the Prince of Orange. But it had all the effect of a real and decisive war.

Our first essay, in America, to establish a federative government had fallen, on trial, very short of its object. During the war of Independence, while the pressure of an external enemy hooped us together, and their enterprises kept up necessarily on the alert, the spirit of the people, excited by danger, was a supplement to the Confederation, and urged them to zealous exertions, whether claimed by that instrument or not; but, when peace and safety were restored, and every man became engaged in useful and profitable occupation, less attention was paid to the calls of Congress. The fundamental defect of the Confederation was, that Congress was not authorized to act immediately on the people, and by its own officers. Their power was only requisitory, and these requisitions were addressed to the several Legislatures, to be by them carried into execution, without other coercion than the moral principle of duty. This allowed, in fact, a negative to every Legislature, on every measure proposed by Congress; a negative so frequently exercised in practice, as to benumb the action of the Federal government, and to render it inefficient in its general objects, and more especially in pecuniary and foreign concerns. The want, too, of a separation of the Legislative, Executive, and Juduiciary functions, worked disadvantageously in practice. Yet this state of things afforded a happy augury of the future march of our Confederacy, when it was seen that the good sense and good dispositions of the people, as soon as they perceived the incompetence of their first compact, instead of leaving its correction to insurrection and civil war, agreed, with one voice, to elect deputies to a general Convention, who should peaceably meet and agree on such a Constitution as "would ensure peace, justice, liberty, the common defence and general welfare."

This Convention met at Philadelphia on the 25th of May, '87. It sat with closed doors, and kept all its proceedings secret, until its dissolution on the 17th of September, when the results of its labors were published all together. I received a copy, early in November, and read and contemplated its provisions with great satisfaction. As not a member of the Convention, however, nor probably a single citizen of the Union, had approved it in all its parts, so I, too, found articles which I thought objectionable. The absence of express declarations ensuring freedom of religion, freedom of the press, freedom of the person under the uninterrupted protection of the Habeas corpus, and trial by jury in Civil as well as in Criminal cases, excited my jealousy; and the re-eligibility of the President for life, I quite disapproved. I expressed freely, in letters to my friends, and most particularly to Mr. Madison and General Washington, my approbations and objections. How the good should be secured and the ill brought to rights, was the difficulty. To refer it back to a new Convention might endanger the loss of the whole. My first idea was, that the nine States first acting, should accept it unconditionally, and thus secure what in it was good, and that the four last should accept on the previous condition, that certain amendments should be agreed to; but a better course was devised, of accepting the whole, and trusting that the good sense and honest intentions of our citizens would make the alterations which should be deemed necessary. Accordingly, all accepted, six without objection, and seven with recommendations of specified amendments. Those respecting the press, religion, and juries, with several others, of great value, were accordingly made; but the Habeas corpus was left to the discretion of Congress, and the amendment against the re-eligibility of the President was not proposed. My fears of that feature were founded on the importance of the office, on the fierce contentions it might excite among ourselves, if continuable for life, and the dangers of interference, either with money or arms, by foreign nations, to whom the choice of an American President might become interesting. Examples of this abounded in history; in the case of the Roman Emperors, for instance; of the Popes, while of any significance; of the German Emperors; the Kings of Poland, and the Deys of Barbary. I had observed, too, in the feudal history, and in the recent instance, particularly, of the Stadtholder of Holland, how easily offices, or tenures for life, slide into inheritances. My wish, therefore, was, that the President should be elected for seven years, and be ineligible afterwards. This term I thought sufficient to enable him, with the concurrence of the Legislature, to carry through and establish any system of improvement he should propose for the general good. But the practice adopted, I think, is better, allowing his continuance for eight years, with a liability to be dropped at half way of the term, making that a period of probation. That his continuance should be restrained to seven years, was the opinion of the Convention at an earlier stage of its session, when it voted that term, by a majority of eight against two, and by a simple majority that he should be ineligible a second time. This opinion was confirmed by the House so late as July 26, referred to the Committee of detail, reported favorably by them, and changed to the present form by final vote, on the last day but one only of their session. Of this change, three States expressed their disapprobation; New York, by recommending an amendment, that the President should not be eligible a third time, and Virginia and North Carolina that he should not be capable of serving more than eight, in any term of sixteen years; and though this amendment has not been made in form, yet practice seems to have established it. The example of four Presidents voluntarily retiring at the end of their eighth year, and the progress of public opinion, that the principle is salutary, have given it in practice the force of precedent and usage; insomuch, that, should a President consent to be a candidate for a third election, I trust he would be rejected, on this demonstration of ambitious views.

But there was another amendment, of which none of us thought at the time, and in the omission of which, lurks the germ that is to destroy this happy combination of National powers in the General government, for matters of National concern, and independent powers in the States, for what concerns the States severally. In England, it was a great point gained at the Revolution, that the commissions of the Judges, which had hitherto been during pleasure, should thenceforth be made during good behavior. A Judiciary, dependent on the will of the King, had proved itself the most oppressive of all tools, in the hands of that Magistrate. Nothing, then, could be more salutary, than a change there, to the tenure of good behavior; and the question of good behavior, left to the vote of a simple majority in the two Houses of Parliament. Before the Revolution, we were all good English Whigs, cordial in their free principles, and in their jealousies of their Executive Magistrate. These jealousies are very apparent, in all our state Constitutions; and, in the General government in this instance, we have gone even beyond the English caution, by requiring a vote of two-thirds, in one of the Houses, for removing a Judge; a vote so impossible, where [1] any defence is made, before men of ordinary prejudices and passions, that our Judges are effectually independent of the nation. But this ought not to be. I would not, indeed, make them dependent on the Executive authority, as they formerly were in England; but I deem it indispensable to the continuance of this government, that they should be submitted to some practical and impartial control; and that this, to be imparted, must be compounded

[1] In the impeachment of Judge Pickering, of New Hampshire, a habitual drunkard, no defence was made. Had there been, the party vote of more than one-third of the Senate would have acquitted him.—T. J.

of a mixture of State and Federal authorities. It is not enough that honest men are appointed Judges. All know the influence of interest on the mind of man, and how unconsciously his judgment is warped by that influence. To this bias add that of the *esprit de corps,* of their peculiar maxim and creed, that "it is the office of a good Judge to enlarge his jurisdiction," and the absence of responsibility; and how can we expect impartial decision between the General government, of which they are themselves so eminent a part, and an individual State, from which they have nothing to hope or fear? We have seen, too, that contrary to all correct example, they are in the habit of going out of the question before them, to throw an anchor ahead, and grapple further hold for future advances of power. They are then, in fact, the corps of sappers and miners, steadily working to undermine the independent rights of the States, and to consolidate all power in the hands of that government in which they have so important a freehold estate. But it is not by the consolidation, or concentration of powers, but by their distribution, that good government is effected. Were not this great country already divided into States, that division must be made, that each might do for itself what concerns itself directly, and what it can so much better do than a distant authority. Every State again is divided into counties, each to take care of what lies within its local bounds; each county again into townships or wards, to manage minuter details; and every ward into farms, to be governed each by its individual proprietor. Were we directed from Washington when to sow, and when to reap, we should soon want bread. It is by this partition of cares, descending in gradation from general to particular, that the mass of human affairs may be best managed, for the good and prosperity of all. I repeat, that I do not charge the Judges with wilful and ill-intentioned error; but honest error must be arrested, where its toleration leads to public ruin. As, for the safety of society, we commit honest maniacs to Bedlam, so judges should be withdrawn from their bench, whose erroneous biases are leading us to dissolution. It may, indeed, injure them in fame or in fortune; but it saves the Republic, which is the first and supreme law.

Among the debilities of the government of the Confederation, no one was more distinguished or more distressing, than the utter impossibility of obtaining, from the States, the moneys necessary for the payment of debts, or even for the ordinary expenses of the government. Some contributed a little, some less, and some nothing; and the last furnished at length an excuse for the first to do nothing also. Mr. Adams, while residing at the Hague, had a general authority to borrow what sums might be requisite, for ordinary and necessary expenses. Interest on the public debt, and the maintenance of the diplomatic establishment in Europe, had been habitually provided in this way. He was now elected Vice-President of the United States, was soon to return to America, and had referred our bankers to me for future counsel, on our affairs in their hands. But I had no powers, no instructions, no means, and no familiarity with the subject. It had always been exclusively under his management, except as to occasional and partial deposits in the hands of Mr. Grand, banker in Paris, for special and local purposes. These last had been exhausted for some time, and I had fervently pressed the Treasury board to replenish this particular deposit, as Mr. Grand now refused to make further advances. They answered candidly, that no funds could be obtained until the new government should get into action, and have time to make its arrangements. Mr. Adams had received his appointment to the court of London, while engaged at Paris, with Dr. Franklin and myself, in the negotiations under our joint commissions. He had repaired thence to London, without returning to the Hague, to take leave of that government. He thought it necessary, however, to do so now, before he should leave Europe, and accordingly went there. I learned his departure from London, by a letter from Mrs. Adams, received on the very day on which he would arrive at the Hague. A consultation with him, and some provision for the future, was indispensable, while we could yet avail ourselves of his powers; for when they would be gone, we should be without resource. I was daily dunned by a Company who had formerly made a small loan to the United States, the principal of which was now become due; and our bankers in Amsterdam, had notified me that the interest on our general debt would be expected in June; that if we failed to pay it, it would be deemed an act of bankruptcy, and would effectually destroy the credit of the United States, and all future prospect of obtaining money there; that the loan they had been authorized to open, of which a third only was filled, had now ceased to get forward, and rendered desperate that hope of resource. I saw that there was not a moment to lose, and set out for the Hague on the second morning after receiving the information of Mr. Adams's journey. I went the direct road by Louvres, Senlis, Roye, Pont St. Maxence, Bois le duc, Gournay, Peronne, Cambray, Bouchain, Valenciennes, Mons, Bruxelles, Malines, Antwerp, Mordick, and Rotterdam, to the Hague, where I happily found Mr. Adams. He concurred with me at once in opinion, that something must be done, and that we ought to risk ourselves on doing it without instructions, to save the credit of the United States. We foresaw, that before the new government could be adopted, assembled, establish its financial system, get the money into the Treasury, and place it in Europe, considerable time would elapse; that, therefore, we had better provide at once, for the years '88, '89, and '90, in order to place our government at its ease, and our credit in security, during that trying interval. We set out, therefore, by the way of Leyden, for Amsterdam, where we arrived on the 10th. I had prepared an estimate, showing that

FLORINS

There would be necessary for the year '88	531,937–10	
'89	538,540	
'90	473,540	

	Total,	1,544,017–10

FLORINS

To meet this, the bankers had in hand,	79,268–2–8	
and the unsold bonds would yield,	542,800	622,068–2–8

Leaving a deficit of	921,949–7–4
We proposed then to borrow a million, yielding	920,000

Which would leave a small deficiency of	1,949–7–4

Mr. Adams accordingly executed 1000 bonds, for 1000 florins each, and deposited them in the hands of our bankers, with instructions, however, not to issue them until Congress should ratify the measure. This done, he returned to London, and I set out for Paris; and, as nothing urgent forbade it, I determined to return along the banks of the Rhine, to Strasburg, and thence strike off to Paris. I accordingly left Amsterdam on the 30th of March, and proceeded by Utrecht, Nimeguen, Cleves, Duysberg, Dusseldorf, Cologne, Bonn, Coblentz, Nassau, Hocheim, Frankfort, and made an excursion to Hanau, thence to Mayence, and another excursion to Rudesheim, and Johansberg; then by Oppenheim, Worms, and Mannheim, making an excursion to Heidelberg, then by Spire, Carlsruh, Rastadt and Kehl, to Strasbourg, where I arrived April the 16th, and proceeded again on the 18th, by Phalsbourg, Fenestrange, Dieuze, Moyenvie, Nancy, Toul, Ligny, Barleduc, St. Diziers, Vitry, Châlons sur Marne, Epernay, Chateau Thierry, Meaux, to Paris, where I arrived on the 23d of April; and I had the satisfaction to reflect, that by this journey our credit was secured, the new government was placed at ease for two years to come, and that, as well as myself, relieved from the torment of incessant duns, whose just complaints could not be silenced by any means within our power.

A Consular Convention had been agreed on in '84, between Dr. Franklin and the French government, containing several articles, so entirely inconsistent with the laws of the several States, and the general spirit of our citizens, that Congress withheld their ratification, and sent it back to me, with instructions to get those articles expunged, or modified so as to render them compatible with our laws. The Minister unwillingly released us from these concessions, which, indeed, authorized the exercise of powers very offensive in a free State. After much discussion, the Convention was re-formed in a considerable degree, and was signed by the Count Montmorin and myself, on the 14th of November, '88; not, indeed, such as I would have wished, but such as could be obtained with good humor and friendship.

On my return from Holland, I found Paris as I had left it, still in high fermentation. Had the Archbishop, on the close of the Assembly of Notables, immediately carried into operation the measures contemplated, it was believed they would all have been registered by the Parliament; but he was slow, presented his edicts, one after another, and at considerable intervals, which gave time for the feelings excited by the proceedings of the Notables to cool off, new claims to be advanced, and a pressure to arise for a fixed constitution, not subject to changes at the will of the King. Nor should we wonder at this pressure, when we consider the monstrous abuses of power under which this people were ground to powder; when we pass in review the weight of their taxes, and the inequality of their distribution; the oppressions of the tithes, the tailles, the corvees, the gabelles, the farms and the barrier; the shackles on commerce by monopolies; on industry by guilds and corporations; on the freedom of conscience, of thought, and of speech; on the freedom of the press by the Censure; and of the person by Lettres de Cachet; the cruelty of the Criminal code generally; the atrocities of the Rack; the venality of the Judges, and their partialities to the rich; the monopoly of Military honors by the Noblesse; the enormous expenses of the Queen, the Prince and the Court; the prodigalities of pensions; and the riches, luxury, indolence and immorality of the Clergy. Surely under such a mass of misrule and oppression, a people might justly press for a thorough reformation, and might even dismount their rough-shod riders, and leave them to walk on their own legs. The edicts, relative to the corvees and free circulation of grain, were first presented to the Parliament and registered; but those for the impôt teritorial, and stamp act, offered some time after, were refused by the Parliament, which proposed a call of the States General, as alone competent to their authorization. Their refusal produced a Bed of justice, and their exile to Troyes. The Advocates, however, refusing to attend them, a suspension in the administration of justice took place. The Parliament held out for awhile, but the ennui of their exile and absence from Paris, began at length to be felt, and some dispositions for compromise to appear. On their consent, therefore, to prolong some of the former taxes, they were recalled from exile; the King met them in session, November 19, '87, promised to call the States General in the year '92, and a majority expressed their assent to register an edict for successive and annual loans from 1788 to '92; but a protest being entered by the Duke of Orleans, and this encouraging others in a disposition to retract, the King ordered peremptorily the registry of the edict, and left the assembly abruptly. The Parliament immediately protested, that the votes for the enregistry had not been legally taken, and that they gave no sanction to the loans proposed. This was enough to discredit and defeat them. Hereupon issued another edict, for the establishment of a cour plenière, and the suspension of all the Parliaments in the kingdom. This being opposed, as might be expected, by reclamations from all the Parliaments and Provinces, the King gave way, and by an edict of July 5th, '88, renounced his cour plenière, and promised the States General for the 1st of May, of the ensuing year; and the Archbishop, finding the times beyond his faculties, accepted the promise of a Cardinal's hat, was removed [September '88] from the Ministry, and M. Necker was called to the department of finance. The innocent rejoicings of the people of Paris on this change provoked the interference of an officer of the city guards, whose order for their dispersion not being obeyed, he charged them with fixed bayonets, killed two or three, and wounded many. This dispersed them for the moment, but they collected the next day in great numbers, burnt ten or twelve guardhouses, killed two or three of the guards, and lost six or eight more of their own number. The city was hereupon put under Martial law, and after awhile the tumult subsided. The effect of this change of ministers, and the promise of the States General at an early day, tranquillized the nation. But two great questions now occurred. 1st. What proportion shall the number of deputies of the Tiers état bear to those of the Nobles and Clergy? And 2d, shall they sit in the same or in distinct apartments? M. Necker, desirous of avoiding himself these knotty questions, proposed a second call of the same Notables, and that their advice should be asked on the subject. They met, November 9, '88; and, by five bureaux against one, they recommended the forms of the States General of 1614; wherein the Houses were separate, and voted by orders, not by persons. But the whole nation declaring at once against this, and that the Tiers état should be, in numbers, equal to both the other orders, and the Parliament deciding for the same proportion, it was determined so to be, by a declaration of December 27th, '88. A Report of M. Necker, to the King, of about the same date, contained other very important concessions. 1. That the King could neither lay a new tax, nor prolong an old one. 2. It expressed a readiness to agree on the periodical meeting of the States. 3. To consult on the necessary restriction on Lettres de Cachet; and 4. How far the press might be made free. 5. It admits that the States are to appropriate the public money; and 6. That Ministers shall be responsible for public expenditures. And these concessions came from the very heart of the King. He had not a wish but for the good of the nation; and for that object, no personal sacrifice would ever have cost him a moment's regret; but his mind was weakness itself, his constitution timid, his judgment null, and without sufficient firmness even to stand by the faith of his word. His Queen, too, haughty and bearing no contradiction, had an absolute ascendency over him; and around her were rallied the King's brother d'Artois, the court generally, and the aristocratic part of his Ministers, particularly Breteuil, Broglie, Vauguyon, Foulon, Luzerne, men whose principles of government were those of the age of Louis XIV. Against this host, the good counsels of Necker, Montmorin, St. Priest, although in unison with the wishes of the King himself, were of little avail. The resolutions of the morning, formed under their advice, would be reversed in the evening, by the influence of the Queen and court. But the hand of heaven weighed heavily indeed on the machinations of this junto; producing collateral incidents, not arising out of the case, yet powerfully co-exciting the nation to force a regeneration of its government, and overwhelming with accumulated difficulties, this liberticide resistance. For, while laboring under the want of money for even ordinary purposes, in a government which required a million of livres a day, and driven to the last ditch by the universal call for liberty, there came on a winter of such severe cold, as was without example in the memory of man, or in the written records of history. The Mercury was at times 50° below the freezing point of Fahrenheit, and 22° below that of Reaumur. All out-door labor was suspended, and the poor, without the wages of labor, were, of course, without either bread or fuel. The government found its necessities aggravated by that of procuring immense quantities of fire-wood, and of keeping great fires at all the cross streets, around which the people gathered in crowds, to avoid perishing with cold. Bread, too, was to be bought, and distributed daily, gratis, until a relaxation of the season should enable the people to work; and the slender stock of bread stuff had for some time threatened famine, and had raised that article to an enormous price. So great, indeed, was the scarcity of bread, that, from the highest to the lowest citizen, the bakers were permitted to deal but a scanty allowance per head, even to those who paid for it; and, in cards of invitation to dine in the richest houses, the guest was notified to bring his own bread. To eke out the existence of the people, every person who had the means, was called on for a weekly subscription, which the Curés collected, and employed in providing messes for the nourishment of the poor, and vied with each other in devising such economical compositions of food, as would subsist the great number with the smallest means. This want of bread had been foreseen for some time past, and M. de Montmorin had desired me to notify it in America, and that, in addition to the market price, a premium should be given on what should be brought from the

United States. Notice was accordingly given, and produced considerable supplies. Subsequent information made the importations from America, during the months of March, April and May, into the Atlantic ports of France, amount to about twenty-one thousand barrels of flour, besides what went to other ports, and in other months; while our supplies to their West Indian islands relieved them also from that drain. This distress for bread continued till July.

Hitherto no acts of popular violence had been produced by the struggle for political reformation. Little riots, on ordinary incidents, had taken place as at other times, in different parts of the kingdom, in which some lives, perhaps a dozen or twenty, had been lost; but in the month of April, a more serious one occurred in Paris, unconnected, indeed, with the Revolutionary principle, but making part of the history of the day. The Fauxbourg St. Antoine is a quarter of the city inhabited entirely by the class of day laborers and journeymen in every line. A rumor was spread among them, that a great paper manufacturer, of the name of Reveillon, had proposed, on some occasion, that their wages should be lowered to fifteen sous a day. Inflamed at once into rage, and without inquiring into its truth, they flew to his house in vast numbers, destroyed everything in it, and in his magazines and work-shops, without secreting, however, a pin's worth to themselves, and were continuing this work of devastation, when the regular troops were called in. Admonitions being disregarded, they were of necessity fired on, and a regular action ensued, in which about one hundred of them were killed, before the rest would disperse. There had rarely passed a year without such a riot, in some part or other of the Kingdom; and this is distinguished only as cotemporary with the Revolution, although not produced by it.

The States General were opened on the 5th of May, '89, by speeches from the King, the Garde des Sceaux, Lamoignon, and M. Necker. The last was thought to trip too lightly over the constitutional reformations which were expected. His notices of them in this speech, were not as full as in his previous "Rapport au Roi." This was observed, to his disadvantage; but much allowance should have been made for the situation in which he was placed, between his own counsels, and those of the ministers and party of the court. Overruled in his own opinions, compelled to deliver, and to gloss over those of his opponents, and even to keep their secrets, he could not come forward in his own attitude.

The composition of the Assembly, although equivalent, on the whole, to what had been expected, was something different in its elements. It had been supposed, that a superior education would carry into the scale of the Commons a respectable portion of the Noblesse. It did so as to those of

Paris, of its vicinity, and of the other considerable cities, whose greater inter-course with enlightened society had liberalized their minds, and prepared them to advance up to the measure of the times. But the Noblesse of the country, which constituted two-thirds of that body, were far in their rear. Residing constantly on their patrimonial feuds, and familiarized, by daily habit, with Seigneurial powers and practices, they had not yet learned to suspect their inconsistence with reason and right. They were willing to sub-mit to equality of taxation, but not to descend from their rank and preroga-tives to be incorporated in session with the Tiers état. Among the Clergy, on the other hand, it had been apprehended that the higher orders of the Hierarchy, by their wealth and connections, would have carried the elec-tions generally; but it turned out, that in most cases, the lower clergy had obtained the popular majorities. These consisted of the Curés, sons of the peasantry, who had been employed to do all the drudgery of parochial services for ten, twenty, or thirty Louis a year; while their superiors were consuming their princely revenues in palaces of luxury and indolence.

The objects for which this body was convened, being of the first order of importance, I felt it very interesting to understand the views of the parties of which it was composed, and especially the ideas prevalent as to the organi-zation contemplated for their government. I went, therefore, daily from Paris to Versailles, and attended their debates, generally till the hour of adjournment. Those of the Noblesse were impassioned and tempestuous. They had some able men on both sides, actuated by equal zeal. The debates of the Commons were temperate, rational, and inflexibly firm. As prelimi-nary to all other business, the awful questions came on, shall the States sit in one, or in distinct apartments? And shall they vote by heads or houses? The opposition was soon found to consist of the Episcopal order among the clergy, and two-thirds of the Noblesse; while the Tiers état were, to a man, united and determined. After various propositions of compromise had failed, the Commons undertook to cut the Gordian knot. The Abbé Siéyès, the most logical head of the nation (author of the pamphlet "Qu'est ce que le Tiers état?" which had electrified that country, as Paine's Common Sense did us), after an impressive speech on the 10th of June, moved that a last invitation should be sent to the Noblesse and Clergy, to attend in the hall of the States, collectively or individually, for the verification of powers, to which the Commons would proceed immediately, either in their presence or absence. This verification being finished, a motion was made, on the 15th, that they should constitute themselves a National Assembly; which was de-cided on the 17th, by a majority of four-fifths. During the debates on this question, about twenty of the Curés had joined them, and a proposition was made, in the chamber of the Clergy, that their whole body should join. This was rejected, at first, by a small majority only; but, being afterwards somewhat modified, it was decided affirmatively, by a majority of eleven. While this was under debate, and unknown to the court, to wit, on the 19th, a council was held in the afternoon, at Marly, wherein it was proposed that the King should interpose, by a declaration of his sentiments, in a *séance royale*. A form of declaration was proposed by Necker, which, while it censured, in general, the proceedings, both of the Nobles and Commons, announced the King's views, such as substantially to coincide with the Commons. It was agreed to in Council, the *séance* was fixed for the 22d, the meetings of the States were till then to be suspended, and everything, in the meantime, kept secret. The members, the next morning (the 20th) repairing to their house, as usual, found the doors shut and guarded, a proclamation posted up for a *séance royale* on the 22d, and a suspension of their meetings in the meantime. Concluding that their dissolution was now to take place, they repaired to a building called the "Jeu de paume" (or Tennis court) and there bound themselves by oath to each other, never to separate, of their own accord, till they had settled a constitution for the nation, on a solid basis, and, if separated by force, that they would reassemble in some other place. The next day they met in the church of St. Louis, and were joined by a majority of the clergy. The heads of the Aristocracy saw that all was lost without some bold exertion. The King was still at Marly. Nobody was permitted to approach him but their friends. He was assailed by falsehoods in all shapes. He was made to believe that the Commons were about to absolve the army from their oath of fidelity to him, and to raise their pay. The court party were now all rage and desperation. They procured a committee to be held, consisting of the King and his Ministers, to which Monsieur and the Count d'Artois should be admitted. At this committee, the latter attacked M. Necker personally, arraigned hs declaration, and proposed one which some of his prompters had put into his hands. M. Necker was brow-beaten and intimidated, and the King shaken. He determined that the two plans should be deliberated on the next day, and the *séance royale* put off a day longer. This encouraged a fiercer attack on M. Necker the next day. His draught of a declaration was entirely broken up, and that of the Count d'Artois inserted into it. Himself and Montmorin offered their resignation, which was refused; the Count d'Artois saying to M. Necker, "No sir, you must be kept as the hostage; we hold you responsible for all the ill which shall happen." This change of plan was immediately whispered without doors. The Noblesse were in triumph; the people in consternation. I was quite alarmed at this state of things. The soldiery had not yet indicated which side they should take, and that which they should support would be sure to prevail. I considered a successful reformation of government in

France, as insuring a general reformation through Europe, and the resurrection, to a new life, of their people, now ground to dust by the abuses of the governing powers. I was much acquainted with the leading patriots of the Assembly. Being from a country which had successfully passed through a similar reformation, they were disposed to my acquaintance, and had some confidence in me. I urged, most strenuously, an immediate compromise; to secure what the government was now ready to yield, and trust to future occasions for what might still be wanting. It was well understood that the King would grant, at this time, 1. Freedom of the person by Habeas corpus: 2. Freedom of conscience: 3. Freedom of the press: 4. Trial by jury: 5. A representative Legislature: 6. Annual meetings: 7. The origination of laws: 8. The exclusive right of taxation and appropriation: and 9. The responsibility of Ministers; and with the exercise of these powers they could obtain, in future, whatever might be further necessary to improve and preserve their constitution. They thought otherwise, however, and events have proved their lamentable error. For, after thirty years of war, foreign and domestic, the loss of millions of lives, the prostration of private happiness, and the foreign subjugation of their own country for a time, they have obtained no more, nor even that securely. They were unconscious of (for who could foresee?) the melancholy sequel of their well-meant perseverance; that their physical force would be usurped by a first tyrant to trample on the independence, and even the existence, of other nations: that this would afford a fatal example for the atrocious conspiracy of Kings against their people; would generate their unholy and homicide alliance to make common cause among themselves, and to crush, by the power of the whole, the efforts of any part to moderate their abuses and oppressions.

When the King passed, the next day, through the lane formed from the Château to the "Hotel des états," there was a dead silence. He was about an hour in the House, delivering his speech and declaration. On his coming out, a feeble cry of "vive le Roi" was raised by some children, but the people remained silent and sullen. In the close of his speech, he had ordered that the members should follow him, and resume their deliberations the next day. The Noblesse followed him, and so did the Clergy, except about thirty, who, with the Tiers, remained in the room, and entered into deliberation. They protested against what the King had done, adhered to all their former proceedings, and resolved the inviolability of their own persons. An officer came, to order them out of the room in the King's name. "Tell those who sent you," said Mirabeau, "that we shall not move hence but at our own will, or the point of the bayonet." In the afternoon, the people, uneasy, began to assemble in great numbers in the courts, and vicinities of the palace. This produced alarm. The Queen sent for M. Necker. He was conducted, amidst the shouts and acclamations of the multitude, who filled all the apartments of the palace. He was a few minutes only with the Queen, and what passed between them did not transpire. The King went out to ride. He passed through the crowd to his carriage, and into it, without being in the least noticed. As M. Necker followed him, universal acclamations were raised of "vive Monsieur Necker, vive le sauveur de la France opprimée." He was conducted back to his house with the same demonstrations of affection and anxiety. About two hundred deputies of the Tiers, catching the enthusiasm of the moment, went to his house, and extorted from him a promise that he would not resign. On the 25th, forty-eight of the Nobles joined the Tiers, and among them the Duke of Orleans. There were then with them one hundred and sixty-four members of the Clergy, although the minority of that body still sat apart, and called themselves the Chamber of the Clergy. On the 26th, the Archbishop of Paris joined the Tiers, as did some others of the Clergy and of the Noblesse.

These proceedings had thrown the people into violent ferment. It gained the soldiery, first of the French guards, extended to those of every other denomination, except the Swiss, and even to the body guards of the King. They began to quit their barracks, to assemble in squads, to declare they would defend the life of the King, but would not be the murderers of their fellow-citizens. They called themselves the soldiers *of the nation,* and left now no doubt on which side they would be, in case of rupture. Similar accounts came in from the troops in other parts of the kingdom, giving good reason to believe they would side with their fathers and brothers, rather than with their officers. The operation of this medicine at Versailles was as sudden as it was powerful. The alarm there was so complete, that in the afternoon of the 27th, the King wrote, with his own hand, letters to the Presidents of the Clergy and Nobles, engaging them immediately to join the Tiers. These two bodies were debating, and hesitating, when notes from the Count d'Artois decided their compliance. They went in a body, and took their seats with the Tiers, and thus rendered the union of the orders in one chamber complete.

The Assembly now entered on the business of their mission, and first proceeded to arrange the order in which they would take up the heads of their constitution, as follows:

First, and as Preliminary to the whole, a general Declaration of the Rights of Man. Then, specifically, the Principles of the Monarchy; Rights of the Nation; rights of the King; rights of the Citizens; organization and rights of the National Assembly; forms necessary for the enactment of Laws; organization and functions of the Provincial and Municipal Assemblies; duties and limits of the Judiciary power; functions and duties of the Military power.

A Declaration of the Rights of Man, as the preliminary of their work, was accordingly prepared and proposed by the Marquis de La Fayette.

But the quiet of their march was soon disturbed by information that troops, and particularly the foreign troops, were advancing on Paris from various quarters. The King had probably been advised to this, on the pretext of preserving peace in Paris. But his advisers were believed to have other things in contemplation. The Marshal de Broglie was appointed to their command, a high-flying aristocrat, cool and capable of everything. Some of the French guards were soon arrested, under other pretexts, but really, on account of their dispositions, in favor of the National cause. The people of Paris forced their prison, liberated them, and sent a deputation to the Assembly to solicit a pardon. The Assembly recommended peace and order to the people of Paris, the prisoners to the King, and asked from him the removal of the troops. His answer was negative and dry, saying they might remove themselves, if they pleased, to Noyons or Soissons. In the meantime, these troops, to the number of twenty or thirty thousand, had arrived, and were posted in, and between Paris and Versailles. The bridges and passes were guarded. At three o'clock in the afternoon of the 11th of July, the Count de La Luzerne was sent to notify M. Necker of his dismission, and to enjoin him to retire instantly, without saying a word of it to anybody. He went home, dined, and proposed to his wife a visit to a friend, but went in fact to his country house at St. Ouen, and at midnight set out for Brussels. This was not known till the next day (the 12th), when the whole Ministry was changed, except Villedeuil, of the domestic department, and Barenton, Garde des sceaux. The changes were as follows:

The Baron de Breteuil, President of the Council of Finance; de la Galaisière, Comptroller General, in the room of M. Necker; the Marshal de Broglie, Minister of War, and Foulon under him, in the room of Puy-Ségur; the Duke de la Vauguyon, Minister of Foreign Affairs, instead of the Count de Montmorin; de La Porte, Minister of Marine, in place of the Count de La Luzerne; St. Priest was also removed from the Council. Luzerne and Puy-Ségur had been strongly of the Aristocratic party in the Council, but they were not considered equal to the work now to be done. The King was now completely in the hands of men, the principal among whom had been noted, through their lives, for the Turkish despotism of their characters, and who were associated around the King, as proper instruments for what was to be executed. The news of this change began to be known at Paris, about one or two o'clock. In the afternoon, a body of about one hundred German cavalry were advanced, and drawn up in the Place Louis XV, and about two hundred Swiss posted at a little distance in their rear. This drew people to the spot, who thus accidentally found themselves in front of the troops, merely at first as spectators; but, as their numbers increased, their indignation rose. They retired a few steps, and posted themselves on and behind large piles of stones, large and small, collected in that place for a bridge, which was to be built adjacent to it. In this position, happening to be in my carriage on a visit, I passed through the lane they had formed, without interruption. But the moment after I had passed, the people attacked the cavalry with stones. They charged, but the advantageous position of the people, and the showers of stones, obliged the horse to retire, and quit the field altogether, leaving one of their number on the ground, and the Swiss in the rear not moving to their aid. This was the signal for universal insurrection, and this body of cavalry, to avoid being massacred, retired towards Versailles. The people now armed themselves with such weapons as they could find in armorers, shops, and private houses, and with bludgeons; and were roaming all night, through all parts of the city, without any decided object. The next day (the 13th), the Assembly pressed on the King to send away the troops, to permit the Bourgeoisie of Paris to arm for the preservation of order in the city, and offered to send a deputation from their body to tranquillize them; but their propositions were refused. A committee of magistrates and electors of the city were appointed by those bodies, to take upon them its government. The people, now openly joined by the French guards, forced the prison of St. Lazare, released all the prisoners, and took a great store of corn, which they carried to the corn-market. Here they got some arms, and the French guards began to form and train them. The city-committee determined to raise forty-eight thousand Bourgeois, or rather to restrain their numbers to forty-eight thousand. On the 14th, they sent one of their members (Monsieur de Corny) to the Hotel des Invalides, to ask arms for their Garde Bourgeoise. He was followed by, and he found there, a great collection of people. The Governor of the Invalids came out, and represented the impossibility of his delivering arms, without the orders of those from whom he received them. De Corny advised the people then to retire, and retired himself; but the people took possession of the arms. It was remarkable, that not only the Invalids themselves made no opposition, but that a body of five thousand foreign troops, within four hundred yards, never stirred. M. de Corny, and five others, were then sent to ask arms of M. de Launay, Governor of the Bastille. They found a great collection of people already before the place, and they immediately planted a flag of truce, which was answered by a like flag hoisted on the parapet. The deputation prevailed on the people to fall back a little, advanced themselves to make their demand of the Governor, and in that instant, a discharge from the

Bastille killed four persons of those nearest to the deputies. The deputies retired. I happened to be at the house of M. de Corny, when he returned to it, and received from him a narrative of these transactions. On the retirement of the deputies, the people rushed forward, and almost in an instant, were in possession of a fortification of infinite strength, defended by one hundred men, which in other times had stood several regular sieges, and had never been taken. How they forced their entrance has never been explained. They took all the arms, discharged the prisoners, and such of the garrison as were not killed in the first moment of fury; carried the Governor and Lieutenant Governor to the Place de Grève (the place of public execution), cut off their heads, and sent them through the city, in triumph, to the Palais royal. About the same instant, a treacherous correspondence having been discovered in M. de Flesselles, Prevôt des Marchands, they seized him in the Hotel de Ville, where he was in the execution of his office, and cut off his head. These events, carried imperfectly to Versailles, were the subject of two successive deputations from the Assembly to the King, to both of which he gave dry and hard answers; for nobody had as yet been permitted to inform him, truly and fully, of what had passed at Paris. But at night, the Duke de Liancourt forced his way into the King's bed chamber, and obliged him to hear a full and animated detail of the disasters of the day in Paris. He went to bed fearfully impressed. The decapitation of de Launay worked powerfully through the night on the whole Aristocratic party; insomuch, that in the morning, those of the greatest influence on the Count d'Artois, represented to him the absolute necessity that the King should give up everything to the Assembly. This according with the dispositions of the King, he went about eleven o'clock, accompanied only by his brothers, to the Assembly, and there read to them a speech, in which he asked their interposition to re-establish order. Although couched in terms of some caution, yet the manner in which it was delivered, made it evident that it was meant as a surrender at discretion. He returned to the Château a foot, accompanied by the Assembly. They sent off a deputation to quiet Paris, at the head of which was the Marquis de La Fayette, who had, the same morning, been named Commandant en chef of the Milice Bourgeoise; and Monsieur Bailly, former President of the States General, was called for as Prevôt des Marchands. The demolition of the Bastille was now ordered and begun. A body of the Swiss guards, of the regiment of Ventimille, and the city horse guards joined the people. The alarm at Versailles increased. The foreign troops were ordered off instantly. Every Minister resigned. The King confirmed Bailly as Prevôt des Marchands, wrote to M. Necker, to recall him, sent his letter open to the Assembly, to be forwarded by them, and invited them to go with him to

Paris the next day, to satisfy the city of his dispositions; and that night, and the next morning, the Count d'Artois, and M. de Montesson, a deputy connected with him, Madame de Polignac, Madame de Guiche, and the Count de Vaudreuil, favorites of the Queen, the Abbé de Vermont her confessor, the Prince of Conde, and Duke of Bourbon fled. The King came to Paris, leaving the Queen in consternation for his return. Omitting the less important figures of the procession, the King's carriage was in the centre; on each side of it, the Assembly, in two ranks a foot; at their head the Marquis de La Fayette, as Commander-in-chief, on horseback, and Bour-geois guards before and behind. About sixty thousand citizens, of all forms and conditions, armed with the conquests of the Bastille and Invalids, as far as they would go, the rest with pistols, swords, pikes, pruning-hooks, scythes, &c., lined all the streets through which the procession passed, and with the crowds of people in the streets, doors, and windows, saluted them every-where with the cries of "vive la nation," but not a single "vive le Roi" was heard. The King stopped at the Hotel de Ville. There M. Bailly presented and put into his hat, the popular cockade, and addressed him. The King being unprepared, and unable to answer, Bailly went to him, gathered from him some scraps of sentences, and made out an answer, which he delivered to the audience, as from the King. On their return, the popular cries were "vive le Roi et la nation." He was conducted by a Garde Bourgeoise to his palace at Versailles, and thus concluded an "amende honorable," as no sovereign ever made, and no people ever received.

And here, again, was lost another precious occasion of sparing to France the crimes and cruelties through which she has since passed, and to Europe, and finally America, the evils which flowed on them also from this mortal source. The King was now become a passive machine in the hands of the National Assembly, and had he been left to himself, he would have willingly acquiesced in whatever they should devise as best for the nation. A wise constitution would have been formed, hereditary in his line, himself placed at its head, with powers so large as to enable him to do all the good of his station, and so limited, as to restrain him from its abuse. This he would have faithfully administered, and more than this, I do not believe, he ever wished. But he had a Queen of absolute sway over his weak mind and timid virtue, and of a character the reverse of his in all points. This angel, as gaudily painted in the rhapsodies of Burke, with some smartness of fancy, but no sound sense, was proud, disdainful of restraint, indignant at all obstacles to her will, eager in the pursuit of pleasure, and firm enough to hold to her desires, or perish in their wreck. Her inordinate gambling and dissipations, with those of the Count d'Artois, and others of her *clique,* had been a sensible item in the exhaustion of the treasury, which called into action the reforming hand of the nation; and her opposition to it, her inflexible perverseness, and dauntless spirit, led herself to the Guillotine, drew the King on with her, and plunged the world into crimes and calamities which will forever stain the pages of modern history. I have ever believed, that had there been no Queen, there would have been no revolution. No force would have been provoked, nor exercised. The King would have gone hand in hand with the wisdom of his sounder counsellors, who, guided by the increased lights of the age, wished only, with the same pace, to advance the principles of their social constitution. The deed which closed the mortal course of these sovereigns, I shall neither approve nor condemn. I am not prepared to say, that the first magistrate of a nation cannot commit treason against his country, or is unamenable to its punishment; nor yet, that where there is no written law, no regulated tribunal, there is not a law in our hearts, and a power in our hands, given for righteous employment in maintaining right, and redressing wrong. Of those who judged the King many thought him wilfully criminal; many, that his existence would keep the nation in perpetual conflict with the horde of Kings who would war against a generation which might come home to themselves, and that it were better that one should die than all. I should not have voted with this portion of the legislature. I should have shut up the Queen in a convent, putting harm out of her power, and placed the King in his station, investing him with limited powers, which, I verily believe, he would have honestly exercised, according to the measure of his understanding. In this way, no void would have been created, courting the usurpation of a military adventurer, nor occasion given for those enormities which demoralized the nations of the world, and destroyed, and is yet to destroy, millions and millions of its inhabitants. There are three epochs in history, signalized by the total extinction of national morality. The first was of the successors of Alexander, not omitting himself: The next, the successors of the first Cæsar: The third, our own age. This was begun by the partition of Poland, followed by that of the treaty of Pillnitz; next the conflagration of Copenhagen; then the enormities of Bonaparte, partitioning the earth at his will, and devastating it with fire and sword; now the conspiracy of Kings, the successors of Bonaparte, blasphemously calling themselves the Holy Alliance, and treading in the footsteps of their incarcerated leader; not yet, indeed, usurping the government of other nations, avowedly and in detail, but controlling by their armies the forms in which they will permit them to be governed; and reserving, *in petto,* the order and extent of the usurpations further meditated. But I will return from a digression, anticipated, too, in time, into which I have been led by reflection on the criminal passions which refused to the world a favorable occasion of saving it from the afflictions it has since suffered.

M. Necker had reached Basle before he was overtaken by the letter of the King, inviting him back to resume the office he had recently left. He returned immediately, and all the other Ministers having resigned, a new administration was named, to wit: St. Priest and Montmorin were restored; the Archbishop of Bordeaux was appointed Garde des sceaux, La Tour du Pin, Minister of War; La Luzerne, Minister of Marine. This last was believed to have been effected by the friendship of Montmorin; for although differing in politics, they continued firm in friendship, and Luzerne, although not an able man, was thought an honest one. And the Prince of Bauvau was taken into the Council.

Seven Princes of the blood Royal, six ex-Ministers, and many of the high Noblesse, having fled, and the present Ministers, except Luzerne, being all of the popular party, all the functionaries of government moved, for the present, in perfect harmony.

In the evening of August the 4th, and on the motion of the Viscount de Noailles, brother in law of La Fayette, the Assembly abolished all titles of rank, all the abusive privileges of feudalism, the tithes and casuals of the Clergy, all Provincial privileges, and, in fine, the Feudal regimen generally. To the suppression of tithes, the Abbé Siéyès was vehemently opposed; but his learned and logical arguments were unheeded, and his estimation lessened by a contrast of his egoism (for he was beneficed on them), with the generous abandonment of rights by the other members of the Assembly. Many days were employed in putting into the form of laws, the numerous demolitions of ancient abuses; which done, they proceeded to the preliminary work of a Declaration of rights. There being much concord of sentiment on the elements of this instrument, it was liberally framed, and passed with a very general approbation. They then appointed a Committee for the "reduction of a projet" of a constitution, at the head of which was the Archbishop of Bordeaux. I received from him, as chairman of the Committee, a letter of July 20th, requesting me to attend and assist at their deliberations; but I excused myself, on the obvious considerations, that my mission was to the King as Chief Magistrate of the nation, that my duties were limited to the concerns of my own country, and forbade me to intermeddle with the internal transactions of that, in which I had been received under a specific character only. Their plan of a constitution was discussed in sections, and so reported from time to time, as agreed to by the Committee. The first respected the general frame of the government; and that this should be formed into three departments, Executive, Legislative and Judiciary, was generally agreed. But when they proceeded to subordinate developments, many and various shades of opinion came into conflict, and schism, strongly marked, broke the Patriots into fragments of very discordant principles. The first question, Whether there should be a King? met with no open opposition; and it was readily agreed, that the government of France should be monarchical and hereditary. Shall the King have a negative on the laws? shall that negative be absolute, or suspensive only? Shall there be two Chambers of Legislation? or one only? If two, shall one of them be hereditary? or for life? or for a fixed term? and named by the King? or elected by the people? These questions found strong differences of opinion, and produced repulsive combinations among the Patriots. The Aristocracy was cemented by a common principle, of preserving the ancient regime, or whatever should be nearest to it. Making this their polar star, they moved in phalanx, gave preponderance on every question to the minorities of the Patriots, and always to those who advocated the least change. The features of the new constitution were thus assuming a fearful aspect, and great alarm was produced among the honest Patriots by these dissensions in their ranks. In this uneasy state of things, I received one day a note from the Marquis de La Fayette, informing me that he should bring a party of six or eight friends to ask a dinner of me the next day. I assured him of their welcome. When they arrived, they were La Fayette himself, Duport, Barnave, Alexander la Meth, Blacon, Mounier, Maubourg, and Dagout. These were leading Patriots, of honest but differing opinions, sensible of the necessity of effecting a coalition by mutual sacrifices, knowing each other, and not afraid, therefore, to unbosom themselves mutually. This last was a material principle in the selection. With this view, the Marquis had invited the conference, and had fixed the time and place inadvertently, as to the embarrassment under which it might place me. The cloth being removed, and wine set on the table, after the American manner, the Marquis introduced the objects of the conference, by summarily reminding them of the state of things in the Assembly, the course which the principles of the Constitution were taking, and the inevitable result, unless checked by more concord among the Patriots themselves. He observed, that although he also had his opinion, he was ready to sacrifice it to that of his brethren of the same cause; but that a common opinion must now be formed, or the Aristocracy would carry everything, and that, whatever they should now agree on, he, at the head of the National force, would maintain. The discussions began at the hour of four, and were continued till ten o'clock in the evening; during which time, I was a silent witness to a coolness and candor of argument, unusual in the conflicts of political opinion; to a logical reasoning, and chaste eloquence, disfigured by no gaudy tinsel of rhetoric or declamation, and truly worthy of being placed in parallel with the finest dialogues of antiquity, as handed to us by Xenophon, by Plato and Cicero. The result was, that the King should have a suspensive veto on the laws, that the legislature should be composed of a single body only, and that to be chosen by the people. This Concordate decided the fate of the constitution. The Patriots all rallied to the principles thus settled, carried every question agreeably to them, and reduced the Aristocracy to insignificance and impotence. But duties of exculpation were now incumbent on me. I waited on Count Montmorin the next morning, and explained to him, with truth and candor, how it had happened that my house had been made the scene of conferences of such a character. He told me, he already knew everything which had passed, that so far from taking umbrage at the use made of my house on that occasion, he earnestly wished I would habitually assist at such conferences, being sure I should be useful in moderating the warmer spirits, and promoting a wholesome and practicable reformation only. I told him, I knew too well the duties I owed to the King, to the nation, and to my own country, to take any part in councils concerning their internal government, and that I should persevere, with care, in the character of a neutral and passive spectator, with wishes only, and very sincere ones, that those measures might prevail which would be for the greatest good of the nation. I have no doubts, indeed, that this conference was previously known and approved by this honest Minister, who was in confidence and communication with the Patriots, and wished for a reasonable reform of the Constitution.

Here I discontinue my relation of the French Revolution. The minuteness with which I have so far given its details, is disproportioned to the general scale of my narrative. But I have thought it justified by the interest which the whole world must take in this Revolution. As yet, we are but in the first chapter of its history. The appeal to the rights of man, which had been made in the United States, was taken up by France, first of the European nations. From her, the spirit has spread over those of the South. The tyrants of the North have allied indeed against it; but it is irresistible. Their opposition will only multiply its millions of human victims; their own satellites will catch it, and the condition of man through the civilized world will be finally and greatly ameliorated. This is a wonderful instance of great events from small causes. So inscrutable is the arrangement of causes and consequences in this world, that a two-penny duty on tea, unjustly imposed in a sequestered part of it, changes the condition of all its inhabitants. I have been more minute in relating the early transactions of this regeneration, because I was in circumstances peculiarly favorable for a knowledge of the truth. Possessing the confidence and intimacy of the leading Patriots, and more than all, of the Marquis Fayette, their head and Atlas, who had no secrets from me, I learned with correctness the views and proceedings of that party; while my intercourse with the diplomatic missionaries of Europe at Paris, all of them with the court, and eager in prying into its councils and proceedings, gave me a knowledge of these also. My information was always, and immediately committed to writing, in letters to Mr. Jay, and often to my friends, and a recurrence to these letters now insures me against errors of memory.

These opportunities of information ceased at this period, with my retirement from this interesting scene of action. I had been more than a year soliciting leave to go home, with a view to place my daughters in the society and care of their friends, and to return for a short time to my station at Paris. But the metamorphosis through which our government was then passing from its Chrysalid to its Organic form suspended its action in a great degree; and it was not till the last of August, that I received the permission I had asked. And here, I cannot leave this great and good country, without expressing my sense of its pre-eminence of character among the nations of the earth. A more benevolent people I have never known, nor greater warmth and devotedness in their select friendships. Their kindness and accommodation to strangers is unparalleled, and the hospitality of Paris is beyond anything I had conceived to be practicable in a large city. Their eminence, too, in science, the communicative dispositions of their scientific men, the politeness of the general manners, the ease and vivacity of their conversation, give a charm to their society, to be found nowhere else. In a comparison of this, with other countries, we have the proof of primacy, which was given to Themistocles, after the battle of Salamis. Every general voted to himself the first reward of valor, and the second to Themistocles. So, asked the travelled inhabitant of any nation, in what country on earth would you rather live?—Certainly, in my own, where are all my friends, my relations, and the earliest and sweetest affections and recollections of my life. Which would be your second choice? France.

On the 26th of September I left Paris for Havre, where I was detained by contrary winds until the 8th of October. On that day, and the 9th, I crossed over to Cowes, where I had engaged the Clermont, Capt. Colley, to touch for me. She did so; but here again we were detained by contrary winds, until the 22d, when we embarked, and landed at Norfolk on the 23d of November. On my way home, I passed some days at Eppington, in Chesterfield, the residence of my friend and connection, Mr. Eppes; and, while there, I received a letter from the President, General Washington, by express, covering an appointment to be Secretary of State. I received it with real regret. My wish had been to return to Paris, where I had left my household establishment, as if there myself, and to see the end of the Revolution, which I then thought would be certainly and happily closed in less than a year. I then meant to return home, to withdraw from political life, into which I had been impressed by the circumstances of the times, to sink into the bosom of my family and friends, and devote myself to studies more congenial to my mind. In my answer of December 15th, I expressed these dispositions candidly to the President, and my preference of a return to Paris; but assured him, that if it was believed I could be more useful in the administration of the government, I would sacrifice my own inclinations without hesitation, and repair to that destination; this I left to his decision. I arrived at Monticello on the 23d of December, where I received a second letter from the President, expressing his continued wish that I should take my station there, but leaving me still at liberty to continue in my former office, if I could not reconcile myself to that now proposed. This silenced my reluctance, and I accepted the new appointment.

In the interval of my stay at home, my eldest daughter had been happily married to the eldest son of the Tuckahoe branch of Randolphs, a young gentleman of genius, science, and honorable mind, who afterwards filled a dignified station in the General Government, and the most dignified in his own State. I left Monticello on the first of March, 1790, for New York. At Philadelphia I called on the venerable and beloved Franklin. He was then on the bed of sickness from which he never rose. My recent return from a country in which he had left so many friends, and the perilous convulsions to which they had been exposed, revived all his anxieties to know what part they had taken, what had been their course, and what their fate. He went over all in succession, with a rapidity and animation almost too much for his strength. When all his inquiries were satisfied, and a pause took place, I told him I had learned with much pleasure that, since his return to America, he had been occupied in preparing for the world the history of his own life. I cannot say much of that, said he; but I will give you a sample of what I shall leave; and he directed his little grandson (William Bache) who was standing by the bedside, to hand him a paper from the table, to which he pointed. He did so; and the Doctor putting it into my hands, desired me to take it and read it at my leisure. It was about a quire of folio paper, written in a large and running hand, very like his own. I looked into it slightly, then shut it, and said I would accept his permission to read it, and would carefully return it. He said, "No, keep it." Not certain of his meaning, I again looked into it, folded it for my pocket, and said again, I would certainly return it. "No," said he, "keep it." I put it into my pocket, and shortly after took leave of him. He died on the 17th of the ensuing month of April; and as I understood that he had bequeathed all his papers to his grandson, William Temple Franklin, I immediately wrote to Mr.

Franklin, to inform him I possessed this paper, which I should consider as his property, and would deliver to his order. He came on immediately to New York, called on me for it, and I delivered it to him. As he put it into his pocket, he said carelessly, he had either the original, or another copy of it, I do not recollect which. This last expression struck my attention forcibly, and for the first time suggested to me the thought that Dr. Franklin had meant it as a confidential deposit in my hands, and that I had done wrong in parting from it. I have not yet seen the collection he published of Dr. Franklin's works, and, therefore, know not if this is among them. I have been told it is not. It contained a narrative of the negotiations between Dr. Franklin and the British Ministry, when he was endeavoring to prevent the contest of arms which followed. The negotiation was brought about by the intervention of Lord Howe and his sister, who, I believe, was called Lady Howe, but I may misremember her title. Lord Howe seems to have been friendly to America, and exceedingly anxious to prevent a rupture. His intimacy with Dr. Franklin, and his position with the Ministry, induced him to undertake a mediation between them; in which his sister seemed to have been associated. They carried from one to the other, backwards and forwards, the several propositions and answers which passed, and seconded with their own intercessions, the importance of mutual sacrifices, to preserve the peace and connection of the two countries. I remember that Lord North's answers were dry, unyielding, in the spirit of unconditional submission, and betrayed an absolute indifference to the occurrence of a rupture; and he said to the mediators distinctly, at last, that "a rebellion was not to be deprecated on the part of Great Britain; that the confiscations it would produce would provide for many of their friends." This expression was reported by the mediators to Dr. Franklin, and indicated so cool and calculated a purpose in the Ministry, as to render compromise hopeless, and the negotiation was discontinued. If this is not among the papers published, we ask, what has become of it? I delivered it with my own hands, into those of Temple Franklin. It certainly established views so atrocious in the British government, that its suppression would, to them, be worth a great price. But could the grandson of Dr. Franklin be, in such degree, an accomplice in the parricide of the memory of his immortal grandfather? The suspension for more than twenty years of the general publication, bequeathed and confided to him, produced, for awhile, hard suspicions against him; and if, at last, all are not published, a part of these suspicions may remain with some.

I arrived at New York on the 21st of March, where Congress was in session.

So far July 29, 1821.

A JEFFERSON CHRONOLOGY

1743—April 13—Born at Shadwell, Albermarle Co. Va.

1748—Attends English school at Tuckahoe.

1752—Attends Douglas Latin School.

1757—August—His father Peter Jefferson dies.

1760—March—Enters College of William & Mary.

1762—April—Graduates from William & Mary—Enters law office of George Wythe.

1767—Admitted to the Bar.

1769—March—Elected a Burgess.

    May—Writes first public paper (Resolutions of the Virginia House of Burgesses).

1770—February—House and library at Shadwell burned.

1772—January—Marries Martha Wayles Skelton.

    September—His first daughter Martha born.

1773—April—Attends Committee of Correspondence meeting.

1774—April—His second daughter, Jane Randolph, born.

    July—Writes "A Summary View of the Rights of British America."

1775—January—Elected member of Albermarle Committee of Safety.

    March—Elected deputy delegate to Continental Congress.

    June—Attends Continental Congress.

    August—Re-elected member of Continental Congress.

1776—June—Drafts constitution for Virginia—Member of Committee to prepare Declaration of Independence—Reports draft of Declaration.

    October—Bill to abolish entails introduced in Virginia Assembly.

1777—May—Son born and dies.

1778—August—Third daughter, Mary Jefferson, born.

1779—June—Elected Governor of Virginia—Bill for Religious Freedom introduced in Assembly—"Revisers" report Code to Assembly.

1780—June—Re-elected Governor of Virginia.

    November—Fourth daughter born.

1781—January—Orders out militia to repel invasion.

    May—Youngest daughter, Lucy Elizabeth, born.

    June—Resigns Governorship and appointed Peace Commissioner by Continental Congress and declines appointment.

1782—Martha Wayles Jefferson, his wife, dies.

1783—June—Drafts Constitution for Virginia—Elected Delegate to Congress.

1784—March—Submits report on Government for Western Territory.

April—Prepares *Notes on a Money Unit.*

May—Reports Ordinance for Western Lands—Elected Minister to France.

July—Sails from Boston on ship *Ceres.*

August—Arrives at Paris.

September—Arranges for publication of *Notes on Virginia.*

1785—November—Youngest daughter, Lucy Elizabeth, dies in Virginia.

1786—January—Prepares notes for M. Meusnier.

March—Leaves Paris for London.

May—Returns to Paris.

October—Made an L.L.D. by Yale.

December—Act for Religious Freedom adopted by Virginia Assembly.

1787—June—Mary Jefferson arrives from America—Sends natural history specimens to Buffon.

December—English edition of "Notes on Virginia" published.

September-December—Endorses new Constitution for the United States but urges inclusion of Bill of Rights.

1788—June—Made an L.L.D. by Harvard.

1789—June—Prepares Charter of Rights for France.

September—Nominated for Secretary of State and confirmed by Senate.

1790—March—Elected member of American Academy of Arts and Sciences.

June—Reports on coinage, weights and measures.

August—Submits opinion on Foreign debt.

1791—February—Submits opinion on National Bank.

May—Endorses Thomas Paine's "Rights of Man."

1792—Announces to President Washington intention to retire from Cabinet.

1793—April—Submits opinion on French Treaties.

August—Drafts cabinet opinion on Genêt's recall.

December—Resigns Secretaryship of State.

1794—January—Arrives at Monticello.

1795—Establishes nailery at Monticello.

1796—Invents mould-board for plough.

November—Elected Vice-President of the United States.

1797—January—Elected President of Philosophical Society.

March—Assumes office of Vice-President.

1798—July—Opposes Alien and Sedition Act.

October—Drafts Kentucky Resolutions.

1800—January—Prints "Appendix" to "Notes on Virginia"—Plans University of Virginia.

February—Prepares Parliamentary Manual.

May—Nominated for President.

1801—February—Elected President of the United States by Congress.

March—Inaugurated as President.

December—Sends first Annual Message to Congress.

1802—March—Approves bill repealing Judiciary Act.

April—Approves bill to repeal Internal taxes—Approves Judiciary Bill.

December—Sends second Annual Message to Congress.

1803—January—Sends special Message to Congress on Lewis & Clark Expedition.

May—Louisiana Treaty signed at Paris.

July—Frames Louisiana Amendment to the Constitution.

October—Sends Third Annual Message to Congress—Louisiana Treaty ratified by Senate.

November—Drafts bill for Government of Louisiana.

1804—April—Daughter, Mary Eppes, dies.

November—Re-elected President of the United States—Sends Fourth Annual message to Congress.

1805—March—Inaugurated as President.

December—Sends Fifth Annual Message to Congress.

1806—February—Warned of Burr's Conspiracy.

November—Issues proclamation against Burr.

December—Sends Sixth Annual Message to Congress.

1807—January—Elected President of American Philosophical Society—Sends message to Congress on Burr's Conspiracy.

March—Signs bill to end slave trade.

July—Issues proclamation against British War-Ships.

November—Sends Seventh Annual Message to Congress—Sends special message to Congress on Burr's Trial.

December—Sends confidential message to Congress on Disputes with Great Britain—Non-Importation Act goes into effect—Embargo Act signed.

1808—March—Drafts supplementary bill for Embargo.

April—Issues proclamation on Embargo.

November—Sends Eighth Annual Message to Congress.

1809—January—Drafts circular letter on Embargo.

March—Signs repeal of Embargo—Retires from Presidency—Arrives at Monticello.

1811—January—Drafts scheme for a system of Agricultural Societies.

1812—January—Renews friendship with John Adams.
1814—September—Offers library to Congress.
1815—January—Outlines University of Virginia.
1819—November—Draws Plan of circulating medium.
1825—December—Drafts Protest for Virginia.
1826—February—Writes Notes on Lotteries.
    March—Executes will—Adds codicil to Will.
    June 24th—Declines invitation to join in celebrating July 4th—Writes last letter.
    July 4th—Dies.